Theory and History in the Human and Social Sciences

Series Editor

Jaan Valsiner
Department of Communication and Psychology
Aalborg University
Aalborg, Denmark

Theory and History in the Human and Social Sciences will fill in the gap in the existing coverage of links between new theoretical advancements in the social and human sciences and their historical roots. Making that linkage is crucial for the interdisciplinary synthesis across the disciplines of psychology, anthropology, sociology, history, semiotics, and the political sciences. In contemporary human sciences of the 21st there exists increasing differentiation between neurosciences and all other sciences that are aimed at making sense of the complex social, psychological, and political processes. Thus new series has the purpose of (1) coordinating such efforts across the borders of existing human and social sciences, (2) providing an arena for possible inter-disciplinary theoretical syntheses, (3) bring into attention of our contemporary scientific community innovative ideas that have been lost in the dustbin of history for no good reasons, and (4) provide an arena for international communication between social and human scientists across the World.

More information about this series at http://www.springer.com/series/15826

Tobias G. Lindstad • Erik Stänicke
Jaan Valsiner
Editors

Respect for Thought

Jan Smedslund's Legacy for Psychology

Springer

Editors
Tobias G. Lindstad
Asker, Norway

Erik Stänicke
Department of Psychology
University of Oslo
Oslo, Norway

Jaan Valsiner
Department of Communication
and Psychology
Aalborg University
Aalborg, Denmark

ISSN 2523-8663 ISSN 2523-8671 (electronic)
Theory and History in the Human and Social Sciences
ISBN 978-3-030-43065-8 ISBN 978-3-030-43066-5 (eBook)
https://doi.org/10.1007/978-3-030-43066-5

This Springer imprint is published by the registered company Springer Nature Switzerland AG
The registered company address is: Gewerbestrasse 11, 6330 Cham, Switzerland

Contents

About the Editors

Tobias G. Lindstad is an independent researcher and a clinical psychologist in Norway. His research concerns the relevance of epistemology and metaphysics for advancing the scientific basis of psychology, psychotherapy research, and mental health care services.

Erik Stänicke is Associate Professor at the Department of Psychology at the University of Oslo, Norway. He has published papers and books on psychotherapy research, psychoanalysis, conceptual research, and philosophy of science. He is a fellow researcher in *An intensive process-outcome study of the interpersonal aspects of psychotherapy* at UiO. He is a psychoanalyst and president of the Norwegian Psychoanalytic Society.

Jaan Valsiner is Professor of Cultural Psychology at Aalborg University, and University Professor at Sigmund Freud PrivatUniversität Wien-Berlin. From 2013 to 2018 he was Niels Bohr Professor of Cultural Psychology at Aalborg University in Denmark, where he created Europe's first Research Centre on Cultural Psychology. He is the founding editor of the journal *Culture & Psychology* and chief editor of *Integrative Psychological and Behavioral Science*. Among his many publications are the recent books *General Human Psychology; Foundations for a Science* and *Sensuality in Human Living; The Cultural Psychology of Affect*.

About the Authors

Jan Ketil Arnulf is a clinical psychologist and Professor of organizational behavior at BI Norwegian Business School, Norway. He has published papers and books on the psychology of leadership and how digital technologies in natural language parsing may assist research on social-cognitive processes in organizations. He is currently editing an issue on language algorithms and survey research in Frontiers in Psychology. He has coauthored the related predicting survey responses: how and why semantics shape survey statistics on organizational behavior. *PLoS One 9: e106361* and the failing measurement of attitudes: how semantic determinants of individual survey responses come to replace measures of attitude strength. *Behavior Research Methods, 50*

Tor-Johan Ekeland is Professor in social psychology at the Faculty of Social Science and History at Volda University College, Norway, and Professor II at Molde University College. He has previously held positions at the University of Bergen and Nordic University of Public Health, Gothenburg, Sweden. Recently, his research has addressed the interplay between epistemology and neoliberal governing and practice in the mental health field, and he has published both empirical and theoretical studies on these themes. He also has clinical experience.

Kenneth J. Gergen is a Senior Research Professor at Swarthmore College, USA, and the President of the Taos Institute. His many publications on psychological theory include the books, *Toward Transformation in Social Knowledge*, *Realities and Relationships: Soundings in Social Construction*, and *Relational Being: Beyond Self and Community*. He is the cofounder of the journal, *Theory and Psychology*.

Davood Gozli is Assistant Professor of Psychology at the University of Macau, China. He teaches courses on cognitive science and theoretical psychology and is concerned with the improvement of clear and critical thinking in psychological research and education. His book, *Experimental Psychology and Human Agency*, offers a comprehensive and detailed critique of experimental psychology.

Line Joranger is Associate Professor at the Faculty of Health and Social Sciences at the University of South-Eastern Norway. She has previously held positions at Department of Psychology at the University of Oslo and Volda University College. She has published papers and books on language, mind and subjectivity, and how language and historical analysis may reveal sociocultural influences on science and psychology. Her latest publications are *"Scientific" Healthcare and the Person: exemplifying relations between general laws and idiographic interpretation. European Journal for Person Centered Healthcare*, and the book *An Interdisciplinary approach to the human mind: subjectivity, science and experiences in change.*

Tobias G. Lindstad is an independent researcher and a clinical psychologist in Norway. His research concerns the relevance of epistemology and metaphysics for advancing the scientific basis of psychology, psychotherapy research, and mental health care services. He is the main editor (with E. Stänicke and J. Valsiner) of a book that critically evaluates Jan Smedslund's contributions to psychology: *Respect for Thought: Jan Smedslund's Legacy for Psychology.*

Michael McEachrane is a visiting researcher at the Raoul Wallenberg Institute of Human Rights and Humanitarian Law in Lund, Sweden, and has published papers on the philosophy of psychology and the need for a priori methods in psychological research. He is coeditor of the anthology, *Emotions and Understanding: Wittgensteinian Perspectives*. He has also published extensively in the areas of postcolonialism, race, human rights, and the African diaspora in Europe and is among other things the editor of *Afro-Nordic Landscapes: Equality and Race in Northern Europe.*

John McLeod is Emeritus Professor of Counselling, Abertay University, Scotland, and has held professorial positions at the Universities of Oslo, Padua, Massey, New Zealand, and Keele, England. He has published widely on such topics as pluralistic and narrative perspectives on counselling and psychotherapy, methodological issues in psychotherapy research, and cultural aspects of counselling, psychotherapy, and mental health care. Recent books include *Using Research in Counselling and Psychotherapy*, *Pluralistic Therapy: Distinctive Features,* and *An Introduction to Counselling and Psychotherapy, 6th edn.*

Mary Kathleen Roberts is an independent scholar with a Ph.D. in clinical psychology and an M.S. in computer science, both from the University of Colorado, Boulder, USA. After a first career as a licensed psychologist, she worked as a computer scientist in artificial intelligence. She has served twice as President of the Society for Descriptive Psychology and is a member of the Editorial Board for *Advances in Descriptive Psychology*. Her publications include *Companions of Uncertain Status* and 13 articles in *Advances in Descriptive Psychology.*

Sergio Salvatore is Professor of Dynamic Psychology at La Sapienza, University of Rome. Italy. He has published books and papers on psychodynamic modeling of mental processes and sociocultural phenomena, psychotherapy research, and psychological intervention. On these issues, he has directed and coedited several projects and publications. He is Editor-in-Chief of the Springer series *Culture in Policy Making. The Symbolic Universes of Social Action* and Associate Editor of *Integrative Psychological and Behavioral Science*. He is coeditor of the recent volume *Symbolic Universes in Time of (Post)Crisis: The Future of European Societies* and has recently published the book *Psychology in Black and White: The Project of a Theory-Driven Science*.

Martin B. Smedlund is an independent scholar with a master's degree in psychology from the University of Iceland, where he has also taught. He now works at the Icelandic Government Agency for Child Protection as an expert on treatment and foster care. One of his main academic interests is the conceptual foundations of psychology.

Jan Smedslund is Professor Emeritus at the University of Oslo, Norway. He has held positions at the University of Bergen and at universities of Geneva, Harvard, Stanford, Colorado, Minnesota, Kansas, New Mexico, Arizona, Oxford, University College London, Cambridge, and as a Fellow at The Center for Advanced Study in the Behavioral Sciences. He has published extensively, and among his books are *Psycho-Logic* and *The Structure of Psychological Common Sense*.

Henderikus J. Stam is Professor of Psychology at the University of Calgary, Canada, the founding editor of *Theory and Psychology*, and former president of the International Society for Theoretical Psychology. He is a former president of the Society for Theoretical and Philosophical Psychology of the American Psychological Association as well as of the Society for the History of Psychology, Division 26 of the American Psychological Association. He has published and coedited several books on theoretical problems and historical foundations of psychology, among these are *Theoretical Psychology: Classic Readings* and the forthcoming *The Sage Handbook of Theoretical Psychology*.

Erik Stänicke is Associate Professor at the Department of Psychology at the University of Oslo, Norway. He has published papers and books on psychotherapy research, psychoanalysis, conceptual research, and philosophy of science. He is a fellow researcher in *An intensive process-outcome study of the interpersonal aspects of psychotherapy* at UiO. He is a psychoanalyst and president of the Norwegian Psychoanalytic Society.

William B. Stiles is Professor Emeritus of Psychology, Miami University, Oxford, Ohio, USA, and Adjunct Professor of Psychology at Appalachian State University, Boone, North Carolina. He has been President of Division 29 of the American Psychological Association and the Society for Psychotherapy Research, and Editor of *Psychotherapy Research* and *Person-Centered and Experiential Psychotherapies*. He has published many papers on psychotherapy and research methods (e.g.,

Responsiveness in psychotherapy research: Problems and ways forward. In J. C. Watson & H. Wiseman (Eds), *Attuning to enhance therapist responsiveness*).

Jeff Sugarman is Professor of Education at Simon Fraser University, Canada. He has published books and papers on the psychology of personhood, the sociopolitical influence of psychology, the psychology of neoliberalism, and the application of historical ontology to psychological inquiry. He is past President of the Society for Theoretical and Philosophical Psychology, former Associate Editor of the *Journal of Theoretical and Philosophical Psychology and New Ideas in Psychology,* and coeditor of *The Wiley Handbook of Theoretical and Philosophical Psychology* and *A Humanities Approach to the Psychology of Personhood.*

Rolf Sundet is Professor in clinical mental health work at the Faculty of Health and Social Science, Institute of Health, Social and Welfare Studies, at the University of South-Eastern Norway. He has published several papers on the use of routine outcome monitoring, family therapy, and descriptions of local practices. Among his publications are feedback as a means to enhance client–therapist interaction in therapy in T. Tilden and B.E. Wampold (Eds.) *Routine outcome monitoring in couple and family therapy: The empirically informed therapist.*

Karl Halvor Teigen is Professor Emeritus at the Department of Psychology, University of Oslo, Norway. He has previously held positions in psychology at the universities of Bergen, Tromsø, and Oslo. His published books and papers are mainly concerned with social cognition, judgment and decision making (e.g., Teigen, K. H. & Keren, G. (2020). Are random events perceived as rare? On the relationship between perceived randomness and outcome probability. *Memory & Cognition*, https://doi.org/10.3758/s13421-019-01011-6), and the history of psychology (e.g., Teigen, K. H. (2002). One hundred years of laws in psychology. *Journal of American Psychology, 115*, 103–118).

Miika Vähämaa holds a Ph.D. in social psychology from the University of Helsinki, Finland, where he now works as a lecturer. He has been Pre-Doctoral Fulbright Fellow at the UNC-Chapel Hill, USA. His prior research asks what kind of roles and conceptualizations "knowledge" gains in our daily interaction as well as within individual reflection. Using data from the major newsrooms in the United Kingdom and Finland, his current research compares journalists' epistemic beliefs of the newsworthiness of religious topics.

Luk Van Langenhove is former founding Director of UNU-CRIS, the Institute for Comparative Regional Integration Studies of the UN University in Bruges and former Vice-President of the International Social Sciences Council. He is now Research Professor at the Institute of European Studies of the Vrije Universiteit

Brussel (VUB) and Academic Commissioner for International Networks and institutes at the VUB. He has published widely on regional integration, international relations as well as on social sciences theory, positioning theory, and psychology. Among his many publications are the monographs *Building regions* and *Innovating the Social Sciences* as well as the coedited books *Positioning Theory*, *Rethinking Psychology*, *People and Societies: Rom Harré and the Designing of the Social Sciences*, and *The EU and Multilateral Security Governance*. He has been coordinator of several EU-funded projects.

Chapter 1
Editorial Introduction

Tobias G. Lindstad

The idea for this anthology on Jan Smedslund's legacy was born after a meeting between the editors in Erik Stänicke's office at the early spring of 2016. Two days later, in his contribution to a seminar held by Jaan Valsiner at the University of Oslo, Smedslund emphasized the importance of the notion of *respect* so strongly that the early working title for the book popped up in Valsiner's mind: *Respect for Thinking: Jan Smedslund's legacy for Psychology*. Almost exactly 3 years later, the title of the book was slightly changed for the better, and the reason why will be clear by further reading.

The book was originally thought to be one possible output from a larger research project, the main aim of which was to clarify the prospect of a priori psychological knowledge. As part of this was to discuss the possibilities for advancing psychological knowledge through deductive reasoning, as suggested by Smedslund (1988, 1991a, 1995), and by abductive reasoning, as suggested by Valsiner (e.g. 2012), a second option for the title of the book came to mind: *Respect for Reasoning*. Unfortunately, despite the repeated overall positive feedback from the Research Council of Norway, the research project has not (yet) been funded. Part of the reason seems to be the controversial status of Smedslund's bold claims that do not only challenge the empirical foundation of psychological science, but that also scream for the need to advance a constructive alternative with ground-breaking consequences for psychotherapy research and clinical practice. Funding is good to have, but for advancing ideas of relevance for real science it is not mandatory. Human thinking about relevant issues never stops and the lack of funding did not stop us from analyzing Smedslund's ideas and then present the discussions to a wider public. We started editing this book in June 2016, and for 4 years we have spent our time in

T. G. Lindstad (✉)
Asker, Norway

T. G. Lindstad et al. (eds.), *Respect for Thought*, Theory and History in the Human and Social Sciences, https://doi.org/10.1007/978-3-030-43066-5_1

a creative and constructive reviewing of psychology in light of Jan Smedslund's seminal suggestions.

In some respects, the editing of this anthology has been a rather lengthy process. Part of the reason is that the main editor had to do the respective work on top a full-time work as a clinician, and also that the process was interrupted for almost a year due to illness and hospitalization. Moreover, the process of finding contributors to the book that do not only have the relevant interest for Smedslund's work, but who also have the courage to assess it from their perspective, is relatively hard. However, we are also happy that the process was less difficult than expected, and as such it has been a pleasure to discover that Smedslund's work has gained the reputation it deserves to a greater extent among scholars working outside of Norway, than within the stipulated borders of his home country. As such, we would like to express our gratitude for the positive responses from those scholars who have had to decline from contributing to the book; and of course, we are no less grateful for the valuable contributions provided by the authors of the chapters of this anthology. For those scholars who managed to finish their chapters rather quickly, we are sorry that they had to wait to see their chapters published, and we are grateful for their patience. On the other hand, we are also grateful to the scholars who patiently maintained their interest even though they could not complete their contributions other than being late in the process. Moreover, it has been great fun that some of the contributors also jumped on the train after having heard rumors about the upcoming book!

Last but not least, we are grateful to Smedslund for his willingness to contribute to the book and for having had the patience to wait to see it published. We had really hoped to see the book completed before his 90th birthday in the springtime of 2019. However, it brings some consolation that it was possible to present and discuss themes from the book with Smedslund and other contributors to the book at the conference of the International Society for Theoretical Psychology (ISTP) in Copenhagen the same year. Relatedly, and as mentioned, we would like to share the little story about how the title of the book was changed for the slightly better. In the celebration of Smedslund's 90th birthday, to which we are honored to have been invited, the main editor gave a speech, and when he was about to mention the title of the book, he simply could not remember which of the two above-mentioned proposals we had landed on: Was the title supposed to be *Respect for Thinking* or *Respect for Reasoning*? At that fateful moment, he landed on the first original option even though the second was the updated version at that time. Apparently recognizing this stumbling maneuvre, Smedslund asked whether a final decision was made on the title. When he heard that it was not, he expressed his momentary opinion that *Respect for Thought* might be more in line with his concerns, as it better accounts not only for reflective reasoning and explicit, declarative thinking, but also for unreflective, implicit, and unconscious thought. The reader is referred to the chapters of the book to see that his suggestion is very much to the point. However, except from this apt proposal and his own contributions, Smedslund has had no impact on the content of the book.

As editors, we have done our best not to express any agreement or disagreement with the viewpoints advanced by the contributors, and have rather tried to contribute to highlight, raise, and sharpen their voices. Part of this has also been to avoid misrepresentations of Smedslund's viewpoints as far as it is possible from our perspectives. In some respects, this threefold strategy is part of an overall aim of avoiding the difficulties and dilemmas described by Smedslund (2020) in the latter paragraph of his first contribution to this volume:

> Looking back, I can see that my work both has profited and suffered from the loneliness of my undertaking. With one exception, I have published around 150 articles and 7 books as single author. This relative isolation has enabled me to avoid being smothered by immediate counterarguments, and, has left me undisturbed to develop some relatively original perspectives. On the other hand, the loneliness has prevented me from profiting from closer cooperation with able colleagues. Only after having already stabilized my own position, have I been able to profit from debates. p. 33.

Our aim as editors has not been to smother any of the ideas of the contributors, but rather to bring their ideas into fruitful debate with Smedslund's ideas. As such, the chapters to follow critically evaluate Smedslund's legacy not only by expanding upon the possibilities opened up by his ideas, but also by exploring the limitations of his work, as well as putting the questions raised in the relevant historical and interdisciplinary context. Our mission with the book can be well expressed by borrowing some words expressed by Henderikus Stam (2020) in his contribution:

> Even for those of us who disagree with elements of the structure of psychologic however, the depth and breadth of Smedslund's efforts to create a psychologic have opened up discussions and possibilities to address the serious shortcomings of the discipline that many of us have called home for the length of a career. p. 146–147.

The discipline that Stam speaks of is psychology, and for those of you who wonders about what *psychologic* is about, you have chosen the right book and that one good place to start reading is the next chapter (Chap. 2). Here, Smedslund provides a prehistory of his current conclusions that largely relates to his efforts to advance the project of psychologic (to which various authors in the book refer by using the abbreviation "PL" or the more nuanced hyphenated name "Psycho-logic"). Indeed, though there are other significant ideas of Smedslund that are discussed in the book, it should be no secret that his work on Psycho-logic is center stage, and most of his other ideas seem to relate to this project in one way or another.

Thus, though Smedslund's (1963) most cited work to date is a seminal paper from the early 1960s, triggering the influential heuristics-and-biases program of Kahneman et al. (1982), from the late 1960s, Smedslund (1970, 1990) challenged the foundation of this program, as well as any other research strand of psychology presuming to be dependent on statistical empirical evidence (1991a, 1995, 2016a). As such, for the growing number of psychologists who have raised concerns about the one-sided emphasis on inductive generalization from accumulations of empirical data in scientific journals, research institutions, and practice guidelines, and that this narrow research paradigm cannot ever pay apposite respect to human mind and experience, Smedslund's work has been, and will be, prominent. Particularly important is the notion of *pseudo-empirical research* denoting investigations in which assertions are put to empirical test that can allegedly be known without it, introduced as part of Smedslund's (1978) seminal critique of Bandura's (1977) influential social learning theory. However, Smedslund's (1988, 1991a, 1995, 1997, 2012c) related efforts to advance the project Psycho-logic, and the descendent proposal of a *bricoleur model* (2009, 2012b, 2016b) of psychotherapy, have not gained the needed attention. This book exists to contribute to provide exactly that.

Organization and Content of Chapters

In what follows, the chapters of the book are shortly presented, and their ordering explained. It should also be noticed that the presentation is based on abstracts written by the contributing authors themselves. To the extent that the abstracts are altered, it is only for combining them with transitionary text. Though the main aims and contents of the respective chapters cluster into the overall themes of the four parts of the book, many of the chapters also deal with themes that are relevant for one or more of the other parts. When they do so substantially, we have attempted to point it out. All sections, except for the third, which is very much an extension of the second, starts out with a respective chapter by Smedslund.

Part I: Smedslund's Work in Historical Perspective

All the four chapters in the first part of the book contribute in various ways to put Smedslund work into historical context. In Chap. 2, **A Prehistory of My Present Position**, ***Jan Smedslund***'s first contribution to the book, Smedslund in fact saved the editors for much work when writing this editorial introduction as it provides no less than what its title says that it does provide. Hence, there is no need to present the prehistory of Smedslund's views here, but only to refer the reader to his chapter.

> First, I describe the early development of my position, influenced by, among others, Piaget, and leading to the formulation of a circular relation between logic and understanding. I, then, describe three debates with Stanford psychologists: I tried to show that Albert Bandura's theory of self-efficacy is necessarily true, whereas Bandura maintained that it was empirical. I still think that the core hypotheses are necessarily true, but that the concrete predictions from the theory are empirical, in so far as they always involve auxiliary hypotheses. I criticized Tversky and Kahneman's distinction between fallacy and misunderstanding because the concepts mutually presuppose each other, and we cannot understand the illogical (fallacy). I still think that errors must always be understood as misunderstandings, but in some contexts (e.g., teaching) they may, for practical reasons, be treated as fallacies. Against Lee Ross, I argued that, for many reasons, practitioners cannot profit from empirical research. I still maintain that this is generally the case, but concede that one can find exceptions, notably when it comes to large-scale interventions. Finally, I summarize the content of recent formulations of my position, notably why psychology cannot be an empirical science, and why the practitioner has to work as a *bricoleur (maximally open-minded and creative).*

Interestingly, from the perspective of the editors of this book, though Smedslund's arguments and conclusions, and also his style of writing, have undoubtedly been developing, his present position still seems to be in line with the title of his early publication from 1969, *Meanings, implications and universals: towards a psychology of man*. However, in a recent e-mail correspondence with the main editor Smedslund explained that in 1969 he had not yet experienced three aspects that have had decisive impact on the further development of his thoughts: (1) The meeting with clients as a clinician, (2) Anna Wierzbicka's work on clarifying the semantic primitives and lexical universals of a purported Natural Semantic Metalanguage (Wierzbicka 1996; Goddard and Wierzbicka 2014), and (3) his efforts to advance Psycho-logic by explicating a purported structure of psychological common sense (Smedslund 1978, 1988, 1991a, 1995, 1997, 2012c).

In the first full version of Psycho-logic, Smedslund (1988) did not only acknowledge the work of Peter Ossorio as something he has profited from reading, but he also argued that his project is related to Ossorio's (e.g., 1985) work with explicating the knowledge and competency of persons living in a world of persons as part of a discipline Ossorio called Descriptive Psychology (Schwartz 2019). In the third chapter, ***Mary K. Roberts*** discusses the extent to which these projects really are as similar as they may appear to be under the apt title **A Place for Persons: The Formal Systems of Smedslund and Ossorio**. This chapter does not only discuss Smedslund's work in relation to one of his relevant historical contemporaries, but also the extent to which their respective work differs and/or are relevantly similar because of their various sources of inspiration from earlier scholars.

> Jan Smedslund of the University of Oslo, and the late Peter G. Ossorio of the University of Colorado, both created innovative conceptual systems for use by behavioral scientists. Smedslund named his system "Psycho-logic" and described it as an axiomatization of "what persons *take for granted about* every person." Ossorio called his system the "Person Concept" and characterized it as a formal system providing access to all the facts and possible facts concerning persons and their behavior. My aim is to show the similarities and differences between these systems with respect to methodology, primary concept, and universality, and to place them in a wider, historical context. Hopefully, the paper will contribute to an appreciation of the value of systematic delineation of fundamental concepts in behavioral science, as well as an understanding of two different ways of going about the task.

In the fourth chapter, ***Karl Halvor Teigen*** writes that a discussion of Jan Smedslund's legacy to psychology would be incomplete without a presentation of his by far most famous paper. We agree. Here is Teigen's abstract for the chapter **The Concept of Correlation in Adults Comes of Age**:

> Jan Smedslund's most cited publication is a landmark study of illusory correlations published in 1963. In two experiments, nurse students received decks of patient cards featuring the presence or absence of a specific disease along with the presence or absence of a specific symptom. Nearly, all participants reported that the symptom was associated with the disease, so that the symptom would be useful for diagnostic purposes, although it occurred equally often in patients with and without the disease. Smedslund concluded that lay people's concept of correlation was severely deficient as the participants of his studies attended mainly to the present-present cell of a 2×2 contingency table. The finding was widely cited

> by Smedslund's contemporaries as an instance of human irrationality in lay statistical thinking. Later research has modified these conclusions by showing that perceived correlations are also dependent on expectations, cell frequencies, and the way data are presented to subjects. We find it perhaps ironical that Smedslund, who has later claimed that human rationality is a basic assumption for psychological research, and that fallacies in thinking cannot be empirically established, was among the first to demonstrate a basic shortcoming in people's ability to perceive statistical independence in a series of observations.

In the last chapter of the first historically oriented section, ***Line Joranger*** boldly argues that Smedslund's work embodies the spirit of a well-known historical forerunner that might have had no smaller academic ambitions than Smedslund. In Chap. 5, **The Socrates of Modern Psychology: A Historical-Socratic View on Smedslund's Common Sense Perspective**, she...

> ...highlights the intellectual relationship between Smedslund's work on Psycho-logic and the ancient philosopher Socrates' "*dialectic method,*" as well as the notions of "*virtue*" and "know thyself." Like Socrates' dialectic, Smedslund's method is divided into a negative and a positive part. The former invokes a process of reasoning to show that the discussed issues are in a state of confusion, inconsistency, and/or contradiction. The positive side of this method is that one should study people by systematically clarifying psychological common sense. Moreover, *virtues* emphasized by both Socrates and Smedslund, such as courage, piety, and self-control, are incessantly relevant in our societies and embody some of the key attributes we continually strive for. But of importance is also their emphasis on *knowing yourself.* To truly know yourself means self-possession and independence. It may enable a person to come to terms not only with his/her limitations but also with his/her potentials, which then can lay the groundwork for realistic therapeutic goals. If a person, be it a psychologist or a patient, does not keep watching over himself/herself, (s)he may impulsively do wrong towards himself/herself or others. To help another person to gain the relevant self-understanding may therefore be an *ethically* relevant goal in a therapeutic setting. However, to get the relevant kind of self-understanding are also of relevance for the psychological researcher; if psychologists neglect clarifying what they know about being a person, the scientific discipline of psychology, may run the risk of being unethical.

As mentioned, even more chapters discuss Smedslund's work in relation to historical developments in psychology, as well as to historical developments within other disciplines, such as various fields of research in philosophy and the social sciences. However, the focal aims of these chapters make it more appropriate to group them into the following sections.

Part II: Psychology as Science: Concepts and Epistemology

The chapters in the second part of the book can all be read as responses to and extensions upon how Smedslund has recently modified and developed his position. As such, they may be read as responses to Smedslund's chapter in the former part of the book. Like several of Smedslund's earlier critics (e.g., see responses to Smedslund 1991a, 1999a) all authors of these chapters comply with Smedslund's call to avoid *pseudo-empiricism.* However, they do not agree about in what the alternative could and should consist, nor about how it can be explained. Probably, this reflects various academic backgrounds and interests. However, it could also be but a sign of aptly critical voices within a promising, but hitherto unestablished, research field in progress. Thus, as editors of this book we do not only believe that further conciliatory work needs to be done, but we suggest that the clarification and grounding of alternatives to pseudo-empiricism ought to be recognized as a significant psychological research field of its own. As such, the next eight chapters of the book could be thought of as representing the current state of the art of this research field, continuing the inquiries that started with earlier exchanges between Smedslund and his previous critics, and as argued by Lindstad (Chap. 12), Ekeland (Chap. 19), and Stänicke and Lindstad (Chap. 22), the implications of this research for psychotherapy research and mental health care services are profound.

In the later decades of the last century, several scholars engaged in critical dialogue with Smedslund (e.g., 1991a, 1999a), and many (e.g., Parrot and Harré 1991; Shotter 1991, Harré 1999; Gergen and Gergen 1999) shared an interest in Wittgenstein's work. Though Smedslund (1991b) first rejected the relevance of their critique, he (e.g., 1997, 1999b, 2012a) later modified his standpoints to accommodate to it or circumvent it. The question remains, however, to which extent these modifications were steps in the right direction and/or whether they have been taken far enough. In Chap. 6, **Meanings of Words and the Possibilities of Psychology: Reflections on Jan Smedslund's Psycho-logic**, ***Michael McEachrane*** builds on his earlier critique (2009) and argues that Smedslund's more recent statements (2011, 2012a, 2012c, 2016a, b) are still open for Wittgensteinian critique:

> This chapter is on the methodology and philosophy of psychology as a science. By reflecting on Jan Smedslund's critique of the empirical research paradigm of scientific psychology as tending towards pseudo-empiricism and lacking sufficient grounding in conceptual analysis and definitions—the chapter investigates the import of meanings of words and reflecting on these to the practices and possibilities of psychology as a science. Specifically, the chapter investigates the role of scientific psychology of reflecting on the meanings of words (i.e., conceptual investigations or analyses); the need in psychology to distinguish conceptual from empirical investigations; the nature of the meanings of psychological terms and statements; and the method of analyzing the meanings of psychological terms and statements. The chapter ends by pointing to ways in which Jan Smedslund's system of Psycho-logic reveals the importance for psychology of reflecting on the meanings of words—but misleads on the nature and implications of such reflections.

In the seventh chapter of the book, **The Case for Psychological Quietism: Wittgensteinian Propaedeutics in Smedslund's Writings**, ***Martin B. Smedlund,***[1] suggests a somewhat more charitable reading of Smedslund's recent work inspired by the philosopher John McDowell's (2009) work on Wittgensteinian quietism. Noticeably, he also projects this understanding to aspects of relevance for the fourth part of the book, that is, psychotherapy. This is the abstract:

---

[1] Like ourselves, the historically interested reader may perhaps like to know that we have been informed by Smedlund (without any "s" in the middle of his name) that at the Department of Psychology in Iceland, from the late 1970s till at least 2017 focal publications of Smedslund (now with the "s") was put on the reading lists for the students on an undergraduate level, and that they are still central for discussion on the master's level. Of course, as editors of this book we cannot help to suggest that any psychology department should consider following the lead of the Icelanders.

> In what follows, I present Smedslund's and Wittgenstein's different ways of conducting conceptual analysis as reflecting two different conceptions of language. I argue that when it comes to the nature of language, Smedslund has it wrong and Wittgenstein has it right. However, due to what appears to be an instrumentalist shift in Smedslund's thinking, it seems possible to adjust his conceptual approach to Wittgenstein's conception of language. Likening conceptual analysis to cartography, I suggest that we view the two as using different methods of projection. I then go on to argue that the project of mapping psychological concepts has a claim to universality, at least partially, since there seem to be psychological facts and principles, common to human beings, that restrain the ways in which human psychology can be conceptualized—a point made by both Smedslund and Wittgenstein. After this, I lay out Wittgenstein's philosophical quietism and demonstrate in what ways Smedslund's a-theoretical view of psychology parallels it. I emphasize that quietism, in both philosophy and psychology, is to be conceived of as a propaedeutic. Finally, I suggest that Smedslund's bricoleur model for psychological practice is an example of the quietist ethos. This brings forth the ethical dimension of quietism, which is the renunciation of dogma.

In the eighth chapter, **Jan Smedslund and Psychologic: The Problem of Psychologism and The Nature of Language**, ***Henderikus J. Stam*** also questions the extent to which Smedslund's recent modifications to his account of Psychologic can succeed as responses to critique from Wittgensteinian quarters. However, he also picks up upon themes of relevance for the first historically oriented part of the book and puts Smedslund's work into further historical and interdisciplinary context in order to explain why he thinks the answer to this question must be negative. Here is the abstract:

> Three issues that are raised by Smedslund's psychologic are addressed in this chapter: First, the analytic-synthetic distinction although briefly addressed by Smedslund himself has not been thoroughly appreciated. I argue that it is crucial to understanding a project like the psychologic. Second, I place Smedslund's work in a historical perspective derived from the debates surrounding psychologism in the late nineteenth and early twentieth century initiative to find human reason on a series of logical laws. I present a short history of this complicated chapter in philosophy. By placing psychologic in a historical perspective, it is clear that Smedslund's notion of an a priori conceptual structure of psychology has some very influential forerunners, even if they constitute a different project in other ways. These historical forerunners provide a number of crucial lessons for contemporary psychologic as well as psychology. Third, I emphasize that following Wittgenstein, the nature of language throws up some serious obstacles to psychologic as it is currently conceived. Although Smedslund has begun to respond to his critics who have noted this problem, Smedslund does not go far enough in addressing this fundamental question. Finally, I agree with Smedslund that much of psychology is pseudo-empirical, but I see this as a result of the nature of psychological theorizing with its commitment to an indeterminate functional ontology.

In contrast to the former three authors, in Chap. 9, **The Linguistic Fore-Structure of Psychological Explanation**, ***Kenneth J. Gergen*** does not discuss whether or not Smedslund has succeeded to respond adequately to earlier critique from Wittgensteinian quarters but turns to expand upon Smedslund's earlier formulations:

> This chapter extends the early work of Smedslund on the common-sense underpinnings of hypothesis testing in psychology. As argued by Smedslund, experiments cannot really test hypotheses about the relationship between psychological process and behavior because any failure to verify them would defy cultural understanding. However, I propose that the intelligibility of psychological phenomena does not rest so much on cultural understandings as

> on *tautological language use*. This is born out of the impossibility of ostensively defining the states of mind presumably giving rise to action. The result is reliance on a logic of *originary resemblance*, that is, *attempts to explain A, will bear a likeness to A*. For instance, explaining a given behavior in terms of a "miniaturized" form of itself displaced within the mind. Further, because each definition of a mental term relies on the meaning of another term for its meaning, we enter a condition of *semiotic slippage*. It is thus possible to account for psychological explanations far removed from simple or transparent tautology. By drawing on *extended tautologies* and extended definitional sequences, we find that any given behavior (or its negation) can be explained by virtually any randomly drawn motive or trait. This includes otherwise counterintuitive or paradoxical explanations. These developments bear importantly on the potentials of psychological research, mental and diagnostic testing, and psychotherapy.

Though the last chapter (Chap. 12) in this second part of the book does engage in critical dialogue with Smedslund's Wittgensteinian critics, the next four chapters do not respond to Smedslund's recent advancements of his position primarily from a Wittgensteinian perspective. However, though the theme picked upon in the tenth chapter are relevant for the discussion with the Wittgensteinian critics, the question asked by ***Miika Vähämaa*** in his title appears to be related to an earlier discussion between Valsiner (1985) and Smedslund (1985): **Can Common Sense Change? Psychologic, Synthetic Thinking and the Challenge of Changing Language**. Smedslund and his Wittgensteinian critics seem to share the conviction that it cannot. Similar to Valsiner's earlier arguments, Vähämaa brings arguments towards the opposite conclusion, but in apparent contrast to Valsiner's (1985, 2014) arguments, Vähämaa does not think of common sense as providing culturally confined limits that ought to be transcended by science, but rather as something to be maintained by synthetic thinking beyond the current scope of Psycho-logic.

> Common sense and common meaning of words are linguistic and psychological elements that enable people to speak and to understand each other with ease. Accordingly, ease and fluidity of interaction do not arise on their own. On the contrary, if we lose common sense and commonly shared language, we face disorderliness, chaos, and misunderstandings in small and large group interactions. This chapter discusses an argument that we now witness potential decay of both common sense and common word meanings, as our mass and social media practices change. Without widely shared common sense and common word meanings, we lose the necessary psychic unity that makes us understandable. To counter the observable loss of "common meaning," I present a critical analysis of these core concepts and an increased effort to regenerate common meanings through synthetic thinking. In synthetic thinking, logically incompatible propositions are used to yield new and unexpected hybrids of meaning. These new hybrids move beyond the current scope of Psycho-logic. Such novel meanings can emerge in group settings, in which language is used to create and reinforce in-group cohesion. While the media "narrow-cast" meanings to small groups of like-minded individuals, such like-mindedness is also at the heart of the process of making something "common" in any sense. Thus, if we become good at reflecting and understanding the base of our common sense and fundamental psychological axioms of our language, we are also better equipped to consider unfamiliar word meanings with flexibility. This would enable new meanings in the maintenance of common sense.

In Chap. 11, **How to Avoid Throwing the Baby Out with the Bathwater: Abduction Is the Solution to Pseudo-Empiricism**, ***Sergio Salvatore*** extends upon his earlier arguments with Valsiner (Salvatore and Valsiner 2010) that though the prevailing reliance on inductive generalization from empirical data cannot deal adequately with the inherent meaningfulness of a great lot of psychological phenomena, neither can Smedslund's emphasis on deductive reasoning. Hence, he provides another solution alluded to in the title of his contribution, *abductive* reasoning:

> In this chapter, I show how important it is for psychology to recognize the semiotic and semantic valence of psychological constructs, and thus, their embeddedness in common sense, which can be drawn from Smedslund's criticism of the pseudo-empirical nature of psychological research. Smedslund has drawn a completely alternative scientific program, *Psycho-logic*, from this criticism. According to him, since psychological constructs are linked semantically, the function of psychology is to make the normative commonsensical meaning underpinning such linkages explicit. However, my thesis is that Psycho-logic is not the solution to the problem he identified. Indeed, it throws the baby (the possibility of empirical psychological knowledge) out with the bathwater (the problematic way empirical research is usually carried out). What is needed is a form of empirical research which is consistent with the semiotic nature of psychological phenomena. Accordingly, the second part of the paper proposes a view of psychological phenomena in terms of inherent formal (rather than efficient) causality and an approach combining dialectically abstract theory with an abductive analysis of local phenomena.

In Chap. 12, **A Priori Afterthoughts: Continuing the Dialogue on Psycho-logic**, ***Tobias G. Lindstad*** aims to continue the critical dialogue on the content, aim, and explanation of Psycho-logic:

> Jan Smedslund has seminally presented *Psycho-logic* as a result of explicating psychological *common sense*, and he has persistently characterized this kind of inquiry as amounting to *a priori knowledge*. However, the question of which psychologically relevant assertions can be known a priori (and how) must not be conflated with the question of which assertions constitute psychological common sense (and how), and pace Smedslund, the former question must be given priority for advancing a needed alternative to empirical psychological research. However, this also calls for a refined and somewhat deflated notion of a priori psychological knowledge that takes issue with a contentious Fregean spirit of Smedslund's arguments. By discussing Smedslund's analysis of the conditions for trust, I argue that a suitably revised notion of a priori psychological knowledge implies not only that these conditions are better conceived of as conditions of trustworthiness, but also that Psycho-logic comprises a far more varied body of knowledge than hitherto recognized. As such, Psycho-logic is not about concepts, words, or common sense, but more fundamentally about possible relations between possible properties of persons.

Part III: Psychology as Science: Research Extensions

The third section of the book shares parts of its title with the second: *Psychology as science*. However, the chapters in this section do not discuss conceptual and epistemological problems of psychology as much as they suggest various ways that psychological research may and should expand upon Smedslund's efforts to advance Psycho-logic, and three of the chapters do even present concrete research extensions in this regard.

However, the first chapter of this section is a notable exception to this, as it does not discuss or present research extensions compatible with Psycho-logic, but research that is purportedly *not*. In this chapter ***Jan Smedslund*** deals with an issue only tangentially touched upon by two other authors in the book (i.e., Henderikus

Stam and Jeff Sugarman in Chaps. 9 and 16). Though controversial, the conclusions that Smedslund makes this chapter have been part of his overall perspective for a long time. However, they have not earlier been spelled out as clearly as here, and arguably, the need for discussing these matters has become more urgent than ever. For bringing his points through Smedslund have, yet again, coined a term that might be suitable for shaking up the corridors of psychological research institutions. The term is aptly used already in the title of his chapter: What is at stake is the currently widespread, but arguably misleading, **Neuro-Ornamentation in Psychological Research**.

> *Neuro-ornamentation* designates the unneeded insertion of references to neuro-science in psychological texts. A text is taken to be more "scientific" when it contains references to brain studies, just as an object is expected to be more "beautiful" when decorated. I give three increasingly powerful examples of neuro-ornamentation. They all presuppose the Correspondence Premise stating that for every psychological event there is a corresponding neural event. The first example shows the distribution of occurrences of the terms "neuro-cognitive" vs. "cognitive" in a psychological text. It appears that the prefix "neuro-" has no other discernible function than emphasizing the ideology that psychology should be based on neuro-science. The second example is the neuro-scientific contribution by Moser & Moser concerning the spatial orientation of rats. It arguably adds nothing to what has been known for many years in psychology. Hence, references in psychological texts to the work of these recent Nobel Prize winners are only neuro-ornamentation. The third example is the use of the term "endogenous depression." This concept refers to psychological phenomena that can allegedly be explained only in terms of neuro-science. This directly contradicts the idea that all psychological phenomena can be psychologically explained and, hence, represents maximally powerful neuro-ornamentation. Finally, I explain the current exodus of psychologists to neuro-science as a result of a deplorable conceptual confusion.

Like in the former chapter in which Smedslund discusses the extent to which various kinds of concepts are relevant for psychological science or not, Chap. 14 could just as well have been put in the former part of the book. However, not as much as because it deals with conceptual issues, but because ***Davood Gozli*** deals extensively with epistemological issues of relevance for psychological science in his chapter called **Experimental Psychology and Distortions of Common Sense**. However, though Gozli is not as dismissive with respect to the value of experiments in psychology as Smedslund (2015, 2016a), his aim is to demonstrate the continuing relevance of Smedslund's critique. Thus, extending on his recent book (2019), Gozli provides arguments to the effect that one significant research extension of Smedslund's work is that his arguments contribute to provide a relevant kind of methodological self-awareness for doing psychologically relevant experimental research.

> This chapter outlines a critique of experimental psychology, based on Jan Smedslund's work on the epistemic status common-sense psychology. The critique is fleshed out with several examples from experimental research on cognitive control, cheating, self-reference bias, and sense of agency. Claims about discovery of surprising or general findings, at least in some cases, depend on neglecting or distorting common-sense psychology. Attention to psychological common sense, therefore, can sensitize us to certain types of error (e.g., pseudo-empirical research, over-generalization), similar to how attention to quantitative research can sensitize us to certain types of error (e.g., the so-called type I and type II

errors). I consider possible objections from the standpoint of experimental researchers, as well as reasons for a prolonged neglect of common-sense psychology.

While the two mentioned chapters in this third part of the book examine the scope and limits of psychological research, the next three creatively suggest and demonstrate intriguing ways to extend upon Smedslund's efforts to advance Psycho-logic in other prolific directions. Thus, though not buying into all the arguments made by Smedslund regarding the axioms of Psycho-logic, ***Luk Van Langenhove*** complies with this format for **Extending Smedslund's Psycho-logic System into a Social Theory**, which is also the title for Chap. 15:

> This chapter proposes to extend Smedslund's axiomatic system of psycho-logic (PL) into a psycho/socio-logic theory that is based upon insights from social theory and from the so-called linguistic turn in the social sciences. It will be argued that developing a conceptual system for psychology as Smedslund did, only makes sense if it is embedded in a broader context of social theory since psychological phenomena cannot be separated from the social realm. Smedslund focuses upon the agency of people, but one needs also to take into account the impact of structures on people. To this end, a reformulation of some of the axioms of PL will be presented that take as a starting point the notion that persons are social and moral beings and that the study of persons should start with the conversational context in which they operate.

In Chap. 16, **Smedslund and the Psychological Style of Reasoning**, ***Jeff Sugarman*** discusses Smedslund's work in light of his recent earlier work (Sugarman 2017) on what he in the wake of Ian Hacking's (2012) work has called "styles of reasoning":

> The chapter presents a critique of "*psychologism*" as a "*style of reasoning*" that has dominated disciplinary psychology from its inception and set the course for how psychological phenomena are made intelligible and investigated. Styles of reasoning comprise distinct disciplinary frameworks for scientific argumentation that set the terms for how phenomena are identified, defined, and understood, thus circumscribing the kinds of questions that can be posed about them and kinds of answers that can be justified. Psychologism as a style of reasoning holds that thought and experience are reducible to internal mental properties, in turn, taken to be manifestations of more primary biochemical and neurophysiological structures and processes. An explanation of styles of reasoning and their common features is followed by description of the characteristics and assumptions of psychologism, how it functions as a style of reasoning, and the ways it creates conditions of possibility in which psychological properties become articulated and attain ontological status. Subsequently, Smedslund's analysis of psychological pseudo-empiricism and, particularly, his insights concerning the miscasting of analytic claims as empirical ones derived from psychological experimentation, are discussed in light of the ways they align with and support the account of psychologism provided. An illustration of the applicability of the analysis is given using the psychological study of self-regulation.

In Chap. 17, **Wittgenstein's Revenge: How Semantic Algorithms Can Help Survey Research Escape Smedslund's Labyrinth**, and extending his earlier work (Arnulf et al. 2018), ***Jan Ketil Arnulf*** creatively claims to have shown through empirical research that...

> ...semantic algorithms can often predict the statistics of survey data *a priori*, particularly in topics like "leadership" and "motivation." In those cases, the survey data reflect the language usages of respondents, not the attitudes towards the topics in question. While this fact seems to bewilder researchers, it opens a computational tool for exploring our semantic construction of psychological reality. Using Dennett's concept "competence without

> comprehension," this article discusses how humans are trapped in a semantic network that we ourselves struggle to understand. Since Smedslund's work and the language algorithms have common roots in formal logics, the computational algorithms may help us explore the cognitively challenging area of a priori assumptions in psychological research. There may be a computational way to test and explore Smedslund's ideas of "pseudo-empiricism," helping science explore the complex area between empirical, logical, and psychological phenomena.

Part IV: Psychotherapy and Psychotherapy Research

In the third part of the book, the authors discuss, criticize, and/or expand upon Smedslund's ideas of relevance for critical practice, the bricoleur model, and its relationship to Psycho-logic and the related concern to advance alternatives to pseudo-empiricism. To set the stage, the section starts with ***Jan Smedslund's*** chapter **Professional Practice Without Empirical Evidence: The Psychologic of Trust**, which is the 18th chapter of the book.

> I begin by summarizing why empirical research cannot support psychological practice. After presenting the non-empirical approach of Psycho-logic and the accompanying bricoleur model, I focus on the central role of trust in psychological treatment. To trust is to think that a person will not harm you. There are five necessary and jointly sufficient conditions of trust: care, understanding, own-control, self-control, and relevant know-how. I discuss some of the challenges that may be encountered in attempting to build trust. The first four conditions are reasonably well defined and in principle manageable. However, since we cannot know the relevant composition of context-bound know-how (skill), we must conclude that we cannot know fully how to teach students to become good psychologists. The task may even be unsolvable because treatment outcomes depend on indefinitely numerous, variable, and partly random conditions.

Like many of the other authors contributing to the book, ***Tor Johan Ekeland*** is also demonstrating important bridges between his own earlier work (e.g., 1999) and Smedslund's. As such, In the 19th chapter of the book, **Psychotherapy: An Illusion that Works**, he points out that mainstream psychology is based on the epistemology that the domain for psychology exists in an independently pre-given reality (ontology) and that truth about such reality is attainable through empirical scientific investigation.

> Mainstream psychology is based on the epistemology that the domain for psychology exists in an independently pre-given reality (ontology) and that truth about such reality is attainable through empirical scientific investigation. This has become a position more or less taken for granted in mainstream psychology and psychotherapy research. Jan Smedslund has challenged this epistemology in a profound way. Inspired by this, the argument in this chapter is not only that this epistemology is false, as convincingly argued by Smedslund, but I also expand on his conclusion about the bricoleur model of psychological practice by contextualizing psychotherapy culturally and historically and thereby classifying it as a kind that belongs to the *art of healing*. Necessary and sufficient conditions for the healing context are discussed. Furthermore, it is argued, this epistemological change could rescue psychotherapy from the problematic mismatch between what psychotherapy pretends to be, and what is really going on in practice.

Likewise, in Chap. 20, ***William B. Stiles*** demonstrates the bridges between his earlier arguments regarding responsiveness in psychotherapy (e.g., 2009) and Smedslund's arguments for a bricoleur model of psychotherapy. However, there are also relevant differences. Stiles has given his chapter the title **Bricoleurs and Qualitative Theory-Building Research: Responses to Responsiveness.**

> In his extended critique, Smedslund suggested that scientific theory and research on psychotherapy are not feasible because (1) people respond to a myriad of constantly shifting determinants, and their behavior (2) evolves in ever-compounding sequences that are not precisely predictable, (3) that is never precisely repeated, and 4) is deeply enmeshed in interactions with other people. Instead, he suggests that therapists should be *bricoleurs*, drawing on psychological common sense, which includes knowledge shared by virtue of being human, understandings acquired through language and culture, and personal familiarity with the client. Smedslund's characterization articulates what I have previously characterized as appropriate responsiveness: therapists strive to do the right thing in response to ever-changing client requirements and emerging context. Despite this challenge, I am more optimistic than Smedslund about theory and research on psychotherapy and distinguish explanatory theories from treatment theories. An explanatory theory describes what things are and how they are related to each other within a domain. They are evaluated by comparing detailed observations with theoretical tenets and derivations. I call this theory-building research. A treatment theory describes the principles and practices that guide clinicians in conducting a therapy. They propose to say what works, and they tell therapists what to do. They are evaluated by assessing whether the treatment is effective. I call this product-testing research, illustrated by clinical trials. I argue that Smedslund was on target for treatment theory and product-testing research but that qualitative theory-building research on explanatory theory offers a strategy that can address Smedslund's critique.

In Chap. 21, **Working with Stuckness in Psychotherapy: Bringing Together the Bricoleur Model and Pluralistic Practices**, ***John McLeod and Rolf Sundet*** also build bridges between their own work on what they call pluralistic practices (McLeod 2018) with Smedslund's bricoleur model.

> The chapter takes the experiences of being stuck, of lack of change, and detrimental development of persons in psychotherapy as its start point. The aim of the chapter is to connect these experiences to the work of Jan Smedslund and show how his ideas not only offer a perspective for addressing such events, but also provide a gateway into the work of other theorists who have similarly contributed to the development of an alternative critical standpoint in relation to professional knowledge and practice. The position being offered does draw on the experience of the authors and their engagement with stuckness. Informed by pluralism the practices highlight how to respond to stuckness, lack of change, and evidence of not being on track. Bringing together the work of Smedslund and pluralistic practice, perspectives on the use of theory and research in practice is developed. Central is Smedslund's critique of generalized knowledge and its lack of focus on individual uniqueness. A relationship between the bricoleur model and pluralistic practices is established, grounded in a reconceptualization of how therapeutic change takes place, away from "interventions" and instead seeing what therapists do as "invitation to respond." The chapter connects these ideas to other authors that can help us expand alternative knowledge of psychotherapy in line with Smedslund's proposed bricoleur model and pluralistic practice. Lastly, the chapter underlines the importance of everyday language and cultural experience, and the value of engaging clients in a process of collaborative inquiry concerning relevant aspects of their everyday lives.

In the final chapter of the book, ***Erik Stänicke and Tobias G. Lindstad*** extend upon earlier ideas of Stänicke et al. (2019); Stänicke and Stänicke (2014), Lindstad,

(2020), and Lindstad's critique of Psycho-logic in Chap. 12 to discuss and compare what they call psychoanalytic *thought-models* and Smedslund's arguments for the bricoleur model. By so doing, they also discuss earlier work on the clinical implications of Psycho-logic by Waldemar Rognes (e.g., 1996) whose large and groundbreaking work is not as known as Smedslund's because he wrote mostly in Norwegian. Here is the abstract for their chapter **The Pragmatic Status of Psychoanalytic Theory: A Plea for Thought-models**:

> We argue that the concepts, notions, and assertions of psychoanalytic theory often constitute *thought-models* that might be practically relevant. Thus, these models are theoretically anchored regulative principles that may be relevant for practice even though the aspects and relations they refer to are not always manifested. As such, they may contribute to ground psychotherapy as a practice where one strives to meet persons as openly and unprejudiced as possible. As this aim is also shared by Jan Smedslund as part of his proposal of a bricoleur model of clinical practice, it is pivotal to discuss the extent to which the perspectives are compatible and may join forces or not. With respect to the bricoleur model, we acknowledge the critique of Salvatore and Valsiner that Smedslund's related efforts to advance Psycho-logic must be broadened so as to include the relevance not only of *deductive reasoning* but also of *abductive reasoning*. However, pace Smedslund and Valsiner, we argue that these reasoning capacities may reveal not only conceptual relations, but also causal relations between dispositional properties of persons. On the other hand, we also argue that this requires that the traditional understanding of psychoanalytic perspectives as primarily based upon experiences of clinical encounters must be broadened so as to acknowledge the aspect of Andre Green's notion of *clinical thinking* that it may comprise theoretical elaborations that may be removed from direct clinical experience.

References

Arnulf, J. K., Larsen, K. R., & Martinsen, Ø. L. (2018). Respondent robotics: Simulating responses to Likert-scale survey items. *SAGE Open, 8*(1), 1–18.

Bandura, A. (1977). Self-efficacy: Toward a unifying theory of behavioral change. *Psychological Review, 84*, 191–215.

Ekeland, T.-J. (1999). Meining som medisin. *Ein analyse av placebofenomenet og implikasjonar for terapi og terapeutiske teoriar* [Meaning as medicine. An analysis of the placebo phenomenon and implications for therapy and theories of psychotherapy]. Doctoral thesis, University of Bergen, Bergen, Norway.

Gergen, K. J., & Gergen, M. M. (1999). Memory as discourse and the future of psychological research. *Scandinavian Journal of Psychology, 40*(Suppl. 1), 31–35.

Goddard, C., & Wierzbicka, A. (2014). *Words & meanings: Lexical semantics across domains, languages, & cultures*. Oxford: Oxford University Press.

Gozli, D. G. (2019). *Experimental psychology and human agency*. Cham, Switzerland: Springer.

Hacking, I. (2012). 'Language, truth, and reason' 30 years later. *Studies in History and Philosophy of Science, 43*, 599–609.

Harré, R. (1999). Commentary on "Psychologic and the study of memory". *Scandinavian Journal of Psychology, 40*(Suppl. 1), 37–40.

Kahneman, D., Slovic, P., & Tversky, A. (Eds.). (1982). *Judgment under uncertainty: Heuristics and biases*. Cambridge: Cambridge University Press.

Lindstad, T. G. (2020). In Anjum, R. L., Copeland, S. & Rocca, E. (Eds). *Rethinking causality, complexity and evidence for the unique patient*. New York: Springer.

McDowell, J. (2009). Wittgensteinian “quietism”. *Common Knowledge, 15*(3), 365–372.
McEachrane, M. (2009). Emotion, meaning and appraisal theory. *Theory & Psychology, 19*, 33–53.
McLeod, J. (2018). *Pluralistic therapy. Distinctive features*. Oxon: Routledge.
Ossorio, P. (1985). An overview of descriptive psychology. In K. Gergen & K. E. Davis (Eds.), *The social construction of the person* (pp. 19–40). Rome, NY: Springer-Verlag.
Parrott, G., & Harré, R. (1991). Smedslundian suburbs in the city of language: The case of embarrassment. *Psychological Inquiry, 2*(4), 358–361.
Rognes, W. (1996). Selvfølelsens Psykologikk. Doktoravhandling. [The Psychologic of Self-esteem]. Doctoral Thesis. SV-fakultetet, Universitetet i Oslo.
Salvatore, S., & Valsiner, J. (2010). Between the general and the unique: Overcoming the nomothetic versus idiographic opposition. *Theory & Psychology, 20*(6), 817–833.
Schwartz, W. (2019). *Descriptive psychology and the person concept; essential attributes of persons and behavior*. Elsevier: Academic Press.
Shotter, J. (1991). Measuring blindly and speculating loosely: But is a “psychologic” the answer? *Psychological Inquiry, 2*(4), 363–366.
Smedslund, J. (1963). The concept of correlation in adults. *Scandinavian Journal of Psychology, 4*, 165–173.
Smedslund, J. (1969). Meanings, implications and universals: Towards a psychology of man. *Scandinavian Journal of Psychology, 10*, 1–15.
Smedslund, J. (1970). Circular relation between understanding and logic. *Scandinavian Journal of Psychology, 11*, 217–219.
Smedslund, J. (1978). Bandura’s theory of self-efficacy: A set of common sense theorems. *Scandinavian Journal of Psychology, 19*, 1–14.
Smedslund, J. (1985). How stable is common sense psychology and can it be transcended? Reply to Valsiner. *Scandinavian Journal of Psychology, 27*, 91–94.
Smedslund, J. (1988). *Psycho-logic*. Heidelberg & New York: Springer-Verlag.
Smedslund, J. (1990). A critique of Tversky and Kahneman’s distinction between fallacy and misunderstanding. *Scandinavian Journal of Psychology, 31*, 110–120.
Smedslund, J. (1991a). The pseudoempirical in psychology and the case for psychologic. *Psychological Inquiry, 2*, 325–338.
Smedslund, J. (1991b). Psychologic: A technical language for psychology. *Psychological Inquiry, 2*(4), 376–382.
Smedslund, J. (1995). Psychologic: Commonsense and the pseudoempirical. In J. Smith, R. Harre, & L. Van Langenhove (Eds.), *Rethinking psychology* (pp. 196–206). London: Sage.
Smedslund, J. (1997). *The structure of psychological common sense*. Mahwah, NJ: Lawrence Erlbaum Associates.
Smedslund, J. (1999a). Psychologic and the study of memory. *Scandinavian Journal of Psychology, 40*(Suppl. 1), 3–17.
Smedslund, J. (1999b). Author’s response: Psychologic in dialogue – Reply to commentaries. *Scandinavian Journal of Psychology, 40*(Suppl. 1), 123–138.
Smedslund, J. (2009). The mismatch between current research methods and the nature of psychological phenomena: What researchers must learn from practitioners. *Theory & Psychology, 19*(6), 778–794.
Smedslund, J. (2011). Meaning of words and the use of axiomatics in psychological theory. *Journal of Theoretical and Philosophical Psychology, 31*, 126–135.
Smedslund, J. (2012a). What follows from what we all know about human beings. *Theory & Psychology, 22*, 658–668.
Smedslund, J. (2012b). The bricoleur model of psychotherapeutic practice. *Theory & Psychology, 22*, 643–657.
Smedslund, J. (2012c). Psycho-logic: Some thoughts and after-thoughts. *Scandinavian Journal of Psychology, 55*, 295–302.
Smedslund, J. (2015). The value of experiments in psychology. In J. Martin, J. Sugarman, & K. Slaney (Eds.), *The Wiley handbook of theoretical and philosophical psychology: Methods, approaches, and new directions for social sciences* (pp. 359–373). Oxford: Wiley-Blackwell.

Smedslund, J. (2016a). Why psychology cannot be an empirical science. *Integrative Psychological and Behavioral Science, 50*(2), 185–195.

Smedslund, J. (2016b). Practicing psychology without an empirical evidence-base. *New Ideas in Psychology, 43*, 50–56.

Smedslund, J. (2020). A pre-history of my present position (Chapter 2, this volume). In T. G. Lindstad, E. Stänicke, & J. Valsiner (Eds.), *Respect for thought: Jan Smedslund's legacy for psychology* (pp. 21–34). New York: Springer.

Stam, H. (2020). Jan Smedslund and psychologic: The problem of psychologism and the nature of language (Chapter 9, this volume). In T. G. Lindstad, E. Stänicke, & J. Valsiner (Eds.), *Respect for thought: Jan Smedslund's legacy for psychology* (pp. 145–162). New York: Springer.

Stänicke, E., & Stänicke, L. I. (2014). Psykoanalytisk terapi. In L. E. O. Kennair & R. Hagen (Eds.), *Psykoterapi – tilnærminger og metoder*. Oslo: Gyldendal Akademiske.

Stänicke, E., Strømme, H., Krisitiansen, S., & Stänicke, L. I. (2019). *Klinisk tenkning i et psykoanalytisk perspektiv*. Oslo: Gyldendal Akademiske.

Stiles, W. B. (2009). Responsiveness as an obstacle for psychotherapy outcome research: It's worse than you think. *Clinical Psychology: Science and Practice, 16*, 86–91.

Sugarman, J. (2017). Psychologism as a style of reasoning and the study of persons. *New Ideas in Psychology, 44*, 21–27.

Valsiner, J. (1985). Common sense and psychological theories: The historical nature of logical necessity. *Scandinavian Journal of Psychology, 26*, 97–109.

Valsiner, J. (2012). *A guided science: History of psychology in the mirror of its making*. New Brunswick, N.J: Transaction Publishers.

Valsiner, J. (2014). *An invitation to cultural psychology*. London: Sage.

Wierzbicka, A. (1996). *Semantics: Primes and universals*. Oxford & New York: Oxford University Press.

Part I
Smedslund's Work in Historical Perspective

Chapter 2
A Prehistory of My Present Position

Jan Smedslund

Seeking further clarification and a coherent overview, I first describe what I learned from the contrast between the analytic philosophy of Arne Næss, American empirical psychology, and the epistemology of Jean Piaget. Then, I describe debates with three prominent psychologists at Stanford University, Albert Bandura, Amos Tversky, and Lee Ross, that helped me to further clarify and consolidate my views. Then, I present abstracts of recent articles leading up to my present position. At the end, I outline some questions I think need to be dealt with by future researchers.

Retrospective Prologue

I remember sitting in my office in Palais Wilson, Geneva, looking out on Lac Leman, the Jet d'eau, and the white speck of Mont Blanc. In the year 1957–1958, the common topic at the Centre International D'Èpistemologie Gènètique was "Learning and Logic." I had arrived from Oslo with my mind filled with American learning theories and analytic philosophy, and I had selected as my topic "can young children learn to become more logical?"; more specifically, can one teach the concept of conservation of weight to children who have not yet mastered it. The short story of the outcome was that, yes younger children could learn to respond correctly to test questions, but they did not *understand* what they had learned (1959). My colleagues at the Center generally agreed, and Piaget's formulation has followed me in the background throughout my later career: "One cannot accommodate to what one has not assimilated."

J. Smedslund (✉)
University of Oslo, Oslo, Norway
e-mail: jan.smedslund@psykologi.uio.no

T. G. Lindstad et al. (eds.), *Respect for Thought*, Theory and History in the Human and Social Sciences, https://doi.org/10.1007/978-3-030-43066-5_2

Upon my return to Oslo, I followed up this line of thought with an experiment in the context of Brunswik's theory of perception as the outcome of probability learning. A complex varying stimulus-material contained two discriminable probabilistic cues with a multiple correlation of +0.90 with a criterion. The majority of the Ss showed *no learning, even after as many as 4800 stimulus repetitions.* I quote from the summary:

> *It was concluded that a simple "photographic impression" theory is inadequate. There seems to exist a circular relationship between learning and perception, such that learning occurs only in relation to the available perceptual schemata, but can reorganize and modify them.* (1961, p. 386).

Inspired by comparing Smedslund (1966), and by two stimulating years, first with Jerome Bruner at the *Center for Cognitive Studies* at Harvard and then at the *Center for Advanced Study in the Behavioral Sciences* at Stanford, I stated my views in a paper entitled *Meanings, implications and universals: towards a psychology of Man* (1969). I quote from the abstract:

> *S-R psychology ignores the nonlawful regions between stimulus and meaning, and between intention and response. Psychology is defined: the science of phenomena as they exist for the individual person. The data in psychology: the public meanings of a person's acts, the meanings shared by all members of the person's community. Mental processes are related by implication rather than causation. Logic is a precondition for efficient mental functioning. Concepts with purely logical connotations (universals) are necessary for all higher mental functioning. No general psychological theory can perhaps exist, only development of already existing a priori conceptual schemata (common sense) and of diagnostic techniques.*

A central point in the preceding publications was further analyzed in a small article entitled *Circular relation between Understanding and Logic* (1970). Again, I quote the abstract:

> *Procedures for determining logicality presuppose understanding, and procedures for determining understanding presuppose logic. One can escape from this circle only by presupposing logicality, in agreement with common-sense thinking. Understanding can then be studied as an empirical variable. Traditional research has been based on the opposite solution: Logicality is treated as an empirical variable, understanding is implicitly presupposed; hence results are obtained which do not 'make sense.' One cannot understand the illogical.*

The preceding summarizes some of the background for the subsequent developments of my thinking.

Three Skirmishes at Stanford

Three debates with researchers from Stanford dealt directly with, and served to clarify, many of the central issues mentioned above.

Bandura

During a stay at the University of Kansas in Lawrence, I came upon an article by Albert Bandura (1977) presenting his theory of *self-efficacy*. It immediately occurred to me that, translated into ordinary English, the entire theory consisted of non-empirical, logically necessary common sense propositions, and I published this in (1978). I quote from the abstract:

> *Bandura's (1977) theory of self-efficacy is translated into non-technical language and is shown to consist of logically necessary rather than empirically testable statements. As an alternative to the dominant empiricist view, it is argued that valid theories in psychology are explications of conceptual relationships embedded in language (common sense). This conceptual network is anterior to both observation and theorizing. The analogy between the tasks of pre-Euclidean geometry and contemporary psychology is explored. The tasks are seen as involving explication of our implicit concepts of respectively space and people. One consequence of the stated view is that much psychological research is pointless since it attempts to verify logically necessary statements by empirical methods.*

Bandura (1978) replied that the theory nevertheless was empirical because it could be tested. He also argued that one must distinguish between logical and empirical verification. A theory can be wrong, even if it is logically necessary. Logical verification does not ensure empirical verification. At first, I simply could not understand Bandura.

However, lately I have come to see one way of interpreting his position that incidentally also throws light on why empirical researchers have generally resisted my arguments (1991b) and (1999). In order to clarify the point, let me use a simpler example than Banduras' propositions, namely "a surprised person has experienced something unexpected." Given ordinary definitions of the terms, it would seem to be unacceptable and meaningless to assert that a surprised person has *not* experienced anything unexpected, or that a person who *has* experienced something unexpected is not surprised. The proposition is non-empirical and indisputably logically true. Yet, if one relies exclusively on observable (behavioral) indices, the ensuing prediction is empirical because it may be wrong. A person may declare that she is surprised, but that she has experienced absolutely nothing unexpected, or state that she has experienced something unexpected, but is not at all surprised. In order to make sense of this, one must assume failure of at least one unstated auxiliary hypothesis.

One obvious possibility is that the person *lies* about one or both propositions. This brings to light one unstated premise, usually taken for granted, namely that the person tells the truth. Another possibility is that the person does not *understand* correctly one or both terms, for example, because she is a newly arrived immigrant. A third possibility is that the person does not pay attention to the question, and a fourth, that she does not hear what is asked and so on. I submit that the number of unstated auxiliary hypotheses taken for granted in making predictions from a psychological proposition is always indefinitely high. This is why predictions even from logically necessary propositions should always be qualified by the reservation, "no other circumstances intervene." Overlooking the qualification allows researchers as Bandura to insist that predictions from analytic theories and hypotheses also are empirical and must be tested. Even in the case of logically necessary hypotheses, every prediction involves indefinite numbers of auxiliary hypotheses. In other words, it does not make sense to test the core proposition that surprised persons always have experienced something unexpected, but one *can* test if the participants lie, misunderstand, fail to perceive, etc. The test results are empirical, but the results only concern the validity of the auxiliary hypotheses, that is, the presumptions about method, technique, and context. Hence, Bandura's argument that all theories must be empirically tested is intelligible, albeit imprecise (Bandura 1978). In the case of analytic propositions, only the auxiliary assumptions are tested. Contrary to Bandura, a necessarily true theory is *not* strengthened or weakened by data.

Already at the time I commented on Bandura, I began to wonder about how often psychological research is *pseudo-empirical* (1991a), that is, how often researchers put psychologically relevant assertions to empirical test that can be known *without* such testing. Discovery of pseudo-empiricality is important because it is a waste of time and resources to put theories to empirical test that can be known a priori. Testing makes sense only if there are reasons to doubt one or more of the auxiliary hypotheses.

Whether an assertion, hypothesis or theory can be known a priori can be checked by asking whether it can be meaningfully negated. However, this question is conspicuously absent from textbooks of psychological research methodology.

One may ask what led Bandura to formulate his theory. May be, he just selected hypotheses that all look plausible, which is also the bench mark of a priori and necessarily true propositions. During my stay in Kansas, I had weekly discussions with Fritz Heider, who had been the first in modern times to systematize common sense psychology and to notice that many common sense propositions are "analytic" (Heider 1958). It should be noticed that Heider used the term as meaning "logically provable," whereas I also include what we necessarily take for granted about humans. I came to think that, perhaps, *all* common sense propositions are a priori and noncontingently true, and that this is why they are common sense. Over the following years, I developed the axiomatic system of *Psycho-Logic (*1988*),* revised in *(*1997a*).*

Seen in retrospect, two circumstances, among other things, support the validity of this large-scale formalization:

The first one is that, to my knowledge, the content has not been challenged over the past decades.

Another is that the large-scale change in structure from 1988 (PL) to 1997(EL), did not change the content: I quote from (1997a, p. x).

> Content has remained remarkably unchanged by the transition from PL to EL over a period of 8 years. …Of the 109 basic propositions in PL (axioms + definitions), 96 are retained in some form in EL (axioms + primitives + definitions). None of the omitted 13 PL definitions are contradicted in EL. Hence the two systems are almost identical in content, and appear to reflect a stable kernel structure in psychological common sense.

Since one may assume that psychologists only select plausible looking hypotheses for testing, and mostly publish confirming results, it is possible that all generally accepted psychological hypotheses have a necessarily true core, even though the predictions from them are empirical because of the ubiquitous auxiliary hypotheses. A picture started to emerge of modern psychology as a science with a hidden a priori and unavoidable framework, and a surface of empirical research, that in fact only tests auxiliary hypotheses.

During my frequent and prolonged stays at Stanford, I also had discussions with Amos Tversky, where the circular relation between logic and understanding reappeared as a central theme.

Tversky

In the 1980s, Tversky and Kahneman published studies of decision-making, where they argued that human reasoning sometimes deviates from classical expected utility theory. Tversky and Kahneman (TK) interpreted the deviations from classical theory, as involving *fallacies* rather than *misunderstandings.* In what follows, I refer to the text in one of their articles (Tversky and Kahneman 1983). As distinguished from Bandura's theory, where the empirical predictions are totally *consistent with* common sense logic, Tversky and Kahneman emphasize apparent *contradictions between* empirical findings and logical derivations. In this widely cited study, participants were given the following background information (p.304):

"Linda is 31 years old, single, outspoken and very bright. She majored in philosophy. As a student she was deeply concerned with issues of discrimination and social justice, and also participated in anti-nuclear demonstrations." The participants were asked to check which of two alternatives was more probable: "Linda is a bank teller (T)" or "Linda is a bank teller and is active in the feminist movement (T & F)." Eighty-five per cent of the respondents indicated that T and F was more probable than T, which was in violation of the conjunction rule (A conjunction cannot be more probable than one of its constituents).

Are these findings a result of *fallacies* or *misunderstandings*? TK do not provide formal definitions of the two concepts, but propose three diagnostic signs to make the distinction:

> A judgment is appropriately labeled a fallacy when most of the people who make it are disposed, after suitable explanation, to accept the following propositions: (a) They made a non-trivial error, which they would probably have repeated in similar problems, (b) the error was conceptual, not merely verbal or technical, and (c) they *should* have known the correct answer or a procedure to find it. Alternatively, the same judgment could be described as a failure of communication if the subject misunderstands the question or if the experimenter misinterprets the answer. Subjects who have erred because of a misunderstanding are likely to reject the propositions listed above and to claim…that they knew the correct answer all along, and that their error, if any, was verbal or technical rather than conceptual" (1983, p. 304).

TK recognize that "the dividing line between fallacies and misunderstandings … is not always clear." This is not surprising, since each of their criteria involves highly complicated and ambiguous distinctions. Criterion (a) can only be decided relying at least on distinctions between "trivial" and "non-trivial," and "similar" and "non-similar." Criterion (b) requires distinction between "conceptual" and "non-conceptual," between "verbal" and "non-verbal," and between "technical" and "non-technical." Criterion (c) can only be decided, given a distinction between "should" and "should not." It is hard to see the resulting distinction between "fallacy" and "misunderstanding" as simple and useful. It would appear that the issue can be clarified only by substituting simple and non-controversial definitions of the two concepts.

I proposed (1990) that the concept of fallacy is defined as a *logical error*, i.e., as an inference in which the conclusion does not follow from the premises. Therefore, a decision about whether or not there is a fallacy can only be made when one can assume that the person has correctly understood these premises, and that the researcher has correctly understood the person's answer.

I also propose the following definition of the concept of misunderstanding: P misunderstands what Q means by expression E, to the extent that P and Q disagree about (1) what means the same as E, and/or (2) what follows from E, and/or (3) what is contradicted by E, and/or (4) what is irrelevant to E.

The proposed definition does not mean that the participants necessarily know *that* they misunderstand each other.

Given these definitions, one feature of the relation between logical fallacy and misunderstanding is definitely *not* recognized by Tversky and Kahneman, namely the circularity I described many years earlier (1970). One cannot decide about misunderstanding, unless one can take it for granted that the person's reasoning is logically correct. Conversely, one cannot decide that the reasoning is logically correct, unless one can take it for granted that the terms are correctly understood. Given the suggested definitions, this means that the kind of error cannot be decided. Cognitive errors can be explained as fallacies or misunderstandings. The circular relation means that the ambiguity must be resolved either by a variable strategy of sometimes using one and sometimes the other concept, or by consistently using only the concept of fallacy or only the concept of misunderstanding. Because of the circularity, it is impossible to implement a variable strategy because one cannot find criteria for deciding *when* an error should be seen as fallacy, and *when* it should be seen as misunderstanding. Also a strategy of *always* treating errors as logical fallacies leads to numerous totally unacceptable interpretations, such as when someone commits error in an unfamiliar language. This *cannot* be seen as a failure of logic. The only remaining defensible solution is a strategy of *always* attributing cognitive errors to misunderstanding. In the case of Linda, this means understanding the majority answers as a result of interpreting "Linda is a bank teller" as meaning "Linda is bank teller but *not* active in the feminist movement." More generally, TK's findings do not mean that people's reasoning sometimes deviates from the classical utility formula, but that sometimes, their conclusions follow from premises *other than* those of the experimenter. This alternative strategy avoids having to explain logical fallacy, which is impossible since the very concept of explanation presupposes logicality. People must always be seen as logical, since otherwise their behavior becomes unexplainable.

Lately, I have come to realize that the distinction between fallacy and misunderstanding, although theoretically indefensible, nevertheless may be useful in many practical contexts. For example, in mathematics, the purpose may simply be to teach certain formalizations to all pupils, disregarding entirely how their "wrong" responses can be explained. Responses are simply treated as "wrong" because in many situations this may be the most expedite solution.

The conclusion is that TK's theory, although formally indefensible, is useful in many practical settings because it summarizes people's most frequent predilections for misunderstanding. However, even though the objective empirical registrations of behavior depend on variation in adequacy of different auxiliary hypotheses (context), the observed behavior always follows logically from the subjective premises of the participants. The findings in the Linda case exactly parallel findings from developmental research in Geneva and elsewhere. When given 12 balls, ten of which are red and two are blue, and asked "Are there more 'balls' or 'more red balls'?" younger preschool children usually answer "red balls, because there are only two blue ones." Again, it is obvious that the children misunderstand, and for the same reason as adults: In everyday life, most simple choices are between perceptually discernible options.

In the years following the debates with Bandura and Tversky, I became increasingly interested in my experiences as a practicing psychologist. This eventually resulted in a third debate that also taught me valuable lessons.

Ross

Recognizing the divide between academic research and psychological practice, my colleague Lee Ross and I undertook to explore our opposing views on this topic (Smedslund and Ross 2014). The following is the abstract of the resulting paper:

> A practitioner (JS) and an academic social psychologist (LR) debate the practical value of empirical psychological research and theory relative to that of reliance on a priori knowledge of humans (*psycho-logic*), and concrete knowledge of individual persons and situations. JS contends that the complexity, and multiplicity of determinants of human behavior, and the time-bound, and context specific nature of research findings and 'middle-range' theories embodying them generally prove to be of little value in psychological practice. He buttresses his contention with examples from his own clinical practice. In reply LR, challenges the assertion that JS and other clinical practitioners fail to make use of research-based advances in knowledge. He further describes specific non-obvious findings and effect magnitudes which he argues add significantly to the sources JS describes, and are of particular value in applied contexts and public policy debates that involve choice and decision-making. The authors then rebut each other's contentions and clarify their own, focusing on issues of temporal stability in findings and aggregate versus individual levels of analysis. In summarizing areas of agreement and remaining disagreement both authors affirm the importance of attending to the specifics of situational context and meanings actors attach to their particular circumstances and choices.

The preceding abstract does not directly specify the remaining important disagreement. As a practitioner, my experience is that I have *not* been able to profit from the findings of empirical research. Lee Ross, who is an academic researcher, but not a practitioner, insists that one *can* profit from empirical research. The exact reasons for this persisting disagreement remained somewhat unclear. We agreed about predictions at the aggregate level. It is indisputable that large-scale statistical tendencies, even if small, may be useful in decisions about social policy. However, psychological practice normally involves *specific* individuals, families, groups, or organizations, and this is the domain of some persisting disagreement.

At first sight, Ross is undoubtedly correct that research findings ought to inform actual practice also with individual cases and influence the choice of treatment. Suppose it is found that procedure A is x percent more likely to succeed than procedure B. This figure is based on computing the mean of measured responses to tests and questionnaires before and after sketchily described treatments of a number of unknown unique individuals in unknown personal life-situations. It should also be remembered that although the average results computed in this way favor treatment A, a minority of the participants may produce equal scores in both conditions, or higher scores in B.

Also, each description of an objective condition and an objective response covers an indefinite number of unstated presuppositions. This follows from what I wrote in the paper from (1969) quoted above about "the unlawful relation between stimulus and meaning and between intention and response." Objective registration of experimental conditions and overt responses tells us nothing definite about what goes on subjectively.

As a consequence, a therapist can justify treating her client in accordance with given scientific findings, only by making a high number of assumptions on shaky grounds. The practitioner must assume that the context of the research and the average characteristics of the participants do not differ in treatment-relevant ways from the situation and characteristics of a particular client. The practitioner must also assume that her individual way of following a manual is in every important way similar to the average ways of the therapists participating in the study. Finally, she must assume that her interpretation of the research findings and of her own client is correct. As a consequence of these numerous untested and practically untestable assumptions, the specific numerical probability of success reported in the research report, evaporates. Hence, the "application" of a research finding to the treatment of a specific concrete client cannot be assigned a definite probability of success. I can only describe such "application" as an act of "faith." I agree that the usefulness of this "faith" can be empirically decidable *post facto* in each case. However, considering that the troubles of each individual derive from that person's history, and since this history is always filled with fortuitous events, I find it hard to rely with any confidence on the small differences in probability provided by formal research.

In view of the above arguments, how can Ross still maintain that, one can profit from controlled statistical research also in individual cases? I think that he can do this to some extent because of the extensive socialization of people and the extensive regularity of the social environment. Even though, the number of factors potentially influencing behavior is infinite, some may be temporarily stable within given cultural contexts. We *reckon* that people in our culture generally share our ways of interpretation and acting as they are socialized into interpreting situations and actions in similar ways. Although everything is potentially changeable in unique ways, this could be successfully ignored in some limited conditions. All kinds of people in unique life-situations may behave relatively similarly in some rule-regulated situations. However, the ubiquitous possibility of innumerable possible variations must never be ignored.

The position of Ross might appear more defensible if one asserts that the practitioner can profit only from the *general insights* derived from the middle-range theories and not from empirical predictions based on specific studies. However, then one encounters the problem that research aiming to test middle-range theories will also tend to be *pseudo-empirical.* I have tried to show this with Bandura's theory of Self-Efficacy, and Kahneman and Tversky's Prospect Theory. Other examples are Frijda's Laws of Emotion (1992), Rognes's (2007) Analysis of Wells Model of Social Phobia, and Geir Smedslund's Analysis of the Theory of Prochaska (1997). These examples appear to indicate that the value of middle-range theories does not derive from their empirical base, but from their power as explications of what we all know a priori. Little substance remains to support the programmatic claim for "empirical evidence."

The three debates at Stanford have been important to me in clarifying the issues and also in making it easier for me to understand the positions of my opponents.

My Recent Position

My recent views have been stated in a cluster of articles, beginning in (2009), continued in (2012a, b), and then in (2015, 2016a). The abstracts of these articles give a bird's eye view of my current position and serve as background for the concluding remarks.

The article from 2009 was intended to be an integrated overview of the basic shortcomings of current empiricist research. The article represents an attempt to understand my own experience after many years of having been both an academic psychologist and a professional practitioner. Increasingly, this has felt as trying to bridge an unbridgeable chasm.

> *Abstract: Psychological research and practice both start from what we all know about being human because we are human, what we know about each other because we participate in shared meaning systems (language and culture), and what we know about unique individuals. Practitioners rely on these three sources of knowledge, but researchers try to establish a fourth kind by looking for a limited number of general and empirically based regularities. However, this project runs aground because of four characteristics of person processes; they are influenced by an indefinitely high number of factors; they are sensitive to outcomes and, hence, always changeable; the regularities that can be found stem from participation in stable meaning systems already implicitly familiar; and they are unique.*

These characteristics are circumvented in the popular randomized control trial research design, but at the expense of practical relevance of the findings.

The next article (2012a) was an attempt to formulate a rationale for a new kind of professional practice, in the light of the failure of the academic tradition, and the accompanying scientist–practitioner (Boulder) model.

Abstract: A bricoleur is a resource person enlisted when conventional procedures in daily life fail to work, and who utilizes whatever is at hand in the given situation to effect a solution. The psychologist- cum bricoleur relies on three sources of knowledge: what we all know about being human because we are human, what we know about others because we participate in particular shared meaning systems (language and culture), and what we know about unique persons. Psychological treatment is seen as composed of three interacting part projects, namely building trust between psychologist and client, modifying the client's behavior, and modifying the client's surroundings. Actual interventions are formed by the concrete treatment situations. Finally, the differences between the bricoleur model and the standard scientist-practitioner model are examined.

The bricoleur model emphasizes openness to the unique, freedom from technical rules, interaction between the psychologist and other persons, and above all the central role of trust.

The last part of the trilogy was an article summarizing some of the content of what we all know about being human that serves as background for the activity of the bricoleur. It regroups and reformulates core aspects of the large-scale axiomatizations in (1988) and (1997).

Abstract: This is the third part of a trilogy. The first article is a critique of current empirical research and the second presents the bricoleur model of practice. Here, I try to describe parts of what follows from what we all know about being human because we are human. This knowledge may be partly inherited: that is, we may have an inborn disposition to understand other members of our species in certain ways. An axiomatic system consisting of nine axioms is presented and discussed. They are labelled as follows: Mentality, Intentionality, Reflectivity, Verbality, Learning, Responsibility, Morality, Feeling, and Vulnerability. The axioms are formulated partly in terms of Wierzbicka's semantic primitives, assumed to be found in all human languages. The usefulness of the axioms is taken to be testable only by general consensus.

The last two articles in the trilogy in *Theory and Psychology* were only printed after a considerable delay and, as a consequence, a broader historical and theoretical overview, written later, was published almost at the same time (2012c) in the *Scandinavian Journal of Psychology*. The partly novel contents are summarized in the abstract:

The main features of the system of psycho-logic and its historical origins, especially in the writings of Heider and Piaget, are briefly reviewed. An updated version of the axioms of psycho-logic, and a list of the semantic primitives of Wierzbicka are presented. Some foundational questions are discussed, including the genetically determined limitations of human knowledge, constructive, moral, and political nature of the approach, the role of fortuitous events, the ultimate limitations of psychological knowledge (the "balloon" to be inflated from the inside), the role of the subjective unconscious, and the implications of the approach for practice.

Finally, the group of recent articles includes two, both published in 2016, that state the ultimate implications for psychological research and practice:

Why Psychology cannot be an Empirical Science. *Integrative. Psychological and Behavioral Science*, 50, 2016a, 185–195.

Abstract: The current empirical paradigm for psychological research is criticized because it ignores the irreversibility of psychological processes, the infinite number of influential factors, the pseudo-empirical nature of many hypotheses, and the methodological implications of social interactivity. An additional point is that the differences and correlations usually found are much too small to be useful in psychological practice and in daily life. Together, these criticisms imply that an objective, accumulative, empirical and theoretical science of psychology is an impossible project

Practicing Psychology without an Empirical Evidence-Base: The Bricoleur-Model. *New Ideas in Psychology*, 2016b, 43, 50–56.

Abstract: The scientist-practitioner model is rejected, based on an earlier critique of the current paradigm for psychological research. Ten cases exemplifying a bricoleur type of practice without a discernible empirical evidence-base are briefly presented. In the absence of useful empirical scientific evidence, the bricoleur model is proposed as a possible rationale for professional psychological practice.

Together, the mentioned articles summarize my present views. It remains to describe what I see as possible steps in the future.

Prospective Epilogue

An obvious task for future researchers is to determine more securely the prevalence of *pseudo-empirical* research in contemporary psychological science. Such research aims to test hypotheses and theories whose opposite or negated content is meaningless or absurd. Only the indefinitely numerous *auxiliary* assumptions are testable. There have been many reports of pseudo-empiricality, but no large-scale systematic and representative studies have so far been conducted. If one can show a high incidence, this will confirm the general importance of logical, conceptual, and semantic analysis, in preventing unnecessary empirical work.

Another task is to determine the exact prevalence of *neuro-ornamentation* (see Chap. 5). The term denotes reference to processes in the brain that can be left out with no loss of psychological content. In my view, publications of this type are becoming increasingly frequent. Apparently, neuro-ornamentation is used to make psychological findings seem more "real" and "scientific." It remains to document the actual frequency.

A third project is to try to determine more exactly *why* pseudo-empirical studies occur. One explanation is that researchers trained in the empiricist tradition always look for empirically testable hypotheses and that they tend to select hypotheses that appear *plausible*. However, the plausibility may stem largely or exclusively from an automatic and unreflective recognition of semantic, that is, meaningful relations.

Let me use a simple example: If you *think* that something is "an approaching lion," and if you *want* to survive you will *feel* "afraid." This follows logically from the meanings of the terms, but it is also empirically true. The semantic relation also indicates an empirical relation, and this means that if a hypothesis appears to be necessary, it will also seem empirically plausible. Therefore, if researchers tend to select plausible hypotheses, they also tend to select necessary ones. This leads one to expect a very high frequency of pseudo-empirical studies.

A consequence of the preceding is that if there is *no* semantic relation between two concepts there is also no necessary empirical relation, and a general hypothesis about an invariant relation is therefore highly implausible. For example, if you think that a person wants to own a sailboat, this is no reason for thinking that he will invariably prefer pears to apples, and this lack of semantic relation also indicates that no invariant or regular relation exists. More generally, we know in advance that semantically unrelated entities are never regularly or invariantly related, and thus also that no empirical research can ever discover such relations. Absence of semantic relations means absence of general empirical relations. Absence of relation means that all four binary combinations are possible. In the given example, one can imagine finding; persons who want to buy a sailboat and prefer pears, persons who want to buy a sailboat and prefer apples, persons who do not want to buy a sailboat and prefer pears, and persons who do not want to buy a sailboat and prefer apples.

One may assume that a human language entails what is necessary, possible, and impossible to observe, in other words, an empirically relevant *psycho-logic*. Does it follow from this that each of the thousands of human languages has its own version of psycho-logic? A preliminary study of this covering the psycho-logic of trust in Arabic, Ewe, Norwegian, Tamil, Turkish, and Vietnamese is reported in (1997b), but more extensive and better analyzed work is needed.

In this chapter, I have repeatedly referred to Anna Wierzbicka's (1996) *Natural Semantic Meta Language*, and particularly to the 60+ conceptual primitives that allegedly are common to all human languages. These primitives form a logical network first noted in modern psychology by Fritz Heider (1958) in the proposition (my reformulation):

If P <u>wants</u> to <u>do</u> A in C at t, and P <u>thinks</u> that P <u>can do</u> A in C at t, and no other conditions interfere, then P will <u>try</u> to <u>do</u> A in C at t.

The English terms for conceptual primitives are underlined, *C* = context, *t* = time.

Many of the conceptual primitives are logically independent, for example, *want* and *think,* but others are logically connected, for example *want, think,* and *feel* (if you *want* something and *think* something about the situation, then what you *feel* follows necessarily.)

Finally, I would like to mention a dilemma that has occupied me throughout my career. It is generally known, and is probably also age-old, but it has kept bothering me, first as an experimenter and then as a practitioner: On the one hand, I have felt an urge to find something *truly genera*l; some stable knowledge to be discovered by controlled research, or at least some stable guidelines in trying to help patients. On the other hand, I have felt an equally strong urge to remain as *open* as possible to the unlimited richness of variation in people and situations that I encounter. This conflict is obviously related to philosophical debates about nominalism versus realism, going on at least since the Middle Ages.

As a student, I admired the ancient mathematicians who discovered eternally valid and practically useful geometrical principles, Newtonian physics and calculus, the periodic table of elements, the double helix, etc. However, I soon came to think that the effort to find "Laws" in psychology has failed entirely because of intrinsic characteristics of the field, and that contemporary "middle range theories" and "models" based on statistical findings are much too weak to support psychological practice. The now popular "qualitative research" does keep close to the rich phenomenological world, but has also failed to produce generally valid knowledge.

Trying to balance generality and openness, my work has, nevertheless, generated two basic principles.

One of them is the circular relation between objective observation and subjective understanding, leaving understanding as the only viable option for psychology. This means that psychology must be the study of what exists *for* persons.

The other is the indefinitely high number of auxiliary hypotheses, or presuppositions (contexts) taken for granted in every psychological hypothesis. This means that one cannot find entirely stable and generally valid propositions in psychology, and that regularities in psychology always reflect temporary *dynamic equilibria* maintained by stable consequences.

Looking back, I can see that my work both has profited and suffered from the loneliness of my undertaking. With one exception, I have published around 150 articles and 7 books as single author. This relative isolation has enabled me to avoid being smothered by immediate counterarguments, and, has left me undisturbed to develop some relatively original perspectives. On the other hand, the loneliness has prevented me from profiting from closer cooperation with able colleagues. Only after having already stabilized my own position, have I been able to profit from debates.

There is probably no definite answer to the question of the relative importance of isolation and cooperation in basic research. I will never know if I could have achieved more by working continuously with others.

In conclusion, I will refer to my last conversation with Ken Hammond who was then 88 years old. We heartily agreed on one thing; it has been fun!

References

Bandura, A. (1977). Self-efficacy: Toward a unifying theory of behavioral change. *Psychological Review, 84*, 191–215.

Bandura, A. (1978). On distinguishing between logical and empirical verification. . A comment on Smedslund. *Scandinavian Journal of Psychology, 19*, 1997–1999.

Heider, F. (1958). *The psychology of interpersonal relations*. New York: Wiley.

Rognes, W. (2007). Well's kognitive modell for sosial fobi: En analyse. *Psykologisk Tidsskrift, 1*, 40–48.

Smedslund, G. (1997). Some psychological theories are not empirical: A conceptual analysis of the "stages of change model". *Theory and Psychology, 1997, 7*(4), 529–544.
Smedslund, J. (1959). Apprentissage des notions de la conservation et de la transitivité du poids. *Études d'Épistemologie génétique, 9*, 85–124.
Smedslund, J. (1961). The utilization of probabilistic cues after 1100 and 4800 stimulus presentations. *Acta Psychologica, 18*, 383–386.
Smedslund, J. (1966). Constancy and conservation: A comparison of the systems of Brunswik and Piaget. In Hammond, K. R. (Ed.) The psychology of Egon Brunswik. New York: Holt, Rinehart and Winston. 382–404.
Smedslund, J. (1969). Meanings, implications and universals: Towards a psychology of man. *Scandinavian Journal of Psychology, 10*, 1–15.
Smedslund, J. (1970). Circular relation between understanding and logic. *Scandinavian Journal of Psychology, 11*, 217–219.
Smedslund, J. (1978). Bandura's theory of self-efficacy: A set of common sense theorems. *Scandinavian Journal of Psychology, 19*, 1–14.
Smedslund, J. (1988). *Psycho-logic*. Heidelberg: Springer-Verlag.
Smedslund, J. (1990). A critique of Tversky & Kahneman's distinction between fallacy and misunderstanding. *Scandinavian Journal of Psychology, 31*, 110–120.
Smedslund, J. (1991a). The pseudoempirical in psychology and the case for psychologic. *Psychological Inquiry, 2*, 325–338. (Target article).
Smedslund, J. (1991b). Psychologic: A technical language for psychology. *Psychological Inquiry, 2*, 376–382. (Author's response).
Smedslund, J. (1992). Are Frijda's "Laws of Emotion" empirical? *Cognition and Emotion, 6*, 435–456.
Smedslund, J. (1997a). *The structure of psychological common sense*. Mahwah, NJ: Erlbaum.
Smedslund, J. (1997b). Is the "psychologic" of trust universal? In S. Niemeier & R. Dirven (Eds.), *The language of emotions* (pp. 3–13). Amsterdam: John Benjamins.
Smedslund, J. (1999). Author's response: Psychologic in dialogue – Reply to commentaries. *Scandinavian Journal of Psychology, 40*(Suppl. 1), 123–138.
Smedslund, J. (2009). The mismatch between current research methods and the nature of psychological phenomena. *Theory & Psychology, 19*, 778–794.
Smedslund, J. (2012a). The bricoleur model of psychological practice. *Theory & Psychology, 22*, 643–657.
Smedslund, J. (2012b). What follows from what we all know about human beings. *Theory & Psychology, 22*, 658–668.
Smedslund, J. (2012c). Psycho-logic: Some thoughts and after-thoughts. *Scandinavian Journal of Psychology, 53*, 295–302.
Smedslund, J. (2015). The value of experiments in psychology. In J. Martin, J. Slugarman & K. Slaney (Eds.). *The Wiley Handbook of Theoretical and Philosophical Psychology: Methods, Approaches, and New Directions for Social Sciences*. Wiley-Blackwell, 359–373.
Smedslund, J. (2016a). Why psychology cannot be an empirical science. *Integrative Psychological and Behavioral Science, 50*, 185–195.
Smedslund, J. (2016b). Practicing psychology without an empirical evidence-base: The Bricoleur-model. *New Ideas in Psychology, 43*, 50–56.
Smedslund, J., & Ross, L. (2014). Research-based knowledge in psychology: What, if anything, is its incremental value to the practitioner? *Integrative Psychological and Behavioral Science, 43*(4), 363–383.
Tversky, A., & Kahneman, D. (1983). Extensional versus intuitive reasoning: The conjunction fallacy in probability judgment. *Psychological Review, 90*, 293–315.
Wierzbicka, A. (1996). *Semantics: Primes and universals*. New York: Oxford University Press.

Chapter 3
A Place for Persons: The Formal Systems of Smedslund and Ossorio

Mary Kathleen Roberts

> [What is the number one? What does the symbol 1 mean? ...] Questions like these catch even mathematicians, or most of them, unprepared with any satisfactory answer. Yet is it not a scandal that our science should be so unclear about the first and foremost among its objects, and one which is apparently so simple? ... If a concept fundamental to a mighty science gives rise to difficulties, then it is surely an imperative task to investigate it more closely until those difficulties are overcome. (Frege 1884/1980, p. ii)

What is a person? What is behavior? *Pace* Frege, we may note that questions like these catch psychologists, or most of us, unprepared with any satisfactory answers. On the whole, the inability to answer these fundamental questions about our subject matter has not been a matter of concern. It has been enough to claim that persons and behavior are what we study. In contrast, for Jan Smedslund and Peter G. Ossorio, it was imperative to give scientifically viable answers.

Because of the chilly reception their work often received, both men valued the mutual respect they shared. In 1983, when Smedslund was beginning to formulate his thoughts about a psycho-logic, he invited Ossorio to do a presentation at the University of Oslo (Smedslund 2013, pp. 86–87). He later acknowledged Ossorio not only as one of the people he had "profited from reading" (Smedslund 1988a, p. *vii*), but also as one of the people whose sympathy enabled him to persevere in the years until his initial version of Psycho-logic was completed (Smedslund 2013, p. 89). Ossorio (1991) recognized Smedslund's achievement, writing, "I am pretty well in complete sympathy with Smedslund's basic position, and I believe his program is valuable and viable" (p. 354).

In the literature, their names have been linked in connection with "common sense accounts of human action" (Shotter and Burton 1983, p. 272); "the non-empirical quality of much social psychological research" (Davis 1995, p. *xiii*); "constructionist inquiry ... directed to the axioms or fundamental propositions underlying descriptions of persons in present-day society" (Gergen 1985, p. 5); "attempts to locate basic suppositions that underlie cultural (and scientific) knowledge about the mind" (Gergen 1987, p. 121); and the "implicit recognition of the

M. K. Roberts (✉)
Independent Scholar, University of Colorado, Boulder, CO, USA
e-mail: tee.roberts@ieee.org

T. G. Lindstad et al. (eds.), *Respect for Thought*, Theory and History in the Human and Social Sciences, https://doi.org/10.1007/978-3-030-43066-5_3

causal networks associated with common terms" (Kelley 1992, p. 19). These descriptions reflect varying degrees of understanding—and misunderstanding—of what they were doing.

For this volume on Smedslund's legacy, I have been asked to write about similarities and differences in the systems they created, Psycho-logic (Smedslund 1988a, 1997, 2002) and the Person Concept (Ossorio 1966/1995, 1982/1998, 2006). In addition, I will place their systems in a wider, historical context in the hope of contributing to a greater understanding of their work. To keep the paper within reasonable limits, I will not be discussing applications of the systems. Psycho-logic has been used successfully in critiquing pseudo-empirical research (Smedslund 2002) and in formulating the bricoleur model for clinical practice (Smedslund 2012c). These applications are discussed by other authors in this volume. The Person Concept has also been used in a range of applications, summarized by Ossorio (1983b).

An additional note of clarification about Ossorio's work may be helpful. Ossorio designates his four-component conceptual system as the "Person Concept," and the social enterprise of using the Person Concept and related formulations as "Descriptive Psychology" (cf. Ossorio 1971/1978, p. xii and p. 15). Because I will be focusing on the conceptual system rather than its use, I will speak primarily of the Person Concept. The capitalization serves to distinguish Ossorio's formal system from the concept of a person we all share.

Methodology

Since antiquity, there have been prescriptions for how to invent and discover new truths ("the context of discovery"), how to justify them ("the context of justification"), and how to present them in a compelling way. For a substantive contribution to be taken seriously by the members of a scientific community, the methodological rules of that community must be followed. In the world of quantitative research, for example, a discovery will not be eligible for the status of "scientific" unless the appropriate experimental methods are used to confirm or refute it, and its probability is reported from a third-person point of view ("It has been shown at the .001 level…"). But what if a scientist is not discovering or justifying new truths? What if the task is presenting a concept that we have all mastered and use every day? How can that be accomplished?

The Axiomatic Method

One time-honored option is to use the axiomatic method. As David Hilbert, the mathematician who achieved the first rigorous axiomatization of Euclidean geometry, expressed it:

> The axiomatic method is now and for all time the instrument suited to the human mind and indispensable for every exact enquiry, whatever its field may be. It is logically unassailable, and at the same time, fruitful. It also preserves for the enquirer the most complete liberty of movement. To proceed axiomatically in this sense is simply to think with knowledge of what one is about. (cited in Kneale and Kneale 1962/2008, p. 684).

This was the method of choice for Smedslund in creating his system. He knew that it was held in "disrepute" by modern psychologists. Nonetheless, he hoped with the help of an analogy to geometry, they would see why it was well suited for his task (Smedslund 1978, pp. 11–13). Instead, the majority reacted strongly to the fact that he was treating his axioms as true in the absence of empirical data.

The battles that ensued over the methodological status of his axioms in some ways mirrored those that had been fought in the early twentieth century over the status of Hilbert's axioms. Were they timeless, eternal truths? Conventions of a particular time and place? Definitions in disguise? Articulations of formal relationships? (cf. Coffa 1991)

For Smedslund's axioms, Harré (1999) proposed using the Kantian terminology of "synthetic a priori" with a Wittgensteinian interpretation: if the axioms are negated, they are not false but senseless. In response to Harré, Smedslund tentatively accepted that suggestion: "The psychologic propositions may, perhaps, best be characterized in terms of traditional philosophical categories as *synthetic* (not analytic) and *a priori* (not empirical)" (1999, p. 124). He affirms in his autobiography that "axioms [are] impossible to deny because their negations do not make sense" (Smedslund 2013, p. 110).

Later, when Kukla's *Methods of Theoretical Psychology* was published, Smedslund resonated to his discussion of the "contingent a priori" and reassigned his axioms to that status. As Kukla (2001) notes, "the major historical contrast in the realm of the contingent a priori is between Kantian and Kuhnian presuppositions. The former are grounded, fundamental, universal, inborn, inflicted, and not revisable. The latter are ungrounded, specific, idiosyncratic, acquired, adopted, and revisable" (p. 225). Smedslund seems to have had the Kantian variety in mind when he made his status assignment.

Conceptual–Notational Devices

In delineating the Person Concept, Ossorio made different choices regarding methodology. Rather than putting forth propositions to be accepted as truths, Ossorio emphasized that he was *presenting a conceptual framework*, for which truth was not an issue.

To help students understand the idea of a conceptual framework, he sometimes used the analogy of a bookkeeping system. In a bookkeeping system for a business, the account sheets in a general ledger have columns such as "date," "item," "debit," "credit," and "balance." Each of these headings holds a place for facts about business transactions. Taken together, the headings organize the facts into a form useful to a businessman. Historical facts that are entered into the ledger can be true or false (e.g., "Is it true that a Stradivarius sold in June for 2.5 million?"), but the form itself cannot be.

Accordingly, there are reminders throughout Ossorio's work that he is reminding, prescribing, instructing, etc., but he is not making true statements. In *"What Actually Happens,"* for example, he emphasizes: "The declarative sentences in the present paper should not be understood as statements, but rather as instructions or exhortations modeled on the lines of 'Notice this … aspect of the conceptual structure I am *presenting herewith'*." (1971/1978, p. 65). In *Meaning and Symbolism*, he writes: "In a preliminary way, let us note that in the absence of propositions there are neither hypotheses nor deductions nor implications" (1969/2010, p. 127). More polemically, he points out in *Persons*: "For concepts no questions of 'true' or 'false' can arise at all, since they are not statements. And because they are not statements, neither can they be derived from any premises… If a concept is *presented* in declarative sentences… that will, in the present account, be generally in the service of delineation rather than an impossible and quite irrelevant claim to Truth" (1966/1995, p. 235).

In lieu of making true statements, Ossorio used a small set of conceptual–notational devices—parametric analyses, calculational systems, paradigm case formulations, and definitions—as resources in formulating and presenting the Person Concept (Ossorio 1979/1981). The use of parametric analysis was familiar to most psychologists because of the Munsell color system, in which colors are distinguished on the basis of Hue, Saturation, and Brightness. These are the parameters of color, i.e., the ways in which one color, as such, can be the same as another color or different from it. Taken together, they constitute a parametric analysis, which can be expressed by the formula <C> = <H, S, B>.

In a parallel manner, a parametric analysis of behavior can be created by answering the question, i.e., "What are the ways in which one behavior, as such, can be the same as another behavior or different from it?" In the Person Concept, the resulting analysis involves eight parameters, presented in Table 3.1. The form of behavior codified in the analysis is identified as Intentional Action (IA), and its

Table 3.1 Parameters of Intentional Action

I	Identity	Whose behavior it is
W	Want	A wanted state of affairs (the "motivational" aspect of behavior)
K	Know	What distinctions are being acted upon (the "cognitive" aspect of behavior)
KH	Know how	The relevant learning history (the "competence" aspect of behavior)
P	Performance	The process that occurs (the "procedural" aspect of behavior)
A	Achievement	Whatever is different in the world by virtue of the occurrence of the behavior (the "outcome" aspect of behavior)
PC	Person characteristic	The person characteristics that the behavior is an expression of
S	Significance	What the person is doing by engaging in the performance (the "meaningful" and/or "ulterior" aspect of the behavior)

formula is <B> = <IA> = <I, W, K, KH, P, A, PC, S>. This formula is used as the initial element in another conceptual–notational device, a calculational system.

The idea of calculational systems dealing with non-mathematical content is not new. In the seventeenth century, Gottfried Leibniz (1646–1716) wrote that "Not all formulas signify quantity. We can conceive of an infinite number of ways of calculating" (quoted in Kneale and Kneale 1962/2008, p. 336). Over the centuries, Leibniz's work inspired others to experiment with calculational systems that had nothing to do with numbers or space. Smedslund (2012b), for example, characterizes his system as a calculus of common sense: "The axiomatic system of psychologic can also be characterized as an attempt to create a calculus from our common knowledge, instead of leaving it an unanalyzed collection or fragments. A calculus is a system allowing one to derive a large number of predictions from a small number of assumptions" (p. 660).

In the Person Concept, calculational systems follow a specific model, the "Element-Operation-Product" model. In this model, (a) when an Operation is performed on an Element, the result is a Product, and (b) whatever is a Product is also an Element (cf. Ossorio 2006, pp. 39–40). The Elements are not assumptions, however, and the Products are not predictions because calculational systems are used to generate forms or structures rather than truths.

In the calculational system for behavior, the Operations are Identity, Substitution, and Deletion, and the initial Element is the Intentional Action (IA) formula. When we perform the initial operation of Substitution, what we substitute is the IA formula, i.e., we use the IA formula as a partial specification of the value of a parameter in that formula. The Product that is generated is itself a parametric analysis, but one of greater complexity than the original. It may in turn be used as an Element or in specifying the value of a parameter. Canonical forms of description that result from Substitution operations are listed in Table 3.2.

When we perform the Deletion operation, either on the original IA formula or on a generated Product, we remove a parameter from consideration, creating a parametric analysis that is simpler than the Element that was used. By calculating recursively and reflexively with the formulas in this way, we can generate forms of whatever degree of complexity is needed for representing facts and possible facts about behavior.

Primary Concept

In delineating the concepts of person and behavior, a system-designer has a choice not only about what methodology to use, but also about which of the concepts to take as primary. If "person" is identified as primary, then behavior can be treated as what a person does. Alternatively, if "behavior" is taken as primary, then a person can be treated as an individual who does that (cf. Ossorio 2006, p. 69). Either approach works because the concepts are so closely connected.

Table 3.2 Calculational system for behavior

Element	Operation	Product
<I, W, K, KH, P, A, PC, S>	Substitution	<I, W, <B>, KH, P, A, PC, S> Cognizant Action formula
"	Substitution	<I, <B>, <B>, KH, P, A, PC, S> Deliberate Action formula
"	Substitution	<I, W, K, KH, P, <B>, PC, S> Social practice formula
"	Substitution	<I, W, K, KH, <B>, A, PC, S> Symbolic behavior formula Significance description
"	Deletion	<θ, W, K, KH, P, A, θ, θ> Agency description
"	Deletion	<θ, θ, K, KH, P, A, θ, θ> Activity description
"	Deletion	<θ, θ, θ, θ, P, A, θ, θ> Performance description
"	Deletion	<θ, θ, θ, θ, θ, A, θ, θ> Achievement description
"	Deletion	<θ, W, K, KH, P, θ, θ, θ> Performative description
"	Deletion	<θ, θ, K, θ, P, θ, θ, θ> <θ, θ, K, θ, θ, A, θ, θ> <θ, θ, K, θ, P, A, θ, θ> Stimulus-response descriptions
"	Identity	<I, W, K, KH, P, A, PC, S> Intentional Action

Person

In formulating Psycho-logic, Smedslund makes the primary identification that of "person." He asks specifically, "What is a person *to another person*?," using the phrase in italics to emphasize that "a person is nothing "in itself," but always as seen by someone, including the person him/herself" (2012a, p. 297). His axioms are answers to that question, expressed in the form, "P takes it for granted that O…," where P and O are both persons.

Fitting with his assignment of the axioms to the status of contingent a priori truths, there is a Kantian quality to his discussion of persons. In his *Critique of Pure Reason*, Kant (1781/1996) claimed that there are pure forms of intuition and understanding that are "in us prior to the perception of any object" (B41). All the objects of which we can have knowledge must conform to these a priori forms because without them, "no experience takes place" (A664/B692).

Similarly, Smedslund (2013) talks about his axioms as expressing "unavoidable inborn views of the characteristics of other persons" (p. 90). He emphasizes that they "do not originate *in* experiences of other persons, but determine *how* these other persons are experienced" (2012a, p. 300). In a more biological idiom, he writes that "our basic conceptual framework regarding people … ultimately depends on genetically constituted characteristics of *Homo sapiens*" (2012a, p. 297).

The substantive content of his axioms is, nonetheless, independent of his belief about what is inborn and/or inherited. As he notes, "One could disregard the question of whether these [axioms] describe inherited characteristics of all members of the species *Homo sapiens*, or merely refer to what all members of this species must learn very early because of commonalities in the life conditions of all humans" (2012b, pp. 665–666).

In light of his formulation of "person," "behavior" is treated as what a person does. His Intentionality Axiom—"P takes it for granted that what O knows, thinks, feels, perceives, says, and does, is partly directed by what O wants."—deals explicitly with the cognitive and motivational aspects of human behavior and provides a framework for understanding the behavior of persons as we take it to be (Smedslund 2012a, p. 297).

Behavior

Instead of taking "person" as primary, Ossorio makes the opposite choice: he takes "behavior" as the primary concept and defines a "person" as an individual who does that. As we have seen, his formulation of behavior is given by a calculational system with the parametric analysis of Intentional Action as its initial Element.

His definition of a Person is "an individual whose history is, paradigmatically, a history of Deliberate Action in a dramaturgical pattern" (Ossorio 2006, p. 69). As shown in Table 3.2, Deliberate Action is one of the forms of behavior generated by use of the Substitution Operation. From the formula <B> = <DA> = <I, <B>, <B>, KH, P, A, PC, S>, we can see that in Deliberate Action, a person knows what he is doing (reflected in the Substitution of a Behavior formula as a partial specification of the Know parameter) and chooses to do it (reflected in the Substitution of a Behavior formula as a partial specification of the Want parameter).

The use of "paradigmatically" in the definition tells us that a Paradigm Case Formulation (PCF)—one of the conceptual–notational devices listed above—is implicitly involved. We need the logic of Paradigm Case Formulation because "what is conceptually necessary to being a person is not literally found universally in persons" (Ossorio 2006, p. 32). In infancy, we do not yet have a history of Deliberate Action. Moreover, throughout our lives there are times when we are exhausted, asleep, intoxicated, etc., and not engaging in Deliberate Action. The "paradigmatically" reminds us not to take the definition as a claim of empirical universality.

Notice, too, that the definition is in terms of a history. Although a poet may find "character isolated by a deed," in the Person Concept the size of the unit for conceptualizing a person is a life history. Thus, in addressing the question of similarities and differences among persons, Ossorio asks, "How can one life history, as such, be the same as another life history or different from it?"

He does not assume that persons are specimens of Homo sapiens. Instead, he introduces the following distinctions:

- A human being is an individual who is a person and a specimen of Homo sapiens.
- An alien being is an individual who is a person and has a biological embodiment other than that of Homo sapiens.
- A robot is an individual who is a person and has a non-biological embodiment.

Given that all the individuals who have been recognized so far by us as persons are human beings, why would Ossorio create placeholders for persons with alternative embodiments?

One reason is that the Person Concept is a system designed to provide formal access to all the facts and possible facts concerning persons and their behavior. If we do not have these alternative embodiments available conceptually as possibilities, we cannot establish them observationally as actualities. The "bookkeeping" therefore includes a placeholder for "Embodiment" as one of the ways that one life history can be the same as or different from another.

In addition to their formal significance, the subcategories had a pragmatic significance for Ossorio. Over the years, he was involved in a variety of artificial intelligence projects through his businesses (e.g., Ossorio and Kurtz 1989; Kurtz et al. 1990). The policy that guided those projects—"Don't treat people as defective computers; treat computers as defective people"—reflected the possibility of creating persons with non-biological embodiment. Moreover, in the years when he was working with scientists and engineers at NASA, there was genuine concern with the question, "If we encounter persons with an embodiment different from ours, how will we recognize them as persons?"

Universality

Formal systems are the products of particular individuals at particular times and places in history making particular design choices. How can their creators claim that their systems are applicable to other times and other places? On what basis does Smedslund say that the axioms of Psycho-logic are cross-cultural truths? On what grounds does Ossorio (1982/1983a) speak of his calculational system for behavior as a "universal formulation" (p. 14)?

Cross-Cultural Truths

Smedslund, challenged on these and related issues by reviewers (e.g., Valsiner 1985; Cushman 1991), formulated the problem in terms of two questions: (a) Is Psycho-logic translatable from English to other languages? (b) Is there consensus among native speakers of other languages that the axioms are true and valid?

In dealing with the question of translatability, Smedslund was drawn to Natural Semantic Metalanguage (NSM), which is made up of more than 60 "universal human concepts" identified on the basis of lexical analysis (Goddard and Wierzbicka 2014). These "semantic primitives"—concepts like "know," "think," "feel," "want," "say," "do"—are said to be present in the lexicons of all natural languages. Smedslund knew that NSM was controversial, but nonetheless decided to rewrite the axioms of Psycho-logic insofar as possible using the primitive concepts of NSM. In this way, he hoped to insure both their translatability and universality (cf. Smedslund 2012b, p. 660).

In dealing with the question of consensus, Smedslund conducted eight studies in which participants were asked to judge the validity or truth of his propositions, as well as to choose between alternative statements inferred from his propositions. Participants in the studies included native speakers of English, Norwegian, Urdu, Ewe, Arabic, Turkish, Tamil, and Vietnamese. Overall, the results showed extremely high consensus, ranging from 92% to 98% (cf. Smedslund 2002, pp. 64–67).

The Multilevel Structure of Behavior

In understanding Ossorio's approach to universality, making the distinction between two of the parameters of Intentional Action—Performance and Significance—is crucial. Performance is the concrete, easily observable, process aspect of behavior, and Significance is what the person is doing *by* engaging in that Performance. For example, if I practice cello *by* playing scales, "playing scales" is a partial specification of the value of the Performance parameter, and "practicing cello" is a partial specification of the Significance parameter of my behavior.

A given Performance can have more than one Significance. If we keep asking, "What is she doing *by* doing that?," we can generate a series of answers.

Q1. What is she doing?

A1. She's playing scales.

Q2. What is she doing by playing scales?

A2. She's practicing cello.

Q3. What is she doing by practicing cello?

A3. She's preparing for rehearsals.

Q4. What is she doing by preparing for rehearsals?

A4. She's preparing for a concert.

Q5. What is she doing by preparing for a concert?

A5. She's making a living.

Q6. What is she doing by doing that?

A6. She's living the life of a professional musician.

Q7. What is she doing by doing that?

A7. She's living the life of a Norwegian, and that's her way of doing it.

This sequence may be represented using the Symbolic Behavior formula, <B> = <I, W, K, KH, <B>, A, PC, S>, in which a Behavior formula is substituted as a partial specification of the Performance parameter. Behaviors higher in the question–answer sequence have as the value of their Performance parameter any or all of the Behaviors lower in the sequence. For example, if we ask, "How does she prepare for a concert?" (A4), the answer may be "by playing scales" (A1), "by practicing" (A2), "by preparing for rehearsals" (A3), or all three.

The Symbolic Behavior formula makes it easy to see human behavior as a multilevel phenomenon with a minimum of two levels involved, both of which are necessary for representing the facts about what a person is doing. In mainstream psychology, when we take it that the Performance is what the behavior *really* is and do not have a placeholder for its Significance, we create confusion because our bookkeeping is inadequate for the facts.

As Ossorio (1982/1983a) writes, "the Significance parameter provides an opportunity to represent the part-whole relation between a given, historically occurring behavior and the historical, societal, and cultural configurations within which it can and does take place… Since every human behavior is *essentially* the historical realization of cultural patterns, understanding the behavior requires a knowledge of what those patterns are and what part the individual behavior has in those patterns" (pp. 15–16).

The Person Concept therefore includes a variety of additional resources for representing cultural patterns. The Social Practice formula, <B> = <I, W, K, KH, P, <B>, PC, S>, in which a Behavior formula is substituted as a partial specification of the Achievement parameter, allows us to represent one behavior as the outcome of another, and to represent patterns involving the behavior of more than one person. When a finer level of detail is needed, Process Representations from the Reality component of the Person Concept are available (cf. Ossorio 1971/1978). For multicultural analysis, there is a parametric analysis of culture (cf. Ossorio 1982/1983a).

Rather than being universal by virtue of specifying truths accepted in every culture, the calculational system for behavior is universal in that it allows us to generate whatever forms we need to distinguish and characterize different behaviors, types of behavior, social practices, ways of living, etc. The specific content that is represented using the forms will depend on a particular culture's own concepts, and of course will vary across individuals, groups, and cultures.

Historical Context

Just as with any choice of behavior, the choices of Smedslund and Ossorio in designing their systems can be understood more fully by understanding the historical and cultural context within which those choices were made. We therefore turn our attention to the wider context in which Psycho-logic and the Person Concept were achieved. After a "slice of history" is presented in this section, connections to Smedslund and Ossorio are made in the next section.

Modern Logic

In the opening decades of the twentieth century, there was intense excitement—as well as intense conflict—about logic. It was not the simple, fixed forms of Aristotelian logic that generated the buzz, of course. It was the new symbolic logic of Gottlob Frege. In his 1879 pamphlet, *Begriffsschrift*, Frege had presented a conceptual–notational system in which it was possible to create forms of unprecedented complexity by calculating with logical symbols. In addition to presenting notational symbols, Frege stated nine simple axioms that governed their use. The use of axioms was not customary in logic, but Frege wanted his logic to be a deductive system like Euclid's, the standard for rigor for two millennia (cf. Kneale and Kneale 1962/2008, p. 530).

Like Euclid, Frege set forth his axioms as necessary truths, not requiring proof because they were clear and obvious, and then proved his propositions by logical deduction from the axioms. In a demand that went "beyond Euclid," Frege (1893/2013) required that *everything* involved be stated explicitly, including the rules of inference (p. vi). His ultimate goal was to prove that all the truths of arithmetic were "timeless truths" and could be derived from logic.

Independently of Frege, Alfred North Whitehead and Bertrand Russell had been working on a similar project, using a notational system invented by an Italian mathematician, Giuseppe Peano. Like Frege, they took Euclidean geometry as the model for their work, but their project was more ambitious. They wanted to demonstrate that all the truths of mathematics, not merely the truths of arithmetic, had their foundation in logic. In 1910, 1912, and 1913, Whitehead and Russell published their axiomatic system in the three-volume *Principia Mathematica*, their title an allusion to Newton's *Principia*.

For Frege, Whitehead and Russell, it was a given that logic was a tool for making deductive inferences. How could it be otherwise? But at the same time they were working out their rigorous, formal proofs, a different conception of logic was gaining traction—logic as a tool for the characterization of structure.

This new understanding was reflected in the work of David Hilbert, a German mathematician. In 1899, Hilbert published a monograph in which he gave an explicit, rigorous formulation of all the axioms of Euclid's geometry. In doing so, he did not presuppose the meanings of concepts like "points," "lines," and "planes." In fact, he wrote to Frege that these words could be replaced by arbitrary symbols, as long as it was understood that he was *defining* the logical relations between them. The ordinary meanings of the terms were irrelevant in Hilbert's approach. What mattered were the relationships expressed in the logical structure created by the axioms, independent of the subject matter in question.

If an axiomatic system is approached in this way, then what are axioms? Are they still true statements? In response to that question, Jules Poincaré, a French mathematician, claimed that we had been fooled by axioms. They had the appearance of being true statements, but they were really operating as undercover definitions, giving meaning to the primitive terms in a geometric system. He created a new status, "definition in disguise," and assigned axioms to that status. In light of the status change—from "necessary truth" to "definition in disguise"—Poincaré (1905/2007) wrote:

> What, then, are we to think of the question: Is Euclidean geometry true? It has no meaning. We might as well ask if the metric system is true, and if the old weights and measures are false; if Cartesian co-ordinates are true and polar co-ordinates false. One geometry cannot be more true than another; it can only be more convenient. (p. 50)

Hilbert championed the new field of metamathematics, devoted to evaluating axiomatic systems. Instead of focusing on truth, metamathematicians asked questions like, "Is the system of axioms complete?" "Are the axioms consistent?" "Are the axioms independent?" Questions regarding the empirical interpretation of axioms and their representational adequacy were set aside for others to address.

Inspired or infuriated by ideas like these, mathematicians and logicians divided into the warring schools of "logicism" (with Frege, Whitehead, and Russell), "formalism" (with Hilbert and Poincaré), and "intuitionism" (with an emphasis on the intuitive nature of mathematics). When Einstein published his general theory of relativity in 1915, conflict between the groups intensified in light of Einstein's use of a non-Euclidean axiomatization of geometry.

Logical Positivists

When Ossorio was born in 1926 and Smedslund in 1929, the Berlin Circle and a closely related group, the Vienna Circle, were working to understand the revolutionary changes taking place in logic, mathematics, and physics. Contrary to the popular stereotype, the interest of these groups in the 1920s and early 1930s was not primarily in empiricism or verification. Their focus was on clarifying the concept of a priori knowledge (Friedman 1999, p. *xv*).

Hans Reichenbach (1920/1965), the leader of the Berlin Circle, appreciated Hilbert's formulation of axiom systems as pure conceptual structures, not connected with any particular empirical content. But for science, Reichenbach (1920/1965) argued, these pure systems must be "coordinated" to concrete, observable phenomena. "Axioms of coordination" must be specified to give meaning to the terms in a formal structure and to create a framework in which genuinely empirical statements can be evaluated. Unlike a priori principles that are universal and "true for all times," coordinating principles are theory-relative and subject to change (1920/1965, p. 48).

Rudolf Carnap, a leader of the Vienna Circle, was initially part of the logistic school but later changed to a formalist approach. After the switch, Carnap treated scientific theories as interpreted axiomatic systems. For the fields of set theory, arithmetic, geometry, physics, and biology, he presented axiom systems written in symbolic logic, emphasizing that the axioms defined the pre-empirical, linguistic frameworks of the respective sciences (Carnap 1958). In his systems, he carefully distinguished between syntax, e.g., rules for the formation of expressions, and semantics, rules for the intended interpretation.

Participants in the Circles used symbolic logic in their discussions as well as in their writing and were almost passionate about its use. For example, Arne Naess, a Norwegian philosopher and member of the Vienna Circle in 1934 and 1935 wrote:

> Why did I use elementary symbolic logic when stating theorems and conceptual structures in *Interpretation and Preciseness*? I did it both for economy of expressions and beauty. Very early in life, I admired *Principia Mathematica* by Bertrand Russell and Alfred North Whitehead. The notation I adopted follows that of David Hilbert and Wilhelm Ackerman's beautiful textbook of symbolic logic (1950). It is a sheer joy to follow their proofs! (2005, p. *lxxi*)

Independently of these developments in Europe, an American psychologist, Clark L. Hull, was developing his own views on the use of logic in psychology. While he was teaching at Harvard in the summer of 1929, Hull had met Alfred North Whitehead, who introduced him not only to *Principia Mathematica* but also to Newton's *Principia* (Smith 1986, p. 165). Inspired by the way Newton had modeled his system on Euclidean geometry, Hull (1935, 1937) published two "miniature systems" that used the deductive method, one for the subject matter of rote learning and one for adaptive behavior. These mini-systems brought him into contact with members of the Vienna Circle, and Otto Neurath and Arne Naess (quoted above) encouraged him in his work. His magnum opus, *Principles of Behavior* (Hull 1943), with its opening chapter extolling the virtues of the axiomatic method, became "one of the most influential books in psychology's history" (Hergenhahn and Henley 2014, p. 414).

Ordinary Language Philosophers

Not everyone was enamored with symbolic logic—an "artificial" or "ideal" language. Ludwig Wittgenstein, who met with some of the members of the Vienna Circle in the 1920s, returned to Cambridge in 1927 and turned his attention to the everyday use of language, i.e., to the pragmatics of language rather than its syntax or semantics. To gain insight into the use of language, Wittgenstein recommended focusing on "language-games"—games like giving orders, telling a story, making a joke, guessing riddles, asking, thanking, cursing, greeting, and praying. He encouraged keeping "the multiplicity of language-games in view" and understanding these language-games as part of a form of life (1958, §23–24).

Wittgenstein rejected a number of tenets of the logical positivists, including the idea that symbolic logic would help reveal the structure hidden beneath ordinary language. He wrote that "Nothing is concealed… Nothing is hidden… Everything lies open to view" (1958, §435 & §126). He also emphasized that ordinary language is not deficient in any way, not vague or misleading, and not in need of rewriting in logical form.

Wittgenstein's ideas, circulating in notes and manuscripts in the 1930s and 1940s, were inspirational for philosophers at Oxford as well as Cambridge. Gilbert Ryle (1949), in *The Concept of Mind*, focused on the ordinary use of psychological terms to show what was wrong with talking about the mind in the same way we talk about the body. J. L. Austin (1955), in *How to Do Things with Words*, emphasized that many utterances are the performance of actions, e.g., to say "I now pronounce you man and wife" is to perform a marriage under the right conditions. P. F. Strawson (1959), in a move away from Wittgenstein, sought "to lay bare the most general features of our conceptual structure" through an analysis of everyday language (p. 9).

Fritz Heider

Fritz Heider was an Austrian philosopher, psychologist, and free spirit. He had contact with the logical positivists in the 1920s and resonated to Carnap's formulation of conceptual explication as a scientific tool. In his *The Psychology of Interpersonal Relations*, Heider (1958) notes: "Carnap (1953) has referred to this task of redefining old concepts as the problem of explication; he points out that making more exact a concept that is used 'in a more or less vague way either in every-day language or in an earlier stage of scientific language' is often important in the development of science and mathematics" (p. 9). Heider developed his own notation "to explicate the conglomerate terms of everyday language," a notation with "some of the features of symbolic logic without pretending to be as exact and systematic" (1958, p. 299, p. 15). He also found the ideas of Gilbert Ryle "stimulating" (p. 12). From the various schools of thought of his time, including some not mentioned here, Heider created a unique synthesis for understanding interpersonal behavior.

Connections

Psycho-logic and the Person Concept are out of joint with mainstream empirical psychology, but fit in the wider historical context we have just sketched. Seeing the connections between these systems and the historical movements we have discussed—logicism, formalism, and ordinary language philosophy—may be a springboard for understanding.

Psycho-logic has a place in the logistic tradition, along with other truth-oriented axiomatic systems—Euclid's *Elements* (written in Greek), Spinoza's *Ethics* (Latin), Newton's *Principia* (English), Whitehead & Russell's *Principia Mathematica* (symbolic logic), and Hull's *Principles of Behavior* (English). This placement fits with the influence of both Arne Naess and Clark Hull on Smedslund's work. As he notes in his autobiography, "I suppose my earlier fascination with Hull's theory, and Arne Naess's thinking about interpretation and preciseness, played a role in this project that developed in total contrast to the surrounding psychology" (Smedslund 2013, p. 96). After he entered the University of Oslo in 1948, he learned symbolic logic from Naess and became "a great admirer" of Hull (pp. 14–15).

The Person Concept is closer to the formalist school. Notice that "formalism" here refers to the movement associated with Hilbert, in which conceptual structures are articulated by rigorous, logical symbolism, and the applicability of the formulation is a separate question. Smedslund, of course, sought to formalize common sense through his axiomatization. But he was not concerned with the distinction between form and content characteristic of the formalists. When Ossorio entered UCLA in 1946, many of his professors were émigrés to the United States who had fled from Europe after Hitler's rise to power. As an undergraduate he had classes in logic with Han Reichenbach, and as a graduate student with Rudolf Carnap. Although he strongly rejected Carnap's semantic approach to language, he appreciated Carnap's formalist systems and included them as "part of the intellectual history of the Person Concept" (Ossorio 1983b).

The strongest influences for Ossorio, however, were the ordinary language philosophers. By the time he received his degree in 1961, Ossorio had "discovered" Gilbert Ryle and P. F. Strawson and references both philosophers in his dissertation, *Meanings in Ordinary Language*. When he completed the initial formulation of the Person Concept in 1964, he wrote that he had been "stimulated by the writings of Wittgenstein (1958), Ryle (1949), Anscombe (1958), Strawson (1959), Gosling (1962), and Carnap (1958)" (Ossorio 1966/1995, p. 223). Smedslund does not seem to have been influenced directly by the ordinary language philosophers, but he was influenced indirectly through his long-time Wittgensteinian friend John Shotter (Smedslund 2012b, p. 298) and the philosopher–psychologist Rom Harré (1999).

Fritz Heider, who visited the University of Oslo in 1961, is identified by Smedslund as "the psychologist who most profoundly influenced my professional career" (2013, p. 37). Two of Smedslund's articles (1988b, 2008) reflect his deep respect for Heider and his work on psychological common sense.

What Things Are

There is much more that could be said about the two systems than space permits. For example, I have talked about the axioms of Psycho-logic, but said nothing about its definitions and corollaries (cf. Smedslund 1988a). Without these, it is not possible to appreciate the differentiation or complexity of Smedslund's system. Likewise, I have touched upon only two of the four major components of the Person Concept—Behavior and Person—but said nothing about the Language and Reality components (cf. Ossorio 1971/1978, 1997). Without these, it is not possible to appreciate the comprehensiveness of the Person Concept.

I have also not mentioned Ossorio's status dynamic maxims, a set of almost one hundred warnings and reminders (Ossorio 1982/1998). The maxims call for comment because they have been mistaken for propositions or traditional axioms. Smedslund (2012b), for example, wrote: "The only other attempt that I know of at something like an axiomatic system in modern psychology, in addition to the well-known one created by Hull (1952), was made by Peter Ossorio (2006), who used the term 'maxims' for what I call axioms: that is, principles that we must take for granted" (p. 659). Describing the status dynamic maxims as "something like an axiomatic system" would have evoked a sharply raised eyebrow from Ossorio because it ignores his repeated reminders that he is not stating propositions (cf. Ossorio 1991, p. 355).

In light of the historical sketch above, we can note that stating truths is a highly respected "language-game." But there are many other language-games that have scientific value—games like giving warnings, offering reminders, presenting commentaries, and providing justification when an important failure in describing persons is at stake (cf. Ossorio 1998, pp. 4–5). The status dynamic maxims are better understood in the spirit of Wittgenstein's "reminders for a particular purpose" (1958, §127) than in the spirit of Frege's "timeless truths" (1893/2013).

Kenneth Gergen (1985, 1987), who described the work of both Smedslund and Ossorio as directed at "fundamental propositions" and "basic suppositions," also overlooked Ossorio's explanation of what he was doing. Smedslund created his system in the time-honored Euclidean tradition of proving propositions from self-evident suppositions. Ossorio did not.

Harold Kelley (1992), of course, misrepresented both systems when he claimed that Smedslund and Ossorio were "implicitly recognizing causal networks" (p. 19). The concept of intentionality and the distinction between causes and reasons, fundamental to both Psycho-logic and the Person Concept, were clearly not recognized by Kelley. (For an attempt to rescue Heider from a similar fate, see Malle and Ickes (2000). For discussions of causality, see Smedslund (2012a) and Ossorio (1973, 1978).

In response to these clarifications, challenges may be raised: "Why can't we just treat Psycho-logic as the implicit recognition of causal networks?" "Why can't we just treat Ossorio's maxims as timeless truths?" "Why can't we just treat Smedslund's axioms as warnings and reminders?" We can do these things, but we run the risk of violating the integrity of the systems as envisioned by their designers. I therefore leave the temptations (and satisfactions) of those kinds of redescriptions and revisions for others.

Conclusion

Jan Smedslund and Peter Ossorio shared an appreciation of the need for a conceptual system to delineate the basic concepts of behavioral science. They also had in common the fortitude to develop their systems, undeterred by the lack of understanding and hostile reactions of colleagues. Ossorio (1980) described his work as "a fundamental intellectual and technical gift … to those in various intellectual communities who grasp it" (p. 950). The same can be said of Smedslund's system. Their gifts have not always been well received, but for those who do appreciate them, they offer a compelling alternative to the widely accepted naturalistic, mechanistic, reductive approaches of mainstream behavioral science.

References

Anscombe, G. E. M. (1958). *Intention*. Oxford: Basil Blackwell.

Austin, J. L. (1955). *How to do things with words*. Cambridge, MA: Harvard University Press.

Carnap, R. (1958). *Introduction to symbolic logic and its applications*. New York: Dover Publications.

Coffa, J. A. (1991). *The semantic tradition from Kant to Carnap: To the Vienna station*. Cambridge, MA: Cambridge University Press. https://doi.org/10.1017/CBO9781139172240.

Cushman, P. (1991). Psychologic or psychological Esperanto? *Psychological Inquiry, 2*, 339–375. https://doi.org/10.1207/s15327965pli0204_2.

Davis, K. E. (1995). *Preface. Persons. The collected works of Peter G. Ossorio* (Vol. I, pp. xi–xvi). Ann Arbor, MI: Descriptive Psychology Press.

Frege, G. (1980). *The foundations of arithmetic*. (J. L. Austin, Trans., 2nd rev. ed.). Evanston, IL: Northwestern University Press. (Original work published 1884).

Frege, G. (2013). *Gottlob Frege: Basic laws of arithmetic*. (P. A. Ebert & M. Rossberg (Eds., Trs.). Oxford: Oxford University Press. (Original work published 1893, 1903).

Friedman, M. (1999). *Reconsidering logical positivism*. Cambridge, UK: Cambridge University Press.

Gergen, K. (1985). Social constructionist inquiry: Context and implications. In K. Gergen & K. Davis (Eds.), *The social construction of the person* (pp. 3–18). Rome, NY: Springer-Verlag.

Gergen, K. (1987). The language of psychological understanding. In H. Stam, T. Rogers, & K. Gergen (Eds.), *The analysis of psychological theory: Metapsychological perspectives* (pp. 115–129). Washington, DC: Hemisphere Publishing.

Goddard, C., & Wierzbicka, A. (2014). *Words & meanings: Lexical semantics across domains, languages, & cultures*. Oxford: Oxford University Press.

Gosling, J. (1962). Mental causes and fear. *Mind, 71*, 289–306.

Harré, R. (1999). Commentary on 'Psychologic and the study of memory'. *Scandinavian Journal of Psychology, 40*(Supplement), 37–40.

Heider, F. (1958). *The psychology of interpersonal relations*. New York: Wiley.

Hergenhahn, B., & Henley, T. (2014). *An introduction to the history of psychology* (7th ed.). Belmont, CA: Wadsworth.

Hull, C. L. (1935). The conflicting psychologies of learning—A way out. *Psychological Review, 42*(6), 491–516. https://doi.org/10.1037/h0058665.

Hull, C. L. (1937). Mind, mechanism, and adaptive behavior. *Psychological Review, 44*(1), 1–32. https://doi.org/10.1037/h0058294.

Hull, C. L. (1943). *Principles of behavior: An introduction to behavior theory*. New York: Appleton-Century-Crofts.
Hull, C. L. (1952). *A behavior system*. New Haven: Yale University Press.
Kant, I. (1996). *Critique of pure reason*. (W. S. Pluhar, Trans.). Indianapolis: Hackett Publishing. (Original work published 1781 and 1787).
Kelley, H. (1992). Common-sense psychology and scientific psychology. *Annual Review of Psychology, 43*, 1–23. https://doi.org/10.1146/annurev.ps.43.020192.000245.
Kneale, W., & Kneale, M. (2008). *The development of logic*. Oxford: Clarendon Press. (Original work published 1962).
Kukla, A. (2001). *Methods of theoretical psychology*. Cambridge, MA: MIT Press.
Kurtz, M., Mussio, P., & Ossorio, P. (1990). A cognitive system for astronomical image interpretation. *Pattern Recognition Letters, 11*, 507–515. https://doi.org/10.1016/0167-8655(90)90087-I.
Malle, B. F., & Ickes, W. (2000). Fritz Heider: Philosopher and psychologist. In G. A. Kimble & M. Wertheimer (Eds.), *Portraits of pioneers in psychology* (Vol. 4, pp. 195–214). Washington, DC: American Psychological Association.
Naess, A. (2005). Author's preface to this edition. In H. Glasser & A. Drengson (Eds.), *The selected works of Arne Naess* (Vol. I, pp. *lxix–lxxi*). The Netherlands: Springer.
Ossorio, P., & Kurtz, M. (1989). Automated classification of resolved galaxies. *Data analysis in astronomy, 40*, 121–128. https://doi.org/10.1007/978-1-4684-5646-2_13.
Ossorio, P. G. (1973). Never smile at a crocodile. *Journal for the Theory of Social Behavior, 3*, 121–140. https://doi.org/10.1111/j.1468-5914.1973.tb00320.x.
Ossorio, P. G. (1978). *"What actually happens": The representation of real world phenomena*. Columbia, SC: University of South Carolina Press. (Original work published 1971 as LRI Report No. 10a).
Ossorio, P. G. (1980). Where the action is. *Contemporary Psychology, 25*, 950. https://doi.org/10.1037/019434.
Ossorio, P. G. (1981). Conceptual-notational devices: The PCF and related types. In K. E. Davis (Ed.), *Advances in descriptive psychology* (Vol. 1, pp. 83–104). Greenwich, CN: JAI Press. (Original work published 1979 as LRI Report No. 22).
Ossorio, P. G. (1983a). A multicultural psychology. In K. E. Davis & R. M. Bergner (Eds.), *Advances in descriptive psychology* (Vol. 3, pp. 13–44). Greenwich, CN: JAI Press. (Original work published 1982 as LRI Report No. 29).
Ossorio, P. G. (1983b). *Why descriptive psychology*. (LRI Report No. 35). Boulder, CO: Linguistic Research Institute. Retrieved from https://scholar.colorado.edu
Ossorio, P. G. (1991). Naive baseball theory. *Psychological Inquiry, 2*, 352–355. https://doi.org/10.1207/s15327965pli0204_7.
Ossorio, P. G. (1995). *Persons. The collected works of Peter G. Ossorio* (Vol. I). Ann Arbor, MI: Descriptive Psychology Press. (Original work published 1966 as LRI Report No. 3).
Ossorio, P. G. (1997). What there is, how things are. *Journal for the Theory of Social Behavior, 27*, 149–172. https://doi.org/10.1111/1468-5914.00032.
Ossorio, P. G. (1998). *Place. The collected works of Peter G. Ossorio* (Vol. III). Ann Arbor, MI: Descriptive Psychology Press. (Original work published 1982 as LRI Report No. 30a).
Ossorio, P. G. (2006). *The behavior of persons. The collected works of Peter G. Ossorio* (Vol. V). Ann Arbor, MI: Descriptive Psychology Press.
Ossorio, P. G. (2010). *Meaning and symbolism. The collected works of Peter G. Ossorio* (Vol. VI). Ann Arbor, MI: Descriptive Psychology Press. (Original work published 1969). Retrieved from https://scholar.colorado.edu.
Poincaré, H. (2007). *Science and hypothesis*. (W. J. Greenstreet, Trans.). New York: Cosimo. (Original work published 1905).
Reichenbach, H. (1965). *The theory of relativity and a priori knowledge*. (M. Reichenbach, Trans.). Los Angeles, CA: University of California Press. (Original work published 1920).
Ryle, G. (1949). *The concept of mind*. New York: Barnes & Noble.

Shotter, J., & Burton, M. (1983). Common sense accounts of human action: The descriptive formulations of Heider, Smedslund and Ossorio. In L. Wheeler & P. Shaver (Eds.), *Review of personality and social psychology* (Vol. 4, pp. 272–296). Beverly Hills, CA: Sage.
Smedslund, J. (1978). Bandura's theory of self-efficacy: A set of common sense theorems. *Scandinavian Journal of Psychology, 19*, 1–14. https://doi.org/10.1111/j.1467-9450.1978.tb00299.x.
Smedslund, J. (1988a). *Psycho-logic*. Berlin: Springer-Verlag.
Smedslund, J. (1988b). Fritz Heider misinterpreted. *Contemporary Psychology, 33*(3), 275. https://doi.org/10.1037/025576.
Smedslund, J. (1997). *The structure of psychological common sense*. Mahwah, NJ: Erlbaum.
Smedslund, J. (1999). Author's response: Psychologic in dialogue — Reply to commentaries. *Scandinavian Journal of Psychology, 40*(Suppl), 123–138. https://doi.org/10.1111/j.1467-9450.1999.tb01462.x.
Smedslund, J. (2002). From hypothesis-testing psychology to procedure-testing psycho-logic. *Review of General Psychology, 6*, 51–72. https://doi.org/10.1037/1089-2680.6.1.51.
Smedslund, J. (2008). From Heider to psycho-logic. *Social Psychology, 39*(3), 157–162. https://doi.org/10.1027/1864-9335.39.3.157.
Smedslund, J. (2012a). Psycho-logic: Some thoughts and after-thoughts. *Scandinavian Journal of Psychology, 53*, 295–302. https://doi.org/10.1111/j.1467-9450.2012.00951.x.
Smedslund, J. (2012b). What follows from what we all know about human beings. *Theory & Psychology, 22*, 658–668. https://doi.org/10.1177/0959354312441512.
Smedslund, J. (2012c). The *bricoleur* model of psychological practice. *Theory & Psychology, 22*, 643–657. https://doi.org/10.1177/0959354312441277.
Smedslund, J. (2013). *From nonsense syllables to holding hands: Sixty years as a psychologist*. Chagrin Falls, OH: Taos Institute Publications.
Smith, L. D. (1986). *Behaviorism and logical positivism: A reassessment of the alliance*. Stanford, CA: Stanford University Press.
Strawson, P. F. (1959). *Individuals: An essay in descriptive metaphysics*. New York: Routledge.
Valsiner, J. (1985). Common sense and psychological theories: The historical nature of logical necessity. *Scandinavian Journal of Psychology, 26*, 97–109. https://doi.org/10.1111/j.1467-9450.1985.tb01147.x.
Wittgenstein, L. (1958). *Philosophical investigations: The English text of the third edition*. (G. E. M. Anscombe, Trans.). Upper Saddle River, NJ: Prentice Hall.

Chapter 4
"The Concept of Correlation in Adults" Comes of Age

Karl Halvor Teigen

A discussion of Jan Smedslund's legacy to psychology would be incomplete without a presentation of his by far most famous paper (Smedslund 1963). Despite appearing in the relatively obscure *Journal of Scandinavian Psychology* it has as of today obtained more than 500 citations, according to Google Scholar, more than twice of any other of Smedslund's contributions. It is still frequently cited and has achieved the status of a classic in judgment and decision-making textbooks, sometimes even reproducing his original data (e.g., Baron 2000; Hardman 2009; Plous 1993).

The title is odd: "The concept of correlation in adults." Why "adults"? Most studies of people's understanding of statistical concepts are done with grown-up participants anyway. Bruner had called his seminal book *A study of thinking* (Bruner et al. 1956), not "A study of adult thinking," and Wertheimer's posthumous work on *Productive thinking* (1945) was not entitled "Productive thinking in adults." But Smedslund was at the time inspired by Piaget's ground-breaking work on thinking in a developmental perspective and had published several papers on logical and mathematical thinking in children. Inhelder and Piaget (1958) had among other topics tried to determine at which stage children come to understand that two observations are contingent, i.e., statistically dependent upon each other. What are their strategies for finding out whether, for instance, a particular eye color (blue or brown) and a particular hair color (light or dark) go together? In the simplest case, we can place eye-hair observations in a 2 × 2 contingency table and claim a statistical connection exists if most blue-eyed individuals are blonde, whereas brown-eyed are generally dark-haired. To draw such a conclusion, all cells in the table must be attended to and compared. For children, this is a demanding task, which

K. H. Teigen (✉)
University of Oslo, Oslo, Norway
e-mail: k.h.teigen@psykologi.uio.no

T. G. Lindstad et al. (eds.), *Respect for Thought*, Theory and History in the Human and Social Sciences, https://doi.org/10.1007/978-3-030-43066-5_4

they only achieve (at best) around 14–15 years of age, when the stage of "formal operations" is within reach. But Piaget's theories can be criticized on at least two accounts: On the one hand for underestimating the logical capabilities of small children (Lourenço and Machado 1996), and for overestimating the rationality of grown-ups, on the other (e.g., Wason 1968). Reading the title of Smedslund's paper, we already suspect he might be siding with the second group of critics.

The ending of the paper is also a bit unusual. We find here, as customary, a list of references. But this list contains only three items, two of which to the work of Piaget and Inhelder. The third is to Peter Wason (1960) and his famous four-card problem, demonstrating that adults, even scientists, test hypotheses about a relationship by checking what they believe are positive, confirming instances, rather than actively looking for negative instances where the proposed relationship does not hold. Interestingly, these three relevant studies are not cited in the introductory section, as background sources, as most authors would have done today, but appear only in the discussion. They are here cited as research findings in support of Smedslund's conclusions, rather than as studies upon which his research was based.

The Experiments

The paper includes two experiments. Participants in both were nurses in training, who were shown a pack of cards representing 100 individual patients, with letter A indicating a target symptom and letter F indicating a target disease. Going through the whole pack one by one, they were asked "to form an impression of the extent to which A is a useful symptom in the diagnosis of F" (Experiment 1) or "whether there is a relationship (connection) between symptom A and the illness F" (Experiment 2).

In Experiment 1, all cards were marked with four symptom letters, including or excluding A, and with four diagnoses, including or excluding F. The other letters functioned as distractors, making it difficult to keep a mental count of co-occurrences, single occurrences, and non-occurrences of the target letters. In the second experiment, the task was simplified by marking cards with +A (symptom A is present) or −A (symptom absent), and with +F or −F (for illness present or absent, respectively). The cards in both experiments could accordingly be sorted in four categories, all of them crucial to determine the existence of a correlation. An elementary task for a researcher with some grasp of statistics, but perhaps not for a nurse leafing through a pack of patient cards.

Participants in Experiment 1 received five different decks of cards in five separate conditions. In three conditions, the symptom was useless, occurring equally often with and without the disease. These conditions differed only in the proportion of patients with diagnosis F: high (70%), low (30%), and medium (50%). Participants in the medium condition, where all four combinations of symptom and disease occurred equally often, were asked to rate the strength of the relationship. Despite a zero correlation, three of 19 participants said it was "strong," ten described it as "medium," only one said zero. When asked to explain their judgments, many gave "particularistic" reasons, apparently thinking that whenever A and F go together, a relationship is present; otherwise, it is absent. More than half of the subjects endorsed a slightly more statistical notion by judging the strength of the relationship from the frequency of AF-observations, but without reference to the other combinations. Not a single subject gave any indication of having understood the role all four cells in determining the relationship.

The experiment has the appearance of being exploratory, by varying deck composition from condition to condition in inconsistent ways, adding different questions in some conditions, and trying out different ways of coding open-ended responses. Participants in four conditions were American student nurses from Denver, Colorado, whereas the medium group referred to above consisted of Norwegian student nurses in Oslo.

Participants in Experiment 1 had found the task abstract and exacting. Experiment 2 was designed "to create optimal conditions for the occurrence of an understanding of the concept of correlation" (p. 170). In addition to simplifying the stimulus material (with only two symbols per card), participants were given a more active role, left free to rearrange the cards, and make written notes, if they wished. They all received the same deck of cards, making the study more transparent also for readers. The composition of the deck can be arranged in a four-fold table as shown in Table 4.1.

It is easy to see from the table that patients with this particular illness has symptom A about as often as not. But the same symptom appears with other patients too, and to a similar extent. So the symptom is useless for diagnostic purposes, at least as far as illness F is concerned. This conclusion was not so easily drawn by nurses who saw the deck card by card. Only two out of 28 thought there was no relationship, against 24 who thought that symptom and illness were related (two gave up). The relationship was typically explained by the fact that the number of +A+F cards was the largest or was large. Well, it was. Readers are not told why these frequencies were chosen in the first place. There are more than twice as many patients with than without F, and slightly more with symptom present than absent, making cell frequencies hard to compare. But only five participants took the opportunity to arrange the cards in four groups, and nobody used the paper and pencil offered, despite complaining that they felt the task hard to understand. The results led Smedslund to conclude "that normal adults with no training in statistics do not have a cognitive structure isomorphic with the concept of correlation. Their strategies and inferences typically reveal a particularistic, non-statistical approach, or an exclusive dependence on the frequency of ++ instances" (p. 172).

Table 4.1 Composition of a pack of cards presented to participants in Experiment 2 (Smedslund 1963)

	+A (symptom present)	−A (symptom absent)
+F (illness F found)	(A) 37	(B) 33
−F (illness F not found)	(C) 17	(D) 13

A Triad of Evidence

Four-fold contingency tables can be adapted to many situations where the relationship between two variables is at stake. Signs and diagnoses are just one of them. Cause and effect relationships are another. Jenkins and Ward (1965) performed a series of studies where participants were asked to judge how well they could control the appearance of a symbol on a screen by choosing one of two available responses. Both active subjects, who made the responses, and spectator subjects, who just observed what was going on, perceived a connection between responses and outcome that was unrelated to degree of contingency. Instead, perceived degree of control was strongly affected by the sheer frequency of target outcome. When the target outcome happened on most of the trials, it was perceived as highly controllable even when unrelated to what the active subject did.

Perhaps they were influenced by prior beliefs that such outcomes "should" be controllable. What would happen in a situation where outcomes are acknowledged to be more chance-dependent and unpredictable? This was tested in a subsequent study where Ward and Jenkins (1965) asked participants to assess the effectiveness of cloud seeding upon rainfall, based on information about rainy and non-rainy days with and without seeded clouds. They also varied the presentation form. Those who received information in tabular form performed much better than those who received the information on a trial by trial basis. Interestingly, the summary tables were not very helpful when given at the end. Ward and Jenkins reiterated Smedslund's conclusion that even educated (but statistically naïve) adults seem to lack a proper notion of contingency when information is presented serially. This is the usual format for learning trials in real life.

This triad of papers, the two by Jenkins and Ward, preceded by the one by Smedslund, have since been cited together as inseparable pieces of evidence casting doubt on people's—especially clinicians—ability to learn from experience. In a one-page "note," Smedslund (1966) was perhaps the first to see it as a source of "certain widespread fallacies in clinical research," like ignoring the antecedent probability of a particular diagnosis or effect (also known as base rate neglect). In a later, much cited paper, Berndt Brehmer (1980) elaborated on clinicians' inability of learning from experience, preserving their beliefs in ineffectual cures:

> The problem of learning about the validity of one's judgment in the present case is basically that of learning about the relation between two dichotomous variables. The judgment dichotomizes the independent variable into two categories: those who do and those who do not get treatment, and the dependent variable is dichotomized into those who succeed and those who do not, e.g., those who get well and those who do not.
>
> This particular learning task has received considerable attention (Jenkins and Ward 1965; Smedslund 1963; Ward and Jenkins 1965). The results show that the subjects, when learning these tasks, tend to focus only on the number of true positives, i.e., they follow the same strategy of using only confirming evidence as we have observed earlier. This is, of course, not very satisfactory from a logical point of view. It makes sense, however, when we consider that under natural circumstances, e.g., when people have to learn about the validity of their judgment, they will not have access to all four outcomes. Thus, it may not be so surprising that people have not learned the optimal way of coping with tasks of this sort (Brehmer 1980, p. 239).

We find towards the end of this quotation a dawning realization that illogical conclusions may have their reasons that reason does not know, to paraphrase Pascal. We will later meet a different attempt to align these conclusions with reason (McKenzie and Mikkelsen 2007).

Man as an Intuitive Statistician

The Smedslund–Jenkins–Ward studies predated (and partly inspired) the new wave of interest for people's "intuitive" estimates of magnitudes that can be compared to probabilistic and statistical norms. The catch phrase "Man as an intuitive statistician" dates back to a paper by Peterson and Beach (1967), which reviewed available studies of how well people perform in summarizing statistical, variable information without the help of calculators and algorithms. Most studies showed inexact, but relatively unbiased estimates of means, frequencies, probabilities, and proportions, the major exception being the Smedslund–Jenkins–Ward studies of correlations. Peterson and Beach speculated that this might be restricted to the 2 × 2 contingency table and expressed a hope that "statistical man" would become more normative when one moved beyond this special case to a more complex stimulus situation.

This hope was not fulfilled. In the following years, statistical man was dethroned and replaced by a far more irrational creature (by some even described as an intellectual "miser" or "cripple"), primarily due to the heuristics-and-biases program of Amos Tversky and Daniel Kahneman. Their original studies in the 1970s concerned primarily lay probability estimates, not correlations. But the idea of mental shortcuts that simplify the estimation process, at the risk of arriving at non-normative, biased estimates, bears a family resemblance to the nurses' biased covariation assessments by overreliance on the present-present cell. Smedslund's contingency studies were accordingly frequently cited in support of the heuristics and biases approach. The classic volume that sums up the first 10 years of Judgment under uncertainty-research (Kahneman et al. 1982) includes one section on "Covariation and control" where Smedslund, Jenkins, and Ward feature prominently as showing an "unflattering portrait" of laypeople struggling with a covariation assessment task that "seemingly was an unusually simple and straightforward one" (Jennings et al. 1982, p. 212). "These results are extremely important, since they say that even when all of the relevant outcome information is available, people don't use it," Einhorn concludes (1982, p. 278).

If people disregard three-fourths of the available evidence, they will easily "detect" correlations where none exist. The term *illusory correlation* was not coined by Smedslund, but by Loren Chapman (1967), who had found that people overestimated the frequency of word-pairs in a paired associates list when the two words in the pair were perceived as belonging meaningfully together. This turned out to be the case in clinicians' reports of diagnostic signs as well (Chapman and Chapman 1967). Both clinicians and lay people "saw" a relationship between certain diagnostic "signs" in projective tests and specific diagnoses, despite being empirically uncorrelated. It was sufficient that an associative link existed between sign and diagnosis in the perceiver's mind. Thus, clinicians' reports of behaviors they have "observed" to go together may simply mirror their prejudices and prior held beliefs.

Smedslund's and the Chapmans' studies differed. Smedslund's symptoms and diseases had neutral labels to prevent specific prior associations to play a role. Moreover, his participants were able to recall the frequencies of all four cells fairly well. Yet "illusory correlations" were observed. Both findings matched well the novel hunt for cognitive biases which placed them in the same chapter, akin with "confirmation bias," by some explained by "availability," by others as instances of "attentional biases" (Baron 2000). Illusory correlations were, in turn, made responsible for well-known phenomena like the halo effect (Matlin 1989), stereotypes (Hamilton 1981), the illusion of control (Langer 1976), and superstitious beliefs (Nisbett and Ross 1980). All of these (and more) peculiarities of thinking depend on selective information processes, where some observations or co-occurrences are highlighted whereas others are not attended to, or seen as unimportant or irrelevant.

Modifying the Picture

It is in the nature of science that ground-breaking studies, with findings that at first look simple, persuasive, and clear, will be followed by more critical research that tries to establish boundary conditions, factors facilitating or attenuating the phenomenon in question, and unravelling the mechanisms on which it depends. Are people always blind to correlations? Will they never take more than the present-present cell into account? Harriet Shaklee and collaborators (Shaklee and Mims 1981, 1982; Shaklee and Tucker 1980) identified four strategies participants may use to assess event covariations. They may pay exclusive attention to Cell A (the present-present cell in the four-fold table), they may compare Cell A and B, they may compare diagonals (A + D vs. B + C), and they may compare the two conditional probabilities, as normatively required. When all information is simultaneously available, most participants in Shaklee's studies used the second and the third of these rules, indicating an imperfect grasp of the concept of correlation, but better than Smedslund's results might lead us to believe. In research and overviews published in the 1980s, several modifying factors were explored.

Expectations. Chapman's illusory correlations demonstrate that signs expected to go together will be more salient and lead to exaggerated reports of how often they have been observed. Nisbett and Ross (1980) suggested a distinction between data-driven and theory-driven correlations. In areas where subjective theories about a relationship exist, observations will be selectively processed, and few confirming instances are needed to "see" the expected relationship in a data set. Without such expectations, data appear messy, and low or even medium correlations may go undetected (Jennings et al. 1982). Smedslund had tried to avoid intrusion of prior expectations by using abstract labels both for disease and symptom. And yet, when asked whether a disease is characterized by a specific symptom, participants may have suspected the existence of a theory proposing such a connection. After all, symptoms are, by default, diagnostic signs of diseases.

Cell frequencies. In Experiment 1, Smedslund had varied the percentages of patients with the target disease, without finding (or reporting) any differences. In Experiment 2, patients diagnosed with F outnumbered control patients, as shown in Table 4.1. Other studies have shown that correlations are exaggerated when the target event occur frequently. Participants feel they can control an event that occurs often, even when not connected to their own responses (Allan and Jenkins 1980; Jenkins and Ward 1965).

Data presentation. In the nurse study, events were presented sequentially, placing demands on memory and requiring more cognitive resources than when frequencies in all cells are made simultaneously available. Performance is better when frequencies are presented in tabular form (Crocker 1981; Jenkins and Ward 1965). Shaklee and Mims (1982) found that the two simplest strategies, the Cell A Strategy and the A versus B Strategy were especially common in the memory condition.

Instructions. Participants are sensitive to what the experimenter asks them to do. In the original study, their attention was explicitly directed towards Cell A, as they were asked "to form an impression of the extent to which A is a useful symptom in the diagnoses of F. In other words, do you think that A is a symptom one should pay attention to in trying to determine whether or not the patient is likely to be diagnosed as F" (Smedslund 1963, p. 164). Shaklee and Tucker (1980) asked instead their participants to determine whether the presence of one factor was related "to the presence or absence of another," suggesting that the task required a comparison of cells. This instruction gave very few Strategy A responses. Beyth-Marom (1982) concludes: "In short, subjects judging relationship appear to do what they are told to do. As a result, different instructions lead to different behavior" (p. 513).

Symmetric vs. asymmetric values. In the original study, patients were described as having or not having a particular disease and a specific symptom. These values are not symmetric, most people would think that occurrences have a higher ontological status and are more important than non-occurrences. Beyth-Marom (1982) found that all cells were used when values were more symmetrically labelled, for instance, if two strains of mice were said to have skin with dark vs. light pigment, rather than pigment present vs. absent. Thus, the perception of a relationship can be a function of the way values are described or framed.

To summarize: Subsequent research has shown that people can, and do, make use of all four cells in a contingency table. But they do not regard them as equally important. Crocker (1982) asked participants explicitly about which information they considered necessary and sufficient for making an accurate judgment of relationship between two variables. Frequencies in Cell A were mentioned by 77%, followed by Cell B (60%), Cell C (40%), and Cell D (26%). A similar *Cell weight inequality* has been found in several studies. To quote Mandel and Lehman (1998): "Perhaps the most consistent finding concerning how people integrate contingency information is that they assign differential importance to each of the four cell frequencies. In absolute terms, people tend to weight A > B > C > D" (p. 271).

Smedslund Revisited

Despite numerous citations and an abundance of studies yielding divergent results, Smedslund's original studies were never scrutinized, analyzed, or replicated until Vallée-Tourangeau, Hollingsworth, and Murphy (1998) made an attempt of doing just that. These authors were not satisfied with Smedslund's conclusions about people's insensitivity to contingencies, and the supreme importance of the present/present cell, which they felt had become "textbook wisdom."

In their analysis of the original studies, they gave Experiment 2 short shrift for being poorly designed, "using a set of frequencies which might have lured subjects to infer the presence of a positive correlation because of the high disease base rate" (p. 223). Even so, a replication attempt might have been in place since this was the most famous of the two experiments and with one single condition most easily reproduced (with no independent variable manipulated by the experimenter, it might technically not be regarded as an experiment at all).

Instead, Vallée-Tourangeau and colleagues modelled their studies after Smedslund's Experiment 1, with the difference that the same subjects were exposed to all five conditions. Two experiments were run. First, participants supposed they were examining the symptoms of five different diseases. The five sets of observations included one positive and one negative correlation between symptom and disease, and three sets of zero correlations, as in the original study. The zero correlation patterns included one with a high proportion of disease, one with a low proportion and one with a medium proportion. Participants rated "the relationship between the symptom and disease" on a scale from −100 to +100. They were also asked to recall how many patients they had seen with or without symptom and with or without disease.

The researchers found that the positive correlation was identified as strongly positive, and the negative as negative (but not equally strong), with the three zero correlations in between, more positive than negative, indicating a bias towards inferring (a weak) correlation even in cases where there was none. With many ill patients, this illusion was stronger than when there were few, confirming earlier findings. Participants also underestimated the number of patients in the absent/absent cell; otherwise, their recall of the number of patients in each category was fairly accurate. In his original study, Smedslund had also asked for frequencies and arrived at a similar conclusion.

A second experiment was run with the same four-fold distributions, but with a scenario unlikely to elicit prior expectations; it was in fact unlikely to be realized anywhere, as it described space ships with laboratory mice going to five different planets. The mice reproduced both on board of the space ships (more vs. less abundantly), and after landings, the question being whether each planet's atmosphere had a stimulating or detrimental effect on their reproductive success. The order of events (on board vs. after landing) was believed to make the task more typical for cause–effect sequences, and the outcome values (high vs. low reproductive success) were more symmetrical than in the case of a disease present or absent.

The results showed again that people clearly, and this time more symmetrically, distinguished between positive and negative correlations, taking all four combinations of outcomes into account. But again, zero correlations with high base rates were perceived as (illusory) positive correlations. With lower base rates, perceived correlations were reduced and even reversed so as to appear negative.

Vallée-Tourangeau and colleagues also objected to Baron's notion of *an attentional bias*, as participants recalled the number of observations in each cell fairly well. Smedslund (1966) seemed to have favored an explanation in terms of associative learning, pointing out that no learning theory assumes that associations are affected by the absence of a signal. But not much later, Rescorla (1968) demonstrated in studies of animal conditioning that such sensitivity exists. So interestingly, later models of associative learning (Pearce and Hall 1980; Rescorla and Wagner 1972) predict a higher sensitivity to contingencies in rats than in Smedslund's adults.

On Fallacies and Misunderstandings

Of all people who have visited or revisited Smedslund's (1963) paper, Smedslund is the most modest one. I have found only one self-citation over a time span of 50 years, as a side remark in a paper about psychologic (Smedslund 1991, p. 332). This is remarkable for an author otherwise not known for shyness.

The reasons are not hard to guess. From about 1970 Smedslund turned away from empirical studies, due to what he perceived to be a basic failure of the S-R approach (Smedslund 1969). He even turned against them, insisting that in most cases findings from psychological experiments are self-evident, small, or both, opinions that he still vocally defends (e.g., Smedslund 2016). Moreover, he must have felt uncomfortable of being associated with the heuristics-and-biases approach, which seemed to portray human thinking as basically flawed. To Smedslund, humans are deeply rational, and even the errors they make can only be investigated and understood by taking logic "in a wide sense" for granted (Smedslund 1970, p. 217).

This is most clearly demonstrated in his critique of Tversky and Kahneman (TK), where he takes issue with these authors' distinction between fallacy and misunderstanding (Smedslund 1990). Fallacies occur when people persist in committing a logical error in a task that is clearly presented to highlight its logical structure. Several of TK's demonstrations of errors in reasoning, including the famous "conjunction fallacy" (where a combination of events is judged to be more likely than one of its constituents) appear to defy elementary logic. To press this point, TK introduced "a series of increasingly desperate manipulations designed to induce subjects to obey the conjunction rule" (Tversky and Kahneman 1983, p. 299), yet the errors persisted. Smedslund argues that even so, we have to assume that the perspectives and evaluations that underlie human actions are logical in order to understand what they are doing and why. In fact, understandings and misunderstandings alike rest on a substrate of explicit or implicit logical inferences.

This discussion may appear as a barren academic exercise if not for Smedslund's analysis of understandings. First of all, to him understanding is a matter of degrees (perhaps surprising, as Smedslund often makes his points, for instance, about logicality and the value of experimental evidence, in categorical terms). This makes the distinction between understanding and misunderstanding less absolute than one may otherwise have thought. Secondly, understanding is conceived as a relational (communicative) concept, namely as a match between the intended and the perceived meaning of a message. You do not simply "understand" a concept or a message, you understand *someone's* (a speaker's) message. Thirdly, the understanding, or agreement between speaker and listener can be analyzed into four components, namely agreement as to what is (1) *equivalent* to, (2) *implied* by, (3) *contradicted* by, and (4) *irrelevant* to what is said (Smedslund 1970, p. 217; 1990, p. 112).

At this point, my personal wish would have been that Smedslund had stopped his crusade against TK's views on fallacies and instead discussed what those who make "conjunction errors" think are equivalent to, implied by, contradicted by and irrelevant to the statements presented to them by the experimenter. It would then be possible to distinguish between misunderstandings at a relatively superficial, linguistic level (which TK claimed to have controlled for) and deviant or deficient understandings at a more fundamental level (which TK, perhaps inappropriately, had labelled fallacies). We can then imagine, for instance, that participants and experimenters would more often agree about what is *equivalent* to a conjunctive statement than about what the *implications* are. A further wish would be that Smedslund (1990) had taken the opportunity to revisit Smedslund (1963) on the concept of correlation to illustrate his novel interpretation of cognitive illusions. His original claim of a missing conceptual structure in the normal, untrained adult mind came very close to the description of a fallacy. Now, armed with a better developed analysis of understanding, it might be possible to discuss participants' interpretations of the task they were exposed to. Perhaps terms like *useful symptom*, *relation*, and *connection* were in their language and in their minds *not* equivalent to the statistically minded experimenter's concept of a *correlation* or a *contingency*. Both the original and subsequent research indicate that naïve participants disagree with the experimenters as to which observations are *irrelevant*. For a researcher, absolute numbers are not relevant, as it is the relative frequencies that count. Many participants held instead that occurrences in Cell D were irrelevant.

Rationality as a Premise

Smedslund has not been alone in his insistence on the basic rationality of thinking. For other voices in the so-called rationality debate, see Cohen (1981), Evans and Over (1996), Gigerenzer (1996), and Stanovich and West (2002), to name a few. In Smedslund's version, logicality must be assumed before any data are collected. That may look like an easy way of settling the issue: thinking is logical almost by definition. But the implications are not so trivial. It could even be converted into a heuristic for psychologists, namely when you observe people doing something apparently illogical and "stupid," try to figure out some premises from which this odd behavior will logically flow. You might then find that the apparent irrationality lies in the premises instead of the conclusions, or perhaps that people import some premises that are not among those explicitly mentioned in the description of the task. It is in fact hard to imagine a task where all relevant premises are fully specified. Even participants who reason correctly according to the book must build on unstated premises, for instance, that they should disregard or "bracket" most of their real-world knowledge of the target theme.

McKenzie and Mikkelsen have in recent years studied people's apparently biased contingency judgments from a similar angle. They argue that prior expectations *should*, even normatively, be taken into account if we view the task as updating previous beliefs with new evidence, as dictated by Bayesian statistics. Moreover, it is normatively correct to find Cell A more informative than Cell D in cases where the presence of a signal, a sign, or a diagnosis must be regarded as more infrequent than its absence. And we know, based on a life-time of experiences, that F is less frequent than non-F (there are fewer patients with F than without F in this world) and, generally speaking, fewer A's than other letters in the alphabet, which should give us good reason to be attentive when F and A go together (regardless of the fact that in this particular sample, the F's were over-represented). In the special case where F and A are generally widespread, the pattern will be reversed and attention is drawn to the Cell D, according to their studies (McKenzie and Mikkelsen 2007).

Then, what remains of *The concept of correlation in adults*? Plous claimed that "Smedslund's basic observations have stood the test of time" (1993, p. 163), whereas Vallée-Tourangeau argued that "Smedslund's influential conclusion … was not supported by his own data" (1998, p. 229). This looks like widely different views. But a closer look reveals that they did not have the same observations, or the same conclusions, in mind. Vallée-Torangeau objected to "an exclusive dependency on the frequency of + + (Cell A) instances" (quoting Smedslund 1963, p. 172), whereas Plous merely referred to people's "difficulties" in assessing covariation and their tendency to "rely heavily" on positive occurrences of both events. In other words, they differed in their understanding of what Smedslund's findings implied. Fifty years of empirical research make both assessments appear reasonable.

The Irony of Science

Smedslund has for more than 40 years been a relentless critic of experimental psychologists for producing mostly trivial results, and for disregarding the basic logicality of the human mind. It is perhaps ironical that his most cited paper is an experimental demonstration of the difficulties people experience in coming to terms with a basic statistical concept. The study cannot be charged with being "pseudo-empirical," as a prior analysis of the concepts involved would make us expect a totally different (more normatively acceptable) pattern of results. Nor were the effects of a trivial magnitude, "much too small to be useful in psychological practice and in daily life" (Smedslund 2016, p. 185), as in fact only two of his participants showed "a dawning understanding of correlation, but not very developed" (Smedslund 1963, p. 171). Moreover, we have seen that Smedslund, and several of his successors, regarded the findings as having profound and far-reaching implications for understanding potential errors clinicians and lay people make, both in their professional practice and in daily life. Subsequent empirical research has, however, modified the original conclusions, and thus to some extent vindicated Smedslund's criticisms against empirical studies: Experimental findings can rarely claim universality, and people's responses may be more context-dependent, and thus also more rational, than the original investigators are tempted to believe. Yet this realization is in itself a product of experimental research, demonstrating the capability of this approach in probing the generality and boundary conditions of its own findings.

Perhaps "the concept of correlation in adults" and later findings inspired by Smedslund's pioneering study can best be understood as manifestations of a basic *simplicity principle* of human cognition (Chater 1999). This principle requires the perceiver, or thinker (and, for that matter: the scientist) to process and summarize their observations in the simplest possible way. But, as Einstein reputedly added: not simpler. This last proviso was evidently overlooked by Smedslund's original subjects. And perhaps sometimes, by Smedslund himself.

References

Allan, L. G., & Jenkins, H. M. (1980). The judgment of contingency and the nature of the response alternatives. *Canadian Journal of Psychology, 34*, 1–11.

Baron, J. (2000). *Thinking and deciding* (3rd ed.). Cambridge: Cambridge University Press.

Beyth-Marom, J. (1982). Perception of correlation reexamined. *Memory & Cognition, 10*, 511–519.

Brehmer, B. (1980). In one word: Not from experience. *Acta Psychologica, 45*(1-3), 223–241.

Bruner, J. J., Goodnow, J. S., & Austin, G. A. (1956). *A study of thinking*. New York: Wiley.

Chapman, L., & Chapman, J. (1967). Genesis of popular but erroneous psychodiagnostic observations. *Journal of Abnormal Psychology, 72*, 193–204.

Chapman, L. J. (1967). Illusory correlation in observational report. *Journal of Verbal Learning and Verbal Behavior, 6*, 151–155.

Chater, N. (1999). The search for simplicity: A fundamental cognitive principle? *The Quarterly Journal of Experimental Psychology, Section A, 52*(2), 273–302.

Cohen, L. J. (1981). Can human irrationality be experimentally demonstrated? *Behavior and Brain Sciences, 4*, 317–370.

Crocker, J. (1981). Judgment of covariation by social perceivers. *Psychological Bulletin, 90*, 272–292.

Crocker, J. (1982). Biased questions in judgments of covariation studies. *Personality and Social Psychology Bulletin, 8*, 214–220.

Einhorn, H. (1982). Learning from experience and suboptimal rules in decision making. In D. Kahneman, P. Slovic, & A. Tversky (Eds.), *Judgment under uncertainty: Heuristics and biases* (pp. 268–283). Cambridge: Cambridge University Press.

Evans, J. S. B. T., & Over, D. E. (1996). *Rationality and reasoning*. Hove, UK: Psychology Press.

Gigerenzer, G. (1996). On narrow norms and vague heuristics: A reply to Kahneman and Tversky. *Psychological Review, 103*, 592–596.

Hamilton, D. L. (1981). Illusory correlation as a basis for stereotyping. In D. L. Hamilton (Ed.), *Cognitive processes in stereotyping and intergroup behavior*. Hillsdale, NJ: Erlbaum.

Hardman, D. (2009). *Judgment and decision making: Psychological perspectives*. Chichester: Wiley-Blackwell.

Inhelder, B., & Piaget, J. (1958). *The growth of logical thinking from childhood to adolescence*. New York: Basic Books.

Jenkins, H. M., & Ward, W. C. (1965). Judgments of contingency between responses and outcomes. *Psychological Monographs, 79*, 1–17.

Jennings, D. L., Amabile, T. M., & Ross, L. (1982). Informal covariation assessment: Data-based versus theory-based judgments. In D. Kahneman, P. Slovic, & A. Tversky (Eds.), *Judgment under uncertainty: Heuristics and biases* (pp. 211–230). Cambridge: Cambridge University Press.

Kahneman, D., Slovic, P., & Tversky, A. (Eds.). (1982). *Judgment under uncertainty: Heuristics and biases*. Cambridge: Cambridge University Press.

Langer, E. J. (1976). The illusion of control. *Journal of Personality and Social Psychology, 36*, 941–950.

Lourenço, O., & Machado, A. (1996). In defense of Piaget's theory: A reply to 10 common criticisms. *Psychological Review, 105*, 143–164.

Mandel, D. R., & Lehman, D. R. (1998). Integration of contingency information in judgments of cause, covariation, and probability. *Journal of Experimental Psychology: General, 127*, 269–285.

Matlin, M. W. (1989). *Cognition*. New York: Holt, Rinehart & Winston.

McKenzie, C. R. M., & Mikkelsen, L. A. (2007). A Bayesian view of covariation assessment. *Cognitive Psychology, 54*, 33–61.

Nisbett, R., & Ross, L. (1980). *Human inference: Strategies and shortcomings of social judgment*. Englewood Cliffs, NJ: Prentice-Hall.

Pearce, J. M., & Hall, G. (1980). A model for Pavlovian learning: Variations in the effectiveness of conditioned but not of unconditioned stimuli. *Psychological Review, 87*, 532–552.

Peterson, C. R., & Beach, L. R. (1967). Man as intuitive statistician. *Psychological Bulletin, 68*, 29–46.

Plous, S. (1993). *The psychology of judgment and decision making*. New York: McGraw-Hill.

Rescorla, R. A. (1968). Probability of shock in the presence and absence of CS in fear conditioning. *Journal of Comparative and Physiological Psychology, 66*, 1–5.

Rescorla, R. A., & Wagner, A. R. (1972). A theory of Pavlovian conditioning: Variations in the effectiveness of reinforcement and nonreinforcement. In A. H. Black & W. F. Prokasy (Eds.), *Classical conditioning II* (pp. 64–99). New York: Appleton-Century-Crofts.

Shaklee, H., & Mims, M. (1981). Development of rule use in judgments of covariation between events. *Child Development, 52*, 317–325.

Shaklee, H., & Mims, M. (1982). Sources of error in judging event covariation: Effects of memory demands. *Journal of Experimental Psychology: Learning, Memory, and Cognition, 8*, 208–224.

Shaklee, H., & Tucker, D. (1980). A rule analysis of judgments of covariation between events. *Memory & Cognition, 8*, 459–467.

Smedslund, J. (1963). The concept of correlation in adults. *Scandinavian Journal of Psychology, 4*, 165–173.

Smedslund, J. (1966). Note on learning, contingency, and clinical experience. *Scandinavian Journal of Psychology, 7*, 265–266.

Smedslund, J. (1969). Meanings, implications and universals: Towards a psychology of man. *Scandinavian Journal of Psychology, 10*, 1–15.

Smedslund, J. (1970). Circular relation between understanding and logic. *Scandinavian Journal of Psychology, 11*, 217–219.

Smedslund, J. (1990). A critique of Tversky and Kahneman's distinction between fallacy and misunderstanding. *Scandinavian Journal of Psychology, 31*, 110–120.

Smedslund, J. (1991). The pseudoempirical in psychology and the case for psychologic. *Psychological Inquiry, 2*, 325–338.

Smedslund, J. (2016). Why psychology cannot be an empirical science. *Integrative Psychological and Behavioral Science, 50*(2), 185–195.

Stanovich, K. E., & West, R. F. (2002). Individual differences in reasoning: Implications for the rationality debate? In T. Gilovich, T. D. Griffin, & D. Kahneman (Eds.), *Heuristics and biases: The psychology of intuitive judgment* (pp. 421–440). Cambridge: Cambridge University Press.

Tversky, A., & Kahneman, D. (1983). Extensional versus intuitive reasoning: The conjunction fallacy in probability judgment. *Psychological Review, 90*, 293–315.

Vallée-Tourangeau, F., Hollingsworth, L., & Murphy, R. A. (1998). 'Attentional bias' in correlation judgments? Smedslund (1963) revisited. *Scandinavian Journal of Psychology, 39*, 221–233.

Ward, W. C., & Jenkins, H. M. (1965). The display of information and the judgment of contingency. *Canadian Journal of Psychology, 19*, 231–241.

Wason, P. C. (1960). On the failure to eliminate hypotheses in a conceptual task. *Quarterly Journal of Experimental Psychology, 12*, 129–140.

Wason, P. C. (1968). Reasoning about a rule. *Quarterly Journal of Experimental Psychology, 20*, 273–281.

Wertheimer, M. (1945). *Productive thinking*. New York: Harper.

Chapter 5
The Socrates of Modern Psychology: A Historical-Socratic View on Smedslund's Common Sense Perspective

Line Joranger

For more than half a century, Jan Smedslund, has questioned modern psychological practices and why psychologists have been so eager to use empirical research methods in order to discover lawful or regular relations. Throughout his academic career, Smedslund has been concerned about fundamental problems of scientific psychology and believes the domain of psychology cannot sustain empirical generalizations. According to Smedslund, there are no psychological laws governing the intentional domain and the way people live their lives. Whenever a person asks a psychologist for help, the psychologist is faced with the unknown, yet, "these social interactions give the practitioner access to information that is not available from structured interviews, questionnaires, tests, manuals or other 'one way' encounters in which the practitioner remains an observer rather than a participant." (Smedslund and Ross 2014, p. 369).

In several publications (Smedslund 1988, 1991a, b, 1997, 2012, 2015, 2016a), Smedslund has convincingly argued that the domain of psychology is very inhospitable to experiments because of irreversibility, infinite numbers of determinants, social interactivity, and the impossibility of impersonal objectivity. Psycho-logic (PL) is the name of the common sense psychology where Smedslund gives contemporary psychologists an alternative way of acting toward their patients by using their everyday life knowledge. To Smedslund, PL and common sense psychology is dealing with cultural and social phenomena people take for granted about each other and themselves (a la Kant). That is, those things that cannot be improved because they are just taken for granted, such as the common meaning behind a shared language or expression: For example, we respect a "no" for a "no" because the meaning behind the concept is shared and normally respected. We intuitively assume without further thinking that someone is hurt when we hear a person cry desperately, or

L. Joranger (✉)
University of South-Eastern Norway, Porsgrunn, Norway
e-mail: Line.Joranger@usn.no

T. G. Lindstad et al. (eds.), *Respect for Thought*, Theory and History in the Human and Social Sciences, https://doi.org/10.1007/978-3-030-43066-5_5

otherwise, we intuitively assume that a person is happy when we hear laughter. However, by investigating these expressions and our own common sense assumptions further, we can improve our understanding of what these expressions entail for this specific person. That is, through systematic reflections and thought experiments, we can turn our common sense assumptions into wisdom and get deeper into the meaning behind a person's "no," a person's cry, and a person's laughter. However, as Smedslund argues, the unique person can never be understood from a number of universal empirical laws. In practice, psychology must always relate to unique persons in a creative way.

Because we are social animals, we have grown up in a culture as part of language communities and have the ability to reflect on ourselves; Smedslund argues that we already, a priori, know a lot about each other and ourselves. Hence, rather than a science whose task is to discover regular or lawful relations by empirical means, the task of psychological science must, according to Smedslund, be to clarify psychological common sense and cultural meanings and conditions. Thus, he proposes to use thought experiments and conceptual analysis to clarify and systematize what we all can and must take for granted when we relate to other people and ourselves, such as our fear of pain or need for love, understanding, acceptance, and safety (Smedslund 2004, p. 7). From Smedslund's writing it even seems that we may derive a professionally and scientifically relevant moral stance: It would not only be professionally and scientifically virtuous to try to clarify a priori psychological knowledge, but it would also be wrong to ignore this possibility.

Smedslund (2012, 2016b) has not been afraid to provoke and has boldly expressed his rejection of the mainstream clinical emphasis on empirically and statistically based diagnostic systems and fixed techniques His bold statement is that the strong emphasis on empirical methods and general laws that we find in current psychological practices often lead to unprofitable use of time, money, and labor. He therefore encourages psychologists to stop trying to validate general causal theories for practice by using statistically supported empirical research methods. Instead of reciting familiar rhetoric on how one should think and cope with symptoms, his notion is that the therapist should clarify and systematize their own concepts and engage the patient with an open mind and careful questioning based on psychological common sense.

Smedslund's Ancient Roots

Epistemologically, Smedslund's discussions point toward the old Cartesian mind–body problem and topics concerning language and logic, scientific ideals, interpretation, and understanding (Joranger 2015). The mind–brain separation relates to the distinction between the nomothetic and idiographic sciences, first outlined by the neo-Kantian philosopher Wilhelm Windelband (1905, 1919). Conceptually, the nomothetic sciences are based on what Kant ([1787]1996) relates to the natural sciences, that is—sciences that can generalize and describe the effort to derive laws and concepts that *explain* objective phenomena in general. Idiographic sciences are based on the humanistic sciences and what Kant describes as a tendency to specify, that is—our efforts to interpret and *understand* the meaning of contingent, unique, and often subjective phenomena.[1]

A related distinction is made by Ian Hacking (1995) and Kurt Danziger (1997), who separate "natural kinds" from "human kinds." Whereas natural kinds are defined as something that exists independently of those studying them (e.g., physical objects and biological species), human kinds are described as defined and constituted by the aims, methods, and practices of human agents. Danziger (1997, pp. 191–192) claims that: "Human kinds... are not natural kinds, but neither are they mere legends. They do refer to features that are real. But it is a reality in which they themselves are heavily implicated, a reality in which they are a part." According to Walsh et al. (2014), psychologists have defined the focal points of their study through this kind of dual thinking. They believe that: "Psychologists with a natural-science orientation typically emphasize the prediction and control of behavior (...). Psychologists with a human-science orientation generally stress *subjectivity* (...)" (Walsh et al. 2014, p. 6).

Smedslund positions his critical views on modern psychology as belonging to the ideographic sciences dealing with language, meaning, and subjectivity. Despite his strong rhetorical and logical argumentation, and despite being one of Norway's most cited psychologists internationally, in his home country he is regarded as an rebel. However, Smedslund's thoughts have not developed like mushrooms from the earth. His theories are extensions of and in continuity with several critical scholars of his time. Intellectual traditions in critical psychology (cf. Brunswik 1956, 1942; Danziger 1997; Hacking 1995; Kvale 1992; Richards 2010; Robinson 1986; Rose 1990; Rose and Abi-Rached 2013; Taylor 1989; Teigen 2002; Tolman and Brunswik 1935), social psychology (cf. Gergen 1973; Harré 2012, Martin and Sugarman 1999, Moghaddam 2003), and cultural psychology (cf. Bruner 1990; Shweder 1991; Valsiner 2014; Vygotsky 1978),[2] are in many ways concerned with the same or related questions that are raised by Smedslund.

Looking back at the history and philosophy of psychology, Smedslund's theoretical notions and his tireless explorations, lead back to ancient time. In the history and evolution of Hellenic thought, we find two tendencies of inquiry, one dealing with what one today would call natural science, that is, the objective manifestations of the universe, and what one today would have called human sciences, that is, the study of mind, language, and meaning. To the former class belong Thales, Anaximander, Anaximenes, Pythagoras, and their attempts to discover principles for the explanation of natural phenomena. The pioneering Greek thinker, Socrates, however, belongs to the other group. Socrates' way of revealing psychologically relevant conditions by defining and asking questions about language and everyday life, without any empirical investigations, makes him one of the fathers of psychology

[1] For American psychology, the terms idiographic and nomothetic were introduced by Gordon Allport in his work *Personality: Psychological Interpretation* (1937).

[2] The traditions are overlapping and not clearly delimited.

and the grandfathers of modern psychopathology, and the first who attempted to study human beings from the point of view of subjectivity.[3]

In the words of Snider (1903, p. 216), "In Socrates, the human mind burst forth into knowing itself as thinking." To Socrates, and one may argue that it is also implied by Smedslund's stance, neither the experience nor the language of specialty can be explained without taking into account how people live their lives. Thus, how people live their lives cannot be removed from the explanandum which requires that the persons involved go into thoughts experiments directed toward themselves and their nature. Zeller (1877, p. 116) very thoughtfully remarks:

> The interests of philosophy being thus turned away from the outer world and directed towards man and his moral nature, and man only regarding things as true and binding of the truth of which he was convinced himself by intellectual research, there appears necessarily in Socrates a deeper importance attached to the personality of the thinker.

Like Socrates, as he is presented in the respective dialogues of Plato and Xenophon, Smedslund may best or advantageously be portrayed as approaching problems relying on "the dialectic method," "the concept of virtue," the notion "know thyself," as well as the metaphoric notion of "midwife."

The Dialectic Method

In Socratic philosophy, the "dialectic method" occupies a lofty position emphasizing reflective questioning and thought experiments, and Aristotle characterizes it as the induction of reasoning and the definition of general concepts. By the dialectic method Socrates penetrated deeply into human nature and experience, and Gomperz (1906) speaks of the great zeal that Socrates exhibited in this method. He believes that a life without cross-examination, that is, without dialogues in which the intellect is exercised in the pursuit of truth, for Socrates is a life not worth living. Schwegler (1877, p. 75) pertinently asserts "that through this art of midwifery the philosopher, by his assiduous questioning, by his interrogatory dissection of the notions of him with whom he might be conversing, knew how to elicit from him a thought of which he had been previously unconscious, and how to help him to the birth of a new thought."

Briefly stated, the dialectic method is divided into two parts, the negative and the positive. The former is known as the Socratic irony. By this method, the philosopher takes the position that he is ignorant and endeavors to show by a process of reasoning that the subject under discussion is in a state of confusion and proves to the

---

[3] The source of information regarding the biography of Socrates and his philosophy comes from two authors, Xenophon and Plato. The former portrays him as a moral philosopher and in his book, *Memorabilia* (Xenophon 1897), he seems to eulogize his master. The latter however presents him as a thinker, and it is maintained by many critics that Plato put into the mouth of Socrates his own ideas. It is lamentable that this great philosopher committed nothing of his monumental work in writing.

interlocutor that his supposed knowledge is a source of inconsistencies and contradictions. On the other hand, the positive side of the method, "the so-called obstetrics or art of intellectual midwifery" (Schwegler 1877, p. 741) leads to definite deductions. To illustrate the two phases of this method, the following example may be taken. A youth of immature self-confidence believed himself to be competent to manage the affairs of state. Socrates would then analyze the general concept of the statecraft, and reduce it to its component parts, and by continuous questions and answers would show to this supposed statesman that he was lacking true knowledge. Again, a young man of mature judgment, but of an exceedingly modest temperament, being reluctant to take part in the debates of the Assembly, Socrates would prove to him that he was fully competent to undertake such a task.

Like Socrates' dialectic method, Smedslund's method is divided into two parts, one negative and one positive (Smedslund 2004). The negative part is provocative and takes the position as ignorant to show by a process of reasoning that the discussed issues are in a state of confusion, inconsistency, and/or contradiction. Like Socrates, through thought experiments and by questioning those who believe that the psychological domain sustains empirical generalizations and fixed techniques, Smedslund make it clear that every person is unique and cannot be reduced to general laws and diagnosis. By analyzing the general concept of "science" and the general concept of "person" and "context" etc., Smedslund finds that one cannot predict a person from any general laws, or place a person under any diagnostic system, or treat a person with any fixed technique. A person must instead be understood in accordance with social rules and by way of clarifying the logic of meanings, and not by causal laws. Finally, everything a person does is sensitive to context and consequences. Hence, by changing context and/or perceived consequences, acting and experience can always be changed. The resulting uniqueness of persons and their contexts means that what persons do cannot be predicted by any general theory, incorporated by any general empirically based diagnostic system, nor dealt with by any general fixed techniques.

The positive side of this method is that one should begin to understand, predict, and deal with people by means of a calculus embedded in all human languages. "The calculus is a formalization of implicit common sense" (Smedslund 2004, p. 7). To Smedslund, one must rely on what follows from the meaning of words, sentences, and nonverbal acts, and one must be open to and deal with the ever-changing uniqueness of the persons and situations one encounters. If someone asks: How can there be a science and a profession dealing with persons, if persons are so changeable and unique? Smedslund would explain to the questioner that people are very predictable because they speak the language and follow the social rules of their group or culture. Since language is shared, we can predict innumerable things about every competent speaker. "For example, everyone will answer, 'yes' to the question 'Is a dog an animal?'" (Smedslund 2004, p. 8).

Smedslund (2004) refers to the Polish linguist Anna Wierzbicka and colleagues (Goddard and Wierzbicka 1994; Wierzbicka 1992, 1996) who claim that there are many basic psychological concepts embedded in any ordinary language, which also appear to be lexically presentenced in all human languages, something that may make psycho-logic a transcultural framework for psychology. Among these concepts are: "I," "you," "can," "know," "think," "want," "feel," "good," "bad," etc. These concepts relate to each other in definite ways, e.g., what a person "feels" in a situation follows from that the person "thinks" and "wants" in that situations. By investigating these and other concepts, one can describe, explain, predict, and control what persons do, "given information about her situation." (Smedslund (2004, p. 8). By this follows that even though the content of psychology does not allow for general causal laws, the existence of a common conceptual basis for human languages and cultures makes it possible, to some extent, to describe, explain, predict, and control what persons do.

In Smedslund's book from 2004, *Dialogues about a New Psychology*, we are witnessing several different dialectical dialogues between the psychologists Manny, Adam, and Eve. Like in Plato's dialogues, they are using thought experiments and examples from everyday life to challenge regular psychological concepts in such a way that they all become illuminated and changed. In one of their discussions (Smedslund 2004, pp. 236–239), Manny and Adam discusses the relationship between psychological praxis and scientific research.

Manny says:

> A colleague of mine recently asked me 'How can you do research without having variables and without quantitative estimates of outcomes?' The question was a reminder of what my mainstream colleague takes for granted. To answer it, the only option is to reject the question itself and its underlying presupposition. So I replied, "If by 'research' you mean 'experimental empirical research where you vary one factor, keeping others constant and observe the variation in the dependent variable,' then the answer is given, and I agree with you. You must have variables and you must have quantitative estimates of outcomes. However, as we have tried to show, the domain of psychology is not very suitable for this kind of research. The deepest reason is that the domain is pre-structured, that is, it must be described in terms of the language of the person investigated. This again means that plausible, subjectively convincing general hypothesis tend to be true, and implausible, subjectively unconvincing general hypothesis tend to be false. The only remaining place for empirical procedures is the testing of local assumptions and procedures. Maybe this should not be given the prestigious title 'research,' but should rather be called 'checking and double-checking,' 'testing,' 'controlling,' etc.

To this, Adam replies:

> Even so, I think it is impossible to stop making quantitative estimates, especially when it comes to conclusions and outcomes. For the proses, for example, of social policymaking, we need to know how many are profiting how much from a certain treatment program compared to a control group. We need to know probabilities. This is true irrespective of whether or not a treatment program is based on previous empirical evidence or on deduction form premises that must be taken for granted, that is, psycho-logic.

And Manny replies:

> At first, both may appear to be subsumable under the conventional hypothetic-deductive model. However, as we have discussed many times, this is not so. The mainstream approach is based on counting, and hypotheses are both generated and tested by observed differences and correlations. This is a strategy for exploring the unknown and meaningless. The new approach is based on explication meanings and deriving implications from them. This is strategy for exploring what is already tacitly known.

During the discussion, Manny and Adam come to a clearer view of the differences between the old and new psychology as having to do with rejection versus acceptance of language-based knowledge. They both agree that language has made us describable, explainable, predicable, and controllable to each other and that psychology can capitalize and build on this, as a systematization and simplification of what we take for granted in the form of the axiomatic system of psycho-logic. They also seem to agree that humans are constituted by social rules that exist independently of us as individuals. What we know about ourselves in a more general sense follows from that we are human and members of a linguistic and cultural communities. The rest of our knowledge is specific and concrete. It may thus be thought strange to label psychological knowledge as scientific, as neither a priori psychological knowledge nor the specific and locally relevant knowledge of unique persons and groups of persons has ordinarily not been acknowledged as scientific. However, to the extent that psychology is a science, this must change.

The example shows that Smedslund's method presents two striking tendencies; one destructive, the other constructive; the former annihilates erroneous conceptions, and the latter aids the building up of functional concepts representing common sense and everyday life. In a broad sense, the dialectic method bears some resemblance to the psychoanalytic, inasmuch as both seek to analyze human nature in the light of individual experience; to find the ultimate and predominating truth underlying such an experience; both attempt to make the individual realize the extent of his limitations and capacity of adjustment by subordinating the antagonistic forces and at the same time aiding the construction of a world of healthy concepts.

Conception of Virtue

Virtue is knowledge because all living things aim for their perceived good; and therefore, if anyone does not know what is good, he cannot do what is good because he will always aim for a mistaken target. However, if someone knows what is good, (s)he will do what is good, because (s)he will aim for what is good. This is the argument presented by Xenophon in his Memories of Socrates (iii, 9, 5). What Socrates maintained was that true virtue must depend upon knowledge about one self and other, through rational reflections and thought experiments. Socrates' thesis "Virtue is knowledge" has the consequence that the one who knows what is good, does what is good, or in other words, the good practitioner is the wise and virtuous practitioner. However, that may apply only when a rational choice is made, for I may also do "the very things I hate" under the unchecked impulse of a bad habit or instinct, not only from ignorance of the good. In short, to Socrates knowledge is the root of moral action, and, on the other hand, lack of knowledge is the cause of vices. In other words, no human being or therapist can voluntarily pursue evil and to prefer evil to good would be foreign to human nature. Hence, in the Socratic sense, in the unconscious lies the root of antisocial deeds, and, as Forbes (1978, p. 191) puts it: "Socratic view of sin, in fact, keeps it in a region subliminal to knowledge. The sinner is never more really than an instinctive man, an undeveloped, irrational creature; strictly speaking, not a man at all."

In the *Meno* (Plato, 380 B.C.E. 1994–2009),[4] Socrates argues further that no one knowingly desires what is bad (*to kakon*). His argument shows that by "bad" he means things that are harmful to the subject, i.e., the one who would desire these things. It is not in human nature for someone to wish to go after what (s)he thinks is bad in place of the good. We can understand this claim in positive terms. Virtue is the chief psychological good; wrongdoing destroys virtue. Therefore, Socrates' strong commitment to virtue reflects his belief in its value for the reflexive mind, as well as the importance of the soul's condition for the quality of our lives.

Since Socrates identified virtue with knowledge, it is evident that education, environment, religion, and conventionality are the determining factors in the cultivation of the conscious. "What may be called institutional virtue," writes Snider (1903, p. 248), "is for Socrates the fundamental and all-inclusive Virtue, the ground of the other Virtues." As such, Socrates believes in the common value of the state, he obeys the laws, performs his duties as a citizen. However, this does not hinder him from seeing defects in the existent state and its laws, and trying to remedy them. Indeed, his whole scheme of training in virtue is to produce a man who can make good laws, and so establish a good state. "What is Piety?" he asks, "not a blind worship of the gods, but worship of them according to their laws and customs, which one must know." (Snider 1903, p. 249). That is, one must know the law of the thing, the time of mere instinctive action and obedience is past.

Compared to Socrates, though Smedslund never uses the notion of the state, he does highlight the common sense of any human citizen belonging to a community. True psychological or therapeutic virtue thus depends upon culture and common sense, and common sense is regarded as a power of human beings that cannot be overturned by empirical inquiries. Hence, common sense encompasses good therapeutic practice as well as good political practice, and opposite; the lack of common sense implies absurdity. According to Smedslund, we can as human beings reflect upon our own psychological concepts and thus come to an improved understanding of what we can and must take for granted about human beings. Psychologists relying on statistically validated empirical generalizations, whether being unwise practitioners and/or mainstream researcher uncritically complying with the current scientific paradigm, can in this sense be compared to an instinctive individual, who does not adapt to the unique persons, and/or the situations, involved by aid of reflective reasoning about what may be possible and impossible for individuals in various situations.

As for Socrates, Smedslund praises the value of common sense, still, that does not prevent him from challenging the institutional virtue, which for Smedslund, in

[4] Meno (/ˈmiːnoʊ/; Greek: Μένων, Menōn) is a Socratic dialogue written by Plato. It appears to attempt to determine the definition of virtue, or areté, meaning virtue in general, rather than particular virtues, such as justice or temperance. Socrates introduces positive ideas: the theory of knowledge as recollection (anamnesis), among other.

some sense, represent the positivistic mainstream psychophysical knowledge. To Smedslund knowledge is dependent on context, culture (conventionality) and common sense knowledge, which for him constitutes the all-inclusive virtue. This all-inclusive virtue is thereby the determining factor of knowledge and conscious mental phenomena. When intellectuals in modern democracies constitute a community of cultural critics, according to Smedslund, psychologists have rarely seen themselves that way, largely because they are so caught up in the self-image generated by positivist science. Psychology, in this view, deals only in objective truths and eschews cultural criticism. Smedslund's point of view is that scientific psychology will fare better when it recognizes that its truths, like all truths about the human condition, are relative to the point of view that it takes toward that condition. It is where psychology starts and wherein it is inseparable from anthropology and the other cultural sciences, psychology then, needs explaining, not explaining away.

To Smedslund (2004), the wise researcher and the wise practitioner will feel at peace and at the height of their practice if they manage to contextualize themselves and their practices because there will be harmony between what he or she does as a professional, and his or her experience of life as human being. The new, wise, and peaceful practitioner will then have the virtue to know oneself and others and to work as what Claude Levi-Strauss called a bricoleur, that is, someone who creatively utilizes whatever possibilities are available in each unique case to solve the problems, but always relying on the calculus of psychologic (cf. Smedslund 2012, 2016a, b).

Know Thyself

The great Socratic maxim, "Know Thyself," is one of the strongest moral precepts in ethics and therapeutic practice. Although the sophists had already called attention to the fact that "man is the measure of all things," however this applied to the individual and not to human nature in general. "But Socrates proclaimed that this self-knowing Ego knows itself likewise as object, as the principle of the world, in which man is to find himself in order to know it." (Snider 1903, p. 234) To know one's self implies calmness of self-possession, fearlessness, and independence. Furthermore, it leads one to a striking realization of one's limitations and shortcomings, which form the foundations of success, and, as Forbes expresses it, "in this self-knowledge is the secret of blessing and success in the handling of human affairs, and right relationship with others." (Forbes 1978, p. 173).

Socrates, such as he is rendered in *Memorabilia* (Xenophon 1897, vol. II, book IV), discusses his maxim with Euthydemus. Through thoughts, experiments, and examples from everyday life, the discussion gives a clear and comprehensive idea of the subject matter:

> "Tell me, Euthydemus," Socrates says, "have you ever gone to Delphi?" "Yes, twice," replied he. "And did you observe what is written somewhere on the temple wall, Know Thyself?" "I did." "And did you take no thought of that inscription, or did you attend to it,

> and try to examine yourself to ascertain what sort of a character you are?" "I did not indeed try, for I thought that I knew very well already, since I should hardly know anything else if I did not know myself." "But whether does he seem to you to know himself, who knows his own name merely, or he who (like people buying horses, who do not think that they know the horse that they want to know, until they have ascertained whether he is tractable or unruly, whether he is strong or weak, swift or slow, and how he is as to other points which are serviceable or disadvantageous in the use of a horse so he), having ascertained with regard to himself how he is adapted for the service of mankind, knows his own abilities?" "It appears to me, I must confess," says Euthydemus, "that he who does not know his own abilities, does not know himself." "But is it not evident," Socrates replies, "that men enjoy a great number of blessings in consequence of knowing themselves, and incur a great number of evils, through being deceived in themselves? For they who know themselves know what is suitable for them, and distinguish between what they can do and what they cannot; and, by doing what they know how to do, procure for themselves what they need, and are prosperous, and by abstaining from what they do not know, live blamelessly, and avoid being unfortunate."

By gaining knowledge of yourself, Socrates (in Xenophon 1897, vol. II, book IV) believes that human beings can form an opinion of other human beings, and, by our experiences of the rest of humankind, obtain for ourselves what is good, and guard against what is evil. But those who do not know themselves, but are deceived in their own powers, are in similar case with regard to other human beings, and other human affairs, and neither understand what they require, nor what they are doing, nor the character of those with whom they connect themselves. Being in error as to all these particulars, they fail to obtain what is good, and fall into evil. On the other hand, they who understand what they take in hand, succeed in what they attempt, and become esteemed and honored.

In the *Dialogues about a New Psychology*, the three participant Eve, Adam, and Manny discusses the meaning of knowing yourself in order to understand another person under the mantra "If you do not understand something, move closer." (Smedslund 2004, pp. 144–147) Moving closer means in this case to get to know a person more completely. It refers to the quality, content, and scope of the interaction. A person can only know another person through an encounter. This involves focus also on the psychologist's person and strategy because what comes out of an encounter depends on both participating persons.

> Quality refers to the degree of openness that depends on the degree of mutual trust of the participant. Content refers to the centrality and relevance of the topics covered, and scope refers to the context of the encounter. (Smedslund 2004, p. 144).

Moving closer and knowing yourself is as such a matter of establishing trust. But it is also a matter of courage. In everyday life, the danger from the other one is always there. But also in professional work moving closer is risky. It will not do for you as a psychologist to remain closed and impersonal because this makes it hard for the client to trust you, not knowing who you are. On the other hand, the psychologist cannot just expose herself in the same way as the client does.

In the discussions (Smedslund 2004, p. 146), Adam says:

> I know practitioners distinguish between being personal and being private, but exactly what is this?

And Eve answers:

> The distinction really builds on the distinction between being 'on duty' and 'off duty' is to be professional, which is, having promotion of the client's best interest as one's superordinate goal. At the same time as being professional, one must move closer, and this entails placing oneself at risk. (...) Case study methodology, using open questions and repeated sessions, as well as being open yourself, helps you to move closer in order to determine what the person wants, thinks, feels, can and does. But even more important is the knowledge that concerns the interactive qualities of the person. A person interacts with other persons. Knowledge about this can only be gained through close encounter. The psychological researcher and practitioner are, or should be, capable of engaging in such encounter in a professional manner.

The virtues, which Socrates and Smedslund emphasize in their dialogues including courage, common sense, piety, and self-control, are continually relevant in our societies and embody some of the key attributes we continually strive for. But also of importance is the emphasis on knowing yourself. To truly know yourself means self-possession, fearlessness, and independence. It enables a person to come to terms not only with his/her limitations but also with his/her potential, which can lay the groundwork for success and realistic therapeutic goals. If a person, be it a psychologist or a patient, does not keep watching over him/herself, forestalling the irrational inclinations to wrongdoing, (s)he will impulsively do what is evil toward him/herself and other, even if (s)he rationally knows what is good. To help another person to gain self-understanding is therefore of high importance and should be a psychological and ethical goal in the therapeutic setting. Using Smedslund's common sense psychology in his doctoral thesis about the psychology of self-esteem, the Norwegian psychologist Waldemar Rognes (1996), clarified that people who systematically have been neglected with ignorance, hostility, and unwontedness, tends to have low self-esteem and self-understanding, and a correspondingly high need to be met with respect, care, and wondering, in the therapeutic setting. Broadly speaking, Smedslund and Rognes view is that any therapist who relies on randomized studies and statistics risks missing out upon various person's unique subjective needs and thereby also fail their ethical and psychological duties as a therapist.

Common Sense

The phrase "a common point of view as to the general nature of psychology" is and has been critical; it turns out to have both strong positive and strong negative results or connotations; it means the widening of the horizons of psychology, as well as the erection of a barrier to the acceptance of these views. By this statement, Smedslund brought himself within the purview of Thomas Kuhn's "structure of scientific revolutions," as described in his book of that title (Kuhn 1962). That is, on the positive side, Smedslund declares himself to be radical and more than "normal scientists," as Kuhn would say it; he has announced himself to be revolutionary. But revolutionaries are unwelcome in science unless they first provide results that lend credence to their views.

The challenge a psychologist meets when (s)he wants to be faithful to subjective experience is to construct a method by means of which reality as we live it is not exchanged for reality as it conforms to a readymade worldview. What Smedslund tries to tell us is that when we turn to experience and learn what it may have to teach us, we cannot do so by a scientific method constructed to exclude it. The wise practitioner, who acknowledges this, must follow his/her common sense, which in the therapeutic sense is an ethical and virtuous duty. Putting Smedslund's psycho-logic and common sense psychology into ethical considerations, a psychologist who holds high ethical and virtuous standards will always try to clarify a priori psychological knowledge in their approach to another human being. The upshot is that there are few fixed regular relations to be found by empirical methods. This is because any study of persons is also inquiry into the necessarily various, ongoing, dynamic processes of interaction. Nevertheless, meaningful distinctions can still be made between sociocultural practices and individual psychological experiences. It is through this never-ending sociocultural transformation that Smedslund's new psychology and bricoleurical method must be lodged.

What impresses me deeply is Smedslund's uncompromising intellectual sincerity and his courage to think through the consequences of his ideas carefully, and to speak out in public even when the scientific community does not want to listen and makes him pay a price for maintaining these standards. Smedslund's struggle as an academic is, in my view just like Socrates, about maintaining ethical and virtuous standards and intellectual integrity in a scientific community in which his ideas fell on hostile ground held by ignorant troops. Great thinkers often learn, to their surprise, that new ideas are less than welcome. Nevertheless, the virtue of "knowing yourself" continue to be relevant today; it does not only represent an important ethical facet of life when it comes to mental health and therapeutic work, but also to psychology as a science and academic discipline.

References

Bruner, J. S. (1990). *Acts of meaning*. Cambridge, MA: Harvard University Press.

Brunswik, E. (1956). *Perception and the representative design of psychological experiments* (2d ed.). Berkeley: University of California Press.

Brunswik, E. F. (1942). *Motivation and behavior*. Provincetown, MA: The Journal Press.

Danziger, K. (1997). *Naming the mind: How psychology found its language*. London: Sage Publications.

Forbes, J. T. (1978). *Socrates*. Folcroft, PA: Folcroft Library Editions.

Gergen, K. J. (1973). Social psychology as history. *Journal of Personality and Social Psychology, 26*(2), 309–320.

Goddard, C., & Wierzbicka, A. (1994). *Semantic and lexical universals: Theory and empirical findings*. Amsterdam/Philadelphia: John Benjamins.

Gomperz, T. (1906). *Greek thinkers: a history of ancient philosophy* (G. G. Berry, Trans. Authorized ed. Vol. 2, book 4: Socrates and the Socratics). London: John Murray.

Hacking, I. (1995). *Rewriting the soul: Multiple personality and the sciences of memory*. Princeton, NJ: Princeton University Press.

Harré, R. (2012). *Psychology for the third millenium integrating cultural and neuroscience perspectives*. Los Angeles, CA: SAGE.

Joranger, L. (2015). *Subjectivity as science and experience: An existential-phenomenological and historical approach to subjectivity, objectivity, and psychology*. (no. 543), Department of Psychology, Faculty of Social Sciences, University of Oslo, Oslo.

Kant, I. ([1787]1996). *Critique of Pure Reason* (W. S. Pluhar, trans.). Indianapolis: Hackett.

Kuhn, T. S. (1962). The structure of scientific revolutions. Chicago: University of Chicago Press.

Kvale, S. (1992). *Psychology and postmodernism*. London: Sage.

Martin, J., & Sugarman, J. (1999). *The psychology of human possibility and constraint*. Albany, NY: State University of New York Press.

Moghaddam, F. M. (2003). Interobjectivity and culture. *Culture and Psychology, 9*(3), 221–232.

Plato. (380 B.C.E.). (1994–2009) Meno. Retrieved from http://classics.mit.edu/Plato/meno.html

Richards, G. (2010). *Putting psychology in its place : Critical historical perspectives* (3rd ed.). London: Routledge.

Robinson, D. N. (1986). *An intellectual history of psychology*. Madison, WI/London: University of Wisconsin Press.

Rognes, W. (1996). *Selvfølelsens psykologikk* (Vol. B. 1). Oslo: Klinikk for psykiatri, Lovisenberg diakonale sykehus.

Rose, N. S. (1990). *Governing the soul : The shaping of the private self*. London/New York: Routledge.

Rose, N. S., & Abi-Rached, J. M. (2013). *Neuro : the new brain sciences and the management of the mind*. Princeton, NJ/Woodstock: Princeton University Press.

Schwegler, A. (1877). *Handbook of the history of philosophy* (6th ed.). Edinburgh: Oliver & Boyd.

Shweder, R. A. (1991). *Thinking through cultures: Expeditions in cultural psychology*. Cambridge, MA: Harvard University Press.

Smedslund, J. (1988). *Psycho-logic*. Berlin: Springer-Verlag.

Smedslund, J. (1991a). The pseudoempirical in psychology and the case for psychologic. *Psychological Inquiry, 2*(4), 325–338.

Smedslund, J. (1991b). Psychologic: A technical language for psychology. *Psychological Inquiry, 2*(4), 376–382.

Smedslund, J. (1997). *The structure of psychological common sense*. Mahwah, NJ: L. Erlbaum Associates.

Smedslund, J. (2004). *Dialogues about a new psychology*. Chagrin Falls, OH: Taos Institute.

Smedslund, J. (2012). The bricoleur-model of psychological practice. *Theory and Psychology, 22*, 643–657.

Smedslund, J. (2015). The value of experiments in psychology. In J. Sugarman, J. Martin, & K. L. Slaney (Eds.), *The Wiley handbook of theoretical and philosophical psychology: Methods, approaches, and new directions for social sciences* (pp. 359–373). Chichester: John Wiley & Sons.

Smedslund, J. (2016a). Why psychology cannot be an empirical science. *Integrative Psychological and Behavioral Science, 50*(2), 185–195.

Smedslund, J. (2016b). Practicing psychology without an empirical evidence-base. *New Ideas in Psychology, 43*, 50–56.

Smedslund, J., & Ross, L. (2014). Research-based knowledge in psychology: What, if anything, is its incremental value to the practitioner? *Integrative Psychological and Behavioral Science, 48*, 365–383. https://doi.org/10.1007/s12124-014-9275-1.

Snider, D. J. (1903). *Ancient European philosophy: the history of Greek philosophy psychologically treated*. St. Louis, MO: Sigma Publishing.
Taylor, C. (1989). *Sources of the self: The making of the modern identity*. Cambridge, MA: Harvard University Press.
Teigen, K. H. (2002). One hundred years of laws in psychology. *American Journal of Psychology, 115*(1), 103–118.
Tolman, E. C., & Brunswik, E. (1935). The organism and the causal texture of the environment. *Psychological Review, 42*(1), 43–77. https://doi.org/10.1037/h0062156.
Valsiner, J. (2014). *An invitation to cultural psychology*. Thousand Oaks, CA: Sage.
Vygotsky, L. S. (1978). *Mind in society: The development of higher psychological processes* (M. Cole ed.). Cambridge, MA: Harvard University Press.
Walsh, R. T. G., Teo, T., & Baydala, A. (2014). *A critical history and philosophy of psychology : Diversity of context, thought, and practice*. New York: Cambridge University press.
Wierzbicka, A. (1992). *Semantics, culture, and cognition : Universal human concepts in culture-specific configurations*. New York: Oxford University Press.
Wierzbicka, A. (1996). *Semantics: Primes and universals*. Oxford: Oxford University Press.
Windelband, W. (1905). *Über Willensfreiheit : zwölf Vorlesungen* (2. unver. Aufl. ed.). Tübingen: J. C. B. Mohr.
Windelband, W. (1919). *Präludien : Aufsätze und Reden zur Philosophie und ihrer Geschichte* (6. unveränderte Aufl. ed.). Tübingen: J.C.B. Mohr.
Xenophon. (1897). Memorabilia: Recollections of Socrates. Retrieved from https://ebooks.adelaide.edu.au/x/xenophon/x5me/index.html
Zeller, E. (1877). *Socrates and the Socratic schools* (O. J. Reichel, trans. 2nd ed.). London: Longmans.

Part II
Psychology as Science: Concepts and Epistemology

Chapter 6
Meanings of Words and the Possibilities of Psychology: Reflections on Jan Smedslund's Psychologic

Michael McEachrane

> *The confusion and barrenness of psychology is not to be explained by its being a 'young science'; its state is not comparable with that of physics, for instance, in its beginnings (...) For in psychology, there are experimental methods and conceptual confusion (...)*
> *The existence of the experimental method makes us think that we have the means of getting rid of the problems which trouble us; but problem and method pass one another by.*
>
> *Ludwig Wittgenstein, Philosophical Investigations*

Jan Smedslund offers two broad criticisms of the empirical research paradigm of scientific psychology. One is that psychologists have had a tendency to produce hypotheses, claims, and findings that are *pseudo-empirical*—i.e., understood as empirical and contingent when they actually are a priori and noncontingent (Smedslund 1991, 2016b). The other is that psychology cannot be an empirical science—at least not in the sense that natural science can—since it is about a domain that lacks invariant empirical conditions and laws (Smedslund 2016b). Underlying both these criticisms is the view that empirical psychology allegedly lacks sufficient grounding in conceptual analysis and definitions of terms on which psychology depends such as awareness, action, belief, and feeling (1991, 1997, 2011). Smedslund's advancements of Psychologic is intended to meet this need by providing a system of analyses and definitions of psychological terms (1988, 1990, 1997, 2012c). It offers an alternative model of psychology where empirical methods and studies are not treated as the exclusive nor even primary sources of knowledge and the goal of finding laws of cause and effect is forsaken (Smedslund 1990, 1991, 1997, 2004, 2011, 2012b, c, 2016b).

In this chapter, I examine four aspects of Smedslund's account of Psychologic—which are all of general import to psychology as a science. First, the role of reflecting on the meanings of words by reflecting on their use to psychology as a science

I would like to thank Tobias Gustum Lindstad for his helpful comments and suggestions on an earlier draft of this chapter

M. McEachrane (✉)
Raoul Wallenberg Institute of Human Rights and Humanitarian Law, Lund, Sweden

T. G. Lindstad et al. (eds.), *Respect for Thought*, Theory and History in the Human and Social Sciences, https://doi.org/10.1007/978-3-030-43066-5_6

(i.e., the role of conceptual investigations or analyses to psychology). This will be explored in the first section of the chapter by reflecting on the not fully recognized role of the meanings and uses of words in Psychologic.

Second, the charge—by Smedslund and before him similarly by Wittgenstein—of *pseudo-empiricality* in psychology and the need to distinguish conceptual from empirical investigations (Wittgenstein 2009/1953; cf. McEachrane 2006, 2009a, b). Smedslund's understanding of the conflation of empirical with conceptual issues in psychology will be both criticized and elaborated on in the second section ("On Pseudo-empiricality).

Third, the nature of the meanings of psychological terms and statements. Smedslund's supposition that psychological terms at minimum have a core meaning of necessary conditions will be examined in the third and the fourth parts of the chapter (respectively, "On the Nature of Meaning" and "Smedslund on the Need for Necessary Conditions").

Fourth, the method of analyzing the meanings of psychological terms and statements. The fifth part of the chapter ("On investigating the Meaning of words….") reviews and finfs wanting the three central methods of Psychologic for justifying its propositions, investigating the meanings of psychological terms and distinguishing between conceptual and empirical matters in psychology.

In the sixth and concluding part of the chapter, I point to ways in which Psychologic importantly reveals the import to psychology of reflecting on the meanings of words—but misleads on the nature and implications of such reflections.

Psychologic has also earlier been criticized by scholars inspired by Wittgenstein (e.g., Shotter 1991, 1994, 1999; Parrott and Harré 1991; Harré 1999; McEachrane 2009b). To some extent Smedslund (1997, 1999b, 2004) has modified his ideas in response to their arguments. However, there is a further argument to be made that neither the critique nor the response to it have been far-reaching enough and that Psychologic needs to be substituted for an alternative form of conceptual investigations and view of the language and possibilities of psychology. The following examination of Smedslund's Psychologic seeks to point towards such a complementary method for and view of psychology as a science (cf. McEachrane 2006, 2009a, b).

On the Roles of Meaning

Among the assumptions of Psychologic is that psychology uses and depends on psychological terms whose meanings are given—by ordinary language or what we take for granted about each other as persons—and determine how psychological data and phenomena can be meaningfully described. Although there is truth to this assumption, especially later iterations of Psychologic construe it in misleading ways.

What especially later versions of Psychologic misconstrues can be summarized as the following five methodological principles of why and how conceptual investigations are relevant to psychology as a science:

1. The most elemental questions that may be asked about statements of psychology as a science are questions about their meanings.
2. Statements of psychology as a science must first make *sense* before they can be true or false.
3. Reflecting on the meanings of words by reflecting on their use is integral to clarifying and determining the meanings of statements of psychology as a science.
4. In clarifying and determining the meanings and uses of terms such as "feeling," "thought," and "want" in psychology as a science we need to take into consideration how such terms are ordinarily used outside of psychology as a science.
5. Methods of conceptual investigations into the scientific and ordinary meanings and uses of words are epistemically primary to determining the (possible) meanings, truth, and falsity of statements of psychology as a science [—whereas experimental and other empirical methods are epistemically secondary to determining the (possible) meanings, truth, and falsity of statements of psychology as a science]. (Cf. McEachrane 2006).

Whereas these principles were at least partly adhered to in earlier versions of Psychologic, in later versions they have been either abandoned or misconstrued (e.g., Smedslund 1988, 2012b). Below is a brief account of this development and how it puts the methodology of Psychologic into trouble.

In earlier versions of Psychologic, it was thought that the meanings of psychological terms are embedded in ordinary language and that uncovering these meanings can provide a conceptual framework for psychology (Smedslund 1988, 1990). This was to be done by offering *definitions* of such terms of ordinary language as awareness, want, belief, feeling, and action. In later developments, Psychologic is envisioned as definitions of technical/scientific terms (so-called *axioms*).[1] Although these definitions no longer have the purpose of defining ordinary language terms, the aim of Psychologic still is to capture the "core" meaning—i.e., the *necessary conditions*—of psychologically relevant natural language (Smedslund 1997, pp. x–xi; 2011, p. 127–133). However, now the objective of the definitions (axioms) of Psychologic is to summarize basic assumptions that go beyond language and that refer to how we as persons (irrespective of our language or culture) automatically *conceive of*, and what we *take for granted about*, every person (Smedslund 2012b, p. 297; 2012c, p. 661). For example, whereas Psychologic previously intended to define *the ordinary concept of "feeling"* as a state of awareness that is determined by the relationship between a person's wants and beliefs (Smedslund 1988, p. 35)—"feeling" is now accounted for as part of an alleged axiom that *every person takes for granted that what any person feels follows from the relation between what they want and think* (2012b, p. 298). This shift is bound up with the idea that Psychologic now is based on *semantic primitives*—meanings which there are terms for in every human language and are expressive of how we conceive of each other as human persons irrespective of language or culture (Smedslund 2012b, c).

[1] Axioms have two defining features: (i) they imply numerous and important other sentences, yet cannot themselves be derived from any more basic sentences; (ii) they are experienced as necessary (Smedslund 2012b, p. 296).

Examples of such semantic primitives are: "I," "you," "someone," "people," "when," "before," "after," "because," "do," "think," "know," "want," "feel," "see," "hear," "good," and "bad" (Smedslund 2012b, pp. 299–300; Wierzbicka 1996). In order to qualify as an axiom in Psychologic, a proposition should be stated in terms of semantic primitives only and should in principle be translatable to any human language (Smedslund 2012b, p. 299).

Whereas earlier versions of Psychologic perhaps gave definitions and "ordinary language" an unwarrantedly reified status in psychology, later versions (e.g., Smedslund 2011, 2012b, c) fail to properly recognize the import to psychology of reflecting on the meanings of words by reflecting on their use. In later versions, Psychologic intends to ground psychology on how we, allegedly, *must* perceive things and Wierzbicka's empirically based theory of "semantic primitives," rather than in descriptions (definitions) of the meanings of words per se. However, it is not obvious that this move has strengthened Psychologic and its contribution of pointing out the import of describing, reflecting on, and clarifying the meanings of psychological words, terms, queries, and statements. For instance, whether or not a statement in psychology is to be understood as an empirical statement to be addressed by empirical means such as experiments and surveys or may actually (perhaps unreflectively) be a statement about the meanings of words. A case in point are the meanings of the axioms of Psychologic. Regardless of any empirical findings of "semantic primitives" to support them, it would seem that their viability depends on the ordinary meanings and uses of words and may be examined by reflecting on these.

Some of the elemental relevance to psychology as a science of reflecting on the meanings of words by reflecting on their use—as outlined above by the five methodological principles—may be demonstrated by turning to the axioms of Psychologic. For example, consider the earlier mentioned axiom about feeling:[2] "P takes for granted that what O feels, follows from the relation between what O wants and what O thinks" (Smedslund 2012b, p. 298). The most elemental questions to be asked about this axiom—or any other statement of psychology—are questions about its meaning. How, if at all, does it make sense to say that "we as persons take for granted that what a person feels follows from the relation between what they want and what they think"? "Take for granted" how? When, in which situations and how do we take this for granted about people's "feelings"/"emotions"? How, if at all, does it make sense to claim that "what a person feels follows from the relation between what a person wants and thinks"? If we understand this axiom—as we probably should (cf. Smedslund 1997, pp. 51, 53, 57)—as claiming that "all emotions are (at least in part) constituted by, and a result of, a combination of what a person wants and believes," then do terms such as "joy," "fear," "disgust," and "sadness" always refer to a combination of beliefs and wants? How does this make sense? This may be examined by reflecting on the use of such terms and in doing so consider how such terms are ordinarily used outside of psychology as a science. Irrespective of the truth of "semantic primitives" on which the later iterations of

[2] I take it that Smedslund by "feeling" in this axiom means the same as "emotions" and does not include sensations/sensory experiences such as the feeling of wind against one's face.

Psychologic are based, in examining the meanings of Psychologic axioms and how they may or may not make sense, we need to turn to how psychological terms ordinarily are used. For instance, by asking ourselves if we always and in every situation to which such terms as "joy," "fear," "disgust," and "sadness" may be applied use and understand such terms in the sense of being a combination of beliefs and wants? If we speak of someone's "joy of a warm summer's day," does this "joy" necessarily refer to belief(s) and a particular relationship between what the person wants and what they believe—say, that one's want to experience a warm summer's day has been fulfilled (see Smedslund 1997, p. 51)? This seems doubtful. It would make perfect sense to speak of such joy as deriving from, say, the warmth, the light, the greenery, and leisurely atmosphere of a warm summer's day rather than any beliefs about these (McEachrane 2009b, pp. 35–36).[3] To this Smedslund might respond that at a minimum such joy would not be joy if there was nothing about the warmth, light, etc., that was experienced as good for the person, and, hence, as something that the person wants. This relates to his so-called "hedonism axiom": "P thinks that O wants to feel good and that O wants not to feel bad" (e.g., 2011, p. 131). Adding the hedonism axiom to the axiom on feeling—joy presumably must involve an evaluation of something as good to the person feeling joy and hence as something that the person desires. Still, this is yet another dubious understanding and necessary condition of what it may mean to feel "joy." For instance, what sort of a presumed evaluation need to be present to enjoy the warmth, the light, etc., of a warm summer's day? "The warmth that I am experiencing now is good for me as I like warm weather" or "this warm weather is good for my physical well-being and health"? Here it would seem to make more sense that what one is taking joy in is not an *evaluation* of the warmth, the light, etc., as good—but rather the warmth, the light, etc., itself; how the warmth feels in one's body and the brightness, colorfulness, and spectacles of the sunlight across the landscape, etc. It may also be the case that even if one evaluates the warm summer's day as good for oneself—one may not be able to take joy in it or experience its goodness as it were since, say, one is in a depressed

[3] Conversely, it would not be a logical contradiction to claim that it is not certain that feelings will follow from any given combination of wants and beliefs. Although not a typical response, a person may believe that they are in grave danger—say because of being in a crashing plane to take an extreme example—and very much want to get out of the danger, yet do not feel fear (or feel little fear). Maybe because the situation gave rise to a razor-like focus and bare presence to the situation or because they are trained to deal with situations of danger or are advanced meditators who can remain calm and collect even in such situations. This may amaze us, but should not strike us as logically contradictory. To this Smedslund may respond that since it is commonplace that the capacity for simultaneous attention is limited, a person may indeed believe that they are in grave danger, but still are not afraid because, say, all of their attention is on getting out of the dangerous situation (cf. Smedslund 1999a, p. 7). This could be an explanation for some cases where there seems to be a given combination of wants and beliefs without a corresponding given emotional response, but not for all such cases. For example, a person may feel no fear or little fear when confronting a situation that they believe that it involves grave danger to their lives and very much would like to avoid—such as facing terminal cancer—and without being distracted, preoccupied, or absorbed by something else, but still not feeling fear because, say, they have resigned themselves to the situation or become so used to it that it no longer scares them or make them feel sad for what the situation means (such as an irrevocable loss to themselves and their loved ones) rather than fear.

mood with dulled senses, a lack of presence, and a preoccupation with ruminations about the past.

In any case, the point here is mostly a methodological one of demonstrating the relevance to psychology as a science—and in this case to examining the axioms of Psychologic—of reflecting on the meanings of words by reflecting on their use. To this Smedslund might respond that Psychologic is a "technical language" that defines how we *must* perceive persons—and that although it captures the core or prototypical meanings of psychological terms it may not capture all ordinary uses of these terms (Smedslund 2011, 2012b, p. 300; 2012c, p. 660). This as a way of defending it against the sort of charge that has just been demonstrated—that, over and above grounding Psychologic in Wierzbicka's empirical theory of "Semantic primitives," the statements of Psychologic need to answer to reflections on their meanings by reflecting on their use and take into consideration our ordinary use and understanding of psychological terms. Nevertheless, if it makes sense to speak of, say, joy in a warm summer's day, phobic fears of spiders one knows can do one no harm, disgust for slimy substances, anger at having stepped on a sharp stone, inexplicable sadness about everything and nothing—as emotions that are not constituted by or the result of beliefs, then it is false to claim that we *must* understand emotions as following from beliefs and that this is something that we as humans *take for granted* about each other (McEachrane 2009b, p. 36). If anything, pointing out that some emotions may be spoken of and understood in terms of beliefs whereas others may not, is to display the variety of emotions that psychology may study and how to understand them as a subject. If psychology is to understand psychological phenomena for what they are—whatever their complexities and nuances—it will not be helpful to replace "ordinary language" with the "technical language" of Psychologic. For example, if by emotion terms like "joy," "fear," "disgust," and "anger" we do not mean what we ordinarily may mean by these terms, then the question arises whether or not the subject matter has been changed or is insufficiently represented, what exactly psychology is studying when it claims to be studying emotions, how and why it differs from what we ordinarily mean by emotion (cf McEachrane 2009b, pp. 36–38). Here, Smedslund may persist that the "technical language" of Psychologic need not overlap or be congruent with "ordinary language" terms for emotion; that the same terms may be used in Psychologic and ordinary language to refer to different things and that if anything it will be relevant to Psychologic to clarify these different senses; maybe with the additional caveat that Psychologic is a *theory* meant to capture core psychological phenomena to which exceptions may be expected and welcomed and accounted for by complementary explanations. However, Psychologic will then need to give up its language of a priori truths, logical implication, necessity, and what we *must* take for granted of psychological phenomena. Instead, it will need to rely on such terms as "typically," "generally," and "in most cases" we take it for granted that, say, what people feel follows from what they want and think. This will then be contingent on empirical claims of frequency (of people's assumptions of each other's psychology). In any case (and, again, emphasizing the methodological point that reflecting on the meanings of words by reflecting on their use is elemental to psychology), Psychologic will need to turn to the garden variety of ordinary language uses of psychological terms to delineate what it means and does not mean, includes, excludes, why and how—by its use and understanding of psychological terms. In contrast to earlier versions of Psychologic, the point here is not that psychological terms are embedded in an "ordinary language" that psychology must uncover and follow to make sense (Smedslund 1988). Rather, references to "ordinary" are here merely meant to point to ways in which we may use words in our daily lives when we are not doing science.

On Pseudo-Empiricality

A hallmark of Smedslund's contribution to psychology is the critique that much of its research is *pseudo-empirical* and misapplies empirical methods such as experiments to queries to which they are not relevant. Although this charge is fair, Smedslund misconstrues it as "research that attempts to test propositions believed to be empirical and contingent but that can be shown to be a priori and noncontingent, given plausible definitions and axioms" (1991, p. 325; cf. also 1990, pp. 53–4; 2016b).

Here too, Smedslund misrecognizes the relevance to psychology as a science of reflecting on the meanings of words by reflecting on their use. His understanding of "pseudo-empiricism" fails to recognize how it is the meanings of words themselves—not whether these can or cannot be formulated as definitions, axioms, necessary conditions, or rules—that determine whether a statement, issue, or question in psychology is to be addressed by conceptual or empirical means or a mixture of the two. Moreover, it treats propositions in psychology as necessarily either conceptual or empirical—whereas they can be a mixture of the two.

An alternative understanding of "pseudo-empirical" research that avoids such issues is as *research that seeks to empirically test what follows from the meanings of words*.

Harking back to the five methodological principles outlined in the previous section—this understanding recognizes that the most elemental questions that may be asked about statements of psychology are questions about their meanings; and that reflecting on the meanings of words by reflecting on their use is integral to clarifying and determining the meanings of the statements of psychology. Faced with a question such as "Do people's emotions follow from what they want and think?" psychology will need to inquire into its meaning to figure out how to address it. In psychology, it may be assumed that such a question is to be addressed by experimental or otherwise empirical means—whereas investigating the meaning of the question may reveal that the answer to the question follows from the meanings of emotion terms (McEachrane 2009a, b). For example, it may follow from what it means for someone in a given situation to be "angry" that their preferences have been thwarted and that they thought something that made them angry. A child may be angry because it thinks that its new ball that it loves has been stolen and this thought and frustration may be part of what makes it "angry." What is of essence here is that thoughts and wants may follow from what it *means* to be angry—not whether or not this meaning can be reduced to, summarized, or encapsulated by definitions or axioms. We do not need to define words or assume certain definitions of words in order to refer to their meanings—it is sufficient that we agree on how words may be used and what these uses may mean (cf. the next four sections below). To determine whether or not the statement, "Thoughts are either internal images or self-talk," is empirical—we do not need an additional axiom for "thoughts." Instead, what we need is to examine whether this statement can be addressed by reflecting on what it may mean to "think" (cf McEachrane 2009a).

Furthermore, the Psychological understanding of pseudo-empiricism may give a false impression that propositions are either categorically empirical and contingent *or* a priori and noncontingent. A categorically "pseudoempirical" proposition could be to seek to empirically test whether "Surprised persons have experienced something unexpected" whereas "to have experienced something unexpected" follows from what it means "to be surprised" (Smedslund 2016b, p. 190). However, other psychologically relevant propositions may be a mixed bag with respect to their conceptual and/or empirical content and we may very well, and indeed should, keep it an open question whether or not, to what extent and how any given proposition is empirical, conceptual, or a mixture of the two. What is of essence to "pseudo-empiricism" as a methodological misstep in psychology is that it is meaningful to distinguish between empirical and conceptual quandaries, and that psychology may misidentify conceptual for empirical quandaries, not that this distinction always must be categorical and cannot sometimes be blurred or overlapping.

An example taken from outside Smedslund's Psychologic—for all I know, he may agree with me on this point—is the proposition, "Persons with low self-esteem are more prone to depression," an empirical one to be studied by surveys and the like, conceptual to be studied by reflecting on the meanings and uses of words or a mixture of the two (cf. Sowislo and Orth 2013)? On the one hand, feelings of worthlessness and other forms of low self-esteem are part of the symptoms, signs, or criteria of clinical depression, and low self-esteem is an essential part of how some psychologists understand what it means to be clinically depressed (cf. American Psychiatric Association 2013; Beck et al. 1990). If having low self-esteem is among the typical elements or criteria of having a depression, this belongs to the clinical understanding or definition of the term "depression," and the term "self-esteem" is understood or defined in the same way with or without it being a part of depression, then it would indeed seem to be an instance of pseudo-empiricism to treat the proposition as empirical whereas it follows from the meanings of the terms that, "Persons with low self-esteem are more prone to depression."[4] On the other hand, even if we

[4] Here—again without presuming that Smedslund would disagree—it would be insufficient to propose as a counter-argument that "low self-esteem" and "depression" are not synonymous; that having "low self-esteem" is not a sufficient or even necessary condition of being depressed; that low self-esteem is a feature of a wide range of other clinical conditions too such as learning disorders, stuttering, and social phobia; or that the correlation between having low self-esteem and being depressed varies across empirical studies, that feelings of worthlessness are present only in a portion of individuals diagnosed with depression and do not belong to the most frequent depressive symptoms (Sowislo and Orth 2013, p. 216). For even if it only is sometimes that people who suffer from depression also suffer from low self-esteem as part of their depression or that people with low self-esteem develop clinical depression during their life time—still, having low self-

were to agree that it can be determined merely by reflecting on the meanings and uses of words that already feeling worthless, inadequate, etc. makes one more prone to clinical depression than not feeling this way—the clinical concept of "depression" as including "low self-esteem" among its defining features or indicators may itself be born of empirical research of the symptoms of people with depressed moods most of the days for at least 2 weeks (i.e., the necessary criteria for clinical "major depression"). For instance, it may be found that—out of many possible symptoms which it could make sense are due to or part of being depressed such as ruminations about the past, negative assessments of present life circumstances, opportunities, or future prospects—feelings of worthlessness stand out as a common feature or symptom of major depression and make one more prone to depression than any of these other possible symptoms (American Psychiatric Association 2013). This central role of low self-esteem as an especially common feature of depression may then be an empirical finding.[5] All this merely to say that rather than treating propositions in psychology as categorically empirical or conceptual—it makes sense to be open to that their content could be a mixed bag.

On the Nature of Meaning

Besides pointing to the role of meaning in psychology as a science and its need to reflect on the meanings of words to determine whether or not, why and how its propositions are empirical—the axiomatic system of Psychologic relies on a specific understanding of the nature of the meanings of psychological terms. This understanding includes at least two controversial assumptions or premises. The first contentious presumption is that the meanings of ordinary psychological terms have a "core or essence" of necessary conditions that the axiomatic system of Psychologic captures. In Psychologic what a word or sentence "means" refers to what "follows from" or is "logically implied" by it and can be expressed by formulaic "if A, then B" propositions with fixed truth-conditions (Smedslund 1997, 2011, pp. 128–129). For example, according to the earlier mentioned Axiom 8 on *feeling,* what a person feels (say, anger) follows from a combination of what the person wants and thinks (say, wanting to keep a job and thinking that they have been unfairly fired from it) (Smedslund 2012b, p. 298; 2012c, p. 664). According to this axiom, "if a person wants to keep a job and thinks that they have been unfairly fired from it, then it is also true that they are angry." Inversely, "if a person is angry, then it is also true that

esteem will increase the probability of having or developing major depression. In addition, with or without the clinical understanding and definition of depression it makes a lot of sense to claim that persons with low self-esteem are more prone to depression and little or no sense to claim that it will make no probable difference or likely make persons *less* prone to depression. For instance, feeling worthless or lousy about oneself as a person, inadequate in living up to basic standards of who one thinks one ought to be and so on—is itself a reason to become or be depressed.

[5] Leaving aside for now issues of psychology as a domain of empirical inquiry such as the empirical status of psychological phenomena and their relative variance or invariance.

they are wanting and thinking something that makes them angry." In other words, what it means "to feel" something (in this case, "to be angry") has certain fixed truth-conditions—such that whenever a person is feeling something it must also be true that they want and think something (that is making them feel what they feel, e.g., angry). The second contentious assumption is that ultimately what makes sense in psychology—allegedly encapsulated by the axioms of Psychologic—follows logically from how we as persons automatically *conceive of*, and what we *take for granted about*, every person (Smedslund 1997, 2012b, c).

None of these assumptions seem to stand the scrutiny of reflecting on the meanings and uses of psychological terms. Regarding the first assumption, it falsely projects logical necessity, implication, and fixed truth-conditions onto the meanings of words. In a nutshell, it falsely insists that words *must* have necessary conditions for their (truthful) application (and, hence, logical implications with fixed truth-conditions). Although psychological terms may have necessary conditions for their application, they do not always—arguably, even usually—have such conditions and at least outside science there is no reason why they should. The second assumption does not fair better in so far as it merely shifts the emphasis from logically necessary *meanings* to *assumptions*. Even if the later iterations of Psychologic claims to have abandoned attempts to define natural/ordinary language terms by seeking necessary and sufficient conditions for their application; even while Psychologic no longer is understood as clarifying conceptual relations between such terms; and the onus now is wholly on what we as humans *must take for granted* (Smedslund, e.g., 1997, p. xi; 2012c, pp. 660–661)—nevertheless, the proposed axioms of Psychologic need to stand the test of whether, how, if at all, they are logically necessary; manage to capture the core or essence of what it means to "think," "feel," "speak," "learn"; and, thus, what the axioms include, exclude, how, why, what are the implications of this and so forth.

In what follows, I will briefly consider the two contentious issues outlined above in more detail with a few reflections on the meanings of some of the purported axioms of Psychologic. According to Axiom 2 on *intentionality*, "P takes it for granted that what O knows, thinks, feels, perceives, says and does, is partly directed by what O wants" (Smedslund 2012b, p. 297). From Smedslund's own explanation of this axiom, it seems clear that it contains three propositions: (i) knowing, thinking, feeling, perceiving, saying, and doing is always directed towards something that it is about; (ii) this something always involves a degree of want, satisfaction, or dissatisfaction; and (iii) our doing always is directed at increasing satisfaction and decreasing dissatisfaction. Proposition (i) seems to suggest that all psychological phenomena are "about something." However, psychological moods and dispositions such as "joyfulness," "depression," and "cheerfulness" may be about everything and nothing in particular.[6] Proposition (ii) suggests that psychological phenomena, thinking and perceiving, always involve a degree of want, satisfaction, or dissatisfaction. Still, we may wake up in the morning and let our gaze wander around the room, without the "perception" of the room involving a degree of want, satisfaction, or

[6] In response to Smedslund's "hedonism axiom" (cf above and 2011, p. 131), neither is it so that, say, or joyfulness or cheerfulness need to be based on any particular evaluation of something or other as good; people may even be joyful or cheerful despite evaluations of something or other as bad and something they do not want (like being turned down on an application or not having a job).

dissatisfaction. We may "know" a lot of things about which we have no particular desire such as the difference between the colors green and red, detailed knowledge of global geography or how many letters there are in the English alphabet. Proposition (iii) suggests that our doings always are directed at increasing satisfaction and decreasing dissatisfaction. Yet, we may "think" disturbing thoughts, say, recollect traumatic experiences that do not seem to be directed at increasing satisfaction nor decreasing dissatisfaction, "make" a mindless remark that turned out to be hurtful while thinking about something else or have a general inclination to "day dream" or "ruminate" regardless of what satisfaction or dissatisfaction it might bring.

According to Axiom 4 on *verbality,* we take it for granted that we can always say something about what we know *that* we know, think, want, feel, perceive, say, and do, and *only* about that (Ibid). Trivial as this may seem, it includes two related points that both allow for exceptions: (i) we cannot speak about what we know, think, feel, etc. *before* it has become explicitly/reflectively known to us; and (ii) we can only say something about what we know *that* we know, think, want, etc. For instance, we may say something about things that we did *not* know that we knew, thought, or felt—such as novel conclusions on a topic while giving a lecture or pointing out complex directions that we did not know that we knew. We may also express more anger or sadness about something in a conversation than we thought or knew that we had and that becomes explicitly/reflectively known to us first *after* we have spoken. Not to mention various forms of tacit knowledge where we may know that we know how to do something, but perhaps cannot say something about it—such as keeping the balance while cycling, imitating people well, or drawing a precise line in a portrait.

Although Axiom 5 on *learning* is supposed to capture the human ability and inclination to learn—it is open to interpretation how this is done by the definition, "P takes it for granted that what O thinks will happen after now, follows from what O thinks happened before now" (Smedslund 2012b, p. 298; cf. 2012c, p. 663). On one interpretation, "learning" consists of thoughts about the future ("what will happen after now") that follow from thoughts about the past ("what happened before now").[7] However, this provides a truncated understanding of the many possible ways in which human beings have the ability to "learn"—even if we limit this ability only to the sort of learning that can be expressed in words and exclude nonverbal kinds of learning (which the axiom does not seem to do). For instance, we may learn facts about history, say, the Mali Empire, the meaning of "modus ponens" in logic, how to fill out a form, why a remark we made at a party was hurtful, and much else that are not thoughts about the future following from thoughts about the

[7] There are two other interpretations that both seem to cancel themselves out as axioms since they are not about the meaning or nature of "learning" per se (i.e. a second and a third interpretation). On a second interpretation, the axiom states that we as human persons take for granted that we have the ability and also the inclination to think that what will happen in the future (after now) follows from what we thought happened in the past (before now)—and that we have an ability and inclination to "learn" in this sense and that we take for granted of each other that we do. On a third interpretation, everything we think will happen in the future (after now) follows from what we think happened in the past (before now) and is a kind of "learning" that we take for granted of each other.

past. Even thoughts about the future need not be derived from thoughts about the past, but could be derived from, e.g., religious convictions about salvation, an optimism that goodness ultimately will prevail, one's current understanding of human nature and the state of world affairs or an advanced understanding of the state of the art and possibilities of Artificial Intelligence.

Axiom 6 is on *responsibility*, "P takes it for granted that O is responsible for what O says and does" (Smedslund 2012b, p. 298). Even if it may be a true (empirical) statement of what most people take for granted about persons in most situations—we need not, and perhaps should not, assume that persons always or even ever are responsible for what they say or do. They may have had a momentary epileptic fit or be on a medication that, although it did not take away their ability to act, made them somewhat incapacitated and drowsy, and therefore, say, turn into a car in the opposite direction and fail to pull the brakes in time. Similarly, people may act while being psychotic or otherwise mentally impaired, out of instinct in situations of severe distress, in ways that unintentionally lead to accidents or they may be too young to act deliberatively. In cases like these, it is at least not obvious if and how we should ascribe responsibility to what people say and do. Perhaps there is even a convincing case to be made that as everything we say or do ultimately is a result of neurophysiological causes or for other reasons is based on an illusory sense of self and experience of ourselves as actors/doers—we cannot take it for granted that people are responsible for what they say and do (e.g., Caruso and Flanagan 2018; Repetti 2017).

According to Axiom 7 on *morality*, "P takes it for granted that O wants to do what O thinks is right, and wants not to do what O thinks is wrong" (Ibid). In Smedslund's own words this "axiom asserts that people think that a desire to do what the person thinks is right always exists" (Smedslund 2012c, p. 663). However, he goes on, the axiom does not exclude that persons may behave in ways that they think are wrong, but when this is the case we assume that the person wants something else more strongly than doing what is right (Ibid). Nevertheless, even with this caveat, the axiom does not express something that we must take for granted; in this case about the nature of "morality," what it means "to be a person" or our beliefs about these. It may make perfect sense to say of someone that "they do not do…," "do not want to do…," or "do not care to do what they think is right." Not because they have a stronger conflicting desire, but because perhaps "they lack integrity," "do not care about doing what they think is right" or "do not have any thoughts or know what to think in terms of right and wrong about what they do or want to do." In addition, rather than taking for granted that human nature and/or the inherent social reality of human beings is such that human persons want to do what they think is right (unless there is a stronger conflicting desire to do otherwise)—some people may take for granted that human persons are self-interested beings who only want to do what they think serves their own interests, including sometimes doing what is deemed "right" (cf. Smedslund 2012b, 298; 2012c, p. 664).

These are merely some examples that put into question either of the premises of Psychologic that its axioms express necessary, logical truths and that the meanings of words must have necessary conditions (older version) or that its axioms are about "what we should take for granted in our understanding of the world" (newer version) (2012c, 660–61).

Smedslund on the Need for Necessary Conditions

Smedslund addresses the sort of objections to the axioms of Psychologic, as outlined above, in at least four ways.

One way is to argue that as science requires necessary conditions for the application of its terms, an invariant component in the use of words must be assumed and necessary definitions be pursued by Psychologic. This is to construct an explicit, meaningful, and definite scientific language for psychology (Smedslund 2011, p. 128). However, even if we were to assume that psychology as a science needs to be able to define its terms, this cannot be made to mean that psychology must assume that words have necessary conditions for their application or that they—even in the technical language of Psychologic—capture what we must take for granted. If anything, this should mean that even if words may not have necessary conditions for their application or stand for what we must take for granted about the world—for scientific purposes psychology needs to *give* them necessary definitions or at least be able to clearly state what they mean in the context of the research. Rather than assuming that words *do* or *must* have necessary conditions or stand for what we must take for granted—it could be the case that psychologists for the sake of doing science use words and describe psychological phenomena in a limited or confined sense. It may then be of interest to the scientific enterprise to clarify how this sense is limited or confined and what about psychological phenomena it captures and what if anything it does not.

Another way Smedslund addresses these sort of objections is to argue that although one may doubt that the ordinary uses of psychological terms can be boiled down to necessary conditions—each word must have some fixed core meaning in order to be useful in language since words with no definite meaning exclude nothing, and, hence, are useless (Smedslund 2011, p. 133). However, to the contrary there is no reason why we cannot learn to both identify many different words as well as different uses of the same words without joint necessary conditions (such as a river "bank" and a monetary "bank").

A similar and third way Smedslund addresses the sort of objections to Psychologic mentioned above is by arguing that the assumption that words have fixed, core meanings explains why the same word may be used in seemingly very different situations (Smedslund 2011, p. 126). In an example borrowed from me (McEachrane 2009b, p. 36), Smedslund points out that,

> You can, for example, be "angry" at a person for treating you without respect, but occasionally also for being irresponsible, cold, a nuisance, dumb, a poor student, or for belonging to

> the wrong ethnic group, worshipping the wrong deity, having poor taste, not trying hard enough, and so on.[8] (2011, p. 126)

How can it be, Smedslund wonders, that the response to all these situations sometimes is described by the *same* particular word "anger"? (Ibid). His response is that unless an invariant component exists in the usage of the word "anger," it becomes a mystery how we all know when this same word can be applied. Although we can speculate that people may learn separately that the same word applies to the way we react to two situations without any relevant similarities in response whatsoever, it remains hard to avoid asking why the reactions to these two situations should be described by the same word, and not by different words. Especially, if we consider a third, fourth situation and so forth; where the "cognitive burden of learning innumerable completely unrelated uses of the same word would rapidly transcend all plausible limits" (Smedslund 2011, pp. 126–127). However, here we need to distinguish *describing* that words lack necessary conditions or how putative necessary conditions are not necessary after all, from *explaining* why the same word may be used in different ways without a joint, necessary condition. What primarily is at stake here is whether or not psychological terms do have necessary conditions, not how we should explain their use if they do not. Still, a possible explanation for the possibility that words may lack necessary conditions for their application yet still be successfully used and understood could be that the similarities of their various uses cluster in a "family" of uses conjoined by overlapping and criss-crossing similarities (like the resemblances between members of a family in build, features, color of eyes, temperament, and so on) (cf. Wittgenstein 2009/1953, §§66–67). Besides, in the spirit of science even if a phenomena or fact may be a mystery yet (or perhaps never) to be explained, this is not an argument against it.

A fourth counter-argument by Smedslund against objections to that words have necessary conditions is that—according to later versions of Psychologic—the meanings of psychological terms ultimately follow from what we (irrespective of our language or culture) *take for granted* about human persons. The axioms of Psychologic are supposed to define these anterior or basic presuppositions underlying the meanings of psychological terms (e.g., Smedslund 1997, 2011, 2012b, c). Since the axioms of Psychologic no longer are understood as based on ordinary language per se, but on anterior and universal human presuppositions—even if the axioms may not encompass all possible meanings and uses of ordinary psychological terms they at least define their core or prototype meanings (Smedslund 2011, p. 127; 2012b, p. 295–299; 2012c, pp. 660–661, 664–665). Notwithstanding this supposed theoretical status of Psychologic to the extent that its axioms at all make sense as being about what we "take for granted" and defining the necessary conditions for, core or essences of, psychological terms—they must stand the test of

[8]This was used by me as an example to put into question an axiom (4.6.4) on *anger,* "P is angry at O, if and only if, P believes that at least one person whom P cares for has, intentionally or through neglect, been treated without respect by O, and P has not forgiven O" (Smedslund 1997, p. 53).

being examined if and how and in which situations it makes sense to say that we as human persons must "take for granted" this or that or that the axioms indeed manage to capture the necessary conditions, core or essences of the meanings and uses of psychological terms.

On Investigating the Meanings of Words and What we (Supposedly) Take for Granted

The propositions of Psychologic mainly rely on three kinds of methods for their justification.

Among these is the empirical and linguistic work of Anna Wierzbicka and others behind the idea that the meanings of some words such as "I," "you," and "do" are "semantic primitives" in common to all languages and based on what we as humans take for granted as given about each other and our world (e.g., Wierzbicka 1996). By formulating Psychologic axioms in terms of "semantic primitives" and their implicit logical relations, Smedslund hopes that the axioms must be necessary and in common to all persons (Smedslund 2012b, p. 298). He admits that Psychologic in its later guise depends on the viability of "semantic primitives" and even concedes that more fieldwork and logical analysis are needed for their justification (Ibid, p. 299).

Nevertheless, despite this later development of Psychologic, propositions on what we supposedly "take for granted" about human persons' needs to make sense as such. The meanings and uses of the words of these propositions can and should be examined as to if, how, when, and under what circumstances they make sense. Smedslund's standing contribution to psychology as a science will likely be pointing out that it intimately depends on and carefully needs to examine the meanings and uses of words. Despite the later developments of Psychologic, it remains his view that "psychology takes its departure in, and consists of reflections about and analyses of, persons in terms of ordinary language" and that the analysis of ordinary language reveals the limits of psychological research (Smedslund 2016b, pp. 186, 190).

To this end, the propositions of Psychologic rely on two conceptual analytical methods, the *negation-test* and the *consensus-test* (e.g., Smedslund 2016b, p. 191; 2012c, p. 665; 2011, pp. 133–134; 2009, p. 783; 1991, pp. 335–336). The "negation-test" is a method to determine both axiomatic and pseudoempirical statements. In keeping with Smedslund, a simple way to determine whether a hypothesis in Psychology is pseudoempirical is to consider if a negation of it is possible and acceptable. If a negation is unacceptable by being absurd or senseless, then the hypothesis is not empirical, but a necessary truth (Smedslund 2016b, p. 191). In Smedslund's view, the negation-test is also the "best method" to evaluate the necessary truths of Psychologic axioms (Smedslund 2012c, p. 665). If an axiom can be negated, it is not an axiom.

However, the negation-test is a misleading method for investigating the meanings of words and their roles in Psychology. First, it presupposes the relevance of axiomatic definitions of psychological terms to psychology and that the meanings of psychological terms have a core or necessary conditions. Yet, this is a presupposition that itself needs to be investigated. As such, a broader method of conceptual investigations into the meanings and uses of words requires this presupposition to at least be bracketed. Second, by exclusively focusing on whether propositions express necessary truths or conditions—the negation-test fails to bring out, point to, and represent the many roles the meanings of words may have in psychology. For example, merely negating the proposition, "What a person feels follows from the relation between what the person wants and thinks"—say, by giving examples of when and how a person may "feel" something that does not follow from a relation between what they want and think—may serve to exclude that the proposition expresses a necessary condition for what it means to "feel" something. But it does not serve to test or otherwise investigate, for instance, whether, why, and how this means that the proposition instead is "empirical" or perhaps partially true of what it in some circumstances *may* mean for a person to "feel" something and how and which circumstances this may be true. Similarly, neither can the negation-test account for an understanding of "pseudo-empiricality" in psychology where what is at stake is *not* whether a proposition is assumed to be empirical and contingent—while it can be shown to be a priori and noncontingent. But rather, whether it is assumed to be empirical—while it can be shown to follow from the meanings of words.

The "consensus-test" is a method that is used to justify statements about the meanings and uses of words (including the negation-test statements). In Smedslund's view, since whether a proposition in psychology is an axiom (by being a non-negatable necessary truth) cannot itself be tested logically or empirically, it can only be tested by *consensus* (Smedslund 2012b, p. 296). Allegedly, if everyone agrees with the formulation and necessity of an axiom, it can be retained and taken for granted. Overall, according to Smedslund, a priori assumptions can only be decided by consensus. For example, if everyone agrees that human behavior is nearly always purposive, so be it, until something convinces us of the contrary (2012a, p. 646). What is to be determined is whether, for instance, "to act" in the ordinary or natural English language implies "to have a purpose," and this can only be determined by way of agreement among English speakers. However, Smedslund seems to waver between whether every speaker needs to agree or merely an indicative sufficient percentage of speakers. On the one hand, he asserts that only if everyone in the scientific community agrees that something must necessarily be assumed should one, provisionally, accept it—and that the ultimate test should be a complete and general agreement (2012c, p. 665). On the other hand, he refers to a number of studies that have been made about the assumptions of Psychologic in various languages, including English, Ewe, Turkish, and Urdu that point to high, near-perfect agreement among speakers on their validity—and, hence, a much stronger verification than is usually obtained in support of psychological theories (Smedslund 1997, p. 57; 2004, p. 47; 2012b, pp. 296–297; 2012c, p. 665).

The consensus-test points to an essential predicament of conceptual investigations into the meanings and uses of words. In the course of such investigations, what, if anything, justifies statements about how words may be used and understood in various contexts? Smedslund's answer is that ultimately such statements can only be justified by way of agreement among competent informants of a language that this is how words may be used and what they may mean in a language. However, this answer seems to pose some methodological dilemmas. What makes consensus a means of justification? Is it that the more informants who agree that this is how words meaningfully are used in a language the more likely it is true that this is how words meaningfully are used in a language? But what makes some uses of words meaningful and others not? Is it simply that that a certain way of using words is common, frequent, or widespread? But how can frequency make it true that a certain use of words makes sense? And can we justify how words *ought to* be used or understood, merely by showing how words *in fact* are used or understood? These are thorny issues for the consensus-test. Yet, we can by pass such issues as misplaced or at least secondary to the practice of conceptual investigations, if we give up seeking to "justify" them by referring to an assumed third-person ordinary or natural language and instead understand references to the meanings and uses of words as reminders that "we" in the first person need to recognize and agree on as making sense to us (cf. McEachrane 2006).[9]

In summary—and in line with Wittgenstein's insight in the introductory quote—a schematic overview of some key differences between empirical and conceptual investigations in psychology could be as follows:

Empirical methods	Conceptual methods
Investigate *third-person observations* of psychological phenomena[a]	Investigate *first-person reminders* of how we (in the first person) use and understand words[b]
Discover psychological *facts*, give (causal or other) *explanations* of psychological phenomena and make psychological *predictions*	Reflect on the *meanings of terms and propositions* in psychology by reflecting on our ordinary and scientific *use and understanding of words*
Determine the *truth or falsity* of propositions in psychology	Determine the *meanings (if any) of propositions* in psychology
Develop psychological *theories*	*Clarify* the meanings of terms and propositions in psychology

[a]Typically third-person observation, but psychology may also include third-person observations of first-person avowals—which is sometimes based on first-person observations of one's own mental states

[b]Cf. Harré & Tissaw 2005 on the relevance of "reminders" to resolving conceptual issues in psychology, pp. 159 and 290

[9]Rom Harré and Michael Tissaw also refer to examples of how words used as *reminders* (Harré and Tissaw 2005, pp. 159, 162). Although they do not say whether such reminders are to be understood in a first-person sense as I do, judging from Harré's social constructionist view on language and psychological terms and for example the following quote by him; it would seem that they would understand such reminders as first- and third-person: "Instead of asking the question, 'What is anger?' we would do well to begin by asking, 'How is the word 'anger,' and other expressions around it, actually used in this or that cultural milieu and type of episode" (Harré 1986, pp. 4–5). Cf. Wittgenstein in *Philosophical Investigations*: "The work of the philosopher consists in marshalling recollections for a particular purpose" (2009/1953, §127).

In Conclusion

As outlined above, Psychologic implies a misleading reduction of the relevance of the ordinary meanings of words for psychology as an academic subject. However, despite its flaws Smedslund's seminal advancements of Psychologic correctly calls on psychology to pay heed to its overextension of empirical methods, the meanings of psychological terms, and the methods needed to investigate them. Thus, if we abandon Psychologic as a system—which this chapter suggests that we should—we will be left to more freely ponder the relevance of the meanings and uses of psychologically relevant terms. As such, we should follow Smedslund's lead on questioning not only whether psychology can ever become a science in the sense that natural science is, but also the extent to which psychological phenomena can be operationally defined so as to be studied in empirical experiments (be it to reveal causal laws or merely regularities) as well as the roles that empirical research can play in guiding the theories and practices of psychotherapy (cf. Smedslund 2016a). However, now with a view that we are examining the *possibilities* rather than the *necessities* of meaning.

References

American Psychiatric Association. (2013). *Diagnostic and statistical manual of mental disorders (DSM-5)*. Washington, DC: American Psychiatric Association Publishing.

Beck, A. T., Steer, R. A., Epstein, N., & Brown, G. (1990). Beck self-concept test. *Psychological Assessment, 2*, 191–197.

Caruso, G. D., & Flanagan, O. (Eds.). (2018). *Neuroexistentialism: Meaning, morals and purpose in the age of neuroscience*. New York: Oxford University Press.

Harré, R. (Ed.). (1986). *The social construction of emotions*. Oxford/New York: Basil Blackwell.

Harré, R. (Ed.). (1999). *The social construction of emotions*. Oxford/New York: Basil Blackwell.

Harré, R., & Tissaw, M. (2005). *Wittgenstein and psychology: A practical guide*. Aldershot/Burlington: Ashgate Publishing.

McEachrane, M. (2006). Investigating emotions philosophically. *Philosophical Investigations, 29*, 342–357.

McEachrane, M. (2009a). Capturing emotional thoughts: The philosophy of cognitive-behavioral therapy. In Y. Gustafsson, C. Kronqvist, & M. McEachrane (Eds.), *Emotions and understanding: Wittgensteinian perspectives* (pp. 81–101). Basingstoke/New York: Palgrave Macmillan.

McEachrane, M. (2009b). Emotion, meaning and appraisal theory. *Theory & Psychology, 19*, 33–53.

Parrott, G., & Harré, R. (1991). Smedslundian suburbs in the city of language: The case of embarrassment. *Psychological Inquiry, 2*(4), 358–361.

Repetti, R. (Ed.). (2017). *Buddhist perspectives on free will: Agentless agency?* New York/London: Routledge.

Shotter, J. (1991). Measuring blindly and speculating loosely: But is a "psychologic" the answer? *Psychological Inquiry, 2*(4), 363–366.

Shotter, J. (1994). Is there a logic in common sense? The scope and the limits of Jan Smedslund's "geometric" psychologic. In J. Siegfried (Ed.), *The status of common sense in psychology* (pp. 149–168). Norwood, NJ: Ablex.

Shotter, J. (1999). From within an external world. *Scandinavian Journal of Psychology, 40*, 81–84.

Smedslund, J. (1988). *Psychologic*. Berlin: Springer-Verlag.
Smedslund, J. (1990). Psychology and psychologic: Characterization of the difference. In G. R. Semin & K. J. Gergen (Eds.), *Everyday understanding: Social scientific implications* (pp. 45–63). Thousand Oaks, CA: Sage Publications.
Smedslund, J. (1991). The Pseudoempirical in psychology and the case for Psychologic. *Psychological Inquiry, 2*, 325–338.
Smedslund, J. (1997). *The structure of psychological common sense*. Mahaw, NJ: Lawrence Erlbaum Associates, Publishers.
Smedslund, J. (1999a). Psychologic and the study of memory. *Scandinavian Journal of Psychology, 40*, 3–17.
Smedslund, J. (1999b). Author's response: Psychologic in dialogue – Reply to commentaries. *Scandinavian Journal of Psychology, 40*(Suppl. 1), 123–138.
Smedslund, J. (2004). *Dialogues about a new psychology*. Chagrin Falls, OH: Taos Institute Publications.
Smedslund, J. (2009). The mismatch between current research methods and the nature of psychological phenomena: What researchers must learn from practitioners. *Theory & Psychology, 19*, 778–794.
Smedslund, J. (2011). Meaning of words and the use of axiomatics in psychological theory. *Journal of Theoretical and Philosophical Psychology, 31*, 126–135.
Smedslund, J. (2012a). The Bricoleur model of psychological practice. *Theory & Psychology, 22*, 643–657.
Smedslund, J. (2012b). Psychologic: Some thoughts and after-thoughts. *Scandinavian Journal of Psychology, 53*, 295–302.
Smedslund, J. (2012c). What follows from what we all know about human beings. *Theory & Psychology, 22*, 658–668.
Smedslund, J. (2016a). Practicing psychology without an empirical evidence-base: The Bricoleur model. *New Ideas in Psychology, 43*, 50–56.
Smedslund, J. (2016b). Why psychology cannot be an empirical science. *Integrative Psychological and Behavioral Science, 50*, 185–195.
Sowislo, J. F., & Orth, U. (2013). Does low self-esteem predict depression and anxiety? A meta-analysis of longitudinal studies. *Psychological Bulletin, 139*, 213–240.
Wierzbicka, A. (1996). *Semantics: Primes and universals*. New York: Oxford University Press.
Wittgenstein, L. (2009/1953). *Philosophische Untersuchungen/Philosophical Investigations*. Chichester: John Wiley and Sons Ltd.

Chapter 7
The Case for Psychological Quietism: Wittgensteinian Propaedeutics in Smedslund's Writings

Martin B. Smedlund

> *The confusion and barrenness of psychology is not to be explained by its being a "young science"; its state is not comparable with that of physics, for instance, in its beginnings... For in psychology, there are experimental methods and conceptual confusion... The existence of the experimental method makes us think that we have the means of getting rid of the problems which trouble us; but problem and method pass one another by. (Wittgenstein 1953/2009, xiv, §371).*

The echo of Wittgenstein's remark on the deplorable state of academic psychology can still be heard in psychology departments from time to time, although the message is easily lost in an ever-sounding siren song of evidence-based theory and practice. Fortunately, however, there are other dissenting voices, and Smedslund's is without doubt one of the more prominent. For decades, he has worked admirably towards a methodologically more sophisticated science; tirelessly drawing consideration to the difference between matters conceptual and matters empirical. His trenchant notion of pseudo-empirical research (cf. Smedslund 1991), that is, research in which assertions, whose truth value can be known without empirical testing, are put to empirical test, underscores—just like Wittgenstein's remark—the unfortunate mixture of conceptual negligence and meticulous data collection that bedevils psychology; problem and method pass one another by.

Now, there are certainly those who would claim that this is as far as the similarities between these two logicians go, for even if Wittgenstein's call for a conceptual awakening within psychology has reverberated powerfully in Smedslund's work, they have two different views on the nature of concepts, which result in two altogether different forms of conceptual analysis. I would like to argue, however, that we have good reason to view Smedslund's overall take on psychology as being of a general Wittgensteinian bent. My rationale for this is twofold: On the one hand, it seems that we can reconcile their different ways of conducting conceptual analysis since Smedslund has detached his analytical approach from his view on the nature

---

M. B. Smedlund (✉)
Reykjavik, Iceland

T. G. Lindstad et al. (eds.), *Respect for Thought*, Theory and History in the Human and Social Sciences, https://doi.org/10.1007/978-3-030-43066-5_7

of concepts; rendering the latter irrelevant to the former. On the other hand—and more importantly—it seems that we can read Smedslund as extending Wittgenstein's philosophical quietism to the domain of psychology.

Famously, Wittgenstein argued that philosophical problems tend to be pseudo-problems—a bewitchment of our understanding—that cease to be problems as soon as we have acquired a clear picture of the meaning of words. Consequently, he thought that philosophy (at least in the metaphysical mode) could not be a growing body of substantive knowledge. It could contain no theses or theories; only aim at the explication of an already established structure of concepts. "It leaves everything as it is." (Wittgenstein 2009, §124). In a similar vein, Smedslund has argued that the answers to questions about general psychological facts and principles are to be found in the logical structure of ordinary language (Smedslund 2016a). Thus, they are not to be answered by constructing theories and putting them to empirical test, but by reminding ourselves of what we already take for granted. Consequently, he thinks that psychology (at least in the intentional mode) cannot be a growing body of empirical knowledge. It has to be a-theoretical (Smedslund 2004). His view of the discipline could, therefore, with proper adjustments, be described as a form of psychological quietism.

In what follows, I present Smedslund's and Wittgenstein's different ways of conducting conceptual analysis as reflecting two different conceptions of language. I argue that when it comes to the nature of language, Smedslund has it wrong and Wittgenstein has it right. However, due to what appears to be an instrumentalist shift in Smedslund's thinking, it seems possible to adapt his conceptual approach to Wittgenstein's conception of language. Likening conceptual analysis to cartography, I suggest that we view the two as using different methods of projection. I then go on to argue that the project of mapping psychological concepts has a claim to universality, at least partially, since there seem to be psychological facts and principles, common to human beings, that restrain the ways in which human psychology can be conceptualised—a point made by both Smedslund and Wittgenstein. After this, I lay out Wittgenstein's philosophical quietism and demonstrate in what ways Smedslund's a-theoretical view of psychology parallels it. I emphasise that quietism, in both philosophy and psychology, is to be conceived of as a propaedeutic. Finally, I suggest that Smedslund's bricoleur model for psychological practice is an example of the quietist ethos. This brings forth the ethical dimension of quietism, which is the renunciation of dogma.

Two Models of Conceptual Analysis

Although Smedslund has diagnosed correctly, as did Wittgenstein, that psychology's problems are conceptual, rather than empirical, they diverge in their conceptual approaches. Smedslund's project of psycho-logic (PL), which is an attempt at "explicating the implicit conceptual system of psychology embedded in ordinary language" (Smedslund 1997, p. ix), has since its inception been situated within what Parrott and Harré (1991) have called a Euclidean model of analysis. This entails the formalisation of our psychological vocabulary into a deductive system with axioms, corollaries and theorems, specifying necessary and sufficient conditions for the meaning of words. Contrary to this, a Wittgensteinian model of analysis does not seek formalisation. It merely describes how words are used in the language and, importantly, does not assume that different uses of the same word must have one thing in common in order to constitute a concept. Instead, it is assumed that they can constitute a concept simply by sharing family resemblance (Wittgenstein 2009, §67), which means that certain features (various similarities and affinities) are typical of them without necessarily being found in all of them. This mode of representing our concepts leaves room for flexibility and multiplicity in a way foreign to the Euclidean model.[1]

Smedslund has, however, never recognised the Wittgensteinian model as a valid option for PL. As a matter of fact, he has stated that "in order to maintain a scientific approach, some invariant component in the use of the same word must be assumed," and subsequently made the requirement that "in a professional (technical) terminology we must be able to specify this component, that is, define the term." (Smedslund 2011, p. 128). His argument for the existence of invariant components goes like this: The use of a word must involve a necessary condition, for if it did not, the word would not exclude anything, and if it did not exclude anything, it could mean literally anything and hence, it would be useless. Now, it is certainly true that without *any* logical relations between the different uses of a word, a scientific PL (or any meaningful PL) would not get off the ground. But it does not follow that there must be *one* invariant component tying *all* the different uses together. In other words, Smedslund's argument is not an argument against the Wittgensteinian model.

Wittgenstein never claimed that there are no logical relations between the different uses of a word. The idea of family resemblance, although discouraging the search for an invariant component, does not imply semantic chaos. Word meanings are not amorphous. Wittgenstein's point is this: In many cases, it is safe to assume that the coherence of a concept turns on, not one, but many logical relations and each of them ties together, not all, but some of the different uses of a word. With a striking simile, he compared the development and formation of a concept to that of spinning a thread by twisting many little fibres: "And the strength of the thread resides not in the fact that some one fibre runs through its whole length, but in the overlapping of many fibres." (Wittgenstein 2009, §67).

Two Conceptions of Language

Looming large behind the conceptual approaches of Smedslund and Wittgenstein are two different views on the nature of language. Smedslund can readily be seen as propounding what Hacker (2013, Chap. 6) has called the calculus conception of language. This is a view that takes language to be a structure reducible to the form

[1] This is also captured by Strawson's (1992, Chap. 2) now widely used distinction between "reductive" analysis (exemplified by the Euclidean model) and "connective" analysis (exemplified by the Wittgensteinian model).

of a meaning calculus and it has been a recognised theoretical framework for a century or so, with advocates ranging from Frege and Russell to Davidson and Chomsky. The young Wittgenstein was also devoted to this view but he later rejected it in favour of an anthropological conception of language (Ibid. Chap. 6). He came to see the sought-after meaning calculus as a chimera and argued that there is no deeper and purer structure to language than what people actually do with words. Language is human behaviour—an irreducible aspect of the human form of life.

Now, much can be said about the differences between these views, but for the present purpose, suffice it to notice that the calculus conception of language assumes a priori that the different uses of words are connected by means of invariant components, whereas the anthropological conception of language does not. The reason that the former is dependent on such firm logical relations is mirrored in its name. Without invariant components fixating the correct uses of words, language would not be a calculus. The axiomatic ideal driving this formalisation project does not allow for a less tight connection. With this in mind, it becomes evident that Smedslund's argument as to why the different uses of a word must contain an invariant component actually is an argument as to what must be the case in order for the calculus conception of language to be true. As soon as we let go of this conception, the argument loses its force. And there is good reason to let go of it, since a proposed definition of a word in ordinary language often can be criticised quite easily in the form of suggested exceptions.

Now, because of such criticism, Smedslund (2012a, p. 660) has acknowledged the problem of definitions. However, since he also argues that words would be useless without invariant components, he is, by parity of his own reasoning, stuck with the calculus conception of language. This puts him in a hopeless situation. Without the notion of family resemblance, it seems that a word *must* have an invariant component that explains how a coherent concept can spring from its different uses. And yet, it seems impossible to formulate definitions that hold invariably. Smedslund's attempted way out of this false dilemma is to assume that the invariant components are "so complex that they cannot be described by any existing language." (Smedslund 2011, p. 127). But this God-of-the-gaps strategy not only fails as a defence of the calculus conception of language, it knocks the bottom out of the very idea, for it turns the purported invariant component into a vacuous notion—a ghost in the machinery of language.

We are told that we know that a word applies to a specific psychological phenomenon, in a number of different situations, because it is anchored by an invariant component. However, we are also told that this logical super fastener cannot be described. This is paradoxical. As competent speakers of a language, we have mastered the different ways of using its psychological predicates. In other words, we know what the criteria are for applying them correctly. And these criteria, these rules of application, could not be hidden from us. If they were, there would be no way of telling whether we had used a psychological predicate correctly or not. Accordingly, if such hidden rules existed, they would have no function in our language. And this means that they could just as well be non-existent. Smedslund's invariant component, which supposedly lies beyond our current reach, is no different. Like Wittgenstein's beetle, it "drops out of consideration as irrelevant." (Wittgenstein 2009, §293).

Smedslund's Instrumentalist Turn

So, we can see how Smedslund's appeal to inexplicable invariant components points the way to a *reductio* argument showing the calculus conception of language to be deeply misguided. Perhaps this has struck him in one way or another, for he has admitted that there is "a lingering uncertainty" (Smedslund 2011, p. 126) with his suggested solutions. However, such speculation apart, there is another side to the postulation of inexplicable invariant components: If there is no way of formulating an exact description of the implicit conceptual system of psychology embedded in ordinary language, then PL cannot be answerable to its exact nature. Of this, Smedslund is very much aware. Therefore, instead of seeing PL as an "explication of parts of an implicit calculus built into language" (Smedslund 1999, p. 4), he now sees it as "an attempt to *create* a calculus from our common knowledge" (Smedslund 2012a, p. 660, italics added). By making this move, he has made the definitions of PL immune to objections that point to counterexamples in ordinary language. The project has made a retreat from ordinary language to a technical one (Ibid. p. 660).

Thus, it seems that PL must be given an instrumentalist interpretation. Its validity lies not in how accurately it represents our common psychological knowledge, but in how well it utilises this knowledge in the form of an axiomatic system. And this view of the project is quite interesting, I think, for it invites a reconciliation between the different views of Smedslund and Wittgenstein. If PL is an approximation to the implicit conceptual system of psychology embedded in language, and not an exact rendering of it, then it matters little whether the underlying conceptual system is a calculus or a complex network of family resemblances. What matters is that psychologists are reminded of important links between concepts. And as I see it, both the Euclidean model and the Wittgensteinian model are of assistance in this regard. Hence, my suggested reconciliation, on which I elaborate further in the next section, consists in acknowledging Wittgenstein's anthropological conception of language as correct while at the same time accepting Smedslund's Euclidean model as an admissible method of projection.[2]

[2] Note that the claim is not that Smedslund's instrumentalist turn makes his position compatible with that of Wittgenstein's because Wittgenstein was an instrumentalist (he was not). The point is that inasmuch as Smedslund has shifted to an instrumentalist understanding of the Euclidean model, the calculus conception of language has become irrelevant to the development of PL. Thus, we can, if we like, simply replace it with Wittgenstein's anthropological conception of language and thus relieve the tension between their different conceptual approaches.

Euclidean Cartography

Early formulations of PL received a somewhat mixed response from scholars working in the tradition of Wittgenstein. In light of the preceding discussion, this should not come as a surprise. Smedslund's call for greater sensitivity to the conceptual structures wherein psychology operates was lauded, but his belief in the Euclidean model as an accurate depiction of these structures was criticised. Shotter, for instance, regarded the "closed textual system" of PL to have a limiting effect on psychology, despite its scientific soundness and rigour, and argued that the true power of the discipline lay in its poetic potential, since words are "open to different uses in different circumstances." (Shotter 1991, p. 365). In a similar vein, Parrott and Harré referred to Wittgenstein's illuminating metaphor of language as an ancient city (Wittgenstein 2009, §18) and claimed that PL was like a rigidly planned modern suburb, removed from "the crooked lanes and irregular plazas of the older areas, whose links with one another are neither rectilinear nor simple." (Parrott and Harré 1991, p. 358).

Now, if we acknowledge that Wittgenstein's idea of family resemblance captures the typical structure of concepts in ordinary language, and if we want to represent the conceptual system of psychology implicit therein as accurately as possible, then, to be sure, the Euclidean model is a rather poor choice. With its axiomatic architecture and insistence on necessary conditions for the illumination of word meanings, it is likely to give a distorted picture of the structure of concepts. However, similarity with regard to its object is not the only criterion by which to assess the validity of a model; another is utility with regard to its purpose. And notably, this was part of Smedslund's response to his early Wittgensteinian critics (cf. Smedslund 1991). His defence of classical definitions notwithstanding (Ibid. p. 378), he admitted that there was more to our psychological reality than could ever be enclosed in his axiomatic system. Rather modestly, he averred that PL was "only intended as an analytic instrument for dealing with limited research and professional problems." (Ibid. p. 381).

In retrospect, then, we can see that Smedslund planted the promising seed to an instrumentalist reorientation of PL very early. The problem, as I have described it, is that although this view of the project has now matured, it is still standing in the barren soil of the calculus conception of language. However, transplanting an instrumentalist reading of Smedslund's PL to the fertile grounds of the anthropological conception of language is not much of a problem. In order to demonstrate how to do this, I want to take issue with Parrott and Harré's interpretation of PL's relationship to the city of language. In my view, they misrepresent the nature of the project rather severely when they portray the Euclidean model as a rigidly planned modern suburb. It is, therefore, somewhat unfortunate that Smedslund, in his rejoinder to them, chose to accept this characterisation. Quite memorably, he consented to the notion of PL as a "linguistic suburb" (Smedslund 1991, p. 380). In fact, he still approves of this metaphorical description of the project (see Smedslund 2011).

The characterisation of Smedslund's programme as the construction of a linguistic suburb may seem apt at first. It is, however, deeply problematic, for it obliterates the distinction between model and reality. The difference between PL and the conceptual structure of our everyday psychological discourse is not that of a rigidly planned modern suburb and the more organically developed areas of an Old Town. Modern suburbs are only adjacently connected to the older parts of a city and do not have to conform to their layout in any way. But PL "is an attempt to make explicit what is already implicit in language" (Smedslund 2012b, p. 297). Accordingly, the project consists in charting a city already built, not in constructing new districts. Inevitably, the Euclidean method of projection does not show all the crooked lanes and irregular plazas of our psychological vocabulary, but it has the potential of providing a well-organised overview of these conceptual areas. Perhaps it should be compared to a map of the type that shows the network of a public transportation system. The intricate structure of the city has been transformed into links that are rectilinear and simple, so that it becomes easier to see important connections. As a case in point, take the concept of anger, which Smedslund (1997, p. 53) has given the following succinct definition:

> *P is angry at O, if and only if, P believes that at least one person whom P cares for has, intentionally or through neglect, been treated without respect by O, and P has not forgiven O.*

This is a straightforward statement of both necessary and sufficient conditions for being angry. The reason is always that someone that we care for (and this includes ourselves) has been treated without respect. Furthermore, we are said to remain angry at the offender until we have forgiven him or her.[3] On our Euclidean map, a rectilinear link connects two points (anger and perceived disrespect) via a third (the absence of forgiveness). In reality, however, matters are not as clear-cut:

> But surely, one can be angry at a person for other reasons, such as being irresponsible, cold, a nuisance, dumb, a poor student, or for belonging to the wrong ethnic group, worshipping the wrong god, having poor taste, not trying hard enough, and much more. Of course, one can also be angry with oneself for, say, allowing oneself to be deceived or for not completing what one set out to do. One need not even be angry with people, but can also be angry at, say, the weather. (McEachrane 2009, p. 36).

McEachrane's suggested exceptions to Smedslund's definition draw attention to the unfeasibility of the idea that one invariant component informs all meaningful uses of the word "anger." However, now that all the emphasis has been put on diversity in the use of the word, we lose track of the fact that the concept displays a pattern. If we stick to the reason(s) for being angry (and disregard the role of forgiveness), McEachrane does not encourage us to think that there is a close connection between anger and perceived disrespect. Instead of a rectilinear link between these two points, his map shows a number of streets connected to only one of them (anger).

[3] Note that PL is about what exists *for* persons. Thus, Smedslund's definition is wholly compatible with the fact that our anger abates, even disappears, when we do not think about the transgression. It only states that whenever we call it to mind, or are reminded of it, we will get angry again, unless we have forgiven the offender.

Smedslund (2011) has tried to rectify this by arguing that at least some of McEachrane's examples concern perceived disrespect. For instance, if I am angry at someone for being cold, it is because I think that I deserve a more sympathetic treatment, and so, I believe that I have been treated disrespectfully. And if I am angry at someone for adhering to the wrong religion, it is because I think that the other person has not recognised my religion in an appropriate way, and hence, has treated me with disrespect. Now, these are interesting interpretations of people's angered reactions, and perhaps it is possible to construe more of McEachrane's examples in this way, but we cannot go too far down this road. The element of perceived disrespect will not turn out to be an *invariant* component of anger. However, on an instrumentalist reading of Smedslund's PL, we do not need it to be an invariant component. We only need the relation between anger and perceived disrespect to be important enough to justify a rectilinear link between them in his Euclidean model. And arguably, this is the case. If we look at Hacker's Wittgensteinian model of anger, it too gives perceived disrespect a prominent place in the structure of the concept (while also recognising many of McEachrane's exceptions):

> Anger is an emotional response to the thwarting of one's will or the flouting of one's authority or instructions; to physical conflict; to an offense to one's status, pride, or dignity; to challenges to one's judgement or opinion on matters close to one's heart; to the offenses of others that one considers to be wicked or otherwise unwarranted; to stupidity and incompetence (of another or one's own). This is not a *definition* of anger, merely a preliminary circumscription of the domain of our conceptual investigation. (Hacker 2017, pp. 239—240).

If Smedslund's definition of anger is elegant due to its brevity and simplicity, then Hacker's preliminary circumscription of the emotion is elegant due to its richness and subtlety. Instead of a map showing a rectilinear link between two points, we now have a map showing crooked lanes and irregular plazas. What we get is a picture of an old and asymmetric area in the city of language. However, the same conceptual reality influences both maps, which is partially evident from the fact that much in Hacker's variegated description of circumstances that arouse anger can be recast (at the expense of precision) into Smedslund's overarching notion of perceived disrespect.

Thus, it seems to me that we can view the Euclidean model and the Wittgensteinian model as two different methods of projection. Of course, this paves the way for a discussion about whether one of them is always preferable to the other, or whether the context of need determines which to choose, or, indeed, whether it can be a question of style. But I have no intent of engaging in such a discussion here. I only wish to point out that on an instrumentalist reading of Smedslund's PL, Wittgensteinian criticism of it must demonstrate that a vital element of a concept is lacking. If it is merely directed at the representation as such, that is, at its axiomatic nature, it seems to boil down to a question of aesthetics. This is not to say that aesthetic considerations about our representational devices are irrelevant, nor that it is just a matter of personal taste, but it shows that our two models are compatible with each other on a functional level. Whether our model is Euclidean or Wittgensteinian, the objective is to produce a "surveyable representation" so that we can arrive at the "understanding which consists in seeing connections." (Wittgenstein 2009, §122).

Restraints on Human Psychology

Shotter once queried whether Smedslund's calculus existed independently of his PL or whether he had created it. "Is it a discovery, or is it simply a possible construction, one among countless others? Does it in fact *underlie* our common-sense reasoning, or is it something that could be used to *overlay* it?" (Shotter 1999, p. 81). Obviously, saying that the calculus underlies our common sense reasoning would be at odds with an instrumentalist view of the project. So, the answer to Shotter's question is that it is a possible construction, something that can be used to overlay our common-sense reasoning; a map of psychological districts in the city of language.

Now, we should note that if we were to take the metaphor of PL as a linguistic suburb seriously, we would also answer Shotter's question by saying that the calculus is a possible construction. However, it would be wrong of us to say that it could be used to *overlay* our common-sense reasoning. Rather, we would have to say that it could be used *alongside* it. And then it would be unclear in what way PL connects to our common-sense reasoning at all. Thus, we can see how the metaphor of a linguistic suburb, not only obliterates the distinction between model and reality, but also contravenes the purpose of the calculus, which is to help us better understand the interlocking of our already established psychological concepts. In construing PL, not as Euclidean city construction, but as Euclidean cartography, we do this purpose justice.

Still, this answer would not have satisfied Shotter. Indeed, he anticipated it and worried that the use of a calculus would be detrimental to our understanding of psychological concepts. It would alienate us from their flexibility; force us to "live in our maps rather than in our cities." (Shotter 1999, p. 84). But this seems to be an unnecessary worry. Since the initial Wittgensteinian criticism, Smedslund has been consistently clear on the limitations of PL: "I have not insisted that we should live with and by psycho-logic only, but merely that it is useful for research and professional purposes." (Smedslund 1999, p. 12). Its "closed textual system" does not threaten a poetic understanding of what it is to be human. What is more, Shotter's (1991) case for psychology as a poetic undertaking is not inherently Wittgensteinian. The tension between poetic licence and scientific rigour in psychological matters is not something on which Wittgenstein picked a side. Hence, neither is the conception of psychology as a scientific project, on which PL rests, inherently anti-Wittgensteinian.

Furthermore, it seems that we are justified in rejecting Shotter's suggestion that Smedslund's calculus, conceived of as a possible construction, would be only one among *countless* others. Smedslund (2012c) argues that Wierzbicka's (1996) discovery of semantic primitives, that is, concepts that cannot be defined by other concepts and that are represented in all human languages, shows that there are characteristics common to all human beings that restrain the ways in which human psychology can be conceptualised. And this is noteworthy, for it brings him into agreement with Wittgenstein, who insisted on a shared human form of life as a prerequisite for language. "It is not only agreement in definitions, but also (queer as this may sound) agreement in judgements that is required for communication by means of language." (Wittgenstein 2009, §242). And "this is agreement not in opinions but rather in form of life." (Ibid. §241).

On its own, Wittgenstein's remark is quite obscure, but Glock (1996) has elaborated on it in relation to the possibility of translating a new and foreign tongue. He argues that in order to do so, we must assume that the behaviour of the speakers abide to some fundamental laws of rationality. We must assume, for instance, that they act logically in accordance with their beliefs and desires (see also Smedslund 1990). But this is not our starting point. Underlying the assumption that these complete strangers are rational is the assumption that they experience the world in a way that is fundamentally like our experience of it—and thus have similar beliefs and comparable desires:

> We cannot even start to translate the natives' utterances unless we can take for granted that they share with us basic *perceptual capacities*. We take for granted that they can survey the scene around them and are aware of what goes on within their perceptual range. And this is a precondition for ascribing to them shared needs and desires. We cannot recognize them, for example, as refusing unpleasant things unless we can assume that they know that they are confronted with a knife rather than a piece of fruit. (Glock 1996, p. 168).

Compare this to Smedslund's (2012a, p. 661) proposed axiom of mentality, which he claims is a prerequisite for our dealings with other people: *"P takes it that O can think, want, feel, perceive and do."* From a Wittgensteinian perspective, we can now add that P assumes, not only that O is capable of all this, but also that P and O will, in many ways, think, want, feel, perceive and do *the same things*. This could readily be included in the axiom, which Smedslund considers tentative at any rate, but the point of interest is, again, that both Wittgenstein and Smedslund argue that there are universal human characteristics restraining the ways in which psychology can be conceptualised.

Of course, commonalities across cultures are compatible with a certain degree of variation and Smedslund (2009) has recognised that we can expect languages to differ somewhat in the structure of their implicit system of psychological concepts. However, this does not change the fact that every language holds within it conceptual truths about the psychological lives of its speakers that predate the arrival of psychology as a science. And this takes us to a rather intriguing question: Are there any general psychological truths to discover that are not already part of language?

Smedslund's Increasingly Radical Position

The received notion of psychology as an empirical science contains the ideal of progression by way of a detached evaluation of hypotheses and theories in light of given data. In reality, things do not proceed as smoothly as such an ideal suggests since there are different schools of thought placing different amounts of emphasis on different types of data. This can lead to disputes, and often it has, but a way to settle the differences, a way that many psychologists prefer, is simply to recognise the differences as differences in point of view and to accept that within the empirical science of psychology there is room for a wide variety of approaches. In other words, although there can be divergence in the explanatory variables chosen, there is unity in the belief that the validity of a psychological assertion hinges on the quality of the data in support of it. Against this background, it is not surprising that when Smedslund has suggested that the validity of certain general psychological assertions has nothing to do with empirical data, but is a matter of logical links between concepts, it has met with little or no understanding from researchers.

Now, add to this disparity the fact that Smedslund's position has, with his own words, become "increasingly radical" (Smedslund 2013, p. 13). He now argues that the analysis of psychological concepts does not so much point the way towards fruitful empirical research as reveal that empirical research is, as a rule, uncalled for; at least if the goal is to unearth general psychological facts and principles. Indeed, Smedslund is inclined to believe that "the task of psychology must necessarily be limited to explication and analysis of what is already implicitly familiar." (Smedslund 2016a, p. 186). If we were to take this statement at face value, it would mean that it is not just the validity of certain general psychological assertions that is a conceptual matter, but the validity of all general psychological assertions. This is a strong statement. And unnecessarily so. Suitably, Smedslund stops short of it in the finer details of his argument: "One cannot categorically exclude that one could formulate general hypotheses in psychology that are neither necessary nor self-contradictory, but simply express probabilities." (2016a, p. 191). Nevertheless, he remains sceptical of the prospects and—pointing to the meagre outcome of more than a 100 years of research—suggests the following: "One may assume that since goal-directed, reflecting human beings have lived in societies over innumerable generations, any practically useful psychological regularity in daily life would have been discovered long ago and also incorporated in language." (Ibid. p. 191).

Thus, what Smedslund has done is nothing less than to articulate an alternative to psychology's prevailing empirical paradigm which turns the examination completely around—to borrow a phrase from Wittgenstein. In brief: We should not expect that empirical research will yield more knowledge of general psychological facts and principles. Instead, we should attend to the logical structure of ordinary language, for we have reason to expect that it will contain those generalisable truths that are of our concern. As noted at the outset, this is reminiscent of Wittgenstein's philosophical quietism, to which I now turn. By giving an account of what it is, I lay down a foundation that will help me spell out what I take to be Smedslund's psychological version.

Wittgenstein's Philosophical Quietism

Wittgenstein's philosophy is commonly divided into an early period and a later period. The early period is exemplified by *Tractatus Logico-Philosophicus*, a book published in 1921. It is an attempt to identify the relationship between language and reality as it pertains to scientific discourse on the one hand and ethical discourse on the other. The later period began in the early 1930s and lasted up until Wittgenstein's death in 1951. It is characterised by a rejection of many of the philosophical assumptions of the *Tractatus* and gets a clear articulation in *Philosophical Investigations*, a book that was first published posthumously in 1953.

Although a sharp line can be drawn between the early Wittgenstein and the later, he always saw his task as that of elucidating the conditions for meaningful language, that is, of developing the analytical tools required for distinguishing between what can be meaningfully stated and what cannot. In the words of Janik and Toulmin (1973, p. 257): "However much else changed in his actual methods of philosophizing, between 1918 and 1948, the fundamental propaedeutic never changed." This fundamental propaedeutic is formulated towards the end of the *Tractatus*:

> The correct method in philosophy would really be the following: to say nothing except what can be said, i.e., propositions of natural science—i.e., something that has nothing to do with philosophy—and then, whenever someone else wanted to say something metaphysical, to demonstrate to him that he had failed to give a meaning to certain signs in his propositions. (Wittgenstein 2001, 6.53.).

As can be seen from this paragraph, already from early on Wittgenstein carried with him the idea that it could not be in the business of philosophy to contribute with substantive knowledge of the world. In the *Tractatus,* he even thought that he had found the definitive solution to the problems of philosophy (p. 4). The effable realm of scientific discourse had been drawn up and beyond it lay the ineffable realm of ethics. This was, once and for all, an unequivocal demarcation between sense and nonsense and hence, the work of a philosopher was done. Staying true to his conclusions, Wittgenstein turned to other things.

However, he was later to return to academic philosophy, and when he did, it slowly dawned on him that, contrary to what he had envisaged, the line between sense and nonsense could not be drawn once and for all. In the *Investigations,* he writes: "The work of the philosopher consists in marshalling recollections for a particular purpose." (Wittgenstein 2009, §127). This paragraph conveys the change in Wittgenstein's view of the philosophical task. A philosopher is to (dis)solve conceptual problems, not by giving a general account of the essence of language, but *by assembling reminders*, from case to case, of the uses of the relevant words in ordinary talk (or in technical talk, if that is where the problem lies). For as Wittgenstein argued: "the meaning of a word is its use in the language." (§43).

The purpose of philosophical enquiry continued, however, to be the clarification of what can be meaningfully stated, not the unfolding of new facts about the world. For the work of a philosopher is said to consist in marshalling recollections, that is, to remind people of something they might have forgotten or overseen for the moment, not to tell them something they did not know; a point underscored by Wittgenstein immediately in paragraph 128: "If someone were to advance *theses* in philosophy, it would never be possible to debate them, because everyone would agree to them." (Ibid. §128) This is so, since, according to Wittgenstein, such theses would convey nothing but the already implicitly recognised use of words, which is not to say that words always have a clear-cut use, nor that it is never the case that people use words differently, that is, mean different things by them. However, when a description of the different applications of a word lies before us, the philosophical problems that surround it should disappear:

> It was correct that our considerations must not be scientific ones... And we may not advance any kind of theory. There must not be anything hypothetical in our considerations. All *explanation* must disappear, and description alone must take its place. And this description gets its light—that is to say, its purpose—from the philosophical problems. These are, of course, not empirical problems; but they are solved through an insight into the workings of our language, and that in such a way that these problems are recognized—*despite* an urge to misunderstand them. The problems are solved, not by coming up with new discoveries, but by assembling what we have long been familiar with. (§109).

This paragraph deepens the point of both paragraph 127 and 128. It also makes clear that philosophy differs from science. In science, hypotheses are formulated and theories constructed which may be true or not, and it might be that their epistemological status remains unknown for some time, since empirical research can be inconclusive. This is not the case in philosophy, for in philosophy the goal is a description of a segment of our language and in language "everything lies open to view" (Ibid. §126). Thus, philosophy is not about making new discoveries, but about assembling various linguistic facts that we have long been familiar with. Its investigations are not empirical but, as Wittgenstein used the term, "grammatical" (§90). They are about "the sense- or meaning-determining rules for the use of words" (Hacker 2010, p. 9). In this way, we can say that philosophy is "a contribution, not to human knowledge, but to human understanding." (Hacker 2013, Chap. 1). "[I]t is ... essential to our investigation that we do not seek to learn anything *new* by it. We want to *understand* something that is already in plain view." (Wittgenstein 2009, §89).[4]

A concrete example of how Wittgenstein's philosophical method can dispel conceptual confusion and thereby sharpen our understanding, an example that connects his philosophy of psychology to that of Smedslund's, can be taken from the part of the *Investigations* usually referred to as the private language argument (Wittgenstein 2009, §§244-315). After a grammatical enquiry into the concept of pain, which, as becomes evident, is supposed to work as a stand-in for psychological predicates in general, Wittgenstein reaches the conclusion that "only of a living human being and what resembles (behaves like) a living human being can one say: it has sensations; it sees; is blind; hears; is deaf; is conscious or unconscious." (Wittgenstein 2009, §281).[5]

---

[4] I think that we can understand and appreciate the relevance of Wittgenstein's point when he contrasts the conceptual domain of philosophy with the empirical domain of science without thereby having to conclude that when we investigate the conceptual foundations of psychology, we are not doing science. I return to this point below.

[5] The concept of pain functions as a stand-in for psychological predicates in general, not in the sense that all such predicates are learnt in the same way (they are not), but in the sense that Wittgenstein uses it to drive home the point that all psychological predicates are logically (grammatically) connected to behaviour.

The profound theoretical impact of this simple point should not be overlooked. Bennett and Hacker (2003) have seized on it and argued that modern-day neuroscience is ridden with conceptual blunders. It does not make any sense, not literally, they claim, to ascribe psychological predicates to parts of a human being, like the brain or networks of neurons, for such predicates apply only to the human being as a whole. The failure of recognising this and entertaining the idea that brains see and know things, make inferences about the environment and so on, which is common in neuroscientific research and theory construction, is to commit a "mereological fallacy."

Wittgenstein's grammatical remark is a reminder of the conditions for the meaningful use of our psychological vocabulary and as such a commentary on, and dissolution of, the mind–body problem. Psychological attributes do not belong to a discrete and hidden entity called the mind but to the *living human being*. Talk about the mind is talk about various actions, conditions and character traits of *persons* (Hacker 2010, pp. 249–256). Hence, the age-old problem of how the mind is connected to the body is a pseudo-problem. This has far-reaching implications, not just for neuroscience, but also for psychology. For instance, it cancels out a widely accepted premise in cognitive psychology, which takes the mind to be a computer programme that runs on the hardware of the brain and causes bodily movements. According to this notion, it is the brain that is the bearer of psychological attributes, and consequently, to the extent that technology allows it, a main object of study in psychology (see Shanker 1998, for the history of this idea).

At this point, Smedslund's views on the nature of the mind can be read as a continuation of Wittgenstein's, when he writes that "psychology is a separate conceptual level, … that … would continue to exist even if we had no knowledge of what goes on inside our heads." (Smedslund 2013, p. 125). Indeed, it is altogether sensible, albeit controversial in the ontological climate of today, to claim, as Smedslund does, that "[m]ost psychologically relevant knowledge can be arrived at independently of neuroscience." (p. 125; see also his Chap. 13 in this volume).

Now, having sketched a picture of the key elements in Wittgenstein's take on philosophical issues, let us back up a bit and look at it from a metaphilosophical perspective. In what way should we characterise it? To be sure, there is more than one way of characterising it. But if we focus on the fact that we cannot seem to describe it, either by pointing to basic substantive claims, or by referring to a novel explanatory framework that is supposed to pave way for new forms of understanding, we can readily fit it into the philosophical tradition of quietism, which, as Macarthur (2017, p. 250) explains, is a "non-doctrinal" and "non-constructive" mode of philosophising. It is not "a philosophical doctrine, as its name perhaps suggests, but a *method* of philosophizing that aims at ridding oneself of philosophical doctrine in one region of thought or another." (Ibid. p. 250). The method of which he speaks is, however, not the same across all forms of quietism. Macarthur labels Wittgenstein's variant "semantic" quietism to distinguish it from Pyrrhonian "aporetic" quietism and describes its basic sentiment in the following way:

> It is a method based on suspicion of the *intelligibility* of metaphysical 'problems' and their 'solutions.' A quietist of this kind engages in the delicate art of *scrutinizing the problems themselves*—rather than working on answers to them—to avoid having to take a stand in metaphysical debates about which theory (say, which realism or anti-realism) is best. The immediate aim of [quietism] in the region of philosophical thought to which it applies is not to debate metaphysical doctrines, which are seen as semantically dubious (non-truth-apt, non-explanatory, etc.), but to attempt to get along without them. (Macarthur 2017, p. 252).

Now, it cannot be emphasised enough that there is no such thing as turning away from philosophical issues in the quietist aim of getting along without metaphysical doctrines. On the contrary, there can be no quietism without a deep involvement with philosophy. Showing that it is fruitless to debate metaphysical theories, as it only *seems* meaningful to do so when we overlook the grammar of our language, demands work. McDowell, who is well-known for his quietist reading of Wittgenstein, is very clear on this:

> There is no guarantee that it will be easy to uncover a forgetfulness of something obvious, underlying the conviction of being under an intellectual obligation to engage in [metaphysical] tasks… So, this kind of philosophy needs a precise and sympathetic appreciation of the temptations it aims to deconstruct. There is no question of quickly dismissing a range of philosophical activity from the outside. (McDowell 2009, p. 372).

It may appear as if quietism is merely reactive; nothing but a deconstruction of misguided metaphysical speculation. It is not. Quietism calls for proactive work as well. McDowell sees its aim as that "of quieting *the felt need* for substantive philosophy." (McDowell 2009, p. 370, italics added). Hence, it is no less part of the quietist agenda to forestall metaphysical speculation by describing the grammatical features of a segment of our language than it is to dismantle it by showing that certain claims are semantically askew.

Finally, we may ask whether it is not necessary to delineate the legitimate scope of quietism. Is it a mode of thought that always applies or are there areas in philosophy where it is out of place? McDowell seems to think that it does not suit the problems of practical philosophy: "Think, for instance, of reflection about the requirements of justice or the proper shape of a political community." (McDowell 2009, p. 367). Thus, he concludes: "[Q]uietism is not a refusal to engage in substantive philosophy in the face of what everyone has to accept as genuine problems." (2009, p. 317). Macarthur, however, takes issue with this demarcation of quietism. To him, it is "a failure to acknowledge that metaphysical thinking can and does characterize ethical, social and political reflection no less than reflections about, say, the mind, propositions, science, mathematics and God." (Macarthur 2017, p. 261). Still, it might be that Macarthur only underscores what is, after all, implicit in McDowell's position, for he does not claim that the quietist method will deliver the final word in every matter philosophical. Not all problems are pseudo-problems. Also he concludes that it is "no part of quietist methodology to turn away from a legitimate problem in philosophy." (2017, p. 255). Therefore, Janik and Toulmin (1973) may have found just the right word when they described this way of doing philosophy in terms of a propaedeutic. That is, the quietist mode of philosophising will always be necessary. However, no claim is made to its universal sufficiency.[6]

Smedslund's Psychological Quietism

The foundation on which to build a case for viewing Smedslund's take on psychology as being in line with Wittgenstein's take on philosophy—and thereby placing it within the philosophical tradition of quietism—has now been laid down. Before I engage in this expository task, however, we need to know exactly what Smedslund means by psychology, for the discipline touches upon many fields of scientific enquiry if it is taken to be any attempt at explaining the cognitive, conative, affective and perceptive behaviour of human beings. It can be instructive, in this regard, to turn to Harré (2002), who has distinguished between three areas of discourse—three different grammars—which he takes to be both psychologically and scientifically relevant. Firstly, there is the everyday discourse of human beings as persons, that is, as purposive and meaning-seeking agents, constantly formed by their experiences and the bearers of moral rights and responsibilities. This kind of discourse he calls P-grammar. Secondly, there is the discourse of human beings as biological organisms that are the product of Darwinian evolution. This he calls O-grammar. Thirdly, there is the discourse of human beings as the outcome of complex molecular activity. This he calls M-grammar. Now, O-grammar and M-grammar can, without doubt, be used to pick out facts that are relevant in a wholesale explanation of human behaviour, but they pertain, primarily and respectively, to the fields of ethology and neurobiology. Smedslund is concerned with P-grammar, or what he likes to call "psychology proper," that is, "domains in which all variables investigated are psychological." (Smedslund 1995, p. 177). Of course, he is talking about the realm of intentionality.[7]

[6] In a recent article, Moyal-Sharrock (2017) criticises "the myth of the quietist Wittgenstein". She attacks those who portray Wittgenstein's philosophy as being purely therapeutic; aiming only at the dissolution of philosophical problems without contributing to our understanding of phenomena in any way. But this does not seem to be the kind of quietism that Macarthur and McDowell have in mind and that has been laid down here, for they do not deny that we seek to sharpen our understanding. Moyal-Sharrock actually comments briefly on McDowell's (2009) interpretation of Wittgensteinian quietism. She accuses him of failing to see that Wittgenstein was not only occupied with diagnosing philosophical pseudo-problems but also in the business of problem-solving. However, I see no reason to believe that McDowell would deny that Wittgenstein not only diagnosed philosophical problems as pseudo-problems but also, in so doing, engaged in the (dis)solution of these very problems. In fact, I read the two articles as being wholly compatible, save for the fact that Moyal-Sharrock is unhappy with the term "quietism".

[7] We should note that Harré's notion of P-grammar does not emphasise intentionality, but normativity. This need not, however, concern us here. Intentionality and normativity are closely related concepts and any differences between them are irrelevant to our discussion.

Thus, we can expound Smedslund's psychological quietism as a non-doctrinal and non-constructive way of doing psychology. It is an a-theoretical approach to the subject matter (cf. Smedslund 2004); a method based on suspicion of the feasibility of constructing general theories and trying to validate them empirically within the context of P-grammar. A quietist of this kind engages in the delicate art of scrutinising any theories and hypotheses put forth—rather than testing them by collecting data—to avoid getting entangled in pseudo-empirical research. The immediate aim of quietism in the region of psychology to which it applies is not to debate theoretical perspectives and their preferred empirical methodology, which are seen as epistemologically dubious, but to show that it is possible to do without theory and data (cf. Macarthur 2017, p. 252). In order for it to be successful, this kind of psychology needs a precise and sympathetic appreciation of the temptations it seeks to deconstruct. There can be no question of quickly dismissing a range of psychological research activity from the outside (cf. McDowell 2009, p. 372).

Instead of empirically informed theory construction, the quietist method involves conceptual analysis and its focal point is the familiar use of words. This subsumes both the reactive task of unmasking pseudo-empirical research and the proactive task of charting the logical geography of psychological concepts. When engaged in these tasks, we do not try to uncover new facts. We make explicit what is already implicit in language. Thus, psychological quietism seeks to understand psychological phenomena, rather than adding to the bulk of psychological knowledge (cf. Hacker 2013, Chap. 1). We are not, in a sense, trying to learn anything new about our psychological reality. Rather, we want to understand something that is already in plain view (cf. Wittgenstein 2009, §89).

A reason to doubt that psychology will discover general psychological facts and principles by means of empirical research is, as noted above, that human beings have lived together in societies for countless generations and hence, it can be expected that those psychological regularities that have emerged—partly by way of a common evolutionary history and partly by way of society-specific enculturation processes—are part of ordinary language already (cf. Smedslund 2016a, p. 191). For a quietist, searching for such regularities today, by means of empirical research, is like the futile task of trying to inflate a balloon from the inside—to follow Smedslund in his recurrent use of Israel's (1982) very telling metaphor. Thus, psychological quietism is a recognition of the peculiar epistemological situation that follows from the fact that the whole enterprise of psychology starts from within an already inflated balloon. Indeed, we could—with a nod to Wittgenstein—say that if someone were to advance theses in psychology, it would never be possible to debate them because everyone would agree to them (cf. Wittgenstein 2009, §128). Or as Smedslund (2016a, p. 190) puts it with regard to the implicitly recognised meaning of words:

> *Given what is taken for granted, hypotheses that make sense are true, and hypotheses that do not make sense are false.*

Now to a pressing issue: We have seen that Wittgenstein contrasted the conceptual domain of philosophy with the empirical domain of science. So, does the quietist view of psychology as a conceptual undertaking mean that the discipline cannot be a venerable part of the scientific community? It seems to me that there is not much to gain from either/or thinking here. If science is both the search for new knowledge and an organisation thereof (attempts at understanding), then psychology is not so much in the business of the former, but most certainly in the business of the latter; the project of PL being an important example. Accordingly, psychology can be deemed a science, even though it is not, predominantly, an empirical science (cf. Smedslund 2016a).

Another pressing issue is whether Smedslund's Euclidean method of projection is compatible with the quietist dictum of leaving everything as it is. Does its forced rectilinear links not interfere with a correct understanding of the structure of concepts? This was, of course, Shotter's worry, but on the instrumentalist reading of PL that I have suggested, the Euclidean mapping of concepts merely works as a reminder of important connections. We recognise that reality is a more intricate place and do not mistake our map for it. It should be noted that in his philosophical investigations, Wittgenstein too did not present a complete grammatical network of the concepts under consideration, but only highlighted those features of them that were significant to solve the philosophical problem at hand. The only thing that we must reject in Smedslund's own description of his work, if we want to uphold a quietist interpretation of it, is the suggestion that his definitions may in the long run improve ordinary language (Smedslund 2011, p. 134). This not only contradicts the idea of leaving everything as it is, it is also mistaken, especially when it comes to the nature of psychological concepts. For, as Wittgenstein noted, the fact that these concepts have loose edges is a consequence of our daily needs. Psychological discourse is indeterminate, to an extent, but this is not a deficiency, for a little indeterminacy makes it flexible, which is fitting. A logically more precise language would not be better for us; not in this domain of human life. Commenting on the attempts at constructing such a language, Wittgenstein mocked: "I asked him for a bread knife, and he gives me a razor blade because it is sharper." (Quoted in Hacker 2013, p. 125).

Psychological quietism is a propaedeutic. Not in the sense that it is a mere stepping stone towards more important matters but in the sense that its necessity does not entail universal sufficiency. It is an approach that severely undermines the current all-embracing empirical programme of psychology, but it is no part of the quietist agenda to turn away from a legitimate empirical issue. It would be beyond the scope of this chapter to discuss the possibilities of conducting fruitful empirical research within the context of P-grammar but we can note that Smedslund (2002) has identified "capacity-testing" as a legitimate field of study. Capacity-testing is research into the boundary conditions of psychological processes, such as perceptual and cognitive biases or the limits of attention and memory. He has also recognised the strictly empirical nature of "hybrid studies" (Ibid.). Such studies begin when we look beyond P-grammar and ask how various non-psychological variables, such as genes, neural networks and the historical conditions of human evolution, relate to psychological variables. If PL is a picture of the inside wall of the psychological balloon (cf. Smedslund 2012b, p. 296), then we can think of hybrid studies as attempts at showing how this picture relates to the outside wall of the balloon.

Finally, something should be said about the quietist sentiment in connection to the possibility of conceptual innovation. As with regard to empirical research, there is no opposition to it in principle, whether it be the possibly fruitful creation of new nodes in the already established conceptual network, or altogether new descriptions of human behaviour. For one cannot categorically exclude that there are aspects of our lives that could gain from such stipulations. However, the quietist will not indulge in conceptual novelties, but keep a temperate and somewhat reserved attitude towards them. Shotter was undoubtedly right when he claimed that there is psychological power in the poetic potential of language, but there is good reason to be careful here, and not get distracted by shiny objects. We must, in the name of scientific parsimony, ask ourselves whether a new and alluring form of representation is truly enlightening or whether it is merely the type of explanation it offers that thrills us. The statements made in various forms of depth psychology do not, for instance, rest upon any empirical discoveries of unconscious mental processes. They simply offer a different way of talking about psychological phenomena. So, the critical question to ask, when facing such approaches, is not (typically) whether there is data in support of the general claims made about people's unconscious drives and motives, but whether these "specialized dialects" of our P-grammar (Harré and Moghaddam 2012, p. 11) add anything to our understanding of the psychological domain. Perhaps they are altogether expendable or even detrimental to a scientifically sound P-grammar.

The Bricoleur Model and the Ethical Dimension of Quietism

Over the last years, Smedslund (2009, 2012b, 2015, 2016b) has levelled heavy criticism at the prevailing Boulder model of the scientist-practitioner, which states that psychological practice is to be based on generalised empirical research. In its stead, he has introduced the bricoleur model. A bricoleur-practitioner is a jack-of-all-trades, who, without a theoretical base in empirical research, responds to the specifics of a person's life-situation when trying to be of help.

Now, as we have seen, Smedslund's rationale for being suspicious of the utility of empirical research at the abstract level of psychological concepts is the likelihood of it being pseudo-empirical, that is, that it will simply move along the conceptual tracks that have already been laid down in language. When he expands this suspicion to the concrete reality of psychological practice, other extra-linguistic factors come into play. Here, at the level of individuals, he rejects the utility of generalised empirical research on the grounds that it cannot capture the important idiosyncrasies of a person to which any treatment must be tailored. To shed light on this, Smedslund (2009, 2016a, b) has tallied four different, but intertwined, arguments.

1. *Infinitely numerous determinants.* An infinite number of possible contexts can determine the nature of psychological processes. Hence, in order to recognise a psychological phenomenon for what it is, it is necessary to know the context in which it is situated. Natural science does not have to deal with this. It can discard the larger context of physical processes since their nature is context-independent. Smedslund illustrates this with the simple example of raising an arm and extending a finger upwards. Neurophysiologically speaking, there is a finite description of the various nerve impulses and muscle contractions that are causally responsible for making such a movement possible. Psychologically speaking, the action of raising an arm and pointing upwards can mean anything depending on the context. It can, for instance, be a threatening gesture, or the signalling of a suddenly gained insight, or a call for attention at something above. Because of the infinite number of contexts that can determine the meaning of psychological processes, theorising about them is difficult, to say the least, since a theory can only have a limited number of variables for it to be workable. What a psychologist needs, in order to be of help, is not theory, but an extensive knowledge of a person's history and life-situation.
2. *Irreversibility.* Psychological processes are strictly irreversible. Every experience, everything a person undergoes, changes him or her in a way that cannot be fully undone. Constancy in an individual's traits and tendencies merely reflects stability in the environment and does not change the fact that psychological phenomena are historical. This makes psychology as the study of individuals inhospitable to regularity-seeking empirical research, which is based on the premise that possible findings can be replicated. Experimental studies of the randomised-control-trial-type are an attempt to circumvent the problem of irreversibility by measuring the average behaviour of different groups of people in objective situations. Ignoring the fact that studies of this type are likely to be pseudo-empirical, they could only ever support conclusions of a general kind, at the cost of knowledge about individual persons.
3. *Uniqueness.* Since people are genetically different, are moulded in a particular historical and socio-economic context and irreversibly learn different things from their experiences, which contain infinitely variable and fortuitous events, they are unique. This is, of course, irrelevant at the aggregate level of statistical regularities—which is a way of ignoring that which is unique—but it is imperative in psychological practice. This creates an unbridgeable gap between generalised empirical research and practice. Knowledge of a population's average behaviour is of little use when we have to respond sensitively to the behaviour of a unique person.
4. *Social interactivity.* Psychological processes are inherently social. The psychological lives of human beings are the result of prolonged social interactions and this means that a psychologist cannot hope to gain access to, and understand, their unique nature, if he or she does not enter the field of study, so to speak, and engage with each person socially. Now, it is probably safe to assume that most psychologists actually work in this way but we should admit that social engagement does not fit well with the idea of a scientist-practitioner, which encourages

the attitude of a detached observer extrapolating predictions about the behaviour of individuals based on people's average behaviour.

Thus, Smedslund concludes that a psychologist has no empirically generalised knowledge of psychological phenomena that he or she can use to explain and predict the behaviour of a person. Of course, he does not deny that a psychologist may be aided by his or her knowledge of local and temporary regularities within a particular population. However, it is an important part of his position that we cannot assume such knowledge to be relevant and hence, it should not figure as a guiding-principle when encountering another human being. Indeed, he makes it clear that a psychologist should always refrain from putting forth any hypotheses about a case (Smedslund 2016b, p. 56) and adopt an initial attitude of *not-knowing* (Anderson and Goolishian 1992). This outright rejection of theory and complete openness to a person's life-situation is diametrically opposed to the avowed goal of mainstream empirical psychology, which is exactly that of applying theories to a person, that is, empirically generalised explanations and predictions (Smedslund 2012a, p. 101).

Now, it is not difficult to see in what way the bricoleur model exemplifies the quietist ethos. We have reason to call it both non-doctrinal and non-constructive, for neither does it rest on substantive claims about the human condition, nor does it ordain a particular procedure. However, as already noted above, we are not dealing with the structure of language, as we are when we engage in PL, but with the highly intricate and unforeseeable possibilities of human life. Are we justified in thinking of the quietist stance in such a way that it becomes an applicable term of art, not only at the abstract level of conceptual analysis, but also at the concrete level of human interaction? If we take into account its ethical dimension, I think we are. Indeed, it then becomes a rather natural move to make.

In his account of philosophical quietism, Macarthur (2017) argues that it is not only a method of concern for academic philosophy, but an important mode of thinking for dealings in everyday life. To begin with, he notes that central to the quietist critique of metaphysics is the charge that it lacks sensitivity to the empirical. Then, he equates this with dogma, by which he means "claims about reality whose truth is taken to be authoritatively established independently of the empirical." (Ibid. p. 265). Therefore, quietism is to be understood as a form of reflection with the ethical goal of renouncing dogma. And this is comparable to the rationale underlying the bricoleur model. For central to the critique of conducting psychological practice on the basis of generalised empirical research is, as we have seen, the charge that it overshoots the important idiosyncracies of a person to which any treatment must be tailored. In other words, and quite ironically, it lacks sensitivity to the empirical, that is, the empirical reality of treatment. Indeed, inasmuch as the bricoleur model warns against the mindless following of evidence-based principles, without thereby encouraging loose speculation on behalf of the psychologist, it can be seen as a model with the ethical goal of renouncing dogma. As such, it is an example of the quietist mode of thinking.

Now, a necessary addendum: Macarthur is undoubtedly on the right track in construing quietism as an attempt to resist dogma by noting that it demands of our thinking that it be properly grounded in the empirical. However, he fails to consider that the quietist critique of metaphysics is no less based on the fact that it is not properly grounded in the conceptual. As we have seen, quietism invalidates the assumption that the mind is an entity in its own right. Partly, this is because the assumption is insensitive to empirical investigation, that is, neither is it possible to support it, nor refute it, with empirical means. But this is not something that could be overcome by, say, technological advancements, for it is a conceptual matter. The notion of the mind as a discrete entity is, first and foremost, invalidated because it is conceptually awry. Hence, quietism must be seen as an attempt to resist dogma, not only with regard to the empirical, but also with regard to the conceptual. In fact, it is only by conducting conceptual investigation that we can come to see whether a particular question is in need of empirical investigation or not; a point that Smedslund has been trying to get through to the psychological community for the last 50 years or so.

Concluding Remarks

By emphasising the ethical dimension of quietism, we have, again, returned to the reason why Janik and Toulmin chose to describe Wittgenstein's anti-metaphysical way of philosophising in terms of a propaedeutic. Duly, they noted that had he renounced metaphysics on the basis of some kind of anti-metaphysical theory, as did, for instance, the logical positivists, he would only have replaced old dogmas with new. But he consciously did not, for his aim was liberation from dogma as such (Janik and Toulmin 1973, p. 256).

Now, identifying dogma as claims not properly grounded in the conceptual and the empirical, there is no getting around the fact that Smedslund is guilty of endorsing one in insisting that the coherency of concepts is dependent on the existence of invariant components. On the face of it, this should make a quietist interpretation of his work difficult to justify. However, I have tried to argue that in Smedslund's case, the dogma has become idle. It is a conception without consequences. Thus, we can charitably disregard it.

In construing Smedslund's work as an offshoot of quietism, I hope that a unifying picture of his critique of empirical psychology has emerged with the particular force that comes with a name. Bringing together the various threads of the argument, we can sum up the quietist reading of Smedslund as, not only a way to acknowledge the a-theoretical nature of his position, but also a way to appreciate his two major contributions to psychology—the project of PL and the bricoleur model—as showing us how to fend off dogmatism. On the one hand, we are urged to mark the meaning of words, so that we do not lose touch with psychology's conceptual reality. On the other hand, we are asked to heed the particularity of every person, so that we do not lose touch with psychology's empirical reality.[8]

[8] I would like to thank Tobias G. Lindstad for invaluable comments on earlier drafts of this chapter.

References

Anderson, H., & Goolishian, H. (1992). The client is the expert: A not-knowing approach to therapy. In S. McNamee & K. Gergen (Eds.), *Social construction and the therapeutic process* (pp. 25–39). Newbury Park, CA: Sage.

Bennett, M., & Hacker, P. M. S. (2003). *Philosophical foundations of neuroscience*. Oxford: Blackwell.

Glock, H. J. (1996). On safari with Wittgenstein, Quine and Davidson. In H. J. Glock & R. L. Arrington (Eds.), *Wittgenstein and Quine* (pp. 144–173). New York: Routledge.

Israel, J. (1982). *Om konsten att blåsa upp en ballong inifrån*. Gothenburg: Korpen.

Janik, A., & Toulmin, S. (1973). *Wittgenstein's Vienna*. New York: Touchstone.

Hacker, P. M. S. (2010). *Human nature: The categorial framework*. Oxford: Blackwell.

Hacker, P. M. S. (2013). *Wittgenstein: Comparisons and context*. Oxford: Oxford University Press.

Hacker, P. M. S. (2017). *The passions: A study of human nature*. Oxford: Wiley Blackwell.

Harré, R. (2002). *Cognitive Science*. London: SAGE.

Harré, R., & Moghaddam, F. M. (2012). *Psychology for the third millennium*. London: SAGE.

Macarthur, D. (2017). On metaphysical quietism and everyday life. In G. D'Oro & S. Overgaard (Eds.), *The Cambridge companion to philosophical methodology* (pp. 249–273). Cambridge: Cambridge University Press.

McDowell, J. (2009). Wittgensteinian "quietism". *Common Knowledge, 15*(3), 365–372.

McEachrane, M. (2009). Emotion, meaning and appraisal theory. *Theory & Psychology, 19*(1), 33–53.

Moyal-Sharrock, D. (2017). The myth of the quietist Wittgenstein. In J. Beale & I. J. Kidd (Eds.), *Wittgenstein and Scientism* (pp. 152–174). Abingdon: Routledge.

Parrott, G., & Harré, R. (1991). Smedslundian suburbs in the city of language: The case of embarrassment. *Psychological Inquiry, 2*(4), 358–361.

Shanker, S. G. (1998). *Wittgenstein's remarks on the foundations of AI*. London/New York: Routledge.

Shotter, J. (1991). Measuring blindly and speculating loosely: But is a "psychologic" the answer? *Psychological Inquiry, 2*(4), 363–366.

Shotter, J. (1999). From within an external world. *Scandinavian Journal of Psychology, 40*, 81–84.

Smedslund, J. (1990). A critique of Tversky and Kahneman's distinction between fallacy and misunderstanding. *Scandinavian Journal of Psychology, 31*, 110–120.

Smedslund, J. (1991). The pseudo-empirical in psychology, and the case for psychologic. *Psychological Inquiry, 2*, 325–338.

Smedslund, J. (1995). Auxiliary versus theoretical hypotheses and ordinary versus scientific language. *Human Development, 38*, 174–178.

Smedslund, J. (1997). *The structure of psychological common sense*. Mahwah, NJ: Ablex.

Smedslund, J. (1999). Psychologic and the study of memory. *Scandinavian Journal of Psychology, 40*, 3–17.

Smedslund, J. (2002). From hypothesis-testing psychology to procedure-testing psychologic. *Review of General Psychology, 6*(1), 51–72.

Smedslund, J. (2004). *Dialogues about a new psychology*. Chagrin Falls, OH: Taos Institute Publications.

Smedslund, J. (2009). The mismatch between current research methods and the nature of psychological phenomena. *Theory & Psychology, 19*, 778–794.

Smedslund, J. (2011). Meaning of words and the use of axiomatics in psychological theory. *Journal of Theoretical and Philosophical Psychology, 31*(2), 126–135.

Smedslund, J. (2012a). What follows from what we all know about human beings. *Theory & Psychology, 22*, 658–668.

Smedslund, J. (2012b). The bricoleur model of psychological practice. *Theory & Psychology, 22*, 643–657.

Smedslund, J. (2012c). Psycho-logic: Some thoughts and after-thoughts. *Scandinavian Journal of Psychology, 53*, 295–302.

Smedslund, J. (2013). *From nonsense syllables to holding hands: Sixty years as a psychologist.* Chagrin Falls, OH: Taos Institute Publications.

Smedslund, J. (2015). The value of experiments in psychology. In J. Martin, J. Sugarman, & K. L. Slaney (Eds.), *The Wiley handbook of theoretical and philosophical psychology* (pp. 359–373). Oxford: Wiley Blackwell.

Smedslund, J. (2016a). Why psychology cannot be an empirical science. *Integrative Psychological and Behavioral Science, 50*, 185–195.

Smedslund, J. (2016b). Practicing psychology without an empirical evidence-base: The bricoleur model. *New Ideas in Psychology, 43*, 50–56.

Strawson, P. F. (1992). *Analysis and metaphysics.* Oxford: Oxford University Press.

Wierzbicka, A. (1996). *Semantics: Primes and universals.* Oxford: Oxford University Press.

Wittgenstein, L. (2001). *Tractatus Logico-Philosophicus.* London/New York: Routledge (orig. German pub. 1921).

Wittgenstein, L. (2009). *Philosophical investigations.* Oxford: Blackwell (orig. pub. 1953).

Chapter 8
Jan Smedslund and Psychologic: The Problem of Psychologism and the Nature of Language

Henderikus J. Stam

> …logic is a psychological discipline since the process of coming-to-know takes place only in the soul, and since that thinking which completes itself in this coming-to-know is a psychological process. …Obviously, no-one claims that psychology dissolves into logic. What separates the two sufficiently is that logic is a sub-discipline of psychology (Lipps 1893, cited in Kusch 2015)

Having followed the work of Jan Smedslund for decades, I can only say what a privilege and pleasure it is to be able to address in some small way the very extensive corpus that he has produced in support of his *Psychologic*. At this juncture, I am going to assume that the reader is familiar in large measure with Smedslund's work and that many of the papers in this volume will have elaborated on the foundational issues as well as the changes in psychologic over the years. I will refer to Smedslund's work as necessary but will not provide a broad overview in order to land on the three interrelated issues I would like to highlight in this chapter.

First, the analytic-synthetic distinction is an important issue that was debated in mid-twentieth century philosophy. I made reference to it in my only commentary on psychologic some years ago (Stam 2000). It is an important issue since Smedslund himself has addressed the question on a number of occasions, for example in 2002, but unfortunately he dismissed it by arguing that this issue could be "bypassed" (Smedslund 2002, p. 55). I will argue that this is too fast, that despite the "complex topics involved" (Smedslund 2002, p. 55), these are questions that are crucial to the project of a psychologic.

I am indebted to Tobias Lindstad for his careful reading and comments which I hope have improved this chapter. I remain responsible for all errors of omission and commission!

H. J. Stam (✉)
University of Calgary, Calgary, Canada
e-mail: stam@ucalgary.ca

T. G. Lindstad et al. (eds.), *Respect for Thought*, Theory and History in the Human and Social Sciences, https://doi.org/10.1007/978-3-030-43066-5_8

Second, I would like to place Smedslund's work in a historical perspective. That is, I wish to relate his efforts to found a psychologic to the late nineteenth and early twentieth century initiative to found human reason on a series of logical laws. This turns out to be a complicated history, and I shall be presenting a very short version of it. My reason for doing so is that I have not seen this commented on in any of the many places that Smedslund's work has been discussed and debated nor have I noted any mention of it by Smedslund himself.[1] By placing psychologic in a historical perspective, we can see that Smedslund's notion of the a priori conceptual structure of psychology has some very influential forerunners, even if they constitute a different project in other ways (I want to be clear that I am not claiming that they are equivalent). These historical forerunners provide us with a number of crucial lessons for contemporary psychologic and psychology.

Third, I wish to emphasize that the nature of language that we have come to understand through the Wittgensteinian tradition throws up some serious limits to psychologic.[2] In both 2002 and more recent work, Smedslund has begun to respond to his critics who have noted this problem as a deep problem for psychologic. In my view, Smedslund does not go far enough in addressing this fundamental question because it will require more than simply making minor changes to the system of psychologic. Nonetheless, this need not be a fatal counterargument.

Before starting, however, I must, like all of those who have read and admired Smedslund's work, acknowledge the tremendous service he has offered to the theoretical endeavors in the discipline and in a sense for psychology as a whole. With deceivingly straightforward titles as "Why psychology cannot be an empirical science" (Smedslund 2016) and "What follows from what we all know about human beings" (Smedslund 2012a), he has advanced a sophisticated and integrated system of developing arguments about the nature of the a priori/noncontigent in psychology and how it must be separated from the empirical/contingent to keep us from doing pseudoempirical research. In this, I can only support the project, for much psychological research is indeed pseudoempirical, sometimes for the reasons articulated by Smedslund but sometimes for other reasons, which I will attempt to examine in my conclusion.[3]

Even for those of us who disagree with elements of the structure of psychologic however, the depth and breadth of Smedslund's efforts to create a psychologic have opened up discussions and possibilities to address the serious shortcomings of the

---

[1] The version of psychologism that I discuss here is the original concerns with psychologism as it was expressed in the late nineteenth century (Kusch, 1995). The use of the term by Sugarman (2017; Chap. 16) is quite different and represents one of the many generalizations of the term in the twentieth century (see Kusch 1995, 2015 for a discussion).

[2] See also chapters by Martin B. Smedlund and by Michael McEachrane (respectively, Chaps. 8 and 9 this volume).

[3] Smedslund (1991, p. 326) provides a formal definition of what is "pseudoempirical" which states, in part, that researchers take propositions to be empirical when they are in fact a priori and noncontingent. I take pseudoempiricism to include tests of hypotheses that cannot possibly be tested because they do not specify precise objects of investigation (see conclusion below).

discipline that many of us have called home for the length of a career. It is not only in his original writings but also in his response to critics that he has shown a sensibility that transcends the simply combative nature of many debates and clarified over the years this project of a psychologic. In addition, he has had to field critiques from die-hard empiricists and drive-by data collectors as well as more philosophically inclined interlocutors who are in some measure sympathetic with the project—as I myself am.

In the meantime, however, Jan Smedslund has also modified his stance slightly, which will be relevant to my comments. I am referring in this instance to his 2012 paper in the *Scandinavian Journal of Psychology* (2012b) wherein he expressed some reservations about earlier claims and doubles down on the work of Anna Wierzbicka, whose notion of a natural semantic metalanguage has been important as a foundation for Smedslund (e.g., Goddard and Wierzbicka 2014). More on this below.

Analytic vs Synthetic Distinction

In a commentary on a paper by Geir Smedslund, I had tried to begin a discussion on the analytic-synthetic distinction and the historical foundations of attempts to ground psychology in logic (Stam 2000). Obviously, I must not have been very clear because in his response to my commentary, Geir Smedslund did not appear to understand what I was trying to do (G. Smedslund 2000). Although this was not an exchange with Jan Smedslund, Geir Smedslund certainly claimed to be representing psychologic. Hence, I refer readers to that earlier commentary and will only provide a brief summary here. The fact that both Jan and Geir Smedslund have responded to this issue, however, will allow me to say something new about the question.

The analytic vs synthetic distinction has been debated for the better part of 200 years. Beginning with Kant, the literature is vast, and the words have certainly been used to refer to different phenomena. According to Kant, an analytic statement is one in which the concept of the predicate is contained in its constituent terms. Logical positivists expressed this in terms of *meaning*, that is, analytic truths are true by virtue of the *meanings* expressed and only the propositions of logic and mathematics fulfill these requirements. So for example, Ayer (1936/1946) argued—following the Vienna Circle—that an empirical hypothesis may not be conclusively verifiable, but "some possible sense-experience should be relevant to the determination of its truth or falsehood" (p. 41). Furthermore, "if a putative proposition fails to satisfy this principle, and is not a tautology, then I hold that it is metaphysical, and that, being metaphysical, it is neither true nor false but literally senseless" (p. 41). Hence, by the middle of the twentieth century, the analytic-synthetic distinction had been championed by the logical positivists to become a distinction between a priori analytic claims, probable hypotheses, and a third category of meaningless statements that were metaphysical.

The classic example of analytic statements that populated philosophy textbooks for generations was "all bachelors are unmarried." Or to use one of Smedslund's examples, "P Becomes Surprised If, and Only If, P Experiences Something Unexpected" (Smedslund 2002). These statements are true because of the meanings assigned to the word "bachelor" or the word "surprise." Synthetic truths are those that are dependent on the way the world is, that is "matters of fact" as David Hume had it. Hence, a statement such as "Jane is married to Tilley" is a synthetic one because its truth is dependent on some characterization of the world.

Among others, Quine (1953) famously argued that the distinction between analytic and synthetic statements could not hold because it could only be defined in a circular manner and that it was dependent on the disputed verificationist theory of meaning. The latter referred to, in short, the notion that propositions could only be known if we could strictly separate meanings from facts. Speaking of science, Quine argued that we do not evaluate statements one at a time since all statements are interconnected. Instead we evaluate the field as a whole, and hence the analytic/synthetic distinction was a false one. In other words, argued Quine, "taken collectively, science has its double dependence upon language and experience; but this duality is not significantly traceable into the statements of science taken one by one" (Quine 1953, p. 42). While others have continued to defend this view on occasion (e.g., Juhl and Loomis, 2010, 2012; Russell 2008), it was for long thought of as fallen by the wayside as a, if not indefensible, certainly difficult to defend notion in practice. What this meant for the philosophy of science, at least for the past 60 or so years, is that theories are viewed as not only resistant to change but they are easily adjusted by making changes at the boundaries.[4] The implications for science were that it was hard to take seriously the notion that a single experimental observation could undermine a theoretical edifice.

If this debate is any indication, the distinction that Smedslund has built psychologic on, between a kind of logic based on semantic primitives, and an empirical research tradition that is deluded by its pseudoempirical contents, is not as clear-cut as it seems. A priori distinctions cannot be rooted in the axioms that Smedslund has argued for but instead are based on local traditions or what Parrott and Harré (1991) called "family resemblances." I think this will become clearer after the next two sections of this chapter but for now I merely wish to argue that the hard line between Smedslund's a priori and empirical propositions does not hold for the simple reason that the distinction between these two is based on an outdated, logical positivist notion of meaning.

To be fair, Smedslund has addressed this issue on at least several occasions, including his major 1991 paper in *Psychological Inquiry* and in his 2002 paper in the *Review of General Psychology.* In 1991, he argued that he prefers the terms "a priori" and "empirical" to analytic and synthetic. This is because the latter two terms are "an amalgamation of purely logical (modal) and epistemic notions and

[4] Further complicating matters is the notion first articulated by Hanson (1958) that data is theory-laden as well as Kuhn's (1962) conception and critique of scientific progress. Although this too has implications for psychologic, I will not address these developments here.

therefore may serve to confuse the issues" (p. 326). Smedslund does not say how they serve to confuse. This usage however is consistent with the general usage preferred by logical positivists such as Ayer. While acknowledging the influence of Quine, Smedslund argues that "this debate need not concern us here. In scientific practice, there will always be a difference between what is presupposed and taken to be removed from direct empirical test and what is taken to be empirically testable. It is implicit in the above that what is to be regarded as a priori or empirical is relative to the axioms and definitions selected" (p. 326). But this is circular, what is regarded as a priori is defended on the basis of what has been selected, a priori. Smedslund dismissed the debate while failing to recognize the profound defeat of logical positivism and its theory of meaning, vestiges of which remain in psychologic.

In 2002, Smedslund argued that, "If 'analytic' is taken to refer to sentences that follow from the meaning of their constituent terms, then what is analytic in a given language can be determined by studying the consensus among native speakers. Later I describe studies that show the extent to which there is consensus about the axioms of psychologic" (p. 55). However, studying the "consensus among native speakers" is historically contingent, not analytic; languages are not set in stone. Just as meanings change (note for example how the terms *subjective* and *objective* have shifted over the past several centuries—Daston and Galison 2007), so can a consensus break down (see how quickly the word *gay* took on multiple meanings in the past 50 years). Certainly, we can agree broadly on the use of words, indeed, we have to, but as Parrott and Harré (1991) note, local conditions of application and core meanings cannot be separated. In sum, the distinction between a priori statements and empirical claims is just not as clear-cut as Smedslund takes it to be.

The Psychologism Debate and Logic in the Late Nineteenth Century Philosophy

I am pleased to be able to raise again the historical issues, this time I will rely on the extensive discussion of the notorious problem of psychologism provided by Martin Kusch (1995, 2015). The traditional account of the history of late nineteenth century psychologism is a debate in philosophy about the place of logic within psychology and the place of psychology within logic.[5] The brief version is that German logicians, such as Theodor Lipps, were impressed by John Stuart Mill's claim that logic was a branch of psychology (Kusch 1995). The Germans held that logical laws were the empirical generalizations of human reason. Kusch in his 2015 article lays out

[5] Kusch's 1995 volume makes clear that this is not an arcane debate about the relationship between psychology and logic but involved the allocation of chairs of philosophy to experimental psychologists. Philosophers fought back to protect their discipline using accusations of 'psychologism' to deter the appointment of psychologists. In the meantime the term "psychologism" came to refer to a wide variety of 'errors.'

just how complex these arguments were, but it was at least clear that psychologism could be seen as the claim that "logic is a part of psychology" or "logic must be based on psychology" (Kusch 2015). Kusch (2015) identifies another version of psychologism that has some relevance to Smedslund's psychologic. Kusch expresses it as follows:

1. The touchstone of logical truth is the feeling of self-evidence.
2. The feeling of self-evidence is a human mental experience.

Ergo, logic is about a human mental experience—and thus a part of psychology.

Kusch attributes this particular version of psychologism to Theodor Elsenhans (1862–1918), one of psychologism's defenders (see also the Lipps quote with which I begin this chapter). Psychologism concerned itself in the first instance by demonstrating that mathematics and logic were part of psychology and that the objects of logic could be explained by psychological observations. This is of course *not* what Smedslund's psychologic claims. Instead, Smedslund has argued that …

> The axioms and definitions of PL get their necessary status from the combination of having a compellingly plausible mass of implications and having unacceptable (senseless or absurd) negations and alternatives. In other words, the axioms and definitions indicate how we must use language to describe and explain psychological phenomena, in order to make sense and be consistent (Smedslund 1991, p. 334).

Smedslund's argument here is that a natural language, having "developed" over "thousands of years" has a "conceptual framework" that is very difficult to change. "A language prohibits an indefinite number of logically possible permutations and combinations of symbols" (Smedslund 1991, p. 334). Hence in its original formulation, psychologic was tied to the structure of language wherein language is the mediating link between psychological phenomena and psychologic.

In 2012, Smedslund reiterated this position but with one addition. After a statement that a "central" feature of psychologic is that it is organized as an "axiomatic system" Smedslund (2012b, p. 296) argues that.

> A search for such a system occurs almost necessarily, when one deals with an unorganized multitude of sentences, and especially if one cherishes the idea that these sentences should form a system as exact (cooperationally precise), neat, and simple as possible. Then, questions about whether or not given sentences do or do not follow from other sentences, easily come to the fore. If a sentence implies numerous and important other sentences, yet cannot itself be derived from any more basic sentences, and, in addition, is experienced as necessary, one has arrived at what is called an axiom. Together, the axioms make up a maximally simple description of how humans construe, or organize their view of, other humans, given an innate conceptual framework.

So far this is much like earlier versions of psychologic. However, Smedslund adds, "Since the axioms cannot be tested logically or empirically, they can only be tested by consensus" (p. 296). Not only is psychologic a system that, according to Smedslund, makes explicit what is already implicit in language and common sense, "the axioms are constructions applying to all human social realities, and should be shared by everyone" (Smedslund 2012b, p. 297).

The same year Smedslund (2012a) described psychologic as a "*proposal* to organize and describe human activity in a certain way" (p. 659, my italics). Rather than a system, it is here a mere "proposal" but Smedslund follows this not with an explanation of what is meant by a proposal, instead it is followed by "*hence*, it is normative, and involves a *suggestion* to talk in a certain way and take for granted certain things about the world" (p. 659–660, my italics). But the "hence," which would normally mean, "consequently" or "therefore," does not follow from what precedes it. It might be better to say that it is a proposal, and that as such, it is also normative or possibly prescriptive, by being a suggestion to talk in a certain way. Smedslund continues, "It is not about the relations between words, but about what we should take for granted in our understanding of the world" (p. 660). At this point, it is not what is "shared by everyone" but rather a tentative suggestion that this might be the case.[6]

The difference between the earlier and later version(s) is that Smedslund has moved away from what appears to be a foundation in logic and grammar to a foundation in the consensual use of language. Harré (1999) has earlier noted that this is like a *psychosemantics*, not a *psychologic*. "A culture is defined by those semantic principles it takes to be consensually self-evident. … There will be a Smedslundian psychosemantics for each community" (p. 38). Unfortunately, Smedslund does not fully develop his point, and it remains for the reader to fill in the details. Nonetheless, this seems to provide the seeds for an important shift that will change the way psychologic is understood.

What is my point here? Smedslund is neither the first nor likely to be the last to argue for the importance of logical foundations to human psychological phenomena. The failure of either Smedslund or his critics to notice this is not particularly surprising given the complex history of this debate at the beginning of the twentieth century. However, as Kusch (1995, 2015) has pointed out on several occasions, there are multiple echoes of the psychologism debate in contemporary psychology and philosophy. For example, there was a call by Quine in the 1960s to return to a form of psychologism through a naturalized epistemology, and there are contemporary philosophers who have revived elements of this debate (Juhl and Loomis 2010, 2012; Kusch 2015; Russell 2008).[7] Indeed, elements of the current penchant for neuroscientific explanations of all things psychological (what Smedslund (2020) in his Chap. 13 in this volume calls "neuro-ornamentation") have a resonance with the psychologism debates. So to note the parallels between nineteenth and early twentieth century philosophical and psychological debates and Smedslund's work is to note that Smedslund's arguments are part of a long series of speculations on the relationship between thought, logic, and action. Of all psychologism's critics, Frege's and Husserl's attacks on psychologism were considerable and extensive and as

---

[6] I am indebted to Tobias Lindstad for pointing me to this passage (despite the fact that I had read it prior to its publication as the editor of the journal that published Smedslund 2012a).

[7] To be clear, contemporary forms of the debate in fact have little in common with late nineteenth and early twentieth century accounts of psychologism save for a family resemblance that appeals to naturalism or materialism as foundational moments for psychology.

Kusch (1995) points out, this was not unrelated to political developments in German philosophy departments at the turn of the nineteenth century. Prior to WWI, psychologists in German-speaking countries had no departments of their own and increasingly occupied chairs in philosophy departments. The charge of psychologism was leveled at psychologist/philosophers in an attempt to return logic (and thus philosophy) to some non-psychological foundation. It was also an attempt to prevent the further incursion of psychologists into philosophy departments. In Husserl's case, the alternative to psychologism would be phenomenology, a foundation for an entirely new philosophy based on the structure of consciousness, not logic.

For Smedslund, however, the attempt to create a psychologic is deeply embedded in the contemporary failure of psychology to develop as a natural science. Here logic as a kind of precursor to meaning is not based on psychological categories but, instead, is the consequence of psychological categories. Natural language consists of "context-influenced" words, according to Smedslund, and "the semantic primitives and the system they form is always resorted to when humans describe what they experience to each other" (Smedslund 2012b, p. 299; see also Smedslund 2011). Furthermore, the axioms of psychologic are unconscious, that is, they are part of a "subjective unconscious" which makes it a kind of grammar (Smedslund 2012b, p. 299). This claim is not surprising since people presumably do not go about formulating the kinds of axioms that Smedslund claims we need to make sense of the world. So an axiom such as the "axiom of mentality" ("P takes it for granted that O can know, think, want, feel, perceive, say, and do, UNLESS, there are indications to the contrary," p. 297) is created unconsciously or sometimes as Smedslund notes, unreflectively. Furthermore, it must be stated in semantic primitives as defined by Wierzbicka (1996). Such "primitives" must be lexically represented in all languages (e.g., I, you, someone, something, etc.).

Smedslund thus places the system of psychologic in a similar class (but not the same) as Chomsky's universal grammar. Perhaps this is far-fetched but in commenting on John Shotter, Smedslund (2012b) argues, "all humans appear to share one particular set of common primitive concepts" (p. 298). Hence, there are features of language (semantically primitive concepts) whose logical relations create psychologic. What Smedslund has done is, in effect, taken part in a long tradition of trying to formulate just what the relationship is between psychology and logic. Does logic depend on psychology or is psychology independent of logic, the origins of which must be sought elsewhere? For Smedslund psychologic is based in language, semantic primitives to be exact, and hence the connection between logic and psychology is once again on the table. What the history of these debates has shown however is that the arguments for linking psychology and logic have not been supported by either science or philosophy (despite the political reasons for the original anti-psychologism movement). Logical laws are not psychological laws was Husserl's argument, and the notion that laws of logic, or for that matter psychologic, are laws "in accordance with which psychology must proceed" (Kusch 2015), was rejected over a 100 years ago as a clear refutation of psychologism. Indeed, if we take logical laws to be the precursor for psychological laws, we deny the autonomy of psychology and place psychology within a rigid framework of a limited set of rules ("primitives") within which it must proceed. The history of psychology itself is proof enough that the discipline will not be limited in this way, even if, according to Smedslund, the discipline is wrong. The vast range of topics and problems discussed in the discipline can hardly be confined to a few primitives. However, that does not mean that the analysis is not useful for other purposes. The notion that there are a number of key semantic primitives is interesting in its own right even if it does not necessarily mean that it serves as a foundation for psychological life. Furthermore, Smedslund's claim that much of psychology is pseudoempirical is an insight that I would not want to jettison despite my misgivings about psychologic.

The Wittgensteinian Bargain

Smedslund's use of semantic primitives and the placement of psychologic within language might seem to escape this problem altogether. As others have noted, however, it raises a second issue, one related to language and what might be called the linguistic turn in philosophy and the social sciences. This too is a historical question; there have been more than 50 years of debate and elaboration on a question that, in this case, Smedslund has actually addressed. I believe this is in part because of the issues raised by Rom Harré and his colleague Gerrod Parrott (Harré 1999; Parrott and Harré 1991) and by John Shotter (1991, 1994).

For Wittgenstein, the meaning of a word is in its use. Parrott and Harré (1991) argue that universal assent is insufficient to create universals, axioms, or theorems. A proposition about embarrassment (used as an exemplar by Parrott and Harré) expresses the "local conditions for the application of concepts from the relevant semantic field…universal assent is not a criterion for a proposition's being an a priori or conceptual truth" (Parrott and Harré, p. 359). Local conditions of application need to be discovered, and the core meanings (the semantic primitives) are not available apart from the local conditions of application. Wittgenstein expresses the difficulty here (1953/1958) as follows:

> "So you are saying that human agreement decides what is true and what is false?"—It is what human beings *say* that is true and false; and they agree in the *language* they use. That is not agreement in opinions but in form of life (§ 241).

I quoted Smedslund above as saying, "since the axioms cannot be tested logically or empirically, they can only be tested by consensus" (2012b, p. 296). Wittgenstein, however, is not interested in overt agreement or in a consensus but in agreement in "form of life." He follows this with "If language is to be a means of communication there must be agreement not only in definitions but also (queer as this may sound) in judgments" (§ 242—a passage also quoted in this context by Parrott and Harré). A "form of life" is a complex project in the *Philosophical Investigations*(PI), but it indicates that our agreements in language are embedded in the pragmatics of everyday life. As Wittgenstein (1953/1958) argues earlier in the PI (§23), language games are part of a form of life, that is, language works because it fits into a pragmatic, contingent way of being in the world.[8] One interpretation of "form of life" is one in which it might be suggested that there is only one universal form of life, a human one (Biletzki and Matar 2018). But even here we do not have a psychologic so much as a multitude of activities that count as human. For to begin to catalogue the numerous ways in which cultures characterize ways of living is beyond the lifetime of any anthropologist, which is not to say that we cannot count on certain regularities or transcultural phenomena. This has been the focus of much debate in philosophy if not anthropology, most particularly around Quine's conception of "radical translation" and Davidson's "radical interpretation" (see Glock 1996). Although Quine takes translation to be indeterminate, in effect Wittgenstein's insight is that any translation requires some overlap in forms of life (Glock 1996, p. 168).

Shotter likewise uses a Wittgensteinian move to address a core issue in Smedslund's work,

> …I suggest, rather than always already having certain undisputable core meanings (as if they only make their appearance within a closed textual system), words in everyday life are best thought of as open to different uses in different circumstances, in other words, as a constant set of forms or means (like the tools in a toolbox) for use in the making of meanings (Shotter 1991, p. 365).

In addition, Shotter (1994) argues against the kind of rigid closure argued for in Smedslund's psychologic. He indicates that the notion that our understanding of closure in language is a moral, practical, and political matter. In the traditions of Vygotsky and Bhaktin, and especially, the understanding of meaning in the Wittgensteinian tradition, Shotter attempts to clarify the ways of sense making that already exist prior to our invention of theoretical frameworks and the like (Shotter n.d.). As Shotter argues,

> To arrive at such a sense, we need, I will argue, to oscillate continually between traditional scientific inquiries of a methodical kind and non-traditional philosophical explorations, aimed at our gaining an *orientation*, a sense of knowing "our way about," as Wittgenstein (1953, no.123) puts it, within each new circumstance we create in the scientific phase of our activities—for in our more practical affairs, rather than simply seeking 'truths' to satisfy our 'minds,' the results we seek are of the kind, as again Wittgenstein (1953) puts it, where we say "'Now I can go on'" (no.154). We need to arrive at a 'directive sense' which, although still not at the level of a certainty, arouses in us the feeling that our next step is the best one available to us in the circumstances in question (Shotter n.d., p. 5).

Shotter spent the better part of a life in psychology working out where this kind of inquiry might lead. He emphasized in numerous writings that in our interactions there is much that is both unreflective and unthinking but always culturally structured. Utterances are filled with responsive reactions to other utterances, Shotter argued, and he called this a "relational-responsive" understanding as opposed to a "representational-referential" understanding that is overtly conscious (e.g., Shotter

---

[8] I am aware that the notion of "form of life" in Wittgenstein's work is in fact a contested notion. However in this case, the question of a language game as an agreement about a form of life rather than an opinion about the contents of language are a propos (see Biletzki and Matar 2018).

1999). Human interaction has a dialogical structure to it, which for Shotter meant that we rely on what Bakhtin called *speech genres*,

> ...it is our actual or imagined ways of us responsively relating ourselves to each other—in what, as already mentioned, Wittgenstein calls our "forms of life"—that are the basis for our ways of talking, which ultimately provide us with our ways of thinking and feeling, valuing and judging (Shotter 1999, p. 80)

Like Smedslund, Shotter considered most of contemporary psychology a kind of pseudoempirical enterprise. Yet his take on the question of what constitutes common sense was far from traditional. He drew a trajectory from Vico through Bakhtin to the present by arguing that we have missed a crucial feature of human practices and that these practices contain within them a social poetics and not a theory to be discovered.

Smedslund acknowledges in several of his articles that both Harré and Shotter have caused him to rethink his work. In response he noted that psychologic "will remain a technical suburb of natural and culture language (Parrott and Harre 1991), because it is adapted to suit professional requirements" (Smedslund 2012b, p. 300). In the same paper he notes that.

> it gradually became clear from the Wittgensteinian view, including the 'intrinsic contestability' of word meanings (Shotter 1994), that ordinary language is resistant to the quest for precision and order. In line with a suggestion of Parrott and Harre´ (1991), I have come to regard psycho-logic as a constructed technical system, that, while taking its explicit departure in the semantic primitives of ordinary language, aims at making more precise, and systematizing, a conceptual framework for psychology (p. 295).

With respect to Shotter, Smedslund simply reiterates his belief that Wierzbicka's semantic primitives are sufficient to make the case for a closed system of the sort that Smedslund espouses. I hope I have made clear here that by doing so he neither acknowledges nor considers in any serious way what Shotter has been arguing. For Shotter, language does not prescribe in the sense that Smedslund wishes us to believe, it does not contain a fixed set of priorities from which springs a psychology, but instead our utterances display a certain heteroglossia. Bakhtin argued that the utterance brushes up "against thousands of living threads" (Bakhtin 1981, p. 276). Through a process he called *ventriloquation* we show where we come from, which world we inhabit and something of our beliefs and ideologies (Wortham 2001). This is a long way from semantic primitives, which may exist but perhaps not in the way Smedslund argues they exist. Instead, common features of language reflect common, embodied experiences in the world. We are historically conditioned in the way we must all find shelter and food, find ways of organizing families or their equivalents so following generations are appropriately inducted into cultural practices, organize our civic life in ways that reflect our priorities, and so on. This does not even begin to take into account the vast technological changes that have been unleashed on human life in the past 400 years, and the way these have changed our ways of interacting. Certainly, there will be semantic primitives in such circumstances if only because we share a bodily existence within similar contexts, opportunities, and challenges. But the number of ways in which we express local conditions are near impossible to count, and their interactions create ever more complex as well as uniform ways of being.

I take seriously Smedslund's (2012b) claim that psychologic is a kind of constructed, technical system. This is indeed a reduced project for psychologic, akin to arguing that it is a technique for interpreting psychological claims rather than a claim that undermines the project of an empirical psychology. Though this may seem to run counter to the project as seminally presented by Smedslund, exemplified to its most extreme by recent titles such as "Why psychology cannot be an empirical science" (Smedslund 2016), this may perhaps nevertheless be a viable way of proceeding for a future project of psychologic.

Conclusion: What Can we Gain from Psycho-Logic

This has been a quick, far too quick, movement through a number of key issues in Smedslund's work. I wish to close with a brief reflection on the problems of psychology and to honor Smedslund's work in a different way.

Many critics of the discipline under a variety of topics have analyzed the pseudo-empirical elements of psychology. For example, psychology is dependent on a deceptive set of statistical practices contributing to the current crisis of replicability. This is fostered by such practices as *p-hacking* (Simmons et al. 2011) among other "Questionable Research Practices" (Shrout and Rodgers 2018), as well as outright fraud, the most infamous of which was that perpetrated by Diederik Stapel in The Netherlands.[9] Smedslund is right to note that much psychological research seems not to move the field forward in any obvious way as one might otherwise expect from a mature science.

While the diagnoses have been legion, the solutions are limited (see Shrout and Rodgers 2018, for a number of commonly suggested solutions). There are several reasons for this; primary among them is, I claim, the nature of psychological theorizing.[10] Our notion of a "theory" is not like a theory in physics nor is it even like the theory of evolution. The conceptual frameworks of psychology are weak insofar as they do not specify clear and well-defined objects of investigation. Instead, objects

[9] Stapel was a professor, and eventually dean, who held positions at two Dutch universities and fabricated data over the length of his career as an academic psychologist. According to the website Retraction Watch, at least 58 of his articles have been retracted from the published literature since the investigations into his activities began in 2011 (see http://retractionwatch.com/category/diederik-stapel/)

[10] The other is the problem of reflexivity, which will need considerably more space to expand on than is available here (however, see Stam 1996). In short, reflexivity (which is yet another contested concept) refers to the claim that in order to understand, research or practice psychology one must be an apt participant in the world/culture/community where psychology makes sense. As such psychological theories are always historically bound claims that are embedded in particular worlds. On such an account, psychologic could never claim to be an absolute set of axioms applicable across time and geography.

of investigation are determined by the functions that create them. A personality trait is the outcome of a score on a scale, it does not exist outside of the completion of that scale. An experimental study of memory is made possible by the creation of a task that requires someone to recall material learned under some standard conditions. We then say we have an example of, say, episodic memory when the person in question can recall what and where she learned the target material. Now the object of investigation is visible. Hence, psychology is wedded to a functional language, a language that is inherently flexible on the one hand and whose objects can be multiplied indefinitely on the other hand. How is this possible? A functional language allows even a neophyte to quickly create "variables" or other psychological objects by simple naming them and creating conditions for their existence.

Let me take an example from a recent issue of the *Journal of Personality and Social Psychology*. Schumpe et al. (2018) claim that "sensation seeking mediated the relation between meaning in life and willingness to self-sacrifice and support for political violence" (p. 1). Each of these four variables was determined using a standardized scale with anywhere from 5 to 21 items ranked from "1" to "5" or "1 to "6" or "1" to "7." Hence, each of these objects of investigation was made visible through the completion of a scale—a set of numbers derived by marking a page after reading a set of statements. I am not interested in such things as validity or reliability here, I assume they are adequate in these regards. The point is that the objects of investigation do not exist until participants have read a set of statements and indicated a number on paper that purports to show their level of agreement or disagreement. There are thousands of such scales in the psychological literature and hence each is an object of investigation that can be manipulated, correlated, or factor analyzed, etc., for some purpose. Such objects, as I said, can be created indefinitely because the theories that generate and "explain" such variables are themselves expressed in a functional language that does not specify the objects of investigation. The study by Schumpe et al. (2018) concerns itself with "Significance Quest Theory" and "Sensation Seeking." The former claims that the "desire to matter and to feel meaningful is a fundamental human need" (p. 1). Sensation seeking is based on the notion that some people need more stimulation than others. Neither of these "theories" specify objects of investigation. They allow the researcher to develop what they need to "test" the theory which can only be "tested" when the variables are made visible through some procedure (filling in a rating scale). Consider the difference with certain other sciences: When I want to know the velocity of an object, Newton's second law of motion specifies precisely what I need to know, i.e., mass and acceleration. But in psychology we define objects as needed based on procedures. Hence, it is inherently flexible, my version of a sensation-seeking scale might be completely different from the standard one even though it is equally reliable and valid. Hence, we can create objects of investigation indefinitely. These functional entities are largely invented anew at a high rate and their relationship to one another appears to be of little concern to the research community. On the one hand, their inherent flexibility and manner of reproduction allows even the neophyte to produce research topics and research studies with very little training or background. Why can second year students design and conduct a study with very little training? Take a variable and break it down into two variables, ask what the relationship between them and some other psychological entity is and you have a simple study. However, it encourages a proliferation of hypothetical entities such that there is little observable progress or concern for the ontological status of these entities.[11] There is no limit to the kind and degree of functional entities that can be introduced, studied in some research context and hence become a legitimate feature of the psychological literature. And the psychological literature is one very large, sprawling morass, the oversight of which is beyond the capabilities of any one person.[12]

This version of functionalism, which I have called "indeterminate functionalism" (see Stam 2004) is also referred to as "role functionalism" (Kim 1998).[13] Theoretical entities are defined, at least in the past 75 years of the discipline's research history, as *functional* entities. This means that psychological objects and properties are not *realistically* but *heuristically* defined. These heuristic, functional accounts can be cognitive, behavioral, or even psychodynamic and are frequently fused to various biological and more recently to neuropsychological accounts. Overwhelmingly committed to a version of theoretical statements in the language of variables, as I noted in my example above, psychologists create these heuristically functional descriptions but make no commitment to any ontological properties. They are functional descriptions of properties that are defined according to how they act rather than what they are. They are functional insofar as their presence *must* be inferred from a set of practices, that is, actions carried out in a laboratory or elsewhere. Indeterminate functionalism is either in danger of sliding into dualism or reductionism. It slides into dualism because it does not commit itself to real properties, but it is in danger of sliding into reductionism because it carries a promissory note that eventually all those functional entities that remain imprecise will be known when science allows.[14]

This does not mean there is no possible value to empirical content. On the contrary, any individual experiment is grounded in a set of genuine observations. Yet, in the long run, this research will run aground in a quagmire of functional entities.

[11] It is not that psychologists have some disagreement about the ontological status of their objects of investigation by, for example, being eliminativists who must first define features of the world in functional terms. It is more that it just is not discussed or debated but taken for granted that the kind of indeterminate functionalism is what counts as psychological theorizing. In this way psychology in general, with notable exceptions, has continued a fuzzy framework of vague ontological entities whose status remains of no immediate concern to the discipline, so long as it can carry on business as usual.

[12] Which is not to deny that there are pockets of regularities, phenomena that recur predictably, and "findings" that are easily reproduced. Mostly, however, they have no relation to a larger frame of psychological understanding.

[13] Kim's aims with his arguments, however, are entirely different from mine and seeks to ground a non-reductive version of physicalism. However, he ultimately concludes that such a perspective cannot account for the so-called phenomenal (qualitative) aspects of mental states.

[14] Perceptual and psychophysical cases are more complex and hence not included in this discussion.

Eventually, the field decides that a particular phenomenon is no longer robust and the investigators move on. Smedslund is right then to note the pseudoempirical nature of this enterprise. That is, there is little progress in the endless chase of new variables when these variables are dependent on ordinary, everyday understandings that are given a new coat in the guise of functional descriptions. Smedslund is right to suspect there is something basic at work in our discipline that smuggles everyday knowledge into a language of variables and experimental designs. I believe that his seminal work on psychologic has alerted us to the nature of some preconceptions we have by virtue of our participation in a community of language users. Such preconceptions, however, are not part of some set of axioms but they are part of shared, mutual existence.

References

Ayer, A. J. (1946). *Language, truth and logic* (2nd ed.). Harmondsworth, UK: Penguin. (Original published 1936).

Bakhtin, M. M. (1981). *The dialogical imagination*. M. Holquist (Ed.). C. Emerson and M. Holquist, trans. Austin: University of Texas Press.

Biletzki, A. & Matar, A. (2018) Ludwig Wittgenstein. *The Stanford Encyclopedia of Philosophy*, E. N. Zalta (Ed.), Retrieved from https://plato.stanford.edu/archives/sum2018/entries/wittgenstein/

Daston, L., & Galiston, P. (2007). *Objectivity*. New York: Zone Books.

Glock, H. (1996). On safari with Wittgenstein, Quine and Davidson. In R. Arrington & H. Glock (Eds.), *Wittgenstein and Quine*. London: Routledge.

Goddard, C., & Wierzbicka, A. (2014). *Words and meanings: Lexical semantics across domains, languages, and cultures*. Oxford: Oxford University Press.

Hanson, N. R. (1958). *Patterns of discovery: An Inquiry into the conceptual foundations of science*. Cambridge: Cambridge University Press.

Harré, R. (1999). Commentary on "Psychologic and the study of memory". *Scandinavian Journal of Psychology, 40*(Suppl. 1), 37–40.

Juhl, C., & Loomis, E. (2010). *Analyticity*. Abingdon, UK: Routledge.

Juhl, C., & Loomis, E. (2012). Analytic truth. In G. Russell & D. G. Fara (Eds.), *The Routledge companion to philosophy of language*. London: Routledge.

Kim, J. (1998). *Mind in a physical world*. Cambridge, MA: MIT Press.

Kuhn, T. S. (1962). *The structure of scientific revolutions*. Chicago, IL: University of Chicago Press.

Kusch, M. (1995). *Psychologism: A case study in the sociology of knowledge*. London: Routledge.

Kusch, M. (2015). Psychologism. *The Stanford Encyclopedia of Philosophy*, Edward N. Zalta (ed.). Retrieved from https://plato.stanford.edu/archives/win2015/entries/psychologism/.

McEachrane, M. (2020). The meaning of words and the possibilities of psychology: Reflections on Jan Smedslund's psycho-logic (Chapter 6, this volume). In T. G. Lindstad, E. Stänicke, & J. Valsiner (Eds.), *Respect for thought: Jan Smedslund's legacy for psychology* (pp. 85–104). New York: Springer.

Parrott, W. G., & Harré, R. (1991). Smedslundian suburbs in the city of language: The case of embarrassment. *Psychological Inquiry, 2*, 358–361.

Quine, W. V. O. (1953). Two dogmas of empiricism. In W. V. O. Quine (Ed.), *From a logical point of view* (pp. 20–46). Cambridge, MA: Harvard University Press.

Russell, G. (2008). *Truth in virtue of meaning: A defense of the analytic/synthetic distinction*. Oxford: Oxford University Press.

Schumpe, B. M., Bélanger, J. J., Moyano, M., & Nisa, C. F. (2018, November 1). The role of sensation seeking in political violence: An extension of the significance quest theory. *Journal of Personality and Social Psychology, 118*, 743. https://doi.org/10.1037/pspp0000223.

Shotter, J. (1991). Measuring blindly and speculating loosely: But is a "Psychologic" the answer? *Psychological Inquiry, 2*, 363–366.

Shotter, J. (1994). Is there a logic in common sense? The scope and the limits of Jan Smedslund's "geometric" psychologic. In J. Siegfried (Ed.), *The status of common sense in psychology*. Norwood, NJ: Ablex.

Shotter, J. (1999). Life inside dialogically structured mentalities: Bakhtin's and Voloshinov's account of our mental activities as out in the world between us. In J. Rowan & M. Cooper (Eds.), *The plural self: Multiplicity in everyday life*. London: Sage.

Shotter, J. (n.d.). Towards a new 'Fluid' common-sense of ourselves as personal beings in relation — And why this issue matters. Unpublished manuscript. Retrieved from https://www.academia.edu/25794805/Towards_a_New_Fluid_Common-Sense_of_Ourselves_as_Personal_Beings_in_Relation_and_Why_This_Issue_Matters.

Shrout, P. E., & Rodgers, J. L. (2018). Psychology, science, and knowledge construction: Broadening perspectives from the replication crisis. *Annual Review of Psychology, 69*, 487–510.

Simmons, J. P., Nelson, L. D., & Simonsohn, U. (2011). False-positive psychology: Undisclosed flexibility in data collection and analysis allows presenting anything as significant. *Psychological Science, 22*, 1359–1366.

Smedlund, M. B. (2020). The case for psychological quietism: Wittgensteinian propaedeutics in Smedslund's writings (Chapter 7, this volume). In T. G. Lindstad, E. Stänicke, & J. Valsiner (Eds.), Respect for thought: *Jan Smedslund's legacy for psychology* (pp. 105–128). New York: Springer.

Smedslund, G. (2000). Psycho-logic: A 'conceptual toolbox' and 'mind sharpener' for health psychologists: A response to commentaries. *Journal of Health Psychology, 5*, 165–171.

Smedslund, J. (1991). The Pseudoempirical in psychology and the case for Psychologic. *Psychological Inquiry, 2*, 325–338.

Smedslund, J. (2002). From hypothesis-testing psychology to procedure-testing psychologic. *Review of General Psychology, 6*, 51–72.

Smedslund, J. (2011). Meaning of words and the use of axiomatics in psychological theory. *Journal of Theoretical and Philosophical Psychology, 31*, 126–135.

Smedslund, J. (2012a). What follows from what we all know about human beings. *Theory & Psychology, 22*, 658–668.

Smedslund, J. (2012b). Psycho-logic: Some thoughts and after-thoughts. *Scandinavian Journal of Psychology, 53*, 295–302.

Smedslund, J. (2016). Why psychology cannot be an empirical science. *Integrative Psychological and Behavioral Science, 50*, 185–195.

Smedslund, J. (2020). Neuro-ornamentation in psychological research (Chapter 13, this volume). In T. G. Lindstad, E. Stänicke, & J. Valsiner (Eds.), *Respect for thought: Jan Smedslund's legacy for psychology* (pp. 221–228). New York: Springer..

Stam, H. J. (1996). Theory & practice. In C. Tolman, F. Cherry, R. V. Hezewijk, & I. Lubek (Eds.), Problems of theoretical psychology (pp. 24–32). Toronto: Captus Press.

Stam, H. J. (2000). Logic or Psychologism: Smedslund's PsychoLogic and health. *Journal of Health Psychology, 5*, 161–164.

Stam, H. J. (2004). Unifying psychology: Epistemological act or disciplinary maneuver? *Journal of Clinical Psychology, 60*, 1259–1262.

Sugarman, J. (2017). Psychologism as a style of reasoning and the study of persons. *New Ideas in Psychology, 44*, 21–27.

Sugarman, J. (2020). Smedslund and the psychological style of reasoning (Chapter 16, this volume).. In T. G. Lindstad, E. Stänicke, & J. Valsiner (Eds.), *Respect for thought: Jan Smedslund's legacy for psychology* (pp. 269–284). New York: Springer.

Wierzbicka, A. (1996). *Semantics: Primes and universals*. New York: Oxford University Press.

Wittgenstein, L. (1958). *Philosophical investigations,* 2nd ed., trans. G. E. M. Anscombe. Oxford: Blackwell. (Original published 1953).

Wortham, S. (2001). Ventriloquating Shakespeare: Ethical positioning in classroom literature discussions. *Working Papers in Educational Linguistics, 17*, 47–64.

Chapter 9
The Linguistic Fore-Structure of Psychological Explanation

Kenneth J. Gergen

We tend to view human beings as meaningful agents, with language serving as the vehicle for inter-subjective sharing. However, if our language is circumscribed by the rules of usage, we are introduced to the possibility that what we can say is not so much an expression of our subjective worlds as an outcome of linguistic convention. In turn, we may raise a more formidable question: to what extent are claims to knowledge determined not by the "world as it is," but by the structure or demands of language? Such a question has gained momentum within disparate enclaves of scholarship. Beginning with Saussure (1974), scholars have explored the character and significance of semiotic systems, including spoken and written language. To speak intelligibly essentially requires embracing a system of meaning already in place. Similarly, with Kuhn's (1970) account of scientific revolutions, we entertain the possibility that scientists function within paradigms of understanding—including both ontology and epistemology. In effect, the scientist enters into experimentation with assumptions already in hand, and these assumptions may guide both what is observed and how it is represented. And with Derrida (1976–1988) we are introduced to the interlocking character of words. In explicating the meaning of any word, we must always defer to other words. In the end, "*Il n'y a pas de hors texte*" (p. 144) ("There is nothing outside of text.") In psychology, inquiries have also been made into the way in which metaphors (Leary 1994) and narrative structures (Gergen and Gergen 1986) are essential to the coherence and intelligibility of psychological theory.

My aim in what follows is not to explore the degree to which knowledge in general is limited or governed by the "rules of the game." More pointedly, however, I

This chapter represents an extended elaboration of Gergen (2018).

K. J. Gergen (✉)
Swarthmore College, Pennsylvania, PA, USA
e-mail: kgergen1@swarthmore.edu

T. G. Lindstad et al. (eds.), *Respect for Thought*, Theory and History in the Human and Social Sciences, https://doi.org/10.1007/978-3-030-43066-5_9

wish to explore the linguistic limits of what can be intelligibly written or spoken about mental process. And more pointedly, can psychological research of any kind ever tell us anything that is not already contained within the existing conventions of language? Is empirical research in psychology redundant? What alternatives might we envision?

For me, it was Wittgenstein's writings (1953, 1992) that initially set the stage. As he asks, for example:

- "How did we ever come to use such an expression as 'I believe…' Did we at sometime become aware of a phenomenon (of belief)?" *PI* 190e
- "What is a *deep* feeling? Could someone have a feeling of ardent love or hope for the space of 1 s—*no matter what* preceded or followed this second.?" *PI* 583
- "Can I separate a visual experience from a *thought-experience*? (And what does that mean)." *LW,* 1, 564

In these simple questions, one begins to confront the limits of both common sense and science. How indeed did we come to make claims about beliefs and deep feelings? Through observation? And why don't we talk about thought-experiences? Because we don't have them? Such questions have long intrigued me and have been pivotal in my writings on social construction. Yet, I owe a major debt to the writings of Jan Smedslund in this case, for he has singularly spoken out to challenge the frameworks of understanding in psychology and the related potentials for empirical research. His work has ignited for me an extended intellectual adventure into the linguistic determinants of claims about mental process. In what follows, I will first recount what for me have been the most dramatic implications of Smedslund's work. This will serve as the springboard to describing three specific inquiries. In these inquiries I will both extend Smedslund's work and open further questions of broad significance.

The Smedslund Challenge

In what for me was a frontal challenge to the experimental tradition in psychology, Smedslund (1978) proposed that Bandura's (1977) highly acclaimed theory of self-efficacy essentially duplicates common sense cultural suppositions. Thus, he argued, the extensive experimental support for the theory was essentially pointless, as failures to support its hypotheses would be unintelligible to English speakers. To expand, Bandura's theory was concerned with people's coping behavior, how long it can be sustained, and whether they would press on in spite of obstacles. The determinants of such activity, Bandura reasoned, are primarily cognitive in nature, with self-expectations playing a critical role. Smedslund subjected the major explanatory propositions to careful conceptual analysis, demonstrating one by one, that not only are the suppositions derived from common sense, but because they cannot be falsified without violating common sense. In effect, they are empirically untestable.

To illustrate, Bandura proposes that a "person's convictions of their own effectiveness is likely to affect whether they will even try to cope with given situations" (p. 193). Smedslund then converts this proposal into a formal theorem: "If P wants to do T in S and if P believes with complete certainty that he can do T in S, and no other circumstances intervene, then P will try to do T in S." (p. 3). He then goes on to demonstrate the unintelligibility of this not being the case: "The alternative to P trying to do T in S is P not trying to do T in S. But P not trying to do T in S is not acceptably explained by P's wanting to do T in S and by P's certainty that he can do T in S. Hence some additional circumstances must be involved." (p. 3). Simply put, if a person is convinced they can do something they want to do, and no other circumstances prevail, then it will make no sense that they will not try to do it. To introduce evidence that they will try to do what they want, knowing they can, is pointless. The contrary would make no sense.

Such analyses are as intriguing as they are profound. Are all our mental explanations lurking within the rules of ordinary language? Can we never uncover the psychological origins of our actions, never find illumination through careful and systematic inquiry? Or more generally, has more than a century of empirical work in psychology been for naught? At times, Smedslund suggests such conclusions. In his 1972 book, he proposes that all psychological theory is derived from a conceptual network embedded in ordinary language. Surely such a proposal would meet with resistance in the discipline of psychology. Its theories often seem to cut against the grain of common sense. For decades, psychoanalytic theory was viewed by outsiders with suspicion, Jungian theory was regarded as a fairy tale, and Skinnerian theory was repugnant—while simultaneously embraced by cadres of serious and well-trained professionals. The most attractive feature of Festinger's (1957) cognitive dissonance theory, was its capacity to make counter-intuitive predictions. Clearly, there is more to be said on the issue of linguistic determination, and this issue cuts to the core of psychology.

From Common Sense to the Necessity of Circularity

For me, one of the most compelling questions triggered by Smedslund's (1978) challenge concerned the origins of logical necessity. Why, in the preceding example, does it make no sense to say that if a person wants to do something, and he can do it, that he won't do it? In this case and others, Smedslund argues that we are compelled by common sense understandings within the culture. Yet, how did these understandings come into being? How did we discover that people have mental processes and these processes influence their behavior? In later publications, Smedslund (2004) draws from the work of Anna Wierzbicka (1996) in proposing that our concept of human action rests on a series of "semantic primitives," amounting to a universal and "complete archetypical conception of human being." (Smedslund 2009, p. 781). As proposed, for example, it is simply axiomatic that people can "know, think, want, *and* feel…" (p. 782).

Although the idea of universally shared conceptions of the person is a fascinating possibility, it is not immediately compelling. There are simply too many historical and anthropological accounts of variations in people's constructions of the person to warrant such a sweeping generalization. Where, for example, in the semantic primitives would one place the soul, nirvana, repression, instinct, or a fractional anticipatory goal response? At the same time, within his various analyses of Bandura's theory, one of Smedslund's (1978) arguments for common sense assumptions struck me as beyond any particular conception of the person. In Theorem 5, he proposes: "If P believes he is capable of handling S and if not other circumstances intervene, then P will behave assuredly…" (p. 4). Smedslund's proof of common sense is that "it follows directly from the meaning of theorems involved. To 'behave assuredly' means to 'behave believing one is capable of handling the situation.'" To describe a person as behaving confidently is not fundamentally different from saying the person is confident. In effect, the explanation is tautological. Believing oneself to be capable is not *a cause* of behaving assuredly; it is essentially a definition of what it is to be assured. The relation between cause and effect is circular. With further effort, it also proved possible to convert virtually all the common sense theorems to a near-tautology. For example, in the earlier illustration, "belief" that one can succeed is part of what it means to "try" to succeed; trying to succeed is premised on the assumption that success is possible. With this move in place, the door is open to considering the more general possibility that most (if not all) psychological explanations are tautological.

Why should one suspect this might be the case? Primarily because there are no public observables to control what may be said about mental states or conditions. Most of us would accept with little question the social psychological proposal that "attitudes toward political candidates affect one's voting." But what precisely is an attitude; what are its properties? Observation provides no guidance. We are left, then, to speculate about its existence. And as well, all we have is speculation about how it affects our actions? Perhaps attitudes have nothing to do with what we vote for, what we eat, drink, etc. How would we know?

In this light, we may ask by what logic one can establish the relationship among mental states or between mental states and the world? Given "the fact of emotion" for example, how can we explain its relationship to other mental states; how it is affected by the outside world; and how does it influence behavior? We cannot derive these relationships from observation (what is an emotion, after all?), so how else can we make sense of such relations? There is no a priori logic that would demand any such connections. Is this not fertile soil, then, for tautological explanations. where plausibility is immediately apparent? In effect, x affects y by virtue of a commonly shared definition.

Consider, then, the possibility of a *principle of originary resemblance*. By this it is meant that *with no other information available, attempts to explain the causal source of A, will bear a likeness to A*. In this case, all propositions concerning the relationship among mental states owe their intelligibility to the degree to which they share definitional space. To illustrate, we have no specific referents for either "emotional arousal" or "rational thought." They are also mutually constitutive, as rational thought is defined in terms of the absence of emotions, and vice versa.[1] As a result, we may plausibly say that "emotional arousal interferes with rational thought," and "by thinking clearly you can calm your anxiety." In effect, if you have *x*, you remove that which is defined as *not x*. Freud's (1933) famous account of the relationship between ego and id hinges on just this form of logic. His concluding statement in Lecture 31 about the effects of psychoanalysis—"where id was, there ego shall be" is essentially a tautology. Circularity also governs the relationship among particular kinds of emotion or thought. Thus, we may intelligibly say that "his grief overwhelmed his feelings of happiness," and "by engaging in mental association we improve our recall." Conversely, we might respond quizzically if someone announced "his thinking overwhelmed his intentions," "her anxiety brought forth rapture," or "his motivation to do it suppressed his desire." There is no immediate overlap in definition.

Dualism in Question

At this point, curiosity begins to kill the cat. The field of psychology essentially emerges from a mind–world dualism with deep roots in Western history. From the nineteenth century laboratories in Germany to the present focus on cognitive process, the vast share of psychological research is devoted to charting the relationship between mind and world. On the one side are longstanding programs of research concerned with the relationship between the external and mental events. Research in perception, information processing, learning, social inference, and motivated perception are illustrative. And on the other, we have equally ambitious programs of research on the relationship between psychological states and individual behavior. We focus, for example, on the effect of attitudes on behavior, mental disease on behavior disturbances, self-esteem on school performance, and so on. Can we not entertain the possibility that: *all propositions concerning the relationship between mental states and the physical world owe their intelligibility to the degree to which they share definitional space?*

To explore, let us first turn first to the relationship between the "stimulus world" and mental representation. The question of how these are related has been a longstanding challenge for both psychologists and philosophers. We ask, for example, how is the world registered in the mind; how is knowledge of the world built up from observation; how does individual mental functioning determine the way we see the world? While conflicting answers to such questions are longstanding in both psychology and philosophy, there are also scholars in both camps who have decried the very assumption of dualism. Following Wittgenstein, for example, J. L. Austin (1962) demonstrates a range of devilish problems created in the long-standing

[1] "Mental states…especially in contrast to reason" as the Farlex Free Dictionary—among others—describes.

presumption that objects in the world are registered in the mind as "sense data."—or in effect, we never see the world directly for what it is, but only have access to the way the world is registered in our senses. Rorty (1981) later goes on to argue that the entire epistemological project in philosophy does not derive from a challenge put to us by nature, but by linguistic traditions. In effect, we have a tradition of "real world discourse" on the one hand and "mental discourse" on the other. We have fallaciously objectified each discourse, and then worried ourselves with how the "real world" gets into the "mental world."

Following this line of reasoning, we may consider the proposition that *every object in what we call the environment or stimulus world can be defined by (or converted into) a mental term*. "*There is* a rabbit" can be restated as "*I see* a rabbit." Or to put it otherwise, there are not two different kinds of rabbit, one in the world and another in the head; there are simply two discourses for the same event. In the same way, the utterance "The ocean is *here before me*" might be reformulated as "*I spy* the ocean." In the late twentieth century, an entire paradigm shift in psychology occurred as psychologists converted "the stimulus situation," to "the perceived situation." Whether beauty is in the world or "in the mind of the beholder, then, is not a substantive question; we simply have two discourses in play.

With this proposition in place, we can then appreciate the potential for tautological understandings of the relationship of world to mind. For example, we cannot plausibly say, "there is a rabbit and I therefore see a duck," or "his intelligence makes me think he is stupid." But we can say without a batting eye, "she is so beautiful; no wonder I am attracted to her." Further, to say that someone has *misperceived* the situation requires that a claim is made to a real-world event, to which the other is responding incorrectly with a report on a mental condition. If one could not make a claim in real-world discourse, one could not justifiably say the other has misperceived. There would only be a contest between two subjectivities.

Turning to psychological research, classical studies on attitude change have demonstrated that characteristics of a communicator will affect attitude change. Thus, for example, if a communicator is an expert, is attractive, or trusted, the empirical evidence suggests that one is more likely to agree with him or her. Yet, in terms of definition, this is to say little more than we agree with what is agreeable, or are attracted to what attracts us. Or, in the case of Werthheimer's (1912) early Gestalt research on apparent motion, it was shown that a string of lights, rapidly illuminated in succession, is experienced by the observer as motion. As if by brain magic the one had been converted to the other. In fact, however, the same event is simply defined by the researchers as "a rapid succession of lights" and by the experimental subject as "motion." They could have both used the same terms, as they are mutually defining. The explanation is thus circular.

Let us turn, then, to the relationship between mental events and subsequent actions. In what degree are intelligible propositions relating the mental world to one's behavior tautological? Or in Descartes terms, how can mental events cause physical events? Here it is useful to consider one of Charles Taylor's (1964) early proposals, that most descriptive terms for human action carry with them an implicit assumption of intentionality. Thus, for example, we cannot say of an individual that he was aggressive, loving, helpful, or devoted without presuming that he acted in these ways intentionally. If he "didn't mean" to be aggressive, for example, but was trying to be helpful, we lose our grounds for saying he was aggressive. If one intends through his helpfulness to exploit, then we can only say that the behavior "seems to be helpful, but it is not." On these grounds, we can see that behavioral descriptors are suffused with psychological content. Being angry, one might say, is no more a state of mind than it is a state of the body. It is indeed this argument that has invited many neuropsychologists to argue that mind and body are isomorphic; the more reductionistic critics have proposed to abandon mental discourse altogether. In any case, one can see here further support for many of Smedslund's (1978) original demonstrations of what he would view as common sense necessities in Bandura's accounts of the relationship between cognition and behavior.

I had initially termed this tautological explanatory relationship between mind and world as the *principle of functional circularity* (Gergen 1987). Such phrasing reflected my background in psychology, where experimentalists refer to casual connections between stimulus-organism-response in terms of functional relations (e.g., mental events are a function of stimulus inputs, and behavior is a function of mental events). At the same time, we can scarcely conclude that the principle of functional circularity has no exceptions. In a certain sense, the question here is empirical. If we survey the vast range of psychological explanations that appear in the research literature, to what extent do they rely on tautology? Here the most extensive work has been carried out by Wallach and Wallach (1994, 1998, 2001). As they find, the vast bulk of explanation in social psychology research relies on near-tautologies. The attendant research is unfalsifiable. And while controversial (Schaller et al. 1995), their conclusions remain robust.

The Extended Tautology: Language on Holiday

If tautological explanations were obvious, they would seldom be used in scientific psychology. It is neither interesting nor illuminating to explain, "he stole the car because he wanted to," or "because he was a thief." However, it does become interesting to say, "he stole the car because he was jealous." So, we ask, why would he do that? And one might explain, "he was jealous of Arthur because he was stealing the affection of his girl friend. So, he stole Arthur's car on the night Arthur was to go out with her." The explanation seems reasonable enough, but precisely because it is an *extended tautology*. The theft of the car was equivalent to an act of jealousy. The explanation acquires its interest by virtue of splitting the definition of the act into two, the jealousy and the theft of the car. The one serves as the cause, and the other as an effect. This potential for multiple definitions sparked a further line of inquiry. Here, it seemed, was an opening to significant plasticity in explanation.

I thus set out on a conceptual exploration into the linguistic limits to what may be said about behavior we index as *aggression* (Gergen 1984). Helpful here were the attempts of Ossorio (1978) and Davis and Todd (1982) to develop a *paradigm case* method for determining the set of ordinary language criteria relevant to the use of a given concept. As I saw it, these were attempts to establish the broader array of assumptions by which an act might be defined as being of a certain kind. I thus proposed that we could take the common assumptions underlying our description of an act such as aggression as establishing what I called an *intelligibility nucleus*. That is, built into the definition of what it takes to call someone's behavior aggressive are assumptions that circumscribe what might meaningfully be said about it. For example, if we take a common definition of aggression as "hostile or violent behavior toward another" we establish at the outset a range of utterances that are irrelevant, congenial, or contrary. In terms of irrelevance, one cannot intelligibly say "violent behavior is green" or "hostility weights three ounces." Color and weight are not assumptions within the nucleus. In contrast, one can appropriately say "people with hostile personalities are more likely to be violent," as the utterance essentially restates the definition. One may also say of aggression that "she intended it, planned it, was conscious of it, felt hostile, tried to accomplish it, and so on.[2] Without further explanation, one cannot sensibly say, however, that "his desire to comfort her caused him to strike her."

However, the case rapidly becomes more complex when we begin to unpack the nucleus. That is, we explore the relationship of terms within the home nucleus to other nuclei. Let us call these *second-order nuclei.* For example, "hostility"—a component of the aggression nucleus—is often defined as an "emotional state." But an "emotional state " will also have within its nucleus a range of other assumptions. These assumptions may be related to the definitional nucleus of aggression, but they are not identical. Thus, by virtue of these common links, we can expand still further what may sensibly be said about aggression. We can see the plausibility in the comment that "emotional arousal can be channeled into aggression." And because emotion is the absence of thought, we would likely resist the comment that "thoughtful people are more aggressive." One may also expand the analysis to include for example, third- and fourth-order nuclei. If war is defined as combat and armies engage in combat, we can intelligibly say that "hostile people are more likely to volunteer for the armed services." The reverse of this proposal would be suspicious.

We can also see that because each nucleus is linked to others through definition, there can be felicitous utterances that do not directly feed from the initial nucleus. For example, if the term "aggression" is also one used to define certain business tactics, it would not be silly to say that "business is generally pro-war." In effect, we have a spreading array of common sense utterances generated by linked definitions. None of them depend on observation; at the same time, they are central ingredients in sustaining society.

Wittgenstein (1953) used the metaphor of language "going on holiday," by which he meant that the meaning of a term is not confined to its usage in a given context. The world may be used metaphorically in other contexts, and as the contexts become

---

[2]This form of definitional unpacking is an alternative to the Smedslund (1978) attempt to establish semantic primitives relevant to all action. At the same time, it accomplishes some of the same work.

diversified, so does the meaning become diffused. Its meaning is set loose from its moorings. I find it useful here to conceptualize this process as *semiotic slippage*.[3] As we have seen, such slippage can expand the range of what may be felicitously said. However, with sufficient slippage we also confront the possibility of impossibility. For example, love may be defined as intense attraction, attraction as intense desire, intense desire as a state of abject need, abject need as a helpless dependency, and helpless dependency as a state of slavery. We might thus conclude that we hate those we love, and love should be abolished.

As this analysis also suggests, while the logic of language may dictate what may plausibly be said about the to and fro of mental life, meaning is also elastic. With the indefinite extension of what a term may mean, so do the potentials for making sense of mental life expand.[4] Through the simple process of free association, we can create a world of intelligible—and even interesting—conversation. Community rides the back of tautology. It is this conclusion that sets the stage for a final adventure.

Escaping Linguistic Determinism?

If mental explanations are fundamentally tautological, then how are we to regard the vast industry of mental testing, assessment, and diagnosis? In all these cases, claims are made to scientific objectivity, based on systematic procedures for test design. With multiple, carefully screened, and inter-related test items, psychologists proceed to inform the world about an individual's level of intelligence, personality, prejudices, abilities, proclivities, state of mental well-being, and so on. Does the methodological rigor with which these tests are constructed thus escape the argument for tautology? It would not appear so.

For example, the popular Beck Depression Inventory features 21 items, asking the individual, whether he/she feels sad, is discouraged about the future, feels like a failure, and so on. Answers are summated, and conclusions are drawn on the level of mental depression. However, the concept of depression is a cultural construct of relatively recent invention. How can we be certain then, that answers to these questions are indicative of depression? Because we have no direct access to the mental state, we cannot. Inevitably, then, we are brought to the conclusion that the pattern of answers on these items is synonymous with what the psychologists calls depression. They do not *measure* depression; they *define what depression means* for the psychologist. By the same token, intelligence test scores do not measure an internal condition of intelligence, but are equivalent to what the investigator means by

[3] See also Derrida (1976–1988) on the concept of *difference*.

[4] In Shotter's (1999) terms, we are free to change the rules of the language games, and the shifting character of context will virtually demand an unpredictability in our forms of talk. This argument is set against Smedslund's (1988) attempt to establish a universal and historically stable definitional system.

intelligence. Whether the culture in general agrees to such interpretations is quite another matter.

But in light of the potentials for semiotic slippage, the plot thickens. How elastic is the relationship between the overt behavior and what we take to be its mental source? Tautologies may be obvious and compelling; few would doubt that an individual who declares he is depressed is feeling depressed. And yet, for psychoanalytic practitioners, such interpretations may be far from obvious. A declaration of depression may be indicative of repressed anger, a hidden but stifled desire to slay one's father. This conclusion does not save the inference from tautology. As in the preceding section, the conclusion is made possible through semiotic slippage. It plays on overlapping definitions. What is commonly called a "declaration of depression" on the one hand is ultimately redefined as "an expression of repressed desire." However, considerable semiotic work must be accomplished to create the intelligibility of this conclusion.

If a psychoanalyst can be successful in showing how an avowal of depression is an expression of hatred for one's father, a further question emerges: are there any constraints on what can intelligibly said about the psychological sources of a given action? Given the liquidity of extending the definition of terms, what I am calling semiotic slippage, could a sophisticated speaker demonstrate how *any psychological state can give rise to any behavior*? Or conversely, given someone's behavior, can it be explained in terms of virtually any psychological state? Turning then to psychological testing, for example, can we conclude that scores on any psychological test may be sensibly attributed to virtually any psychological state or condition? The implications are substantial.

To explore these possibilities, I set out with two of my students—Alexandra Hepburn and Debra Fisher—to examine the explanatory limits of scores on a popular personality trait test.[5] Numerous investigators had used the Rotter internal-external (I-E) control scale to assess the degree to which individuals see themselves as responsible for their actions and their consequences, as opposed to external world conditions. Agreement with an item such as "There is a direct connection between how hard I study and the grades I get," would be indicative of an internal locus of control. To agree that "Unfortunately, an individual's worth often passes unrecognized no matter how hard he tries." would reveal a tendency to see one's outcomes as controlled by external circumstances.

The first step in the exploration was to determine the extent to which one could trace responses on these items to virtually any psychological trait. We thus enlisted a group of two dozen undergraduate students in a series of "interpretation puzzles." As one of their challenges, we asked if they could show how it would make sense for someone who had a given trait, to agree with a given item from the Rotter scale. The traits were randomly drawn from a list of some 500 common traits.

As we found, the participants rarely encountered difficulty. For example, it was explained that a *lonely* person would say that who gets to be boss is a matter of luck

[5] Gergen et al. (1986).

(external) because "A lonely person lacks self-confidence and thus believes his actions will make no difference in the outcome." A person who is *impulsive* would agree that an individual's worth passes unrecognized no matter how hard he tries because "he might very well need to justify his feelings of staying too short a time with one project or another by believing that no matter how persevering he remains, he won't be acknowledged anyway." An independent group of research participants also rated these explanations (along with others) as "plausible" to "highly plausible."

We then found that our participants could take the same trait and show how it could be expressed in two *opposing* items from the I-E scale. A *broad-minded* person could easily understand why "well-prepared students" would say "there are no unfair tests" (an Internal indicator). The broad-minded person would also say that we are "victims of forces out of our control" (External) because the "broad-minded person would not try to blame world events on a particular politician or groups." Further research revealed that the various rationales employed by participants seldom duplicated each other. In other words, there were multiple and intelligible ways in which a given response on the Rotter scale could be explained in terms of a given psychological trait. And further, participants had little difficulty in relating any given psychological trait to a group of multiple and contradictory items on the Rotter scale. Such alacrity in explanation, even among young college students, suggests that there is no decidable relationship between an action and our attributions to its psychological source. Claims that psychological testing (including psychodiagnostics) can illuminate the psychological sources of behavior are groundless.

However, there remains one further question concerning the character of the participants' explanations. Specifically, much has been said now about the dependency of psychological explanations on tautology—either direct, or extended through semiotic slippage. Do their explanations—with their enormous variations—depend on tautology? By and large the answer is yes. Consider, for example, the explanation that a *lonely* person would say that who gets to be boss is a matter of luck because "A lonely person lacks self-confidence and thus believes his actions will make no difference in the outcome. Thus, lonely is defined as low self-confidence and is defined by believing one's actions make no difference. The explanation is an *extended tautology*. In effect, through semiotic slippage, definitions can be extended in such a way that we may locate the tautological basis for the inteligibility of all psychologically based explanations.

Yet, there was one commonly used form of explanation that does expand our understanding of "making psychological sense." We may term this rhetorical maneuver *value reversal*, and its implications for the freedom of explanation are substantial. Simply put, value reversal is represented in redefining what is *bad* as *a good* (or the reverse), with the result that one opens new and often more plausible explanations. To illustrate, how could one explain why a lazy person takes up rock climbing. One can explain that the lazy person is distressed with his way of life, and thus takes up an active sport. In effect, the lazy state is redefined as a motivator for its negation (effectively: laziness is redefined as motivation to be active). This capacity for value reversal enabled research participants to inject plausibility into numerous cases of otherwise non-sensical connections between trait and behavior.

It is also by this means that Freud could suggest that moral people should not be trusted: the super-ego (moral control) represses one's instinctual energies. Through value reversal, the explanatory world is richly expanded.

Let us now draw together the implications of these excursions.

Collecting Threads for an Emerging Tapestry

In one of his most delightful short stories, *The library of Babel*, Jorge Luis Borges (1944) describes a library that contains all that may be sensibly expressed, in all languages. Anything that can plausibly be written—all combinations of words and sentences—can be found in its volumes. By implication, anyone could visit this library and locate the story of his or her life; no lives could be lived that were beyond the available descriptions. And, by implication, everything that could be said about the human mind would have a place in the library. In the present analysis, we have not quite approached this imaginary space, but we have come to grips with substantial ways in which the means of our making sense place a grip over the sense that we can mean.

Surveying the results of these explorations, what conclusions now seem warranted? How are we placed in the unfolding dialogue so powerfully stimulated by Jan Smedslund? What are the implications for the future of psychological inquiry—in theory, research, and practice? Let us first consider major conclusions that seem warranted by the preceding.

On the Linguistic Limits to Psychology

There is a preliminary sense in which Wittgenstein is correct in his proposal that the limits of our language are the limits of the world. At this point in Western history, what largely counts as knowledge is propositional. That is, we more or less presume that knowledge of the world can be represented in propositional form (possibly with graphic accompaniment). As we say, our libraries are repositories of knowledge. It follows that there is no knowledge outside that which can be articulated. Or to put it otherwise, if there are psychological processes that are not amenable to linguistic representation, we shall never know them.

There is also a more restricted sense in which the Wittgensteinian surmise is correct. To the extent that we employ language as a means of communicating about the nature of the world, we fall victim to its systemic constraints. These are first of all grammatical and syntactic constraints. But this is not insignificant. For example, a reliance on nouns and pronouns will commit us to an atomized account of the world (i.e., a world of independent entities). We also fall heir to various rhetorical and literary traditions, and these traditions will also place significant demands over our theories and descriptions. Recall the earlier comment on the centrality of metaphor and narrative in psychology and other sciences as well.

However, when turning the specific case of the constraints on psychological explanation, the present explorations suggest the following:

- With limits yet to be established, Smedslund's initial contention that the Bandura explanations are both constrained by the everyday logics of language, and essentially untestable, remains in place.
- The linguistic demands on psychological explanations in the profession do not lie so much in their origins in common sense, as in their tautological character. Commonly shared assumptions within the culture certainly affect psychological theory, but simultaneously the understandings generated among professional psychologists affect the culture.
- Tautology stands as perhaps the chief means of explaining the relationship among mental states or entities (e.g., between reason and emotion).
- Tautology also stands as the chief means of explaining the relationship between the "external world" and "the mind." In forming explanations of how the mind and world are related, we approach a condition of *functional circularity,* with all causally related units owing their intelligibility to tautology. The extent to which explanations in psychological research are circular is open to continuing inquiry.
- The tautological character of such explanations is largely hidden because of the polysemous character of all terms within a given definition. That each term within a definition can be defined in multiple ways, and each term within these further definitions may be defined in still further ways, creates the conditions for *semiotic slippage*. The meaning of all terms is malleable. Owing to semiotic slippage, a vast and sensible world is made available to a culture, a world that does not depend on observation, and which may be crucial to our sense of coherence.
- Because of the unprincipled potential for redefinition, attempts to establish foundational logics governing the creation of meaning are unpromising.
- There is nothing to warrant claims that psychological testing and diagnostics tell us anything about the nature of a mental world. Owing to semiotic slippage, any test item can be explained in terms of virtually any psychological state or condition. Inferring psychological conditions from a public action is a rhetorical achievement and depends on the linguistic ability of the speaker.
- Attempts to explain a person's actions by virtue of its psychological underpinnings are redefinitions of the action. To say, for example, that a person's expressions of love are driven by sexual desire is to redefine his expressions. Explanations through extended tautologies thus serve a pivotal function in the pragmatics of social life.

Implications for Inquiry and Practice

There is much to be said about the implications of this discussion for the future of psychological science. The issues are both complex and substantial in significance. At this juncture, I shall simply focus on several critical points with the hope of seeding further dialogue.

With respect to psychological science, this essay both supports and expands on Smedslund's critique of hypothesis testing in psychological research. However, it is important to note that these arguments are not lodged against all empirical inquiry. Rather, the chief focus is on research that attempts to establish lawful explanations about the relationship of mind to world—relationships between what is in the world and what takes place in our heads, or what is in our heads and what we do. As we find, such explanations cannot fundamentally be falsified because they are tautologies.

While Smedslund has much to say about future directions of inquiry (see, for example, 2004, 2009), my constructionist leanings here are toward a pragmatic vision of future research (Gergen 2015). In this case, the general aim of psychological science to establish abstract, psychological laws of behavior should be abandoned in favor of working on concrete problems in society. Rather than warring encampments of theorists with allegiances to competing explanations (e.g., cognitive, psychodynamic, neurological, behaviorist, humanist), research would be stimulated by the major challenges of living together harmoniously with each other and the planet. Research that would enhance peace, reduce injustice, contribute to flourishing forms of life, for example, would replace the attempt to prove general laws of mental life. The natural sciences gain their importance in the world not primarily because of their general theories, but by virtue of accomplishments that matter to people. So it should be for psychology as well.

A commitment to a pragmatic vision is also a commitment to deliberation on "the good." To ask about what is useful, is simultaneously to raise such questions as, for whom is it beneficial and in what ways, and who or what may be harmed? It is here, for example, that questions may be raised about psychological testing and diagnostics. As we have seen, such tests tell us nothing about the mental conditions of those under examination. They tell us a great deal, however, about the assumptions of those who design or administer the tests. The question of who benefits and who suffers from these practices is of major social significance.

Finally, there is the more general question of linguistic constraints. To be sure, all that we can communicate in spoken and written language will be limited by this mode of representation. However, psychologists are not alone in their inattention to the demands of the modality over how we understand ourselves and our world. It is in this vein that psychologists should welcome the movement toward arts-based inquiry (Leavy 2015) emerging across the humanities and social sciences. Elsewhere we find researchers employing photography (Dikovitskaya 2006), film (Jones 2011), short stories (Diversi 1998), theatrical performance (Gray and Sindling 2002; Saldaña 2011), music (Barrett 2012), poetry (Neimeyer 2008), pastiche (Lather and

Smithies 1997; Spry 2016), and more.[6] With each new mode of representation, we expand our sensitivities and open new avenues of action. What might be written about drug addiction, for example, can be vitally enriched by photography, video, mime, and even music. Given the limits of the logocentric tradition of communication, new and exciting vistas are on the horizon.

These scarcely exhaust the issues of emerging from this discussion. Little has been said here on the attendant problems of dualism, the linguistic imposition of atomistic metaphysics, the pragmatics of psychological discourse, the potentials of differing linguistic traditions, the Western conception of knowledge, or the practical implications for therapists, educators, peace-builders, or policy makers. There may be exciting times ahead.

References

Austin, J. (1962). *Sense and sensibilia*. London/New York: Oxford University Press.

Bandura, A. (1977). Self-efficacy: Toward a unifying theory of behavioral change. *Psychological Review, 84*, 191–215.

Barrett, F. (2012). *Yes to the mess: Surprising leadership lessons from jazz*. Cambridge, MA: Harvard University Press.

Borges, J. L. (1944). *Ficciones*. Buenos Aires, AR: Editorial Sur. (Published in English, 1962, Grove Press).

Davis, K. E., & Todd, M. J. (1982). Friendship and love relationships. In K. E. Davis & T. O. Mitchell (Eds.), *Advances in descriptive psychology*. Green-wich CT: JAI Press.

Derrida, J. (1976–1988). *Of grammatology* (Translator G. C. Spivak) Baltimore, London: Johns Hopkins University Press.

Dikovitskaya, M. (2006). *Visual culture: The study of the visual after the cultural turn*. Cambridge, MA: MIT Press.

Diversi. (1998). Glimpses of street life: Representing lived experience through short stories. *Qualitative Inquiry, 4*, 131–137.

Festinger, L. (1957). *A theory of cognitive dissonance*. Stanford, CA: Stanford University Press.

Freud, S. (1933). *New introductory lectures on psychoanalysis*. New York: W.W. Norton.

Gergen, K. J. (1984). Aggression as discourse. In A. Mummendey (Ed.), *The social psychology of aggression: From individual behavior to social interaction*. Heidelberg: Springer-Verlag.

Gergen, K. J. (1987). The language of psychological understanding. In H. J. Stam, T. B. Rogers, & K. J. Gergen (Eds.), *Metapsychology and the analysis of psychological theory*. New York: Hemisphere.

Gergen, K. J. (2015). From mirroring to world-making: Research as future forming. *Journal for the Theory of Social Behaviour, 45*, 287–310.

Gergen, K. J. (2018). The limits of language as the limits of psychological explanation. *Theory and Psychology., 28*(6), 697–711.

Gergen, K. J., & Gergen, M. (1986). Narrative form and the construction of psychological science. In T. R. Sarbin (Ed.), *Narrative psychology: The storied nature of human conduct*. New York: Praeger.

Gergen, K. J., Hepburn, A., & Comer, D. (1986). The hermeneutics of per-sonality description. *Journal of Personality and Social Psychology, 6*, 1261–1270.

[6] The specific application of arts-based inquiry to psychology is explored in Gergen and Gergen (2012).

Gergen, M. (2012). In K. J. Gergen (Ed.), *Playing with purpose: Adventures in per formative social science*. New York: Routledge.
Gray, R., & Sindling, C. (2002). *Standing ovation: Performing social science research about cancer*. Walnut Creek, CA: AltaMira Press.
Jones, K. (2011). *Rufus Stone*, Vimeo.com/109360805.
Kuhn, T. (1970). *The structure of scientific revolutions* (2nd ed.). Chicago, IL: University of Chicago Press. (First published in 1962).
Lather, P., & Smithies, C. (1997). *Troubling with angels: Women living with HIV/AIDS*. Boulder, CO: Westview.
Leary, D. (1994). *Metaphors in the history of psychology*. Cambridge, MA: Cambridge University Press.
Leavy, P. (2015). *Method meets art: Art-based research practices* (2nd ed.). New York: Guilford Press.
Neimeyer, R. A. (2008). The poetics of experience. *Journal of Constructivist Psy chology, 21, 288–297.*
Ossorio, P. (1978). *What actually happens: The representation of real world phe- nomenon*. Columbia, SC: University of South Carolina Press.
Rorty, R. (1981). *Philosophy and the mirror of nature*. Princeton, NJ: Princeton University Press.
Saldaña, J. (2011). *Ethnotheatre: Research from page to stage*. Walnut Creek, CA: Left Coast Press.
Saussure, F. (1974). *Course in general linguistics, (*First published 1916.*)* London: Fontana.
Schaller, M., Crandall, C. S., Stangor, C., & Neuberg, S. L. (1995). `What kinds of social psychology experiments are of value to perform?' Comment on Wallach and Wallach (1994). *Journal of Personality and Social Psychology, 69*, 611–618.
Shotter, J. (1999). From within an external world. *Scandinavian Journal of Psychology, 40*(Suppl), 81–84.
Smedslund, J. (1978). Bandura's theory of self-efficacy: A set of common sense theorems. *Scandinavian Journal of Psychology, 19*, 1–14.
Smedslund, J. (1988). *Psycho-logic*. New York: Springer.
Smedslund, J. (2009). The mismatch between current research methods and the nature of psychological phenomenon: What researchers must learn from practitioners. *Theory and Psychology, 19*, 1–17.
Spry, T. (2016). *Autoethnography and the other: Unsettling power through utopian performatives*. New York: Routledge.
Taylor, C. (1964). *The explanation of behavior*. London: Routledge Kegan Paul.
Wallach, L., & Wallach, M. A. (1994). Gergen vs. the mainstream: Are hypotheses in social psychology subject to empirical test? *Journal of Personality and Social Psychology, 67*, 233–242.
Wallach, L., & Wallach, M. A. (2001). Experiments in social psychology: Science or self-deception. *Theory and Psychology, 11*, 451–473.
Wallach, M. A., & Wallach, L. (1998). When experiments serve little purpose: Misguided research in mainstream psychology. *Theory and Psychology, 8*, 163–194.
Wertheimer, M. (1912). Experimentelle studien uber dass sehen von bewegung. Experimental studies of the perception of movement. *Zeitschrift fur psychologie, 61*, 161–265.
Wierzbicka, A. (1996). *Primes and universals*. London: Oxford University Press.
Wittgenstein, L. (1953). *Philosophical investigations*. (translated by G.E.M. Anscombe) Oxford, UK: Blackwell, Oxford.
Wittgenstein, L. (1992). Last writings on the philosophy of psychology: The inner and the outer. *Vol. 2*. (Edited by G. H. von Wright & H. Nyman) (Translated by C. G. Luckhardt & Maximilian A. E. Aue) Oxford, UK: Blackwell.

Chapter 10
Can Common Sense Change? Psycho-logic, Synthetic Thinking, and the Challenge of Changing Language

Miika Vähämaa

This chapter considers the notion of *common sense* from the viewpoint of shared *language*. At the most basic and relevant level, a shared language implies an agreement among the way people assign shared meaning across contexts by using same words for the same or at least similar purpose. Over time and repetition, an agreement upon word meanings becomes widely accepted. In this way, an agreement upon word meanings creates the ability for humans to communicate with ease; thus, they create commonly held meanings in the things they perceive within a commonly held sense of the world. This *Weltanschauung* is a sort of common sense of things, a common sense which also works as the linguistic basis of the psychological research project Psycho-logic (PL), first proposed by Jan Smedslund (1988, 1997, 2008, 2012). From such a linguistic viewpoint, sensible reasoning in the framework of PL has been taken to rely upon commonly comprehensible word meanings. As an example of such commonly understandable words, I discuss semantic primes with regard to their ability to remain as mental constants, or, conversely, to appear as liminal, passing, transitional notions of the day in psychological language (see also Smedslund 2012; Wierzbicka 1996).

Commonly understandable word meanings, such as semantic primes, are linguistic and psychological key elements that enable people to speak and to reason with each other with ease and without conscious effort. Purportedly, if we lose primitive basic components of language, such as semantic primes, we lose common sense, which resides in commonly shared language, and will thus face disorderliness, chaos, and misunderstandings in small- and large-group interactions. In fact, despite that Smedslund (e.g., 1985, 2011) has persistently argued that psychological

M. Vähämaa (✉)
Media and Communication Faculty of Social Science, University of Helsinki, Helsinki, Finland
e-mail: miika.vahamaa@helsinki.fi

T. G. Lindstad et al. (eds.), *Respect for Thought*, Theory and History in the Human and Social Sciences, https://doi.org/10.1007/978-3-030-43066-5_10

common sense is relatively stable; some such negative developments seem already to be emerging in our era of digitalized communication. One may justifiably wonder if the ease and fluidity of communication and reasoning are merely an epiphenomenon of language which arises without a continuous and conscious effort.

I argue that we are now witnessing a potential decay of both common sense and common word meanings as our mass and social media practices keep changing (Oeberst et al. 2016, p. 105–106). While the media in our postmodern Web 2.0 world "narrow-cast" meanings to small groups of like-minded individuals, word meanings become more and more idiosyncratic in these small groups and circles to describe what something means in these particular contexts (Baresch et al. 2011, p. 18; Flaherty 2011, p. 1302–1303). Importantly, though, in any case, such like-mindedness is also at the heart of the process through which meanings can become "common." Thus, small groups have a crucial role not only as repositories of stagnant and commonplace meanings, but as birthplaces of new common meanings.

The creation and continuation of shared meanings is crucial, since without the necessary psychological key notions of common sense and common word meanings, the psychic unity necessary for social functioning decreases, as Jan Smedslund's (1988, 2008, 2012) PL posits. If shared meanings are lost, the emerging social problems and disparities posit both serious challenges and new opportunities. As an antidote to the disorderliness and the loss of common meaning we observe in our postmodern societies, I propose not only a critical analysis of the core concepts of common sense, language (in the sense of commonly understandable word meanings) and semantic primes, but an increased effort to regenerate common meanings.

As a way to regenerate common meanings, and in turn, common knowledge, I discuss *synthetic thinking* and consider how new meanings occur through reasoning. Synthetic thinking is a type of *creative* thinking which allows multiple cognitive interpretations for the same object to exist mentally at the same time and place. Synthetic thinking, therefore, enables the creative use of language and conversation. In such manner, synthetic thinking, accompanied with conversation, can generate new meanings in the social regulation of common language and interaction. Such effort, I posit, could help people to better understand each other across social groups and avoid "talking past one another."

What may remain puzzling throughout this chapter is my claim that the notions of *common sense,* shared *language* (commonly understandable word meanings) and *semantic primes* are entirely, or, at least increasingly, in a state of swift change (e.g., Strauss 1989; Virilio 1997). If that is the case, how is it, then, that despite what are commonly described as rapid media and communication developments we continue to communicate in our quotidian lives, but still manage to make sense of our casual, yet at times psychologically demanding, interactions?

The linguistic research of Wierzbicka (1996, 1999, 2001) and Goddard (1998), among others, provide a basis for a compelling answer. Their reductionist proposals and findings about a core of all human languages give some credence to the idea that the semantic primes may form the basis of a psychologically universal language which, in turn, could be presented through axioms and formal logic. The notion of cross-cultural universals of affective meaning is by no means novel (cf. e.g., Osgood et al. 1975; Wierzbicka 1996), but it is Smedslund's research in the recent era which provides a formalized project upon which such research can build. Smedslund relies on constant and invariant core meanings of words and promotes the use of semantic primes as a basis in the formalized project of PL that depicts the common-sense nature of psychological language and reasoning (Smedslund 2011, 2012). Claims regarding a universally applicable internal conceptual language are bold. Do some rudimentary linguistic notions, such as semantic primes, capture and store the complexity of our contemporary language, or in particular, psychological language that we use in interaction and thought?

Common Meaning as Premise of Common Sense

Linguist Anna Wierzbicka (1996, 1999, 2001) has posited that all languages use similar types of semantic primes, a set of few primary words. Smedslund (2008, 2011, 2012) additionally posits that these primary words can form the basis for human reasoning and for psychological reasoning. One example of such a semantic prime is the term "is" or "exists." Other examples are, inter alia, some fundamental substantives such as "I," "you," "someone/person," and "people" or mental predicates such as "think," "know," "want," "feel," "see," and "hear" (Smedslund 2012; Wierzbicka 1996). Through semantic primes, it is possible to find semantic equivalencies in languages all around the globe (Wierzbicka 1996, 1999, 2001). In general terms, it is not hard to imagine that contemporary languages would have universal roots. Some of these roots are the semantic primes that in some manner provide, on their part, the elements of universal building blocks of language. After all, we do have common ancestors who were able to speak, regardless of the exact nature of such primary language, or *Ur-sprache*, which will likely forever remain as a mystery (Whitrow 1988). Yet, one might wonder, how could it be that semantic primes, or any cultural and linguistic concepts and words, could truly provide us with persisting, psychological knowledge that makes sense across cultures?

Purportedly, psychological common sense, language (commonly understandable word meanings) and semantic primes are profoundly relevant to humans, especially with regard to regulating and organizing social interaction and enabling psychological reasoning. I use the conceptualizations of these notions as they are presented in relation to the advancements of PL (Smedslund 1988, 1997, 2008, 2012). PL presumes that we, as psychologists, thinkers, and laymen, continue to express common sense through common word meanings (Smedslund 1988, 2011, 2012), meanings which could be seen as dating back to some sort of *Ur-sprach,* or to when changes in environments or technologies necessitated the development of new words or concepts. The project of PL makes use of the general assumption that words have invariant core meanings for all competent users of a language. As Smedslund (2008, p. 160) summarizes:

> There must be invariant components in word meaning in order to explain the usefulness of languages and their function in social life. If words were completely transparent, that is, their meanings completely determined by context, the orderliness of social life could not be explained. Part of the function of language is precisely to ensure communication with little contextual support.

While this statement outlines clearly the necessity of shared word meanings, some suspicion arises whether word meanings actually *are* such that there *must* be invariant components to word meanings. This idea becomes particularly contentious once we reflect upon the continuous change in media, and in particular the notion of "narrow-casting." What we see happening in mass and social media point to a communicative realm in which word meanings are increasingly variable, if not totally devoid of invariant, or at least core, components. Since this development is a common source of comment, it seems that the premise of invariability of word meanings, in the sense that Smedslund (2008, p. 160) posits it, requires critical analysis. In the current postmodern era, as some have suggested, there appears to be a cultural trend where words only have particular meanings in particular contexts. Hence, the frequently lamented disorderliness of social life seems to be a result (Baudrillard 1988; Virilio 1997), and while we might bemoan the disorder, it seems to cast doubt upon the notion of semantic primes.

As an example, how would a psychologist persist in an argument for the continuity of invariability of word meanings after the US President Bill Clinton attempted in the proceedings of Clinton–Lewinsky scandal to deflect prosecution for sexual misconduct by saying that whether he had had intercourse with a woman depended on "what 'is' is." Through such events the notion that there always are and will be constant word meanings and these meanings must be generally sensible on some principal basis, including "semantic primes," became questionable. Are there then, one should ask, words that all agents skilled in a language know ab initio—or are we entering a different type of semantic reality altogether? (Baudrillard 1988; Wierzbicka 1996, 1999, 2001)

In my view, it can be reasonably claimed that *common sense* is a sum of multiple higher psychological and societal functions; common sense, so defined, involves a set of goal-oriented behaviors and, therefore, to some extent. It involves the ever-changing phenomenon in ordinary and extraordinary life conditions, such as the above description of a nonsensical use of language in the global communicative public sphere. The extraordinary, or absurd, may actually be more descriptive of our present general state concerning common sense, as I argue that group-based meanings are potentially overriding what once was beyond doubt common sense, or in a sense, are becoming the new "common" or rather "idiosyncratic sense" which may not fulfill the criteria of "common" in the past sense of the word.

While the notion of common sense may have become problematic along with the general loss of invariant or universal components in word meanings, the notion of common sense is and remains at the core of PL (Smedslund 1988, 2012). Common sense, as posited in PL, provides the individual and groups with necessary psychological knowledge, enabling them to get along with each other and make enough sense of the social world to be able to get through at least the most basic mental or everyday interactions with ease and fluidity (Smedslund 1988, 1997, 2008, 2012). Common sense is conceptualized in PL as a culture that is the collective source of knowledge and rationality. To view human rationality as a function of common sense highlights, the fact that most of what people know is fundamentally social and acquired through socialization—a process to which humans are biologically predisposed (Smedslund 2011). That is what Dwyer (1990) calls sociability, the ability to get along with others.

Common sense, as the notion itself suggests, is common in the sense that it is a sensibility acquired from the collective social world, a world to which there is shared *access*. It cannot be a hermetic cognitive effort created in the isolation of an individual mind. Furthermore, individuals do not need a specialized skill to acquire common sense. The only thing necessary is a common language, as both Smedslund (1988) and Habermas (1994, p. 116) suggest—and as is obvious to gain the ability to perform everyday reasoning; no formal training in formal reasoning is required.

In short, the creation of common sense requires people to interact and talk with one another, and in turn, this path of socialization teaches people common sense. As a result of our ability to speak and understand language, we can generally hold that humans are logical to the extent that they can make sense of each other. Therefore, Smedslund pursues axiomatic psychological assumptions as derivatives of common culture, shared language, and common sense (Smedslund 1988, p. 5, 1997, 2012, p. 295–297). A similar line of thought, regarding the interrelationship of language and common sense, is presented in Jürgen Habermas' theory of communicative action (Habermas 1984, p. 11). But if language is becoming less universal, both Smedslunds and Habermas' positions are challenged since the grand conceptual premise of shared language stands before both all interpersonal communication and all notions of an interior psychological language.

As argued, a major challenge to the claims that common sense and the shared core meanings of our languages will remain permanent, unchanged, to some extent invariable, and constant, come from changes in *media* practices—and, based on those changes, in the ways in which we use language (Oeberst et al. 2016, p. 105–106). We are in a world in which Web 2.0 applications have become a primary source of news (Gottfried Shearer 2016) and the main social media app Facebook has led to a situation in which "your friends choose your news" (Baresch et al. 2011, p. 18; Flaherty 2011, p. 1302–1303).

Can My Common Sense Be Your Nonsense?

If we observe an increase in variations of word meanings and idiosyncratic expressions, we face new and serious dilemmas. For instance, when we reflect and reason, especially about matters regarding our personal issues in psychological interpersonal communication, for instance, in therapeutic sessions, we cannot in full confidence rely on derivatives of common culture, shared language, and common sense (Smedslund 1988 p. 5, 1997, 2012, p. 295–297) or on the Habermasian notion of open and forthright persuasion (Habermas 1984, p. 11). What makes sense to me may not make sense to you, despite our earnest wish to communicate, even in a therapeutic situation in which there is an assumption of shared language in a matrix of common sense.

Both Smedslund and Habermas make assumptions for maintaining shared epistemic values and the continuing potential of humans to create universally shared knowledge. These are noble ideas, but are they concomitant with our reality? I raise this concern, particularly in consideration of smaller groups and their inter-group communication, where much of the talk is emotional and intended to sustain interpersonal relationships (Ellison et al. 2011). In these intimate and smaller contexts, conflict due to misunderstandings arises easily, and the only way to ensure understanding is to be open for clarifying misunderstandings (Smedslund 1990).

PL assumes that in small-group settings we aim to be logical in the sense of being coherent with *our* understanding of the world and how we imagine it exists for us in momentary conceptual frameworks (Smedslund 1988, 2012, p. 295). In the postmodern Web 2.0 world, the momentary conceptual framework is increasingly idiosyncratic due to the developments of the Internet, communicative media, and the subsequent and dramatic increase in the circulation of group-produced knowledge (Oeberst et al. 2016, p. 105–106). The common aspects of shared language underlying the notion of common sense may simply seem less "common" today than at the initiation of PL as a theory. Smedslund'*s Psycho-logic* was first published in 1988, and at that time the current trends of language use and multiple reference groups per each individual may have been hard to imagine.

Furthermore, in 1988, Jean Baudrillard anticipated an increasing decay of common sense (1988, p. 145). In 1988, Baudrillard's world of "hyper-reality" in which signs have become—at least to some extent—unhinged from any signified (Baudrillard 1988, p. 145) seemed like an unrealistic dystopia. Today, the traditional media (i.e., television, radio, newspapers, magazines) as well as social media (i.e., Twitter, Facebook, Instagram, Reddit) "narrow-cast" to small groups of like-minded individuals. In such a way, the common sense of one group may become nonsense to the others that acquire their shared meanings elsewhere. The interactive web technologies have led to a massive increase in the circulation of group-produced and group-targeted knowledge (Oeberst et al. 2016, p. 105–106). Web 2.0 platforms like Facebook and Twitter often produce "fake news." Such material satisfies the Enlightenment universal regulatory practice of knowledge of "justified true belief," one of the epistemic aspects of common sense of psychological theory, only in that it is believed (Goldman 1999). This is an obvious challenge to common sense with serious consequences. Some of the online material can be psychologically and physically harmful. For example, viewers of pro-anorexia websites have worse outcomes for the disorder than do non-viewers (Bardone-Cone and Cass 2007, p. 541–542). In the United States, anti-vaccine websites and related complaints have led 21 of 50 states to enact opt-out legislation such that, in those states, only 70% of children are now vaccinated (Bean 2011, p. 1874). What can be seen as loss or decay of common sense through our ways of using the Internet has resulted in real public health challenges (Betsch et al. 2012, p. 3729).

In my view, the belief that vaccines like the one for polio is a danger because "vaccines are biological poisons, harmful to health, and a contributing factor in childhood illness" (Kata 2010, p. 1711) is an example of common sense turned into nonsense. Here, we see that communication across epistemic differences and across social-psychological in-groups has become difficult (Bergin 2001; Tajfel 1982). How does one find the common ground for reasoned arguments in such a debate?

Communication can function only because of common sense. As Habermas (1994, p. 116) and Smedslund (1988) argue, holding a shared language leads individuals to develop a common sense of meaning in the groups within which they communicate. Via this *sensus communis*, individuals can still operate with ease and fluidity in the symbolic realm. Our shared common sense, now and in the future, is inescapably bound to social groups. Our necessary social nature has various consequences. For instance, already-acquired schemata define what sorts of knowledge can be assimilated (Piaget 1972; Smedslund 2012, p. 296). This is the continuing basis for common sense. Yet, if people decreasingly acquire information outside small groups, there is less ground for an overarching common sense to which individuals would orient themselves to once "their friends select their news." In this scenario, the ability to communicate reasonably both psychologically and epistemologically outside one's familiar groups would be significantly impaired.

Social Groups Continue to Create Common Sense

The example of the US President Clinton and his absurd failure to agree what "is" means can be seen as an example of an era, as envisioned by Strauss (1989, p. 93) and Baudrillard (1988), where the texts of the day have ceased to signify. At the same time, we continue to go about our quotidian lives as we always have, even though truth in some common sense meaning may have vanished, even though 30% of the children in some schools are not vaccinated against polio—all of this implying the decay of what something "is" in some shared sense (Virilio 1997). Eventually, if no effort is given to regenerate common word meanings, serious health consequences may occur regarding the individual well-being—psychological and somatic (Phadke et al. 2016). Disruptions to common sense are causing direct consequences on our well-being. Common sense need not be entirely lost to create an effect; even a small disruption to common sense seems to be creating real effects upon our social well-being.

Upon examining the challenges to common sense, one can ask whether or not we can credibly now claim that invariant elements of language exist so that common sense can remain common. To what extent do words have elements that do not require a reasonably described context for the words themselves to be understood? Is the available solution a type of hyper-specialized individual who is able to understand and speak in some specialized or technical language? How do we find common meaning despite the developments of different forms of mass and social media and their related language-use practices? In my view, these questions are part of the answer. Paying attention to such developments, and to language use as a whole, is itself a starting point from which to regenerate language and to maintain shared meanings. Secondly, linguistic research on semantic primes and the formalized structure of languages in general, and with regard to specific questions, can offer further answers.

One of the assumed goals of studying semantic primes is to discover, or rather to *rediscover*, the invariant elements in word meanings (e.g., Smedslund 2012; Wierzbicka 1996, 1999, 2001). The goal of such a rediscovery of an already existing a priori and axiomatic psychological language could then potentially apply universally in actual conversations and reasoning. In this way, the study of semantic primes reveals a general theory of a universal psychology. The discovery of semantic primes shows, as well, that human communication is goal oriented. The reason one can argue this is that the primes can only be learned through practice as a part of a child's learning of language, which itself is a goal-oriented effort toward a skill. The maintenance of the knowledge of a basic corpus of any human language, by necessity, must continue to emerging as a goal-oriented human practice, with the adult learning new and novel concepts through his or her immersion in a culture.

Therefore, in line with Smedslund's seminal arguments (2008, 2011), we can argue that common meanings and language have some fundamental and constant basis to them. Since this can be shown to be true, we must then ask how one should treat the elliptical, ephemeral, and idiosyncratic meanings that we see being created in small-group interpersonal communication? These group-based meanings are difficult to study in a formalized manner although their significance is apparent. It is small-group communication that matters most with regard to our emotional well-being and our continued felt sense of being reasonable members of our communities (Vähämaa 2013a, p. 13–14).

Semantic primes, as our core and most primitive vocabulary, will be discoverable, even when languages and meanings change over time since they are the deep core of the formalized syntax of our natural languages. A good point of reflection is this text at hand. For this text to be readable, it must be the case that for all readers of this text that there remains an always-extant and invariant corpus of word meanings. When that corpus of signifiers disintegrates, the semiotic realm itself will dissipate, with consequences we actually cannot imagine—since imagination itself exists in the semantic realm (Tateo 2015).

These changeless components of our language are now discoverable in *specialized* settings—as in carefully curated articles like the one you are reading, among sports team members or among groups of professionals. Simultaneously, invariant components of word meanings have become increasingly more difficult to discover and touch upon in more universal and non-particular settings. In the contemporary plural public sphere, mainly due to the specialized "narrow-casting" to their particular and self-selected audiences the media also choose and determine—even if in synchrony with its audience—what is considered common and what something means. Meanings of words have become increasingly enriched by the multitude of social groups that redefine meanings for themselves. To master a language and to get a grasp of common sense, thus, is more demanding than ever before.

Semantic Primes and Rediscovery of Common Language

The previously mentioned Presidential sex scandal suggested that even semantic primes can come into question, even if they do not change (Wierzbicka 1996, 1999). Thus, these semantic primes have the ability to function as mirrors and fundaments to provide something constant in our language that enables us to understand the constant changes in word meanings (Tateo 2018).

Natural language, as the domain of semantic primes, has a structure that enables modeling semantic primes, and we have the skills and technology, if we so will, to reduce to core words even the most complex psychological sentences in a formal manner. As semantic primes do appear universally, their formal research continues yielding interesting results from the viewpoint of cultural psychology and reveals important and reason-based commonalities in our languages.

On the one hand, the increasing lack of shared social ground for common word meanings brings into question the ability of the a priori research approaches to offer comprehensive enough knowledge of psychological language. Everyday talk, its idioms, elliptical meanings, and playfulness may require the psychologist to increase context-dependent approach toward reasoning. Purely generic approaches may become less and less helpful if one is willing to understand the discontent and pure unhappiness we see as outcomes of some of the current Internet discourses as we seek like-minded groups for the better and worse (Bardone-Cone and Cass 2007, p. 541–542; Hewstone 1990).

On the other hand, the discovery of a potentially increasing body of semantic primes in different languages contributes significantly to the a priori cultural psychological knowledge. Such a formal project is an ambitious and specialized project that may locate what makes something in psychology or culture constantly "common," as a formalized presentation of psychological language increases our ability to reflect the basis of our psychological reasoning and the connection of that linguistic base to the fast-changing idiosyncrasies. These idiosyncrasies, in-group references, usage of idioms, playfulness, elliptical, and emotional vividness and ephemeral sayings are not easily found in psychology textbooks, as the everyday psychological language develops at a fast pace. Therefore, the "going back to basics" through semantic primes can be of meaningful help: semantic primes can provide a reflective mirror to the fast-paced changes in psychological language.

This might be particularly valuable if we believe that we actually now live, as Baudrillard (1988, p. 145) suggested, in an era of "hyper-reality," in which signs have become unhinged from any signified; words and things are no longer connected, and words are defined only by other words and have no invariant components left as discussed by Resch (1992) and considered by Smedslund (1988, 2012) as a fundamentally impossible dystopia.

Even in our era, the condition of a limited language having a defined and agreed-upon reference for meanings of its words is still possible. Consider that religious discourses, which persist across nations, contain symbolic *catechisms* in which the meaning of all the terms in the *primary text* is determined. Perhaps, in some sense, our linguistic catechism may be found, to some limited extent, in semantic primes and within their connections to universally understandable sentences as the research unfolds.

The points made thus far imply that epistemic agreements, agreements of what we regard as relevant, even as knowledge, are tightly connected to the notion of common sense. As the fundaments of reasoning, the notions of common sense and common knowledge are practically inseparable. Common sense requires the felt sense of holding common knowledge. To illustrate this epistemic viewpoint, I will next present a scenario of an imaginary prehistoric social interaction as an example of how unavoidable common sense and knowledge are in terms of social interaction. After these considerations, I offer a view of synthetic thinking as a way to deal with both the constant and changing elements of language.

Basics of Psychological Reasoning: A Prehistoric Illustration

Groups are necessary to the formation of knowledge; humans do not form knowledge outside of social structures. In order for groups to exist, they must themselves have an epistemic structure. Some things must be regarded as knowledge to enable communication (Vähämaa 2013a). The nature of social groups makes it necessary to have some sort of initial criteria of knowledge. As I have posited elsewhere (Vähämaa 2013b, p. 26):

> Very much in the very same way as every written argument must start with a letter, must every group start with an epistemology—at least some sort of lay theory of understandable and nonsense sentences.

Following this train of thought, it is apparent that in order for any social group to exist there needs to be some sort of group-based epistemology—a primitive language with common sensibility enabling the group to agree upon things—right at the very genesis of a group. A nascent—or a newborn—social, group-generated, epistemology is largely based in our social needs and their fulfillments (Vähämaa 2015). In order to achieve any social ends or goals to create common meaning, one needs paradoxically to have a group epistemology even *before* joining a group in order to start to generate knowledge through such group-based epistemology. My view on this paradox is the following: the history of man, or *Homo sapiens*, and language are equally long and, therefore, the genesis of the first group was simultaneously the genesis of first linguistic and epistemic agreements—the nascent group epistemologies.

To imagine how such an elementary level of epistemic praxis may evolve, we could think of two human beings meeting each other for the first time in prehistoric times in order to achieve some shared meanings to communicate. As the natural history has it, people have throughout time formed groups and sought out other people to meet individual needs through collective action. Consequentially, as people group together, they at once have some common "language" or signaling system.

This type of a "cave man" epistemology may be a far-fetched example as such, but it does underline the reciprocity of groups and group-based ways of founding what is common sense or common knowledge. Or, in philosophical terminology, how an epistemology emerges. One cannot have one without the other. A group has an immediate set of some level of epistemic standards to enable exchange of sensible communication, and as the group evolves, it generates more knowledge about the world "out there."

To look even further back, in the past eras before language as we now understand it, the items of perception—birds, trees, food, and dwellings, as well as the presumable "fellow men" in the perceptible world—would have be given a set of meanings that are not merely based in perceptions but based in social *meanings* due to the social *reciprocity* the group members would have had (Vähämaa 2015). In contemporary cultural psychological research, this assumption is widely credited and conceptualized as a reciprocal presupposition between continuity and discontinuity in meaning-making processes (De Luca Picione and Freda 2014, 2016; Esposito et al. 2015; Freda 2011; Freda and Esposito 2017). Simply put, continuity means that the same old ideas are in some sense left behind as these ideas become told and circulated via new narrations.

The imaginary prehistoric men would not speak merely of "the big dwelling," that exists (as a semantic prime), we would posit. They would speak of "the big dwelling where our leader, the boss, lives," yielding immediately an expression with a social dimension. Here, we see a cultural psychological implication of an initial unity of psyche and language-based orderliness (Smedslund 2012; Vähämaa 2015, p. 54–56).

All of that, I presume, would result in an elementary "regulation" of knowledge that would enable both of our imaginary cave-dwellers to make observations of the world and, through dialogue with the other group members, to develop social meanings—common sense—about the world. The imaginary *Ur-sprache* would, in its most primitive form, have to be social since it would have to be a shared effort. The primary language, *Ur-sprache,* would be a rudimentary basis of a group epistemology as being simultaneously a set of shared and common meanings.

The important point, regardless of the actual historical development of early regulatory group epistemologies, persists. Groups arise to form meanings, and in the process, they form group-based epistemologies. No knowledge, thus, exists without groups and no groups exist without a reasonable degree of *common sense*.

To Imagine Things Anew: Synthetic Thinking and Regeneration of Common Meanings

If we take the above claims to be true, or plausible with regard their conceptual value, we are struck with the notion of common sense and the need for it because we live and use language unavoidably in social groups. Here, the emphasis can be on the *sense* part of the notion, underlining our continuing ability to reason while *common* meanings may appear "lost" or at least laborious to find as "common" is now more scattered to different loci and hard to rediscover.

How do we, as laymen, thinkers, and cultural psychologists, prepare ourselves for the presented disparities and discontents that relate to the challenges of common sense and language and, yet, depend on reasoned psychological thought and action? My answer goes as follows. In addition to seeking answers from a priori psychological knowledge, we must turn to *synthetic thinking* which relies on imagination as a resource to self-reflect, as a resource to attain new ideas and knowledge. Synthetic thinking allows us to change perspectives as it allows multiple meanings for the same object at the same time and place simultaneously. (Harris 2000; Tateo 2015, 2016.)

By *synthetic thinking*, I refer to a type of thinking where, in addition to a priori knowledge and known and easily inducible or deductible facts, one has to draw on not only facts present in the sentences at hand as in formal logic, but also use and engage in *imagination* as a relevant source of knowledge. Imagination, as a cultural psychological concept, is defined as "a fundamental higher psychological function that is devoted to the manipulation of complex wholes of iconic and linguistic signs," following Luca Tateo's definition (Tateo 2015, p. 146; see also Brinkmann 2015; Harris 2000).

A priori axiomatic and logical reasoning may prove insufficient to yield new and common word meanings because they may not address directly the role of imaginative processes even though imagination has more open-ended possibilities, and it allows co-existence of different meanings for the same objects. This view comes close to the ideas of Piaget (1972), as he assumed that while one may be "incorrect," one is still always "logical" with regard to one's own personal schemata of things and objects (see also Smedslund 2012).

The approach of PL, by itself, as a way to gain non-empirical psychological knowledge has granted us plenty of psychological knowledge. Thus, we cannot say that our difficulties in finding common meanings would be a result of lack of psychological knowledge per se. If anything, we know now more than before. In sum, we have an abundance of theoretically sound psychological knowledge embedded in our culture, stored in our books. Why, then, is there the felt need for non-axiomatic reasoning in—similar non-empirical, reflective, fashion? In simple terms, we can see from the example below that we need to rely on imagination when we reflect on different scenarios, logical or not.

For instance, we could imagine notions of "depression" and "total control of depression"—when we think synthetically. The basic principle, as already implied, is that in synthetic thinking a layperson or a psychologist gives the familiar object multiple co-existing new meanings at the same time and same place using imagination (Harris 2000; Tateo 2016, p. 437–440). A therapist in a session—or a friend in a conversation—will consider the verbalized or visualized object of thought as two or more different things at the same time and at the same place and share it through conversation. Such an *act*, the act of an expressed thought, cannot be true or false—since actions, by default, are validated rather by their functionality, not their epistemic truth-value (Kock 2009).

Here, we could imagine that an individual *E* considers, illogically, that he/she has "depression" and "total control of depression"—both at the same time and place. Such paradox can create a novel and non-logical thought for *E* that can be called having "mixed feelings," or it can produce a thought where depression and control of depression mixed together gets a new meaning altogether. For instance, *E* could imagine or reflect on a thought where depression and control of depression form a hybrid where the felt sense of depression and the felt sense of its total control co-exist.

Such hybrids are not only interesting products of psychological reflection but are important to consider if we want to find common meanings and functioning intersubjectivity once again (De Luca Picione et al. 2017). The individual who is psychologically functional generates hybrids which lead to new understandings and better behavioral outcomes. The individual who is not psychologically functional generates hybrids which lead to "stuckness," impaired behavioral outcomes, mental conundra, and the like. (De Luca Picione and Valsiner 2017)

Cultural psychologist, Raffaele De Luca Picione, posits that if an individual truly attempts to talk with others about new creative ideas—to *narrate* such views to others—some existing semiotic borders have to be crossed between the old and the new, thus creating a novel, future-oriented idea (De Luca Picione 2015a, b). If we do not use language creatively and do not cross over semiotic borders, we remain stuck with repetitious narrations and can not find new psychological meanings. As Raffaele De Luca Picione and Jaan Valsiner (2017, p. 541) say:

> In fact, when the border becomes too rigid, we observe forms of repetition of the same narration, a saturation of sense-making processes and a sclerotization of relations based on opposition systems.

A synthetic idea like the hybrid described above overcomes this type of "saturation" and "sclerotization"—or, stuckness—and allows new meanings to emerge. Such newfound meanings are neither repetitive narrations nor are they entirely blurred by subjectivity in a manner that would make them incomprehensible to others (De Luca Picione and Valsiner 2017). A synthetic idea occurs when none of the imagined "objects" of thought are ignored or negated but they inspire a *new* idea: an interpretation, in this example, of the verbalized or visualized object drawn from an imaginative process which allows such multiplicity and co-existence or co-genesis of projections. To enable such thinking to flourish requires considering both logic and imagination in psychological reasoning and reflection. Equally important is a congenial environment, an epistemic community, to exchange these newfound thoughts and ideas to regenerate common understanding, or, common sense.

An epistemic community, at its genesis, requires only two individuals to exist and to generate shared meanings and shared common sense. To conclude, I hold that if we simply become good at reflecting and understanding fundamental semantic primes and basic psychological axioms of our language, we are also better equipped to consider unfamiliar word meanings with flexibility and imagination. In this way, we would enable new meanings in the social regulation of common language, common sense, and interaction between people who would otherwise "talk past one another."

Conclusions

Synthetic thinking skills allow the psychologist, the thinker, and the laymen alike to draw on their imaginative processes and intuition and allow the co-existence of multiple, uncommon, and even contrarian meanings for the objects at hand. This further yields new and novel ideas. Once these ideas are brought into conversations and interpersonal interactions, we acquire new synthetic knowledge expressed as newfound and shared meanings and regenerate at some level common sense. In the final analysis, there may not be a route besides the route of small groups to maintain and regenerate common sense as the continuing principle—even if sometimes not achieved—of our interactions.

Knowledge gained in this way enables intersubjectivity. Thus, it helps to see things as the *other* does. As cultural psychological research shows, our regulatory practices embedded in our culture, e.g., understanding, empathy, concern, control, regret, and the like, can be improved as we regain some of the lost psychic unity we can not have without a sense that we have common meanings. Ideally speaking, regulation of meaning and interaction becomes easier, between friends and acquaintances and beyond our familiar groups even though there may not be common vocabulary at the beginning of the process.

It is important to understand that the use or adaptation of language and knowledge, for instance, to come up with a novel thought and express it in a conversation, cannot be true or false as such. This is the case because *actions,* such as thinking and speaking (in contrast to propositions of thought), cannot be either true or false. In this manner, the presented approach expands the logical scope of PL. While the explication of common-sense nature of psychological language must rely on logic, some of the changes in our language use can be made visible by considering how we use our language and sensibility in an illogical manner. Illogical and novel use of language in social interaction is part of the process that may both reinforce common sense for those who interact and also challenge the boundaries of common sense. While common sense as a general principle of interaction and language may not change, some of the misunderstandings in small group interaction may be avoided by considering how individuals may express uncommon and novel thoughts and meanings by being illogical and breaking the boundaries of common sense. Therefore, it is important to encourage bold thinking, imagination, and playfulness in our language use. It is equally relevant to constantly consider the more permanent, primary aspects and key notions of our language such as the reviewed semantic primes, common sense, and the interesting changes in word meanings.

References

Bardone-Cone, A., & Cass, K. M. (2007). What does viewing a pro-anorexia website do? An experimental examination of website exposure and moderating effects. *International Journal of Eating Disorders, 40*(6), 537–548.

Baresch, B., Knight, L., Harp, D., & Yaschur, C. (2011). Friends who choose your news: An analysis of content links on Facebook. *ISOJ: The Official Research Journal of International Symposium on Online Journalism, 1*(2), 1–24.

Baudrillard, J. (1988). The hyper-realism of simulation. In M. Poster (Ed.), *Jean Baudrillard: Selected writings* (pp. 143–147). Stanford, CA: Stanford University Press.

Bean, S. J. (2011). Emerging and continuing trends in vaccine opposition website content. *Vaccine, 29*(10), 1874–1880.

Bergin, L. (2001). The role of truth when communicating knowledge across epistemic difference. *Social Epistemology, 15*(4), 367–378.

Betsch, C., Brewer, N. T., Brocard, P., Davies, P., Gaissmaier, W., Haase, N., Leask, J., Renkewitz, F., Renner, B., Reyna, V. F., Rossmann, C., Sachse, K., Schachinger, A., Siegrist, M., & Stryk, M. (2012). Opportunities and challenges of web 2.0 for vaccination decisions. *Vaccine, 30*(25), 3727–3733.

Brinkmann, S. (2015). Imagining cultural psychology. *Culture & Psychology, 21*(2), 243–250.

De Luca Picione, R. (2015a). The idiographic approach in psychological research. The challenge of overcoming old distinctions without risking to homogenize. *Integrative Psychological and Behavioral Science, 49*(3), 360–370.

De Luca Picione, R. (2015b). *La Mente come Forma. La Mente come Testo. Un'indagine semiotico-psicologica sui processi di significazione*. Milan, Italy: Mimemis Edizioni.

De Luca Picione, R., & Freda, M. F. (2014). Catalysis and morphogenesis: The contextual semiotic configuration of form, function, and fields of experience. In K. R. Cabell & J. Valsiner (Eds.), *The catalyzing mind: Beyond models of causality* (pp. 149–163). New York: Springer.

De Luca Picione, R., & Freda, M. F. (2016). Borders and modal articulations: Semiotic constructs of sensemaking processes enabling a fecund dialogue between cultural psychology and clinical psychology. *Integrative Psychological & Behavioral Science, 50*, 29–43.

De Luca Picione, R., Martino, M. L., & Freda, M. F. (2017). Modal articulation: The psychological and semiotic functions of modalities in the sensemaking process. *Theory & Psychology, 28*(1), 84–103.

De Luca Picione, R., & Valsiner, J. (2017). Psychological functions of semiotic borders in sense-making: Liminality of narrative processes. *Europe's Journal of Psychology, 13*(3), 532–547.

Dwyer, J. (1990). The imperative of sociability: Moral culture in the late Scottish enlightenment. *Journal of Eighteenth Century Studies, 13*(2), 169–184.

Ellison, N. B., Steinfield, C., & Lampe, C. (2011). Connection strategies: Social capital implications of Facebook-enabled communication practices. *New Media & Society, 13*(6), 873–892.

Esposito, G., Freda, M. F., & Bosco, V. (2015). Examining perception of competency through practicum competencies outline. *European Journal of Training and Development, 39*(8), 700–720.

Flaherty, D. K. (2011). The vaccine-autism connection: A public health crisis caused by unethical medical practices and fraudulent science. *Annals of Pharmacotherapy, 45*(10), 1302–1304.

Freda, M. F. (2011). Understanding continuity to recognize discontinuity. *Integrative Psychological & Behavioral Science, 45*, 335–346.

Freda, M. F., & Esposito, G. (2017). Promoting reflection and reflexivity through narrative devices: Narrative mediation path qualitative multimodal method. *Qualitative Research Journal, 17*(1), 2–19.

Goddard, C. (1998). Bad arguments against semantic primitives. *Theoretical Linguistics, 24*(2–3), 129–156.

Goldman, A. I. (1999). *Knowledge in a social world*. New York: Oxford University Press.

Gottfried, J., & Shearer, E. (2016, May). *News Use Across Social Media Platforms 2016* (Publication by Pew Research Center). Retrieved from http://www.journalism.org/2016/05/26/news-use-across-social-media-platforms-2016/
Habermas, J. (1984). *The theory of communicative action. Reason and the rationalization of society* (Vol. 1). London: Heinemann.
Habermas, J. (1994). *The past as future*. Cambridge, MA: Polity Press.
Harris, P. L. (2000). Understanding Children's worlds. In *The work of the imagination*. Malden: Blackwell Publishing.
Hewstone, M. (1990). The "ultimate attribution error"? A review of the literature on intergroup causal attribution. *European Journal of Social Psychology, 20*(4), 311–335.
Kata, A. (2010). A postmodern pandora's box: Anti-vaccination misinformation on the internet. *Vaccine, 28*(7), 1709–1716.
Kock, C. E. J. (2009). Choice is not true or false: The domain of rhetorical argumentation. *Argumentation: An International Journal on Reasoning, 23*(1), 61–80.
Oeberst, A., Kimmerle, J., & Cress, U. (2016). What is knowledge? Who creates it? Who possesses it? The need for novel answers to old questions. In U. Cress, J. Moskaliuk, & H. Jeong (Eds.), *Mass collaboration and education* (Computer-Supported Collaborative Learning Series) (Vol. 16, pp. 105–124). Cham: Springer.
Osgood, C. E., May, W. H., Miron, M. S., & Miron, M. S. (1975). *Cross-cultural universals of affective meaning* (Vol. 1). Champaign, IL: University of Illinois Press.
Phadke, V. K., Bednarczyk, R. A., Salmon, D. A., & Omer, S. B. (2016). Association between vaccine refusal and vaccine-preventable diseases in the United States: A review of measles and pertussis. *Journal of the American Medical Association, 315*(11), 1149–1158.
Piaget, J. (1972). *The principles of genetic epistemology*. London: Routledge and K. Paul.
Resch, R. P. (1992). *Althusser and the renewal of Marxist social theory*. Berkeley: University of California Press.
Smedslund, J. (1985). How stable is common sense psychology and can it be transcended? Reply to Valsiner. *Scandinavian Journal of Psychology, 27*, 91–94.
Smedslund, J. (1988). *Psycho-logic*. Berlin: Springer-Verlag.
Smedslund, J. (1990). A critique of Tversky and Kahneman's distinction between fallacy and misunderstanding. *Scandinavian Journal of Psychology, 31*, 110–120.
Smedslund, J. (1997). *The structure of psychological common sense*. Mahwah, NJ: Erlbaum.
Smedslund, J. (2008). From Heider to psycho-logic. *Social Psychology, 39*(3), 157–162.
Smedslund, J. (2011). Meaning of words and the use of axiomatics in psychological theory. *Journal of Theoretical and Philosophical Psychology, 31*(2), 126–135.
Smedslund, J. (2012). Psycho-logic: Some thoughts and after-thoughts. *Scandinavian Journal of Psychology, 53*(4), 295–302.
Strauss, L. (1989). The three waves of modernity. In H. Gildin (Ed.), *An introduction to political philosophy: Ten essays by Leo Strauss* (pp. 81–98). Detroit: Wayne State University Press.
Tajfel, H. (1982). Social psychology of intergroup relations. In M. R. Rosenweig & L. W. Porter (Eds.), *Annual review of psychology* (pp. 1–39). Palo Alto, CA: Annual Reviews.
Tateo, L. (2015). Giambattista Vico and the psychological imagination. *Culture & Psychology, 21*(2), 145–161.
Tateo, L. (2016). Toward a cogenetic cultural psychology. *Culture & Psychology, 22*(3), 433–447.
Tateo, L. (2018). Affective semiosis and affective logic. *New Ideas in Psychology, 48*, 1–11.
Vähämaa, M. (2013a). Groups as epistemic communities: Social forces and affect as antecedents to knowledge. *Social Epistemology, 27*(1), 3–20.
Vähämaa, M. (2013b). A groups epistemology is a group necessity: A reply to Fallis and Mathiesen. *Social Epistemology, 27*(1), 26–31.
Vähämaa, M. (2015). Groups as epistemic communities – Studies on the role of groups in forming and circulating social knowledge. *(Doctoral dissertation). Retrieved from Dissertations and Theses database*. Retrieved from http://urn.fi/URN:ISBN:978-951-51-1012-1
Virilio, P. (1997). *Open sky*. New York: Verso.

Whitrow, G. J. (1988). *Time in history: The evolution of our general awareness of time and temporal perspective*. London: Oxford University Press.
Wierzbicka, A. (1996). *Semantics: Primes and universals*. New York: Oxford University Press.
Wierzbicka, A. (1999). *Emotions across languages and cultures: Diversity and universals*. Cambridge: University Press.
Wierzbicka, A. (2001). *What did Jesus mean? Explaining the sermon on the mount and the parables in simple and universal human concepts*. New York: Oxford University Press.

Chapter 11
How to Avoid Throwing the Baby Out with the Bathwater: Abduction Is the Solution to Pseudo-Empiricism

Sergio Salvatore

Introduction

Few scholars can be said to have provided the scientific community with such a clear and simple idea that also has the disruptive power to outline a paradigm shift in psychology. Jan Smedslund is one of them, having given us the notion of *Pseudoempirical Research* (Smedslund 1991; see also 1982, 1988, 1992, 1995, 2016). Pseudoempirical research is the research that empirically tests a hypothesis that can be known from reasoning on what is conceptually implied by the knowledge grounding the hypothesis itself.

"The sum of a triangle's angles is 180°" is a paradigmatic instance of a priori and noncontingent proposition provided by Smedslund. Research aimed at measuring the angles of a triangle would be pseudoempirical because it is already known that their sum is 180° since this is logically implied in the definition of triangle itself.

The notion of pseudoempirical research has critical implications for psychology as it makes us recognize what a huge amount of pseudoempirical research there is within the discipline, and the naivety of efforts to ground the scientificness of the discipline on the accumulation of "empirical evidence." This is so because, as Smedslund, as well as many other authors (e.g., Harrè and Secord 1972; Valsiner 2007; see also Heft 2013 and Salvatore 2016a, b) have shown, psychological phenomena are made of (broadly speaking) semantic and semiotic relations rather than cause–effect relations. And this means that the relation between psychological

S. Salvatore (✉)
La Sapienza, University of Rome, Rome, Italy
e-mail: sergio.salvatore@unisalento.it

T. G. Lindstad et al. (eds.), *Respect for Thought*, Theory and History in the Human and Social Sciences, https://doi.org/10.1007/978-3-030-43066-5_11

elements is already given, implied in the normative cultural context, and it therefore needs to be tested empirically as much as the statement that the sum of a triangle's angles is 180°. For instance, take a person who is insulted and takes offense. Now, the relation between insult and offense is not of cause–effect type—the insult is not the cause of the person's feeling of being offended. Indeed, cause–effect relations require an exchange of energy, something that is not given in the case of the relation insult-offense. To say that the relation between two such elements is semantic/semiotic means that the latter is the meaning of the former—the feeling of being offended is the way the person interprets the fact of being insulted. In the same vein, one could say that stopping at the traffic light is not the effect of the red light, but its (normative) meaning; the lack of motivation is not the cause of dropping out from school, but its definition, and so on and so forth.

The notion of pseudo-empiricism is a very brilliant one. Its place should be one reserved for ideas that are cornerstones like primary process, assimilation and accommodation, mediation and gestalt. Actually, it has something more: it is a concept *about*, not only *of* psychology—if considered seriously, it leads to a deep shift in the way of thinking of and doing science in psychology.

Smedslund himself has drawn a completely alternative scientific program—Psycho-logic (PL)—from his criticism of the pseudoempirical nature of psychological research (Smedslund 1988,1995). According to him, since psychological constructs are linked semantically, the function of psychology is to make the normative commonsensical meaning underpinned such linkages explicit.

Psycho-logic adopts an axiomatic form of reasoning, the one that is useful to identify the connections between meanings that are part of the semantic network of common sense. In his view, this means that psychology has to work as an analytic science, like geometry—e.g., Pythagoras' theorem is not a matter of empirical investigation just as the relation between the length of the sides and the hypotenuse is not a fact that needs to be detected empirically, but a conceptual implication deduced logically from the general axioms of geometry. Accordingly, psychology should get rid of the illusory idea of discovering empirical facts and should rather devote themselves to the explicit formalization of common sense.

In this chapter, I acknowledge the merit of the notion of pseudo-empiricism. On the other hand, my thesis is that the *construens* part of Smedslund's program (PL) is not the solution to the problem he identified. In my view, PL throws the baby (the possibility of empirical psychological knowledge) out with the bathwater (the problematic way empirical research is usually carried out); as it seems to me this is why Smedslund's vision has had an impact on psychology which is not consistent with its outstanding value. In the second part of this paper, I briefly outline a different *construens* program, aimed at saving the baby: a methodological approach that considers the semantic valence of psychological constructs as the grounds and the target of empirical knowledge in psychology, rather than the condition that makes it impossible to pursue it.

Pseudo-Empiricism in Semiotic Key

Smedslund's criticism of pseudo-empiricism gains even deeper implications when psychological phenomena are viewed through the lens of the semiotic-cultural theoretical approach (Salvatore 2016a; Valsiner 2007). According to this view, mental processes are ongoing dynamics of sensemaking. Sensemaking consists of processes of interpretation of the world that shape the experience. Four basic characteristics of these processes of interpretation are worth highlighting here.

First, according to Peirce's theory of the sign (Peirce 1897/1932a, 1902/1932b), interpretation consists of a following sign that establishes backwardly how the previous sign works as the interpretant of the ones before it. For instance, consider a person that states: "What a beautiful day!" and the addressee "Yes, the sun is shining and is so warm." In so doing, the addressee interprets the addresser's sign "What a beautiful day!" as a statement about the weather.

Second, signs are not only ideas, images, and words—behaviors and affective states are signs as well.

Third, the processes of interpretation are guided by generalized, affect-laden meanings that reflect the cultural milieu and that work as basic embodied assumptions concerning the world—what it is and how it works (Ciavolino et al. 2017; Salvatore 2016a).

Fourth, these assumptions are not separate entities that work on the signs from the outside. Rather, they are immanent to the way things work, as their inherent propension to combine with each other in a certain way. To give an analogy, the relation of immanence between specific signs and generalized meanings is the same as that between molecules of water and a vortex. Molecules are not something different from the vortex. The vortex does not come before the molecules, as its cause. Rather, molecules *are* the vortex, their dynamic reciprocal linkages are what make up the vortex.

Insofar as one regards these four characteristics of sensemaking as constitutive of mental processes, one has to conclude that the relation between states of the mind and behaviors are semiotic: each following state of mind (be it a behavior, an idea, an affective state) is not the effect of the previous one, but its interpretation. Paradoxically enough, the direction of the influence is reversed as any sign works backwards on its previous signs. Moreover, one has to recognize that the relation between signs is not a one-to-one linkage; rather, each sign works as the interpreter of the previous sign due to the whole system of generalized meanings. This means that the sensemaking works as a field dynamics, namely a single process whose instant global state—i.e., the state of the relations among its elements—determines the following global state (Ciavolino et al. 2017).

In sum, the view of the mental process in a semiotic key leads to view the relations among psychological occurrences (i.e., cognition, feelings, affective state, behavior) as *pars-pro-toto relations of semiotic implications,* in the sense that occurrence *a* implies occurrence *b* as its interpretant (semiotic implication) because of the specific position that both *a* and *b* hold within the overall dynamics of sensemaking, in other words, due to the meaning that *a* and *b* have in the context of the process of interpretation (*pars-pro-toto* relation).

Some Examples

Some examples can help to clarify in what sense constructs referring to psychological processes are associated with each other in terms of pars-toto relations of semiotic implications.

Consider the following instances of psychological research.

1. Psycho-social analyses of medical setting have shown that patient's compliance decreases with the complexity of medical regiments, treatment duration (e.g., Claxton et al. 2001) as well as when disease is asymptomatic and ego-syntonic (Grant et al. 2003; Vlasnik et al. 2005).
2. The Health Action Process Approach (HAPA; e.g., Schwarzer and Luszczynska 2015) focuses on the role played by intentional and self-regulatory factors in initiating and maintaining health behavior change. More particularly, the HAPA considers that self-regulatory processes consist of behavioral intentions, self-monitoring, and planning—these factors work in synergy to make the motivation a habitual action.
3. Studies on attachment have shown that secure attachment has a positive effect in adolescents, and it is associated with lower incidence of acting-out behaviors—e.g., theft, drug use, vandalism (Noom et al. 1999), as well as aggressive behavior (Laible et al. 2000).
4. Community psychology has highlighted that the *sense of community*—i.e., the subjective sense of belonging to an organized collectivity—have a positive effect on a variety of participatory behaviors (Talò et al. 2014)—e.g., community engagement and political commitment—as well as well-being (Albanesi et al. 2007), life satisfaction (Hombrados et al. 2013), and quality of life (Rollero et al. 2014).
5. In their extensive review of the literature on the cross-cultural differences and their impact on psychological process, Oyserman et al. (2002) write that "One of the central claims of cultural psychology is that IND COL [individualism-collectivism] cultural frames set up characteristic ways of making sense of the self, and, indeed, 30 studies examined aspects of this claim. This area of research shows promise; COL does make salient social, collective, and related aspects of the self-concept, at least under some measurement conditions" (p. 33).

Consider now how these instances are seen when viewed through semiotic lens.

Take studies that, as in the case of patient's compliance (cf. point i above), connect the psychological construct with external factors, assumed as determinants (e.g., complexity of the therapeutic regimens, treatment duration, and so on). In cases like these, one has to take into account that what is usually intended as an external factor in the final analysis is the marker of a peculiar global state of affairs that is culturally associated with a normative social meaning. For instance, to be involved in a complex and/or long-term treatment shapes a specific state of relation between patient and practitioner, therefore specific trajectories of sensemaking with respect to others—e.g., the treatment has to be interpreted by the patient in its being more intertwined with daily life; and this is the reason why certain ideational/behavioral patterns interpretable as low/high compliance are more likely to be enacted as interpretants of the experience of the cure.

Now consider the HAPA model (cf. point ii). Similarly to what was said about the linkage between working alliance and efficacy of psychotherapy, the linkage that this model envisages between motivation and habit through the chain of behavioral intentions, self-monitoring and planning must not be seen as false. Rather, the point is how to conceptualize it. Indeed, from a semiotic standpoint, behavioral intentions, self-monitoring, and planning are not independent, self-contained mechanisms that act on each other through a causal transference of energy. Rather, they are part of a pattern of intertwined guiding signs that the cultural milieu provides for people so they can properly maintain their actions. They are meanings concerning the representation of the self, not autonomous, self-contained mechanisms.

As to studies on secure attachment and its positive effect on adolescent's acting-out behaviors (cf. point iii), it has to be noted that the construct is the way of describing a behavioral pattern (and/or a narrative pattern concerning the representation of early relationship—this depends on the instrument adopted to detect it). Thus, also in this case the point is that such a pattern consists of social scripts embedded within the cultural milieu, rather than the cause–effect bond between an inner mechanism and its behavior effect. The same can be said for the low probability that can be associated with acting-out behaviors. To give an analogy, it would be easy to show empirically that regarding a person as a friend reduces the risk of producing acting-out behaviors toward him/her. Yet this does not mean that in the subject's mind there is an isolated module of "friendship," and that the more this module works, the less the subject acts out. Rather, to consider someone a friend is a cultural format that channels certain sequences of signs, making other kinds of signs (and among them acting-out behavior) less probable.

Similarly, from a semiotic-cultural standpoint the concept of "sense of community" (cf. point iv) is not viewed as an independent factor acting from the outside on constructs and phenomena as participatory behaviors, community engagement, sense of well-being, life quality, and satisfaction. Needless to say, the conceptual and operative definition of the construct does not refer to such other facets; yet all of them can be viewed as elements of the same cultural pattern—a vision of life in terms of engagement in a meaningful, positive, interpersonal bond that generates a sense of identity and belongingness.

This is even more evident in the case of cross-cultural studies like those reviewed by Oyserman et al. (2002) (cf. point v): the fact that "COL[lectivism] does make salient social, collective, and related aspects of the self-concept" can be conceived of as a causal relation only insofar as one assumes that collectivism is an independent characteristic of the cultural milieu that, as such, acts upon the individual's sense of self. On the other hand, if one resists the seductive temptation to multiply entities, one can recognize that what appears at a certain level as collectivism is nothing but a pattern of elements, with a certain form of the sense of self among them. Accordingly, collectivism and "social, collective, and related aspects of the self-concept" are not two different "things" that the research discovers have an empirical connection, but two ways of seeing the same process, based on different units of observation.

The Black Box Issue

The vast majority of empirical research in psychology does not assume the relation among constructs in terms of semiotic pars-pro-toto implications. Rather the more or less implicit assumption is that constructs refer to entities (i.e., mechanisms/characteristics/factors) that are endowed with their own functioning and are independent of each other, and can therefore be considered in terms of a cause–effect relation.

This approach must not be considered lacking value—it would be mindless to take all the psychological empirical knowledge produced over decades and put it in a bucket of epistemic waste. Rather, the point is to recognize that the theoretical (and practical) status of this knowledge must be different from what is traditionally presumed. Thus, any regularities that might be detected by empirical studies are not due to the invariant functioning of underpinning psychological processes; rather, they are the phenomenic manifestation of cultural patterns of sensemaking. Accordingly, empirical psychological research is a way of describing a cultural world, rather than of explaining psychological events. It is a form of *cultural epidemiology*: a mode of research that makes explicit the implicit cultural meanings comprising the common sense of various populations. Again, this function is relevant because these linkages are not necessarily clear before they are made explicit; sometimes, they can even prove to be surprising (though often studies seem to discover the best thing since sliced bread). For instance, a study carried out recently in Kenya—in a context where many households reported a lack of cash as an impediment to investing in preventive health products, such as insecticide-treated mosquito nets—showed that just providing people with a lockable metal box, a padlock, and a passbook that a household simply labels with the name of a preventive health product, led to a 66–75% increase in savings and investment in these products (Dupas and Robinson 2013).

On the other hand, this cultural epidemiology is not enough, as it hides, rather than overcomes, the fundamental need for understanding the causal mechanism underpinning the alleged cause–effect relation between purportedly discrete entities. This need is both theoretical and practical. From a theoretical standpoint, the detection of empirical regularities tells us little or nothing about the processes and mechanisms by which these regularities occur, the way and the circumstances where they occur. In other words, the empirical analysis of the co-variation among variables leads, at the most, to see *what* happen, but not *why*. We see the relation between input and output, but their relation remains locked in the *black box*.

An instructive example of this methodological issue is provided by the research on the psychotherapy process. The last three decades have been devoted to analyzing the co-variation between specific characteristics of the psychotherapeutic exchange (e.g., work alliance, narratives, characteristics of the patient and therapist, level of motivation) and outcome. In so doing, a huge amount of factors that have been shown to affect the outcome of psychotherapy have been listed. Yet, why these factors play the role they play is not clear, or, if it is, it is for commonsensical reasons. In order to understand this properly, we must model the processes as such, namely as an overall dynamics whose ways of working enable certain factors to be structured into patterns detectable by empirical research. Physics provides a clear example of what this means for explicative theory-building. Indeed, when gravity was discovered, it had a descriptive valence; it stated that bodies have a specific reciprocal relation of attraction, mapped by the Newtonian formula. Einstein' theory of general relativity went beyond such a descriptive level, clarifying that the phenomenon of gravitational attraction is due to the curvature of space. And after Einstein, the current effort is to identify the particle (graviton) mediating gravity, and in so doing taking a step ahead in the direction of opening the black box.

As mentioned, the need to take a peek inside the black box is a practical necessity too. Indeed, it is the only way to develop a theory of change that frames psychological interventions (Salvatore 2016b). Needless to say, a certain state of affairs can be modified by trial and error or through the generalization of methods that proved to be efficacious in other contexts; yet a scientific approach to change should consist of the development of methods designed to affect the causative mechanism underpinning the target phenomenon. The difference between the two approaches is the same as that alchemy and chemistry.

Psychology is not unaware of the risk of remaining at a descriptive level if the box remains black. Yet the main solutions that have been found—or at least the solutions that are currently up-to-the-minute—are, on the one hand, to search for intermediate constructs mediating the relation between independent and dependent variables, and, on the other hand, to leave neuroscience the task of looking for determinants. In the former case, the effort of opening the black box proved to be a Sisyphean task, because, since the logic of a causal link among separate entities is maintained, the problem of understanding the mechanisms returns asymptotically any time a mediator effect is detected. As to the latter case, as is also pointed out by Smedslund in this volume, even without discussing the enormous theoretical problems associated with such a reductionist approach, in the final analysis it is a kind of epistemic suicide—psychology surrenders to the actually complex, yet central mission of building explicative models and delegates such as a mission into another scientific field.

Semantic and Semiotic Relations Are, However, Empirical Facts

The considerations made above leads to the question, is there an alternative? How can psychology escape from the Scylla of descriptivism and the Charybdis of neuroscientific reductionism? Smedslund's response, PL, provides a brilliant and consistent strategy since psychological phenomena are set in the network of meanings embedded in psychological common sense, psychology should focus on making explicit this commonsensical framework. Yet, though this answer has the merit of indicating the strategy, it does not provide all that is needed to accomplish it. This is so for two main reasons.

First, it implies a monolithic view of common sense, as if it were a single, invariant self-contained, internally consistent block of meanings that can be described in formal terms. From a theoretical standpoint, this view involves reifying the meaning, as if it were an entity with its own life, independent of, and coming before, the dynamics of the sensemaking embedded in it (for a discussion of this view of meaning and its limits, see Salvatore 2016a, cap. 1–2). From a methodological standpoint, such a view prevents the possibility of recognizing the dynamicity and situatedness, and thus, the heterogeneity, of the cultural milieu (Ciavolino et al. 2017): Through their ongoing interpretative activity, people make specific areas of meaning pertinent—backgrounding many other potential alternatives—and they do so as the way of shaping, keeping stable, mediating, and regulating their relation with the world. Thus, even concepts that may seem primitive and basic (e.g., intention, emotion, motivation) are inherently polysemic, in the sense that they are signs open to a variety of uses and in so doing they acquire their local meaning. In sum, common sense is not a self-contained semantic and semiotic structure—it is an ongoing dynamics of interpretative activity. Hence, a formal system is able to grasp it just as clumsily as a fork can catch a cake of soap.

Second, to assume that psychology cannot be an empirical science means throwing the baby of empirical research out with the bathwater of the research model based on detecting a cause–effect relation among separate variables. Beyond the metaphor, making the commonsensical meaning underpinning psychological processes explicit is an important task, but it is only half the story. Psychology must also take on the task of understanding *why*, and *from what conditions*, commonsensical meaning gets its form in the circumstances where people make sense of their experiences. And this means that semantic and semiotic relations are not empirical when one considers them in their content but once the inherent plurality of common sense is recognized, they are empirical in being contingent acts of meaning performed within situated activity of interpretation (Austin 1962). To use an analogy with geometry, the relation between the properties of a triangle of having three sides and having 180° as the sum of their angles is not empirical because both are (broadly speaking) implied conceptually by the term "triangle." Thus, we do not need to calculate any correlations between these properties over a set of empirical instances of triangles to know it. Yet, if one takes into account that geometry is not a monolithic block, but can take many forms and in accordance to different spatial models (i.e., non-Euclidian spaces), it should be possible to recognize that to claim the relations between three sides and the sum of angles = 180° in any triangle is a contingent act making a given form of geometry pertinent with respect to the others. As such, it is an empirical fact that needs to be explained in terms of the identification of the causes that determine its condition of existence.

Thus, psychological science should neither confine itself to describing or making daily life meanings explicit; it has to go beyond common sense in order to explain its local organization and manifestations. This mission is central, and it appears even more relevant if one takes into account that psychological science aims to develop models of intervention (Salvatore 2016b) designed to promote psychological change.

We Have to Choose the Right Form of Causation, Not to Eliminate It

As said, the explanation of the semantic and semiotic relation (in their being acts of interpretation) does not lend itself to be investigated in terms of cause–effect linkages. This is so for the evident reason that, as we have said above, acts of interpretation are not bodies that exchange energy with each other, but they interact with each other in terms of the pars-pro-toto semiotic relation.

However, by recognizing the inadequacy of cause–effect logic, one is not committed to absolutely eliminate the notion of causation nor the view of psychology as empirical science. Rather, it leads to rely on a different form of causation: immanent and constitutive (formal causation, in Aristotelian terms). According to this view, understanding a psychological process means modeling its immanent dynamics, namely the way its organization constrains/guides its evolution through time, due to the field conditions in which it is embedded (for a discussion of psychosocial process in terms of constitutiveness, see Heft 2013).

This means that one moves from searching for cause–effect linkages between discrete elements to modeling how the process as a whole works and in so doing defines temporal relationships between its local spatial-temporal states. To use an image, if one wants to understand the movements of a couple of dancers, it would be senseless to consider the movement of one as the (efficient) cause of the partner's following movement; instead, one should understand the inner dynamic organizational pattern making up the dance— whether it is a tango, a waltz, or the like; the movements of the dancers will acquire meaning when projected over this dynamic pattern. The study of the psychotherapy process provides an example of this approach.

Although the dominant trend in psychological research has been to focus on the search for discrete factors presumed to have a causal impact on outcome, some researchers (e.g., Rocco et al. 2017; for a review, see Salvatore and Gennaro 2015) have provided models of the global functioning of the clinical exchange, namely a map of the dynamic organization underpinning its phenomenical course. The understanding of this dynamic organization enables us to make an explicit hypothesis as to why certain psychotherapies are efficacious whereas others are not, as well as why certain factors play a role in making the difference.

Incidentally, the idea of immanent formal causation does not mean that some form of teleological view is adopted. Indeed, the recognition of the immanency of the sensemaking dynamics implies that its ongoing reproduction is not a purpose, motivating and orienting the process from the outside. In other words, the dynamics is reproduced not as the way of pursuing a purpose, but just because the immanent organization of the dynamics is the constraint that determines its following state. The organization simply works and the fact that it works enables the observer to describe it as being reproduced over time.

To use an analogy, the reproduction of the process looks like the reproduction of a language over time—people do not use the language in order to keep it alive. Rather, people speak within the constraint of the language organization (the semantic and syntactic relations which make that language just that language and not another) and in so doing the language works and can be recognized by the observer as reproducing itself over time.

The Complementarity of Abstraction and Abduction for Empirical Psychology

It has to be recognized that to investigate sensemaking in terms of formal causation requires a different methodological approach than the one generally adopted in psychology. In my view, what is required is to combine dialectically abstract theory and abductive analysis of local phenomena (for details, see Salvatore 2017; Lauro-Grotto et al. 2009; Salvatore et al. 2009; Salvatore and Valsiner 2010).

Abstract theory is abstract in the sense that it is made up of *intensional* concepts, that is, concepts that model specific forms of relation among potentially infinite empirical occurrences. For instance, the content of the notion of "sign" consists of the relation "X stands for Y", regardless what X and Y are. The abstraction is required because the formal causation (i.e., the dynamics underpinning the phenomenical occurrences) has no empirical content; indeed, it is the particular relation (what Maturana and Varela (1980) call "organization") that remains invariant through the ongoing change of the phenomenical occurrences (the "structure," as Maturana and Varela call it). For instance, the organizational pattern "to count" reproduces over time as the relation (n+1) that remains the same through the variation of the phenomenic occurrences (i.e., the sequence of numbers). In other words, abstraction enables theory to encompass the (potentially infinite) variability of phenomenical occurrences and to explain such variability in terms of the whole dynamics (i.e., the form) underpinning it.

It should be pointed out that abstract theory is by definition unable to provide an understanding of the concrete, idiosyncratic psychological phenomena, as they occur in the situated circumstances of life. Indeed, due to its intensional nature, abstract theory is focused on the invariant dynamics underpinning the many different contents the psychological process can assume. Here one can find the complementary role of abduction, in the sense of the particular logic of investigation for psychology (Salvatore and Valsiner 2010). According to Peirce, abduction is the form of reasoning that infers the cause from the effect, through the reconstruction of the dynamics mediating between the former and the latter (e.g., Peirce 1897/1932a, 1902/1932b). Thus, abduction is empirical, in the sense that it starts from the datum (the phenomenical occurrences alleged as the effect of what has to be inferred) and it aimed to provide an understanding of it. In this it is similar induction and different from deduction—i.e., the form of reasoning that Smedslund (1991) sees as the cornerstone of psycho-logic. On the other hand, unlike induction, abduction does not consider the datum as informative in itself. The phenomenic occurrences become significant only when in terms of the reconstruction of the dynamics linking it to the inferred cause.

Here, one can recognize both the peculiar function of abstraction and abduction as well as their dialectical complementarity. On the one hand, abstract theory models the fundamental dynamics (i.e., the formal cause) underpinning psychological processes, regardless by whom, where, when, for what, the latter are produced. In so doing, it provides the general (intensional) rules framing the abductive interpretation of the psychological phenomena in their local, situated specificity—namely the understanding of why and due to what conditions the dynamics of sensemaking has assumed the exact idiosyncratic configuration it shows in the context of investigation (e.g., a certain relation between two variables). On the other hand, due to the very fact that abduction needs to be framed by abstraction, the former systematically challenges the general theory and in this way enables the latter to develop, in terms of its capacity to satisfy the demand to understand the local phenomenon (Salvatore and Valsiner 2010).

In sum, while it is true that formal causation requires abstraction, it is also true that abstraction is not an end in itself—it is the ground of the empirical, abductive investigation of the psychological phenomena as they manifest locally, in the situated circumstances of life. Common sense, and more in general sensemaking, needs to be studied both in its basic organization and in the contingent forms it assumes within and because of the historical, situated conditions where it unfolds.

Beyond Empiricism

Contemporary psychology tends to consider the objectivity of the datum as the main assurance of scientific validity. Be their behaviors, responses to questionnaires, neuro-images, and the like, the basic idea underlying most psychological research is to leave the empirical occurrences to speak for itself. Theory is seen as the ordered collection of what data have said.

There is a subtle, but highly significant, difference between inductive idea of letting the data speak and the abductive modality of speaking through data. In the latter case, data are used by theory, in order to challenge its heuristic valence and in so doing to develop it (Salvatore and Valsiner 2010). Vygotsky, Piaget, and Freud, just to refer to some of the giants whose shoulders we are standing on, elaborated their theoretical framework as the conceptual tool enabling them to understand the surprising event that data presented them with. Thus, they did not eliminate data, even if they did not use data as the conveyor of self-evident information; rather, they used data as a source of constraint and challenge to their efforts of theory-building: The hysterical symptom was interpreted in the light of the theory of the unconscious, rather than vice versa; the child's cognitive development was interpreted at the light of the general abstract notion of assimilation and accommodation, and so forth.

Today the situation is rather different—a lot of psychological theories are more or less the generalization of the empirical hypothesis surviving the rejection of the null hypothesis. For instance, we know that the therapeutic alliance is important in psychotherapy because studies showed that the greater the former, the better the latter; we know that customer satisfaction fuels loyalty because the empirical association between these two empirical variables is high and significant. Again, we know that a good school climate is a protective factor against dropping out because studies have showed that measures of both constructs are related. And so on and so forth. In the final analysis, psychological theory is less and less a matter of thinking and more and more a matter of measurement and computation—a cognitive bureaucracy.

The combination of abstraction and abduction envisages a different approach, which goes beyond the empiricism of most current psychological research. Indeed, abduction is based and triggered by empirical data; yet, the abductive interpretation implies the theory-driven construction and interpretation of data (Salvatore 2016a). Each datum does not speak for itself, but acquires meaning because of how the general theory frames it. And this means that it is the theory that informs the datum, rather than the datum informing the theory. The theory remains bound to empirical investigation, but not as its direct input. Rather, the theory develops through systematic and recursive efforts to provide relevant resources for interpreting new challenging sets of data.

Conclusion

From the recognition of the semantic and semiotic nature of psychological phenomena, Smedslund has concluded that the core mission of psychological science must be to explicate and systematize common sense. In so doing, he has outlined a research program that makes psychology into an analytic science, like geometry.

In this chapter, I have argued that to recognize the semiotic and semantic valence of psychological constructs, and thus their embeddedness in common sense, is not the same as committing oneself to reduce psychology into some geometry-like inquiry, rejecting the very possibility of empirical knowledge of psychological phenomena. Rather, the recognition of the pseudoempirical nature of psychological constructs provides room to rethink the form of empirical research, in order to make it consistent with the semiotic nature of psychological phenomena.

References

Albanesi, C., Cicognani, E., & Zani, N. (2007). Sense of community, civic engagement and social well-being in Italian adolescents. *Journal of Community and Applied Social Psychology, 17*, 387–406.

Austin, J. (1962). *How to do things with words*. Oxford: Oxford University Press.

Ciavolino, E., Redd, R., Avdi, E., Falcone, M., Fini, V., Kadianaki, I., Kullasepp, K., Mannarini, T., Matsopoulos, A., Mossi, P., Rochira, A., Sammut, G., Santarpia, A., Valsiner, J., Veltri, G. A., & Salvatore, S. (2017). "Views of context". An instrument for the analysis of the cultural 1 milieu. A first validation. *Electronic Journal of Applied Statistical Analysis, 10*(2), 599–628.

Claxton, A. J., Cramer, J., & Pierce, C. (2001). A systematic review of the associations between dose regimens and medication compliance. *Clinical Therapeutics, 23*(8), 1296–1310.

Dupas, P., & Robinson, J. (2013). Why Don't the poor save more? Evidence from health savings experiments. *American Economic Review, 103*(4), 1138–1171.

Grant, R. W., Devita, N. G., Singer, D. E., & Meigs, J. B. (2003). Polypharmacy and medication adherence in patients with type 2 diabetes. *Diabetes Care, 26*(14), 08–12.

Harrè, R., & Secord, P. F. (1972). *The explanation of the social behaviour*. Oxford: Oxford University Press.

Heft, H. (2013). Environment, cognition, and culture: Reconsidering the cognitive map. *Journal of Environmental Psychology, 33*, 14–25.

Hombrados Mendieta, I., Gómez-Giacinto, L., Dominguez-Fuentes, J. M., & García-Leiva, P. (2013). Sense of community and satisfaction with life among immigrants and the native population. *Journal of Community Psychology, 41*, 601–614.

Laible, D., Carlo, G., & Raffaelli, M. (2000). The differential relations of parent and peer attachment to adolescent adjustment. *Journal of Youth and Adolescence, 29*, 45–59.

Laura-Grotto, R. P., Salvatore, S., Gennaro, A., & Gelo, O. (2009). The unbearable dynamicity of psychological processes: Highlights of the psychodynamic theories. In J. Valsiner, P. Molenaar, M. Lyra, & N. Chaudhary (Eds.), *Dynamics process methodology in the social and developmental sciences* (pp. 1–30). New York: Springer.

Maturana, M. R., & Varela, J. F. (1980). *Autopoiesis and cognition. The realization of the living*. Dordrecht, NL: Reidel Publishing.

Noom, M., Dekovic, W., & Meeus, W. (1999). Autonomy, attachment and psychosocial adjustment during adolescence: A double-edge sword. *Journal of Adolescence, 22*, 771–783.

Oyserman, D., Coon, H. M., & Kemmelmeier, M. (2002). Rethinking individualism and collectivism: Evaluation of theoretical assumptions and meta-analysis. *Psychological Bulletin, 128*, 3–72.

Peirce, C. S. (1932a). Harvard lecture on pragmatism. In C. Hartshorne & P. Weiss (Eds.), *Collected papers of Charles Sanders Peirce (Volume II)*. Cambridge, MA: Harvard University Press. [Original version: 1902].

Peirce, C. S. (1932b). On sign. In C. Hartshorne & P. Weiss (Eds.), *Collected papers of Charles Sanders Peirce (Volume II)*. Cambridge, MA: Harvard University Press. [Original version: 1987].

Rocco, D., Gennaro, A., Salvatore, S., Stoycheva, V., & Bucci, W. (2017). ClinicalMutual attunement and the development of therapeutic process: A preliminary study. *Journal of Constructivist Psychology, 30*(4), 371–387. https://doi.org/10.1080/10720537.2016.1227950.

Rollero, C., Gattino, S., & De Piccoli, N. (2014). A gender lens on the quality of life: The role of sense of community, perceived social support, self-reported health and income. *Social Indicators Research, 116*, 887–898.

Salvatore, S. (2016a). *Psychology in black and white. The project for a theory driven science*. Charlotte NC: Information Age Publishing.

Salvatore, S. (2016b). The contingent nature of psychological intervention. From blind spot to basic resource of psychological science. In G. Sammut, J. Foster, S. Salvatore, & R. Andrisano-Ruggieri (Eds.), *Methods of psychological intervention* (*Yearbook of Idiographic Science Series*) (Vol. 7, pp. 13–54). Charlotte NC: InfoAge Publishing.

Salvatore, S. (2017). The formalization of cultural psychology. Reasons and functions. *Integrative Psychological and Behavioral Science, 51*(1), 1–13. https://doi.org/10.1007/s12124-016-9366-2.

Salvatore, S., & Gennaro, A. (2015). Outlines of a general semiotic and dynamic theory of the psychotherapy process. The clinical exchange as communicational field: Theoretical considerations and methodological implications. In O. Gelo, A. Pritz, & B. Rieken (Eds.), *Psychotherapy research* (pp. 195–212). Berlin: Springer.

Salvatore, S., Lauro-Grotto, R., Gennaro, A., & Gelo, O. (2009). Attempts to grasp the dynamicity of intersubjectivity. In J. Valsiner, P. Molenaar, M. Lyra, & N. Chaudhary (Eds.), *Dynamics process methodology in the social and developmental sciences* (pp. 171–190). New York: Springer.

Salvatore, S., & Valsiner, J. (2010). Between the general and the unique: Overcoming the nomothetic *versus* idiographic opposition. *Theory & Psychology, 20*(6), 817–833.

Schwarzer, R., & Luszczynska, A. (2015). Health action process approach. In M. Conner & P. Norman (Eds.), *Predicting health behaviours* (3rd ed., pp. 252–278). Maidenhead, UK: McGraw Hill Open University Press.

Smedslund, J. (1982). Commons sense as psychosocial reality. A reply to Sjöberg. *Scandinavian Journal of Psychology, 23*(1), 79–82.

Smedslund, J. (1988). *Psycho-logic*. Heidelberg: Springer-Verlag.

Smedslund, J. (1991). The pseudoempirical in psychology and the case of psychologic. *Psychological Inquiry, 2*(4), 325–338.

Smedslund, J. (1992). Are Frijda's "laws of emotion" empirical? *Cognition & Emotion, 6*, 435–456.

Smedslund, J. (1995). Psychologic: Common sense and the pseudoempirical. In A. Smith, R. Harré, & L. V. Langenhove (Eds.), *Rethinking psychology* (pp. 196–206). London, UK: Sage.

Smedslund, J. (2016). Why psychology cannot be an empirical science. *Integrative Psychological and Behavioural Science, 50*(2), 185–195.

Talò, C., Mannarini, T., & Rochira, A. (2014). Sense of community and community participation: A meta-analytic review. *Social Indicators Research, 117*, 1–28.

Valsiner, J. (2007). *Culture in minds and societies. Foundations of cultural psychology*. New Delhi: Sage Publications.

Vlasnik, J. J., Aliotta, S. L., & DeLor, B. (2005). Medication adherence: Factors influencing compliance with prescribed medication plans. *The Case Manager, 16*(2), 47–51.

Chapter 12
A Priori Afterthoughts: Continuing the Dialogue on Psycho-Logic

Tobias G. Lindstad

Re: Person I knew
—Bill Evans

Sometimes our answers are not quite right because not all the questions we have asked are quite right either. This may even be so when our major conclusions are groundbreakingly bold and on the right track. Jan Smedslund's (1988, 2012b) efforts to advance Psycho-logic (PL) is a significant case in point, or so I argue. The problem is that PL has been portrayed not only as *a priori knowledge*, traditionally characterized as justified independently of empirical evidence, but also as *psychological common-sense*, what any person takes for granted about any person. However, the question of which assertions are knowable a priori must not be conflated with the question of which assertions constitute common-sense. These questions must be dealt with separately, and pace Smedslund, the former must be given priority.

However, in line with a growing number of psychologists (e.g., Harré 1999; Valsiner 1999, 2012; Martin et al. 2003; Brinkmann 2011; Salvatore 2016), I welcome Smedslund's seminal critique (1991a) of pseudo-empirical research; indeed, we should not mindlessly put assertions to empirical test if they are knowable by other means. One must also notice that although this request is put in negative terms, it is not the result of pursuing destructive aims. Conversely, it paves the way for a constructive alternative by liberating psychology from a restrictive paradigm that exclusively emphasizes empirical research.

However, characterizing PL as common-sense does not sufficiently explain how the assertions of PL are a priori knowable. Thus, I propose a revised account that rests on more fundamental capacities to reflect on the possible relations between the properties of what our concepts refer to, regardless of whether assertions about these relations are already taken for granted or not. This calls for a revised notion of a priori psychological knowledge that takes the recent philosophical discussion on the roles of experience in a priori justification into account (Casullo and Thurow 2013; Jackson 2015). It also implies that PL comprises a more varied body of knowledge than hitherto recognized. Hopefully, this may not only convince the

T. G. Lindstad (✉)
Asker, Norway

T. G. Lindstad et al. (eds.), *Respect for Thought*, Theory and History in the Human and Social Sciences, https://doi.org/10.1007/978-3-030-43066-5_12

scholars who have acknowledged Smedslund's critique of pseudo-empiricism also to recognize his positive contribution but may also lead researchers raised by the empirical zeitgeist to open their minds for a prolific alternative.

Dialogue Continued: Thinking of Persons

Calling for cooperational preciseness, Smedslund (2012b) has always been eager to specify what he means and not, and as such, he has been well aware that the notion of common-sense psychology has often been used in ways that differ from his. Thus, although different in content, Smedslund's use of the term is clearly in line with G. E. Moore's (1925) overall characterization of common-sense as including only those assertions that all of us believe and find absurd to deny and not every culturally fashioned proverb and superstitious belief that has been commonly believed. Accordingly, my claim is not that Smedslund has conflated a priori knowledge with scientifically dubious assertions. What I call into question is the extent to which we must take for granted that every person always takes every assertion of PL for granted. Pace Smedslund (2012a), I think we must not, because, if we do, we do not only demand too much of human beings for them to count as conceptually competent, but we also underestimate their potentials for inquiring into the world they inhabit.

Although PL was initially presented as an attempt to make explicit the implicit conceptual system embedded in ordinary language and common-sense thinking (Smedslund 2012b), Smedslund has continuously worked to improve his understanding of PL, and partly, through engaging in critical dialogue. In response to critique from Wittgenstein-inspired scholars (e.g., Shotter 1994; Parrott and Harré, 1991) Smedslund (1997) abandoned his initial aim to provide so-called classical definitions of natural language terms by clarifying sufficient and necessary conditions for their proper use. However, his fascination for the linguistic work of clarifying semantical primitives and lexical universals purportedly common to all ordinary languages (Goddard and Wierzbicka 2014) later led Smedslund (2008, 2011) to maintain that a scientific approach requires that there are invariant components in the use of the same words and that we must specify these in our scholarly terminology via definitions.

Moreover, responding to Harré's (1999) suggestion that many propositions of PL are not analytic but synthetic a priori, and also taking into account the arguments of Kukla (2001) that a purported Kantian notion of a priori contingent belief is needed for grounding psychology as a science, Smedslund (1999, 2012a, p. 660—1) confessed that his initial account of PL did not sufficiently differentiate between logical relations built into language and basic assumptions that do not follow from the meaning of natural language terms. This move was already anticipated by his earlier claim that the task is not to study the embodiment of psychological concepts in language, but the intuitions expressed by means of language (Smedslund 1993, p. 10). What is clear, however, is that he no longer understands PL solely as an attempt to clarify conceptual relations between natural language terms and that he has increasingly focused on basic assertions that must, purportedly, be taken for granted, although they do not follow from the meaning of terms involved. Thus, on Smedslund's latest account PL is not about relations between words or semantic regularities but about what we do and must take for granted in our understanding of the world.

I suggest modifying the project even more radically by downplaying the relevance of the notion of common-sense. Thus, I depart from Smedslund's (2002, p. 69) account of Psycho-logic (PL) as an explication of what we all know implicitly about psychology. This may seem to run counter to the very project as he has not only emphasized the notion of psychological common-sense from before the term Psycho-logic (PL) was coined, but he has done so even more strongly in later publications. By contrast, I argue that PL is not only not about words, but it is also not about common-sense. What matters is to make sense of persons, and as such, what is *potentially* a priori *knowable* may in principle exceed what is already known.

If Not Common-Sense, Then What?

In his book from 1972 (p. 78, my italics), Smedslund mentioned three features of his understanding of psychological common-sense that seem to have stayed with him since: (1) It is normally *unreflective* (unconscious), (2) it is *shared by all ordinary* persons, and (3) *when made explicit, it is* compellingly *self-evident*. At this stage, Smedslund did not characterize the third feature as having to do with common-sense being a priori but variously explained its purported self-evident character by characterizing it as comprising tautologies or analytic assertions. Although he (Smedslund 1991a) later changed this, there is a question to what extent this change was substantial or whether it was simply a change of vocabulary. Moreover, in relation to this early characterization of psychological common-sense, Smedslund (1972) seems to have argued that it is only *when* it is *made explicit* that it is self-evident. However, although it is indeed hard to realize that anything is self-evident without considering it explicitly, it is unlikely that Smedslund meant that it is *only if* psychological assertions are made explicit and recognized as self-evident that they are common-sense. On the contrary, as mentioned, he has persistently characterized PL as taken for granted, at least implicitly, by any person.

Furthermore, already when presenting the first full-version of PL, Smedslund (1988, p. 68) did not only characterize PL as shared by all ordinary persons, but he also contended that persons believe that all persons share the complete system of valid psychological propositions understood as common-sense psychology. Not long after, (Smedslund 1990, p. 50, my italics) he also added that PL, although formulated so as to refer to what exists for persons, is exclusively concerned with what *all competent* persons regards as correct, and this has been emphasized even more strongly in later versions. Thus, in earlier versions (Smedslund 1988, 1990, 1997; 2004; 2009) all assertions were formulated so as to be about every person (P), whereas later (Smedslund 2011, 2012a, b) these were reformulated so as to be about what every person (P) thinks about any person (O). For instance, the so-called hedonism-axiom was originally formulated as "P wants to feel good and wants not to feel bad" (Smedslund 1997, 2009) whereas in later versions as "P thinks that O wants to feel good and that O wants not to feel bad" (Smedslund 2011, p. 131). Apparently, this relates to the following characterizations of PL:

> the axioms do not describe what persons are, but what [persons] *take for granted about* every person. [PL] is about how persons view persons, that is, about subjective phenomena (Smedslund 2012a, p. 661).

> [PL] is an attempt to make explicit what is already implicit in language and common sense … the axioms are constructions applying to all social realities, and should be shared by everyone … It should be noted that they refer to how we automatically conceive of persons, rather than to what persons are (Smedslund 2012b, p. 297).

However, these characterizations are too restrictive, and the added clause " … thinks that O" is a change in the wrong direction: There's no need to avoid inquiring into what persons are like and exclusively inquire into what persons take for granted. Relatedly, although Smedslund (2012a, p. 300) has admitted that the following paragraph may sound problematic, it is unclear whether his reasons for thinking so are the same as mine:

> An axiom should not only be subjectively necessarily true, but it should also describe how people really are … It should describe persons in a way that we must subscribe to, because we are persons, but the descriptions should also be veridical. In other words, the axioms should describe predispositions to conceive of humans correctly. …[PL] is a project attempting to describe the basic features of how we must perceive persons, which also is how we agree about what persons really are … [PL] does not originate in experiences of people's behaviour, but describes how we must experience people (Smedslund 2012b, p. 300).

Could it be that Smedslund has thought that *how* something really is, and *what* it is, are different questions, and thus, that his claim that PL should describe *how* people really *are* (p. 300, my italics) does not contradict his claim that PL does *not* refer to or describe *what* persons *are* (p. 297, my italics)? However, pace Smedslund, I do not only think that what persons *are* is (at least partly) determined by *how* they really *are*, but I also find it problematic to assume that persons simply happen to conceive of themselves in ways that are necessarily correct. It is not that PL should speak the truth about persons that is problematic, but rather the idea that this is a competency any person simply has.

Thus, to the extent that PL describes persons correctly, I have no quarrel with characterizing it as a body of knowledge that we *ought* to subscribe to. I also accept that parts of PL are about subjective phenomena, in the sense that they describe what persons may think and want. What I find dubious is that PL is about how persons necessarily view persons and that all parts of PL belong to what Smedslund (1997, 2002) has called social reality, that is, what everyone thinks (more or less explicitly) that everyone thinks that everyone thinks. I agree with Smedslund (2011, p. 134) that PL should describe real characteristics of persons, but where he has argued that these characteristics concern what all persons take for granted about persons, I argue that PL is, and should be, concerned with what persons are like, whether anyone takes it for granted or not. This also seems compatible with Smedslund's (2002, p. 69) earlier claims that persons encountering something unexpected really become surprised, and persons perceiving someone as lacking self-control really become less trusting. However, this is true of persons whether any person takes it for granted or not. Accordingly, I rather defend the first version of the hedonism-axiom than the later one: Persons want to feel good and want not to feel bad[1]. However, this is not only part of *how* persons are, but is also partly constitutive of *what* persons are; any person *is* something that wants to feel good and wants not to feel bad.

Notice, however, that it is not that Smedslund (1972, 2011) cannot be right that psychological common-sense can exist as a relatively stable structure. He might even be right that we are predisposed to conceive of each other in line with such a structure from a very early age. However, these are empirical questions and not something that we can take for granted that everyone takes for granted that everyone takes for granted. The only sense in which one *must* think this comes from wanting to know what is true about persons. Although the hedonism-axiom may be one among more examples of assertions that may very likely amount to common-sense, other parts of PL could just as well amount to *uncommon sense*. A prominent example to be discussed in below section "Conditions of Trustworthiness" is Smedslund's frequent assertion that there are five necessary and sufficient conditions for trust to occur.

Beyond Spectacles and Balloons

In a recent publication on what follows from what we all know about human beings Smedslund (2012a, p. 658) has argued that it is likely that the axioms of PL reflect *a shared inborn* disposition to understand persons in a certain way. On the other hand, Smedslund (2012a, p. 668) has also raised the intriguing question of whether some persons do not rely on all the axioms in some situations. Although this question is explicitly about axioms, it should be noticed that Smedslund's (1988, p. 68, 2012b) characterization of PL as common-sense concerns not only the axioms of PL but the complete system of valid psychological propositions, including the theorems of PL. Thus, supposed Smedslund is right that all persons take all axioms of PL for granted, there is still a question whether all persons also take the theorems that can allegedly be deduced from the axioms for granted.

[1] Of course, persons can want to feel bad when this involves, or is expected to involve, something experienced as good. Masochism, self-harming, self-flagellation and saving others at the expense of oneself are thus not counterexamples. However, would someone knowing that they will never gain anything positive out of it still want to be in extreme, all-encompassing, and endless physical and psychic pain? If such a person can exist, I guess this will count as a counterexample.

The possibility that some persons do not rely on all axioms has admittedly decreased with Smedslund's (2004, 2011) efforts to reduce the number of axioms from 56 in the 1997-version to eight in the latest presentation (2012b). Interestingly, the hedonism-axiom is no longer on the list, and even if Smedslund as late as in 2011 (p. 134) argued that we cannot think that persons do not attribute vulnerability to each other, the vulnerability-axiom has also been removed. However, this is clearly not because he now rejects that persons want to feel good and not bad, and that this can be prevented from happening, but rather because he has considered it possible to deduce these assertions from other axioms. However, although I do assert that persons *are* vulnerable[2], and also think that we tend to learn this very early in our lives, it is still possible not only to think wrongly about persons but also not to take for granted everything that is true about persons. Actually, this is to be expected.

Although the chances for bumping into someone more than two years old who does not know that persons are vulnerable is vanishingly small, it is quite unrealistic to think of knowers in general as logically omniscient beings who know all the deductive consequences of all they know. Ordinary people, even extraordinary people, do not believe all the logical consequences of their beliefs (Stalnaker 1999, p. 241—2). Thus, the metaphor often borrowed by Smedslund (e.g., 2012b) from Israel (1979) that the task of clarifying what can be known a priori about persons is like inflating a balloon from the inside is misleading. Although Smedslund is right that there are limits to what we can come to learn about people, the possibility of clarifying what is a priori knowable does not depend upon that all of us already know all about all the details that might be revealed (on inside surfaces of dilating balloons). Some assertions can in principle be *knowable* a priori even if our cognitive limitations have hitherto prevented us from knowing them (Soames 2010, p. 137). For instance, that the Pythagorean theorem is a priori knowable does not entail that it is already tacitly familiar to us all. This point extends well beyond mathematics and geometry to psychological theories and psychotherapy research; that is, many psychologically relevant assertions can be a priori *knowable* even if not yet a priori *known*.

A striking example is the notorious claim of Wampold and Imel (2015) that the empirical data falsifies the so-called Medical Model of psychotherapy. Nothing is wrong with this conclusion, except that it is*pseudo-empirical*[3]. That psychotherapy can be studied and practiced as if it was a specific pill with specific, context-transcending, regular, and statistically replicable effects is nonsense. Yet, it is unfortunately not common-sense. For instance, Kennair et al. (2002, p. 9) have claimed that though there are variations between humans, there is also a relatively uniform human nature, which purportedly means that interventions working on large groups

[2] Being both physically and psychologically invulnerable is hardly possible as it requires not bothering about whether any of one's wants are fulfilled or not. Accordingly, what was described in the hedonism- and vulnerability axioms can be treated as corollaries of a more fundamental mentality-axiom; persons think and want something (cf. Smedslund 2012b).

[3] This is also pointed out by Ekeland (2020) Chap. 19, this volume.

of persons will probably work for random individuals. The point here is not so much to prosecute this claim (however, see Lindstad (2020, forthcoming) and Stänicke and Lindstad (2020)) as it is to demonstrate that people may not only believe things that contradict PL but may also deny what PL implies. However, had the larger community of psychological researchers acknowledged the relevance of avoiding pseudo-empirical research they would probably have known that psychotherapy cannot ever become anything like a context-transcending pill with regular and replicable effects. This is aptly demonstrated by Smedslund's (2009) argument that RCTs cannot ever deal adequately with the fact that persons are someone for whom something exists. Here is a shortened version: None of us will ever make sense of things from the exact same perspective as any other, and no experience can ever be undone. As we are also continuously susceptible to change by attaching new meanings to things from within ever-evolving and irreversibly unique contexts, we cannot take for granted that persons will react in the same ways on the same event. Hence, there is no other option than to qualify our services one therapy-process at the time. Alas, no matter how convincing this argument is, it is not common-sense.

Thus, in contrast to Smedslund's (1988, p. 275; 1991b, p. 382) characterization of PL as a project aiming to understand the glasses through which we look at psychological phenomena and not these phenomena as such, we can do more with vision than look at eyeglasses (cf. Williamson 2007, p. 46). There is more to sight than staring at spectacles, and PL is more properly understood as an attempt to calibrate our concepts so as to cut psychologically relevant properties of persons at its joints. This calls for a refined notion of a priori knowledge that takes issue with Smedslund's Fregean rationalism (see the below section "Moderating Inclinations Toward Descriptivism"). However, to pave the way for this argument, the Wittgensteinian critique of PL must first be addressed.

If Not in Language Nor in Common-Sense, Then Where?

According to Hacker (1996), the views of Wittgenstein and Quine converged in the dictum "Don't ask for the meaning, ask for the use" and the related denial that ordinary languages are calculi with determinate rules that fix necessary and sufficient conditions for the application of meaningful expressions. Similar contentions seem to have influenced the earlier critique of Smedslund's views. As mentioned, Smedslund has responded to this critique not only by (i) abandoning attempts to classically define natural language terms but also (ii) by replying that PL is not about relations between words but rather (iii) about what we take for granted in our understanding of the world. I approve of both of the first two steps, but find the third to be questionable, not least because Smedslund (2012b, p. 297, my italics) has also postulated that the axioms of PL are *inborn* in the sense of being shaped by complex interactions between early experiences and genetically endowed tendencies. Let me explain:

In certain passages, Wittgenstein (1953, p. 75[e]) seem to have argued that agreements not only in how we use words but also in judgments and forms of life, are required for language-based communication. Relatedly, Glock (1996, p. 166—8) has argued that hermeneutical processes require sharing not only cognitive but also conative and affective features, such as the refusal of unpleasant things. However, this is different from Smedslund's (2012b, p. 297) contention that the axioms of PL cover attributions normally made by every member of Homo sapiens to every other member and that they are inborn. That these aspects must be shared for understanding to take place does not mean that all persons must know about these aspects. Thus, although I agree with Smedslund that PL is not primarily about how we use words, neither is it about what everyone takes for granted. As mentioned, this does not mean that the assertions of PL cannot amount to common-sense, but that this is not necessarily the case, and that PL is more fundamentally about the relations between properties of persons. By not having taken this full step toward a realist picture of PL, Smedslund also seems to have been prevented from taking a full step away from basing PL on classical definitions and ordinary language. On the one hand, he (Smedslund 2012b, p. 295) has confessed that his original understanding of PL ignored that ordinary language is resistant to the precision he requested. On the other hand, he has upheld PL as an attempt to make explicit what is already implicit not only in common-sense but also in language (p. 297). As such, he has argued that instead of leaving the purported structure of psychological common-sense unanalyzed, PL represents an attempt *to create a calculus* and *a technical language*, a general *deductive system,* from a purported *conceptual framework* of psychological common-sense (Smedslund 2002, p. 69; 2012a, p. 660; 2016b, p. 56). This also accords with his upheld contentions that a scientific approach requires that we specify invariant components in our professional terminology (Smedslund 2011).

Probably, Wittgensteinians will be happier with Smedslund's original aim of clarifying assertions embedded in ordinary language than with his later characterization of PL as not about the relations between words. As they will also emphasize Wittgenstein's notion of family resemblance that there are rarely invariant core components tying all uses of ordinary language terms together, they will probably argue that no more than clarifying word usage is needed for avoiding pseudo empirical research. As such, I agree with McEachrane (2009, 2020) that it is often not needed to clarify invariant components in ordinary language to avoid pseudo empirical research. Yet, pace McEachrane, there is more to gain from the notion of pseudo-empirical research than that we should remind ourselves of how we use words. Importantly, there is a further question of what our *concepts* are for and not. As there is no current consensus on what concepts are (Laurence and Margolis 2019), notice that as I use the term, I'm not so much concerned about whether or not concepts are building blocks of thoughts, kinds of mental representations, abilities to use or produce representations, abilities to classify, or abilities to follow rules of language. More fundamentally, I consider concepts to be abilities to *recognize* and *keep track of* phenomena. Thus, pace the Wittgensteinians, scrutinizing how we use words does not exhaust our abilities to avoid pseudo-empirical research, and pace Smedslund, what PL is about is more fundamental than purported common-sensical structures. Rather, *PL concernsa priori knowable relations between properties of the world that might, or must necessarily, belong to persons.*

In contrast to what has been argued both by Smedslund and Wittgensteinian[4] scholars (e.g., McEachrane 2009, 2020; Smedlund 2020), this implies that PL may in principle concern what is not already familiar. It is not that Danziger (1997, p. 5) was wrong that most psychologically relevant terms were in use long before anyone used them to identify objects of psychological research. Conversely, Smedslund's (1988, p. 2) call to get rid of the illusion of doing empirical research in unknown domains is to the point. Yet, although I fully comply with Smedslund's (2012b, p. 301; 2016a, p. 186) characterization of PL as concerned with clarifying what it is possible to know about persons without gathering more empirical data, there is no reason to delimit PL to clarifying a skeleton system of concepts underlying ordinary languages (cf. 1988, p. 2) or an already implicitly familiar structure of common-sense (cf. 1997). Rather, PL is about recognizing and keeping track of features in the real world. To fortify these conclusions, it is needed to take issue with Smedslund's Fregean inclinations.

Moderating Inclinations Toward Descriptivism

A kind of Fregean spirit seems to permeate Smedslund's writings on PL. An illustrative example is his (Smedslund 1991a, p. 327–8) early discussion of how people acquire the ability to label their own and others' state of sadness correctly. Like Smedslund, I find this question intriguing, and I agree that we often speak of sadness as something that may exist without behavioral or bodily display and that such expressions only indicate feelings (crying may indicate sadness, but one may not only be sad without crying, one may also cry when not sad). However, Smedslund also argued that the solution was to provide a conceptual definition containing logically necessary and sufficient criteria of sadness[5], and though he later abandoned this idea of providing classical definitions of ordinary language terms, he has maintained that a scientific approach requires that we specify invariant components defining our scholarly terms. Thus, his arguments seem persistently (perhaps unknowingly) to have been confirming to a description theory of which Frege was an early proponent.

The descriptivist model was initially proposed to account for the meaning of singular terms[6] and has later been extended to general terms[7]. In this model, words refer in virtue of being associated with a specific descriptive content that serves to identify a particular object or individual; the *referent*. Descriptivism thus combines

[4] cf. Wittgenstein (1953, §109, p. 40)[e]

[5] Purportedly, how we feel when something we want is seen as unattainable or irrevocably lost.

[6] Applying to one particular thing such as proper names and definite descriptions. like "Smedslund" and "the author of Psycho-logic".

[7] Applying to more than one thing, such as natural terms like "gold" and psychological terms like "sad".

(i) a psychological claim that for various kinds of terms, there is for each term a description that all speakers who understand the term tacitly associate with it and (ii) a semantical claim that the referent of each term is partly determined by this specific description. Thus, purportedly, whatever any term refers to, its use must satisfy a specific description that all speakers who understand the term tacitly associates with it. This description corresponds to what Frege spoke of as the *sense*[8] of the term, which has often been thought of as shared by competent speakers of a language (Spicer 2010; Robertson 2012; Michaelson and Reimer 2019).

Something strikingly similar to descriptivism has underlain Smedslund's arguments from his (1972) early characterization of psychological common-sense as *shared* by all *ordinary* persons to his (2011) later argument that a scientific approach requires that we specify invariant components in our terminology. Relatedly, at transitional stages, he (1990, p. 51; 1991a, p. 335) argued that the ability to specify such invariants is assured by researchers being *relevantly informed* as *competent* speakers of ordinary languages, and thus, that PL is a system of psychologically relevant implications taken for granted and shared by *all competent* users of such languages.

However, Kripke (1980) seminally challenged descriptivism by arguing that definite descriptions such as "the author of Psycho-Logic" and the name "Smedslund" cannot have the same content and cannot express the same proposition. Allegedly, this is because the sentence "the author of Psycho-Logic is the author of Psycho-Logic" is necessarily (noncontingently) true while the sentence "Smedslund is the author of Psycho-Logic" is only possibly (contingently) true as it describes something that could have been otherwise. It has also been argued that the first sentence is knowable a priori while the second is not, and that if the semantical claim of descriptivism that descriptive content determines reference is right, then the content of "Smedslund" cannot be the same as the content of "the author of Psycho-Logic" (cf. Robertson 2012). Moreover, as pointed out by Soames (2003, p. 367), it is not clear that speakers invariably have implicitly in mind, among all the descriptions they might associate with a given name, some precise reference-fixing description for it. As intriguingly put by Millikan (2005):

> I can recognize my daughters Aino … and Natasha … in hundreds of different ways. Now … you can use their names too, but are you able to recognize them in any of my ways? True, both of us now know them as my daughters. But … [t]hat there must be some inner psychological state common to all who comprehendingly use a proper name seems entirely out of the question (p. 133).

Relatedly, in response to the attempts to extend the description-theory from singular terms to general terms, it has been replied that we must allow for minimal requirements on semantic competence (Russell 2010, p. 190). For instance, Williamson (2007) has argued that:

> A complex web of interactions and dependencies can hold a linguistic or conceptual practice together even in the absence of a common creed that all participants at all times are required to endorse. ... although disagreement is … easier to negotiate and … more fruitful

[8] In German: Sinn.

> against a background of extensive agreement, it does not follow that any particular agreement is needed for disagreement to be expressed in given words (p. 125).

However, there is no current consensus on how all kinds of terms refer, and neither neo-descriptivists accounts nor any causal accounts seem able to solve all puzzles about reference and meaning on its own. As argued by Dickie (2015, p. 5) both ways of determining reference may achieve a relevant focus on the world, and it might be that various models of reference and various ways of combining them are needed for completing the picture (Michaelson and Reimer 2019).

Thus, although this is not the place to solve these issues, we should not simply take for granted that descriptivism provides a firm ground for all aspects of PL, if any at all. At least, we should not ignore Kripke's argument that if something is necessary, this may have nothing to do with anyone's knowledge of anything; that something is necessary does not immediately entail any epistemological or semantic conclusions as it could be something about which all humans could be mistaken or ignorant (Sullivan 2018, p. 5).

One may argue that the subjective necessities Smedslund (2012a, 2012b) has been concerned with are not of the kind that people can ignore, but are rather prescriptive normative principles that people must comply with to function socially and/or that they represent contingently inborn conceptual structures that ordinary persons cannot but take for granted. I don't deny these possibilities, it is just that they do not exhaust all relevant possibilities. At least, since large parts of the world are the way they are independently of our conceptions, could it not be that PL describes facts about persons that are real independently of any conception, stipulation or linguistic competency? If so, Smedslund's (2012b, p. 300) claim that PL describes constraints that do not originate *in* experiences of other persons but determine *how* they are experienced is—if at all true – too restrictive, not only on behalf PL but also on behalf of human capabilities.

Often enough, our ability to form an identifying description *follows from* being able to refer, rather than preceding it (Spicer 2010, s. 230), and although I agree with Smedslund (1991a, p. 328) that individuals are not taught to *identify* sadness with external indicators such as crying, such cues do offer ways to *recognize* what we refer to with our terms. That is, knowing what identifies something is not always needed for recognizing it; people may recognize water without having in common that they know that the H_2O-molecule is necessary for water to be what it is, and persons may competently agree that someone is sad without sharing any knowledge about what identify sadness. This is neither to deny that a central function of our language capabilities is to make communication possible via conventions (cf. Millikan 2005), nor that there are limits to which descriptions can identify what something is and is not.

Despite their different views with regards to the relevance of clarifying and/or stipulating invariant components in the use of terms, the Wittgensteinians (cf. Glock 1996) and Smedslund (2012a, b, 2013, p. 86) seem to have come together on the answer that this comes from human beings being innately disposed to engage in social interaction so that our conceptual constructions might converge. However, to the extent that this is true, one may wonder about the criteria on which our concepts might converge, and also what may secure their correspondence with the world. One relevant possibility, or so I argue, is that the possibility of a priori psychological knowledge rests more fundamentally on our capacities to recognize contradictions among representations of facts lying beyond immediate perception and to make corrections in thought accordingly (cf. Millikan 2006, p. 120). Although this notion of the a priori may be considered to be a rather deflated notion (see sections "A Priori Afterthoughts" and "Continuing the Dialogue on Psycho-logic"), it has the advantage of accounting for a priori psychological knowledge regardless of whether this knowledge is already shared or not. Thus, it has a wider scope than Smedslund's (1990; p. 51) understanding of PL as the explication of common-sense by checking tentative formulations against what one ordinarily already knows. For instance, the necessary conditions of trustworthiness to be discussed in the next section.

Conditions of Trustworthiness

Smedslund (e.g., 1997, p. 72) has often argued that five conditions must be satisfied for any person (P) to trust any other person (O). Purportedly, P trusts O if and only if P thinks that O *cares* for and *understands* P and that O has *own-control* (is autonomous), has *self-control* and has practically relevant *know-how*. However, before questioning the Fregean impulse underlying this theorem, it should be noticed that the involved notion of trust does not cover all the ways the respective term is ordinarily used. At least, it seems that many, if not all, of these ways, refer to the tripartite relation X trusts Y to do Z which is also the case with Smedslund's (p. 69) definition: "P trusts O" is allegedly equal to "P thinks O will not harm (do something bad for) P". By allowing Y to refer to P Smedslund (p. 81) has also relevantly defined "self-trust". However, we also ordinarily allow for Y to refer to social institutions or inanimate things (democracies to rule fairly, roofs not to fall, etc.). The PL-definition also restricts the Z-factor to the negative part of the hedonism-axiom. However, we may also trust someone to make us feel good, and often we specify more precisely what we trust someone to do (mechanics to fix engines, schoolchildren to do their homework, etc.).

What is clear, however, is that Smedslund's definition captures aspects of interpersonal processes where the vulnerability axiom is relevant. As such, it is related to what Hardin (2002) has characterized as *encapsulated interest*, that is, when what we want is also part of (encapsulated by) the wants of someone we find to be trustworthy. This also fits with one of the aspects that Smedslund (1997, p. 70) has claimed to be necessary for trusting someone, namely that we think that someone *cares* for us. However, here Smedslund's Fregean spirit pops up again: He seems to have conflated necessary features of trustworthy persons with what trusting persons necessarily think.

As noted by Hardin (2002, p. 29), the literature on trust has rarely discussed trustworthiness[9], even when it is primarily about trustworthiness rather than trust. Smedslund's publications make no exception, as the abovementioned theorem is not about any necessarily shared notion of trust, but about the necessary conditions for persons to be trustworthy. Notice that I am not trying to make the absurd point that we cannot trust someone when the conditions of the theorem are satisfied. Conversely, if someone really understands and cares for us, and also has own-control, self-control, and relevant know-how, then indeed, conditions that are necessary for someone to be *trustworthy* are fulfilled. It is just that the thought that these conditions are fulfilled is not something that every person must share when they trust someone in the sense defined by Smedslund. That is, we may come to think that someone (O) will not do us any harm for other less reliable reasons, for instance, that we have never experienced that O has done anything harmful and/or that O has so far only acted in ways that make us feel good. Thus, it is false that we trust someone *if, and only if,* we think that the five conditions clarified in the theorem are fulfilled.

However, if Smedslund's arguments about the five necessary conditions of trust are converted to arguments about trustworthiness they are quite convincing. Yet, I don't think his argument that they are also sufficient for trust can be converted to trustworthiness. That is, though O cannot be trustworthy for P (no matter what P thinks) if O does not care about whether P feels good or bad, does not understand what is good or bad for P, cannot prevent O from acting wrongly, cannot act autonomously (independently of other person's wants), and/or do not know how to act to avoid harming P, these conditions are still not sufficient when satisfied. For instance, even when O's care for P is all-encompassing (cf. Smedslund 1997, p. 62) O may want something that is incompatible with P's well-being even more (for instance, divorcing P).

Notice also that we should be reluctant about construing the conditions of trustworthiness as *necessitating* the emergence of trustworthiness. That is, although they are *necessary enabling conditions* for trustworthiness, there are reasons to doubt not only that these conditions necessarily cause trustworthiness, but also that they logically imply that trustworthiness is the case whenever the conditions are satisfied. This is because these conditions are causal dispositions (cf. Mumford and Anjum 2011) and as such, they are neither causal variables regularly linked as by way of any strict causal law, nor simply conceptually linked by way of prescriptive language conventions or stipulation. Thus, even if all conditions were satisfied something could always intervene to prevent them from producing the effect they dispose toward. For instance, O's want to divorce P prevents O from becoming trustworthy, even if O's care for P is all-encompassing. I discuss these issues in somewhat more detail elsewhere (Lindstad 2020, forthcoming; Stänicke and Lindstad 2020). What matters at this point is to notice that aspects of the world that are necessary for something to occur, can still be knowable by other means than gathering further empirical data, also when this is not necessarily something that is already taken for granted.

[9] I make no presumptions about what has happened after Hardin's publication.

Before Logos There Was Light

Although my earlier argument is indeed related to Kripke's critique of descriptivism, my focus is a bit different. Kripke's critique paved the way for an influential reminder not to conflate the notions of a priori, analytic, and necessary (noncontingent) truths. And since then, it has become commonplace to think of them as part of separate distinctions, an epistemological one between a priori and empirical truths, a semantical one between analytic and synthetic truths, and a modal one between noncontingent and contingent truths. Notice, that this does not imply that there cannot be necessary truths that are a priori knowable because they are analytic and true in virtue of their meaning; for instance, that "surprised persons have experienced something unexpected". However, as mentioned, Smedslund has professed that PL is not so much about such semantic relations as it is about what every person takes for granted about persons, and accordingly, that though it is a priori and necessary from the perspective of persons, the fact that this is so is, purportedly, a priori and contingent (2004). This is different from, Harré's (1999, p. 37) argument that the assertions of PL are a priori and synthetic, rather than analytic, because their truth depends not on logical form, but on what we take the involved terms to mean, and allegedly, that we could have used them differently. First, except for in a few rhetorical passages (2008), Smedslund (1991a) has departed from his earlier (1972) characterization of PL as analytic, apparently (2002) to sidestep Quine's (1953) influential critique of the analytic-synthetic distinction. Secondly, although we should take our departure in how ordinary language terms are used, PL is, pace Harré, not the study of what we ordinarily take words to mean. According to Smedslund, PL is about what we take for granted about persons, regardless of whether this is reflected in how we use words.

One may wonder, however, whether Smedslund has overlooked two aspects of PL that have traditionally been seen as what makes synthetic assertions different from analytic ones, namely that a significant part of the assertions of PL is not only true in virtue of language-independent matters of fact but are also potentially ampliative in that they may expand one's knowledge beyond what is already familiar. Interestingly, these features accord with what Kripke called *metaphysical* possibility and necessity. However, where Kripke's discussions focus on necessities that are not a priori (for instance, that water is H_2O), my concern is that something may be a priori knowable also when it is not already known. This requires a revised notion of a priori psychological knowledge that demands less for being conceptually competent and offers a more generous portrayal of our capacities to inquire into the world.

A Priori Afterthoughts

Philosophical issues are often contentious to their bone. A paradigmatic example is whether the traditional epistemological distinction between a priori and empirical knowledge is viable or not. However, just like the terms "analytic", "synthetic", "necessary" and "contingent" have each been used to refer to more than one phenomenon, there has been more than one way to understand the traditional epistemological distinction. In earlier publications, Smedslund (1984, 1991a) followed Bradley and Swartz (1979) who defined empirical knowledge as what it is possible to know only experientially and a priori knowledge as what it is possible to know other than experientially, that is, independently of, and without appeal to, experience. However, although there is nothing wrong with telling what PL is not, this is just as uninformative as other purported traditional negative characterizations of a priori knowledge, for instance, as knowledge whose justification is independent of experience (Russell 2014; Casullo 2012) and/or independent of empirical evidence, that is, evidence from sense experience (Jenkins 2008; Mares 2011). For one thing, one may wonder what the purported independence of empirical evidence or experience amounts to and may argue that a positive story about how a priori knowledge is possible is needed (cf. Jenkins 2012; Devitt 2014).

However, Smedslund has not only sought to define what PL is not, he has also unceasingly maintained that a priori psychological knowledge can be gained by explicating what is already implicitly taken for granted. However, this story does not only conflate a priori with common-sense, but it also involves ideas that depart from how a priori knowledge has been traditionally conceived. For one thing, although Smedslund has constantly maintained that PL hinges upon socialization, he has also argued that its axioms are inborn (2012a, 2012b) in the sense of being shaped by interactions between early experiences and genetically endowed tendencies. However, this controversial idea that what is a priori is also innate has not been part of all traditional conceptions of the a priori.

For instance, Mares (2011) distinguishes nativism from Aristotelian accounts of the a *priori* that emphasizes capacities for abstracting concepts from experience and gaining knowledge from reflecting on these concepts. Moreover, Dogramaci (2012) and O'Shea (2012) point out that Kant (1781) rejected not only that beliefs can neither be had, nor justified, *totally* independently of experience, but also that a priori knowledge consists in the possession of innate ideas that lie ready to be awakened by sense experiences. For Kant, it was arguably not a priori knowledge that is innate but rather the powers of the mind that enable us to acquire such knowledge. Accordingly, O'Shea (2012, p. 21—2) argues that Kant's "*a priori*" does not mean "*prior to* sense experience *in time*", but rather "*independent* of sense experience as to its source of justification", and thus that assertions can become a priori known in different ways depending on each person's experiential history. Yet, once the relevant concepts have been acquired by whatever means, it can be shown that the truth of a priori knowable assertions hold independently and irrespective of *any* such experiential history. This is different from Smedslund's (2012b, p. 300) conception of PL as *not* originating in experiences of people's behavior, but as already taken for granted.

However, not only is Smedslund's conception of the a priori different from Kant's, but it is also needed to evaluate Smedslund's conception concerning the recent discussions on how experience is part of a priori knowledge and justification (Casullo and Thurow 2013, Jackson 2015; Jenkins 2012). Although many relevant aspects of these resurgent discussions must be dealt with in future work, a few statements can still be made. For instance, the traditional conception of a priori justification has sometimes been taken to imply that a priori knowledge is not indefeasible by sense experience. This idea is related to Smedslund's conception of PL as unavoidably taken for granted by all competent persons. However, as argued by Jenkins (2008, p. 437), no matter how good your intuitions, analyses, or deductions are, if everyone else rather trusts some other evidence (empirical or non-empirical) that implies that you must have made a mistake, your putative justification will and should be defeated. Notice, however, that this is no argument against the feasibility of a priori justification, only an argument for characterizing a priori knowledge as defeasible (Jenkins 2012).

On the other hand, several of the currently most significant critics of the notion of a priori knowledge has expressed views that might not be incompatible with a notion of the a priori that is significant for psychological science, as long it is suitably revised and relevantly deflated: For instance, Millikan (2005, p. 67) has not only meant to launch an attack on conceptual analysis, but she (2010, p. 44-5) has claimed that a priori analysis is not the right tool for examining meanings of empirical terms, that is, terms that we have *not* learned to use via particular manners of thinking that are purportedly common to all competent users of the relevant terms. However, notice that in line with my earlier argument, trustworthiness is probably best conceived of as such an "empirical term", although the conditions for being trustworthy still ought to be characterized as a priori knowable. What is wrong is thus not to characterize some justificatory routes concerning the referents of empirical terms as a priori, but rather to exclude the referents of such terms from the scope of a suitably revised notion of the a priori.

Interestingly, for the aim of clarifying such a notion Millikan's arguments seem to provide valuable resources. Not only has she (2006, p. 217) provided convincing arguments for considering humans as animals capable of testing their abilities to recognize and reidentify phenomena independently of pragmatic successes and failures, but she has also argued that humans are ordinarily capable of fulfilling some of their purposes by trial and error with inner representations in thought: Allegedly, rather than wasting time on dozens of observations (2000, p. 31), trying things out in our heads might be quicker and safer than trying them out in the world (2006, p.118—25). As such, our abilities to recognize contradictions among representations of facts lying beyond immediate perception help us to make corrections in our thoughts accordingly. Indeed, the capacity to adjust beliefs until they are consistent is needed primarily by an animal that reconstructs in thought large portions of its world that it has not yet dealt with in practice (cf. Millikan 2006).

Relatedly, on the one hand, Devitt (2014) has criticized the notion of the a priori by arguing that the typical philosopher, like most others, knows little about concepts, but finds out about the world by examining *it*, and that the intuitions that philosophers come up with in armchairs are not a priori ones about concepts but empirical ones about kinds. Yet, on the other hand, he (2011) does not deny the striking epistemological differences between observing and inferring, nor that armchair intuition has a role in philosophy, only that this role has to be seen as a priori

(p. 15—6). From yet another angle, Williamson (2007, p. 165) has challenged the distinction between the a priori and the empirical by arguing not only that in our imagination-based knowledge of assertions about what could have been the case or not (so-called counterfactuals) sense experience can play a role that is neither strictly evidential nor purely enabling, but also (2013, p. 294) that the a priori—a posteriori distinction does not cut at our epistemological joints. Yet, on the other hand, he does not deny that there are clear cases where the distinction applies, and he still defends traditional philosophical "armchair methods" as remaining by far the most reliable and efficient available (2007, p. 7).

So, where does this leave us? For one thing, the arguments of Williamson, Devitt, and Millikan are all controversial, and the last word regarding the nature and existence of a priori knowledge is hardly spoken (Casullo 2012; Jenkins 2012; Jenkins and Kasaki 2015; Sullivan 2018). Moreover, even if we (reluctantly or not) grant that Williamson is right that the traditional a priori—a posteriori distinction is superficial, and that Devitt is right that what philosophers come up with in armchairs are not a priori, and also that Millikan's view that making viable corrections in thought by recognizing contradictions among representations of facts lying beyond perception has nothing to do with a priori justification, - we still need a notion that cuts at the epistemological joints between psychological research that is pseudo-empirical and research that is not pseudo-empirical. And as such, Devitt's confession that "armchair intuitions" has a role to play, Williamson defense of "armchair methods" and Millikan's argument that trying things out in one's head by recognizing contradictions among representations of facts lying beyond immediate perception may give us just what it takes. However, it should be noticed that in the philosophical discussions on the nature and existence of a priori knowledge one has almost exclusively discussed examples drawn from mathematics, formal logic, and semantics. Thus, one may wonder whether these discussions had turned out differently had it been recognized that the discussion is not only relevant for psychology, but also mental healthcare services (Smedslund 2009, 2016b; Stänicke and Lindstad 2020; Lindstad 2020, forthcoming).

What is clear, however, is that the notion needed is not only different from Smedslund's conception, but also traditional philosophical conceptions of the a priori. At least, we should consider the abovementioned Aristotelian conception (Mares 2011). Relatedly, Jenkins (2012) argues that a viable notion of the a priori must differ from traditional conceptions by taking into account how our concepts are epistemologically related to the *empirical input* we get from the world and that by so doing we may combine a need for accounting for knowledge of the mind-independent world with a traditional conception of a priori knowledge as related to examining our concepts. However, one may wonder (cf. Devitt 2014) how characterizing a priori justification as consisting of concept-examination might take us to the real world. Yet, (cf. Williamson 2007) putting our interest in worldly matters is not incompatible with emphasizing issues of semantical structure. Conversely, to make our reasoning instruments more reliable, we must investigate those instruments themselves, even when they are not the ultimate objects of our concern (p. 6). Yet, the envisaged method allegedly involves reflection *with* our concepts and is thus a reflection *on* whatever our concepts happen to refer to, which is only rarely concepts themselves (p. 76).

Thus, what matters for advancing an alternative to pseudo-empirical research is not that our concepts are common sense, but that when we think with our concepts about persons, *we don't need to gather any new empirical data to reach viable conclusions*. As such, rather than portraying all aspects of PL as already implicitly familiar before investigation, we may in line with the abovementioned Kantian view even characterize a priori justification as *afterthought*; that is, *after* we have formed concepts that enable us to recognize various properties of persons (for instance, whether they understand us and cares for us, are autonomous, relevantly competent, etc.), we may use these concepts for reflecting on which combinations these properties may possibly enter into and not (for instance, whether they may combine to make persons trustworthy). If we do not, we do not only run the risk of doing pseudo-empirical research, but we also ignore scientifically relevant capacities of the species Homo Sapiens.

Abductively Reaching for Axioms

Moreover, it seems relevant to consider the revised notion of a priori justification sketched above as compatible with Millikan's (2006, p. 125) arguments about what it amounts to be a creature designed to be able to map the world according to the principle of non-contradiction: In a world like ours, not all properties fit together, and in this world, we exist as creatures that are able not only to recognize some of these properties but also to recognize that many properties exclude one another. For such a being consistent assertions might become a strong test of conceptual adequacy, and thus, our abilities to recognize contradictions among representations of facts lying beyond immediate perception might not only help us to make corrections in thought, but they may also help us recognize that we do not always have to make something actual to show that it is possible or necessary.

However, a further upshot for the proposed notion of "a priori afterthought" is that it may incorporate Salvatore and Valsiner's (2010; see also Valsiner 2012; Salvatore 2020) critique of Smedslund's deductive account of PL by emphasizing the relevance of abductive reasoning. One thing is to demonstrate that something is possible or necessary without making it actual. Abductive inference, however, is to explain what is a fact by adding or modifying one's assumptions about what properties are compatible or incompatible with it to preserve consistent thinking. For instance, and as further argued by Stänicke and Lindstad (2020), if P does not trust O, even though P does experience O as caring for P, then P's lack of trust may, for instance, be explained by that P experiences O as not understanding P, and cannot be explained by that P experiences O as autonomous.

As such, I am certainly inclined to believe that Nussbaum (2013) is right that noncontradiction functions not only as an internal test for consistency of beliefs, but also as a principle for real-world property incompatibility (for instance, lacking self-control is incompatible with being trustworthy), Yet, I also think that Millikan (2013) is right that our reasons for thinking that the principle of non-contradiction cannot get a grip in a world where properties do not exclude one another, is not that the principle has been abstracted from experience. Rather, one may think of the principle as an abductively inferred theory evidenced by the fact that we have been able to construct indefinitely many kinds of consistent concepts by using it. Indeed, learning how not to find oneself in contradiction is a practice that is viable because it has been successful in practice (cf. Millikan 2013, p. 193–4).

This is also what I think PL is all about; *learning – via reflection on the properties that our psychologically relevant concepts refer to – how not to find oneself in contradiction when thinking about persons*. Though this kind of reflection is empirically tuned and informed, it does not depend on gaining any new experiences or gathering any further empirical data. Smedslunds efforts to advance PL has seminally demonstrated that such reflection is possible on a large scale when thinking about persons. However, pace Smedslund, what may become knowable in this way is not necessarily something that is already known. Rather, PL is the result of trying to stay tuned to the real world by avoiding contradiction. Though Smedslund may be right that parts of PL (some axioms are probably good candidates) are normally learned early in life, this is certainly not the case for all of PL (typically theorems). Interestingly, such a possibility for reaching the axioms of PL via abductive inference seems to be in line with Valsiner's (2012, p. 13-4) idea of axiomatic systems as tools for creating new knowledge by allowing for their reconstruction, rather than as systems taken for granted as unchangeable orthodoxy.

Continuing the Dialogue on Psycho-logic

In summary, I present some tentative conclusions: Acknowledging the relevance of a notion of pseudo-empirical research implies that we should specify a proper alternative, and Smedslund has seminally proposed that the notion of a priori knowledge is relevant for this aim. However, his account of PL has been too restrictive by exclusively emphasizing what is already taken for granted by everyone. A viable notion of a priori psychological knowledge should include not only what is already known, but also what is potentially knowable.

Accordingly, I propose a revised notion of the a priori that takes advantage of our natural human capacities to be empirically informed via various senses to attain concepts that enable us to recognize which features of the world are compatible and not, and thus to adjust our concepts in accordance with the principle of non-contradiction. This is expedient for an animal capable of thinking about phenomena that it has not yet dealt with in practice and is needed for recognizing when we are not sufficiently informed to avoid contrary assertions. However, it is also convenient for recognizing when we are sufficiently informed for achieving this aim. In the former case, we need to use our senses to gather more information. In the second case, this is not needed as reflecting on the properties that our concepts refer to is sufficient for concluding whether our assertions are consistent or not.

However, in contrast to traditional conceptions of the a priori, such conclusions are not indefeasible, and in contrast to Smedslund's account of PL, they do not require that the concepts involved are shared by anyone (though how we use words could bring relevant indications). The upshot is that the capacity in question comprises both deductive and abductive reasoning. It also implies that PL may not only comprise assertions about what is already familiar, inborn, necessary, conceptual, semantical, language-based, common-sense and/or mind-dependent, but also what is mind-*in*dependent, possible without being necessary, dispositional and thus also causal, learned by experience, and uncommon sense by being cognitively additive and informatively new. Such a revised notion of the a priori may seem somewhat deflated compared to traditional conceptions. However, it may still be worthy of its name as it may contribute to explain why it is not always needed to gather any new empirical data to conclude whether our assertions about persons are consistent or not.

Probably, the above proposal engenders more questions than it answers. However, such marvels are heartedly welcome. Indeed, if we do not wish them welcome, we risk neglecting parts of what makes us human. However, this is also what psychology risks if Smedslund's efforts to advance PL is ignored. Being a person in our world normally entails that we can scrutinize many of our psychological assertions via thorough reflection and in critical dialogue. Indeed, the possibility of a priori psychological knowledge might not only have significant implications for psychological science but may in itself be significant knowledge about human beings. Though this possibility is hardly all that matters for psychology, its implications are extensive and have only been hinted at here. Yet, some of its implications for psychotherapy and psychotherapy research is discussed by Stänicke and Lindstad (2020) and Lindstad (2020, forthcoming), not to mention in Smedslund's pioneering publications.

References

Bradley, R., & Swartz, N. (1979). *Possible worlds: An introduction to logic and its philosophy*. Oxford, England: Blackwell.

Brinkmann, S. (2011). Towards an expansive hybrid psychology: Integrating theories of the mediated mind. *Integrative Psychological and Behavioral Science, 45*, 1–20.

Casullo, A. (2012). *Essays on a priori knowledge and justification*. New York: Oxford University Press.

Casullo, A., & J. Thurow J. (Eds.). (2013). *The a priori in philosophy*. New York, Oxford University Press.

Danziger, K. (1997). *Naming the mind. How psychology found its language*. London: Sage Publications.

Devitt, M. (2011). No place for the A priori. In M. J. Schaffer & M. L. Veber (Eds.), *What place for the a priori* (pp. 9–32). Chicago & La Salle: Open Court Publishing Company.

Devitt, M. (2014). We don't learn about the world by examining concepts: A response to Carrie Jenkins. In I. R. Neta (Ed.), *Current controversies in epistemology* (pp. 23–33). London: Routledge.

Dickie, I. (2015). *Fixing reference*. Oxford: Oxford University Press.

Dogramaci, S. (2012). Apriority. In G. Russell & D. G. Fara (Eds.), *The Routledge companion to philosophy of language* (pp. 768–781). New York & London: Routledge.

Ekeland, T. J. (2020). Psychotherapy: An illusion that works (Chapter 19, this volume). In T. G. Lindstad, E. Stänicke, & J. Valsiner (Eds.), *Respect for thought: Jan Smedslund's legacy for psychology* (pp. 327–342). New York: Springer.

Glock, H. J. (1996). On safari with Wittgenstein, Quine and Davidson. In H. J. Glock & R. L. Arrington (Eds.), *Wittgenstein and Quine* (pp. 144–173). New York: Routledge.
Goddard, C., & Wierzbicka, A. (2014). *Words & meanings: Lexical semantics across domains, languages, & cultures*. Oxford: Oxford University Press.
Hacker, P. (1996). Wittgenstein and Quine: Proximity at a great distance. In H. J. Glock & R. L. Arrington (Eds.), *Wittgenstein and Quine* (pp. 1–38). New York: Routledge.
Hardin, R. (2002). *Trust & trustworthiness*. New York: Russell Sage Foundation.
Harré, R. (1999). Commentary on "Psychologic and the study of memory". *Scandinavian Journal of Psychology, 40*(Suppl. 1), 37–40.
Israel, J. (1979). *The language of dialectics and the dialectics of language*. Copenhagen: Munksgaard.
Jackson, M. B. (2015). Introduction to the special issue "The roles of experience in a priori knowledge". *Synthese*, 2695–2699.
Jenkins, C. S. (2008). A priori knowledge: Debates and developments. *Philosophy Compass, 3*(3), 436–450.
Jenkins, C. S. (2012). A priori knowledge: The conceptual approach. In A. Cullison (Ed.), *The continuum companion to epistemology* (pp. 180–198). London, Continuum Press.
Jenkins, C. S. I., & Kasaki, M. (2015). The traditional conception of the a priori. *Synthese, 192*(9), 2725–2746.
Kant, I. (1781). *Critique of pure reason*. N. Kemp Smith (1929, transl.). Basingstoke: Palgrave.
Kripke, S. (1980). *Naming and necessity*. Cambridge: Harvard University Press.
Kennair, L. E. O., Aarre, T. F., Kennair, T. W., & Bugge, P. (2002). Evidence-based mental health—The scientific foundation of clinical psychology and psychiatry. *Scipolicy™ The Journal of Science & Health Policy, 2*(1), 1–300.
Kukla, A. (2001). *Methods of theoretical psychology*. Cambridge: The MIT Press.
Lindstad, T. G. (2020). The relevance of dispositionalism for psychotherapy and psychotherapy research. In R. L. Anjum, S. Copeland, & E. Rocca (Eds.), *Rethinking causality, complexity and evidence for the unique patient*. Springer Publ. (forthcoming).
Mares, E. (2011). *A priori*. Acumen.
Margolis, E. & Laurence, S. (2019). Concepts. In E. N. Zalta (Ed.) *The Stanford encyclopedia of philosophy* (Summer 2019 Edition), https://plato.stanford.edu/archives/sum2019/entries/concepts/.
Martin, J., Sugarman, J., & Thompson, J. (2003). *Psychology and the question of agency*. Albany, NY: State University of New York Press.
McEachrane, M. (2009). Emotion, meaning, and appraisal theory. *Theory & Psychology, 19*(1), 33–53.
McEachrane, M. (2020). Meanings of words and the possibilities of psychology: Reflections on Jan Smedslund's psycho-logic (Chapter 6, this volume). In T. G. Lindstad, E. Stänicke, & J. Valsiner (Eds.), *Respect for thought: Jan Smedslund's legacy for psychology* (pp. 85–104). New York: Springer.
Michaelson, E. & Reimer, M (2019). Reference. In Edward N. Zalta (ed.) *The Stanford Encyclopedia of Philosophy* (2019 edition). https://plato.stanford.edu/archives/spr2019/entries/reference/.
Millikan, R. G. (2000). *On clear and confused ideas: An essay about substance concepts*. New York: Cambridge University Press.
Millikan, R. G. (2005). *Language: A biological model*. Oxford: Oxford University Press.
Millikan, R. G. (2006). Styles of rationality. In S. Hurley & M. Nudds (Eds.), *Rational animals?* (pp. 117–126). Oxford: Oxford University Press.
Millikan, R. G. (2010). On knowing the meaning; with a coda on swampman. *Mind, 119*(473), 43–81.
Millikan, R. G. (2013). Reply to Nussbaum. In D. Ryder, J. Kingsbury, & K. Williford (Eds.), *Millikan and her critics* (pp. 193–197). Chichester: Wiley-Blackwell.
Moore, G. E. (1925). A defense of common sense. In G. E. Moore (Ed.), (1959). *Philosophical papers* (pp. 32–59). London: George Allen & Unwin Ltd. New York: The Macmillan Company.
Mumford, S., & Anjum, R. L. (2011). *Getting causes from powers*. Oxford: Oxford University Press.

Nussbaum, C. (2013). Craning the ultimate skyhook: Millikan on the law of non-contradiction. In D. Ryder, J. Kingsbury, & K. Williford (Eds.), *Millikan and her critics* (pp. 176–192). New York: Wiley-Blackwell.

O'Shea, J. R. (2012) *Kant's critique of pure reason*. Acumen.

Parrott, W. G., & Harré, R. (1991). Smedslundian suburbs in the city of language: The case of embarrassment. *Psychological Inquiry, 2*, 358–361.

Quine, W. V. O. (1953). Two dogmas of empiricism. In W. V. O. Quine (Ed.), *From a logical point of view* (pp. 20–46). Cambridge, MA: Harvard University Press.

Robertson, T. (2012). Reference. In G. Russell & D. G. Fara (Eds.), *The Routledge companion to philosophy of language* (pp. 189–198). New York & London: Routledge.

Russell, G. (2010). Analyticity in externalist lnguages. In S. Sawyer (Ed.), *New waves in philosophy of language* (pp. 186–205). Palgrave MacMillan.

Russell, B, (2014), A priori justification and knowledge. In E. N. Zalta (Ed.), *The Stanford Encyclopedia of philosophy*. Retrieved from http://plato.stanford.edu/archives/sum2014/entries/apriori/.

Salvatore, S. (2016). *Psychology in black and white: The project for a theory driven science*. Charlotte, NC: Information Age Publishing.

Salvatore, S. (2020). How to avoid throwing the baby out with the bathwater: Abduction is the solution to pseudo-empiricism (Chapter 11, this volume). In T. G. Lindstad, E. Stänicke, & J. Valsiner (Eds.), *Respect for thought: Jan Smedslund's legacy for psychology* (pp. 181–194). New York: Springer.

Salvatore, S., & Valsiner, J. (2010). Between the general and the unique: Overcoming the nomothetic versus idiographic opposition. *Theory & Psychology, 20*(6), 817–833.

Shotter, J. (1994). Is there a logic in common sense? The scope and limits of Jan Smedslund's geometric psychologic. In J. Siegfried (Ed.), *The status of common sense in psychology* (pp. 149–168). Norwood, NJ: Ablex.

Smedlund, M. B. (2020). The case for psychological quietism: Wittgensteinian propaedeutics in Smedslund's writings (Chapter 7, this volume). In T. G. Lindstad, E. Stänicke, & J. Valsiner (Eds.), *Respect for thought: Jan Smedslund's legacy for psychology* (pp. 105–128). New York: Springer.

Smedslund, J. (1972). *Becoming a psychologist. Theoretical foundations for a humanistic psychology*. Oslo: Oslo University Press.

Smedslund, J. (1988). *Psycho-logic*. Heidelberg: Springer-Verlag.

Smedslund, J. (1990). Psychology and psychologic: characterization of the difference. In K. J. Gergen & G. R. Semin (Eds.), *Everyday understanding: Social and scientific implications* (pp. 45–63). London: Sage.

Smedslund, J. (1991a). The pseudoempirical in psychology and the case for psychologic. *Psychological Inquiry, 2*, 325–338.

Smedslund, J. (1991b). Psychologic: A technical language for psychology. *Psychological Inquiry, 2*(4), 376–382.

Smedslund, J. (1993). How shall the concept of anger be defined? *Theory and Psychology, 3*(1), 5–33.

Smedslund, J. (1997). *The structure of psychological common sense*. Mahwah, NJ: Lawrence Erlbaum Associates.

Smedslund, J. (1999). Author's response: Psychologic in dialogue – Reply to commentaries. *Scandinavian Journal of Psychology, 40*(Suppl. 1), 123–138.

Smedslund, J. (2002). From hypothesis-testing psychology to procedure-testing psychologic. *Review of General Psychology, 6*, 51–72.

Smedslund, J. (2004). *Dialogues about a new psychology*. Chagrin Falls, OH: Taos Institute Publications.

Smedslund, J. (2008). From Heider to psycho-logic. *Social Psychology, 39*(9), 157–162.

Smedslund, J. (2009). The mismatch between current research methods and the nature of psychological phenomena: What researchers must learn from practitioners. *Theory & Psychology, 19*(6), 778–794.

Smedslund, J. (2011). Meaning of words and the use of axiomatics in psychological theory. *Journal of Theoretical and Philosophical Psychology, 31*(2), 126–135.

Smedslund, J. (2012a). What follows from what we all know about human beings. *Theory & Psychology, 22*, 658–668.

Smedslund, J. (2012b). Psycho-logic: Some thoughts and after-thoughts. *Scandinavian Journal of Psychology, 55*, 295–302.

Smedslund, J. (2013). *From nonsense syllables to holding hands: Sixty years as a psychologist*. Chagrin Falls, OH: Taos Institute Publications.

Smedslund, J. (2016a). Why psychology cannot be an empirical science. *Integrative Psychological and Behavioral Science, 50*(2), 185–195.

Smedslund, J. (2016b). Practicing psychology without an empirical evidence-base. *New Ideas in Psychology, 43*, 50–56.

Soames, S. (2003). *Philosophical analysis in the twentieth century* (The age of meaning) (Vol. 2). Princeton University Press.

Soames, S. (2010). *Philosophy of language*. Princeton University Press.

Spicer, F. (2010). Kripke and the neo-descriptivist. In J. Langkau & C. Nimtz (Eds.) *New Perspectives on Concepts. Grazer Philosophische Studien; International Journal for Analytic Philosophy. 81*, Amsterdam, New York: Rodopi.

Stalnaker, R. (1999). The problems of logical ominscience. In R. Stalnaker (Ed.), *Context and content* (pp. 240–254). Oxford: Oxford University Press.

Stänicke, E. & Lindstad, T. G. (2020). The pragmatic status of psychoanalytic theory: A plea for thought models (Chapter 22, this volume). In T. G. Lindstad, E. Stänicke, & J. Valsiner (Eds.), *Respect for thought: Jan Smedslund's legacy for psychology* (pp. 377–400). New York: Springer.

Sullivan, A. (2018). *The constitutive a priori: Developing an extended epistemological framework*. Lexington Books.

Smedslund, J. (1984). What is necessarily true in psychology? In J. R. Royce & L. P. Mos (Eds.) *Annals of Theoretical Psychology, 2*, 241–272.

Valsiner, J. (1999). Eliminating pseudoempiricism from psychology: A return to science. *Scandinavian Journal of Psychology, 40*(Suppl. 1), 93–94.

Valsiner, J. (2012). *A guided science: History of psychology in the mirror of its making*. New Brunswick, NJ: Transaction Publishers.

Wampold, B. E., & Imel, Z. E. (2015). *The great psychotherapy debate: The evidence for what makes psychotherapy work*. London: Routledge.

Williamson, T. (2007). *Philosophy of philosophy*. Oxford: Blackwell Publishing.

Williamson, T. (2013). How deep is the distinction between a priori and a posteriori knowledge. In A. Casullo & J. Thurow (Eds.), *The a priori in philosophy* (pp. 291–312). Oxford: Oxford University Press.

Wittgenstein, L. (1953). Philosophical Investigations. The German Text, with a Revised English Translation. Blackwell Publishing.

Part III
Psychology as Science: Research Extensions

Chapter 13
Neuro-Ornamentation in Psychological Research

Jan Smedslund

I have coined the term "neuro-ornamentation" to designate the insertion of references to neuroscience in psychological texts with the intention of strengthening their scientific impact. I chose the term "ornamentation" to emphasize the similarity to decorating an object in order to strengthen its appeal. A text is supposed to become more scientific when it contains references to brain studies (McCabe and Castel 2008), just as an object is expected to become more beautiful when decorated. In this article, I propose to examine the logic of three different variants of neuro-ornamentation and argue that the belief that neuroscience can contribute to psychology may have little foundation in fact and may consist mainly of programmatic ideology.

However, first, I introduce and comment on what can be labeled "The Correspondence Premise" which forms part of the background for the subsequent analysis.

The Correspondence Premise

This premise may be stated as follows:

For every psychological event there is a corresponding neural event.

The Correspondence Premise goes far beyond what can be concretely demonstrated. For the most part, one has no or only very sketchy knowledge of what goes on in the brain during a psychological event. Even so, it would be strange to deny that

J. Smedslund (✉)
University of Oslo, Oslo, Norway
e-mail: jan.smedslund@psykologi.uio.no

T. G. Lindstad et al. (eds.), *Respect for Thought*, Theory and History in the Human and Social Sciences, https://doi.org/10.1007/978-3-030-43066-5_13

there *is something*, at least this makes no sense in within our modern naturalistic frame. According to this widely acknowledged frame, it is impossible to understand that people can experience and act unless *something* goes on in their brains, whatever that is. This Correspondence Premise is a general background for all research aimed at revealing more specific correspondences between psychological and neural events. However, it also leads to a question about the autonomy of psychology. Must a finding in one of these fields lead to a change in the other? Here, I will limit my discussion to whether or not and in what way it is possible for neuroscience to change psychology. The answer will also influence how we regard neuro-ornamentation. I pursue the question by discussing three types of such ornamentation. I conclude that they are misleading, because research and practice of psychology can go on *without any knowledge of the brain,* and that adding such knowledge cannot change psychology and the ways human beings have always known each other.

My stance in interpreting The Correspondence Premise is monistic and "two-language." I take it that there is one world described in two basically different types of language. The psychological language describes the world as it exists *for* persons in one sort of conceptual framework, and the physical language describes the world as it exists *independently* of persons, and within another type of conceptual framework. These differences in conceptual framework are related to the traditional distinction between "subjective" and "objective," but this article is not the place to comment on and discuss even parts of the immense relevant philosophical literature.

The Correspondence Premise Cannot be Implemented

The difficulties of implementing the principle stem from the vast difference between the two kinds of language. Ordinary languages have developed over eons of time as part of human life. There are thousands of special languages, but they all appear to have a common semantic core (Wierzbicka 1996) and are acquired early and very rapidly by children everywhere. I find it virtually impossible to conceive of a theoretical or practical psychology that does not take its departure in the basic conceptual framework of ordinary language. This language enables us to talk about both thoughts and feelings, our perception of external objects and the body, and interpersonal relations. On the other hand, the technical language of neuroscience involves physical–chemical terms and special concepts such as fMRI, PET SCAN, and Neuro-transmitter and is anchored exclusively in instrument readings. However, just as we cannot use psychological terms to fully describe neurological and biochemical events, neuroscience is incapable of describing psychological phenomena. This can be illustrated by the following simple example:

The setting is a dark road with no other persons. "Excuse me for bothering you, Miss" said the man and stepped closer, "but could you tell me what time it is." "My watch has stopped and I don't want to miss the last train."

The vast amount of information conveyed to English-speaking persons by this description can easily be formulated and handled in terms of psychological interpretations and opens for many possibilities and probabilities to be explored in terms of ordinary language. On the other hand, the corresponding neuroscientific formulations would have to be based on complicated technical instrumentation and even this possibility is totally ephemeral and programmatic. It would involve an inconceivably difficult translation process from meanings to physical and chemical measurements. One is forced to conclude that while The Correspondence Premise must be accepted, it does not offer any useful alternative to ordinary language when it comes to psychological practice and understanding. The measurements of neural activity can increase our knowledge of the brain but are not very helpful in describing and understanding the full range of what goes on within and between people.

I find it illuminating to think of the distinction between the neural and the psychological as in some ways analogous to the distinction between hardware and software in computers. For every instance of software, there must be an instance of hardware, but the belief that a study of the hardware will lead to better understanding of the software is as ephemeral as believing that psychology will be advanced by studying brain processes.

To repeat, it would seem that the psychological and neural languages cannot be manageably translated into each other, which means that the Correspondence Premise cannot be practically implemented.

I now turn to three types of neuro-ornamentation of psychological texts. The first involves frequent use of the prefix "neuro-"(as in "neurocognition"). The second concerns the insertion of references to neuroscientific studies, and the third one is the introduction of the concept of "endogenic depression" that, per definition, has *only* neural explanations.

Occurrences of the Prefix "Neuro-"in a Psychological Text

A recent review of research on schizophrenia (Rund 2015) contains numerous instances of the terms "cognition" and "neurocognition". It is hard to ascribe any empirical content to this distinction, since according to The Correspondence Premise *every* instance of cognition corresponds to something neural. Nevertheless, I have tried to investigate whether the two terms are perhaps used in different contexts, involving respectively psychological or neuroscience methods and data and, hence, describe different types of content.

The outcome is presented in Table 13.1.

Table 13.1 The relation between type of term and type of data

	Cognitive	Neurocognitive	Total
With neuro-data	5	13	18
With psychological data	30	26	56
Total	35	39	74

What do these findings tell? First, that terminology is not very reliably linked to type of data, even though the prefix "neuro-," not unexpectedly, is more frequent when there is actual measurement of brain processes. Second, in the case of purely psychological data, the two terms are equally and seemingly haphazardly distributed. Given The Correspondence Premise, it cannot be that the term "neurocognitive" is used to refer to cognition involving brain processes, whereas the term "cognitive" is not. Since the terminological difference cannot be taken to be totally meaningless, it is hard to avoid the conclusion that the prefix "neuro-" is used intermittently merely to emphasize a belief that psychology should move in the direction of neuroscience. Hence, the prefix "neuro-" may be taken to look more "scientific." Further investigation of occurrences of the prefix "neuro-" in other texts may or may not support my interpretation that the prefix has no factual, but only ideological, content.

The next example involves a genuine neuroscientific study. It is argued that inserting references to this study in psychological texts would not change or add to psychological understanding but would serve only as ornamentation.

The Spatial Orientation of Rats

The Nobel Prize was recently awarded to two researchers (Moser et al. 2014) for their discoveries of neural processes underlying the spatial orientation of rats. Their work represents an undisputable neuroscientific advance but does not improve psychological understanding. Already Tolman (1948) and his coworkers demonstrated by purely psychological methods that rats have "cognitive maps." For example, they observed that, when the ordinary route to food in a familiar environment was blocked, rats selected the shortest available alternative route. These results were arrived at by purely psychological methods and without any knowledge of brain processes. The findings coincide with what can be predicted from our shared common sense knowledge that both rats and humans have cognitive maps of familiar locations. By "psychological common sense," I mean "what follows from the shared meanings of the concepts involved," and not empirical "folk psychology" that may or may not be correct (Smedslund 1997).

The hypothetical example of inserting reference to Moser and Moser in a psychological text describing spatial orientation in rats illustrates why neuroscientific advances cannot contribute to psychology. The neuroscientific findings only reveal some of the content of the Correspondence Premise, namely, how rat brains manage spatial orientation. The fact that rats have cognitive maps is already known to psychologists. The general question is whether there are or can be neuroscientific findings that contradict or add to psychological knowledge. If a neuroscientific finding has psychological implications, these can also be independently established by psychological methods and explained psychologically. To deny this appears impossible. Therefore, one can develop psychology without neuroscientific knowledge, and "neuro-ornamentation" can be recognized as a purely cosmetic process.

Apparent exceptions to the preceding are effects of neural damage to the brain (strokes and accidents). They involve discovery of correlates between psychological and neural effects of head trauma and hence provide some content to The Correspondence Premise. However, since the Premise cannot be implemented in everyday life and in psychological practice, one can continue to believe in the independence of psychology relative to neuroscience.

My third example is use of the concept of "endogenous depression."

Endogenous Depression

By definition, this concept has *no* psychological but *only* neuroscientific explanations. Hence, insertion of the concept in a text has a strong neuro-ornamentation effect.

Use of the concept of endogenous depression means that the psychological approach is seen as insufficient and must be supplemented with neuroscience. The concept and the related one of *bipolar disease* have been widely used and have been the subject of much theorizing. People are seen as depressed (and manic) solely because of altered brain processes. The idea that this variant of depression cannot be psychologically explained sets it apart from our vast commonsense knowledge about depression, including such self-evident elements as hopelessness induced by consistent personal failures and consistently adverse surrounding conditions. Some people certainly appear to be depressed without any known psychological explanation. However, this conclusion may be based on insufficiently extensive investigation of the total psychological context.

The concept of *endogenous* depression and the related more inclusive concept of *bipolar disease* implies that some *psychological* phenomena cannot be *psychologically* explained. Allegedly, only physical–chemical intervention is possible. It differs from cases of accidents or strokes, and where treatment (re-training) is only psychological.

I would like to emphasize that none of the above threatens the autonomy of psychology. Depressed and stroke victims can and must be understood and treated from a psychological point of view and with psychological methods, especially since the alternative of pharmacological treatment is becoming increasingly questionable (Rose 2003; Whitaker 2010; Goetzsche 2013).

A general argument for a psychological approach is that since human beings generally function without fixed constraints ("laws"), the observed regularity of depressive behavior must reflect *dynamic equilibria*, maintained by stable consequences. This means that when a psychologist encounters a depressed client, he or she should always search for the *psychological* conditions that *maintain* the depressive state. The search for and selection of efficient procedures can go on unaffected by knowledge of the concurrent neural processes. It follows that the neuro-ornamentation effect of referring to "endogenous" depression has only ideological content.

Conclusion

The three cases cited of neuro-ornamentation have increasingly strong persuasive power: The first one contains intermittent reference to neuroscience in the form of the prefix "neuro-." There is no clear empirical content, and the prefix merely appears to serve as a reminder of the alleged importance of neuroscience in psychology.

The second case involving spatial orientation contains reference to undisputable and substantial neuroscientific findings that make the text appear very "scientific." However, this does not change psychology. The neural studies demonstrate how rat *brains* function, but psychological studies demonstrate how *rats* function.

The third case concerns the concept of "endogenous depression" that it, per definition, requires a neuroscientific explanation. The person is seen as depressed because of neural processes without a psychological explanation. This case is the most powerful ornamentation, because it not only emphasizes the neural but also directly excludes the psychological.

In summary, the first case of neuro-ornamentation has no empirical content whatsoever, the second case involves neuroscientific advance but does not add to psychological knowledge, and the third case is highly disputable since it excludes psychology by simple definition.

In all three cases, it still remains to understand *why* psychologists are turning increasingly toward neuroscience and indulging in neuro-ornamentation of their texts.

I think the current mainstream trend builds on an unrecognized contradiction between a *monistic materialist* and a *dualistic* position. On the one hand, one takes it that there is one world, and it is material, and the relations in this world are causal. On the other hand, the predominant view is that neural states *cause* psychological states. However, this dualistic position is replete with intrinsic difficulties because causation presupposes *two* separate entities, in this case, a brain state and a psychological state. I think the confusion originates in, and is maintained, because there actually appears to be two clearly different sets of findings, the brain measurements and the introspective reports and test results. From a materialist position, one can in principle explain that the first cause the second, i.e., that neural processes cause the vocal cord movements and sound waves in verbal reporting. However, this does not explain the "meaning" of the verbal reports, and hence, the position of psychologists as brain researchers remains engulfed in an unsolved mystery.

In contradistinction to this, I take it that there is one world described in two very different languages. This means that there are two kinds of conceptual frameworks for describing the same world and that the relation between the neural and the psychological is a matter of *translation* rather than *causation*. A neural state may coexist with psychological depression, but this does not show one- or two-way causality, but only correct translation. Suppose that the same event is described both in Swahili and Urdu, an observed change described in Swahili may be closely mirrored by the observed change described in Urdu, but the first change does not *cause* the second or vice versa. The covariation merely indicates correctness of translation between the two languages. Much confusion and useless speculation originates in the failure to distinguish between causality and translation. As I see it, the attempt to understand how a neural state can "cause" a psychological state or vice versa is misdirected. The instrument-based neuroscientific research discovers neural correlates of psychological processes. The two-language assumption reduces the problem to one of mapping the details in the covariation between the psychological language that has developed to serve human social life and the recently developed physical–chemical instrument-based measurements of neuroscience. No causation is involved; there is only one subject matter and two conceptual frameworks.

The neuroscience conceptual framework developed by applying physics and chemistry to the brain by means of instruments cannot cope with the richness of ordinary language developed over eons. Translation is, therefore, virtually impossible, and neuro-ornamentation of psychological texts raises a false hope. It is simply inconceivable to me for the reasons given above, that further study of the brain can importantly revise or add to psychological understanding and practice.

Disregarding the subtle philosophical problems involved, what is at issue is the autonomy of the discipline of psychology. I take it that everything psychological can be studied by psychological methods and that a psychology can exist and develop independently of neuroscience. If this is the case, then neuro-ornamentation not only has no factual content but also promotes a misleading idea. Psychologists have falsely come to believe that the neuroscientific findings can explain psychological phenomena, and that physio-chemical measurements of brain activity may engender contributions to psychology.

Finally, I would like to add that when it comes to psychology as an independent discipline, psychologic (Smedslund 2012) takes a special position compared to other approaches. This is because *meaning* is a general basic concept in all of psychology, and the meaning of something is what follows (logically) from that something (Smedslund 1970). The study of meanings is a discipline far removed from neuroscience.

References

Goetzsche, P. C. (2013). *Deadly medicines and organized crime*. London: Radcliffe Publishing.

McCabe, D. P., & Castel, A. D. (2008). Seeing is believing: the effect of brain images on judgments of scientific reasoning. *Cognition, 107*, 343–352.

Moser, E., et al. (2014). Grid cells and cortical representation. *Nature Reviews Neuroscience, 15*, 466–481.

Rose, N. (2003, November/December). Neurochemical selves. *Society, 41,* 46–59.

Rund, B. R. (2015). Schizofreni er en nevrokognitiv forstyrrelse. *Tidsskrift for Norsk Psykologforening, 52*(4), 323–333.

Smedslund, J. (1970). Circular relation between understanding and logic. *Scandinavian Journal of Psychology, 11*, 217–219.

Smedslund, J. (1997). *The structure of psychological common sense*. Mahwah, NJ: Lawrence Erlbaum.

Smedslund, J. (2012). Psycho-logic: some thoughts and after-thoughts. *Scandinavian Journal of Psychology, 55*, 295–302.
Tolman, E. C. (1948). Cognitive maps in rats and men. *Psychological Review, 55*(4), 189–208.
Whitaker, R. (2010). *Anatomy of an epidemic*. New York: Crown.
Wierzbicka, A. (1996). *Semantics: Primes and universals*. Oxford, New York: Oxford University Press.

Chapter 14
Experimental Psychology and Distortions of Common Sense

Davood Gozli

Mainstream psychology provides its own methods of self-critique. These methods include replication efforts, meta-analyses, and estimating effect sizes and the frequency of false positives (Open Science Collaboration 2015). Using a signal-detection metaphor, we could describe these methods as "filters." Research findings that fail to pass the filters are regarded as "noise"; those that pass the filters count as "signal," believed to correspond to features of the psychological domain, which could be reproduced or recovered using the required methods. Typically, these take the form of relationships among variables. The "noise," on the other hand, reflects accidents or intentional misconducts in the guise of discovery. The signal detection metaphor—which implies a dogmatic faith in the presence of "signal" and the methods that produce it—is also reflected in the two types of error with which all students become acquainted: Mistaking noise as genuine signal (type I error) and missing a genuine signal (type II error).

The mainstream approach implies that, aside from replicability, the "signal" (favored research) and "noise" (disfavored research) can be similar in other respects. Accordingly, the merits of empirical research can only be evaluated once we have sufficient *empirical* grounds for our evaluation. By identifying the preferred manner in which one can be critical of research findings, the mainstream preserves the faith in more fundamental aspects of research, including the general approach to subject-matter, assumptions, methods, validity, and relevance. By formulating our aim in terms of increasing the signal-to-noise ratio of research findings (filtering out unreplicable research), we would be neglecting the possibility that an unquestioned faith in the "signal" may be ill-founded, and that more empirical work may not be the only method of critique (Kukla 1989).

D. Gozli (✉)
Department of Psychology, Faculty of Social Sciences, University of Macau, Macao, China
e-mail: gozli@um.edu.mo

T. G. Lindstad et al. (eds.), *Respect for Thought*, Theory and History in the Human and Social Sciences, https://doi.org/10.1007/978-3-030-43066-5_14

We might consider the possibility that, at least in some cases, the replication crisis does not result from an overly permissive "filter" but is, instead, an outcome of the ways in which we produce the "signal" in the first place. Testing the replicability of the findings would be beside the point, if the research questions are ill-posed or the methods are inappropriate. Such possibilities are considered by writers whose work addresses the foundations of psychological research, including Jan Smedslund (Smedslund 1978, 1979, 1987, 1991, 1997a, 2012b, 2016; see also, e.g., Billig 2013; Giorgi 2013; Hibberd 2014; Lamiell 2003; Mammen 2017; Slaney 2017; Teo 2006, Teo 2018; Tissaw and Osbeck 2007; Valsiner 2012, 2017; Wallach and Wallach 2001). Smedslund has called for a more reflective approach to psychology and its relation to common sense. While calling into question the underlying assumptions of empirical research, and the kinds of image they portray of human beings, his critique invites a self-understanding that has room for our autonomy, responsibility, openness in human interaction, and a sensitivity to how we are shaped, in part, by the kinds of beliefs and theories we have about ourselves (Smedslund 2013; see also, Brinkmann 2010; Dalrymple 2015; Sellars 1963).

In the present chapter, my aim is to demonstrate the continuing relevance of the style of critique developed by Smedslund, particularly in experimental psychology. I begin with an overview of Smedslund's critique with reference to the conceptual structure of common sense, which he has worked to explicate in the axiomatic system called Psychologic (PL) (Smedslund 1988, 1991, 1997b, 2012b). I then consider some concerns and possible misunderstandings from the perspective of experimental psychologists. I flesh out the critique with reference to a few examples from experimental research. I will end with considering some reasons for resisting psychologic.

Common-Sense Critique of Experimental Psychology

Broadly formulated, the critique is based on three premises. First, the questions of experimental psychology arise from a conceptual structure. This structure consists of a set of interrelated concepts. Understanding each concept comes with knowing where that concept stands in relation to other concepts (Smedslund 1997b; Strawson 1992). For instance, to pose a research question about *human action*, one needs to understand related concepts, such as *intention* and *ability*. Understanding those related concepts is necessary for understanding human action and, therefore, necessary for posing a research question about human action.

Second, the relations among the concepts do not only include category membership (the way "spoon" is related to "fork") or synonymy (the way "brightness" is related to "illumination"), but also axiomatic relations (the way "action" is related to "intention" and "ability"). Accordingly, the statement, "human action is intentional," is not a statement to be confirmed by any particular observation (at least not for competent language users). It is a statement of meaning—it expresses something about the meaning of human action and intention. Therefore, the conceptual structure, which enables posing a research question, might very well contain the answer to the question. In such cases, treating the question ("is human action intentional?"), as empirical would be to neglect the meaning of the concepts. Thus, a line of research might aim to answer a question by empirical means, when the question could be answered by explicating the meaning of concepts. Smedslund called such research*pseudo-empirical* (Smedslund 1979, 1991, 1994).

Third, pseudo-empirical research results from an erroneous management of attention on our part as researchers, when we focus primarily on designing experiments and quantitative analysis, while neglecting the meaning of concepts. We tend to "focus on the phenomena and procedures [...] and to use language unreflectively in describing and explaining them. The phenomena and procedures are apprehended in terms of a language, but the language itself is not in focus" (Smedslund 1997b, p. ix). As a consequence, we tend to pursue questions that can be answered through reflection on, and explication of, what we tacitly understand.

Our understanding of concepts affects what we can take to be true. Having understood the concepts of *daydreaming, work*, and *motivation,* for instance, we are inclined to evaluate people who routinely daydream at their work as relatively unmotivated to perform their work-related tasks, compared to people who rarely daydream during work. At the same time, our understanding is flexible enough to make room for exceptions, such as the case of artists who intentionally daydream as part of their creative work. The case of the daydreaming artist does not contradict our concept of *daydreaming* or *work*. Nor does it contradict our general assumptions about daydreaming at work. In each case, what we are inclined to believe is constrained by our concepts. Conversely, when our beliefs about what is true change, we might be forced to adjust our concepts. Ceasing to believe in the existence of *witches*, for instance, impacts our understanding of a human person. The concepts that enable us to pose psychological questions include the concepts we use (enact) in our social interactions.

Smedslund's identification of the pseudo-empirical research should be viewed in light of the long-standing philosophical discussions over the meaning and function of analytic statements (Juhl and Loomis 2010) and the distinction between a priori and empirical statements (Casullo, and Thurow 2013; Smedslund 1979, 1987, 1994). Smedslund has taken a rather radical position with regard to analytic (axiomatic) statements, according to which our possession of certain concepts implies tacit and unavoidable commitment to a set of identifiable propositions. If we explicate these concepts and their axiomatic interrelations, he argues, we will end up with a system of propositions, which we then ought not to treat as empirical. However, less radical treatments of analyticity are possible that nevertheless seem to remain consistent with Smedslund's overall approach and, in particular, with his identification of pseudo-empirical research. For instance, according to Juhl and Loomis (2010) the question, "What is an analytic statement?" should be addressed with reference to particular programs of inquiry.

In a given inquiry, there are propositions that are—at least for the time being—taken for granted and, implicitly or explicitly, regarded as true. When researchers ask about the effect of motivation level on daydreaming during a task (Seli et al. 2018), they have accepted that task performance is associated with some degree of motivation and that motivation can vary; when researchers ask about the interaction between perception and thought (Firestone and Scholl 2016), they have accepted some degree of independence between the two (Hibberd 2014). When researchers study variations in a type of behavior, such as creative problem solving, they assume that their methods of assessment correspond to the type of behavior and can capture variations in the behavior (De Houwer 2011). In general, the questions that motivate a given project rest on a set of taken-for-granted propositions. By pursuing the line of inquiry, the propositions are treated as axiomatically true. From this perspective, we do not need to accept axiomatic statements either in terms of special linguistic or conceptual features or in terms of timeless and universal truths. What we recognize, instead, is our ability to *regard*, or stipulate, certain propositions axiomatically in a given context (cf. Juhl and Loomis 2010). The taken-for-granted propositions might become the target of investigation in different programs of research, but that does not undermine their use as axiomatic in the original context of inquiry.

The axiomatic function of beliefs can be extended to our analysis of social interactions. In most of our social interactions, we are committed to a set of shared axioms (Ossorio 2006; Smedslund 1997b). We hold that people's action follow from their beliefs and intentions; we hold that people wish to be respected and cared for. We might set aside these presuppositions, when our observations violate the assumptions, in clinical cases when we encounter a breakdown of personal agency, and when causal explanation (appealing to sub-personal processes) seems more plausible. Nonetheless, in most interactions, including our interactions with research participants in the context of experimental research, we deal with fellow human beings, relying on a shared set of presuppositions. PL is an attempt to make our psychological concepts reflectively present and demonstrate their logical consequences. A research question implies a set of accepted propositions. Hence, even without accepting that certain statements are analytic in their own right, we could take analytic or axiomatic statements to be those that are presupposed, for the time being and in a given program of inquiry (Juhl and Loomis 2010).

Dialogue

A one-sided critical engagement with experimental psychology would be much less preferable to a dialogue. Some adversarial relationships are worth nurturing, and I believe an on-going dialogue between PL and the experimental approach would benefit both sides. The domain of common sense and the problem of pseudo-empirical research are points of contact between the two (Smedslund and Ross 2014). An advantage of engaging with multiple perspectives is that each perspective can detect the errors and limits of the other. Left to its own devices, sensitivity-to-error in experimental psychology will remain confined to those related to replicability (recall the type I and II errors). Another dimension of error opens up when we regard common-sense psychology. One type of error, representing one end point of this dimension, is committed by the "armchair psychologists," who overstate the role of common sense and ignoring the value of novel empirical work, while a *complementary* type of error involves neglecting common-sense psychology and conducting pseudo-empirical research (Smedslund 1997a; Smedslund and Ross 2014). In the following subsection, I consider some possible objections from the perspective of experimental research. Having been trained in experimental psychology, these have been some of my own concerns in studying PL and its critique of empirical psychology.

Is Withdrawing from Empirical Work, and Turning to Conceptual Analysis, Not a Form of Withdrawing from Reality?

Concepts and their logical connections are not withdrawn from reality. They have been, and continue to be, shaped by reality over a larger timescale than the timescale of any given empirical research (recall the example of *witches*). When we describe a point of view as withdrawn from reality, we are describing it as nonresponsive to new observations. The *stability* of conceptual structures should not be mistaken with non-responsiveness to observation. Rather than seeing PL in terms of disengagement, it would be more accurate to see it as grounded in a wealth of personal and collective engagement with reality. By virtue of being social, linguistic, and cultural beings, we have an unreflective–practical understanding of the outcome of that engagement. Furthermore, we have reflective access to that understanding, and the possibility of explicitly formulating it.

Smedslund's exposition of PL, which takes the form of a set of initial axioms and deductively derived theorems, can give the impression of an immutable and fixed conceptual structure, with fixed relations among concepts that could be navigated *deductively*. Others have critiqued Smedslund's approach in this regard, favoring stability over rigidity (Stam 2000; Valsiner 2012, p. 176–177). A stable (but not rigid) conceptual structure would be responsive to novel observations and innovative analyses; a stable structure will accommodate new concepts (concepts such as *collective agency* and *unconscious drives*) and will allow one to challenge or redraw existing boundaries. With a flexible conceptual system, for instance, one could argue against the independence of perception from action (Dewey 1896; Noë 2004) or against the independence of thinking from action (Melser 2004). Going beyond deductive reasoning, the responsiveness of a conceptual structure—its ability to accommodate novel observation and conceptual innovations—enables *abductive*reasoning (Valsiner 2012, 2017). For the present purpose, we could set aside this issue. What matters is that (a) the conceptual structure within a context of inquiry is most often stable, (b) analytic statements that are implicit can be explicated from the conceptual structure, and (c) treating propositions that can be analytically derived—taken-for-granted in the context of inquiry—as empirical questions would be erroneous (pseudo-empirical research).

To emphasize the link between analytic statements ("human action is intentional") and empirical statements ("Peter intentionally raised his voice"), we might wish to see them as belonging to a single continuum. We might consider that analytic statements are those that are confirmed by a large set of observations, while empirical statements are confirmed by a small set of observations. Accordingly, a statement confirmed by ten observations is *more* analytic than a statement confirmed by one. This view is inadequate, because analytic and empirical statements serve different functions (Juhl and Loomis 2010). An empirical statement requires taking for granted a set of analytic assumptions. The difference between analytic and empirical statements, therefore, is not just a matter of stability or quantity of empirical observation, but epistemic priority—one has to be presupposed ("an activity is associated with a motive") prior to evaluating the other ("a given activity's motive is reduced in a particular condition") (Bergner 2010, 2016). With regard to both analytic and empirical statements, we can consider the possibility of error, but that is not the same as rejecting their different functions.

The concern about withdrawing from reality is shared by proponents of conceptual analysis (Hibberd 2014, 2016). Neglecting the underlying conceptual structures in empirical research runs the risk of neglecting necessarily present parts of what is under investigation. For example, with reference to the experimental work on ethical decision making, Smedslund has shown how neglecting the analytic assumptions results in formulating logically incomplete statements, regarding the impact of one factor (e.g., reward) on participants' decision (e.g., helping behavior). Any statement in the form, *reward increases the likelihood of helping behavior,* is "incomplete in the sense of failing to include logically necessary and invariably present constituents of action, such as cognitions of outcome and of own ability, personal want and moral evaluation, etc." (Smedslund 1979, p. 139).

Is Common Sense Not Scientifically Naive? Do We Not Wish to Arrive at More Sophisticated Ways of Describing and Explaining Behavior and Experience?

Hommel and Colzato (2015) wrote that the search for definitions has been a drawback in psychological research. At the outset of a research program, "phenomena are originally described in everyday language, which is highly context-dependent and scientifically naïve" (Hommel and Colzato 2015, p. 2). Their rejection of definition at the outset of research is reasonable, though it is important to be precise with what is being rejected (the proverbial bathwater). The type of definition they reject consists of drawing boundaries around a concept, based on some essential features, which would then allow identifying correct and incorrect uses of the concept. Axioms of PL are not meant to serve this function.

When we refer to common sense as a conceptual structure, we are not referring to a set of fixed definitions (i.e., limited domain of use associated with any given term). Instead, we are recognizing that the flexibility of concept use is constrained by the relations between the concepts (Strawson 1992). Smedslund's account of PL makes use of a set of primitive concepts that are explicitly undefined (Smedslund 1997b). Axioms are relations, including relations among primitive concepts, that are explicitly stated (Smedslund 1997b). Instead of setting strict boundaries around the use of concepts, axioms express the ways in which the meaning of concepts is constrained in terms of their relation to each other (Smedslund 1997b).

> an axiom stipulates that the term shall have a fixed relation to one or a few other terms, but except for this, leaves its meaning open (X, if, and only if, Y). Hence, moving from definition to axiom means moving from freezing the total meaning of a term to freezing its relation to one other term only. (Smedslund 1997b, p. xi).

Misunderstanding can arise from thinking PL offers contingent (empirically testable) statements. For example, Kelley (1992) pointed out that common-sense evaluations only succeed when they are presented after the fact. "One wonders whether a person who labels a proposition 'obvious' could have explicated the hypothesis in advance" (Kelley 1992, p. 13). Kelley points out the presence of contradictory aphorisms, such as "birds of a feather flock together" and "opposites attract," arguing that common sense can be taken as support of statements that are mutually inconsistent. The aim of PL, however, is not to offer contingent statements, but to explicate the conceptual structure that underlies contingent statements (Smedslund 2012a). By sharpening the distinction between contingent and noncontingent propositions, PL (a) helps identify pseudo-empirical research and (b) helps cultivate a not-knowing attitude toward possible (contingent) states of affairs. The not-knowing attitude opposes, not only the type of prejudice that might come from cultural aphorisms ("opposites attract"), but also the kind of prejudice that comes from overgeneralizing the findings of empirical psychology ("reward increases the likelihood of helping behavior") (Smedslund 1979, 2012a, 2013).

The "naive" starting point of common sense, therefore, is not an obstacle against scientific progress. Our use of concepts can be reflective or unreflective. If our aim is going beyond common sense, then a reflective treatment of concepts seems to be a better starting point. We would not go beyond the "naive" viewpoint by disregarding what we already understand.

A related concern might be expressed in terms of the wish to innovate. *If we fall back on common sense, would we not stagnate? What would be left to do?* A systematic approach to the psychological common sense, exemplified in PL, does not have to be stagnant. In addition to contributing to a more reflective approach to practice (Smedslund 2012a), PL helps reorient empirical psychology toward other goals (Smedslund 2002, 2009). These include investigating the effect of interventions in groups, demonstrating the limits of human judgment, and showcasing psychological principles in the form of concrete observations (Smedslund and Ross 2014). Moreover, given that common-sense understanding of the psychological domain is best suited for events at the personal and interpersonal level (also referred to as the "middle level" or "mesolevel," contrasted with micro- and macro level), and given that processes at other levels inevitably "intrude" into the psychological domain, empirical research is needed to build bridges between the different levels of analysis (Dennett 1988; Kelley 1992), adding both biological and historical-cultural dimensions to the psychological domain.

By Abandoning Common Sense, We Are Being Open to Surprises in the Data. Prioritizing Common Sense Would Close the Door for Genuine Discovery

We must disentangle distinct meanings of such an objection. First, the sentiment regarding surprise applies in domains of inquiry such as particle physics and evolutionary biology. We are not tacitly competent in particle physics *before* studying the world by empirical investigation. The same cannot be said about psychology. Most, if not all, of our psychological concepts are gained by being a participant in the social world. We are unreflectively competent common-sense psychologists *before* studying psychology, which drastically reduces the likelihood of surprise in the psychological domain, compared to other domains.

Second, when we discover connections between the psychological domain and a neighboring domain (e.g., physiology), we delve into the unknown. We might find out, for example, that cortical blindness in some cases spares the ability to identify emotional expressions (Striemer et al. 2017), which goes beyond our intuitive understanding of vision. Similarly, our intuitions about emotions are silent when we hear that stimulating the anterior cingulate cortex can make the person laugh (Caruana et al. 2015). It is important to note, however, that these examples represent experiences in which PL ceases to offer an account. In the domain of common sense, we regard persons as being able to become reflectively aware of the emotional expressions they encounter, and we regard them as having reflective and/or unreflective reasons for laughter in their experiences (Smedslund 1997b; Stam 1990). As such, it is not the case that common sense offers incorrect explanation in the cases of neurophysiological disorders or interventions. Rather, it recognizes them as beyond its scope and in need of alternative conceptual structures—structures which treat a person's experience and expressions as subject to causes.

Third, it is true that we can, in the domain of psychology, be surprised by contingent (particular) observations. We can be surprised by what someone does; we can be surprised by trends, opinions, and decisions in groups and communities. Common sense recognizes the possibility of these *local* surprises, which entails the understanding that they usually do not shatter our conceptual structures, nor compel us to extrapolate psychological laws. In a large number of psychological studies, however, a sense of surprise is manufactured by distorting common sense, providing a biased or incomplete representation of the study, or taking a contingent observation as a general law-like regularity (Smedslund 1979, 1991, 1994). As an example, let us consider a research paper that argued romantic love can detrimentally affect our cognitive functions.

Van Steenbergen et al. (2014) recruited participants who had recently fallen in love. Participants first completed a questionnaire that assessed their romantic feelings (Passionate Love Scale; Hatfield and Sprecher 1986). Next, the experimenters attempted to prime thoughts and feelings related to romantic love, through imagination, writing, and self-selected music. Participants then performed a computer tasks that required selective attention to targets and ignoring distractors. Important to the authors' argument, the impact of distractors was found to be positively correlated with the measure of passionate love, which they took as evidence for reduced cognitive control in passionate lovers. A critical evaluation of this study can begin by pointing out that passionate love is not merely a domain of feelings and thoughts, but also a domain of goals and actions. When we ask participants to think about their romantic love, we are evoking the associated goals, which have nothing to do with the experimental tasks designed to measure cognitive control. By mistakenly separating romantic love from goals, we would presuppose that participants' desire to engage with the computer task (intended measure of cognitive control) remains the same, regardless of their strong romantic feelings, while their cognitive control is reduced. This rhetorical strategy would enable us to manufacture a sense of surprise. If, on the other hand, we recognize the association between romantic feelings and goals related to romantic love, we would end up with a much less surprising claim. Rather than stating, "cognitive control is reduced in passionate lovers," we would have to state, "people perform poorly when asked to pursue goals about which they care little, especially after we remind them of something else about which they care very much."

Common Sense Is too Imprecise. What We Wish to Offer Is Precision. Perhaps PL Can Say There Is a Relation Between X and Y, but What Is the Exact Relationship? How Could We Characterize the Relation in Precise Quantitative Terms?

Lack of precision is hardly a limitation of PL. Rather, PL emphasizes relevant conceptual and semantical precision where quantitative precision is beside the point (Smedslund 1987, 1997a). Any quantitative imprecision of PL, which only describes psychological phenomena on an ordinal scale, reflects the intrinsic complexity of the psychological domain. Quantitatively precise relations cannot be obtained due to the involvement of potentially infinite variables (Smedslund 2016). To obtain quantitatively precise estimates we rely on repeated measurements, but participants tend to adapt to both stable and transient features of a task (Akçay and Hazeltine 2008), which means the repeated measurements can change what is being measured. Psychological processes are irreversible (Smedslund 2009, 2016).

An experimental psychologist might object at this point: Even if we grant the irreversibility of psychological processes, what we assume is that the processes are repeatable *in the relevant sense*. Those few relevant features that are taking place under the controlled conditions of the laboratory task, the experimenter contends, will not be affected by repetition. In response to this objection, we should consider Watson's (1916, p. 97) observation regarding simple reflexes—Even an unconditional reflex seems irreversible. Specifically, the first instances of a reflex response tend to be a full-body reaction, whereas later instances during the experimental session become increasingly localized and circumscribed. If there are isolable building blocks in psychological processes that can be repeatedly elicited and measured, they are in part the creation of experimental procedures that shape the processes through repetition (Gozli and Deng 2018).

Returning to the issue of estimating effect sizes, we face the question of the proper setting in which the effect should be estimated. This has been puzzling even in the case of relatively simple priming studies, which present participants with a pair of consecutive stimuli, "prime" followed by "target," testing the effect of the former on participants' responses to the latter. Priming effects are sensitive to the type of language, semantic context, prime-target delay, whether the prime is itself relevant to the task, not to mention individual differences (Estes and Barsalou 2018; Petrova et al. 2018). How should one design the conditions in which an effect size is estimated? The list of factors that influence the effect is, in principle, endless. Researchers interested in the replicability of an effect might wish to introduce as many variations in the experimental setup as possible, whereas researchers interested in modulating the effect might design the study in such a way that the effect is strongest and most reliable. The two types of research diverge in their aims and they very likely end up working with different effect sizes.

Rethinking Experimental Findings

The following examples range in topics from cheating behavior, self-reference bias, and sense of agency. In reviewing them, my aim is to disclose the researchers' mistaken emphasis (albeit implicit) on the discovery of general regularities, the potential for pseudo-empirical research, incomplete statements (leaving out conceptually necessary parts of the situation), and the presentation of surprising findings against the background of a distorted common sense.

Detecting Cheaters

Hilbig and Thielmann (2017) reported a set of experiments in which participants could cheat in a task that involved throwing a dice and reporting the outcome. They manipulated the reward of cheating throughout the experiment to test whether the probability of cheating is sensitive to reward (see also, Fischbacher and Föllmi-Heusi 2013). Based on their findings, they classified four types of participants. First, there were participants who cheated regardless of reward, "brazen liars." Second, there were participants who cheated more frequently with low reward, "small sinners." Third, there were participants who cheated more frequently with high rewards, "corruptibles." Finally, there were the "honest" participants who did not cheat or cheated infrequently.

We should note that Hilbig and Thielman observed all logically possible combinations with regard to reward variations and cheating probability (aside from intermediate states). Varying the reward, people either cheat, do not cheat, cheat with low reward, or cheat with high reward. The findings preclude any statement that relates cheating frequency and reward in a simple manner. What is, then, the contribution of the study? The study's contribution rests on the claim that the researchers have identified four types of participants. If we attribute the patterns of behavior to stable character traits, assuming that under different circumstances the participants' behavior would be predicted based on their behavior in this experiment, then the study can be regarded as a discovery. Thus, the presence of the second and third groups ("small sinners" and "corruptibles") can be taken to show that cheating behavior can change, and that it is sensitive to some specific regularly present factors (including reward).

But if the frequency of cheating changes in some of the groups, why can we not assume that it could change in all of the groups, *under a wider range of manipulations* (not limited to monetary reward)? Furthermore, the statement, "there are four types of individuals when it comes to the relation between reward and cheating," would be a case of a logically incomplete statement. Identifying a conclusion as logically incomplete means the conclusion has excluded relevant and necessarily present attributes, such as the participants' understanding of the task, and the meaning of cheating in this particular context. When considering other variables, we are forced to see the findings as open to additional interpretations.

Consider, for instance, the following claims: "Participants can be grouped in several categories. First, there were participants who found it acceptable to cheat in an experiment that they understood to be about cheating. They assumed cheating would be ethically acceptable in this situation, because it was cheating that interested the researchers. Second, there were participants who found it acceptable to cheat in an experiment that they understood to be about cheating, but they refrained from cheating when it involved a high financial cost for the researchers." And, so on, we can continue to redescribe the other two groups. What makes my alternative interpretation uninteresting is that it lacks the character of a general claim about character traits of the participants. It is not about discovering something that is fixed in the participants. My alternative claim is about the (potentially changing) relation between participants and the experimental situation (Valsiner 2017). The way someone understands an experimental task can change with reflection or further instructions.

According to axiom 1.3.9 of PL, a person wants to do what he or she believes is right (Smedslund 1997b, p. 8). Considering the role of beliefs in action, our capacity to reflect and account for our decisions (including the capacity to rationalize unethical action), and the possibility that our beliefs might change, renders the character–trait interpretation of the findings less plausible than the interpretation based on the acceptability (belief) of cheating during the experiments. Note, for instance, that experimenters might have implicitly encouraged participants to cheat by emphasizing the fact that their responses would not be monitored, which might have led some of the participants, identified as "brazen liars" to *comply* with this implicit instruction. If participants had believed that a behavior is norm and expected, in the context of the experiment, they might have been likely to cheat (Axiom 1.3.11; Smedslund 1997b). Thus, the findings of Hilbig and Thielmann (2017) do not constitute general regularities, but rather a description of a particular state of affairs. The interpretation based on stable character traits is not the only interpretation, although it is one that has the unfounded rhetorical advantage of presenting the findings as empirical discovery.

Self-Serving Bias

Experimental research might be an effective way to showcase possible errors in human reasoning (Smedslund and Ross 2014). Let us turn to one such study. Gregg et al. (2017) divided their participants into two groups and were told about a theory about some species on an imagined planet. In one group, the participants were asked to assume the theory was proposed by them, while the other participants were asked to assume the theory was proposed by another person. Both groups were presented with a series of "facts," some of which were inconsistent with the theory. After the presentation of each fact, the participants were asked to estimate the truth likelihood of the theory. The authors found that, in addition to the participants' sensitivity to facts, the group who related the theory to themselves rated the theory more favorably.

According to Axiom 2.2.3 of PL, a person wants to believe what is the case (see also, Theorems 3.6.4 and 3.6.5, which highlight the affective dimension of having one's theory confirmed or disconfirmed). Thus, this axiom can be taken in two ways. It could be taken in terms of one's attitude in forming new beliefs. Given two options, I will pick the belief that better corresponds to evidence. But the axiom could also be taken in terms of our attitude towards already formed beliefs as we face new evidence. Given the option to accept or discard a piece of evidence, I will choose to discard it if it does not match my belief. In other words, Gregg et al.'s findings could be derived from PL axioms, which we take for granted in interacting and understanding each other.

We can assume that wanting to hold true beliefs would make participants responsive to disconfirming facts, and this was observed by Gregg et al. (2017). On the other hand, reevaluating theory against evidence is an effortful process. Assuming that people generally wish to minimize exertion (Axiom 2.4.8, Smedslund 1997b), they might rely on self-reference as a strategy to evaluate theories quickly. It is crucial to note that Gregg et al. informed their participants that "there were no right or wrong answers" (p. 999). Combined with their anonymity as research participants, and the lack of any serious consequence in providing rationally weak responses, it is not surprising that the disconfirming facts were not the *only* variable to which participants' responses were sensitive.

In short, the potential for a self-serving bias in evaluation of theories, especially under circumstances in which there is no urgent demand for strictly rational evaluation, can be derived from the axioms of PL. Presenting such a self-serving bias either as a universal regularity, subject to exact quantification, or as a surprising phenomenon, would require distorting common sense. It would involve proposing a logically incomplete statement, relating self-reference and theory evaluation, excluding necessarily present attributes involved in theory evaluation, such as the context of theorizing, what is at stake, level of expertise, and so forth.

Effort and Sense of Agency

Experimental research on sense of agency relies on situations in which participants cannot clearly judge whether a given event is the outcome of their action. The ambiguity enables researchers to test the effect of variables that might sway the sense of agency one way or another (Gozli 2019). One of these variables that has been tested is the amount of effort. Minohara et al. (2016) used button-press tasks, with the buttons requiring relatively more or less force. With a variable delay after the button-press, a visual event was presented (a box moving up and down on the screen). Participants were asked to report whether they felt this visual event was the outcome of their button-press action. The researchers found that more forceful button presses were associated with slightly higher degree of sense of agency.

Axiom 2.2.3 of PL relates action to the person's ability to perform the action: "P does A, if, and only if, P can do A, and P tries to do A" (Smedslund 1997b, p. 20). Assuming that the person wants to press a button, and attempts to do so, then he or she will complete the button-press, if, and only if, he or she has the ability. From this axiom, we can make inferences about *single actions*, which vary in their degree of effort. We can do so in order to replace ability (as a relatively stable factor) with effort (as a relatively transient factor). Instead of talking about a person acting or not acting, we can say: an action is either completed as planned, or it fails be to be completed. Assuming that the agent wants to perform the action, and attempts to do so, then the action is more likely to be completed if more effort goes into the action. Negating this—or treating it as an empirical statement—would contradict with our concept of *effort* and *action*. Accordingly, if a given task retains its level of difficulty, while more effort goes in the action, then our estimate of likelihood regarding action completion increases. A variant of this statement is the assumption of monotonicity, summarized as "larger forces lead to larger results" (Gärdenfors et al. 2018, p.3). The concept *effort* includes more attributes than simple force, such as increasing accuracy, patience, number of attempts, or focusing on learning.

If an action does not yield any outcome, then increasing effort might increase the actor's expectation for the outcome. Consider an event that is ambiguously seen as the outcome of my action (e.g., my cat turns toward me 3 seconds after I call him). If I have put more effort into calling him, the same ambiguous outcome is more likely to be perceived as the outcome of my action (e.g., my cat turns after I shout vs. after I whisper). In cases of ambiguity, when our ability is marginally sufficient for the action, or when there is something unusual about the outcome (e.g., delay), we might rely on our own effort to disambiguate the relation between action and outcome. The ability to do so is embedded in our practical understanding of action.

The findings from another study might appear more surprising. The surprise lies in the claim that the researchers tested the role of effort on the sense of agency in an "independent task" (Demanet et al. 2013). The task over which sense of agency was tested was performed with the right hand (using the computer mouse), while the left hand was holding a stretched rubber band with high or low effort. The authors found that the force applied to the stretched band increased sense of agency. The claim is that the influence of effort was not limited to where exactly the effort is directed. The two hands, the authors reasoned, were performing two independent tasks. Yet, increased effort in one of them affected the sense of agency in the other. If this claim is taken at face value, it introduces something that goes beyond common sense understanding of effort and action. The question is, can we take the claim at face value? In particular, can we assume that the left and right hands in Demanet et al.'s (2013) study were performing two independent tasks?

What would be our criteria for regarding two tasks as independent? Demanet et al.'s two tasks clearly overlap in time, but that might not be an appropriate criterion. I can drive and have a conversation at the same time, and the two can be regarded as independent activities. A better criterion is whether the two tasks are serving one superordinate goal. Driving and conversation are typically not serving the same superordinate goal. Another way to ask this question would be: If one of the tasks is interrupted or fails, can the other task continue? If a conversation stops, driving can continue; if the car stops, the conversation can continue. In Demanet et al.'s study, the two tasks were serving one superordinate goal (fulfilling the requirements of the experiment). Had participants failed at one of the two tasks (letting go of the rubber band or the computer mouse), the other task would have lost its significance. The criteria for inclusion in the experiment include simultaneously performing both tasks. Therefore, the two cannot be regarded as independent.

Regarding two subtasks as independent is a distortion of common sense that results from suspending our view of the broader context—task instruction, criteria for inclusion, and evaluation of research participants—of the experimental setup (Gozli 2017). Once we regard the two components as belonging to the same task, i.e., required for being included as participants in the experiment, then the same reasoning, applied to Minohara et al. (2016), also applies to the study by Demanet et al. (2013). The relation between effort and outcome is rooted in our common sense understanding of the concepts. It runs through, and is prior to, the very conceptual structure that supports designing and interpreting an experiment. As such, it does not require experimental verification.

It should be emphasized that the propositions we derived from PL, with respect to effort and the sense of agency, do not necessitate the conclusions of the aforementioned studies (Demanet et al. 2013; Minohara et al. 2016). Instead, they imply that certain (contingent) empirical observations would be possible, if their required conditions are satisfied. Although some might think the experimental studies give certainty and precision to common-sense statements, the studies might actually take away what is valuable about our common-sense statements, namely their openness, ambiguity, and flexibility. The statement "effort increases sense of agency" is incomplete; it can be true or false under different circumstances (recall Smedslund's critique of the statement, "reward increases helping behavior"). If we overgeneralize the experimental findings that support the statement, desensitizing ourselves to the role of context and possible exceptions, we would be trading the flexibility of common sense, not for precision, but for rigidity.

Sense of Agency and Goals

Another variable whose effect on sense of agency has been tested is the presence of goals. We should distinguish between distal and proximal goals (Gozli and Dolcini 2018; Pacherie 2008). *Pushing* the door is a more proximal goal, relative to *opening* the door. Pressing a light switch is more proximal than turning on the light. What we call "proximal" and "distal" can change based on our frame of reference. In reviewing the following studies, the term "goal" is used in reference to relatively distal goals, identified by the experimenters. The proximal goals are necessarily involved as the means by which participants attempt to fulfill the distal goals.

Wen et al. (2015) demonstrated that pursuing a goal can reduce participants' sense of agency over otherwise similar actions. They instructed participants to try to control the movements of a cursor using two keys. In one set of condition, participants were instructed to simply try to move around the cursor ("no goal"), which enabled them to explore the relation between the keys and cursor movements, and in another set of conditions they were instructed to try to direct the cursor into a box ("goal"), which required them to use the key–cursor relation. Like other studies on the sense of agency, the relation between the keys and the cursor movement was ambiguous. On average, participants reported lower sense of agency over the movements of the cursor in the "goal" condition.

The study by Wen et al. (2015) should be contrasted with another study (Kumar and Srinivasan 2014), which showed that achieving a goal can *increase* participants' sense of agency, regardless of the more detailed (proximal) attributes of the performance. Kumar and Srinivasan found that if participants hit a designated target, they were (a) more likely to report higher sense of agency and (b) they were more likely to ignore their *actual* sensorimotor ability afforded by the task.

Together, the findings suggest that the presence of distal goals can either decrease or increase the sense of agency. We might say, in light of the findings, that a relatively easy goal (or one that is achieved) can increase participants' sense of agency, whereas a relatively difficult goal (or one that is not achieved) can reduce the sense of agency. Similar statements can be derived from common-sense axioms. Successfully performing a given action is associated with the ability to perform the action, wanting to perform the action, and attempting to do so (Axioms 2.2.3–5, Smedslund 1997b). If one believes one's action to be successful after an attempt, then one understands that one had the ability (agency) to perform the action. Negating this assumption would contradict our understanding of action and ability.

Summary

By isolating a subset of relevant variables (cheating and reward; self-reference and evaluation; sense of agency and effort; sense of agency and goal), an incomplete description of a task can be formulated and as its full conceptual implications are not clarified it is mistakenly treated as in need for empirical testing. Once the statement obtains its empirical expression, it can be regarded as a general regularity ("effort increases sense of agency"), rather than an observation that is contingent on the particular experimental conditions. The controlled conditions of a given experiment might play a role in obtaining the relation between the variables. We considered this in the case of informing participants that their behavior is not being monitored (Hilbig and Thielmann 2017), that there were no right or wrong answers (Gregg et al. 2017). We also considered this in cases where judgments of agency cannot be made unambiguously, rendering participants' sense of agency prone to manipulation. We could include, in this list, the difficulty of achieving the goal, or the difficulty of the means by which participants could pursue the goals, in the studies on sense of agency (Wen et al. 2015; Kumar and Srinivasan 2014). The common role for these factors is that (a) they stay in the background as accidental features of the experimental setup and (b) they help produce a pattern of relation that could not otherwise be obtained. As such, they help presenting incomplete and contingent statements as generalized discoveries (Smedslund 1979, 1991, 1994).

Resisting Common Sense

Why would experimental psychologist not engage more reflectively with common-sense psychology? Part of the answer has to do with the disciplinary training and the current academic culture that emphasizes productivity (number of publications) and self-promotion over reflection and critique (Billig 2013). Experimental psychologists typically begin their career as research assistants, which are, among other things, a gradual process of distorting one's common sense (Smedslund 2013). Many of us are trained in institutes that have already cut off the influence of philosophy, history of psychology, and critical psychology from our education. Not knowing what correctives are available in philosophy, phenomenology, history of psychology, sociology of knowledge, and common-sense psychology, the research assistants who become principal investigators will perpetuate the distortions into the next academic generations (Hibberd and Gozli 2017; Mammen and Gozli 2018).

The correctives are necessary, not in order to impede psychological studies, but to guide them. PL is one corrective, especially against certain types of error (overgeneralization; pseudo-empirical research), but it cannot be the only guide. Taken by itself, PL might lead to disconnecting the psychological field from other fields. As Engelsted put it, "you cannot have a special science of psychology if *everything* is psychological and *only* psychological; if it is to be *explanandum* and not merely *explanans*, psychology must have roots and causes in a non-psychological world" (Engelsted 2017, p. 26). Empirical research could combat the errors of "armchair psychology", when connecting the psychological field with the micro and macro levels of analysis (Kelley 1992), and prevent the drowning of all inquiry into a false "common sense." The fact that common sense can become overconfident or be swayed by certain scientific myths (Lilienfeld et al. 2010) is itself an indication that our common sense requires the right kind of resources. What PL offers is precisely one such guide. Conversely, without the guidance of PL, empirical psychology might lose sight of its own domain. Rather than reflectively pursuing empirical research projects, and being mindful of critical perspectives, psychologists might develop defensive styles of discourse to justify their existing and ongoing research (Billig 2013). Defensive discourse, about science, is not the same as science itself, although the discourse can help preserve flawed lines of research against valid criticism.

As an example of defensive discourse of science, take Ross and Nisbett (2011), who write in the introduction of their influential book on experimental social psychology, "We may never be able to predict how particular people will respond to novel situations. […] Situations are highly complex, and so are people's interpretations of them" (p. 17). So far, their sentiment seems compatible with common sense (Smedslund 2016). They continue to say, however, that they "are neither apologetic about these limits to prediction nor distressed by their practical implications." The unapologetic attitude appears, again, after acknowledging the vast number of factors that enable or influence any given behavior, "the discovery and description of the sources of such inherent unpredictability […] is hardly a cause for apology" (p. 18). A few pages later, the unapologetic attitude seems to be replaced by a disregard, when the authors begin an overview of the book:

> people from different backgrounds, people with different beliefs, even people with apparently different personalities, must understand and react to some situations rather uniformly. … [T]here are at least some important respects in which human beings prove to be more alike than we generally reckon them to be (Ross and Nisbett 2011, p. 24).

Scientists are not generally requested to apologize for the limitation of their work, but it is a clever rhetorical tactic to conflate *apologizing for* something and *having regard for* something, and then refusing both under the reasonably guise of refusing to apologize. Let us take a look at one more example of defensive meta-scientific discourse. In a joint paper, Smedslund and Ross (2014) discuss their opposing views with respect to the value of empirical research in psychology. In defense of empirical research, presumably voicing out Ross's position, we read:

> it would seem perverse to argue that knowledge of the research [...] is of no incremental value to the more general knowledge one has about human judgment and decision-making from ordinary everyday experience and deduction from more abstract principles. (Smedslund and Ross 2014, pp. 377–378).

The word, "perverse," serves a rhetorical purpose, dismissing the opposing view without substantial argumentation. We would be less inclined to adopt, or even seriously consider, a position that is described as "perverse" by an academic authority.

Similar strategies are likely to continue, as long as they help psychologists excel according to the current standards of a successful career. An unreflective science of psychology should be considered with regard to an evolutionary theory of science (Smaldino and McElreath 2016), and the selective pressures that favor productivity and self-promotion. Even if we level the playing field, such that, starting from tomorrow, theoretical–philosophical psychologists and empirical psychologists have equal career opportunities, we will eventually arrive back to the present situation, unless we collectively obtain an alternative set of standards for our scholarly contribution. I believe Smedslund's work promotes a genre of critique that could help improve those standards.

Regardless of the fate of our discipline, common sense and ordinary language have a place for human persons and communities as part of the real world; there is a place for the mental life of persons and their rational engagements with each other (Sellars 1963; Strawson 1992). The natural–scientific reasoning challenges this position when it points to our occasional fallibility. The reasoning goes wrong, however, when human fallibility is used as means of totally undermining our sense of autonomy. The view rooted in common sense and ordinary language, or at least one we should strive to maintain and renew, is one that does have room for human fallibility without throwing away the regard for our rationality, autonomy, and responsibility.

Smedslund's work is the outcome of reflective engagement with common sense, and it affords further reflection. It belongs in the domain, which Sellars (1963) called, the *manifest image* of human beings, standing resistant to the fragmentation seen in the *scientific image*. The manifest image includes the recognition of ourselves as the kind of creatures whose nature is partly determined by what we think of ourselves (Dalrymple 2015; Sellars 1963). An unreflective distortion of concepts, in the service of promoting the status of psychology as a natural science, continues to be a degenerative force in our self-understanding.

Acknowledgments I am grateful to Tobias G. Lindstad and Jaan Valsiner for their very helpful comments on an earlier draft of this chapter.

References

Akçay, Ç., & Hazeltine, E. (2008). Conflict adaptation depends on task structure. *Journal of Experimental Psychology: Human Perception and Performance, 34*(4), 958–973.

Bergner, R. M. (2010). What is descriptive psychology? An introduction. In K. Davis, F. Lubuguin, & W. Schwartz (Eds.), *Advances in descriptive psychology* (Vol. 9, pp. 325–360). Ann Arbor, MI: Descriptive Psychology Press.

Bergner, R. M. (2016). What is behaviour? And why is it not reducible to biological states of affairs? *Journal of Theoretical and Philosophical Psychology, 36*, 41–55.

Billig, M. (2013). *Learn to write badly: How to succeed in the social sciences*. Cambridge: Cambridge University Press.

Brinkmann, S. (2010). *Psychology as a moral science: Perspectives on normativity*. New York, NY: Springer.

Caruana, F., Avanzini, P., Gozzo, F., Francione, S., Cardinale, F., & Rizzolatti, G. (2015). Mirth and laughter elicited by electrical stimulation of the human anterior cingulate cortex. *Cortex, 71*, 323–331.

Casullo, A., & Thurow, J. C. (Eds.). (2013). *The a priori in philosophy*. Oxford: Oxford University Press.

Dalrymple, T. (2015). *Admirable evasions: How psychology undermines morality*. New York: Encounter Books.

Dennett, D. C. (1988). Précis of the intentional stance. *Behavioral and Brain Sciences, 11*(3), 495–505.

Dewey, J. (1896). The reflex arc concept in psychology. *Psychological Review, 3*, 357–370.

De Houwer, J. (2011). Why the cognitive approach in psychology would profit from a functional approach and vice versa. *Perspectives on Psychological Science, 6*(2), 202–209.

Demanet, J., Muhle-Karbe, P. S., Lynn, M. T., Blotenberg, I., & Brass, M. (2013). Power to the will: how exerting physical effort boosts the sense of agency. *Cognition, 129*, 574–578.

Engelsted, N. (2017). *Catching up with Aristotle: a journey in quest of general psychology*. Cham: Springer.

Estes, Z., & Barsalou, L. W. (2018). A comprehensive meta-analysis of spatial interference from linguistic cues: Beyond Petrova et al. (2018). *Psychological Science* (Online first).

Firestone, C., & Scholl, B. J. (2016). Cognition does not affect perception: Evaluating the evidence for 'top-down' effects. *Behavioral & Brain Sciences, e229*, 1–77.

Fischbacher, U., & Föllmi-Heusi, F. (2013). Lies in disguise—An experimental study on cheating. *Journal of the European Economic Association, 11*(3), 525–547.

Gärdenfors, P., Jost, J., & Warglien, M. (2018). From actions to effects: Three constraints on event mappings. *Frontiers in Psychology, 9*, 1391.

Giorgi, A. (2013). Reflections on the status and direction of psychology: An external historical perspective. *Journal of Phenomenological Psychology, 44*(2), 244–261.

Gregg, A. P., Mahadevan, N., & Sedikides, C. (2017). The SPOT effect: People spontaneously prefer their own theories. *The Quarterly Journal of Experimental Psychology, 70*(6), 996–1010.

Gozli, D. G. (2017). Behaviour versus performance: The veiled commitment of experimental psychology. *Theory & Psychology, 27*, 741–758.

Gozli, D. G. (2019). *Experimental psychology and human agency*. Cham: Springer.

Gozli, D. G., & Deng, W. (2018). Building blocks of psychology: On remaking the unkept promises of early schools. *Integrative Psychological and Behavioral Science, 52*, 1–24.

Gozli, D. G., & Dolcini, N. (2018). Reaching into the unknown: Actions, goal hierarchies, and explorative agency. *Frontiers in Psychology, 9*, 266.

Hatfield, E., & Sprecher, S. (1986). Measuring passionate love in intimate relationships. *Journal of Adolescence, 9*(4), 383–410.

Hibberd, F. (2014). The metaphysical basis of a process psychology. *Journal of Theoretical and Philosophical Psychology, 34*(3), 161–186.

Hibberd, F. J. (2016). Is conceptual analysis only an inquiry into rules for the use of concepts? *Theory & Psychology, 26*(6), 815–822.

Hibberd, F. J., & Gozli, D. G. (2017). Psychology's fragmentation and neglect of foundational assumptions: An interview with Fiona J Hibberd. *Europe's Journal of Psychology, 13*, 366–374.

Hilbig, B. E., & Thielmann, I. (2017). Does everyone have a price? On the role of payoff magnitude for ethical decision making. *Cognition, 163*, 15–25.

Hommel, B., & Colzato, L. S. (2015). Learning from history: The need for a synthetic approach to human cognition. *Frontiers in Psychology, 6*, 1435.

Juhl, C., & Loomis, E. (2010). *Analyticity*. Abingdon: Routledge.

Kelley, H. H. (1992). Common-sense psychology and scientific psychology. *Annual Review of Psychology, 43*(1), 1–24.

Kukla, A. (1989). Nonempirical issues in psychology. *American Psychologist, 44*(5), 785–794.

Kumar, D., & Srinivasan, N. (2014). Naturalizing sense of agency with a hierarchical event-control approach. *PLoS One, 9*(3), e92431.

Lamiell, J. T. (2003). *Beyond individual and group differences: Human individuality, scientific psychology, and William Stern's critical personalism*. Thousand Oaks, CA: Sage Publications.

Lilienfeld, S. O., Lynn, S. J., Ruscio, J., & Beyerstein, B. L. (2010). *50 great myths of popular psychology: Shattering widespread misconceptions about human behavior*. Chichester: Wiley-Blackwell.

Mammen, J. (2017). *A new logical foundation for psychology*. Cham: Springer.

Mammen, J., & Gozli, D. (2018). Rebellion, theory, and dialogue: an interview with Jens Mammen. *Human Arenas* (Online first).

Melser, D. (2004). *The act of thinking*. Cambridge, MA: MIT Press.

Minohara, R., Wen, W., Hamasaki, S., Maeda, T., Kato, M., Yamakawa, H., Yamashita, A., & Asama, H. (2016). Strength of intentional effort enhances the sense of agency. *Frontiers in Psychology, 7*, 1165.

Noë, A. (2004). *Action in perception*. Cambridge, MA: MIT Press.

Open Science Collaboration. (2015). Estimating the reproducibility of psychological science. *Science, 349*(6251), aac4716.

Ossorio, P. (2006). *The behavior of persons*. Ann Arbor, MI: Descriptive Psychology Press.

Pacherie, E. (2008). The phenomenology of action: A conceptual framework. *Cognition, 107*(1), 179–217.

Petrova, A., Navarrete, E., Suitner, C., Sulpizio, S., Reynolds, M., Job, R., & Peressotti, F. (2018). Spatial congruency effects exist, just not for words: Looking into Estes, Verges, and Barsalou (2008). *Psychological Science, 29*(7), 1195–1199.

Ross, L., & Nisbett, R. E. (2011). *The person and the situation: Perspectives of social psychology*. Pinter & Martin Ltd. (Originally published in 1991).

Seli, P., Schacter, D. L., Risko, E. F., & Smilek, D. (2018). Increasing participant motivation reduces rates of intentional and unintentional mind wandering. *Psychological Research* (Online first).

Sellars, W. (1963). *Science, perception, and reality*. Austin, TX: Ridgeview Publishing.

Slaney, K. (2017). *Validating psychological constructs: Historical, philosophical, and practical dimensions*. New York, NY: Springer.

Smaldino, P. E., & McElreath, R. (2016). The natural selection of bad science. *Royal Society Open Science, 3*(9), 160384.

Smedslund, J. (1978). Bandura's theory of self-efficacy: A set of common sense theorems. *Scandinavian Journal of Psychology, 19*(1), 1–14.

Smedslund, J. (1979). Between the analytic and the arbitrary: A case study of psychological research. *Scandinavian Journal of Psychology, 20*(1), 129–140.

Smedslund, J. (1987). The epistemic status of inter-item correlations in Eysenck's Personality Questionnaire: The a priori versus the empirical in psychological data. *Scandinavian Journal of Psychology, 28*(1), 42–55.

Smedslund, J. (1988). *Psycho-logic*. Heidelberg: Springer-Verlag.

Smedslund, J. (1991). The pseudoempirical in psychology and the case for psychologic. *Psychological Inquiry, 2*, 325–338.

Smedslund, J. (1994). Non-empirical and empirical components in the hypotheses of five social psychological experiments. *Scandinavian Journal of Psychology, 35*(1), 1–15.

Smedslund, J. (1997a). The ambiguity of covariation: A conceptual note. *Scandinavian Journal of Psychology, 38*(1), 35–38.

Smedslund, J. (1997b). *The structure of psychological common sense*. Mahwah, NJ: Lawrence Erlbaum.

Smedslund, J. (2002). From hypothesis-testing psychology to procedure-testing psychologic. *Review of General Psychology, 6*(1), 51–72.

Smedslund, J. (2009). The mismatch between current research methods and the nature of psychological phenomena: What researchers must learn from practitioners. *Theory & Psychology, 19*(6), 778–794.

Smedslund, J. (2012a). The bricoleur model of psychological practice. *Theory & Psychology, 22*(5), 643–657.

Smedslund, J. (2012b). Psycho-logic: Some thoughts and after-thoughts. *Scandinavian Journal of Psychology, 55*, 295–302.

Smedslund, J. (2013). *From nonsense syllables to holding hands: Sixty years as a psychologist*. Chagrin Falls, OH: Taos Institute Publications.

Smedslund, J. (2016). Why psychology cannot be an empirical science. *Integrative Psychological and Behavioral Science, 50*(2), 185–195.

Smedslund, J., & Ross, L. (2014). Based knowledge in psychology: What, if anything, is its incremental value to the practitioner? *Integrative Psychological and Behavioral Science, 48*(4), 365–383.

Stam, H. (1990). What distinguishes lay persons' psychological explanations from those of psychologists? In W. J. Baker, M. E. Hyland, R. van Hezewijk, & S. Terwee (Eds.), *Recent trends in theoretical psychology* (Vol. II, pp. 97–106). New York: Springer-Verlag.

Stam, H. (2000). Logic or psychologism: Smedslund's psychologic and health. *Journal of Health Psychology, 5*(2), 161–164.

Strawson, P. F. (1992). *Analysis and metaphysics*. Oxford: Oxford University Press.

Striemer, C. L., Whitwell, R. L., & Goodale, M. A. (2017). Affective blindsight in the absence of input from face processing regions in occipital-temporal cortex. *Neuropsychologia* (Online first).

Teo, T. (2006). *The critique of psychology: From Kant to postcolonial theory*. Dordrecht: Springer Science & Business Media.

Teo, T. (2018). *Outline of theoretical psychology: Critical investigations*. New York, NY: Palgrave.

Tissaw, M. A., & Osbeck, L. M. (2007). On critical engagement with the mainstream: Introduction. *Theory & Psychology, 17*(2), 155–168.

Van Steenbergen, H., Langeslag, S. J., Band, G. P., & Hommel, B. (2014). Reduced cognitive control in passionate lovers. *Motivation and Emotion, 38*, 444–450.

Valsiner, J. (2012). *A guided science: History of psychology in the mirror of its making*. Abingdon: Routledge.

Valsiner, J. (2017). *From methodology to methods in human psychology*. New York, NY: Springer.

Wallach, L., & Wallach, M. A. (2001). Experiments in social psychology: Science or self-deception? *Theory & Psychology, 11*(4), 451–473.

Watson, J. B. (1916). The place of the conditioned-reflex in psychology. *Psychological Review, 23*, 89–116.

Wen, W., Yamashita, A., & Asama, H. (2015). The influence of goals on sense of control. *Consciousness and Cognition, 37*, 83–90.

Chapter 15
Extending Smedslund's Psycho-Logic System into a Social Theory

Luk Van Langenhove

This chapter develops in four steps.[1] First, the conceptual universe of Smedslund's psycho-logic (PL) is briefly presented along with some of its basic assumptions. Secondly, a number of flaws and limitations of PL will be discussed. Next it will be advocated that Smedslund's theory could and should be turned into a psycho/socio-logic theory. For this, a number of insights from social theory, especially from the multidisciplinary work of Rom Harré, will be presented. Moreover, it will be argued that it makes sense to bring in some elements from quantum physics as metaphors to help understand how psychological and social phenomena are entangled. In the final section, some elements of such a theory will be presented to illustrate how Smedslund's theory can be linked to the linguistic turn in the social sciences. This will include a discussion on how speech acts form the substance of psychological and social phenomena, how they give rise to moral and knowledge fields and how they create local positions taken by persons. Finally, attention will go to the consequences of the abovementioned for theorizing persons.

Institute of European Studies at the Vrije Universiteit Brussel and United Nations University Institute for Comparative Regional Integration Studies.

[1] This chapter is part of a larger project of the author to re-think the ontology of the social sciences (see Van Langenhove 2007). It draws heavily upon Van Langenhove (2017) where the reader can find more details about what is said here about the centrality of 'speech-acts' for social theory and about 'moral fields'.

L. Van Langenhove (✉)
Institute of European Studies of the Vrije Universiteit Brussel (VUB), Brussels, Belgium
e-mail: luk.van.langenhove@vub.be

T. G. Lindstad et al. (eds.), *Respect for Thought*, Theory and History in the Human and Social Sciences, https://doi.org/10.1007/978-3-030-43066-5_15

The Conceptual Universe of Smedslund

With remarkable continuity of thinking, Jan Smedslund has since the 1970s been working on an attempt to explicate and systematize the psychology used in everyday life commonsense thinking. This culminated in the 1988 book 'Psycho-logic', but until today, Smedslund has been updating and reformulating his project continuously (see for instance: Smedslund 1995, 1997, 2012, 2016). Smedslund defines psycho-logic as *'an approach to psychology, starting from ordinary language and common-sense psychology'* (Smedslund 2012, p. 295). He also referred to it as *'an attempt to systematize and make precise the conceptual psychological framework embedded in ordinary language'* (Smedslund 1995, p. 203). Common sense is thereby regarded as *'the set of all implications taken for granted by all members of a culture'* (Smedslund 1988, p. 5). The outcome of Smedslund's life–work is a system of definitions of psychological concepts and a set of axioms of the system. From the definitions and the axioms, a number of propositions have been derived that take the form of theorems and corollaries. The result is an elaborate set of concepts for which Smedslund has high hopes: His ultimate goal is that the system allows 'one to predict behavior, given sufficient information about antecedent conditions' (Smedslund 1988, p.3). But later, he also stated that:

> the task is not –, as formerly thought, to discover hitherto unknown laws, but to explicate and systematize what we already know … You cannot predict what a particular person will do next because you don't know the person and his or her subjective situation sufficiently well. The better you know the person and his or her situation, the more accurate are your predictions. There are no laws to be discovered. (Smedslund 1995, p. 206)

With this, Smedslund implicitly puts himself on the side of those who reject the idea that nomothetic laws are possible in psychology and along those who favour the development of idiographic knowledge about single cases (see Smith et al. 1995).

The idea to build a conceptual framework for psychology based upon common sense is certainly an interesting and challenging concept. It is in-line with Alfred Schutz's observation that a distinction needs to be made between first- and second-order theories: The first ones are theories constructed by the common-sense thinking of people in their daily lives, the second ones are the social scientists' theories that cannot ignore that first-degree theorizing (Schutz 1953). According to Schutz, social scientists should not dismiss the knowledge, and perhaps the wisdom, that people have about their own situation and how they cope with it. Hence, it seems to make a lot of sense to try to map common sense as Smedslund does.

Smedslund's system of psycho-logic of concepts is a welcome change to much of the empiricist and positivist mainstream approaches to psychology that by now have been criticized by many. In their seminal book, *The Explanation of Social Behaviour*, Harré and Secord (1974) have already pointed to the need to develop a conception of psychology that treats people not as subjects but as persons who have the capacity to talk about what they are doing and why they do it. The same volume also advocated replacing the naive empiricism of many experimental psychologists by a theory led inquiry. Since then, many scholars have followed suit and pleaded for more theory in psychology (Van Langenhove, 2012). But by and large, the discipline of psychology still suffers *'from a gross and systematic underestimation of the scope, variety, and import of theoretical work'* (Kukla 2001, p. xi). Smedslund's work is, therefore, a laudable exception to this trend. But notwithstanding all my sympathy for Smedslunds's approach, a number of critical remarks need to be made.

Flaws and Limitations

First of all, there is the issue to what extent one can build such a conceptual psychological framework upon only 'common sense', without taking explicitly into account insights from psychological theories and research. On the one hand, the question is if a strict separation between common-sense and scientific thinking is even possible. Often insights from psychology permeate into society and become part of what is regarded as common sense. A classic example is the spread of Freudian terminology and related thinking in Western societies (Moscovici 2008). But there are also many other concepts that have found their way from psychology to everyday life. 'ADHD' for instance, or 'burn out', these are diagnostic terms that are now widely used by laypersons and perhaps not always in a correct way. And even a concept such as 'attitude', has its origins in psychological research but is now used as an everyday concept. Interestingly, the notion of attitude does not figure in Smedslund's system, although he uses it in Smedslund (1988, p. 96) when discussing drug habits. On the other hand, it could well be that some of the common-sense ideas that people hold are false without people realizing their error. It could also be that people have appropriated scientific knowledge that makes them realize that their common sense is not correct. For instance, people all over the world see everyday the sun rising and moving until sunset. It is therefore only natural to assume from a common-sense perspective that the sun rotates around the earth. But since Galileo, we know better and people informed by science do realize that the reverse is true: It is the earth that rotates around the sun. There is thus scientific knowledge that goes against common sense as what concerns the physical realm. I see no reason not to believe that the same holds for psychological or social phenomena. The work of Kahnemann (2011) for instance, contains many examples of how common-sense thinking fails to grasp dealing with statistical probabilities. So, one may question the extent to which Smedslund's (e.g. Smedslund 1995) partial departure from common sense in designing a technical language for psychology is wise. But then statistical probabilities are hardly the only way to make sense of the world, there is also a heuristic way to make sense of the world. It should also be noticed that Smedslund thinks of PL as the explication of something inherently coherent and sound and as such psychological common sense, as Smedslund uses the words, is thus not co-extensional with failures to grasp statistical probabilities.

Secondly, Smedslund takes the individual person as a point of departure of his conceptual framework. This is of course totally in line with our common sense as we are all persons that perceive the world, including ourselves as well as other persons. Smedslund (2012, p. XX) states that a person takes for granted that other persons can do the same as (s)he does. While I believe this observation is true, without the relevant supplements, it opens the door to an atomized and inaptly decontextualized view of psychology. This results in a functional approach where psychological phenomena are seen as purely individual phenomena. But since Lev Vygotsky's seminal work in the 1920s and 1930s, we know that the distinction between what is personal and social is not a dichotomy, but an interplay between two logically independent dimensions: The public–private axis and the individual–collective axis. Situating psychological phenomena has to be done on the Cartesian product of both dimensions. As a result, psychological phenomena can be situated in four quadrants: From public and collective to private and individual. In a way, this resonates with Smedslund's remark that 'In the simplest possible way, my agreement with social constructionism can be described as follows: Since Kant, one must agree that we cannot know "das Ding an sich". Therefore, a person must rely on the *interpretation* of the world ("construction"). However, since persons depend on each other for survival and procreation, their interpretations (constructions) must converge (constructions must be shared). Therefore, social constructionism in a broad sense is necessarily true' (Smedslund 2013, p. 86).

Thirdly, Smedslund's conceptual scheme also downplays the importance of language. While the attention goes to defining concepts, he has not clarified in sufficient detail the role of how words are used in creating social reality and how for instance analogies and metaphors shape our thinking (see Hofstadter and Sander 2013). Smedslund seems to have been primarily focused on the *semantic* aspect of concepts, and to a lesser extent the *pragmatic* aspect of using concepts. However, the concepts of PL may not only serve a representational function, but they may often also be used for presentational purposes. For instance, saying 'I am in love with you' is not only a description aiming to represent how one feels, but it is often also a message that aims to trigger a response from someone else.

Finally, there is a normative aspect to Smedslund's thinking as his axioms describe '*how we, as humans, must conceive of other humans*' (Smedslund 2012, p. 296). However, one of the basic normative beliefs in our society is that human beings have to be regarded as persons, that is as beings that are autonomous and sovereign agents. While morally this makes a lot of sense, the question is if it also holds scientifically as it implies a conceptual demarcation between psychological phenomena associated with persons and the social environment in which persons operate. This closes the door for explanations of psychological phenomena that are essentially social, even if they are perceived as individual and therefore psychological.

Bringing in Social Theory and Some Quantum Theory

The abovementioned critics to Smedslund's ideas are not insurmountable and may even be regarded as in line with some of his own proposals. As such, I believe it is possible to expand his conceptual scheme so that it provides a more general and more transdisciplinary conceptual system to look at people and societies. In the remaining part of this chapter, I will provide a first attempt to present the axiomatic basis of my version of a psycho/social–logic system. It is grounded in three sets of insights, taken from social theory and quantum theory: (1) a definition and description of what constitutes the observable social realm, (2) a claim that speech acts are the substance of that social realm and (3) a proposal to use the notion of field as a metaphor to think about the unobservable social realm. The whole exercise is inspired by the so-called linguistic turn in philosophy as advocated by Rom Harré (see Van Langenhove 2011 for an overview of Harré's work on psychology and social sciences). Furthermore, reference is also made to some ideas from quantum physics that are used as a metaphor to grasp the counter-intuitive reality of psychological phenomena.

The Observable Social Realm

Let's start by picturing what a common-sense view of the social realm entails. What do we experience that is 'social'? One way to think about it is to see 'social' as referring to everything that would not exist without human interference. In other words, there is nothing social in the human world that has not been or is not related to what persons are doing. The next question then is what is there in the world that follows this common-sense definition?

First, there are all kinds of material *artefacts* that would not exist without having been created by human beings and are therefore of a social nature. This includes cities, roads, landscaped gardens, Korean food, wine, books, sheets and so on The list is sheer endless, and in today's world, almost everything on the whole planet is in a way social. A mountain is a purely natural phenomenon while a Terrill is the result of human mining and thus a social phenomenon. And even natural mountains are changing due to tourism and human-induced climate change. This has made geologists propose to call the present era the Anthropocene. Mind you, humanity has only made shortly such an impact on the planet and the number of social artefacts has long been much lower. In the middle ages, for instance, the social environment of most people consisted out of far less such artefacts.

Next to the artefacts, we are all surrounded by *people*. All of these people are persons, and that is only possible because they are treated as persons. True, some of them we ignore as we do when being in an elevator with a stranger. Other people are definitely part of our social environment as we constantly interact with them, even if we cannot have a 'proper' conversation with them, as is the case with babies.[2] And then there all those people with whom we never have a conversation with, but to whom we are connected in complex chains of collaboration. For example, somewhere in China, people have been working on assembling the PC that I am using

[2]The importance of such 'conversations' between persons and babies is that it is through that process that babies become persons. See p. xx.

right now. And much of the software on this PC has been developed by people in California. I do not know any of these people, but still, we are somehow socially connected. People are for that matter the only species on earth that have organized themselves in such large and global networks. Other social animals only have local collaborations.

Finally, there are *conversations* between people. People talking to each other is perhaps the most important aspect of the observable social realm. It is through talking that people are connected to each other. There is, for instance, a chain of conversations between myself and those involved in designing and manufacturing my PC. Probably thousands of conversations have been taking place starting with the conversation between the guy who decided to fabricate this type of PC and say the investors he persuaded, up to the one guy at the counter of the shop to whom I paid when purchasing this PC and with whom I did have a conversation. Not only is this chain of conversations connecting people, but it also makes possible that things happen that need to happen if one wants to build and sell a PC. However, the main feature of this is that I do not have to know how to design a PC for using it. So, my brain is not the only tool I use for doing things, I have access to the brainpower of many others. The instrument for this is the speech act that requests others to do something. For long, the only actors that could produce speech acts were people. Today we are also told to do things by machines as well. Think of the navigation system in your car that tells you when to turn right.

Together, artefacts, people and conversations form the observable social umwelt in which persons operate. All three categories do have a material substance that allows us to perceive them through our senses. And, as material things, they can all be situated in space and time. It is that observable social realm that has been studied by many different social sciences disciplines according to a division of labour. The conversations are the providence of linguistic and communication studies. Artefacts are studied by disciplines such as cultural studies (art), economy (money and factories), sociology (institutions) and law (the judicial system). Persons are the subject of psychology. But the link between the object of study and the discipline is never straightforward and there are enduring debates on how the different disciplines relate to each other. This is especially true for how the ontology of the social realm is regarded. For some, the basic building block of society is the person. However, others will call this reductionistic as it illustrates methodological individualism. They will claim that the substance of society is to be found in structures, which are artefacts of a special kind. Both approaches have in common a way of looking at the social world from a perceptual perspective that situates persons and structures in time and space. They use the same ontological grid like the one used in the natural sciences to locate objects: Every material object can be situated in time and space, and the interactions between objects follow Newtonian and Humean laws. But the question is if this is the best ontological grid to study the social realm. Within the natural sciences, it is now understood that the time/space grid only makes sense on the level of macroscopic objects and events. At the quantum physical level that grid does not work to understand what is going on. So why suppose that that grid is also working for the social realm? It is the credit of Rom Harré that he challenged the use of the time/space grid as a suitable ontology of the social realm. According to Harré, one should use another grid to make a better sense of social reality: A grid of persons and conversations (Harré 1984). Within that grid, one can locate speech acts and not persons or structures as the substance of the social realm.

Fields as the Non-visible Social Realm

If one accepts that persons, artefacts and conversations are the three observable elements of the social reality, the question is whether this is an exhaustive description of what the social realm is? Let us take another look at the material world: With our senses, we can observe a good chunk of it, but we know there is more. Radio waves, for instance, are a particular part of the physical reality and they are surrounding us at all times, but we cannot perceive them unless we have a device that transforms the radio signals in sound. I argue that the same holds for the social reality: There are social 'fields' that are as such not directly visible, but they are there and they do have a profound impact on what people do and on how a society function. One essential social field is the moral orders that give rights and duties to people. Another one is the distributed knowledge that exists (and of which most of it is now available on the www) and that is used in daily life.

Thinking of these invisible parts of the social reality in terms of 'fields' is a metaphor, so let's first take a closer look at what fields are in the natural sciences. The technical term 'field' has its origins in physics, more precisely in the mid-19th-century efforts to blend electricity and magnetism into one theory of electromagnetism based upon the notion of magnetic fields (McMullin 2002). From there, the theory developed with the help of mathematics the concept of 'vector fields'. Today, our understanding of interactions between fundamental particles is also based upon the notion of fields. Particles are considered to be an excitation (called a 'quantum') of a certain field. Such fields are said to have wave properties and those waves can 'collapse' into particles. This is the subject of quantum theory, a mathematical framework to predict the outcomes of experiments at the sub-atomic level. Behind the mathematics of quantum field theory, there still lies the notion of an 'area of influence' (McMullin 2002, p. 14).

The most revolutionary aspect of quantum theory is perhaps that the probabilities of finding certain properties in experiments are linked to the act of measurement. Wave functions (which are the expression of the quantum probabilities) are therefore regarded as 'potential realities, not actual ones' (Wendt 2015, p. 3). The mathematics behind this thinking is huge. But the essence can be captured as follows: Sub-atomic phenomena such as electrons can be regarded both as a particle and as a wave. But the conclusion of many experiments is, as Wendt noted, that '*as long as the electron is not being observed, it behaves as if it is a wave, and as soon as it is observed it behaves as if it is a particle*' (Wendt 2015, p. 46). So, the act of observing influences what is observed. This sounds familiar to many social scientists. Not surprisingly then, the terms 'field' and 'quantum', stripped from their mathematical foundations, made their way to the social sciences.

Lewin (1938, 1921/1951) can be credited for introducing field theory in psychology and social theory. But it was Bourdieu (1993: 72–77) who popularized the notion of field amongst social sciences scholars. Since then, several other scholars have also attempted to apply quantum thinking to the understanding of psychological and social phenomena (see for instance: Zohar 1991; Zohar and Marshall 1994). Wendt (2015) even defended the claim that people are in fact quantum systems, which is something that seems doubtful. But it shows that using the quantum world grammar to think about social and psychological realm is tempting. Nevertheless, in contrast to Wendt, I believe that one should not forget it is only a metaphor: The laws of the quantum domain do not apply to our everyday lives where objects and events can be assigned exact locations and time. This in contrast to the quantum realm where elementary particles can only be described by probability distributions.

A good way to explore the power of the metaphor is to imagine that fields surround us at all times and infuse what people do. As Musser puts it: "We are swimming in it and it is always tugging upon us. We never see it directly, but it makes its presence felt by communicating forces from one place to another" (Musser 2015, p. 72). Within the material realm, the flow of time is going in one direction and objects can only take one single place in the time/space. The Newtonian and Humean laws apply and causal effects can only take place in the present and influence the direct future. For the social realm, the situation is however different: Speech acts can have delayed or even backward effects and as such, they play a crucial role in shaping the social realm. People can indeed influence the future: The speech acts in a will, for instance, can have effects even after a person's death. And what we call history is always a reconstruction of the past based upon selections of speech acts.

Time and space are looked at by the scientists today in a different way from how they have been conceived since Newton: Space does not exist independently from time. As Rovelli noted: 'the present is like the flatness of the Earth: an illusion' (Rovelli 2017, p. 59). Moreover, fields and particles are the same thing: 'Not only are the particles in a certain sense diffused in space like fields, but the fields interact like particles' (Rovelli 2017, p. 59). The same seems to hold for speech acts (Buhler 1934; Austin 1962). On the one hand, certain speech acts can become a field under certain circumstances. For instance, when a head of state declares war on another country, both states are entering a new field that will alter both societies. On the other hand, institutional entities that are fields can interact with each other as speech acts. For instance, the EU can issue a statement such as: "Belgium needs to control its government budget". Obviously, the EU—which is not a living human being as such—cannot *utter* such a speech act, but someone can speak on behalf of the EU. And someone can react on behalf of Belgium. As such, a conversation emerges between two entities that are fields. They interact with each other *as if* they were two persons.

So far for a small excursion on how quantum thinking can perhaps shed new light upon old debates in the social sciences. It makes this author conclude that it illustrates that we need to rethink the grammar of our understanding of the social world. And this is something where a Socio/Psychologic System could be of help.

Elements of an Extended Socio/Psycho-Logic System

The argument so far has been that social reality is twofold: Next to the social realm of artefacts, human beings and conversations that are located in space-time, there is also a social realm that is non-spatial and non-temporal in the sense that they are comparable to fields that cannot be situated in one space-time location. However, speech acts can make fields collapse into a local order. It is then when structures have an impact on the agency of persons. On top of it, the speech acts are also creating the persons and so-called institutional facts.

The abovementioned has major consequences for the psycho-logic system: In my view, such a system needs to address explicitly the social environment that envelops people. The social and the psychological are totally entangled and there is no reason to keep the historically grown divide between the disciplines of psychology and sociology. In this section, I will, therefore, try to extend Smedslund's Psycho-Logic system in such a way that it captures the above-outlined ontology of the social realm. I will do so by first presenting a number of axioms that together describe an ontology for the social sciences where the social and the psychological realm are completely entangled and treated as two sides of the same coin. Much as in quantum physics where light is regarded as being both wave and particle. Secondly, I will outline what an extended psycho-logic system could look like and develop one aspect of it, personality, in some more detail.

Axioms of a Socio/Psycho-Logic System

The notion of 'social' as used in 'social sciences' is seldom made explicit. It seems not really an object of contemplation. Hence the difficulties to define what social sciences are. Earlier, a common-sense definition of 'social' was already proposed. Here I take the scientific perspective and propose as a starting point the following axiom:

Axiom 1: Social refers to everything that escapes the explanatory capacity of the natural sciences.

This implies that there is a special place for social sciences, including psychology, that cannot be tackled directly by the natural sciences. Neither the old Newtonian mechanistic model nor the new quantum model can serve as a model for doing social sciences research. But this does not prevent the social sciences to look at analogies and treat some aspects of the natural sciences as metaphors that can help to understand the social realm.

Furthermore, I state that what we refer to as psychological phenomena are so entangled with social phenomena that:

Axiom 2: The social and the psychological can analytically not be separated from each other.

Thinking about the nature of persons and societies has since long been hampered by two main dichotomies: The mind–body dichotomy and the person–society dichotomy. Traditionally, scientists and philosophers have regarded the mind as a product of the physical brain and its neurons. But more and more scholars regard the mind as something that extends beyond our physical brain. According to Siegel (2017) mind is both embodied and relational and cannot be completely disentangled from our interactions. Siegel backs his claim by referring to lots of research from several different disciplines and concludes that in our modern society the common sense is that the mind is equal to brain activity and hence the self is a separate entity. But according to Siegel, the mind extends beyond our physical selves which makes it impossible to completely disentangle our subjective view of the world from our interactions.

The above has implications for our thinking about persons: Persons (P) are not to be conceived as organisms that are first 'made' and then dipped in a society (S). They are social beings right from the outset. Actually,

(a) Without S, human beings cannot become P
(b) Without S, P cannot function as agents
(c) Without P, there exists no S
(d) Without P, the S could not change

If one agrees that the individual psyche (mind), nor the social (society) can be taken as the basis of the social realm, then it follows that one cannot take either persons or structures as basic entities. So, the next question is: What is the substance of social reality? The answer I propose, based upon Harré (1984) and Searle (2009), is:

Axiom 3: The substance of the social realm consists out of speech acts in a web of conversations that is species-wide and history-long.

The idea that the 'substance' of social reality is made-up out of speech acts has been an enduring theme in linguistic philosophy ever since Austin (1962). Rom Harré and John Searle have been at the forefront in defending this claim. For Harré, '*the fundamental human reality is a conversation, effectively without beginning or end, to which, from time to time, individuals may take contributions*' (Harré 1984, p. 20). Such a species-wide and history-long conversational web is regarded by Harré as the 'primary' social reality. This implies that persons and structures are to be regarded as a 'secondary' reality: they are products of the conversational reality that is constituted out of speech acts (Van Langenhove 2011).

According to Searle (2009), there is even one specific formal linguistic mechanism that acts as a single unifying principle that constitutes any institutional structure. The principle underlying the ontology of the social realm is the capacity of persons to '*impose functions on objects and people where the objects and the people cannot perform the function solely in virtue of their physical structure*' (Searle 2009, p.7). Searle calls this 'status functions' as they imply a collectively recognized status. A piece of paper will count as a 20 EUR bill only if people give that status to that piece of paper. Status functions also carry what Searle calls 'deontic power'. This is where the moral perspective comes in as deontic powers are all about 'rights, duties, obligations, requirements, permissions, authorizations, entitlements, and so on' (Searle 2009, p. 9). Deontic powers are according to Searle created by a specific sort of illocutionary speech acts, namely 'declarations'. Saying 'this property is mine' is a declaration that expresses a status function and gives the speaker a whole set of rights as well as duties. At the same time, that speech act also holds deontic powers towards other people, who are supposed to respect the property rights.

For Searle, the whole of social structures and the institutionalized reality that goes with it is created by declaration. And he adds that since the invention of written language, declarations can take the form of 'standing permanent speech acts' (Searle 2009, p. 88). The importance of Searle is that he has introduced along with the notion of deontology the issue of morality into the institutional reality of structures, while at the same time linking structure to speech acts. In this way Searle is capable of explaining what exactly is the 'construction' in social construction: '*the only reality that we can create is a reality of deontology. It is a reality that "confers rights, responsibilities, and so on*' (Searle 2009, p. 89).

Axiom 4: Speech acts create both an observable and unobservable social realm that together forms the social umwelt in which people live their lives.

The observable social realm consists out of (1) the primary social reality, that is: conversations and (2) the secondary social reality, that is people and social artefacts. The unobservable social realm consists out of social fields of (1) knowledge fields and (2) fields of moral right and duties.

Knowledge Fields

At any time, persons are embedded in an environment that consists of artefacts that are there because somewhere there has been knowledge, which is being used to fabricate them. For instance, I have limited knowledge of how to operate the PC that I use to write this chapter, but I know very little about the production processes of this PC or about the physics behind the operating system. Actually, I am using a device that I am almost totally ignorant of. That is OK because somewhere that knowledge exists and other people have been working on fabricating this machine. We all live our lives in a world that we hardly understand and take for granted. We are not experts in most areas of modern life, but we use the expertise of others. And that expertise is stored in books, patents and so on. At the same time, persons have also some knowledge of what to do when they need extra knowledge. When my PC blocks, I know that I can find some help on the internet, or in the manual or I can call the IT person at the office and ask him to fix it. And if he can't solve the problem, he will call colleagues who do have the necessary expertise.

The knowledge used to fabricate the social world in which we live envelops us as a field that influences our capabilities of doing things and acts as an agent. When things work well, we hardly need to know how and why it functions. But when something does not function, we need to tap into the available knowledge. A fundamental characteristic of people, therefore, is that we all possess knowledge on how to get access to knowledge. Part of that knowledge deals with understanding how the social realm functions. The field of knowledge that so to speak surrounds us and influences what we can do, also has another dimension: That field only exists because of a huge network of collaborations between people. In other words, the capacity of a person to act depends as much upon his/her brain than upon the brains of others.

Moral Fields

Next to knowledge fields, we are also surrounded by moral fields. These fields concern not the capacities people have to do things, but the rights and duties people have to do those things. Taking again the example of my PC: Actually, it is not mine, but the property of the university. Being employed by the university gives me the right to take this university property back to my home to work with. And, when my labour contract ends, it is my duty to return it.

When Searle presents the essence of social structures as being a deontological and therefore of a moral nature, he places himself in a long tradition of looking at the social sciences as moral sciences and of referring to moral orders in the theorization of the social realm (see Van Langenhove 2017). It was Harré (1984) who had developed the first systematic theory of moral orders in his attempt to describe how the rights and duties of people differ from situation to situation and from context to context. For Harré, moral order is an organized '*system of rights, obligations and duties obtaining in society, together with the criteria by which people and their activities are valued*' (Harré 1987, p. 219). In Harré's view, a moral order has two dimensions: The first represents the moral rights people have in a given situation, the second is about the physical locations in space and time that a person can (legitimately) occupy. For instance, when in a pub, it gives me the right to order a drink and consume it at the bar, but it does not give me the right to stand next to the barman behind the bar. If a person occupies the moral and physical places he or she is allowed to occupy, then that person acts in a socially conformist way. Any act that puts one in an 'improper' place is, on the contrary, a socially deviant act. Harré pictures society as comprising of different moral orders, some of them rather stable, others more modest in size and only occasional convened (Harré 1984, p. 246). In other words, while some moral norms can be very universal in a given society, others are the result of locally constructed understandings of rights and responsibilities.

As a result, any given culture contains a multiplicity of interacting and complementary moral orders (Harré 1987, p. 220). Moral orders are thus a set of rules and habits that shape what people can and will do in a certain situation. Together they form a social field in which people act and interact. Whether an act is labelled as socially confirming or as socially deviant depends on both the meaning assigned to that act in reference to a certain moral order and on the knowledge the assessor has about justifications or excuses for that act (Semin and Manstead 1983).

From such a combined Searle/Harré perspective, moral orders can be regarded as sets of rights and duties created by declarations with deontic powers. At any given moment people live their lives in a multitude of overlapping moral orders. Some of those moral orders are of a very general nature and hardly linked to space and time. Other moral orders can be very specific and active only in specific spaces and/or for limited time slots only. In both cases (general or specific) moral orders can be latent or active. Latent moral orders are not 'in use' in a certain episode. Van Langenhove (2017) has identified different types of moral orders: General cultural orders, legal moral orders, institutional moral orders, conversational moral orders and personal moral orders. Together, the above five varieties of moral orders constitute the invisible moral space. Moral orders can thus be regarded as fields that surround people at any given time. It is therefore perhaps better to speak about moral fields rather than about moral orders as this allows us to emphasize that they are at the same time both a background to people, as well as a consequence of conversations between people.

It could be that one has to treat one type of moral order as being special, that is, the legal order and the related institution of a state. The same holds for natural fields as Einstein noted: The gravitational field is not just any field. Says Musser: '*all other fields are selective: the electromagnetic field for instance acts only on charged objects*' (Musser 2015, p. 82). But the gravitational field acts equally on all objects. States might play a similar role in the social realm as their legal order applies to all its citizens.

Axiom 5: The ongoing and species-wide web of conversations can be divided into meaningful chunks in time and space, that can be called episodes.

The is a species-wide and history long conversation in which speech acts are launched is not 'one' conversation, but a multitude of conversations between a limited amount of people. These conversations are structured as meaningful entities for the participants. These structures can be called 'episodes' (see Harré 1979 for a discussion of the concept). Episodes have a beginning and an end, sometimes very formal, sometimes rather fuzzy. Episodes can also overlap, both as nested episodes or as different episodes that overlap partly. A football game, for instance, is for the players and audience an episode that lasts 90 minutes of play and about 15 minutes of break between the first and second half. The two-playing half's and the break can each also be regarded as an episode. Or the period before and after the marking of the first goal. Going to watch a game, takes much longer for the supporters as it includes the travel to the stadium and perhaps the drinks in the pub afterwards (meanwhile the pub visit can be regarded as an episode in itself. Being a fan of a team, can also be seen as an episode.

For the players, the game can be regarded as part of a larger episode, for instance, the competition of that year and so on. All of these episodes have in common that some fields will influence the acts performed, including the conversations about what is happening.

Elements of a Socio/Psycho-Logic System

I believe that, based upon the earlier axioms, it must be possible to extend Smedslund's system in such a way that it better reflects the entanglement between the social and the psychological realm. But this is a formidable exercise that cannot be achieved within the limits of this contribution. In the next paragraphs, I will limit myself to outlining what I think could be the structure of such a psycho/social-logic system and illustrate how a more detailed set of definitions could look like.

(a) The starting point should be **speech acts** as they can be said to be the substance of the social (and psychological) realm. Smedslund builds his system upon the notion of 'being aware and active', but awareness cannot be dissociated from speech acts. I would even argue that consciousness is not possible without speech acts. Smedslund (1988) states in his axiom 1.3.4. that 'a person can describe that of which he or she is reflectively aware and only that' (p. 11).[3] I would argue that is the reverse: One can only be aware of something if it can be described in language.

    Next to developing a good definition of speech acts, attention should go to all the possible effects of speech acts, as well as to how speech acts are organized in episodes of conversations.

(b) The rest of the system would then elaborate on all the social 'things' that are created by speech acts, namely **persons**, **moral fields**, **knowledge fields** and **collaborative networks**, **institutional facts** and **social artefacts**.

    For each of these concepts, a set of definitions and corollaries needs to be worked out and where possible integrated with Smedslund's system. As mentioned before, there is no space in this contribution for developing all this. I will, therefore, limit myself to elaborate on the concepts of persons and personality in some detail below. Interestingly, the concept of 'personality' is not present as such in Smedslund's work, although he does mention on several occasions what he calls 'characteristics of persons' (see Chap. 5 of Smedslund 1988).

(c) The point of departure is my axiom that persons and the social realm can logically not be treated as separate areas of study. This is in line with Harré (2016)

[3] It should be noted that Smedslund has published several versions of PL. Axiom 1.3.4 in the 1988 version corresponds to Axiom 1.4.11 in the 1997 version (Smedslund 1997, p. 10). He also made later revisions (e.g. 2012), but these were not full presentations of the entire system.

who argued that persons are both the products and the producers of social acts. Persons are born in a social environment and it is only because other persons treat them as persons, that they will become persons. This happens through what can be called 'personification': Speech acts that attribute personhood to persons. Becoming a person through personification also involves the appropriation of parts of the available knowledge fields as well as being socialized in certain moral fields.

The following conceptual scheme about persons is inspired by the personality theory developed by De Waele and Harré (1976) and builds upon an attempt to systematize it by Van Langenhove (1986). The format follows Smedslund's approach that distinguishes between definitions, corollaries and notes. References to Smedslund's presentations of PL all refer to his original exposition in Smedslund (1988).

Definition 1.0:	**Persons are distinguished from non-persons by personhood.**
Note 1.1:	Personhood is what distinguishes persons from non-persons. Personhood can be regarded as constituted by four basic characteristics:
	(a) the person is a system of intentional acts
	(b) the person is a rational system in the sense that he or she has the capacity to set goals and mobilize means to achieve those goals
	(c) the person is a reciprocal achievement, meaning that persons are persons because they are treated as such by other persons and
	(d) the person is a generator and communicator of meanings
Note 1.2:	Smedslund (1988) does not mention personhood. However, in his note 5.0.0. (p. 55) he talks about characteristics shared by all persons, by virtue of being persons. He argues that most of these characteristics have to do with the wants of persons, for example, their ubiquitous wants for respect, care, understanding and control.
Definition 2.0:	**Persons act in order to cope with given episodes and attempt to give meaning to actions as social performances by monitoring one's own actions.**
Note 2.1:	This resonates with Smedslund's axiom 2.5.1. and corresponds to axiom 1.3. in the 1997 version (p. 8).
Definition 3.0:	**The acting of a person is given form and meaning as social performances through his/her personality which can be seen as a set of resources upon which a person can draw.**
Note 3.1:	This set of resources are appropriated form moral and knowledge fields and can be organized into cognitive schema's that recognize four major components of social competence:
	(a) knowledge on how to present oneself in social situations
	(b) knowledge to recognize situations
	(c) recognition of the possibility of a judgement of the appropriateness of a performance and
	(d) knowledge about rules or conventions that apply in a given situation
Note 3.2:	Smedslund does include in his Psych-logic system several axioms and definitions that resonate with this. See for instance his axioms 2.5.5 and 2.5.7. about what is morally right and wrong.

Definition 4.0:	**A person's particular resources are a product of his/her social background and biographical development.**
Note 4.1:	persons are individuals that are socialized in a specific 'milieu' and that belong to different social groups. This will influence the knowledge and moral fields to which the person is exposed. But persons also have a specific biography that allows them to change their stance towards those fields and seek new social umwelts
Note 4.2:	Smedslund (1988, 1997) devotes a whole chapter of his Psycho-logic to 'personal change' in both PL-versions. However, the concept of biography seems to be absent. Except that in Smedslund's axiom 1.5.15 (1997, p. 16) it is stated that: 'P's awareness of the future consists of extrapolations from P's awareness of trends in the past'. In the 1988 version, this corresponds to axiom 6.1.7 (p. 71)

Conclusions

The above conceptual excursion did not intend to demonstrate that Smedslund is either right or wrong. Its main purpose was to show that other axiomatic systems are possible, not only for psychology but for the whole of the social sciences. As such, this contribution can also be regarded as a plea for more social theorizing. This not only entails that we need more theories but also more debates between different theoretical viewpoints. And above all, there is a need for more attempts to synthesize what both common-sense and social sciences can tell us about the social realm. It is the credit of Smedslund to have done an extraordinary and pioneering effort in showing how this can be achieved.

References

Austin, J. (1962). *How to do things with words*. Oxford: Clarendon Press.

Bourdieu, P. (1993). *The field of cultural production: Essays on art and literature*. New York: Columbia University Press.

Buhler, K. (1934). *Sprachtheory. Die Darstellungsfunktion der Sprache*. Jena: Gustav Fischer Verlag.

De Waele, J. P., & Harré, R. (1976). The personality of Individuals. In R. Harré (Ed.), *Personality* (pp. 189–246). Oxford: Basil Blackwell.

Harré, R. (1979). *Social being*. Oxford: Basil Blackwell.

Harré, R. (1984). *Personal being*. Oxford: Basil Blackwell.

Harré, R. (1987). Grammar, psychology and moral rights. In *Meaning and the growth of understanding* (pp. 219–230). Berlin: Springer.

Harré, R. (2016). Persons as the products and the producers of social acts. *Culture & Psychology, 22*(4), 534–546.

Harré, R., & Secord, P. (1974). *The explanation of social behavior*. Oxford: Basil Blackwell.

Hofstadter, D., & Sander, S. (2013). *Surfaces and essences*. New York: Basic Books.

Kahneman, D. (2011). *Thinking fast and slow*. New York: Farrar, Straus and Giroux.

Kukla, A. (2001). *Methods of theoretical psychology*. Cambridge, MA: MIT Press.

Lewin, K. (1938). *The conceptual representation and measurement of psychological forces*. Durham, NC: Duke University Press.
Lewin, K. (1921, 1951) Field theory in social science: Selected theoretical papers. Dorwin Cartwright (Ed.). New York: Harper and Row.
McMullin, E. (2002). The origins of the field concept in physics. *Physics in Perspective, 4*, 13–39.
Moscovici, S. (2008). *Psychoanalysis, its image, its public*. London: Polity Press.
Musser, G. (2015). *Spooky action at a distance: The phenomenon that reimagines space and time–and what it means for black holes, the Big Bang, and theories of everything*. Macmillan.
Rovelli, C. (2017). *Reality is not what it seems: The journey to quantum gravity*. Penguin.
Schutz, A. (1953). Common-sense and scientific interpretation of human action. *Philosophy and Phenomenological Research, 14*, 1–37.
Searle, J. (2009). *Making the social world: The structure of human civilization*. New York: Oxford University Press.
Semin, G., & Manstead, A. (1983). The accountability of conduct: A social psychological analysis. In *European monographs in social psychology, European Association of experimental social psychology*. Academic Press.
Siegel, D. (2017). *Mind: A journey to the heart of being human*. New York: Norton.
Smedslund, J. (1988). *Psycho-logic*. Springer Verlag.
Smedslund, J. (1995). *Psychologic: Common sense and the Pseudo empirical*
Smedslund, J. (1997). *The structure of psychological common sense*. Mahwah, NJ: Lawrence Erlbaum Associates.
Smedslund, J. (2012). Psycho-logic: Some thoughts and after-thoughts. *Scandinavian Journal of Psychology, 53*, 295–302.
Smedslund, J. (2013). *From nonsense syllables to holding hands: Sixty years as a psychologist*. Chagrin Falls, OH: Taos Institute Publications.
Smedslund, J. (2016). Practicing psychology without empirical evidence-base: The bricoleur model. *New Ideas in Psychology, 43*, 50–56.
Smith, J., Harré, R., & Van Langenhove, L. (1995). Idiography and the case-study. In J. Smith, R. Harré, & L. Van Langenhove (Eds.), *Rethinking psychology*. London: Sage.
Van Langenhove, L. (1986). De Waele's ethogenic personality theory. An attempt at a systematic formulation. In L. Van Langenhove, J. M. De Waele, & R. Harré (Eds.), *Individual persons and their actions*. Brussels: VUB Press.
Van Langenhove, L. (2007). *Innovating the social sciences*. Vienna: Passagen Verlag.
Van Langenhove, L. (2011). *People and societies*. London: Routledge.
Van Langenhove, L. (2012). Theorizing theoretical psychology. *Theory & Psychology, 15*(1), 134–135.
Van Langenhove, L. (2017). Varieties of moral orders. *Frontiers in Sociology*. https://doi.org/10.3389/fsoc.2017.00009.
Wendt, A. (2015). *Quantum mind and social science*. Cambridge: Cambridge University Press.
Zohar, D. (1991). *The quantum self*. New York: William Morrow and Company.
Zohar, D., & Marshall, I. (1994). *The quantum society*. New York: William Morrow and Company.

Chapter 16
Smedslund and the Psychological Style of Reasoning

Jeff Sugarman

I first encountered the ideas of Jan Smedslund almost 30 years ago as a doctoral student studying educational psychology. Noted educational theorist, Kieran Egan, prescribed his 1983 book, *Psychology and Education*, as an antidote for the belief that disciplinary psychology had a foundational role in informing educational design. Among the barrage of arguments Egan marshals in his scathing attack on the psychologizing of education, are those borrowed from Smedslund's writings published in the 1970s regarding psychology's pseudoempiricism. Smedslund's insights concerning the miscasting of analytic claims as empirical ones derived from psychological experimentation came as nothing short of a revelation for me. Having been firmly enculturated into the canon of psychological empiricism, the persuasive manner by which Smedslund delivered and substantiated his allegations resulted in a state of utter disorientation toward the discipline. Smedslund's analysis left a powerful impression and, three decades later, I find myself returning to it in formulating an expanded critique of psychology that I will outline herein and augment with the help of Smedslund's ideas.

The critique I have developed (Sugarman 2017) centers on explicating "psychologism" as a style of reasoning that has dominated psychology from its inception and set the course for how psychological phenomena are made intelligible and investigated. However, psychologism, as a style of reasoning, is not merely an epistemological doctrine. It also bears ontological implications by the ways in which it contributes to constituting the phenomena psychologists seek to know. I will begin

The author extends his appreciation to Jack Martin and Tobias G. Lindstad for their comments on an earlier draft of this chapter.

J. Sugarman (✉)
Simon Fraser University, Burnaby, BC, Canada
e-mail: sugarman@sfu.ca

T. G. Lindstad et al. (eds.), *Respect for Thought*, Theory and History in the Human and Social Sciences, https://doi.org/10.1007/978-3-030-43066-5_16

by explaining "styles of reasoning" and their common features. This will be followed by describing characteristics and assumptions of psychologism that fulfill the requirements of a style of reasoning and how these characteristics and assumptions, along with particularities of the procedures of psychologism, create conditions of possibility in which psychological properties become articulated and attain ontological status. I will then consider Smedslund's critique of psychological pseudo-empiricism. Lastly, I will show its applicability to psychologism using the example of self-regulation.

Styles of Reasoning

"Styles of reasoning" originate with Crombie's (1994) remarkable historical study, *Styles of Scientific Thinking in the European Tradition: The History of Argument and Explanation Especially in the Mathematical and Biomedical Sciences and Arts,* which charts the development of scientific thought beginning with the ancient Greeks and culminating in the nineteenth century. Navigating an immensity of historical detail, Crombie documents six distinct forms or "styles" of argumentation into which scientific thought has coalesced through the ages. Styles of thinking function as frameworks through which the regularities of phenomena are identified, defined, and understood, thus circumscribing the kinds of questions that can be posed about them and kinds of answers that can be justified. The six styles that Crombie discerns are: (1) mathematical postulation, (2) experimentation, (3) hypothetical-analogical modeling, (4) taxonomy, (5) probabilistic and statistical analysis, and (6) historical derivation.

Hacking (2002, 2012) has extended Crombie's analysis, replacing the terminology of "styles of thinking" with "styles of reasoning." For Hacking, "thinking" puts science "too much in the head" (2002, p. 182). Scientific inquiry involves not just thinking, but also, demonstrating, experimenting, arguing, and consensus. The conduct of science is as much public as it is private. Styles of reasoning are publicly sanctioned approaches to gaining knowledge. They set the criteria for judgments of truth and falsity. This does not imply that styles of reasoning are objective. Rather, they provide the terms for what we mean by objectivity. However, as Hacking (2002) elaborates, styles of reasoning pertain not just to epistemology and methodology. By providing the conditions for how phenomena "show up" for inquirers, styles of reasoning also can create possibilities for the occurrence of new kinds of phenomena. For example, with the advent of probability theory and statistics in the latter half of the seventeenth century came the possibility of a new form of evidence (i.e., the data gathered and recorded by public and private institutions), the concepts of population and normal distribution, equations for variance and standard deviation, techniques such as representative sampling, laws including the central theorem limit and the law of error, and objects like the quincunx and statistical software. One need not look far to see how probability theory not only has shaped profoundly our thinking about phenomena—from physics to politics and health—but also made possible a spate of new material innovations.

There are several other interrelated features common across the variety of styles of reasoning, six of which I will note for the purposes of my analysis. First, styles of reasoning are *conditions of possibility*, not causes (Elwick 2012). To claim that A depends on, or is necessary for, B is not the same as claiming that A causes B. As Elwick illustrates, modeling and experimental styles of reasoning provided conditions of possibility for initiating the science of experimental embryology. However, it would be a gross oversimplification to say that these styles of reasoning are what caused Wilhelm Roux to begin poking hot needles into frog embryos in 1866. The distinction between possibility and cause creates explanatory room for contingency and agentive action to be considered. Second, styles of reasoning are *self-authenticating*. This is because they comprise their own criteria for objectivity and validity. This also effectively makes them self-contained and seemingly unassailable by criticism from outside their borders. The circularity between setting internal criteria and accepting as valid only those claims that fit them provides styles of reasoning with much of their *stability* over time; stability being a third common characteristic. Fourth, this stability also is bolstered by the *reciprocal relation* between the techniques of a style of reasoning and the subject matter to which they are applied, which is also another way in which styles of reasoning are self-authenticating—a point that will be elaborated later in discussing the self-authenticating character of psychologism. Fifth, styles of reasoning are *autonomous*. Although they arise in particular historical contexts, as a consequence of their general applicability, they can become extricated from their origins and persist even through seismic social transformations. They also are autonomous in that they are not allied with specific theories, but rather, are prerequisites to theory construction. It is only once a class of phenomena is identified through the framework of a style of reasoning that theories can be developed to account for it. Sixth, styles of reasoning are *combinatorial*. For instance, Hacking (2002) proposes the "laboratory style" as an amalgam of the modeling and experimental styles. Other styles of reasoning have been suggested. For example, Forrester (1996) has defended "thinking in cases" as a style of reasoning and Davidson (2001) has described a "psychiatric style" of reasoning. In line with the foregoing features, I offer "psychologism" to denote a distinctive style of reasoning that has dominated psychological theorizing and research over the past century.

Psychologism as a Style of Reasoning

"Psychologism," as a term of art, was introduced by Erdmann 1866 in his objection to Beneke's attempt to reduce philosophy to features of the mind (Kusch 1995). In the tradition of Kant, Beneke believed in apriori sources of human knowledge and experience furnished by mental properties. He was also convinced that these sources could be revealed empirically by psychology positioned alongside the natural sciences, all of which were to be founded on positivism. According to Beneke, metaphysical, epistemological, ethical, logical, and mathematical questions should be understood as artifacts of the physiology of psychological processes that inevitably would yield to empirical research. In the ensuing debate, Beneke's all-encompassing naturalism fell victim to much criticism, most notably, the attacks of Frege and Husserl who argued, respectively, that logic was independent of context and philosophical truth was necessarily universal. The critiques were persuasive and most philosophers dismissed psychologism as a flagrant philosophical error (Kusch). However, the premise of psychologism has been resuscitated more recently with the promise of neuroscience and, especially, enthusiasm for new technologies (e.g., fMRI) many think are revealing the biophysical substratum and ultimate causes of all human thought, including philosophical thinking[1].

While psychologism has been formulated variously (Kusch 1995), it preserves the common premise that thought and experience are reducible to internal psychological characteristics. Martin and McLellan (2013) recently have adopted the term to highlight how this premise has been instantiated in psychology. As they define, "The core feature of psychologism is the attribution of the primary causes of the perceptions, experiences, knowledge, and actions of individuals to structures, processes, and/or operations internal to their mental lives" (Martin and McLellan, p. 158). My use of the term follows their definition.

As the prevailing instrument of psychology, psychologism has steered psychological explanation to inner mental properties assumed, in turn, to be manifestations of more primary biochemical and neurophysiological structures and processes. From the inception of disciplinary psychology and over the course of its history, psychologism has been remarkably durable. Generations of varieties of structuralists and functionalists embraced psychologism as the guide to psychological explanation. Notwithstanding its renouncement by behaviorists, psychologism populated the theoretical landscape and can be seen to operate across such diverse schools of thought as depth psychology, Gestalt psychology, humanistic psychology, cognitivism, and neuroscience. This evidences both its stability and autonomy.

Like all styles of reasoning, psychologism has generated its own specific procedures (see Sugarman 2017) and takes the following form. It begins with observations of persons' everyday activities and experiences. A putative feature of their observed actions or reported experience is identified and isolated. The assumption is made that the source of the feature is a discrete interior psychological structure or process. The structure or process is named and assigned deterministic causal force by which the observed action or experience is produced. Thus, for example, the person's apparent monitoring of her activity is caused by self-regulation, her opinion of herself is caused by self-esteem, her degree of confidence is caused by self-efficacy, her conception of herself is caused by self-concept, her failure to attempt tasks is caused by fear of failure, and so forth. It should be noted that something cannot be the cause of itself, a logical error that is conveniently overlooked.[2]

---

[1] Many are less sanguine about this promise, including Smedslund (2020).

[2] A similar point has been raised recently by Valsiner and Brinkmann (2016) in their admonishment to avoid delusive causal variables in psychology; for example, claiming that depression is the cause of feeling depressed.

Once dissected and conceptualized in this way, frequently an instrument is constructed that is inferred to target and measure the hypothesized inner psychological property. It should be noted in passing that the use of the term "measure" here is at least very loose, if not entirely misleading. As Martin and McLellan (2013) argue, it is highly debatable whether psychological instruments perform measurement in any meaningful scientific sense of the term. Scientific measurement relies on standard units or metrics that stand independent of the thing being measured. So too with most of the measures we use in daily life whether it is in cooking, carpentry, or calculating weather. Not only are metrics of size, speed, distance, temperature, and so forth, independent of the particular things being measured, but so too are the devices by which measurements are indicated. However, psychologists have no such standard units or devices for the measurement of psychological phenomena and, therefore, they perform only "pseudomeasurement".

As Martin and McLellan distinguish, counting is not measuring. We might be able to count frequencies of ideas. But we can't measure ideas with standard units like we measure length in centimeters or electrical current in amperes. Human thought, action, and experience do not come in discrete independent units. Individuals' ratings of particular questionnaire items or reactions to stimuli are subject to the tremendous variability of idiosyncratic impressions and subjective judgments, individuals' capacities to observe and report on their experiences accurately, their moods and circumstances, and their manner of responding, all of which are contextually constituted and interrelated, undermining the possibility of discrete standardized units of psychological measurement. While it might be argued that measures of blood flow in the brain provide an instance of bona fide psychological measurement, establishing a clear relationship between specific psychological states and neurophysiological activation is notoriously problematic.

Most commonly, psychological instruments require individuals to introspect and self-report on particular thoughts, actions, or experiences believed to reflect the psychological property under investigation. However, whether the instrument employs introspection or behavioral observation, whether it is the Rorschach Technique, Weschler Intelligence Scales, The Self Esteem Inventory, or brain imaging techniques (which also depend on subjects' introspection to establish correlations between psychological phenomena and the neurophysiological structures assumed to produce them), the data generated are admitted as evidence of the existence of the hypothesized psychological phenomenon. Such evidence is considered sufficiently valid that it has spawned a prodigious array of phenomena and programs of research. In fact, it could be argued that the success of psychologism was key to providing psychology with its own distinctive subject matter and attaining status as a sui generis academic discipline.

Conceived thusly, psychologism operates as a style of reasoning. First, it provides conditions of possibility for the appearance of new phenomena: Intelligence, creativity, motivation, personality traits, attitudes, "self" characteristics, psychological disabilities, and psychopathologies, are just a few examples. However, importantly, psychologism sidesteps the question of whether the phenomena conceived through its assumptions and procedures actually exist. The issue here is not simply whether the phenomena already are there waiting to be discovered or if they are artifacts manufactured by the assumptions and procedures of psychologism. The matter is more complicated. Psychological terminology, description, and classification interact with their objects creating what Hacking (1995) has called a "looping effect."

The looping effect designates the ontological implications of a dynamic interaction between our practices of naming and the things named (see Sugarman 2009, 2015a). More specifically, in describing ourselves psychologically, persons are uniquely capable of reacting to the ways we are described such that we can constitute or reconstitute how we understand ourselves. We come to define and act toward ourselves under psychological descriptions and, in the process, form and alter the kinds of persons we are. The looping effect begins with a psychological description or classification that prompts changes to an individual's self-understanding. This change in self-understanding enables new interpretations, intentions, actions, and experiences. New interpretations, intentions, actions, and experiences, in turn, can lead to revised descriptions and classifications or the invention of new ones. These fresh descriptions and classifications are then appropriated, sparking new self-understandings, interpretations, intentions, actions, and experiences, and so on, looping recursively. It is in creating a relation with ourselves through psychological descriptions—defining ourselves in the terms they provide—that we make ourselves intelligible. However, when the looping effect occurs and persons change the ways they describe and understand themselves, they are no longer quite the same persons they were before. By providing conditions of possibility for new forms of psychological descriptions and self-understandings to emerge, psychologism can have ontological consequences.

Second, psychologism is self-authenticating. The existence of a psychological property is accepted if individuals are able to give self-reports of it or exhibit behaviors believed caused by it. In this way, there is circularity between the objectivity and validity of claims and methods on the basis of which claims are derived. What justification is there that a psychological property exists? Because people can report on it or we can observe its behavioral manifestation. Why are people able to make self-reports of it or behave accordingly? Because it must exist. Third, this circularity between the methodologies of self-report, behavioral observation, and brain imaging, and the phenomena they supposedly reveal, also gives psychologism much of its stability. The credibility of the methods relies on the assumption of an inner psychological realm that can be detected by them and, reciprocally, the assumption of an inner psychological realm lends the methods their legitimacy. Fourth, not only has psychologism been resistant to criticism from outside its boundaries, but it also has been autonomous in traveling far past its origins and finding application across a wide variety of psychological schools of thought. It is not allied with any specific psychological theory but, nevertheless, has served instrumentally in producing an entire class of phenomena on which these schools of thought and their theories have been founded. Fifth, psychologism, while a distinct style of reasoning, is combinatorial having incorporated elements of experimental, modeling, statistical, taxonomic, and historical styles of reasoning.

Smedslund and Psychologism

Since the 1970s, Smedslund (1978a, 1978b, 1979, 1988, 1991, 1994, 1995, 2002, 2008) has made a compelling case that many, if not most, empirical claims derived from psychological research are already established by prior conceptual relationships and, consequently, should be seen as only "pseudoempirical." According to Smedslund, what often are taken to be empirical findings from psychological research are the misleading result of confusing "analytic" with "arbitrary" aspects of research design. Smedslund terms "analytic" propositions those made true by definition or logical necessity.[3] In analytic or apriori propositions, the concept of the predicate is entailed implicitly in the concept of the subject such that negating the proposition results in a logical contradiction. In other words, the analytic structure of the proposition ensures the relationship between the two things under consideration. "Arbitrary" refers to contingent circumstantial features, particularities of the context of the specific research being conducted that are legitimately empirical, but have little generalizability beyond the confines and unique features of the research setting. As Egan (1988) simplifies with a clear, if somewhat trite, example of the problem Smedslund insinuates:

> "all unmarried men in Vancouver are bachelors" is true as a matter of logical necessity or by definition. We could treat the question "Are all unmarried men in Vancouver bachelors?" as an empirical question. We could design a tight survey, run it with great care, and analyse the results by the most sophisticated statistical methods. We could then announce that we had empirically established that 100% of the bachelors in Vancouver are unmarried. And, by such a procedure, we would indeed have established the truth of the proposition empirically. The empirical research is, of course, unnecessary; and we need feel no caution in generalizing our results to Chicago or Paris. The connection between bachelors and unmarried men is established by analysis or definition. (p. 71)

Smedslund argues that empirical research in psychology is rife with such analytic entailments the consequence of which is to render the research unnecessary,

---

[3] It should be noted that while Smedslund used the term "analytic" in his writings in the 1970s, in subsequent publications, he tended to avoid it, opting instead for "a priori," "noncontingent," and "nonempirical" (e.g., Smedslund 1991, pp. 325–326) and, more recently, "a priori and contingently true" (Smedslund 2012a, p. 300). This shift in terminology owes to Smedslund's (2002) attempt to sidestep philosophical difficulties with the Kantian analytic-synthetic distinction voiced by Quine (1951) and, also, recognition that in his attempt to articulate a system of "psychologic," he did not differentiate sufficiently between "logical relations built into language and basic psychological assumptions that go beyond language" (Smedslund 2012b, p. 661). As Smedlund (2012b) explains, the latter do not follow strictly from the lexical meaning of words and, thus, are not semantic. Rather, they pertain to functions of persons that are assumed (e.g., learning from experience, having feelings). Consequently, although Smedslund does not take psychologic to pertain exclusively to conceptual relations, he nonetheless interprets its aim to make explicit what he alleges is a conceptual framework implicit in language and psychological common sense. In this light, analyticity still appears to have relevance for the specific aspects of Smedslund's thought on which I am drawing, and I have retained use of the term with limited reference to those propositions the truth or falsity of which is determined by analysis in contrast to those requiring empirical test for validation.

redundant, and delusive. Thus, we should not be impressed when researchers conclude that individuals are likely to be surprised when an alternative outcome is expected (Choi and Nisbett 2000), that individuals tend to help only when they notice a situation requiring help and think that helping would be useful (Latané and Darely 1970), that those predisposed to taking risks are more prone to practicing unsafe sex (Farley 1991), that individuals who have had a history of repeated failure are less likely to attempt tasks (Sears 1940) and those who are confident about their ability to do them successfully are more likely to attempt them (Bandura 1977), that we tend to repeat activities we find pleasurable (Thorndike 1932), or children who have yet to develop the idea of one-to-one identity are unable to determine if two different placements of the same number of items are equivalent (Piaget and Szeminska 1952). It is difficult to see how the outcomes could be otherwise. If the experimental outcomes did not confirm their hypotheses, we would not question the hypotheses. Rather, we would suspect something faulty owing to the experimental conditions, methods and procedures, or broader context that was corrupting the data. Smedslund concludes that such studies are pseudoempirical because the hypotheses under investigation masquerade as empirical propositions but, in fact, need not be verified by any empirical test whatsoever.

Smedslund (2008) credits Heider (1958) for drawing his attention to the observation that common sense is composed of conceptual relations for which validation by empirical study is not required. Smedslund saw three major implications for psychology. First, common sense psychology is a system of meanings contained by concepts and axioms that have established connections among the mental terms of ordinary language (e.g., believe, desire, do, intend, hope, fear, sadness). Second, these meanings can be comprehended by conceptual analysis and without empirical investigation. And consequently, third, psychology must include the study of ordinary language. We think, act, and experience through the descriptions given in language. Not only do people describe, understand, and explain their conduct and experiences using shared ordinary language, but so do the psychologists who study them. In order for the discipline of psychology to exist, a language for understanding ourselves psychologically already had to be in place. The development of language has occurred over millennia during which myriad psychological concepts have been developed to lend meaning to our thoughts, actions, and experiences, making them intelligible and allowing individuals to address themselves reflexively and conceive of others psychologically. If these meanings and a psychological common sense were not already in place, psychologists would have had nothing to study (cf. Danziger 1997).

Furthermore, in order to have any social currency, psychologists' concepts, theories, and research must make contact with the terms and meanings of everyday ordinary language conveys. However, as Smedslund deciphers, ordinary language sets constraints on the logical possibilities by which words and symbols can be combined and there are specific restrictions regarding the deployment of psychological concepts. For example, to say "I am delighted that I never get what I want" doesn't make sense. At the very least, the statement calls for something to be added in order for it to be made meaningful. Further illustrating the point, the game of chess cannot be defined or understood as something independent of the rules that constitute it. I can consider a host of strategies about how the game can be played, but these strategies depend on adhering to the rules of the game. If a strategy violates the rules of the game, it ceases to have a relevant or meaningful application. The same is true of psychological terms. If they violate the rules of ordinary language, they cease to have relevant or meaningful applications. Even if we modify the rules to accommodate a new term or new usage of a term, these rules still are apriori to, and provide constraints on, any meaningful empirical examination of them we might conduct.

Anyone immersed in psychological literature will find little discussion of these matters among psychologists and much confusion of the analytic with the arbitrary. As Smedslund (1991, 1994) attests, such consideration is rare because psychologists, by and large, are inclined to treat all meaningful hypotheses as if they are empirical. There is little attention to defining concepts formally rather than just operationally and, consequently, to distinguishing apriori from empirical propositions. The origin of the problem, as Smedslund (1991) recounts, is that right from the start, there was a fervent belief that psychological knowledge rested on developing methods of acquiring and representing data in highly reliable ways, the accumulation of which eventually would result in scientific advance.

In this light, it is easy to see why Bridgman's (1952) operationalism was received by psychologists as a godsend. But while Bridgman recommended operational definitions only as aids or cues to comprehending the meaning of concepts, psychologists treated operational definitions as if they were exhaustive of conceptual meanings (Koch 1999; Martin et al. 2003). The operational definition was wielded like a wand with which all the conceptual complexity of psychological phenomena could magically be made to disappear and the reliability of methods and data assured. Operationalism ascended and conceptual analysis quickly went out of fashion. However, as Smedslund (1991) has been at pains to point out, rarely is it addressed explicitly exactly what features of an item on an instrument make it an indication of the hypothesized psychological property being studied. It is simply taken for granted that everyone knows what the words mean and the connection between the item and the psychological property is assumed to be intuitively obvious. However, in the absence of adequate conceptual analysis, concepts are applied loosely, an explicit link is never established between operationalized item and response, and phenomena are reduced narrowly to the terms given by specific procedures, materials, and responses.

Smedslund's analysis of pseudoempiricism is highly applicable to psychologism. First, pseudoempiricism contributes to conditions of possibility for the emergence of new phenomena. In the absence of establishing a clear relation between the conceptualized phenomenon and the instruments by which it is investigated, the phenomenon can simply be assumed to exist, evidenced by the self-reports and behaviors of experimental subjects. Second, pseudoempiricism strengthens psychologism as self-authenticating. The ways psychological propositions are analytically entailed not only result in empirical research being merely restatements of what already resides in everyday language and understanding, but also ensures that experimental outcomes appear as validations of empirical hypotheses. Defining phenomena operationally also abets the self-authenticating character of psychologism. Narrowing and simplifying concepts by defining them operationally renders them more amenable to the (unnecessary) empirical test by furnishing means (e.g., pseudomeasurement) by which procedures and outcomes can appear more easily interpreted. Third, analytic, semantic, and/or conceptual entailment ensures the success of psychological hypothesis testing, and continued success lends psychologism stability. Fourth, as the examples mentioned earlier show, pseudoempiricism provides for the autonomy of psychologism, both in its persistence over time and its application in the highly diverse arena of psychological hypotheses and theories.

The Psychologism of Self-Regulation

As promised in the introduction, I now turn to sketch briefly an illustration of psychologism using the currently popular psychological concept of self-regulation, but also incorporating Smedslund's critique.[4] Self-regulation is so prized in psychology that philosopher Stuart Shanker (2017) asserts it will be as consequential for the discipline in the twenty-first century as intelligence was in the twentieth century. While some trace the origins of the scientific study of self-regulation to cybernetics (Carver and Scheier 1998), and others to information processing models of cognitive psychology (Weinstein et al. 2000), the notion that people have, and ought to cultivate, the capacity for self-control can be traced to the ancient Greeks. As early as the sixth century BCE, Heraclitus lauded the virtue of self-mastery and rational control in ruling one's passions (Baloyannis 2013), an admonition reiterated throughout the succeeding centuries. So prominent is this characteristic of the human condition, what Smith (1976/1759) called "the great school of self-command" (p. 145), that almost every major enlightenment, romantic, and modern philosopher has had something to say about it (cf. Seigel 2005).

Given such a rich history, we might expect present studies of self-regulation to be guided by a clear conception of what it is and methods properly suited to its investigation. However, such is not the case. Scanning the psychological literature reveals a host of terms by which it has been conceptualized, including self-control, self-management, self-regulated learning, effortful control, effortful attention, problem-solving, behaviour management and control, goal-directed behavior, conscious impulse control, mood control, delay of gratification, willpower, agency, metacognition, principled structure, central governor, and executive function. While some researchers are highly specific in their use of these terms, others use them interchangeably (Martin and McLellan 2013). Often conceptualizations are tied to specific theoretical frames. There are neo-cybernetic perspectives that comprehend

[4] Elsewhere (Sugarman 2017), I have detailed another example; specifically, how the psychological study of attitudes has been built on psychologism.

regulatory processes in terms of feedback loops, goal states, and error detection; neuroscience approaches that theorize an executive function produced by neural processes; systems theoretical perspectives that highlight the dynamics of self-organization; and cognitive theories emphasizing processing and representational features of impulse control and delay of gratification, or metacognitive skills, behavior skills, personal beliefs, motivation, or ego depletion. This diversity of terms and approaches has led Zeidner et al. (2000) to remark, "there are almost as many definitions and conceptions of self-regulation as there are lines of research on the topic" (p. 750).

On Martin and McLellan's (2013) reading, it would take Herculean effort to clarify the meanings of these terms and ways they are employed. Nevertheless, in the absence of such conceptual work, as they state,

> the entire area of self-regulation risks a solipsistic fragmentation in which each researcher or research team works with concepts, frameworks, and methods that defy translation across programs of research that may be united only in so far as they employ some rubric tied loosely to "self-regulation." (p. 137)

In their critical analysis of the self-regulation literature, Martin and McLellan (2013) detect that sometimes self-regulation is treated as something in the mind; other times, as an activity. Sometimes it is treated as an aptitude; other times, as an event. Sometimes self-regulation is used to designate regulation of the self; other times, regulation by the self, which raises the all too infrequently addressed question of what the self is that is doing the regulating. Relatedly, how is the regulation of activity and learning different from the self-regulation of activity and learning? As Smedslund might ask, in what ways might the activity of persons not be self-regulated? Aren't most of the things we do the result of at least some modicum of purposeful planning and deliberative action? A major issue, according to Martin and McLellan, is that there appear little grounds for distinguishing those actions that are self-regulated from those that are not. As Martin and McLellan elaborate, how can anyone, including researchers, be sure when thoughts, emotions, and motivations are self-determined in ways that transcend the operations of bodies, brains, and contextual constraints? And, further, are neurophysiological processes and structures hypothesized to be causally influential to be considered part of the self or external to it?

While most researchers appear content to work within their chosen paradigms and ignore the conceptual and theoretical morass, some have attempted to address the problem. Martin and McLellan (2013) identify two proposed solutions, both of which they regard as defective. One strategy has been to reconcile what are clearly incompatible definitional and conceptual differences through some kind of integration. However, this approach courts incoherence by mixing apples with oranges. The second strategy looks at empirical research to solve the problem. However, this approach falls victim to precisely the kinds of issues Smedslund has raised. As an example, Winne and Perry (2000) have employed both strategies. In their integrative model, Winne and Perry suggest that self-regulation "has dual qualities as an aptitude and an event… and manifests itself in recursively applied forms of metacognitive monitoring and metacognitive control that change information over time as learners engage with a task" (p. 563). Examining the techniques researchers have employed in studying self-regulation, Winne and Perry further offer that "self-report questionnaires, structured interviews, teacher judgments, think aloud measures, error detection tasks, trace methods, and observations of performance—foreground different components of conditions, cognitive operations, standards, and event-related change" (p. 563). What Winne and Perry seem to be suggesting is akin to the fable of six blind men touching an elephant. They assume all of these things can be integrated as pointing to a singular phenomenon of self-regulation. But, as Martin and McLellan rightly respond, this doesn't solve the problem. It simply evades it. For instance, Winne and Perry fail to clarify how, as both aptitude and event, self-regulation can be one thing.

Furthermore, by contending that empirical "measurement is akin to model building and testing" (p. 563), Winne and Perry (2000) are guilty of pseudoempiricism. Empirical inquiry cannot solve conceptual problems. On its own, empirical inquiry cannot generate a conception of what one is attempting to study. Before something can be studied empirically, there needs to be in place some conception of the phenomenon that stipulates what the phenomenon is and what counts as a case of having seen it. Otherwise, how would a researcher be able to identify it in the first place? As Smedslund would admonish, what is needed is not empirical research, but rather, conceptual clarification of the concept's rules of correct employment that warrant its application to phenomena of interest.

Nevertheless, tacitly assuming a unified conception of self-regulation, researchers have delivered a spate of pseudoempirical claims. For example, the recently published third edition of *Handbook of Self-Regulation: Research, Theory, and Applications* (Vohs and Baumeister 2016) is replete with studies cited as evidence for such claims: "self-regulation plays an important role in inhibiting undesirable impulses from influencing behavior in many situations encountered in everyday life" (p. 62), "self-control requires prioritizing more valued, distal outcomes over smaller yet immediate ones" (p. 146), "self-directed behavioral change usually occurs when individuals perceive discrepancies between their goals or ideals and their current standing on these goals/ideas" (p. 284), "low trait self-control significantly predicted more imprudent behaviors" (p. 49), "use and abuse of alcohol and drugs often result from self-control failure and, likewise, are largely predicted by low self-control" (p. 47), "restraining oneself from expressing sexual thoughts and behavior requires self-control" (p. 48), "some people feel a similarly strong impulse to shop, so self-control is necessary to resist such overspending or impulsive buying" (p. 48), "impulsivity and risk taking that result from low self-control are also important factors in gambling behavior" (p. 49), and "the lower an individual's self-control, the more likely he or she is to engage in risky behaviors, commit a crime, or be imprisoned" (p. 49). The obvious analytic entailments of such claims obviate the need for any empirical research whatsoever.

Self-regulation, like all mental constructs is considered latent and directly unobservable. Consequently, a number of instruments have been devised to operationalize it. The most widely used instrument for assessing self-regulated learning is the

Motivated Strategies for Learning Questionnaire (MSLQ) containing 81 items scored using a 7-point Likert-type scale (Dunn et al. 2012). The *MSLQ* consists of two primary scales—Motivation and Learning Strategies—and 15 subscales. The Motivation Scale is intended to tap goals, beliefs, skills, and anxiety. The Learning Strategies Scale targets cognitive strategies and resources management skills. Two of the subscales are designed specifically to assess self-regulation: The Metacognitive Self-Regulation Subscale and Effort Regulation Subscale (Duncan and McKeachie 2005). These subscales contain such items as "During class time I often miss important points because I'm thinking of other things," "When I become confused about something I'm reading for this class, I go back and try to figure it out," "I work hard to do well in this class even if I don't like what we are doing," and "When I study for this class, I set goals for myself in order to direct my activities in each study period." As Smedslund would argue, hypotheses and outcomes are logically entailed. How could subjects giving positive ratings to such items not be self-regulated?

The structure of the *MSLQ*, like the *Learning and Study Skills Inventory* and other instruments used to investigate self-regulation are predicated on the assumption that self-regulation can be distilled into a set of distinct components that can be isolated from each other and from an integral human being functioning in the world. This assumption is where psychologism begins. Observing the dispositions persons express in their everyday actions—dispositions to plan and act intentionally—psychologists isolated these features and moved them inward, invoking self-regulation as an inner mental property that explains and determines conduct and experience. However, the assumption of such an inner property or entity is neither a logical necessity nor is it made persuasive by the results of psychological study.

As a function of psychologism, the invention and administration of instruments designed to measure self-regulation circumvent the ontological question of whether it exists. The data obtained by such instruments simply are assumed to represent the influence of an inner psychological property or entity. As the study of self-regulation evinces, there is self-authentication and stability created by the reciprocally reinforcing relation between methods and the phenomena of investigation. Instruments such as the *MSLQ* and fMRI studies favor the assumption that there is an interior property or entity of self-regulation to be measured, while belief in the internality of self-regulation lends legitimacy to the instruments. There is also a looping effect. Psychologists measuring self-regulation have promoted ideals of the self-regulated person and self-regulated student, and people are learning to understand themselves and be the kinds of persons who are or who are not self-regulated to varying degrees. By drawing attention to certain individual attributes, claiming to measure and classify them, and making visible what might have remained concealed or vexatiously complex, psychologists have provided conceptual and material means by which we may examine ourselves and others, especially how we or others might deviate from the majority. As Smedslund persistently has argued, such means have been readily adopted largely because they already jive with our psychological common sense.

However, the effect of emphasizing self-regulation as a presumed individual interior feature not only has been to influence our self-understanding, but also to make ourselves and others more readily susceptible and subject to forms of expert intervention and management. For example, schools and other educational institutions now abound with practices designed to encourage students to conceive of and assess themselves in particular ways; more specifically, as autonomous, self-governing, self-responsible and self-reliant individuals. And, it appears as no coincidence that such values are consistent with those of contemporary neoliberal democracies (see Martin and McLellan 2013; Sugarman 2015b).

Conclusion

As Smedslund's work reveals, much of the success of psychologism owes to the ways in which it enables the research practices of psychologists to capitalize on psychological common sense by recapitulating what already is contained and expressed in everyday language and understanding. However, as I have intimated, such practices can transcend what is given and have profound ontological implications by redefining, transforming, and supplanting everyday psychological phenomena. The fundamental problem of psychologism is more than pseudoempiricism. It is that psychologists have located their explanations in cognitive, affective, and volitional structures internal to individuals without adequate consideration of the historical, social, cultural, moral, ethical, political, and economic contexts within which we develop and are constituted as persons. By neglecting the constitutive influence of these contexts, psychologists frequently have attributed features of persons to an inner psychological nature rather than to characteristics of the contexts and interactions within and through which we become persons. We might do well to ask whether self-regulation and other supposed individual psychological properties are simply part of what it is for integral, fully functioning persons to act purposefully in the world given the conditions of possibility and constraint afforded by the contexts in which they develop and live, and not inner psychological antecedents separate from their acting (Martin et al. 2003).

Clearly, the kind of reconsideration called for would require a significant departure from psychologism as an investigative and explanatory style of reasoning. It is beyond the scope of this chapter to detail a style of reasoning appropriate to psychology. However, as a gesture in this direction, a style of reasoning adequate to psychology's purposes would create a space of possibility for, and orientation to, persons acting in worldly contexts; in which key constituents of personhood that transcend the boundaries of an assumed psychological interiority—language, culture, society, history and human relationality—are not ignored or given only cursory treatment.

References

Bandura, A. (1977). Self-efficacy: Toward a unifying theory of behavioral change. *Psychological Review, 84*, 191–215.
Bridgman, P. W. (1952). *The nature of some of our physical concepts*. New York: Philosophical Library.
Baloyannis, S. J. (2013). The philosophy of Heracletus today. *Encephalos, 50*, 1–21.
Carver, C. S., & Scheier, M. F. (1998). *On the self-regulation of behavior*. Cambridge, England: Cambridge University Press.
Choi, I., & Nisbett, R. (2000). Cultural psychology of surprise. *Holistic theories and recognition of contradiction. Journal of Personality and Social Psychology, 79*, 890–905.
Crombie, A. C. (1994). *Styles of Scientific Thinking in the European Tradition: The History of Argument and Explanation Especially in the Mathematical and Biomedical Sciences and Arts*. London, UK: Gerald Duckworth & Company.
Danziger, K. (1997). *Naming the mind: How psychology found its language*. Thousand Oaks, CA: Sage.
Davidson, A. (2001). *The emergence of sexuality: Historical epistemology and the formation of concepts*. Cambridge, MA: Harvard University Press.
Duncan, T. G., & McKeachie, W. J. (2005). The making of the motivated strategies questionnaire. *Educational Psychologist, 40*, 117–128.
Dunn, K. E., Lo, W.-J., Mulvenon, S. W., & Sutcliffe, R. (2012). Revisiting the *Motivated Strategies for Learning Questionnaire*. *Educational and Psychological Measurement, 72*, 312–331.
Egan, K. (1983). *Education and psychology: Plato, Piaget and scientific psychology*. New York: Teachers College Press.
Egan, K. (1988). The analytic and the arbitrary in educational research. *Canadian Journal of Education, 13*, 69–82.
Elwick, J. (2012). Layered history: Styles of reasoning as stratified conditions of possibility. *Studies in History and Philosophy of Science, 43*, 619–627.
Farley, F. (1991). The type t personality. In L. P. Lipsitt & L. L. Minick (Eds.), *Self-regulatory behavior and risk taking: Causes and consequences* (pp. 371–382). Norwood, NJ: Ablex.
Forrester, J. (1996). If p, then what? Thinking in cases. *History of the Human Sciences, 9*(3), 1–25.
Hacking, I. (1995). The looping effect of human kinds. In D. Sperber, D. Premack, & A. J. Premack (Eds.), *Causal cognition: A multidisciplinary debate* (pp. 351–383). Oxford, UK: Clarendon.
Hacking, I. (2002). *Historical ontology*. Cambridge, MA: Harvard University Press.
Hacking, I. (2012). 'Language, truth, and reason' 30 years later. *Studies in History and Philosophy of Science, 43*, 599–609.
Heider, F. (1958). *The psychology of interpersonal relations*. New York: Wiley.
Koch, S. (1999). *Psychology in human context: Essays in dissidence and reconstruction*. Chicago: University of Chicago Press.
Kusch, M. (1995). *Psychologism: A case study in the sociology of philosophical knowledge*. London: Taylor & Francis.
Latané, B., & Darely, J. M. (1970). *The unresponsive bystander: Why doesn't he help?* New York: Appleton-Century-Crofts.
Martin, J., & McLellan, A. M. (2013). *The education of selves: How psychology transformed students*. New York: Oxford University Press.
Martin, J., Sugarman, J., & Thompson, J. (2003). *Psychology and the question of agency*. Albany, NY: State University of New York Press.
Piaget, J., & Szeminska, A. (1952). *The child's conception of number*. New York: Humanities Press.
Quine, W. V. O. (1951). Two dogmas of empiricism. *Philosophical Review, 60*, 20–43.
Sears, P. S. (1940). Levels of aspiration in academically successful and unsuccessful children. *Journal of Abnormal and Social Psychology, 35*, 498–536.

Seigel, J. (2005). *The idea of the self: Thought and experience in Western Europe since the seventeenth century*. Cambridge, England: Cambridge University Press.
Shanker, S. (2017, April). How smart is my child? *Psychology Today*. Retrieved from https://www.psychologytoday.com/blog/self-reg/201704/how-smart-is-my-child
Smedslund, J. (1978a). Bandura's theory of self-efficacy: A set of common sense theorems. *Scandinavian Journal of Psychology, 19*, 1–14.
Smedslund, J. (1978b). Some psychological theories are not empirical: reply to Bandura. *Scandinavian Journal of Psychology, 19*, 101–102.
Smedslund, J. (1979). Between the analytic and the arbitrary: A case study of psychological research. *Scandinavian Journal of Psychology, 20*, 1–12.
Smedslund, J. (1988). *Psycho-logic*. New York: Springer.
Smedslund, J. (1991). The pseudoempirical in psychology and the case for psycho-logic. *Psychological Inquiry, 2*, 325–338.
Smedslund, J. (1994). Non-empirical and empirical components in the hypotheses of five social psychological experiments. *Scandinavian Journal of Psychology, 35*, 1–15.
Smedslund, J. (1995). Psychologic: Common sense and the pseudoempirical. In J. A. Smith, R. Harré, & L. van Langehove (Eds.), *Rethinking psychology* (pp. 196–206). London: Sage.
Smedsund, J. (2002). From hypothesis-testing psychology to procedure-testing psychologic. *Review of General Psychology, 6*, 51–72.
Smedslund, J. (2008). From Heider to psycho-logic. *Social Psychology, 39*, 157–162.
Smedslund, J. (2012a). Psycho-logic: Some thoughts and afterthoughts. *Scandinavian Journal of Psychology, 55*, 295–302.
Smedslund, J. (2012b). What follows from what we all know about human beings. *Theory & Psychology, 22*, 658–668.
Smedslund, J. (2020). Neuro-ornamentation in psychological research (Chapter 13, this volume). In T. G. Lindstad, E. Stänicke, & J. Valsiner (Eds.), *Respect for thought: Jan Smedslund's legacy for psychology* (pp. 221–228). New York: Springer.
Smith, A. (1976). The theory of the moral sentiments. In D. D. Raphael & A. L. Macfie (Eds.), *The Glasgow edition of the works and correspondence of Adam Smith* (Vol. 1). Oxford, England: Oxford University Press. (Original work published 1759).
Sugarman, J. (2009). Historical ontology and psychological description. *Journal of Theoretical and Philosophical Psychology, 29*, 9–15.
Sugarman, J. (2015a). Historical ontology. In J. Martin, J. Sugarman, & K. Slaney (Eds.), *The Wiley handbook of theoretical and philosophical psychology*. Wiley: Oxford, UK.
Sugarman, J. (2015b). Neoliberalism and psychological ethics. *Journal of Theoretical and Philosophical Psychology, 35*, 103–116.
Sugarman, J. (2017). Psychologism as a style of reasoning and the study of persons. *New Ideas in Psychology, 44*, 21–27.
Thorndike, E. L. (1932). *The fundamentals of learning*. New York: Teacher College.
Valsiner, J., & Brinkmann, S. (2016). Beyond the "variables": Developing metalanguage for psychology. In S. H. Klempe & R. Smith (Eds.), *Centrality of history for theory construction in psychology, annals of theoretical psychology* (Vol. 14, pp. 75–90). Cham: Springer.
Vohs, K. D., & Baumeister, R. F. (2016). *Handbook of self-regulation: Research, theory, and applications*. New York: Guilford Press.
Weinstein, C. E., Husman, J., & Dierking, D. R. (2000). Self-regulation interventions with a focus on learning strategies. In M. Boekaerts, P. R. Pintrich, & M. Zeidner (Eds.), *Handbook of self-regulation* (pp. 728–747). San Diego: Academic Press.
Winne, P. H., & Perry, N. E. (2000). Measuring self-regulated learning. In M. Boekaerts, P. R. Pintrich, & M. Zeidner (Eds.), *Handbook of self-regulation* (pp. 532–629). San Diego: Academic Press.
Zeidner, M., Boekaerts, M., & Pintrich, P. R. (2000). Self-regulation: Directions and challenges for future research. In M. Boekaerts, P. R. Pintrich, & M. Zeidner (Eds.), *Handbook of self-regulation* (pp. 750–768). San Diego: Academic Press.

Chapter 17
Wittgenstein's Revenge: How Semantic Algorithms Can Help Survey Research Escape Smedslund's Labyrinth

Jan Ketil Arnulf

Since more than three decades, Jan Smedslund has been publishing a series of studies on pseudo-empiricality (Smedslund 1978, 1987, 1988, 1994, 1995, 2012, 2015). Through his analysis of psychological experiments and measurement instruments, he has shown how we are already in possession of the knowledge that the studies claim to uncover. Taken literally, the actual studies should be superfluous as they tell us nothing new. It seems justified to say that his criticism has gone largely unheeded by the research community. While his ideas have generated some debate, the wider research community does not seem to bother, and research practice, therefore, does not seem to change. References to the problem of logical and semantic structures in research remain hard to publish, keeping psychology trapped in what I henceforth will refer to as "Smedslund's labyrinth": Rediscovering what we already know through research designs that merely illustrate what is reasonable.

The purpose of the present chapter is to look at Smedslund's description of pseudo-empiricality and test some of his central claims using computing science. I will show that some of Smedslund's ideas are compatible with general principles of computing science as embedded in programming languages and high-level algorithms and that they share common roots. Computing science used in conjunction with psychology might, therefore, offer a possible way out of Smedslund's labyrinth.

If we can use computing algorithms to prove some of Smedslund's ideas experimentally, we can possibly also turn this research agenda into a true psychological endeavor: Why are his warnings so difficult to grasp, even to highly trained researchers? If Smedslund is right, why do we not know what we already know? If the pseudo-empirical studies only explore what is given in the research questions, why are we so unskilled at meta-linguistic inferences about knowledge? Therefore, it

J. K. Arnulf (✉)
BI Norwegian Business School, Oslo, Norway

T. G. Lindstad et al. (eds.), *Respect for Thought*, Theory and History in the Human and Social Sciences, https://doi.org/10.1007/978-3-030-43066-5_17

may be justified to propose that if we can simulate Jan Smedslund's claims about Psychologic (PL) (Smedslund 1995, 2012), we can make our subjective blindness the object of psychological research, paradoxical though it may seem. Through their roots in philosophy and formal logics, some assertions of PL could be demonstrated through the use of computer algorithms. We can actually show empirically that prevalent practices in psychometric research produce data that are predictable a priori. To put it bluntly, we can to some extent know what people will answer in Likert-type scale surveys before obtaining their answers.

At the moment of writing, this type of research has been documented in a number of publications (Arnulf and Larsen 2015; Arnulf et al. 2014; 2018a, b, c; Gefen and Larsen 2017; Nimon et al. 2015), but is still widely unrecognized by the scientific community. There are probably two main reasons for this. The first is that methodological paradigms in science tend to perpetuate themselves through publication practices (van Schuur and Kiers 1994). The second reason is more psychologically interesting: The sometimes amazing cognitive capabilities of the human brain are also affected by restrictions that make us error-prone and blind to shortcomings. We find it hard to believe statements that are counterintuitive and require cognitive efforts in understanding (Kahneman 2011; March and Simon 1958; Todd and Gigerenzer 2003). For decades now, we have used computers to overcome our more obvious shortcomings in memory and calculating power. Further progress in analytical techniques may help us overcome even more advanced types of restrictions. Computers can simulate our cognitive structures and make us aware of what we know by implication of what we already know.

This is where I think psychology may even escape some of Smedslund's most dire predictions by accepting the truth of his theory. When he claims that "psychology can never be an empirical science" (Smedslund 2016), there is now a new twist to this: We may overcome this problem by exposing our cognitive shortcomings through digital algorithms. By exploring the borderline between logical and empirical problems using digital tools, we may actually push philosophy back a few steps and make our own mental restrictions accessible to empirical research. Recent research on cognitive systems (Dennett 2012) now emphasizes the distinction between competence (what the system can achieve) and comprehension (what the system can explain about itself). By exploring the difference between competence and comprehension (the performance of our linguistic capabilities and our understanding of it) we may find answers to why it is so difficult to know what we already know.

The present chapter will first display some existing empirical findings that support the abovementioned claims. These findings sometimes seem confusing to people and require some detailed theoretical explanations. To capture and keep the readers' interest, however, this chapter will begin with the findings so far, and work its way backward through the explanations. Along the way, contributions from various traditions and ages will be presented. In the final paragraphs, I will try to integrate some of the viewpoints of the various theoretical explanations offered, and also outline a possible agenda for future research.

Digital Algorithms in Psychology, Status 2017

In 2014, I thought I had discovered a disturbing finding for research using Likert-type scale surveys. Together with my coauthors Kai Larsen, Øyvind Martinsen, and Chi How Bong, we published a study in the peer-reviewed journal *PLoS One* showing how more than 86% of the variation in the statistics from survey responses was predictable a priori (Arnulf et al. 2014). I was excited and thought that others would be, too. While I did not think people would readily embrace the method itself, I hoped for a surprised recognition of the simple fact that the findings of a major research paradigm were obtainable in advance. There were a few initial reactions, but the scientific community has so far been silent, even as the findings have been corroborated in independent studies (Gefen and Larsen 2017; Nimon et al. 2015).

The study analyzed data from some of the most commonly used survey instruments in organizational psychology. In this field, there are literally hundreds or even thousands of studies that explore leadership and motivation with the survey instruments we used, such as the MLQ (Avolio et al. 1995), the LBDQ (Stogdill 1963), or scales measuring various types of motivations (Kuvaas 2006). These instruments have for many years been the gold standard of "measurement" in this research area, a prerequisite to publish in high-ranked journals (Bagozzi 2011; Michell 2013; Yukl 2012). The respondents comprised four big samples from different organizations, making sure that the findings were no coincidence.

While the exact mechanisms will be explained in more detail later, I will explain here in a simple way what we found: Surveys used in organizational psychology usually explore relationships among "constructs" such as different types of leadership, different types of motivation, and their effects on work processes in an organization. The researchers typically want to know if one type of leadership is more effective than another, and which psychological processes are involved in producing these effects. Typical research design may, therefore, imply asking participants in organizations about their perceptions of their managers, how they think about themselves and their motivations, and about the quality and intensity of the work they are doing.

The usual way to analyze these data is to make statistical explorations of the way that these answers are linked together, using correlations, regression equations, or complex structural equation models (SEM) that render quantitative descriptions of how the constructs are linked together (Bagozzi 2011; Jöreskog 1993; MacKenzie et al. 2011; Podsakoff et al. 2012).

By contrast, our semantics project begins by using only the questions from the survey questionnaires themselves, their "items" as they are termed. We feed them as input to digital semantic algorithms that can estimate to which degree these sentences have overlapping meaning. Such algorithms will usually give a number between 0 and 1.0 that indicates if the sentences share meaning in their content.

We use the numbers we get from the algorithms to predict or "guess" what the correlations between the survey items would be. The results were beyond my initial expectations. Depending on the assumptions, we could predict the correlations among leadership, motivation, and the outcomes in the surveys quite accurately. The semantic values captured in the best case 86% of the variation in correlations, but more importantly: in regression equations, this level of explanation was enough to predict the actual correlations as they were created by human respondents down to 2 decimals.

I remember showing the tables of correlations to the British professor in organizational psychology Adrian Furnham. He looked puzzled at it for a moment, then asked: "But if the numbers simply support what we already found, isn't that just a confirmation of our original results?" "Yes, in a way," I replied, "but if we could obtain the numbers simply by running the questions through a machine, we wouldn't need to ask people, would we?" I could see him reflect for a moment, and then nod. "Quite," he agreed.

Working with the findings throughout the analytical process, I had constantly sought someone to prove me wrong. The numbers were simply too good, and I was constantly expecting that someone could point to a flaw in the arguments, showing that the match between semantics and survey statistics would be an artifact or a product of a mistaken sort of analysis. That person never appeared.

Instead, I met a number of researchers who kept reminding me of Jan Smedslund. Most of them would be his previous colleagues or students. Whenever I called on a statistician, a methodologist or a psychological researcher, they would chew on my findings for a while, not coming up with a better explanation, and then shrug: "It reminds me of some of Jan Smedslund's stuff, the sort of ideas he has always been talking about. Maybe you should ask him."

I will return to the relevance of Smedslund's ideas in later sections, but first a few words about the reviews that we got as the first article made its round in attempts at publication. As the article was reviewed in journals addressing organizational psychology, the reviewers generally omitted to mention the fact that commonly reported findings could be reproduced without empirical materials. For all their methodological sophistication, this fact seemed to be the unmentionable elephant in the room. Instead, they usually recommended a rejection of the article because of its unconventional method of using digital text algorithms.

I want to quote three reviewers as their viewpoints shed interesting light about why we do not know what we already know, the a priori truths in pseudo-empirical research. One reviewer stated openly that he had no idea what "semantic algorithms" were, and so he had googled it. What he had read on Google, he said, was unconvincing to him, and so he suggested that the manuscript should be rejected. I replied to the editor that the reviewer paradoxically had been using a text algorithm (Google search) to investigate text algorithms, leading him to declare a disbelief in text algorithms because of what he found with through the use of one (the editor agreed, and asked me to resubmit, but to wait until he himself had quit his post).

Another reviewer made a better and more informed attempt, which we have met over and over again: Maybe we were misinterpreting the findings when we claimed that they contested the empirical research. Maybe the replication of the data structures instead supported their truthfulness. In other words, we had just found what research has already established, and so it wasn't the research findings, but instead, it was *our* research that was superfluous and did not deserve to be published.

Yet a third reviewer added that the text algorithms probably only reflected what people know because the research findings had been disseminated. In other words, we had used language research to find that people had already adopted the findings from leadership research.

Unawares, these three reviewers were articulating an explanation, not for our results, but for why we struggle to understand what we already know. This is a meta-linguistic phenomenon called "competence without comprehension" that we know how to use the language without knowing exactly how it works. I will return to this phenomenon in a later section.

First of all, the reviewer who googled the algorithms seemed to take computerized tools for granted without reflecting on what they really do. Computers are machines that apply the calculating powers of language, known as formal logics, to derive answers we are looking for from what we already know. It is sometimes hard for people to understand this, but formal logics is by its nature truth-preserving. Logical processes can strictly speaking not create new. A computer can only draw conclusions from the information already available to it. Often, we draw on this information because it is accumulated by others and so is new to the user. But most of the time, we let ourselves be amazed by how the computer is thinking in a different way from humans, more systematically and more stringently. The computer works by systematically exploiting what it already knows. One may compare it to a thinking phone book. In my younger years, possessing a phone directory, I "knew" all the phone numbers in Oslo in the sense that they were in my possession. I still had to look them up, at the risk of not finding the number I was looking for. If programmed correctly, a computer will arrive at the right number through a rigid application of the same procedure, proving that it always knows what it already knows.

The second reviewer's reply revealed that he judged our findings to be valid replications of empirical research, but that he was obviously indifferent to whether knowledge is derived from empirical methods or logical deductions. A bit curious for a trained researcher, it still reflects a long-lasting controversy between rationalists and empiricists in philosophy. Whatever one's position on this debate, it testifies to the fact that humans are just as surprised to learn what is logically derived as what is empirically detected. We seem to want or need the information precisely because it isn't obvious to us. We do not care how it was derived as long as there is some validity to it. At this point, reviewer 2 was voicing a version of scientific psychology that Jan Smedslund has been fighting for years. It is a discipline that at great cost goes to great lengths to tell us what we already know, what Jon Elster (2011) has called "hard obscurantism" and a waste of time and efforts in science. The a priori given answer is provided through a method so opaque to most people that they are barred from disputing it.

The third reviewer's comment is more intricate from a scientific point of view. He thought that the language algorithms could have detected and reproduced knowledge structures in language that had been transported there by empirical research in the first place. In other words, he thought of language as a sort of library that contains not only words but complex statements from science too. In this world view, science will enrich our vocabulary by truths as people read the research and import the ideas they read into their everyday language. This is probably not possible, as language is a tool allowing us to propose and think anything and everything, and the idea is generally considered as refuted in linguistic science (Lovasz and Slaney 2013). It actually explains why we need science to help us differentiate among fact, fiction, and nonsense.

Still, this is exactly where there may be a way out of Smedslund's labyrinth. The idea came to me as another colleague, on asked what he thought about the semantics project, mentioned another name that came to his mind: That of Gottlob Frege.

Frege, Wittgenstein, and the Programming Languages

Gottlob Frege was a late nineteenth century German philosopher and logician. He is famous for three contributions to logics (Blanchette 2012; Frege 1884, 1918). First of all, Frege was a pioneer in creating a system of notations in formal logics that made it possible to calculate with words. Through his system, Frege was able to prove that sentences may contain degrees of similar meaning, even where the sentences do not share any words. His system was possible because he made a difference between functions in language and the arguments that the functions take. This was very important because Frege showed that there is a difference between the intrinsic logic of propositions and the content, the stuff we talk about.

The British logician George Boole had already devised a system for turning logics into a calculating system (Boole 1847). However, Boole's project was first and foremost a mathematical project that took the conceptual contents of propositions for given. Frege's approach was more radical. He adopted an explicit linguistic position and claimed that the meaning of a sentence resides in the proposition of the sentence, not in every single word. He wanted to create a system for calculating truths that did not stop with the logical basics, but that was also sensitive to the contents of the sentences—what the sentence is "about", that is, the semantic properties of propositions (Sluga 1987).

Although his own system did not actually survive, he was an important pioneer in showing that language contains logical functions that lend themselves to complex calculations. It had originally been proposed by the seventeenth-century philosopher Gottfried Leibniz, who had conceived the term "*calculus ratocinator*" (Sluga 1987), a calculating machine that would be "an algorithm which, when applied to the symbols of any formula of the characteristica universalis, would determine whether or not that formula were true as a statement of science" (Rogers 1963, p. 934). This tradition has today evolved into programming languages, complex sets of instructions that allow computers to do efficiently and quickly what was to Frege and his contemporaries long and tedious work by hand (Wiener 1948, p. 214).

His second claim to fame came because his system was so promising that he tried to explain algebra as a branch of logics, but this effort is today judged as unsuccessful.

Still, he showed that quantification and mathematical operations are strongly linked to our linguistic capabilities.

The third feature of his historical position has direct relevance to survey research. As he tried to represent the meaning of sentences through formal symbols, Frege noticed that we sometimes use different words or terms that refer to the same existing facts, but that still may convey different meanings. Consider the case of authors with pseudonyms. The three expressions "Mark Twain," "Samuel L. Clemens," and "The author of Huckleberry Finn" all refer to the same historical person. Yet these expressions could also have slightly different meanings, one name being more tightly associated with writing while another name with a postal address or a family.

For this reason, Frege proposed a distinction between "Sinn" and "Bedeutung", that is, meaning and reference. The three expressions earlier all refer to the same person, but they also have separate meanings that allow speakers to concentrate on one aspect of the person.

Frege's logical discoveries went unheeded by the social scientists who followed Likert (1932) in exploring social realities through calculating numerical responses from surveys. A closer reflection on Frege's claims points to the possibility that people who are apparently talking about different things, such as leadership and motivation, are really talking about the same thing, and that there will exist semantic relationships between these concepts by the way they are entered into arguments. It is these semantic relationships that create the mathematical (or statistical) relationships in the survey data. The big methodological problem was already coined at an early stage by Thorndike (1904), after whom it is called the "jingle/jangle fallacy": In a "jingle," there will be two groups of researchers who think they are researching different things. Closer logical scrutiny will show that they have simply developed a differing terminology, and they are actually working on the same subject. A "jangle" is the opposite, a situation where groups of researchers think they are in the same field, but their words have actually developed different references and they are no longer working on the same subject (Kelley 1927).

A large study using semantic algorithms on the items that define constructs in social sciences was able to document the existence of widespread jingle/jangle problems in published research traditions (Larsen and Bong 2016). The jingle/jangle fallacies are almost as predicted by Frege's ideas, as summed up by Patricia Blanchette (2012): "from the Fregean perspective, two sets of sentences can have radically-different syntactic properties and hence be 'logically' inequivalent … while expressing exactly the same set of thoughts and hence being, from Frege's point of view, logically indistinguishable. Similarly, two sets of sentences can be indistinguishable except for the choice of atomic terms … and yet express sets of thoughts that have, from the Fregean point of view, significantly different logical properties."

Frege was looking for a purely propositional language that could allow a clear, unequivocal representation of a proposition or a judgment, and that would allow a comparison of how similar other expressions would be in terms of their underlying meanings.

At a time when scientists were still very much concerned with the difference between empirical and logical truths, Frege had a pupil who sought to solve this problem in a radical way. His name was Ludwig Wittgenstein and the book where he proposed his solution is called "Tractatus Logico-Philosophicus" (Wittgenstein 1922). His main concern was to create a philosophy of science that could clarify the nature of testable empirical propositions. His main aim may not have been successful (also according to himself), but that is of no concern here. The important part of the role of semantics in survey research is that Wittgenstein and his other mentor Bertrand Russell needed to create a way to talk about language, facts, and propositions.

As shown by Wittgenstein and Russell (Russell 1922, p. 17), we can differ between different kinds of facts. Three types of facts are of particular relevance here. As a "fact," we usually think of (1) empirical facts, as to whether it is raining or not. However, the reason we want to check whether it rains or not is that we can have different opinions on the subject. Whether someone believes it to be raining or not could be called a (2) psychological fact. However, to believe something and discuss it, as if it is raining or not, this belief must exist in the form of a proposition that can be communicated. One may call this a (3) "logical" fact—a proposition that someone is capable of believing, or discussing with others, and ultimately check for its truth. This was central to Wittgenstein's "mirror theory," the assertion that there must be a systematic relationship between what we propose and the facts that we use to support or reject a theory.

Our findings when we explore survey statistics with semantics are perfectly explainable through these three types of facts. The researchers set out to explore the empirical nature of their constructs, such as "leadership" or "motivation." They do this by obtaining records of "psychological" facts, the reported attitudes of subjects as scores on Likert-type scales. Eventually, when the statistics are performed, the psychological information is filtered out and the statistical patterns are no longer dependent on the individuals contributing to them. But instead of being descriptive of the empirical domain called "leadership," the numbers are simply reflecting the semantic (or logical) relationships between the item texts.

This capability in a language is the tool that helps us instruct computers today. The mechanical precursors to computers were textile-producing equipment using punch cards, as shown by the engineer Charles Babbage. But as computers got more sophisticated, they needed more systematic tools to instruct their operations, commonly referred to as "programming languages." The pioneers of these, such as Herman Zuse, drew extensively on the groundbreaking work of logical calculations and notations developed by Frege and his British predecessor, Boole (Rojas et al. 2000; Sluga 1987). There is an intrinsic relationship between computer languages and formal logic such that "when a [logical] specification completely defines the relations to be computed, there is no syntactic distinction between specification and program … The only difference between a complete [logical] specification and a program is one of efficiency. A program is more efficient than a specification" (Kowalski et al. 1984, p. 345). Computing languages are instructions to computers to systematically do what humans can only follow for a short while, taking full and systematic account of "what we already know."

This is the unpleasant fact that the reviewers from the survey research tradition seem unable to realize. Our capability to detect, decode, or construct logical "facts" is also tightly linked to our own meta-linguistic handicaps and the reason why computers are useful tools that help us overcome our cognitive limitations.

One of Wittgenstein's pressing arguments was that in order to be empirically testable, a proposition needs to be unequivocal (Russell 1922). In Wittgenstein's own words (Wittgenstein 1922, p. 23), "What can be said at all can be said clearly; and whereof one cannot speak thereof one must be silent." If not, we cannot fixate the relationship between the proposition in the language (the "logical fact") and how things are (the "empirical fact"), a problem that has also been discussed by Smedslund (2002). Lack of precision in this respect creates ambiguities and discrepancies between theory and empirical observations. In other words, we must seek the strictest possible ways to fix the meaning of propositions.

Both Wittgenstein and Russell knew and had improved on Frege's work. They were aware, not only of the computational possibilities in formal logics, but also of Frege's project trying to make the meaning of sentences primary to the logical calculus. Looming above this was also the awareness of the human limitations in making these sorts of arguments. Not only do people use language in imperfect ways, as Frege frequently pointed out but the logicians themselves become entangled in confusing conflicts that are difficult to resolve. In his foreword to the Tractatus, Russell (1922, p. 19) explicitly mentions that logical calculations and derivations are exceedingly difficult to follow, even for a trained mathematician: "As one with a long experience of the difficulties of logic and of the deceptiveness of theories which seem irrefutable, I find myself unable to be sure of the rightness of a theory, merely on the ground that I cannot see any point on which it is wrong." Or, as Patricia Blanchette (2012) sums up Frege's contributions: "It is hard to say what, exactly, separates a good analysis from a failed attempt." This echoes a much older lamentation from Heraclitus, the original inventor of the word "logics": That ideally, the laws of logics should be the same to everyone, even though in practice, it seems that everyone has his own (Graham 2015).

The invention and development of logic have always followed a double-sided, almost paradoxical track: On the one hand, we are expressing ourselves in a language so precise and rule-oriented that everything we say may concomitantly invoke a host of other facts that we can infer. On the other, we easily get lost, stuck, or cannot agree on these inferential steps. It is hard for us to make use of what we actually know.

Interestingly then, we have been able to create tools to help us here, precisely by turning the rules of logic into computers and programming languages. The digital algorithms are therefore giving us a possible mirror, not only to what we can achieve through logical computations but also through exposing our lack of meta-capability. Let us turn to the text algorithms themselves.

Latent Semantic Analysis and Other Text Algorithms

The close relationship between programming languages and natural languages has kept the computing community continuously interested in making computers deal with text (Schank and Abelson 1977). Readers old enough to remember the early DOS interface of PCs also remember the cumbersome task of instructing the computer via its own language. System developers have always wanted to emulate natural languages, even after Apple and later Microsoft adopted graphical icons as substitutes for weird lines of commands.

The quest to make computers understand or produce human-like language has been labeled "Natural Language Processing" (NLP). It has made great progress in recent years as numerous digital appliances are now equipped with voice-controlled interfaces. Even if the digital gadgets are not yet matching humans entirely, Apple lets you talk to its digital assistant Siri on the iPhone, a Tesla car will find addresses, call people, or play music to your verbal commands, and Amazon's Alexa will talk to you about shopping. NLP is used for tasks like automatic translation, indexing of information in large bulks of texts, or for easing the interface between machines and human users. Our future use of artificial intelligence (AI) will be dependent on successful NLP.

A strange obstacle for NLP has been our lack of meta-cognitive abilities as described earlier. The first attempts at making computers relate to natural language consisted of a chase for rules that would allow the computer to analyze or create meaning in language, such as grammar and syntax.

Some approaches to NLP still make use of such information. One such that we have been using is an algorithm termed MI (Mihalcea et al. 2006). The MI algorithm will look up words in a lexical database called WordNet (Miller 1995; Poli et al. 2010). WordNet is like a digital dictionary, but instead of alphabetical listings, it is a database where words are indexed for their semantic proximity to others. "Wolf" and "dog" will appear as more closely related to each other than, for example, "ship." In determining the meaning of a sentence, MI will identify the so-called parts-of-speech and map the meanings of single words within these parts.

In this sense, MI behaves a little like a human trying to learn a foreign language—it looks up words in a dictionary (albeit an electronic one) and in a sense determines the meaning of a text by taking account of their syntactic relationships.

A possibly less intuitive approach is called Latent Semantic Analysis (LSA) and was developed as a purely mathematical approach to text analysis. One of its pioneers, Thomas Landauer, even claimed that it probably simulates the way language is learned and represented in the brain (Landauer and Dumais 1997). While it may not be an accurate copy of the actual cerebral mechanisms, it certainly comes very close to a mathematical explanation. For this reason, some more attention will be given to LSA than to other existing algorithms. The overview of LSA given here still needs to be brief and superficial, so interested readers will have to look up the original sources to find more details (Dennis et al. 2013; Gefen et al. 2017).

LSA is a pure "bag-of-words" approach, meaning that it does not use information about grammar or syntax at all. In one sense, this both echoes and contradicts Frege's skepticism against using single words as sufficient containers of meaning. Frege claimed that the proposition in the sentence has priority over the single words (Sluga 1987), seemingly contradicting a "bag-of-words"-approach. However, instead of "knowing" meanings of single words, LSA draws mathematical inferences from a huge universe of texts, called "semantic spaces." In practice, a semantic space will have to be established by people, for example, by groups of researchers. These texts may consist of thousands of excerpts from newspapers or books. The whole purpose of this text collection is to give the algorithm access to language as it is actually used by people. For example, in our own research, we have used thousands of articles from American newspapers. A semantic space is then generated from hundreds of millions of words, repeated over and over again in many contexts. The semantic space, however, is not the words themselves, but a statistical reduction applied to the relationships between all the words included in the materials.

LSA creates statistical relationships between words and the contexts in which they appear. It is this extraction of semantic relationships from the usage of words that made Landauer call LSA a mathematical theory of meaning. He thought that this process might be similar to what the brains of children do when they are exposed to the use of words in the conversations of people around them (Landauer 2007; Landauer and Dumais 1997). LSA creates statistical relationships between words and the contexts in which they appear. In this way, the "meaning" of any word is represented as the degree to which it can replace another word in similar contexts. LSA will estimate this similarity as a number, using the following calculating steps (the reader who is uninterested in the statistical analysis may skip the following paragraph):

First, LSA constructs a matrix called the "document-term" matrix (TDM), where each row is a word and each column is a document where this word appears. This is a huge matrix in which each cell contains the number of times this word appears within each document. The TDM is then treated with a statistical technique called "Single Value Decomposition" (SVD), which is akin to factor analysis. This step turns the big matrix into three smaller ones, usually referred to as the U, Σ, and V matrices where TDM = $U \times \Sigma \times V$. These matrices contain information about the documents (U), words (V), and the singular values (Σ). The singular values are now truncated to simplify the analysis. This step is important because the truncation determines the number of dimensions used to analyze texts later on. The result of the truncation is usually denoted as "k," the number of singular values made up to describe the matrices. The number of k will determine how simplified the semantic space will be, compared to the original texts, and the significance of this will be explained further down.

LSA and similar algorithms have been used in empirical research on survey data (Arnulf et al. 2014; 2018a, b, c; Gefen and Larsen 2017; Nimon et al. 2015). In this case, the algorithm "projects" each item into a semantic space and estimates how it is represented in the triangular structure of $U \times \Sigma \times V$. The output is then the cosine of this relationship, a number between 0 and 1. The closer to 1, the more similar the meaning of the two terms. For the two sentences "Causes have effects" and "Effects have causes," LSA will return a cosine of 1.00 (if the reader wants to give it a try, an LSA engine can be accessed at the website lsa.colorado.edu).

In the research tradition of using Likert scales, the focus has historically been on the relationships between items or groups of items called scales. Building on the works of Cronbach and Meehl (1955), these scales have been taken as operationalizations of constructs, such as various types of "motivation," "leadership," and similar theoretical objects. Over the years, a number of statistical procedures have been developed that analyze the quantitative properties of such scale relationships, such as principal component analysis (PCA) of structural equation modeling (SEM) (Jöreskog 1993; Kline 2005), that are purportedly able to make precise mathematical estimates of the nature of these construct relationships.

However, the Achilles' heel of all these types of statistical modeling is that they use the co-variation between the items as their point of departure. All of them are applying correlations or covariance between the scores on the scale items as the input to the calculations. In other words, all the relationships in the models are simply iterations of the similarity among items in statistical terms.

In our research on survey statistics, we applied LSA to a series of commonly used questionnaire items. For the most part, we were able to show that the cosines computed by LSA can predict (Arnulf et al. 2014; 2018a, b, c) and thus even replace the correlations (Arnulf et al. 2018c; b; c). While LSA is not as proficient as a human speaker in understanding language, it comes very close, and the "measurement scales" of the researchers have been constructed to ensure performance in the statistical models. The result of this is that the needs of the researchers and of LSA converge in the way Likert-type scale surveys are constructed. We have been able to recreate the PCA and SEM models using semantic information alone (Arnulf et al. 2014; 2018a, b, c; Arnulf and Larsen 2015), and such findings have been confirmed in independent studies (Gefen and Larsen 2017; Nimon et al. 2015).

To put it bluntly, the statistical models of survey research will most likely reproduce the brain's assessment of similarity between these survey items. In the language of Wittgenstein and Russell, the researchers collected information about "psychological facts"—what people believe about their bosses—to make computational models of "empirical facts"—the relationships between leadership behaviors and employee performance. Instead, they ended up with information about the "logical facts," the numbers describing language processing in the brains of the respondents.

Almost paradoxically, the semantic algorithms provide an empirical proof of what Smedslund's original claims (Smedslund 1987), as explicated in a response to a critic (Smedslund 1988, p. 150): "that the inter-item correlations are produced exclusively by shared logical-semantic relations, given the taken-for-granted commonsense conceptual system and the taken-for-granted contextual assumptions."

The fundamental question is why this comes as a surprise to us, masquerading as an empirical finding that seems useful even if it only explicates what we already know. It is this incredulous resistance that keeps reoccurring in our reviewers' rejections. It is the very same intellectual fog that Smedslund's argumentation tries to lift.

Competence Without Comprehension

But how is it possible that we know without knowing that we know?

This is a topic that has frequently been addressed in psychology as "meta-cognition," the demonstration that we are usually much better at doing things than explaining HOW we do them. Language is itself the best case in point: While most adults are quite able speakers of their native languages, they have a much harder time explicating the rules that apply. Foreign students of German are frequently able to quote grammar rules that sound baffling to native speakers, who apply them without giving it a thought.

This phenomenon is the core point of a recent essay by the American philosopher Daniel Dennett where he compares Darwin's theory of evolution to the development of Artificial Intelligence as proposed by the logician Alan Turing (Dennett 2012). Dennett finds that the two share a common explanation, that of "competence without comprehension." This signifies how intelligent systems develop capabilities that the system itself cannot explain. In fact, from a computational point of view, the output of the computations usually shows no resemblance to the machinery that brought the computations about.

Specifically, the DNA code of species can be compared to computer algorithms. Alan Turing laid the foundations of computing science in 1936 by proving that "It is possible to invent a single machine which can be used to compute any computable sequence." The building blocks of the Turing machine were simple pieces of information (0's and 1's) with rules of combinations, very much inspired by the works of Frege (Beeson 2004, p. 6). In the same way, the DNA molecule stores and expresses information by long combinations of the simple base-pairs of G–C (guanine–cytosine) and A–T (adenine–thymine).

In other words, observable biological phenomena—such as the brain's ability to produce language—are products of calculations, but the calculations themselves are usually not apparent to the speakers.

The experience of invariant calculations still appears to the speakers now and then. The notion of "logic" is one such phenomenon. The Greek philosopher Heraclitus living around 500 BC is usually credited with coining the term. He observed how the universe seemed structured as a universally consistent language because there seems to be a lawful consistency in meticulous descriptions of nature. As he pointed out, the way up and the way down is the same way. It was our tendency to lose this out of sight (and hence the need to remind us of their identity) that made him issue the warning already quoted earlier, that although "this Word is common, the many live as if they had a private understanding" (Graham 2015).

This seemingly dual nature of logic has haunted our intellectual efforts ever since: One the one hand, there appears to be an independent lawfulness of the relationships of words and expressions to each other. On the other hand, it is as if the individual always struggles and frequently fails to live by these rules. Although as children we are quick to absorb and use the regularities of language, most of us struggle to use them perfectly. And, most importantly, we seem not to entirely grasp the full implication of the logical linkages that language provides, as per Russell's comment in his foreword to Wittgenstein's *Tractatus*, that stringent scrutiny of a logical theorem was tough even to a trained logician.

This struggle has kept philosophy in a continuous pendulum between logical rationalism—the claim that observation is unnecessary as most problems can be solved through thinking—to theory-rejecting empiricism that distrusts products of the mental apparatus, trusting only what can be measured (Markie 2017). One core proposition in Smedslund's work is that psychology will always be entangled in the intricacies between logical and empirical questions, where researchers keep looking for empirical questions, only to rediscover what was logically necessary.

This is where I believe that our discoveries using text algorithms may help us forward. Text algorithms like LSA take a purely calculative approach. Even if these calculations themselves take only seconds in a prepared semantic space, they may model the way a child's brain calculates the meanings of words during the years of exposure to its native language. Landauer already pointed out how LSA can solve "Plato's paradox"—the fact that children can know so many words for things that they have never actually encountered in real life (Landauer and Dumais 1997). These words are calculable from their semantic networks with other words. An increasing vocabulary implies an increasing differentiation and resolution of details.

In the tradition of Frege and Wittgenstein, it is interesting to ask the seemingly hopeless question: "How many things are there in the universe?" The answer is that it depends on the respondent's conceptual richness. A simple answer may be that there is only one—the universe. Any attempt at specifying more numbers will depend on words that differentiate—round things, blue things, heavy things, small things, and so on.

The practical implication of this is that our level of details in linguistic competence may drown speakers in the details of language, losing its inherent calculative relationships out of sight. Because, as my son once pointed out to me, "there may be many things in the universe that do not have words attached to them, but all words will also be related to other words." To be a meaningful word, any word needs to be defined in terms of others. Our language is thus a huge semantic network where all words are by necessity logically linked to others, however distantly. As our vocabulary increases, we can keep reiterating statements and fall victim to the idiosyncrasies as noted by Heraclitus and Russell and finally look bewilderedly for empirical facts to support our arguments and settle our disputes. We are locked inside Smedslund's labyrinth.

One may think of our semantic network as an enormous crossword puzzle where all words are fixed in their mutual relationships. With our cognitive constraints, we cannot see this—which is why most people find crosswords difficult to solve when the fields are empty, but recognizable as correct when the letters are filled in. In reality, it may be more like a giant Sudoku, where the meaning of any expression will be mathematically fixed by its relationship to all other measures. Psychological theories, then, are frequently not theoretical generalizations of empirical observations. Instead, they may simply be logical iterations of already given propositions. As theory is argued by its authors, the concepts involved are defined in terms of each other, and the relationships become self-evident or tautological (Semin 1989; Smedslund 1988, 1994, 2015; van Knippenberg and Sitkin 2013). The authors and their readers are unaware of the fact that they are merely iterating truths given by the conditions. Like solvers of crossword puzzles, they do not see the solution as self-evident, but simply sense their own cognitive effort paired with a feeling that the line of thinking is reasonable.

At this point, I want to return to the issue of the k dimensions in LSA, as described in the section earlier. If the number of k is very low, the LSA algorithm will tend to simplify everything and estimate higher degrees of similarity between texts, such as sentences. If the number of k is very high, the algorithm may fail to detect similarities until texts become very similar.

Consider the following examples:

If we enter the sentences "Your dog is loose and runs around," "Your hound is roaming about," and "A rabbit sleeps in its hole," the LSA algorithm will detect the differences between them. If we set k to 300, the algorithm will find the sentences with the synonyms "hound" and "dog" very similar, as their cosine will be 0.75, while only 0.40 or 0.33 with the sentence about a sleeping rabbit. However, if we reduce the number of k to 10, the similarity between the two first sentences increase to 0.95, but the rabbit is now also estimated at 0.82 with the sentence about the dog. It is as if LSA looks meticulously at sentences and determines that they are related but not the same when k is set to 300. When k is reduced to 10, LSA seems to make less differentiated, almost sloppy judgments—these are all sentences about some kind of animal in a location.

Using $k = 300$	Your dog is loose and runs around	Your hound is roaming about	A rabbit sleeps in its hole
Your dog is loose and runs around	1	0.75	0.40
Your hound is roaming about	0.75	1	0.33
A rabbit sleeps in its hole	0.40	0.33	1

Using $k = 10$	Your dog is loose and runs around	Your hound is roaming about	A rabbit sleeps in its hole
Your dog is loose and runs around	1	0.95	0.82
Your hound is roaming about	0.95	1	0.67
A rabbit sleeps in its hole	0.82	0.67	1

The effects of the differences in *k* dimensions of LSA are reminiscent of the jingle/jangle fallacies mentioned earlier, where similar concepts exist under different names, and similar names refer to very different concepts. It is also relevant to Frege's distinction between Sinn and Bedeutung (meaning and reference): The precise meaning of a word in the sense of its reference may in practice be a matter of precision. A roaming hound may mean something different from a running dog. Depending on the context, it may also mean the same—even being similar to a rabbit sleeping in a hole.

This calculative capacity of language is exercised whenever we are trying to solve a crossword puzzle. Expressions may mean the same or be distinct, but it frequently requires an intellectual effort to determine this as the calculations of linguistics do not always come as effortless options (Kahneman 2011).

The semantic calculations of the brain are remarkably flexible and precise at the same time. It seems that they are capable of loosening the semantics restrictions almost entirely, as when forming poetry and allegories. The meaning of an allegory is precisely not what it is "about," as in Shakespeare's famous sonnet: "Shall I compare thee to a summer's day?" We can enter this in LSA (helping the modern day algorithm by replacing "thee" with "you"), and test its similarity with two interpretations: One is a poetic transcription, "I find you warm, bright, and lovely," the other a more concrete explication: "Your name may be June." Although LSA sees a possibility that Shakespeare is addressing someone named June (cosine = 0.40), it finds it more likely that the poet refers to the personality of the interlocutor (cosine = 0.67).

Our linguistic capabilities are thus at the same time a product of precise and complex calculations but also leave us mostly aware of probabilistic results with wide room for error and individual interpretations. Being competent without comprehension, in Dennett's words, we find ourselves locked in a labyrinth of semantic networks that appear as logical lawfulness, without being able to overlook it.

Our languages are collective, cultural accumulations of words in which all statements need to be implicitly locked into all other statements to be intelligible. The individual does not have access to this complexity due to lack of meta-cognitive capacity—we merely have competence, but not comprehension. In the statistical models created by the responses to Likert-type scale items, the machinery of the competence reappears as patterns of correlations. This is an instance of "the wisdom of crowds" because it will be the mean response pattern that carries the signal. Individual response protocols seem to contain a lot of semantic noise, as Heraclitus would have recognized.

In our data, it usually takes a few hundred respondents to approximate the structures suggested by the algorithms. If we use only native speakers of English, they will approximate the LSA results quicker than speakers of other languages, but hundreds of Norwegians and even Chinese eventually arrive at the same quantitative structures as predicted by algorithms in American English.

There may even be a linguistic relativity phenomenon in here somewhere: Chinese responding in Chinese are slower to approach the LSA-predicted semantics than Chinese in English (Arnulf & Larsen 2020). Chinese as a language is far looser in its semantic restrictions than Indo-European languages (Harbsmeier 2007), while Germans responding in German seem to comply with the LSA-predicted semantics far quicker than even native English speakers. That may be one reason why German speakers like Frege and Wittgenstein were pioneers in analytical philosophy, and why Chinese do not even actually have an indigenous word for "logic" (Nisbett et al. 2001; Norenzayan et al. 2002). Instead, ancient Chinese philosophy articulated a skepticism toward language as a tool, seeing that it has only limited capability to contain truths about the world (Feng 2015). Some languages may simply structure the output in ways that makes the computational underpinnings more obvious to the speaker than others, making the ancient Greeks like Plato embrace idealism while the Chinese discarded it.

Wittgenstein's Revenge as a Way out of Smedslund's Labyrinth

I have titled this chapter "Wittgenstein's Revenge" because despite his and Russell's fame in the 1920s, their call for more stringent philosophical cleaning of research questions went unheeded, at least in psychology. While the behaviorist movement did call for a more skeptical treatment of non-observable phenomena, these were re-introduced from physics (Bridgman 1927) through the concept of "operationalism" (Boring 1945). Operationalism allowed constructs to be defined through the procedures used to measure them. This instigated Cronbach and Meehl to introduce a 50-year long hegemony of empiricism, sanctioned explicitly by the methodological conventions of the American Psychological Association (AERA et al. 2014; APA 1954; Slaney 2017; Slaney and Racine 2013).

This empiricism gained momentum from the increasing access to advanced statistical models in computing that made factor analysis and structural equations the preferred tools of any researcher who wanted to gain tenure in quantitative research. The need to resort to painful philosophical reflections on the empirical versus logical nature of the research questions seemed to be omitted. One could simply turn any question into a 7-point Likert-type scale, gather responses and begin the computing. It did not, and still does not seem to matter that the nature of the numbers—the *what* of what's being measured—is usually not a part of the discussion and harder to explain than the statistical operations themselves (Lamiell 2013; Mari et al. 2017; Maul 2017).

It is therefore ironic that the main heritage of Boole, Frege, Wittgenstein, and their contemporaries was kept alive in the computing tools themselves—in hardware as well as in the software. As all human work processes are increasingly becoming subject to digitalization, the original projects of the logician pioneers seem reintroduced into the research process itself. The phrase "Wittgenstein's revenge" may be overly catchy, but I believe there is an opportunity to reappraise his tradition in empirical research through the digitized tools of formal logics (hence the idea that he is coming back with a vengeance).

At first glance, it may seem as if our empirical research, in supporting Smedslund's argumentation, maybe just as much a vindication of Frege. However, I think there is a line of development from Boole through Frege to Wittgenstein that is so far unexploited in psychology. Boole saw that logical operation could be formalized into computations. From there, Frege moved on from mere operators to the calculated analysis of propositions—analyzing not only logical but semantic relationships. Finally, while he recognized these previous attempts, Wittgenstein was not satisfied with remaining in the field of logic. He raised the question about the limits of language as a container of scientific knowledge, saying that "In logic nothing is accidental: If a thing can occur in an atomic fact the possibility of that atomic fact must already be prejudged in the thing" (Wittgenstein 1922, prop. 2.012). Furthermore: "The proposition is not a mixture of words (just as the musical theme is not a mixture of tones)" (prop. 3.141). Words cannot be haphazardly blended, but will only be meaningfully combined in combining the logical/semantic properties that are already given in the definitions of the words themselves. The possible combinations of relationships are vast, but in themselves fixed. Wittgenstein located the "mysterious" in realities that certainly exist but that defy logical description, and famously warned against discussing it. This is a locked universe of meaning that we cannot escape.

Or maybe we can. Russell commented (Russell 1922, p. 18) that "after all, Mr. Wittgenstein manages to say a good deal about what cannot be said, thus suggesting to the skeptical reader that possibly there may be some loophole through a hierarchy of languages, or by some other exit." One reason for our lack of escape from Smedslund's labyrinth has probably been our lack of an impartial, third-party judgment of logical or semantic truths. Now that the algorithms have come closer than ever to Leibniz's dream of the "*calculus ratocinator,*" they could provide a tool for exploring the no-man's land between the semantic and the empirical, targeting and describing our cognitive barriers.

Toolmaking has helped humans overcome many types of shortcomings before, increasing our physical strength and our traveling capabilities. As we are improving our cognitive tools, we may also be expanding our empirical reach into what was earlier the exclusive realm of philosophy. As we improve our capability to apply digital analytics not only to the observations but to our theories and research questions themselves, we may be making real progress in differing between logical and empirical questions.

It may also help us explore the fascinating details of why we fail to comply with semantic and logical guidelines. A growing body of psychological knowledge has documented our cognitive shortcomings and driven the notion of "rational man" out of economics, a field covering two Nobel prizes in economics (Kahneman 2011; Simon 1957; Todd and Gigerenzer 2003; Tversky and Kessell 2014). The semantically expected is not uninteresting, whether in itself as documenting the brain's seemingly effortless and yet very precise linguistic parsing capabilities (Michell 1994), or even more as an impartial yardstick for assessment of our failure to comply (Gebotys and Claxton-Oldfield 1989; Kahneman and Tversky 1973; Tversky and Kahneman 1974).

Conclusion: Does it Matter?

This chapter started out describing the disbelief of reviewers confronted with the fact that their research objects were predictable a priori. My interpretation of their individual reactions was that they were being "competent without comprehension." The bigger challenge—that of the scientific community—has been its entanglement in a failure to recognize the difference between logical and empirical problems as described by Smedslund. As we and other researchers have shown repeatedly in recent years, we now actually may have the tools that could help us explore these questions, clear unnecessary confusion, and make way for real progress in psychology.

As a small practical example toward the end, I just want to share the way that I personally apply this new type of knowledge as a practical approach to one of my teaching fields, leadership development.

During the introductory part of the session on leadership with experienced managers, I will frequently introduce myself as a researcher on leadership. I then ask the audience if they think it is meaningful to do research on whether good leadership creates better results in organizations. The usual response is a solemn acceptance of this kind of research. I ask them to define "leadership," and most definitions they come up with contain "results" in them, typically in the form of "achieving goals by cooperation" or something like it. In that case, I say, they should also endorse doing research on what it is about Mondays that creates Tuesdays. If "achievement" is part of the definition, one cannot research whether leadership creates some kind of achievement. We have already decided that as part of the definition (van Knippenberg and Sitkin 2013).

One could easily ridicule the management field for falling victim to thoughtless fads and types of "consultant speech," but this fails to recognize the more important point that we are all competent without comprehension. We become trapped in real problems and get locked inside versions of Smedslund's labyrinth by being competent without comprehension. The resistance of the reviewers when faced with these possibilities may have been fueled with a sense of rejection, that the efforts were all in vain as instances of "hard obscurantism" (Elster 2011).

I believe that the human mind is locked in behind its own cognitive limitations. These limitations may not have played a big role in the natural habitat where homo sapiens emerged. As we have placed ourselves in an increasingly complex system of behavioral, technological, and economic feedback loops, there may be a real need for us to understand these limitations (Harari 2015; Senge 2000; Soros 2006). Our digital crutches are evolving fast and playing into most areas of social decision-making. Psychological research aimed at understanding how our cognitive limitations relate to our new tools will hopefully contribute in keeping the developing technology a servant instead of a master.

References

American Educational Research Association, American Psychological Association, Joint Committee on Standards for Educational, Psychological Testing (US), & National Council on Measurement in Education. (2014). *Standards for educational and psychological testing*. Washington, DC: American Educational Research Association.

American Psychological Association, American Educational Research Association, & National Council on Measurement in Education. (1954). Technical recommendations for psychological tests and diagnostic techniques. *Psychological Bulletin, 51*, 1–38.

Arnulf, J. K., & Larsen, K. R. (2015). Overlapping semantics of leadership and heroism: Expectations of omnipotence, identification with ideal leaders and disappointment in real managers. *Scandinavian Psychologist, 2*(e3). https://doi.org/10.15714/scandpsychol.2.e3.

Arnulf, J. K., Larsen, K. R., Martinsen, O. L., & Bong, C. H. (2014). Predicting survey responses: how and why semantics shape survey statistics on organizational behaviour. *PLoS One, 9*(9), e106361. https://doi.org/10.1371/journal.pone.0106361.

Arnulf, J. K., Larsen, K. R., & Dysvik, A. (2018a). Measuring semantic components in training and motivation: A methodological introduction to the semantic theory of survey response. *Human Resource Development Quarterly, 30*(1), 17–38.

Arnulf, J. K., Larsen, K. R., & Martinsen, Ø. L. (2018b). Respondent robotics: Simulating responses to likert-scale survey items. *SAGE Open, 8*(1), 1–18. https://doi.org/10.1177/2158244018764803.

Arnulf, J. K., Larsen, K. R., Martinsen, O. L., & Egeland, T. (2018c). The failing measurement of attitudes: How semantic determinants of individual survey responses come to replace measures of attitude strength. *Behavior Research Methods*, 1–21. https://doi.org/10.3758/s13428-017-0999-y.

Arnulf, J. K., Larsen, K. R. (2020). Culture blind leadership research: How semantically determined survey data may fail to detect cultural differences. *Frontiers in Psychology 11*(176).

Avolio, B. J., Bass, B. M., & Jung, D. I. (1995). *Multifactor leadership questionnaire technical report*. Redwood City, CA: Mind Garden.

Bagozzi, R. P. (2011). Measurement and meaning in information systems and organizational research: Methodological and philosophical foundations. *MIS Quarterly, 35*(2), 261–292. https://doi.org/10.2307/23044044.

Beeson, M. J. (2004). The mechanization of mathematics. In C. Teuscher (Ed.), *Alan turing: Life and legacy of a great thinker* (pp. 1–54). Berlin: Springer Verlag.

Blanchette, P. A. (2012). *Frege's conception of logic*. New York: Oxford University Press.

Boole, G. (1847). *The mathematical analysis of logic, being an essay towards a calculus of deductive reasoning*. London, England: Macmillan, Barclay, & Macmillan.

Boring, E. G. (1945). The use of operational definitions in science. *Psychological Review, 52*(5), 243–245. https://doi.org/10.1037/h0054934.

Bridgman, P. W. (1927). *The logic of modern physics*. New York: Macmillan.

Cronbach, L. J., & Meehl, P. E. (1955). Construct validity in psychological tests. *Psychological Bulletin, 52*(4), 281–302. https://doi.org/10.1037/h0040957.

Dennett, D. (2012). *A perfect and beautiful machine': What darwin's theory of evolution reveals about artificial intelligence*. The Atlantic.

Dennis, S., Landauer, T. K., Kintsch, W., & Quesada, J. (2013). *Introduction to latent semantic analysis*. Denver, CO: University of Colorado.

Elster, J. (2011). Hard and soft obscurantism in the humanities and social sciences. *Diogenes, 58*(1–2), 159. https://doi.org/10.1177/0392192112444984.

Feng, Y. (2015). *A short history of Chinese philosophy*. Beijing: Foreign Language Teaching and Research Press.

Frege, G. (1884). *Die Grundlagen der Arithmetik: eine logisch-mathematische Untersuchung über den Begriff der Zahl*. Breslau: W. Koebner.

Frege, G. (1918). Der Gedanke. Eine logische Untersuchung *Beiträge zur Philosophie des deutschen Idealismus I* (pp. 58–77).

Gebotys, R. J., & Claxton-Oldfield, S. P. (1989). Errors in the quantification of uncertainty—A product of heuristics or minimal probability knowledge base. *Applied Cognitive Psychology, 3*(3), 237–250.

Gefen, D., Endicott, J. E., Miller, J., Fresneda, J. E., & Larsen, K. R. (2017). A guide to text analysis with latent semantic analysis in R with annotated code: Studying online reviews and the stack exchange community. *Communications of the Association for Information Systems, 41*(11), 450–496.

Gefen, D., & Larsen, K. (2017). Controlling for lexical closeness in survey research: A demonstration on the technology acceptance model. *Journal of the Association for Information Systems, 18*(10), 727–757. https://doi.org/10.17705/1jais.00469.

Graham, D. W. (2015). Heraclitus. In E. N. Zalta (Ed.), *The Stanford Encyclopedia of philosophy* (Fall 2015 Edition ed.).

Harari, Y. N. (2015). *Sapiens: A brief history of humankind*. New York: Harper Collins.

Harbsmeier, C. (2007). *Globalisation and conceptual biodiversity*. Paper presented at the Union Académique Internationale, Oslo.

Jöreskog, K. G. (1993). Testing structural equation models. In K. A. Bollen & J. S. Long (Eds.), *Testing structural equation models* (pp. 294–316). Newbury Park: Sage.

Kahneman, D. (2011). *Thinking, fast and slow*. New York: Farrar, Straus and Giroux.

Kahneman, D., & Tversky, A. (1973). On the psychology of prediction. *Psychological Review, 80*(4), 237–251.

Kelley, T. L. (1927). *Interpretation of educational measurements*. New York, NY: World Book.

Kline, R. B. (2005). *Principles and practice of structural equation modeling* (2nd ed.). New York: Guilford Press.

Kowalski, R., Jackson, M. A., Rogers, M. J., Shepherdson, J. C., Sannella, D., & Lehman, M. M. (1984). The relation between logic programming and logic specification [and Discussion]. *Philosophical Transactions of the Royal Society A: Mathematical, Physical and Engineering Sciences, 312*(1522), 345–361. https://doi.org/10.1098/rsta.1984.0064.

Kuvaas, B. (2006). Performance appraisal satisfaction and employee outcomes: mediating and moderating roles of work motivation. *International Journal of Human Resource Management, 17*(3), 504–522. https://doi.org/10.1080/09585190500521581.

Lamiell, J. T. (2013). Statisticism in personality psychologists' use of trait constructs: What is it? How was it contracted? Is there a cure? *New Ideas in Psychology, 31*(1), 65–71. https://doi.org/10.1016/j.newideapsych.2011.02.009.

Landauer, T. K. (2007). LSA as a theory of meaning. In T. K. Landauer, D. S. McNamara, S. Dennis, & W. Kintsh (Eds.), *Handbook of latent semantic analysis* (pp. 3–34). Mahwah, NJ: Larence Erlbaum Associates, Publishers.

Landauer, T. K., & Dumais, S. T. (1997). A solution to Plato's problem: The latent semantic analysis theory of acquisition, induction, and representation of knowledge. *Psychological Review, 104*(2), 211–240. https://doi.org/10.1037//0033-295x.104.2.211.

Larsen, K. R., & Bong, C. H. (2016). A tool for addressing construct identity in literature reviews and meta-analyses. *MIS Quarterly, 40*(3), 529. https://doi.org/10.25300/Misq/2016/40.3.01.

Likert, R. (1932). A technique for the measurement of attitudes. *Archives of Psychology, 140*, 1–55.

Lovasz, N., & Slaney, K. L. (2013). What makes a hypothetical construct "hypothetical"? Tracing the origins and uses of the 'hypothetical construct' concept in psychological science. *New Ideas in Psychology, 31*(1), 22–31. https://doi.org/10.1016/j.newideapsych.2011.02.005.

MacKenzie, S. B., Podsakoff, P. M., & Podsakoff, N. P. (2011). Construct measurement and validation procedures in mis and behavioral research: Integrating new and existing techniques. *MIS Quarterly, 35*(2), 293–334.

March, J. G., & Simon, H. A. (1958). *Organizations*. New York: Wiley.

Mari, L., Maul, A., Irribarra, D. T., & Wilson, M. (2017). Quantities, quantification, and the necessary and sufficient conditions for measurement. *Measurement, 100*, 115–121. https://doi.org/10.1016/j.measurement.2016.12.050.

Markie, P. (2017, Fall). Rationalism vs. empiricism. In E. N. Zalta (Ed.), *The Stanford Encyclopedia of philosophy* (2017 ed.). Stanford, CA: Stanford University.

Maul, A. (2017). Rethinking traditional methods of survey validation. *Measurement-Interdisciplinary Research and Perspectives, 15*(2), 51–69. https://doi.org/10.1080/15366367.2017.1348108.

Michell, J. (1994). Measuring dimensions of belief by unidimensional unfolding. *Journal of Mathematical Psychology, 38*(2), 244–273. https://doi.org/10.1006/jmps.1994.1016.

Michell, J. (2013). Constructs, inferences, and mental measurement. *New Ideas in Psychology, 31*(1), 13–21. https://doi.org/10.1016/j.newideapsych.2011.02.004.

Mihalcea, R., Corley, C., & Strapparava, C. (2006). Corpus-based and knowledge-based measures of text semantic similarity. *AAAI, 6*, 775–780.

Miller, G. A. (1995). Wordnet—A lexical database for English. *Communications of the ACM, 38*(11), 39–41. https://doi.org/10.1145/219717.219748.

Nimon, K., Shuck, B., & Zigarmi, D. (2015). Construct overlap between employee engagement and job satisfaction: A function of semantic equivalence? *Journal of Happiness Studies, 17*(3), 1149–1171. https://doi.org/10.1007/s10902-015-9636-6.

Nisbett, R. E., Peng, K., Choi, I., & Norenzayan, A. (2001). Culture and systems of thought: holistic versus analytic cognition. *Psychological Review, 108*(2), 291–310.

Norenzayan, A., Smith, E. E., Kim, B. J., & Nisbett, R. E. (2002). Cultural preferences for formal versus intuitive reasoning. *Cognitive Science, 26*(5), 653–684. https://doi.org/10.1207/s15516709cog2605_4.

Podsakoff, P. M., MacKenzie, S. B., & Podsakoff, N. P. (2012). Sources of method bias in social science research and recommendations on how to control it. In S. T. Fiske, D. L. Schacter, & S. E. Taylor (Eds.), *Annual review of psychology* (Vol. 63, pp. 539–569). Palo Alto: Annual Reviews.

Poli, R., Healy, M., & Kameas, A. (2010). WordNet. In C. Fellbaum (Ed.), *Theory and applications of ontology: Computer applications* (pp. 231–243). New York: Springer.

Rogers, H. (1963). An example in mathematical logic. *American Mathematical Monthly, 70*(9), 929. https://doi.org/10.2307/2313050.

Rojas, R., Göktekin, C., Friedland, G., Krüger, M., Langmack, O., & Kuniss, D. (2000). *Plankalkül: The first high-level programming language and its implementation*. Retrieved from Berlin.

Russell, B. (1922). An introduction to the tractatus logico-philosophicus. In L. Wittgenstein (Ed.), *Tractatus logico-philosophicus*. London: Kegan Paul.

Schank, R. C., & Abelson, R. P. (1977). *Scripts, plans, goals, and understanding: An inquiry into human knowledge structures*. New York: Routledge.

Semin, G. (1989). The contributon of linguistic factors to attribute inference and semantic similarity judgements. *European Journal of Social Psychology, 19*, 85–100.

Senge, P. (Producer). (2000). The leadership of profound change. *SPC INK*. Retrieved from http://66.102.9.104/search?q=cache:elAoLNjJDcgJ:www.spcpress.com/ink_pdfs/Senge.pdf+SPC+INK,+2000,+%231.&hl=en&ct=clnk&cd=1&gl=no

Simon, H. A. (1957). *Models of man, social and rational: Mathematical essays on rational human behavior in a social setting*. New York: Wiley.

Slaney, K. L. (2017). *Validating psychological constructs: Historical, philosophical, and practical dimensions*. London: Palgrave Macmillan.

Slaney, K. L., & Racine, T. P. (2013). Constructing an understanding of constructs. *New Ideas in Psychology, 31*(1), 1–3. https://doi.org/10.1016/j.newideapsych.2011.02.010.

Sluga, H. (1987). Frege against the Booleans. *Notre Dame Journal of Formal Logic, 28*(1), 89–98.

Smedslund, J. (1978). Banduras theory of self-efficacy—Set of common-sense theorems. *Scandinavian Journal of Psychology, 19*(1), 1–14. https://doi.org/10.1111/j.1467-9450.1978.tb00299.x.

Smedslund, J. (1987). The epistemic status of inter-item correlations in Eysenck's Personality Questionnaire: The a priori versus the empirical in psychological data. *Scandinavian Journal of Psychology, 28*, 42–55. https://doi.org/10.1111/j.1467-9450.1987.tb00904.x.

Smedslund, J. (1988). What is measured by a psychological measure. *Scandinavian Journal of Psychology, 29*(3-4), 148–151. https://doi.org/10.1111/j.1467-9450.1988.tb00785.x.
Smedslund, J. (1994). Nonempirical and empirical components in the hypotheses of 5 social-psychological experiments. *Scandinavian Journal of Psychology, 35*(1), 1–15. https://doi.org/10.1111/j.1467-9450.1994.tb00928.x.
Smedslund, J. (1995). Psychologic: Commonsense and the pseudoempirical. In J. Smith, R. Harre, & L. Van Langenhove (Eds.), *Rethinking psychology* (pp. 196–206). London: Sage.
Smedslund, J. (2002). From hypothesis-testing psychology to procedure-testing psychologic. *Review of General Psychology, 6*, 51–72.
Smedslund, J. (2012). Psycho-logic: Some thoughts and after-thoughts. *Scandinavian Journal of Psychology, 55*, 295–302.
Smedslund, J. (2015). The value of experiments in psychology. In *The Wiley handbook of theoretical and philosophical psychology* (pp. 359–373). New Jersey: John Wiley & Sons, Ltd..
Smedslund, J. (2016). Why psychology cannot be an empirical science. *Integrative Psychological & Behavioral Science, 50*(2), 185–195. https://doi.org/10.1007/s12124-015-9339-x.
Soros, G. (2006). *The age of fallibility: The consequences of the war on terror*. London: Weidenfeld & Nicolson.
Stogdill, R. M. (1963). *Manual for the leader behavior description questionnaire, form XII*. Columbus, OH: Bureau of Business Research, Ohio State University.
Thorndike, E. (1904). *An introduction to the theory of mental and social measurements*. New York: Columbia University: Teachers College.
Todd, P. M., & Gigerenzer, G. (2003). Bounding rationality to the world. *Journal of Economic Psychology, 24*(2), 143–165. https://doi.org/10.1016/S0167-4870(02)00200-3.
Tversky, A., & Kahneman, D. (1974). Judgment under uncertainty: Heuristics and biases. *Science, 185*(4157), 1124–1131. https://doi.org/10.1126/science.185.4157.1124.
Tversky, B., & Kessell, A. (2014). Thinking in action. *Pragmatics & Cognition, 22*(2), 206–223. https://doi.org/10.1075/pc.22.2.03tve.
van Knippenberg, D., & Sitkin, S. B. (2013). A critical assessment of charismatic—Transformational leadership research: Back to the drawing board? *The Academy of Management Annals, 7*(1), 1–60. https://doi.org/10.1080/19416520.2013.759433.
van Schuur, W. H., & Kiers, H. A. L. (1994). Why factor analysis often is the incorrect model for analyzing bipolar concepts, and what models to use instead. *Applied Psychological Measurement, 18*(2), 97–110.
Wiener, N. (1948). *Cybernetics*. New York: Wiley.
Wittgenstein, L. (1922). *Tractatus logico-philosophicus*. London: Kegan Paul.
Yukl, G. (2012). *Leadership in organizations* (8th ed.). Harlow: Pearson Education.

Part IV
Psychotherapy and Psychotherapy Research

Chapter 18
Professional Practice Without Empirical Evidence: The Psychologic of Trust

Jan Smedslund

In several recent papers (Smedslund 2009, 2012a, b, 2016a, b) I have argued that empirical research cannot support psychological practice and that instead one has to rely on a nonempirical approach. In this article, I give an example by analyzing the central concept of *trust.*

I begin by summarizing why empirical research cannot support psychological practice. Then, I describe the nonempirical approach of *psychologic* (Smedslund 1988, 2012c) and the accompanying *bricoleur model.* Finally, as an example, I focus on the role of the psychologic of *trust* in treatment.

Features of Contemporary Research

The empirical search for general principles of psychology that began more than a century ago immediately encountered two obstacles. The first was that one could not exactly replicate findings because individuals *remembered and were changed by* the first occasion. This is the *irreversibility* of psychological processes. The other obstacle was that attempts to replicate the findings from one individual in other individuals yielded ambiguous outcomes due to *individual differences.* The result of encountering these obstacles was that, in order to create approximately equal conditions, psychological research had to turn to comparison of *group averages.* First, one tried to compare groups that were equal on presumably relevant variables. However, it soon became evident that the number of such variables was too large to

J. Smedslund (✉)
University of Oslo, Oslo, Norway
e-mail: jan.smedslund@psykologi.uio.no

T. G. Lindstad et al. (eds.), *Respect for Thought*, Theory and History in the Human and Social Sciences, https://doi.org/10.1007/978-3-030-43066-5_18

be manageable when trying to construct matched groups. The number of factors influencing psychological processes is *indefinitely high.*

Confronted with constantly and irreversibly changing phenomena influenced by indefinitely numerous determinants, psychological researchers have turned from exact laws to statistical tendencies.

Today, studies generally cluster around the RCT format, that is, they tend to involve comparisons of average performance of groups randomly drawn from the same population and tested in situations differing only in one dimension. The knowledge assembled by this approach is alone supposed to provide sufficient support for professional treatment, but, for a number of reasons, I think it cannot do so.

First of all, empirical research fails to acknowledge the full extent and implications of what we already *know* and *must take for granted* about psychology. This includes that humans are continuously active, goal directed, perceive, and remembering. An important consequence of remembering is *irreversibility*. Persons are continuously changing and remain stable only as long as the consequences of their actions appear to be unchanged. A metaphoric analogue is the whorls in a stream. They remain stable only as long as the stones on the bottom and the water supply remain unchanged. In psychology, stable conditions cannot be taken for granted because humans are so active, goal-directed, and ever open to new experiences. Hence, the idea of an accumulative psychological science leading to discovery of static principles or laws is unrealistic. For the most part, the regularities that may nevertheless be found in empirical psychological research depend directly or indirectly on stable human-made linguistic–societal environments. These include things such as word meanings, grammatical rules, traffic rules, laws, contracts, appointments as well as values, ethical norms, etc. All of these, as well as individual traits, involve *dynamic equilibria* maintained by temporarily stable consequences and change whenever these consequences change.

Prediction of behavior is vastly complicated because we continuously perceive, and take into account, a practically indefinite number of distinctions and sequences. In addition, the events we encounter in life are to a considerable extent random, that is, just happen unpredictably.

A consequence of the mentioned human characteristics is that individuals, starting with different genetic endowment, perceive and learn from indefinitely variable, partly fortuitous, life experiences and become and remain unique.

If psychological processes had been strongly related to a few dominant variables, instead of being weakly related to indefinitely many variables, one could perhaps have disregarded or moderated the preceding considerations. However, since research findings in psychology typically reveal only small statistical tendencies, rather than exact relationships, practical application becomes problematic. The reason is that *one cannot base any practice on findings that are just slightly above pure chance, just as one cannot live a life based on laws, contracts, and appointments that are honored only a trifle better than random guesses.*

Since controlled studies tend to produce empirical results that hover just slightly above the purely random (in contrast to some physical domains where the error variance of experiments is small), psychological research does not provide certain, or even practically useful, “empirical evidence.” This implies an ethical obligation for the practitioner to be wary of relying exclusively on research findings. Conversely, it implies an obligation to be sensitive to the rich and unique features of every individual client and life situation. This conclusion is further strengthened because the context of research findings nearly always is so different from the contexts of individual cases that generalization becomes a hazardous and ethically marginal undertaking. Clients usually make distinctions that are incompatible with those made by researchers. Cf. George Kelly's "personal constructs" (Kelly 1969).

Another problem is how to infer from average findings to individual cases. Even if the outcome of one treatment procedure is on the average superior to another, it may well be that a number of individuals display the opposite effect. Therefore, unless the comparative findings are solidly and consistently nonoverlapping, research outcomes are of uncertain help in deciding the type and form of intervention in the individual case.

The previous considerations only cover genuinely empirical research. The numerous instances of *pseudo-empirical* studies obviously do not fall under the heading of "empirical evidence," since they only describe what is self-evident, that is, follows from the meanings of the words involved. An example of a pseudo-empirical theory is presented in Smedslund (1978). Since the theory is pseudo-empirical, this also applies to the hundreds of experiments that, allegedly, have tested specific predictions from the theory.

Hypotheses appear particularly plausible, and worthy of testing, when they involve logically related concepts. Apparently, one very seldom checks for pseudo-empiricality by asking whether the negation of a hypothesis is at all meaningful. This may explain the high frequency of pseudo-empirical studies in psychology and why they mostly report confirmation.

In summary, a general psychological hypothesis about a logically necessary connection is always empirically true, and a general hypothesis linking logically unrelated variables is always false, that is, always has exceptions. This is not the place for speculation about the origin of the conceptual primitives and the grammar of human language. However, it should be noted that all truly empirical general psychological hypotheses are relative to and change with a context. The outcome of more than a century of research has failed to yield exceptions (Roediger 2008; Teigen 2002).

For the given reasons, I conclude that the outcomes of contemporary empirical scientific research are unfit, or at least grossly insufficient, to guide practical work.

What Then Guides Practical Intervention?

In the absence of reliable support from scientific data and theory, and encountering irreversibly changing persons influenced by innumerable, often random, events, the psychological practitioner must adopt a maximally flexible strategy. He or she must strive to be open to the unpredictable individual case and at the same time rely on the two sources of information that are always available, namely, the a priori knowledge we all have of what it means to be human and the acquired knowledge of the relevant language and culture.

Since each case is unique and contains much that is unpredictable, this justifies a *tentative* approach in close contact and cooperation with the client. This means attempting to secure what is tried lies within what the client deems possible and promising. The opposite procedure, namely, relying exclusively on research findings and professional authority, is fraught with unacceptable consequences. The most important is that it risks disregarding unique characteristics of the client that influence the treatment and, therefore, *must* be taken into account.

Relying only on professional authority virtually ensures that treatment effects are less likely to be maintained in the client's future life. A reason is that trying to rely on the psychologist's authority alone is likely to strain, go beyond, or contradict the client's own accumulated life experience and engrained ways of being and functioning. The clients' engrained ways of perceiving and acting, and the engrained ways of perceiving and acting of the surrounding persons, mutually support each other. Psychologists focusing exclusively on what goes on in the treatment sessions frequently tend to underestimate the stability of these interaction patterns in daily life.

Actual treatment cannot be directly "evidence-based" in the sense of being empirically supported, since, as I have argued above, there is rarely any reliable and useful empirical "evidence." On the contrary, focusing on empirical data and preconstrued theory may distort the "listening" to unique details that are essential in helping the individual client.

It remains to describe the content of an alternative, nonempirical, approach. I have selected to focus on the role of *trust* in treatment.

Treatment Seen as Psychologic

In describing psychological treatment, I take my departure in what I have labeled as *psychologic* (Smedslund 1988, 1997, 2012c). The term refers to what follows from the shared structure of basic concepts in all human languages. I have argued that one must take this structure for granted because to deny it makes no sense. Psychologic describes what is valid for us and cannot be otherwise because we are human and given the way humans must talk. This knowledge is the only thing that is common and stable in psychological practice, where one is dealing with indefinitely varied unique cases and without reliable empirically based guidelines. Psychologic is an attempt to formulate the implicit knowledge that everyone shares and is contained in all human languages. Psychological analysis helps practitioners recognize the invariant structure of their encounters with ever-new concrete cases. Here, I focus on a view of psychological treatment, where the building of *trust* is an integral part.

Before analyzing the role of trust, it is necessary to give a brief general introduction to psychologic.

Psychologic refers to the network of conceptual relations that are logical, that is, are necessarily true for speakers of a given language. The first example used by Heider (1958) was "If someone *wants* to do something, and *thinks* he *can* do it, then he will *try* to *do* it."

Every language contains indefinitely numerous logically necessary relations. Users of a language implicitly take them for granted. When explicitly formulated, they, therefore, appear highly plausible, and the plausibility frequently lures psychological researchers to test them empirically. It appears that people unreflectively take it that empirical verification is more convincing than logical necessity as a test of reality. The result is an abundance of *pseudo-empirical* hypotheses and research that one could have avoided by simply asking if the outcome could possibly have been otherwise (Smedslund, 1978, 1991).

The logically necessary relations in language can be organized in a general axiomatic system of psychologic (Smedslund 1988, 1997) and can be seen as built on a system of (60+) *primitive concepts* that appear to be common to all human languages (Wierzbicka 1996). The primitive concepts contained in the example from Heider presented earlier are *want, think, can, try,* and *do*. The logical relations in the system of primitive concepts are valid for all speakers of a human language. Psychologic would change only if the basic structure of human language changed, which is almost unthinkable.

Psychological statements express relations between *shared* meanings in language and jointly constitute what may be characterized as *psychological common sense*. As I understand this notion, it refers to the system of all logically valid statements in a language as well as what follows from what we take for granted about persons because we are human. Thus, I understood the notion of psychological common sense is different from "folk psychology," which also includes empirical opinions that may or may not be correct. Psychologists have spent much time testing such "folk psychologies" and have especially been searching for "counterintuitive" facts that allegedly advance psychology by showing that what people generally believe is not always true. This empirical research in folk psychology does not concern psycho-logic and common sense as defined here.

In this article, I take my departure in psychologic and view that psychological practice must go on without empirical research evidence. I limit the discussion to the psychologic of trust in professional practice. Personal trust is seen as a total response, transcending isolated acts and specific situations. The extensive literature on trust, much of it condensed by Hardin (2002), covers most of what we all know. The approach of psychologic differs from Hardin's by focusing only on the conceptual structure involved.

The Psychologic of Trust

Among the things we all take for granted, there is one fact that explains the importance of the concept of trust, namely, that every person thinks other persons can harm her. People are *vulnerable*. Therefore, since everyone wants to avoid harm, degree of *trust* is an ingredient in every human relation. To trust someone is to think that the other person will not harm you.

Trust is a *subjective* phenomenon that may or may not correspond to reality; trust can be more or less justified. We all try to avoid being hurt, and if we do not trust a person, we become closed and defensive, and cooperation will suffer. Since cooperation is necessary in treatment, this will also suffer in the absence of trust. It follows that the psychologist practitioner should *always try to avoid harming the client.*

This follows directly from the psychologist's professional obligation to be of help. However, with further consideration, it becomes apparent that the rule is not always simple to implement; other aspects of interpersonal relations and variations in the surrounding circumstances always come into play.

Consider what can happen when the psychologist simply tries to build trust by consistently attempting not to harm the client: Many aspects of the professional role directly *facilitate* the building of trust. A professional relation always involves a *contract* with legal, financial, and ethical implications. A contract facilitates the building of trust in several ways. First, and foremost, it defines a role for the psychologist that the client usually takes for granted. When formulated directly, the professional role goes like this: "You shall try to be of help to your client." The role makes the psychologist trustworthy by definition.

A second important part of the treatment situation is *confidentiality*. This makes it easier to talk about and try out new things without having to consider responses from other persons than the psychologist. This may also contribute to the impression that the psychologist retains what I have called own control as discussed in more detail subsequently. That is, the psychologist will be perceived as trustworthy when his actions are not seen as dictated by any third party. Thus, the confidentiality restriction adds to the trustworthiness of the situation by eliminating many possible threats.

Third, the contract involves a mutual obligation to uphold rights and duties, concerning time and place, payment, and any auxiliary arrangements, such as changes in schedule, way of payment, communication outside sessions, etc.

Together, the formal components of the contract create a predictable and safe situation for the client in which to talk about his or her life situation and to cooperate in trying to improve it. Given the preceding facilitating circumstances, let us now consider what other conditions are involved when the psychologist tries to pursue a strategy of not harming the client in order to build trust.

Openness

One general factor is the *openness* with which the psychologist benevolently communicates with the client. The positive effect of being open is that it is usually less frightening to *know* what the psychologist thinks about you than to be a victim of uncontrolled fantasies about this. Hence, it appears that the psychologist should try to be open. However, this turns out to be a rather demanding requirement.

In order to feel safe, the client wants to know as much as possible about what the psychologist thinks and wants. Therefore, an important part of building safety is always to be honest in answering questions like "what is my diagnosis?"; "Do you think I will ever get better?"; "Do you think I should do this?"; etc. Being open in these and other matters may make it easier for the client to develop trust. Since one should not give advice based on professional or personal views and yet remain open, these are tricky questions. When the client asks, "what do you think I should do," the answer should be to try to take into account how the client views his or her situation and how he or she will understand the psychologist's answer. Hence, this answer could consist in attempting to recapitulate the alternatives and consequences as the client sees them and what the client sees as possible solutions and consequences. It is natural to maintain a wondering attitude that demonstrates understanding of the client's uncertainty. Essentially, it is a matter of taking the client's point of view and judge what openings are available. The psychologist is honestly trying to help while knowing that the only advice that will penetrate is what is very close to or stimulates the client in their world. Communication may also be improved by declaring, "I will always try to tell you what I think, *as soon as it becomes clear enough to be stated in an intelligible way,*" and" I will always be willing to *try* to share my thoughts about how I understand you." One can answer the question about diagnosis by referring to the symptoms initially mentioned by the client, and one's *preliminary and tentative* questions about them, if any, and repeat that it is a joint task to find out what they mean and how to eliminate them. One should always raise questions and thoughts about possibilities and, in general, try to ensure that psychologist and client have running access to each other's thoughts. It is difficult to build trust without openness because clients are often inclined to wonder about what the psychologist "really" thinks and tend to feel safer when this is clarified.

When one adheres to a strategy of trying to avoid harming the client, one must also deal with a number of other possible complications. These stem from the task of establishing and maintaining several necessary and jointly sufficient conditions of personal trust (Smedslund 1997, pp. 68–73).

Respect

A necessary part of a strategy of building trust is to always treat the client with *respect*, that is, according to his or her so*cietally defined rights and duties.* Other terms whose meanings are related to this notion of respect are to be considerate, correct, courteous, polite, and just.

Everyone wants to be respected, and it is painful to be treated without respect, in other words to be *humiliated.*

Because many clients have rarely or never experienced interacting with an open and consistently respectful professional in a confidential setting, this can in itself be a powerful way to strengthen trust.

Note that, although perceiving someone as respectful appears to be necessary for trusting them, this is a logical consequence of two even more basic necessary factors, namely, perceived *care* and *understanding*. With care and understanding, respect follows because if you care for someone you do not want to hurt (humiliate) that person, and if you understand her, you know how to avoid what would hurt. Conversely, if you do *not* care about someone and/or do *not* understand someone, you will not always treat the person with respect.

There are five basic conditions of trusting (seeing someone as trustworthy). Each one is necessary, and jointly, they are sufficient. They all refer to subjective phenomena and not the objective reality.

Care

Perceived care is an important precondition for trusting someone. To think that someone cares for you implies believing that this person always wants and tries to benefit you and avoid hurting you. For general trust, the relevant want to benefit someone is also relatively global and long term and not restricted to a particular situation or point in time. Care is necessary for trust because a caring person tries to protect you from harm, and a person who does not care for you is either *indifferent* or *malevolent.* An indifferent person may hurt you unintentionally, and malevolent person may hurt you intentionally. Therefore, neither of them is trustworthy. Hence, perceived care is a necessary condition of trust. However, it is not sufficient because even caring persons may sometimes hurt you. For example, they may do it unintentionally because they do not understand you.

Understanding

Understanding may be defined it as follows:

> *P understands what O means by saying or doing A, if, and only if, and to the extent that, P and O agree about what follows from A for O.*

You cannot trust someone who you think does not understand you because this may have unpleasant and even serious consequences. Examples range from when an offer to help humiliates an elderly person who is trying to maintain self-sufficiency to serious cases where the psychologist fails to understand that a client contemplates suicide. The experience that a caring person deeply and precisely understands you creates trust. Conversely, the experience that an uncaring person understands you can be frightening. Hence, the project of building trust necessarily requires both perceived care and perceived understanding.

When we encounter a new client as professionals, we may not only be naturally inclined to interpret their activity but may also be inclined to organize our impressions into professional categories. This involves focusing on symptoms and, gradually or rapidly, this leads to an overall picture of the person. The process can sometimes take the form of a "cognitive avalanche" because it may rapidly cover everything and thus may color all interpretations of what goes on afterward. In other words, the "avalanche" freezes the picture. Novice psychologists are led to focus on certain phenomena, for example, restlessness, or hearing voices, as possibly indicating, respectively, "ADHD" or "schizophrenia, and this may bias their succeeding perceptions and prevent alternative or more nuanced interpretations.

In addition to such professional biases, numerous ordinary cultural indices, such as wearing a hijab or having dark skin, activate fixed kinds of expectations. The net outcome may be to distort and limit the understanding of the client. This is serious considering that every client is unique and wants to be understood as the unique person she or he is. Therefore, it is clear that such a combined natural and professional attitude, usually serving to simplify our dealings with others, may also be a threat to a sufficiently correct understanding.

In order to counteract any tendency to categorize and distort, practitioners have suggested preventive remedies. Freud proposed an attitude of "free-floating attention," and Anderson and Goolishian (1988) suggested that the psychologist should adopt an attitude of "*not knowing*" when encountering a new client. This is a necessary way to understand unique other persons because, by definition, any fixed set of categories is bound to distort uniqueness to some extent. Human beings have a vast capacity to get to know persons they encounter, although one cannot fully describe the underlying process in words. This is what Kahnemann (2007) labels System 1. The free-floating, not-knowing attitude allows intuitive nonverbal processes to take place with minimal interference. Only in retrospect can one try to put words on and communicate the outcome. The problem is that verbal communication *about* the process necessarily impoverishes and distorts what we know intuitively. We can communicate our understanding only by means of language, but then we have to be selective and simplify what we experience. This applies to all verbalized understanding of another person.

From the preceding it follows that in order to trust someone, it is necessary that you think the person understands you. However, even if you think that the person also cares for you, there may still be situations where you cannot trust the person.

Own Control

A therapist's goal of getting someone to trust her or him is never fully achieved only by being consistently respectful, caring, and understanding. Additionally, the therapist has to make certain that the person understands that her or his actions are not in important ways controlled by *other* persons or circumstances. This means to have what I have called *own control.*

P has own control of act A If, and only if, P does or does not do A, according to P's own wants and thoughts, and independently of the wants and thoughts of other persons.

An important specification should be made here. P has own control of act A even while considering the wants and thoughts of other persons as long as P takes responsibility for (chooses) act A. In cases where P is *forced* to do or not do A, P does not have own control and is not trustworthy.

A psychologist may not have complete own control, for instance, if she participates in a scientific study and, in one situation, is obliged to conform to the treatment manual, against own judgment. In general, the process of building trust may be halted or destroyed if the psychologist is forced to harm a client. A psychologist has optimal work conditions only to the extent that she can conduct a treatment without interference from bosses, commanding officers, creditors, formal obligations, loyalties, etc. These are "impersonal" conditions of trust, since they do not directly concern the personal relation between the psychologist and the client. However, this is a reminder that working conditions may also interfere with the process of building trust.

In summary, respect, care, understanding, and own control characterize any really trustworthy person. However, there still remain instances where a respectful, caring, and understanding person with own control is not trustworthy.

Self-Control

Trust is threatened whenever a person lacks *self-control*. The concept can be defined as follows:

P has self-control regarding act A if, and only if, P does A only when P thinks it is right and does not do A when P thinks it is wrong.

If a person does things interacting with a client, even when she thinks they are wrong, this means lack of self-control and adversely influences the building of trust.

The definition links self-control to professional *ethics*. Discussing the many intricate distinctions involved goes beyond the scope of the present paper.

Finally, even when all the mentioned conditions are present, there may still be no trust because the psychologist is seen as lacking the expected *know-how*.

Know-How

A sixth condition of trust, namely, *relevant know-how*, presupposes the previous factors and also goes beyond them. The client cannot trust a psychologist who appears to lack professional skill. The criterion of skill is usually amount of success. This is similar to the criteria of a good teacher, a good doctor, a good leader, etc. Success always tends to build trust, even when the exact constituents of the requisite skill are more or less unknown.

If a client feels improved, he or she may typically attribute this to the psychologist's professional skill. Conversely, if the client thinks he or she does not get better or gets worse, he or she may think this reflects the psychologist's lack of skill.

Each of the mentioned five basic conditions is necessary for personal trust, and it can also be proved that, taken together, the conditions are jointly sufficient (Smedslund 1997, p. 72). When all are present, there is trust.

However, the joint logical sufficiency of the conditions is only helpful to a limited extent. Although we know the content of four of the conditions, we do not know what constitutes the additional "skill" needed to make the conditions jointly sufficient. It remains an open question what leads to success or failure in building trust. Even when there is care, understanding, own control, and self-control, we do not know what more we have to teach, in order to ensure success. Psychologic helps, but the fifth condition (relevant know-how) leaves an open area of uncertainty originating in the subtle interplay between a unique psychologist and a unique client in a unique situation.

Challenges for Teachers of Psychology

Although the conditions of personal trust are known, with the exception of the contents of "know-how," there remain intricate teaching problems.

For each of the five conditions it appears that if a novice is not already "prepared" to satisfy them, we may not know exactly how to teach them.

Consider the following questions:

1. How can you teach a student to treat a client respectfully if she is not already prepared to respect?
2. How can you teach a student to treat a client caringly if she is not already prepared to care?
3. How can you teach a student to treat a client with understanding if she is not already prepared to understand?
4. How can you teach a student to treat a client adequately if she does not have own control?
5. How can you teach a student to treat a client adequately if she does not have self-control?
6. How can you teach a student to treat a client correctly if she lacks the relevant know-how?

Usually, most students start out by trying to be respectful, caring, and understanding and trying to secure own control, exercise self-control, and strive to acquire relevant know-how. Even so, each of the questions opens up for more or less extensive and intractable challenges that merit a closer analysis.

Failure to Respect

In a world where people of different cultural origins meet with increasing frequency, the importance of treating clients with respect (i.e., to treat them as having the rights and duties of the members of a given society) has become increasingly salient. The psychologist can only try to treat the client with respect according to the rules of the given society, but the immigrant may not recognize or adopt these rules and, hence, may not come to trust the psychologist. A hypothetical example could illustrate this: A young male client may come from a society where unmarried women are legitimate targets and may try to treat a female psychologist accordingly. The psychologist now comes to see the client as a potential rapist, whereas the client merely sees himself as a normal young man. There is no mutual respect. Such mutual inability to respect can only begin to be resolved by increased cross-cultural *understanding*. Cross-cultural understanding can only be achieved by recognizing human *sameness*. The psychologist must realize that the client at every moment adopts what *he* thinks is the right point of view because it is most consistent with the total of what he has until now experienced. Focusing on human sameness also activates a universal human ethics that transcends all cultures and makes it easier to treat all clients with respect. An essential part of this ethics is precisely the recognition that every human strives for self-preservation and always takes what he or she thinks is the right point of view because it is most consistent with the total of what she has experienced. Problems arise at points where the world views of the psychologist and the client clash. If the psychologist is unable to cope with this, then the project of maintaining respect may falter. The way ahead is to continue to develop better understanding of why the client thinks and feels as she does and what the client can see, or can be brought to see, as possible ways of moving ahead, achieving integration with the new culture. The present concept of building trust presupposes recognition of the client's original point of view as a starting point of a process leading to a state where the client comes to recognize and accepts the rights and duties of being a member of the current surrounding society. At the same time, this involves renouncing earlier views, at least where they clash with the ethics of the current environment. Occasionally, a client ends up deciding to reject the ethics of the surrounding society and leaves. Treating the client respectfully throughout this process is not easy but remains a necessary condition for building trust. A client-centered form of treatment appears to be the only possibility.

Failure to Care

Caring is a feeling that is normally and automatically activated when you sense that another person is suffering and helpless. It is especially strong when you encounter a baby without a caretaker. Care is aroused by encountering suffering clients and normally grows by getting to know a client better and sensing their pain. Exceptions may occur when a client is persistently unwilling to disclose own suffering or behaves in a threatening and abusive way that evokes fear, disgust, or exasperation. One example of what may work is to try to get the client to talk about own experiences and suffering as a child. This may evoke the psychologist's care. There are also cases where lack of care for clients (indifference or aversion) may be the result of being engrossed in private difficulties or by a state of professional "burnout." These problems go beyond what will be discussed in the present chapter.

Faking care is unethical.

Care is the most potent and central condition of trust. To think that someone cares for you means, among other things, that you think he or she will actively *try* to protect you. Whether or not he or she actually *can* protect you depends on other factors reflecting that while care is necessary it is not sufficient for trusting someone.

Failure to Understand

To understand an act of a person is to know what, for that person, the act follows from and what follows from performing the act. In other words, what the act *means* for the person. Understanding why persons do or not do something means understanding what they want to achieve and/or what they want to avoid, in other words, what they take to be good and bad. If the psychologist does not understand this, she may unwittingly come to harm the client or fail to respond helpfully and intelligibly and hence undermine trust. It goes without saying that complete trust and trustworthiness are ideals that may never be fully achieved. The only remedy is to continue to try and to continue to express willingness and interest to understand better. In proceeding, try to avoid professional categories and listen attentively to what the client tells and to her response to your questions and suggestions. Be patient, let your intuition and your reflections unfold, and be tolerant of the unending ambiguity.

In addition, understanding the client should not be seen as an exclusively intellectual task. It also involves not only the client's but also your own feelings. Since the client may not only hope to have his suffering relieved, but may also be afraid of the change needed for improving, focus must be on the strategies by which he or she *avoids* disclosure and possibilities and changes that appear too painful. Some clients may even try to prevent being understood by distracting and attacking the psychologist ("attack is the best defense"). They try to hurt the psychologist by consistently rejecting all initiatives by showing doubts about the psychologist's professional competence, by irony, etc., all signs that the client either still does not trust the psychologist and/or does not want to change.

We all know much of the common sense of how to create trust, but it serves the beginner psychologist well to also recognize the important, possibly disturbing, role of own vulnerability and feelings of threat to own image as a competent professional. It is important to take into account one's own feelings of hurt and try to cope with them. Occasionally, but not always, one may show one's vulnerability to the client, confirming one's openness and humanity. Professional ethics may also help to maintain focus on the client's situation and continue to try helping.

Understanding is necessary for building trust but can also be very threatening to the client, especially if combined with perceived lack of respect and/or perceived lack of care. Clients want to be understood only if, and to the extent that, they see the psychologist as respectful and caring.

Perceived respect, care, and understanding are the core components of *personal* trust because they reflect the other person's attitude to oneself. If you do not respect me, care for me, and understand me, I cannot trust you. If you do not respect me, I feel humiliated; if you do not care for me, I feel rejected; and if you don't understand me, I feel alone and exposed.

Failure of Own Control

It is immediately apparent that you cannot trust a person, even though respectful, caring and understanding, if that person can be forced to harm you by superior officers, bosses, creditors, by existing laws, or by personal obligations and promises. It follows that the professional psychologist should try to secure her autonomy when it comes to treatment. This does not only include factors from outside the treatment situation but also inside determinants. For example; if a participant in a family therapy calls the psychologist the evening before a session, and wants her to promise *not* to introduce a certain topic in the forthcoming session, the psychologist should not make the promise because this would reduce her own control in the treatment and also make her less trustworthy.

Failure of Self-Control

A person without self-control is not trustworthy because she is unpredictable and may act unprofessionally according to her momentary wants. Hence to act consistently in treatment requires self-control. Professional treatment is also an ethical undertaking. Acting without self-control is therefore unethical.

Maintaining and improving self-control is a complicated theme and lies outside the present paper but is widely acknowledged as important. It may be much more personally demanding than securing own control. To keep doing what is *right*, ethically and rationally, may be personally demanding even when supported by reading and reflection about professional ethics and psycho-logic.

Failure of Relevant Know-How

The remaining condition of trust is *relevant know-how*. The only direct cue for clients is their subjective experience of improvement. If a client senses improvement, this is usually attributed to the skill of the psychologist who therefore is also regarded as more trustworthy. If clients fail to improve, they may attribute the failure to themselves or to the psychologist's lack of skill, but it may also be attributed more specifically to a failure of one or several of the other necessary conditions. The factor labeled "relevant know-how" always contains *more* than securing the other five conditions. Therefore, the concept of "good (competent) therapist" is equally difficult to analyze as the concept of "good (competent) teacher" or "good (competent) leader." Empirical analyses have generally failed to yield more than small statistical tendencies. The reason may be that success in treatment, just as in teaching or in leadership, is mostly a result of the accidental fit between psychologist-, client-, and situation characteristics. This means that "good therapist" may be useless as a general term and therefore, to some extent, also *unteachable.* How can you teach a student how to "walk in the fog?"

Conclusion

Many years ago, I presented a logical proof that the necessary factors, taken together, are sufficient to evoke trust (Smedslund 1997, Theorem 5.5.25, p. 72). The first four factors are conceptually clear but, in the cases where the novice is "unprepared" (see above), they may be hard to teach. However, the complex and indeterminate character of the factor "relevant know-how" limits the practical usefulness of the logical analysis even further.

The preceding leads to the conclusion that although we can argue strongly for the necessary role of care, understanding, own control, self-control, and "know-how," these are only logically, but not in practice, jointly sufficient to ensure the building of trust. This is because the content of the factor of "relevant know-how" is hard to pinpoint. Consequently, there are limits to what we can confidently teach psychology students.

Instead, we are led toward another view of how to practice psychology, namely, by adopting a strategy for dealing with ever-new, indefinitely variable and therefore unique cases. Such a strategy requires an initial attitude of "free-floating attention" and "not-knowing" and the subsequent unconventional and creative activity of a "bricoleur". I have borrowed the term from Levi Strauss (1966). One can describe a "bricoleur" as a "Jack-of-all-trades," improvising solutions in ever-new settings. Practitioners have to familiarize themselves with each separate case and improvise interventions based on this local knowledge. This means that one must teach students to adopt an *attitude* rather than to follow any specific *rules*. One should add that one always relies on what we all know about the basic features of being human and on what we know about the language and culture of the client.

The currently dominating scientific psychology advocates the following *strategy*: Treat individual clients based on average findings of empirical studies. If tests show that a client belongs to category X, one should treat the client with methods validated for category X, albeit allowing for informal "adjustments" to the particular circumstances.

The strategy advocated here goes as follows. Get to know the unique case by taking a not-knowing attitude. Then, proceed to deal with the case by acting as a tentatively improvising "bricoleur" in close cooperation with the client.

This chapter has dealt with the psychologic of building trust in psychological treatment. The psychologist and the client can work together only when there is a high degree of mutual trust. Sometimes, establishing trust *is the* treatment. Since one cannot solve unique problems by conventional means, one must strive to be maximally sensitive to uniqueness ("not-knowing") and maximally creative in developing unique solutions (the "bricoleur" model). One cannot teach this kind of practice by referring to specific methods but only by introducing and practicing a meta-strategy.

References

Anderson, H., & Goolishian, H. (1988). Human systems as linguistic systems: Preliminary and evolving ideas about the implications for clinical theory. *Family Process, 27*, 371–393.
Hardin, R. (2002). *Trust and trustworthiness*. New York: Russell Sage Foundation.
Heider, F. (1958). *The psychology of interpersonal relations*. New York: Wiley.
Kahnemann, D. (2007). *Thinking, fast and slow*. New York: Farrar, Straus, and Giroux.
Kelly, G. (1969). *Clinical psychology and personality. The selected papers of George Kelly*. New York: Wiley.
Levi-Strauss, C. (1966). *The savage mind*. Oxford: Oxford University Press.
Roediger, H. L. (2008). Relativity of remembering: Why the laws of memory vanished. *Annual Review of Psychology, 59*, 225–225.
Smedslund, J. (1978). Bandura's theory of self-efficacy: A set of common sense theorems. *Scandinavian Journal of Psychology, 19*, 1–14.
Smedslund, J. (1988). *Psycho-logic*. Heidelberg: Springer-Verlag.
Smedslund, J. (1991). The pseudoempirical in psychology and the case for psychologic. *Psychological Inquiry, 2*, 325–338.
Smedslund, J. (1997). *The structure of psychological common sense*. Mahwah, NJ: Erlbaum.
Smedslund, J. (2009). The mismatch between current research methods and the nature of psychological phenomena. *Theory & Psychology, 19*(6), 778–794.
Smedslund, J. (2012a). The bricoleur model of psychological practice. *Theory & Psychology, 22*(5), 643–657.
Smedslund, J. (2012b). What follows from what we all know about human beings. *Theory & Psychology, 22*, 658–668.
Smedslund, J. (2012c). Psycho-logic: Some thoughts and after-thoughts. *Scandinavian Journal of Psychology, 55*, 295–302.
Smedslund, J. (2016a). Why psychology cannot be an empirical science. *Integrative Psychological and Behavioral Science, 50*(2), 185–195.
Smedslund, J. (2016b). Practicing psychology without an empirical evidence-base: The bricoleur-model. *New Ideas in Psychology, 43*, 50–56.
Teigen, K. H. (2002). One hundred years of laws in psychology. *American Journal of Psychology, 115*, 103–118.
Wierzbicka, A. (1996). *Semantics: Primes and Universals*. Oxford: Oxford University Press.

Chapter 19
Psychotherapy: An Illusion That Works

Tor-Johan Ekeland

When Sigmund Freud, the modern father of psychotherapy, wrote his 1927 work, *The Future of an Illusion*, it was, unfortunately, religion and not his own system that he had in mind. Freud had the great ambition to create what he called "a physic for the soul," and psychoanalysis was his research method (Freud 1953–1974; p. 359). Although Freud later revisited this modernistic ambition, he was thinking in accordance with Danziger's (1990) idea that science is not the story of Sleeping Beauty, an idea that characterizes the epistemology for mainstream psychology and psychotherapy. That is, psychology deals with objects that are present fully formed in nature, and it is the job of the prince/investigator to find them with the magic kiss of research.

This epistemology presupposes that the domain for psychology exists in an independently pregiven reality (ontology) and that truth about such reality is attainable through scientific investigation. This has become a position more or less taken for granted in mainstream psychology and psychotherapy research. The aim of the science of psychology then becomes uncovering this reality and its machinery—namely, how it works and under what laws it operates—while in agreement with the modernistic dream of transferring that knowledge to a technology for the soul (Ekeland 2012). In practical research, this means to relate behavior (considered as the dependent variable), whether it is environmental, biological, or cognitive, to causes (which are viewed as independent variables). This regulative theory of causality has been (and still is) an obsession in psychology—the implication being that without causality there is no science.

The obsession with causes and laws can be understood from the perspective of psychology's technological imperative to predict and control. When thinking in

T.-J. Ekeland (✉)
Volda University College, Volda, Norway
e-mail: tor-johan.ekeland@hivolda.no

T. G. Lindstad et al. (eds.), *Respect for Thought*, Theory and History in the Human and Social Sciences, https://doi.org/10.1007/978-3-030-43066-5_19

causal terms, one also thinks in schemes of reversibility—that is, beyond time and place. Then the technological (practical) imperative seems easy: If science could demonstrate that *if A then B* (or with the probability *p*), then one can do *A* if one wants to accomplish *B*. However, even if psychological processes have a certain degree of regularity, this does not necessarily mean causality. It could, as Jan Smedslund (1995) has showed, simply reveal semantic regularities that behaviors are governed by semantic rules. However, rules are not causes, and they can be changed and opposed and they are historically and culturally situated.

Because of this state of affairs in the domain of mainstream epistemology, there has been a great deal of research about behavior, mental states, cognition, and responses and reactions but little about action, mentality, meaning, and agency. Psychology has pictured individuals as more or less passive, mechanistic stimulus-response devices driven by unconscious or biological forces, or information-processing devices in which behavior can be split into variables. Individuals as agents acting within a world and a moral ecology and a cultural web of meaning, which they strive to master, are just the surface. The machinery and mechanisms below, in the realm of causality, which make individuals tick and go, are what matter.

This is a psychology without a subject, which I, inspired by the works of Bateson (1979), shall characterize as an epistemological error. The problem with epistemological errors, according to Bateson, is that it is difficult to oppose them by experience because they also govern experience. In addition, they cannot easily undergo empirical testing. However, in the end, epistemological errors will reveal themselves through inadequate and problematic practices. As I shall show in this chapter, mainstream psychotherapy is built on such an epistemological error. Following Jan Smedslunds thinking, as I will discuss, can be a way out of this error.

A Rescue Plan

The epistemology outlined here has been taken for granted in the history of psychotherapy research. Inspired by Jan Smedslund, I shall in this chapter not only argue that this epistemology is false (as Smedslund does) but also expand on his conclusion about the bricoleur model 1 of psychological practice (Smedslund 2012) by contextualizing psychotherapy culturally and historically and thereby classifying it as a kind that belongs to the *art of healing*. Furthermore, because I hold psychotherapy, at its best, to be a legitimate and humanistic way to help individuals who suffer, I shall argue for a rescue plan. It is needed because the expansion of psychology and therapeutic thinking in Western society in our time has created a problematic mismatch between what psychotherapy pretends to be, what it actually does, and what it could be.

It is pretended that psychotherapy is scientific and objective; however, as a practice, it is normative. Not only is it driven by values but it also creates values. Its language explains and attributes to causality (*erklären*) to give explanations, but what is going on in practice is an interpretative and hermeneutic discourse (*verste-*

hen). The existing research knowledge about human beings comes from decontextualized statistical aggregates of individuals ("samples" from hypothetical "populations"), while a therapist meets unique subjects and persons who are impossible to know in advance. This mismatch plays an ideological function by legitimizing psychotherapy as psychology's greatest scientific contribution to modern society. As a profession, one can, a bit cynically, argue that this mismatch does not matter as long as practice is popular. However, in my opinion, psychotherapy as an enterprise institutionalized in society, wherein humans heal humans through dialogue will not continue unless it tries to legitimate itself in a new way, in a way that does not mystify what this kind of practice is. We in fact need a new deal, and to create this, we must start by speaking the truth, which is the unified imperative in what we call science. The truth about psychotherapy must start with a contextualization in history.

From Practice to Science

Until the 1950s, psychotherapy was synonymous with a practice rooted in a psychoanalytic or psychodynamic tradition. Since World War II, it has expanded from a kind of esoteric private practice to its implementation in public health-care systems—especially in America, where the Menninger Foundation and Johns Hopkins Medical School were great proponents (Garfield and Bergin 1994). The introduction of client-focused therapy by Rogers (1942) marked a deviation from the analytical tradition. However, this deviation was within a humanistic epistemology. A more profound challenge came from behaviorism, which was based on a physicalist epistemology that was promising for those who longed for psychology to become a real objective science. Within many academic departments of psychology, psychoanalysis occupied an ambiguous position (particularly where behaviorism ruled), and the development of behavior therapy, as initiated by Wolpe (1958) in his book *Psychotherapy by Reciprocal Inhibition,* promised a scientific direction for the future. An implication of this expansion was that it became compellingly necessary to legitimize psychotherapy in academic society and in relation to governments and stakeholders as well as in society.

This scientific ambition found its explicit imperative at the 1949 Boulder Conference, where the profession of psychotherapy declared its allegiance to the goal of integrating science and practice and cast the field in the scientist–practitioner model, which has since been adopted by most professions in psychology in the Western world (Frank 1984). This attempt to bridge science and practice gave academic psychology a central mission on behalf of the profession of psychology: to accumulate scientific knowledge so as to guide practice and strengthen clinical service, in fact be the Prince which with the magic kiss of research awakened the truth and the Sleeping beauty.

The following questions must be answered before psychotherapy can be put on a scientific footing: Does psychotherapy work and if it does, how and why? Interest in answering the first question arose after Eysenck (1952, 1969), a dedicated behaviorist, caused a stir in the 1960s by making the following claim: Psychotherapy has no scientific proven effect, and psychoanalysis could even have negative effects. This claim, derived from his evaluation of 24 effect studies, became the basis for the conclusion that psychotherapy should not be integrated (research and training) into academic institutions. Eysenck's stance generated much research and debate (see, e.g., Luborsky et al. 1975; see also an overview in Bergin and Garfield 1994). A turning point occurred with the publication of Smith and Glass's (1977) article titled "Meta-Analysis of Psychotherapy Outcome Studies" in *American Psychologist*. The sensation created by this study did not simply stem from the documentation that Eysenck was wrong (psychotherapy does indeed work, with many reviews and single studies supporting this) but rather from the fact that the conclusion was based on the first meta-analysis—a statistical analysis seen as a breakthrough in scientific studies of treatments. Although this answer to the question of whether psychotherapy works was celebrated and enthusiastically discussed, a veil of silence fell over another conclusion in the same article. Smith and Glass pointed this out stating, "Despite volumes devoted to the theoretical differences among different schools of psychotherapy, the results of research demonstrate negligible differences in the effects produced by different therapy types" (p. 760). This statement, which concerns the *why* question, was, as we shall see, a profound epistemological challenge to psychotherapy's ambition to be scientific.

Although the conclusion drawn by Smith and Glass (1977) about effect was debated in the years that followed, it was ultimately strengthened by research. In Bergin and Garfield's fourth edition of *Handbook of Psychotherapy and Behavior Change,* Lambert and Bergin (1994) concluded,

> There is now little doubt that psychological treatments are, overall and in general, beneficial, although it remains equally true that not everyone benefits to a satisfactory degree. (p. 144).

However, as we have seen, documenting effect is just a necessity but not a sufficient condition if one wants to fulfill the ambition to be scientific. It is also needed to ask *why it works and how*? How can therapies designed from very different theoretical models apparently have similar effects? The paradoxical findings of outcome equivalence and content equivalence present a serious dilemma to the ambition to be scientific because they seem to imply that no matter what a therapist does, the results will be the same. However, the possibility that psychotherapy could not have specific effects was not a new allegation. Frank (1961) argued for this in his book *Persuasion and Healing: A Comparative Study of Psychotherapy*, and as early as 1936, Saul Rosenzweig made the same claim in an article when he alluded to the verdict of the Dodo bird in *Alice's Adventures in Wonderland*, whereby the Dodo bird declared, "Everybody has won, and all must have prizes."

In a review of empirical studies, Luborsky et al. (1975) drew a similar conclusion as that previously made by Rosenzweig, canonizing the term *Dodo bird verdict* in psychotherapy. The Dodo bird verdict represents a fundamental threat to the ambition of psychotherapy to be scientific. Extensive evidence in the history of empirical research on psychotherapy has tried to falsify it but without success. Furthermore, evidence shows that specific theories and techniques have relatively little to do with effectiveness in psychotherapy; rather, common factors, and particularly human factors, are the primary agents of change (see, e.g., Baldwin and Imel 2013; Duncan et al. 2010; Elkins 2007, 2012; Lambert and Barley 2002; Norcross 2011; Wampold and Imel 2015).

Evidence and the Ambition to be Scientific

As shown, the empirical documentation for nonspecificity in psychotherapy has been available for a long time. Despite this, the editors of *Handbook of Psychotherapy and Behavior Change* concluded that there is massive evidence that psychotherapeutic techniques do not have specific effects, yet there is tremendous resistance to accepting this finding as a legitimate one (Bergin and Garfield 1994, p. 822). This situation has not changed—probably because the evidence-based wave has intensified the hunt for a psychotherapeutic antibiotic (Asnaani and Foa 2014). The ambition to be scientific seems to have implied more than the imperative to seek the truth. It has taken for granted that it is possible, by scientific means, to develop what we may call a "technology for the soul" and that it is possible to develop a specific cure, which is causal for curing specific problems. Bruce Wampold (2001) has denoted this a medical model, and it is a model because the aim in biomedical medicine has been to develop a context-free medicine, a medicine that not only works but also works independent of who the doctors are, of who the patients are (except what is associated with their disease), and of the context for the treatment—in other words, a medicine that presupposes an acceptable, stable, and repetitive causal link between the medicine (input) and the effect (output). It is in this respect that I call psychotherapy an illusion because there is no acceptable evidence for such causal links. If we have followed Smedslunds legacy, we could have saved us the trouble since such empirical research is pseudo-empirical.[1] Anyway, if we, as a thought experiment, see the medical model as a hypothesis about psychotherapy, which was put forward at the 1949 Boulder Conference, it is now, after nearly 70 years of empirical research, falsified. However, Karl Popper has not achieved hero status in mainstream psychotherapy. The hypothesis seems to be adored more than the empirical facts. Scholars are jumping aboard the evidence-based practice bandwagon on which the design of the hypothesis is based (Ekeland 2009).

From a historical perspective, this "resistance" is understandable. The evidence challenges the identity of psychology and the ambition to become a positive science and to fulfill its legitimized position as a profession. In an evaluation of psychology as a science, which was conducted on behalf of the American Association for the Advancement of Science and the American Psychological Association (APA) in the 1950s, Koch (1959–1963) characterized the modern history of academic psychol-

[1] This is also argued by Lindstad (2020), Chap. 12 this volume.

ogy as "a ritualistic endeavor to emulate the forms of science in order to sustain the delusion that it already is a science." This characterization continues to have relevance. Mainstream psychology can still be accused of having offered the phenomenon and forcing reality to surrender to theory so as to save its own methods and epistemological positions (Ekeland 2012). Koch's (1959–1963) recommendation was to reorient psychology within the humanities. It remains a good advice.

Psychotherapy: A Contextual Perspective

In one of the most thorough summaries of empirical research on psychotherapy, Wampold (2001) concluded that the medical model should be replaced with a contextual model. In discussion of what a contextual model could be, he is leaning heavily on Jerome Franks analysis (Frank 1961). Smedslund (2012) reached the same conclusion based not on the empirical data but rather on an epistemological analysis. As Smedslund (2009) showed, empirical-based general laws explaining human behavior cannot exist; hence, the empirical search for causal and universal regularities in psychological phenomena is a waste of effort. The data will anyway be pseudo-empirical. Possible regularities can stem from participation in particular shared meaning systems (language and culture). By implication, Smedslund's (2012) way of understanding psychotherapy is within a contextual model, exemplified by *bricolage—a* term borrowed from Lévi-Strauss (1962/1966) who used it to describe a way of thinking that he called "a science of the concrete" (Smedslund 2012).

The conclusion that psychotherapy is a contextual practice says more about what psychotherapy is *not* rather than what it is. What does it mean? First, a contextual model cannot be a model in the strict sense of the word because it is foremost a way of thinking—a way of thinking, which, according to Wilden (1972), is underestimated in Western episteme and makes us suffer from ecological ignorance. Research on psychotherapy builds on the taken-for-granted epistemology that it is possible to study therapy as something separate from the context that forms it. This is ecological ignorance. However, when referring to context, we are talking about complexity, and if we try to build models, we have to specify at which level we operate. Usually, we are short-sighted in the sense that we only focus on the relevant context, that is, contexts as situations. The treatment room is *now*, and we forget that this now is structured by culture beforehand, that is, ignorance on a higher level.

The Art of Healing

So, what is it then about the illusion that works? First, I think it is necessary to remind ourselves of the fact that psychotherapy, defined as treatment that is mediated through a human relationship, is not a scientific creation. On the contrary, it belongs to our oldest wisdom that human suffering can be comforted and healed through words, symbols, and meaning staged by a co-suffering and trustworthy helper in an atmosphere of trust and warmth. The prehistory of psychotherapy is synonymous with the art of healing. From the oracle in Delphi and the long period of time when the temple of Asclepios was the model for healing in Europe, the methods that were employed to cure were nonspecific and holistic. The aim was to create a healing context, a context that (as I see it) stimulates the self-healing potential that is innate in every organism. This is what the poorly understood placebo phenomenon is about; it is generically psychotherapeutic, and the evidence that placebos work is overwhelming (Ekeland 1999). Knowledge from various disciplines thus shows that humans are evolved to give and receive emotional healing through social means and that what we in the West call psychotherapy an expression of this evolutionarily derived ability to heal one another emotionally through human interaction (Elkins 2015). This means that the genealogy of psychotherapy leads us to conclude that psychotherapy belongs to the "family" of esoteric healing (e.g., Romanucci-Ross et al. 1983), which means that it has "uncles and aunts" within the field classified as alternative medicine and shares lineage with wise women (and some men), with those who lay on hands and other magicians, with esoteric healers, and with shamanism, which continues to be a healing tradition for large numbers of the world's population. This does not mean that psychotherapy is a kind of shamanism; rather, they are both healing rituals that work through mental processes, which depend on cultural meaning systems. Shamanism can only work within a shamanistic culture, whereas psychotherapy can only work within a psychotherapeutic culture.

When endeavoring to answer the question of what works when psychotherapy works, we are misled by the medical model to think that what is going on is treatment and that it contains the ingredients of a kind of medicine. However, psychotherapy has no specific essence (nor has shamanism), and the therapist does not treat. What is going on is meaning making in dialogue; it is the transformation of meaning within a cultural web of meaning. The therapeutic component in psychotherapy is not in the therapy as such; rather, it is in the healing context, and such a context is necessarily part of a cultural landscape.

We can express it this way: *The treatment must be seen as a text within the context of the culture*. Forms of treatment are part of the meaning systems of a culture. The potential effect may involve an interplay between culture and individuality as a precondition. If one is to understand the effect, one must first understand the meaning, and if one is to understand the meaning, one must understand the culture. In nonliterary cultures, for example, shamanistic cultures, such meaning systems are often general and comprehensive images of the world. In highly developed cultures, the differentiation and fragmentation will be far greater. The point is still the same, meaning systems about illness, healing, and treatment must, as with other meaning systems in a culture, be seen as cultural evolution and adaptation, as products of the struggle of humans to master the various domains of existence. Cultural legitimization and healers in legitimized roles are the decisive reasons for the concrete treatment as a figure. When a patient and a therapist meet, they have already met in a sense because they are both woven into the institutionalized web of meaning created by cultural development or what can be denoted diachronic adaptation (Ekeland 1999). Individual suffering is phenomenologically a kind of loss of meaning, and when a certain treatment is initiated, it is the synchronic and individual adaptation (search for meaning) that punctuates this cultural adaptation.

Psychotherapy's Scenery: The Historical Context

Analyzing psychotherapy as a contextual practice involves applying perspectives on a pattern of intervened levels, where the cultural context is the first prerequisite. Put simply, psychotherapy can work because it exists—because it is institutionalized in the society and part of a cultural epistemology that accepts and naturalizes the discourse about the psychic, its maladies and curability.

In Western culture, modern psychotherapy established itself during a 20- to 30-year period spanning the turn of the twentieth century as a project of modernity, born out of the trust and optimism in science and the new individualism in which the secular human has an inner life—not only a soul but also a psyche. The optimism created by the potential of science to restrain nature spilled over to an ambition by scientific means to improve humans and society as well. Although the idea was born within a European context, it is no surprise that it achieved its breakthrough in the United States, the country whose citizens can become self-made. Freudian psychoanalysis is the first epistemological model of humans to depart from a magical–religious explanation; instead, it is a coherent secular model that builds on a psychological rationality. Psychoanalysis opens up the individual and creates a language about the subject; the individual is seen not only from above as in the religious discourse but also from *within*. This happens in a period when the culture is ripe and is longing for a narrative that can repair the loss of meaning, which Weber (1973) denoted as the *entzauberung der welt*. Historically, psychoanalysis is the scenery of psychotherapy—what is there and what shapes our experiences in a way we take for granted. The couch and the secret room become both an asylum for the subject to free himself from a repressive society and a location to be created (*sub*jected) to be a "psychological man"—a man whose goal in life is no longer salvation but rather gratification (Rieff 1987).

When Freud in 1909, disputed and marginalized at this time in Europe, visited Clark University in the United States, he was embraced with enthusiasm, and his presence garnered a great deal of publicity. Within a few years, psychodynamic theory (descended from psychoanalysis) dominated the discourse in the mental health field and was taken up in popular culture as well.

The rise and expansion of psychology in the Western world cannot be understood as a success evolved from the timeless pursuit of understanding the human mind but rather as contingent and historical processes in the emergence of modernity (Ekeland 2012). Psychology and psychotherapy have developed in symbiosis with a culture of individualism and liberal freedom and acquired a particular significance within contemporary Western forms of life, which have come to celebrate the values of autonomy and self-realization that are essentially psychological in form and structure. Individualization, which has played a central role in modernity and the rise of the West, has given birth to the inward-looking, isolated, self-sufficient individual for whom truth is neither collective nor sacred but personal (Rose 1999).

According to Rose (1999), this development in Europe and North America since the late nineteenth century has been intrinsically linked to transformations in the exercise of political power in contemporary liberal democracies. To govern in a modern liberal way is to reconcile two principles: the danger of governing too much and the danger of not governing enough. One needed a language that enabled human subjectivity to be translated into the new language of government—ruling people through their freedoms and their choices. The exercise of power, according to Rose, then becomes a therapeutic matter. Rose also stated that "freedom … is enacted only at the price of relying upon experts of the soul." To live as free individuals is to subordinate to a form of therapeutic authority and language and to construe our lives in psychological terms of adjustment, the art of self-scrutiny, self-evaluation, and self-regulation, not by an alien gaze but through reflexive hermeneutics under the constant gaze of our own suspicious reflexivity, tormented by uncertainty and doubt. The power of psychology in courtrooms, factories, prisons, schoolrooms, and bedrooms involves more than controlling, subduing, disciplining, normalizing, and reforming people; it is also about making them wiser, happier, and healthier as well as more intelligent, virtuous, productive, docile, enterprising, fulfilled, self-confident, and empowered. Psychology has no "church" of its own, but its language and techniques (its expert terminology) and ideas concerning nature and the psyche have infiltrated everyday language and have come to infuse, dominate, or displace the claims of God and religion over time. The psychological becomes norms of truth (Rose 1999).

An important feature of humans is that they can exert effects on themselves; they are affected by their classification and can interact with their classification in ways that affect the classification itself (Hacking 1999; Smedslund 2009). As self-conscious moral agents, humans can become aware of how they are understood and classified and can experience themselves in particular ways as a consequence of this discourse. Because human psychology changes as culture changes, and because psychology is taken up in culture, psychology actually fabricates subjects. Psychology then becomes not only what psychology is but also what it does (Rose 1999). And what it does is to create the meaning system and therapeutic subjects, which are prerequisites for the healing potential in its own therapeutic discourse.

Psychotherapy as Meaning Mending

The contextual model demystify what psychotherapy is. It is a kind of interpersonal healing, and such healing can arise in different interpersonal encounters. Moreover, psychotherapy is a kind of discourse constituted by institutionalized roles and contexts, whereby variations and dilemmas in our culturally situated human lives can be explored. As emphasized also by Smedslund (2012), such a discourse can only be accounted for in a language and systems of meaning where the therapist and the client are both embedded. This embeddedness, I have argued here, is a necessary prerequisite for psychotherapy to work, but is it sufficient? The simple answer is of course not. The healing context, as framed by the psychotherapeutic culture, must obviously have some specific qualities. For instance, there should be a "method," at least an idea about "doing this will be good for that," but as the Dodo bird verdict and nonspecificity from psychotherapy research imply, the scientific validity of the theory or method that guides the therapy is irrelevant. What counts is its relevance in dialogical meaning making. In that sense, even scientific false theories could create therapeutic effects. This troublesome finding is, however, meaningful if we see such theories as languages. The task of language is to make and communicate meaning. In this regard, one language is not in itself truer than another; they cannot be compared on such a basis. The different therapeutic perspectives, theories, and models could be seen as different languages or meaning systems that coordinate communication and actions. What is therapeutic about psychotherapy is its meaning to mend. The therapeutic potential of a theory/perspective is a function of its ability, as a language, to create a meaning that has the cultural preconditions to function adaptively.

Can Meaning Heal?

As emphatically emphasized also by Smedslund (e.g., 2009), we are symbolic animals that are goal-directed, rule-governed, changeable, and historically and socially situated creatures. We compulsively create, react to, and act on meaning. However, the individual's search for meaning (or adaptation) at a given point in time can never be understood as pure subjectivity. If we study meaning as subjectivity, we are simultaneously studying intersubjectivity and culture. Culture is a meaning context whereby one is never on the outside. As repeatedly emphasized also by Smedslund (e.g., 2012), one cannot climb out of one's own language. If we are studying the mental, we are also studying culture or the way in which culture is punctuated by the individual. The mind *is* social. Individual mentality thus becomes a text within the context of culturally possible texts.

Placebo

The best evidence for meaning that can heal is the placebo phenomenon (Ekeland 1999). The placebo effect is generic psychotherapy, and how it heals is exemplary of healing through symbols and meaning. It is similar to how the feeling of national pride does not come from the flag as an object but rather from its meaning and how the power of money to elicit energy in humans is not incarnated in the copper or fine paper that carries its value. The healing force of a placebo pill is not in the pill itself but rather in its potential in the body as a symbol, as something in which the body finds meaning. The individual will attribute the experienced effect to the pill as a substance because we in everyday life do not usually behave like structural linguists and distinguish between things and the names of things. The pill's placebo potential thus lies in its condensed meaning—the condensing of hope and belief in relief and healing that pills symbolize in our culture. It is the meaning that heals. In the hands of a good doctor, the pill is not only chemistry but also sacrament. In a similar way, we can substitute the pill with the different remedies, oaths, and rituals of shamans and other healers, and it is not these remedies as substances but rather their meaning that activates the mental processes that produce the experienced effect. The individual will attribute the effect to the remedies (and rituals) and experience them to have magical power. However, the power is not *in* the remedy as an object. It is already *in* the organism, activated by the remedy as a symbol. This is how meaning mends and how psychotherapy works.

The Healing Process

A healing process is, however, something more comprehensive. It is always an implicit part of illness and suffering. All life has its own preservation as an innate imperative. "The wisdom of the body" was Claude Bernard's way of expressing this as far as it is applied to the body's self-regulating mechanisms. The body also has mentality, and mental processes are similarly a part of the total healing process. This healing is thus a process not simply in the body as biology but in the body's biosemantic ecology. We can only understand this entirety by punctuating it. Therefore, we study illness from biological, psychological, social, and cultural viewpoints. However, we encounter problems in putting the whole thing together again. This is a problem in epistemology, not in the body itself, because this knowledge is how the body works. This implicit knowledge has been gained through evolution's long—and culture's far shorter—learning processes.

An interpersonal process guides the healing in psychotherapy. This interpersonal process must develop some relational qualities, as well as content and a language, which can transform the client's symptoms and problems from the diffuse realm of meaningless into something understandable and manageable. This is a process of negotiation in which the client's own interpretation—his or her self-diagnosis—is the necessary point of departure. The therapist's ability to transform this "diagnosis" into therapeutic language depends not only on his or her rhetoric ability but also on whether the transformation is within a shared epistemology. In this case, the therapist is in need of a "therapeutic theory" or a model. Mainstream psychotherapy holds the model as being therapeutic for the client, but I contend that, therapeutically, the method or model works foremost for the therapist. This is a necessary precondition to enable the therapist to create something therapeutic. Theory and the language of theory make it possible for the therapist to talk to himself or herself about the suffering in a meaningful way (the inner dialogue) and in turn converse with the client to create meaning (the outer dialogue). Without this inner dialogue, the dialogue with the client will soon break down. It is the therapist's mastery of the dialogue and his or her aptitude as a knower that is the sacrament in therapy and the client's hope.

In relation to the client's world, the sacrament must contribute something that creates news—news of hope and possible healing. The therapeutic situation has in itself a communicative redundancy as far as the therapist accepts the client as he or she is and remains present. Through the therapist's language on suffering, he or she administers the sacrament and must, of course, believe in this sacrament. The therapist and the client must share fundamental preconditions in the meaning system of which the sacrament is a part. This corresponds to the situation in which the believer and the minister share the belief in the dogmas of the faith. If we are talking about psychotherapy, the dogmas belong to science. This is a necessary, but insufficient, precondition to allow something therapeutic to be put into effect.

The use of sacrament as a metaphor is not coincidental because religious rituals are prototypes for a healing context. If we continue with such metaphors, "the pact" is the next necessary precondition for the healing context. The pact presupposes, as we have seen, the epistemological union: psychology as a taken-for-granted language used to describe a human being's inner life. Furthermore, the pact is the alliance between the therapist and the client, and this presupposes relational elements that have to do with empathy and care: The client confidently offers his or her suffering into the care of the other person, and the therapist accepts the client without fear and conditions. Empathy, as all research on psychotherapy shows, is a prerequisite for a working therapy. It is not the empathy the therapist experiences that is important but rather it is the client's experience of the therapist's experience of empathy—in other words, empathy as it is communicated. As communication, empathy conveys two messages from the therapist: I can recognize your pain and problems in myself (telling the patient that they are of the same kind), and this is also recognition (telling the patient that his or her problems are acceptable and legitimate) that a patient's problems could even have a name (diagnosis) within the expert knowledge system. Empathy, seen in this way, creates a communion between the client and the therapist, a pact devoted to defeat the devil, which, in our culture, is represented by the symptoms. We could perhaps dare to talk of love and of meeting another person unassumingly. It is, however, a love that must not bind but be set free. It does so only when nothing is demanded in return except hope and trust in the healing. Therefore, the client can give himself or herself up with responsibility for nothing other than himself or herself. None of this is present of its own accord, only as preconditions. The whole thing must be staged and actualized, and the therapist is responsible for this liturgy.

Our point of departure was the question of what is therapeutic about therapy. The analysis implies a shift of focus. What therapies say that they are doing by way of their theories is just one element in the therapeutic process. To answer the question about what therapy *is* in the ontological sense is just as meaningless as explaining what is totemic about a totem pole. Just as it is the context and the initiated that make the sculpture a totem pole, it is the context and the clients that make the therapy therapeutic.

The therapeutic aspect of therapy is not in the magic of therapy itself but rather in a self-healing capacity within the client. It can be realized by the contextual pattern, which promotes mending meaning in a caring, empathic, and trustworthy relationship. Now, we can continue our conversation about our liturgies, techniques, and methods—about how we, in good and bad ways, create the healing context and about how we do even better so that the healing power is strengthened and released. We, as therapists, must humbly admit that we do not have this power. Rather, this power is already present in the client. The same applies to the power of faith. It does not come from without; it is only delivered from there. My allusions to a religious discourse are not coincidental, for it was in the temple of Asclepios where healing with words and meaning began.

Concluding Remarks

The contextualization of psychotherapy is, in a way, to demystify what it is. Demystifying therapy should lead to the demystification of mental problems as well. Mainstream psychotherapies tend to camouflage that individual problems are also cultural problems. Rather than providing an account of the psychopathology of the culture in terms of the inadequacies of individuals in living up to the demands of the times, mainstream psychology has concentrated on describing the inadequacies of the individual. Time changes and so does our approach to living. In Freudian culture, it was important for the subject to disguise; repression became the strategy for managing the gap between the manifest and the latent, and symptoms popped up as a consequence of either too much or too little repression. The situation today seems to be the reverse. In a situation where identity is no longer something given but rather a challenge to be created by the individual, what counts is to be seen, to create a personal brand in the social market. Living as a free individual in this neo-liberal period without authorities to obey other than the obligation to fulfill one's potential presupposes self-technologies to construe one's life in psychological terms of adjustment. In this culture, the rise of cognitive-behavior therapy (CBT) as the cutting-edge and top product in the therapeutic market is understandable. Its language is compatible with dominant neo-liberal discourse: *you* have a problem, there is a fix, and *you* can use it by repairing how you think.

A new deal, or a rescue plan as suggested here, should take epistemological responsibility and promote a psychology that is more honest and relevant to life as it is lived, and by this correct for epistemological errors, as Bateson warned about. A description of what is relevant in human life—wishes, desires, feelings, and actions—can only be accounted for in language and systems of meaning, where the actor and observers are embedded. Therefore, no technical–scientific first-order descriptions of psychological phenomena can exist. Therefore, Smedslunds "bricoleur" is a relevant metaphor for what psychotherapy is. Psychology and psychotherapy will never provide readymade materials and prescriptions for ethical life. It will never tell us just what to do ethically nor just how to do it. It could, however, afford us with insight into the conditions that control the formation and execution of aims—with insight into what could be good or bad given that we want to create forms of living that expand humanity in culture as well as in personal life.

References

Asnaani, A., & Foa, E. B. (2014). Expanding the lens of evidence-based practice in psychotherapy to include a common factors perspective: Comment on Laska, Gurman, and Wampold. *Psychotherapy, 51*(4), 487–490.

Baldwin, S. A., & Imel, Z. E. (2013). Therapist effects: Findings and methods. In M. J. Lambert (Ed.), *Bergin and Garfield's handbook of psychotherapy and behavior change* (6th ed., pp. 258–297). New York, NY: Wiley.

Bateson, G. (1979). *Mind and nature: A necessary unity*. New York, NY: Dutton.

Bergin, A. E., & Garfield, S. L. (1994). Overview, trends, and future issues. In S. L. Garfield & A. E. Bergin (Eds.), *Handbook of psychotherapy and behavior change* (4th ed.). New York, NY: Wiley.

Danziger, K. (1990). *Constructing the subject: Historical origins of psychological research*. Cambridge, England: Cambridge University Press.

Duncan, B. L., Miller, S. D., Wampold, B. E., & Hubble, M. A. (Eds.). (2010). *The heart and soul of change: Delivering what works in therapy* (2nd ed.). Washington, DC: American Psychological Association.

Ekeland, T.-J. (1999). *Meining som medisin. Ein analyse av placebofenomenet og implikasjonar for terapi og terapeutiske teoriar [Meaning as medicine. An analysis of the placebo phenomenon and implications for therapy and theories of psychotherapy]*. (Doctoral thesis). Bergen: University of Bergen.

Ekeland, T.-J. (2009). Hva er evidensen for evidensbasert praksis? [What is the evidence for evidencebased practice?]. In H. Grimen & L. I. Terum (Eds.), *Evidensbasert profesjonsutøvelse [Evidence based professional practice]* (pp. 145–169). Oslo: Abstrakt Forlag.

Ekeland, T.-J. (2012). Sjelens ingeniørkunst. Om psykologien og psykologenes selvforståelse [The engineers of the soul. Psychology and psychologist self-understanding]. *Tidsskrift for Norsk psykologforening, 49*, 746–752.

Elkins, D. N. (2007). Empirically supported treatments: The deconstruction of a myth. *Journal of Humanistic Psychology, 47*, 474–500.

Elkins, D. N. (2012). Toward a common focus in psychotherapy research. *Psychotherapy, 49*, 450–454.

Elkins, D. N. (2015). *The human elements of psychotherapy: A nonmedical model of emotional healing*. Washington, DC: American Psychological Association.

Eysenck, H. J. (1952). The effectiveness of psychotherapy: An evaluation. *Journal of Consulting Psychology, 16*, 319–324.

Eysenck, H. J. (1969). *The effects of psychotherapy*. New York, NY: Science House.

Frank, G. (1984). The Boulder model: History, rationale, and critique. *Professional Psychology: Research and Practice, 15*, 417–435. https://doi.org/10.1037/0735-7028.15.3.417.

Frank, J. D. (1961). *Persuasion and healing: A comparative study of psychotherapy*. Baltimore, MD: Johns Hopkins University Press.

Freud, S. (1953–1974). On the origins of psychoanalysis. In J. Strachey (Ed.), *The standard edition of the complete psychological works of Sigmund Freud* (Vol. 1). London, England: Hogarth Press. (Original work published 1895).

Garfield, S. L., & Bergin, A. E. (1994). Introduction and historical overview. In A. E. Bergin & S. L. Garfield (Eds.), *Handbook of psychotherapy and behavior change* (4th ed.). New York, NY: Wiley.

Hacking, I. (1999). *The social construction of what?* Cambridge, MA: Harvard University Press.

Koch, S. (Ed.). (1959–1963). *Psychology: A study of a science* (Vol. 1–6). New York, NY: McGraw-Hill.

Lambert, M. J., & Barley, D. E. (2002). Research summary on the therapeutic relationship and psychotherapy outcome. In J. C. Norcross (Ed.), *Psychotherapy relationships that work* (pp. 17–32). Oxford, England: Oxford University Press.

Lambert, M. J., & Bergin, A. E. (1994). The effectiveness of psychotherapy. In S. L. Garfield & A. E. Bergin (Eds.), *Handbook of psychotherapy and behavior change* (4th ed.). New York, NY: Wiley.

Lévi-Strauss, C. (1966). *The savage mind.* Chicago, IL: University of Chicago Press. (Original work published 1962).

Lindstad, T. G. (2020). A priori afterthoughts: Continuing the dialogue on psycho-logic (Chapter 12, this volume). In T. G. Lindstad, E. Stänicke, & J. Valsiner (Eds.), *Respect for thought: Jan Smedslund's legacy for psychology* (pp. 195–220). New York: Springer.

Luborsky, L., Singer, B., & Luborsky, L. (1975). Comparative studies of psychotherapies: Is it true that "everybody has won and all must have prizes"? *Archives of General Psychiatry, 32*, 995–1008.

Norcross, J. C. (Ed.). (2011). *Psychotherapy relationships that work: Evidence-based responsiveness* (2nd ed.). New York, NY: Oxford University Press.

Rieff, P. (1987). *The triumph of the therapeutic. Uses of faith after Freud.* Chicago, IL: University of Chicago Press.

Rogers, C. R. (1942). *Counseling and psychotherapy: Newer concepts in practice.* Boston, MA: Houghton Mifflin.

Romanucci-Ross, L., Moerman, D. E., & Tancredi, L. R. (Eds.). (1983). *The anthropology of medicine.* South Hadley, MA: Bergin & Garvey.

Rose, N. (1999). *Governing the soul: The shaping of the private self* (2nd ed.). London, England: Free Association Books.

Rosenzweig, S. (1936). Some implicit common factors in diverse methods of psychotherapy. *American Journal of Orthopsychiatry, 6*, 412–415.

Smedslund, J. (1995). Psychologic: Common sense and the pseudoempirical. In J. A. Smith, R. Harré, & L. Van Langenhove (Eds.), *Rethinking psychology.* London, England: Sage.

Smedslund, J. (2009). The mismatch between current research methods and the nature of psychological phenomena: What researchers must learn from practitioners. *Theory & Psychology, 19*, 778–794.

Smedslund, J. (2012). The *bricoleur* model of psychological practice. *Theory & Psychology, 22*, 643–657.

Smith, M. L., & Glass, G. V. (1977). Meta-analysis of psychotherapy outcome studies. *American Psychologist, 32*, 752–760.

Wampold, B. E. (2001). *The great psychotherapy debate: Models, methods, and findings.* Mahwah, NJ: Erlbaum.

Wampold, B. E., & Imel, Z. E. (2015). *The great psychotherapy debate: The evidence for what makes psychotherapy work.* New York: Routledge.

Weber, M. (1973). *Den protestantiske etikk og kapitalismens ånd [The Protestant Ethic and the Spirit of Capitalism].* Oslo, Norway: Gyldendal. (Original work published 1904).

Wilden, A. (1972). *System and structure: Essays in communication and exchange.* London, England: Tavistock.

Wolpe, J. (1958). *Psychotherapy by reciprocal inhibition.* Stanford, CA: Stanford University Press.

Chapter 20
Bricoleurs and Theory-Building Qualitative Research: Responses to Responsiveness

William B. Stiles

I have framed this chapter as a response to Smedslund's critique of psychological research in his 2016 bricoleur paper (Smedslund 2016a). He described this as a summary and elaboration of an argument "based on an extensive earlier critique of the current paradigm of psychological research" (Smedslund 2009, 2012a, b, c, 2015, 2016b) (p. 50). So this was a convenient summary of a major strand of his work. His critique and his bricoleur model addressed issues that have interested me for many years (e.g., Stiles 1983, 1988, 2009a, b, 2013, in press; Stiles et al. 1998; Stiles and Horvath 2017).

Smedslund's Critique and Human Responsiveness

Smedslund (2016a) began by saying his

> critique ultimately rests on a consideration of the implications of four very general characteristics of psychological phenomena. It appears that due to these four characteristics, empirical research becomes severely curtailed and cannot support the work of the practitioner. (p. 50)

These four very general characteristics were:

1. that human behavior has infinitely many determinants,
2. that behavioral sequences are irreversible, unlike, for example, chemical reactions, and hence never precisely replicable,
3. that each behavior or interaction is unique and,

W. B. Stiles (✉)
Glendale Springs, NC, USA
e-mail: stileswb@miamioh.edu

T. G. Lindstad et al. (eds.), *Respect for Thought*, Theory and History in the Human and Social Sciences, https://doi.org/10.1007/978-3-030-43066-5_20

4. that people are inherently interactive, and much essential information about a social interaction is available only to an active participant in it. And "more generally, … persons are influenced by innumerable fortuitous and unique social events, ,,, [and] they respond to these events and, in turn, influence the other persons who then respond, and so on" (p. 52).

Smedslund summarized, "the psychological practitioner cannot expect much direct help from academic research … [because] first, that stability which is a precondition for empirical research is generally lacking and, second, that the results (differences and correlations) are generally too weak to be applicable in daily life" (p. 52). He concluded:

> The failure of the empirical research project in psychology explains why psychological practice cannot be "evidence-based." It means that it is hard to find general enough and stable enough outcomes of research that could legitimate and guide actual decisions in practical work with individuals. (p. 55)

I think Smedslund's four general characteristics can be understood as congruent with what I have called *responsiveness* (Kramer and Stiles 2015; Stiles 2009b, 2013, in press; Stiles et al. 1998; Stiles and Horvath 2017), which refers to behavior being influenced by emerging context. Human behavior is responsive on timescales ranging from months to milliseconds. That is, the behavior of all people, including therapists and clients, changes constantly in response to what they and other people do and whatever else happens or exists around them. For example, therapists are being responsive when they choose treatments based on presenting problems, plan strategies based on progress, choose interventions adapted to client needs and requirements, and adjust phrasing of interventions in progress depending on the apparent uptake. Thus, (1) people respond to myriad, constantly shifting determinants, (2) behavior evolves in ever-compounding sequences, sensitively dependent on previous events and therefore not precisely predictable, (3) is never precisely repeated, and (4) is deeply enmeshed in interactions with other people.

Following his critique, Smedslund (2016a) offered ten clinical examples from his own practice, each of which had commonsense explanations that did not require recourse to psychotherapy theory and was addressed with relatively simple interventions that, he suggested, were not part of standard treatments. He then proposed that a therapist should be a bricoleur, a jack-of-all-trades who relies on what is at hand to solve problems (the term came from Levi-Strauss 1966). "Given the uniqueness and the importance of context in every case, the bricoleur tries to be as open as possible in two ways … an initial attitude of not-knowing … [and] openness to unconventional and unusual possibilities for intervention" (Smedslund 2016a, p. 54). Instead of relying exclusively on a particular evidence-based approach, a bricoleur draws on his or her psychological common sense (see also Smedslund 2012b, c), which includes knowledge shared by virtue of being human (including self-knowledge), understandings acquired through language and culture, and personal familiarity with the particular individual or individuals being treated (Smedslund 2009).

Responsiveness is not necessarily benign, but in general, therapists try to be helpful. We can call this appropriate responsiveness (Stiles, in press; Stiles and Horvath 2017). So for therapists, being appropriately responsive means: *do the right thing*. I think in recommending that therapists are and should be bricoleurs. Smedslund was arguing that they are and should be appropriately responsive. They should use their best human instincts, professional judgment, and creativity to do the right thing.

I agreed with much of what Smedslund (2016a) said. I concurred that the critique identified and articulated problems that challenge or even invalidate some of the main premises of psychotherapy research-as-usual. On the other hand, I am more optimistic than Smedslund about theory and research on psychotherapy. To explain, I begin with a distinction between two kinds of theory and, in parallel, two kinds of research.

Explanatory Theory and Treatment Theory

In discussing theories of psychotherapy, I think it is important to distinguish explanatory theories from treatment theories. These two types of theories have different functions. Briefly, explanatory theories describe what things are and how they are related to each other. They seek to explain how some aspect of the world works; they may inform practices, but they do not prescribe practices. Treatment theories describe the principles and practices that guide clinicians in conducting therapy; they tell therapists what to do.

Treatment theories are sometimes based on or informed by explanatory theories, and some familiar theories (e.g., psychoanalytic theory, cognitive theory) aspire to be both. However, the two are evaluated by very different sorts of research: Explanatory theories are evaluated by comparing detailed observations with derivations from the theory. I call this theory-building research. Treatment theories are evaluated by assessing whether or not the treatments based on the theories are effective. I call this product-testing research (Stiles et al. 2015).

As I explain later, I think Smedslund's (2016a) critique of psychological research is on-target and important for treatment theories and product-testing research. However, I think the critique is off-target when it comes to explanatory theories and theory-building research, although it does usefully set puzzles for theory-building research.

Explanatory Theory/Theory-Building Research

In speaking of explanatory theory, I am thinking of what Kuhn (1970) described as a *paradigm*. In what Kuhn called normal science, a paradigm is the theory that is generally accepted within the community of researchers, together with cardinal examples, methods and practices, and problems to be addressed. Examples of paradigms include plate tectonics in geology, the standard model in physics, which incorporates relativity theory and quantum theory, and the Darwinian theory of natural selection in evolutionary biology. Paradigms guide research, setting puzzles for scientists to solve. Scientists interpret their observations within the paradigm, and they use their results to refine and elaborate the paradigm. Particular studies are typically directed toward solving the puzzles, checking derivations of the theory against observations, modifying the theory in light of unexpected observations, or extending the theory into new areas.

This sort of puzzle-solving in normal science is the activity I'm calling theory-building research. Theory-building is a purpose, not a method, and many methods can serve this purpose. The aim is to increase the theory's generality, precision, and realism (cf. Levins 1968). Researchers work to explain a wider range of phenomena, to specify the theory in greater detail, and to reconcile the existing theory with new observations.

As an illustration of theory-building research in normal science, consider the famous early test of Einstein's general theory of relativity by Dyson et al. (1920). General relativity theory describes gravity as a bending of space–time geometry. According to one derivation, the light of a star passing close to the sun would follow a curved path. It would appear to be bent inwards by the sun's gravity by a predictable amount, so that the star could be seen from Earth even though it was actually behind the edge of the sun. Usually it is impossible to see such starlight because the sun is so bright. However, during the solar eclipse of 1919, Dyson et al. took a photograph of such a star, showing a deflection that was in reasonably precise agreement with Einstein's prediction. The result made headlines.

The light-bending study illustrates how theory-building research normally addresses small puzzles, not the whole theory. It also illustrates why explanatory theories must be logically coherent, with no internal contradictions and different parts logically interrelated, so observations on one part of the theory bear on other parts. That is, light-bending is not the main point of general relativity theory, but merely a logical derivation from it. Seeing the star that was on the other side of the sun added confidence to the whole theory because the prediction was logically linked to the theory.

Psychotherapy research does not have a generally accepted paradigm, and the theories it has are less interlinked logically than general relativity theory. But, any explanatory theory that is accepted, even tentatively, within a community of researchers can be the focus of theory-building research.

Treatment Theory/Product-Testing Research

Treatment theories are evaluated by comparing the outcomes of their clients with the outcomes of clients who were not treated or who were treated in other ways (e.g., studies reviewed by Lambert 2013; Wampold and Imel 2015). This is what I'm calling product-testing research. Some treatment theories are based on explanatory theories. However, the coherence of and empirical support for the explanation is secondary, so long as the therapists who use it obtain good outcomes.

The gold standard in product-testing is the randomized controlled trial (RCT). RCTs are a statistical adaptation of the experimental method. The logic of the experiment is that if all conditions except one (the independent variable) are held constant (controlled), then any differences in the outcome (the dependent variable) must be attributable to the independent variable. For example, if one client is given a therapy that another identical client is not, but they are treated identically in all other respects, then any differences in their outcomes must have been caused by the therapy. However, no two clients are identical (so one client cannot serve as a control for another), and even if they were, they could not really be treated identically in all respects except one (the independent variable). In an RCT, clients are randomly assigned to treatment groups. Although clients' outcomes will vary within groups (because clients are not identical), any mean differences between groups beyond those due to chance should be attributable to the treatment difference. RCTs are difficult and expensive, but the controlled experiment is the closest science has come to a way to demonstrate causality, in this case, to show that the treatment caused the improvement. So, it is argued, the effort put into RCTs is worth the effort and difficulty.

In contrast to theory-building research, however, clinical trials do not change the theory. They do not test or elaborate the explanations of psychological change or the mechanisms of therapy. Whereas, theory-building research investigates descriptive theoretical accounts, for example, how changes occurred in irrational cognitions, internal conflicts, secondary emotions, or unassimilated problematic experiences; clinical trials only try to show that some treatment package works better than another treatment package or no treatment. (However, responsiveness undermines the internal logic of RCTS, as discussed in a later section.)

The number of clinical trials of psychotherapy reported in the literature has increased exponentially over the past several decades (Carey and Stiles 2016; Wampold and Imel 2015). Because clinical trials are so difficult and expensive, they have virtually monopolized academic talent and financial resources, leaving much less available for theory-building research.

Generality in Theory-Building and Product-Testing

The distinction between theory-building and product-testing research can be illustrated by their different understandings of generality. In theory-building research, generality is the range of events the theory claims to explain. Particular studies examine only small aspects of a theory. Their results may increase or decrease confidence in the theory, but the findings themselves are not meant to be generalized.

In product-testing research, generality is often understood as external validity, a term invented by Campbell (1957), based on an analogy with statistical sampling. It refers to the range of people and circumstances to which a study's results might be expected to apply, analogous to the population from which a statistical sample was randomly drawn.

Research in normal science does not require external validity. For example, the point of the Dyson et al. (1920) light-bending study was not to generalize to other stars that are behind the sun. The generality of general relativity theory is part of the theory itself, just as the generality of cognitive theory is part of cognitive theory. In showing that the star's light was bent as predicted, Dyson et al. supported the whole theory, in all its generality.

Responsiveness Undermines Product-Testing

In this section, I want to amplify Smedslund's critique as it applies to product-testing research in psychotherapy, particularly RCTs. RCTs for psychotherapy have many problems (see, e.g., Carey and Stiles 2016), but I focus on concerns regarding their independent and dependent variables that are at least partly traceable to responsiveness (Stiles 2013).

Responsiveness Clouds the Independent Variables

Among the problems that responsiveness causes for RCTs, perhaps the most intractable is that it undermines the meaning of the independent variable. For the results of a controlled experiment to be meaningful, the independent variable must be clear and explicit. But because of therapist responsiveness, clients in the same treatment condition of an RCT each receives a different, individually tailored treatment. In each moment, new conversational and psychological requirements emerge, and therapists try to respond appropriately. As a result, treatment conditions with the same name (e.g., "cognitive therapy" or "short-term psychodynamic therapy") vary from study to study, from therapist to therapist, from client to client, from session to session, and from minute to minute. Such variability impairs the study's conclusions because the conclusions use the treatment names, and the names have no stable meaning. What can it mean to say that "cognitive therapy is more effective than short term psychodynamic therapy" when each instance cognitive therapy or short-term psychodynamic therapy is different from every other instance? Smedslund (2016a) made a similar point:

> A further complication is that it is almost impossible to ascertain that a practitioner is actually working in conformity with the scientist practitioner model and also that a bricoleur is not relying directly or indirectly on scientific evidence. (p. 54)

Treatment manuals were meant to specify the independent variable (Luborsky and DeRubeis 1984), and they are essentially required in state-of-the-art RCTs. The better ones offer fine-grained descriptions of treatment approaches, but they do not and cannot overcome the huge variation. Manuals do not give rigid instructions but describe repertoires of interventions and suggest how they might be used. They emphasize building rapport, clinical judgment, timing, tact, and adapting the approach to clients and clinical situations. That is, they specify that therapists should be appropriately responsive, with all the multiple influences, lack of replicability, uniqueness, and social interactivity that responsiveness entails. Likewise, clients are not passive recipients but active participants who make their own sense of interventions, respond in their own way, and adapt what they learn to the context of their own lives (cf. Valsiner and Brinkmann 2016). The implication that treatment manuals provide standard definitions for levels of an experimental independent variable is illusory or even deceptive.

A truly standardized script for a psychotherapeutic intervention would be absurd and unethical. The individualization achieved through responsiveness is clinically and humanly appropriate. But, as Smedslund (2009, 2015) has also noted, this is disastrous for the logic of experiments. Because responsiveness is ubiquitous, the meaning of each level of the independent variable in treatment outcome research changes across clients and contexts. As a gross example, clients with overinvolved attachment styles were treated systematically differently than clients with underinvolved attachment styles, even when treated by the same therapists in the same experimental condition (Hardy et al. 1998). To carry on a coherent interaction, therapists must continually make similar and much finer adaptations to clients and circumstances.

Of particular concern, therapists responsively adjust their treatment (the independent variable) in light of their perceptions of client progress or lack of progress (i.e., outcome, the dependent variable). That is, the supposedly independent variable is dependent on the dependent variable, violating the most fundamental principle of the experimental method.

These entanglements are more serious than uncontrolled variability in extraneous conditions because they cannot be overcome by randomization (Smedslund 2009; Stiles 2009b). That is, responsiveness (and with it, Smedslund's four problematic characteristics) is not a confounding variable; it is an essential element of any sensible psychotherapeutic treatment, and it is specified in treatment manuals. Improved experimental design and more careful execution will not make it go away.

The effect of appropriate responsiveness on the results of RCTs and other treatment comparisons is not simply to add random error or noise; it specifically undermines any systematic differences in effectiveness between treatments: To the best of each therapist's and client's ability, each moment of each treatment is responsively adjusted to the client's ever-changing requirements. That is, participants seek to optimize each moment of treatment for that client and circumstance. To the extent this succeeds, each client improves to an optimum degree, and all treatments appear more-or-less equivalently effective. This is what the Dodo has been saying about psychotherapy outcome research for more than 80 years (e.g., Luborsky et al. 1975; Rosenzweig 1936; Stiles et al. 1986; Wampold and Imel 2015).

Smedslund's (2012a, 2016a, b) description of the bricoleur therapist is a description of appropriate responsiveness. Rigid protocols cannot accommodate to changing circumstances, and therapists have responded appropriately. This may entail deviating from treatment principles, but training, supervision, and manuals all enjoin therapists to adapt appropriately, and treatment theories generally offer or allow a broad range of responses.

Evaluation Dominates the Dependent Variables

The dependent variables in product-testing research seem characterized by a nearly exclusive focus on evaluation. Indeed, the term psychotherapy outcome is used almost synonymously with such explicitly evaluative terms as benefit, improvement, effective, efficacious, worked, helped, and so forth. That is, the measures all assess how good it was, as contrasted with what happened descriptively.

Research using evaluative measures has a receptive audience, and a focus on evaluation seems appropriate for product-testing research. Consumers and providers want to know how well a therapy works, whether they will feel better, whether they will be satisfied with the results. Evaluative measures are also robust, I think, because evaluation is a common denominator in people's diverse experiences and understandings, perhaps a manifestation of what Rogers (1959) called the organismic valuing process. Indeed, good outcomes may be descriptively very different across clients; actualized people may become more differentiated rather than more similar (Stiles 1983). But most people seem to have firm convictions about what they think is good, how they feel, and what they like.

The evaluative measures include total scores or summary scores from symptom intensity inventories, as well as global indexes of severity or distress, which may be completed by clients, therapists, or observers. Scales named for symptoms, like the Beck Depression Inventory, or the Hamilton Rating Scale for Depression, or the State-Trait Anxiety Inventory, appear more specific, but a closer look suggests large evaluative loadings. Much of their variance is general distress. And for analyses, even nominally symptom-specific subscales are usually combined into a total score, interpreted as measuring improvement or effectiveness.

Evaluative indexes also dominate process measurement in process–outcome research. For example, most of the variables on Norcross's (2002, 2011) list of "evidence-based" elements of effective therapeutic relationships were evaluative: alliance, group cohesion, empathy, goal consensus and collaboration, positive regard, congruence/genuineness, *repair* of ruptures, management of countertransference, and *quality* of relational interpretations (emphasis added). These elements represent achievements or desired results rather than specific conditions or volitional behaviors (Stiles and Wolfe 2006).[1]

[1] Many descriptive process measures have been developed (e.g., Brauner et al. 2018; Worthington & Bodie 2018). However, these are generally not statistically associated with the evaluative outcome measures, presumably because therapists use them responsively, and hence approximately optimally, so they contribute negligibly to the prediction of outcome (Stiles 1988, 2013; Stiles et al. 1986, 1998). That is, because of responsiveness, statistical association of a process compo-

Evaluative measures of both process and outcome seem to reflect appropriate responsiveness (Stiles, in press; Stiles and Horvath 2017). That is, they assess whether the interventions were desirable or appropriate to the circumstances. The specific attitudes and behaviors that yield the high process ratings, like the specific life changes that successful clients achieve in treatment, differ across cases and times, as therapists do the right thing in response to clients' emerging needs and circumstances. Consumers and practitioners of psychotherapy are appropriately responsive because they seek good outcomes, as Smedslund (2012a, b, c, 2016a) underlined in the bricoleur model. That is, treatments work, in large part, because the participants do their best to ensure they work.

Research that tests the effects of appropriately responsive treatments on global evaluations shows that if participants do the right thing, they tend to be successful. But research focused on such evaluations does not show which specific activities predict or comprise which of therapy's specific effects. Finding that a therapy worked or was effective begs many questions about what changed and how it changed. The focus on evaluation is appropriate in product-testing research. But condensing therapeutic effects and therapeutic relationships into global evaluative dimensions fails to inform us about the specific conceptualizations that scientific research is meant to test.

Explanatory Theory-Building Accommodates Responsiveness

To review, Smedslund (2016a) suggested that psychology, and particularly psychotherapy, is too complex and ephemeral to be adequately represented in theory or research. His critique focused on four major characteristics of psychological processes. First, "psychological processes can be influenced by literally anything [past, future, fantasy], whereas physical science is restricted to the momentary and local" (p. 50). Second, "[p]sychological processes are strictly irreversible, meaning that one can never return to a starting point, [which] prevents genuinely accumulative empirical research" (p. 51), including the possibility of replication. Third, because of each individual's distinct genetics and personal history, "[p]sychological processes are unique, and … persons can only be understood by taking this uniqueness into account" (p. 51). And fourth, "[p]sychological processes … are inherently social, … the outcome of a prolonged process of interacting with other persons" (p. 52), so that much information about a person is available only through prolonged, intense personal interaction with him or her.

---

nent with client improvement tends to be unrelated to the clinical importance of that component in producing that improvement. Nevertheless, because descriptive process measures have not predicted outcome, they have tended to be discounted.

Does Psychology Require Too Many Variables?

As a result of these characteristics, Smedslund (2016a) argued, "theorizing becomes difficult, since a theory can only have a limited number of variables in order to be manageable; … the infinite number of determinants in itself prevents the formulation of practically useful empirical theories in psychology" (p. 51). As I have explained and amplified, I thought the critique was on target for treatment theories and the product-testing research that is used to evaluate them. However, I am more optimistic for explanatory theories and theory-building research, as I explain in this section.

Smedslund's presumed restriction of scientific theory and research to small numbers of variables is imposed, I think, not by the nature of scientific theory but by the statistical requirement for many observations on each variable. In statistics, a large N is required for stable estimates of central tendency and variability. Describing theory and research as aimed at explaining variance presumes some sort of (statistical) regression model predicting a criterion variable. This is a reasonable characterization of product-testing research aimed at assessing determinants of an evaluative outcome–improvement, effectiveness, how well the treatment works. The logic of clinical trials in general and RCTs, in particular, is fundamentally statistical and therefore subject to this restriction.

But explanatory theories are generally not built around predicting a single criterion. An explanatory theory of psychotherapy (e.g., psychoanalytic theory) can seek to explain many aspects and use as many words (or numbers) as are needed. Explanatory theories are limited only by the capacity of language.

Furthermore, strictly speaking, psychology is not uniquely complex or ephemeral. No two things in the natural world are exactly alike and no event is ever repeated exactly. Each star or continent or tree or tiger or rock or snowflake has its own unique characteristics and multitude of influences acting upon it. Gravity waves, predicted by Einstein's theory, are arguably as ephemeral as any observation of human behavior. Like psychological processes, all natural events can be understood as the product of a long history of influences or causal sequences.

Conversely, psychological processes can be understood as the product of contemporaneous determinants. That is, the historical influences on experience and behavior, along with goals for the future, are present here and now in some form. We find it more feasible, however, to describe influences on human experiences and behavior in terms of past and future events rather than in terms of the currently active subconscious experiential processes or neurological traces that are the proximal mediators of those influences.

But even if psychological events are not uniquely complex or ephemeral, psychotherapy's focus on a particular person's life and on subjective experience brings some distinctive intricacies and observational uncertainties. And it does make distinctive demands on explanatory theory. Physical theorists are often content with describing simplified or ideal cases, whereas psychologists, particularly clinicians, must be concerned with the particulars of individuals and hence with the rich tapestry of influences on their lives and their sometimes quirky and convoluted subjective experience. It would also be challenging to describe what determined the details of the shape of a particular tree or a particular snowflake, but biologists and meteorologists are content to describe such things in general terms. I think this leaves a somewhat softened conclusion from Smedslund's critique: Theorists have not been able to simplify an understanding of psychological systems enough to identify a statistically manageable number of variables without oversimplifying or glossing over the phenomena of interest.

Smedslund's Critique as a Challenge to Explanatory Theory

Even a softened version of Smedslund's (2016a) critique poses a challenge. An adequate explanatory theory has to respect the complex, ephemeral nature of the phenomena we want to understand. Attempting to build a statistically researchable theory of psychotherapy by neglecting the complexities will inevitably be misleading or disappointing. We have many oversimplified studies, published on the strength of their internal validity, that ring hollow to practitioners. In order to be accurate, a theory has to explain the sorts of observations that pointed Smedslund to the bricoleur model, illustrated by the striking recoveries in his ten example cases. If common sense leads to effective solutions, an explanatory theory should explain what common sense is, where it comes from, and how it operates.

As I use the term, a theory is a semiotic construction, made of words, numbers, diagrams, and so forth. Like any semiotic construction, theories may be misunderstood or understood differently by different people. A goal of explanatory theory, however, is to be understood in the same way by everybody. I think this helps to account for the attraction of numbers, which are more likely than words to be understood similarly by readers (Stiles 2006, 2009a). But the virtue of numbers is that they are a means to precision and communication. To insist on quantification in theories is to confuse a means with the end of representing an accurate understanding of the target phenomena. If the phenomenon is a product of hugely many determinants, irreversible, unique, and socially interactive, then a theory must seek to represent those characteristics, however many words it takes. And research methods must be developed to study it, even if they are not easily amenable to statistical techniques.

Theory-Building Qualitative Research

I think theory-building qualitative research (Stiles 2007, 2009a, 2017) offers an alternative strategy that can address Smedslund's (2016a) critique and the problem of responsiveness. In qualitative research, investigators observe and describe many aspects of the target phenomenon rather than just one or a few variables. To use these qualitative observations for theory-building, investigators compare each of many aspects of the theory with one or a few of their observations. They do this by describing their observations in terms of the theory, in effect, assessing how the theory fits or does not fit. At issue is the correspondence of theory and observation—how well the theory describes details of the observations. Each detail may be observed only once, but many details are observed.

For such familiar reasons as selective sampling, low power, and investigator biases, the change in confidence in any one theoretical statement, considered in isolation, may be very small. But, because many theoretical aspects can be compared with observations in a qualitative study, the gain (or loss) in confidence in the theory as a whole may be as large as from a statistical hypothesis-testing study. Campbell (1979) described these multiple observations as analogous to multiple degrees of freedom in a statistical hypothesis-testing study.

As Smedslund (2016a) pointed out, statistical hypothesis-testing's requirement of gathering many observations on the same few variables leads to overlooking or distorting the phenomena that are most of interest to psychotherapy researchers. In contrast, theory-building qualitative studies can use any observations that can be described in theoretical terms. The major theories that seek to explain psychotherapy, such as the various psychodynamic theories and theories of cognitive therapy, offer rich accounts of clinical phenomena. By comparing the rich theoretical descriptions with rich case observations, theory-building case studies can empirically assess theoretical precision and realism and accumulate improvements (Stiles 2009a, 2017).

Classically, empirical research can only increase or decrease confidence in a theory. But Peirce (e.g., Peirce 1985) pointed out that when an investigator encounters an observation that does not fit the theory, he or she can rationally change, elaborate, or extend the theory to account for the observation. Of course, like all theorizing, such an amendment is tentative. It must be logically reconciled with the rest of the theory, and it is always subject to further research. Peirce called this creative logical operation *abduction*. The amendments cannot be made lightly because the amended theory must continue to explain all the observations it previously explained.

Through abduction, a theory can be gradually built to accommodate continuing developments in research (Rennie 2012; see also Salvatore and Valsiner 2010). Findings of any research, including hypothesis-testing, can lead to improvements through abduction, but qualitative research is particularly valuable in this regard because it can yield a far greater variety of observations and is thus more likely to find places where the theory needs modifying or could be elaborated or extended. Moreover, in qualitative theory-building case studies, the observations and abductions can capitalize on investigators' clinical knowledge and skills as well as their logical and scientific skills.

In principle, qualitative theory-building research need never lead to formal hypothesis-testing, though of course it may do this. Successive studies can make detailed qualitative observations, formulated in theoretical terms, confirming some aspects of the theory and suggesting abductions that tweak or extend the theory in small ways, with occasional synthetic reviews to help maintain theoretical coherence (i.e., internal consistency and explicit interrelatedness of the tenets). As an example, I offer the assimilation model (Stiles 2001, 2011, 2018; Stiles et al. 1990), a developmental theory of psychological change in therapy that has been built primarily from qualitative and mixed-method case studies (e.g., Basto et al. 2018; Brinegar et al. 2006; Caro Gabalda and Stiles 2013; Honos-Webb et al. 1998; Leiman and Stiles 2001; Stiles et al. 1991). Each case has added confidence by supporting some aspects of the theory and suggested abductions through novel or unexpected observations.

Of course, qualitative case studies involve many potential threats to reliability and validity. Just calling case observations *qualitative research* does not overcome these issues; the familiar cautions regarding observer bias, uncertainty, and variability still apply. But, as I have indicated, human responsiveness and the characteristics of human behavior enumerated in Smedslund's critique pose equally serious problems for statistical hypothesis-testing in psychotherapy research, so the problems of qualitative research may seem more tolerable and worth addressing, and the virtues may loom larger.

Common Sense as a Scientific Resource

In justifying the bricoleur model, Smedslund (2016a) said, "It could be argued that even if practitioners rarely rely directly on research findings, they may frequently rely on very general theoretical insights assumed to ultimately derive from empirical research" (p. 55). But, he continued, most such general theoretical insights were already available from common sense and cultural lore (Smedslund 2009, 2012b, c).

My reply is, yes, culture and common sense offer a wealth of insights into human nature and relationships, but theory-building research is needed to sort the valid and relevant insights from those that are wrong, misleading, or irrelevant. My implicit theory will be different from your implicit theory. Although some common sense can solve clinical puzzles, other common sense can lead to clinical disaster. Common sense must be used sensitively and selectively, and not everyone's common sense can be trusted.

On the other hand, sensitive and selective application, whether of common sense or theoretical principles, is the core skill of the bricoleur and the essence of appropriate responsiveness. Even in presenting his examples, Smedslund (2016a) emphasized selectivity (e.g., "Obviously, this particular intervention was suitable only for this particular woman under these particular circumstances and for this particular psychologist," p. 52; "This intervention worked under these special circumstances, but with otherwise uncertain outcome, given the unknown context," p. 53). I suggest that explicit theory and theory-building research can address the content of common sense and the process of selective application. The challenge is building theories that respect the observed richness, uniqueness, and responsiveness of human interaction in psychotherapy.

Smedslund formalized his common sense in a set of principles and axioms (e.g., Smedslund 2009), meant to specify what we know about helping clients with their psychological problems by virtue of being human, of sharing a culture and language. He suggested that the knowledge needed to practice psychotherapy could be derived from this base, in concert with becoming personally acquainted with the client. In my view, this formalization is an achievement, built not only on Smedslund's humanity, language, and culture, but also on his distinctive acumen and his long career of observing and thinking about the human condition and the process of psychotherapy. In my opinion, the principles and axioms constitute the basis of a theory, indeed, a strong and carefully considered one. But I do not agree that all therapists share this knowledge by virtue of their common humanity, language, and culture. The substantial variation in their effectiveness (Castonguay and Hill 2018) testifies against this. Nor do I agree that research cannot improve it, though I do agree that RCTs are unlikely to help much.

In particular, I think that qualitative theory-building case studies could increase the generality, precision, and realism of Smedslund's theory, as it could improve any theory of psychotherapy. Systematic case observation could be compared with his formalization and derivations from it by describing clinical cases in the terms of the axioms. I suspect that the results would strengthen the confidence in most of Smedslund's formulations. I think they would also suggest abductions: better ways to phrase some aspects, ways to elaborate some tenets, and opportunities to extend the theory into areas not yet explicitly addressed.

Practicing therapists have much to contribute to this sort of research. As bricoleurs, they seek to be more appropriately responsive as they gain expertise and can draw on their professional experience as well as on their training, supervision, cultural heritage, and social skills. As I noted earlier, a bricoleur-like appropriate responsiveness is built into treatment protocols in the guise of rapport-building, adapting techniques, timing, and the like. But explanatory theories have a different purpose—not specifically to guide treatment, but to give a general, precise, and realistic account of psychological change. What is the relation of the bricoleur model to explanatory theory? Here, Smedslund (2009) "argue[d] that it is mostly the other way around and that researchers must listen to and learn from what goes on in practice" (p. 779). I agree (Stiles 1992). The successes and failures of bricoleur practitioners offer an opportunity to build explanatory theory.

The clinical observations that underpin the bricoleur's actions as well as observations of the actions and their effects are grist for the theory-building mill. They can be cast in theoretical terms and compared with others' observations that have accumulated in the tenets and phrasing of the chosen explanatory theory. And they can change the theory, increasing or decreasing confidence or suggesting abductions.

To put this another way, if clinical, personal, and self-observation are formally recorded, cast in theoretical terms, and logically reconciled, they can be abductively incorporated into theory. What is required is consistent use of theoretical terms and continual work to keep the theory logically coherent, that is, internally consistent and logically interlinked.

So my advocacy of qualitative theory-building research may not be so different from Smedslund's (2009) characterization of therapists as practical scientists. The main additional requirement is that the process of reconciling new observations with past ones be explicit and public, so that clinical insights can become theoretical abductions. That is, it requires a written, elaborated theory that can successively incorporate the observations and formulations of clinicians, making these available to the extended community.

References

Basto, I., Stiles, W. B., Bento, T., Pinheiro, P., Mendes, I., Rijo, D., & Salgado, J. (2018). Fluctuation in the assimilation of problematic experiences: A case study of dynamic systems analysis. *Frontiers in Psychology, 9*, 1–10. [1119]. https://doi.org/10.3389/fpsyg.2018.01119.

Brauner, E., Boos, M., & Kolbe, M. (Eds.). (2018). *Cambridge handbook of group interaction analysis*. Cambridge: Cambridge University Press.

Brinegar, M. G., Salvi, L. M., Stiles, W. B., & Greenberg, L. S. (2006). Building a meaning bridge: Therapeutic progress from problem formulation to understanding. *Journal of Counseling Psychology, 53*, 165–180.

Campbell, D. T. (1957). Factors relevant to the validity of experiments in social settings. *Psychological Bulletin, 54*, 297–312. https://doi.org/10.1037/h0040950.

Campbell, D. T. (1979). "Degrees of freedom" and the case study. In T. D. Cook & C. S. Reichardt (Eds.), *Qualitative and quantitative methods in evaluation research* (pp. 49–67). Beverley Hills, CA: Sage.

Carey, T. A., & Stiles, W. B. (2016). Some problems with randomized controlled trials and some viable alternatives. *Clinical Psychology and Psychotherapy, 23*, 87–95. https://doi.org/10.1002/cpp.1942.

Caro Gabalda, I., & Stiles, W. B. (2013). Irregular assimilation progress: Reasons for setbacks in the context of linguistic therapy of evaluation. *Psychotherapy Research, 23*, 35–53.

Castonguay, L., & Hill, C. E. (Eds.). (2018). *How and why are some therapists better than others? Understanding therapist effects* (pp. 71–84). Washington, DC: APA Books.

Dyson, F. W., Eddington, A. S., & Davidson, C. R. (1920). A determination of the deflection of light by the sun's gravitational field, from observations made at the solar eclipse of May 29, 1919. *Philosophical Transactions of the Royal Society A, 220*, 571–581.

Hardy, G. E., Stiles, W. B., Barkham, M., & Startup, M. (1998). Therapist responsiveness to client interpersonal styles during time-limited treatments for depression. *Journal of Consulting and Clinical Psychology, 66*, 304–312.

Honos-Webb, L., Stiles, W. B., Greenberg, L. S., & Goldman, R. (1998). Assimilation analysis of process-experiential psychotherapy: A comparison of two cases. *Psychotherapy Research, 8*, 264–286.

Kramer, U., & Stiles, W. B. (2015). The responsiveness problem in psychotherapy: A review of proposed solutions. *Clinical Psychology: Science and Practice, 22*, 277–295.

Kuhn, T. S. (1970). *The structure of scientific revolutions* (2nd ed.). Chicago: University of Chicago Press.

Lambert, M. J. (2013). The efficacy and effectiveness of psychotherapy. In M. J. Lambert (Ed.), *Bergin & Garfield's handbook of psychotherapy and behavior change* (6th ed., pp. 169–218). New York, NY: Wiley.

Leiman, M., & Stiles, W. B. (2001). Dialogical sequence analysis and the zone of proximal development as conceptual enhancements to the assimilation model: The case of Jan revisited. *Psychotherapy Research, 11*, 311–330.

Levins, R. (1968). *Evolution in changing environments: Some theoretical explorations*. Princeton, NJ: Princeton University Press.

Levi-Strauss, C. (1966). *The savage mind*. Chicago, IL: University of Chicago Press.

Luborsky, L., & DeRubeis, R. J. (1984). The use of psychotherapy treatment manuals: A small revolution in psychotherapy research style. *Clinical Psychology Review, 4*, 5–14.

Luborsky, L., Singer, B., & Luborsky, L. (1975). Comparative studies of psychotherapies: Is it true that "everyone has won and all must have prizes"? *Archives of General Psychiatry, 32*, 995–1008.

Norcross, J. C. (Ed.). (2002). *Psychotherapy relationships that work: Therapist contributions and responsiveness to patient need*. New York: Oxford University Press.

Norcross, J. C. (Ed.). (2011). *Psychotherapy relationships that work: Evidence-based responsiveness* (2nd ed.). New York: Oxford University Press.

Peirce, C. S. (1985). The proper treatment of hypotheses: A preliminary chapter, toward an examination of Hume's argument against miracles, in its logic and in its history. In C. Eisele (Ed.), *Historical perspectives on Peirce's logic of science. A history of science* (Vol. 2). Berlin: Mouton Publishers.

Rennie, D. L. (2012). Qualitative research as methodical hermeneutics. *Psychological Methods, 17*, 385–398. https://doi.org/10.1037/a0029250.

Rogers, C. R. (1959). A theory of therapy, personality, and interpersonal relationships as developed by the client-centered framework. In S. Koch (Ed.), *Psychology: A study of a science* (Formulations of a person and the social context) (Vol. Vol. III, pp. 184–256). New York: McGraw-Hill.

Rosenzweig, S. (1936). Some implicit common factors in diverse methods of psychotherapy. *American Journal of Orthopsychiatry, 6*, 412–415.

Salvatore, S., & Valsiner, J. (2010). Between the general and the unique: Overcoming the nomothetic versus idiographic opposition. *Theory & Psychology, 20*, 817–833.

Smedslund, J. (2009). The mismatch between current research methods and the nature of psychological phenomena. *Theory & Psychology, 19*, 778–794.

Smedslund, J. (2012a). The bricoleur model of psychological practice. *Theory & Psychology, 22*, 643–657.

Smedslund, J. (2012b). What follows from what we all know about human beings? *Theory & Psychology, 22*, 658–668.

Smedslund, J. (2012c). Psycho-logic: Some thoughts and after-thoughts. *Scandinavian Journal of Psychology, 53*, 295–302.

Smedslund, J. (2015). The value of experiments in psychology. In J. Martin, J. Sugarman, & K. L. Slaney (Eds.), *The Wiley handbook of theoretical and philosophical psychology* (pp. 359–373). Oxford: Wiley Blackwell.

Smedslund, J. (2016a). Practicing psychology without an empirical evidence-base: The bricoleur model. *New Ideas in Psychology, 43*, 50–56.

Smedslund, J. (2016b). Why psychology cannot be an empirical science. *Integrative Psychological and Behavioral Science, 50*, 185–195.

Stiles, W. B. (1983). Normality, diversity, and psychotherapy. *Psychotherapy, 20*, 183–189.

Stiles, W. B. (1988). Psychotherapy process-outcome correlations may be misleading. *Psychotherapy, 25*, 27–35.

Stiles, W. B. (1992). Producers and consumers of psychotherapy research ideas. *Journal of Psychotherapy Practice and Research, 1*, 305–307.

Stiles, W. B. (2001). Assimilation of problematic experiences. *Psychotherapy, 38*, 462–465.

Stiles, W. B. (2006). Numbers can be enriching. *New Ideas in Psychology, 24*, 252–262.

Stiles, W. B. (2007). Theory-building case studies of counselling and psychotherapy. *Counselling and Psychotherapy Research, 7*, 122–127.

Stiles, W. B. (2009a). Logical operations in theory-building case studies. *Pragmatic Case Studies in Psychotherapy, 5*(3), 9–22. https://doi.org/10.14713/pcsp.v5i3.973. Available: http://jrul.libraries.rutgers.edu/index.php/pcsp/article/view/973.

Stiles, W. B. (2009b). Responsiveness as an obstacle for psychotherapy outcome research: It's worse than you think. *Clinical Psychology: Science and Practice, 16*, 86–91.

Stiles, W. B. (2011). Coming to terms. *Psychotherapy Research, 21*, 367–384. https://doi.org/10.1080/10503307.2011.582186.

Stiles, W. B. (2013). The variables problem and progress in psychotherapy research. *Psychotherapy, 50*, 33–41.

Stiles, W. B. (2017). Theory-building case studies. In D. Murphy (Ed.), Counselling Psychology: A Textbook for Study and Practice (pp. 439-452). Chichester, UK: Wiley.

Stiles, W. B. (2018). Assimilation of problematic voices and the historicity of signs: How culture enters psychotherapy. In A. Konopka, H. J. M. Hermans, & M. M. Goncalves (Eds.), *Handbook of dialogical self theory and psychotherapy: Bridging psychotherapeutic and cultural traditions* (pp. 56–72). London: Routledge.

Stiles, W. B. (in press). Responsiveness in psychotherapy research: Problems and ways forward. In J. C. Watson & H. Wiseman (Eds), Attuning to enhance therapist responsiveness. Washington, DC: APA Books.

Stiles, W. B., Elliott, R., Llewelyn, S. P., Firth-Cozens, J. A., Margison, F. R., Shapiro, D. A., & Hardy, G. (1990). Assimilation of problematic experiences by clients in psychotherapy. *Psychotherapy, 27*, 411–420.

Stiles, W. B., Hill, C. E., & Elliott, R. (2015). Looking both ways. *Psychotherapy Research, 25*, 282–293. https://doi.org/10.1080/10503307.2014.981681.

Stiles, W. B., Honos-Webb, L., & Surko, M. (1998). Responsiveness in psychotherapy. *Clinical Psychology: Science and Practice, 5*, 439–458.

Stiles, W. B., & Horvath, A. O. (2017). Appropriate responsiveness as a contribution to therapist effects. In L. Castonguay & C. E. Hill (Eds.), *How and why are some therapists better than others? Understanding therapist effects* (pp. 71–84). Washington, DC: APA Books.

Stiles, W. B., Morrison, L. A., Haw, S. K., Harper, H., Shapiro, D. A., & Firth-Cozens, J. (1991). Longitudinal study of assimilation in exploratory psychotherapy. *Psychotherapy, 28*, 195–206.

Stiles, W. B., Shapiro, D. A., & Elliott, R. (1986). Are all psychotherapies equivalent? *American Psychologist, 41*, 165–180.

Stiles, W. B., & Wolfe, B. E. (2006). Relationship factors in treating anxiety disorders. In L. G. Castonguay & L. E. Beutler (Eds.), *Principles of therapeutic change that work* (pp. 155–165). New York: Oxford University Press.

Valsiner, J., & Brinkmann, S. (2016). Beyond the "variables": Developing metalanguage for psychology. In S. H. Klempe & R. Smith (Eds.), *Centrality of history for theory construction in psychology* (Annals of theoretical psychology) (Vol. 14, pp. 75–90).

Wampold, B. E., & Imel, Z. E. (2015). *The great psychotherapy debate: The evidence for what makes psychotherapy work* (2nd ed.). London: Taylor & Francis.

Worthington, D. L., & Bodie, G. D. (Eds.). (2018). *Sourcebook of listening research methodology and measures* (pp. 605–611). Hoboken, NJ: Wiley.

Chapter 21
Working with Stuckness in Psychotherapy: Bringing Together the Bricoleur Model and Pluralistic Practices

John McLeod and Rolf Sundet

A philosophical problem has the form: "I don't know my way about".

—Wittgenstein (1953/2009)

Perhaps the greatest challenge and worry for any practitioner of psychotherapy is to be stuck, to experience a lack of change or more seriously, detrimental development of the person and/or persons you are working with. While theory and research in psychotherapy primarily seeks to identify the processes and interventions that contribute to positive outcomes, there is substantial evidence that failure and stuckness represent a recurring theme within the professional literature, for example in respect of ruptures in the client–therapist relationship (Safran and Muran 2000), client experiences of disappointment with therapy (Werbart et al. 2015) and negative effects (Curran et al. 2019). We believe, therefore, that failure and stuckness comprise significant aspects of the landscape of therapy mental health practice. Our aim in this chapter is to connect this concern to the work of Jan Smedslund and to show how his ideas not only offer a perspective for addressing such events but also provide a gateway into the work of other theorists who have similarly contributed to the development of an alternative critical standpoint in relation to professional knowledge and practice.

For each of us, the relationship to Smedslund was for many years one of lack of interest. Although operating in different professional and academic environments, our responses to first reading about psycho-logic (Smedslund 1988) were very similar. We recall having a sense that Smedslund's contribution was hard to follow and mainly focused on issues in the development psychology and philosophical issues in psychology, was not relevant to therapy practice, and too different from anything else we had been taught. Only now, and much later, have we come to realise that

J. McLeod (✉)
Abertay University, Dundee, Scotland

R. Sundet (✉)
University of South-Eastern Norway, Drammen, Norway
e-mail: rolf.sundet@usn.no

T. G. Lindstad et al. (eds.), *Respect for Thought*, Theory and History in the Human and Social Sciences, https://doi.org/10.1007/978-3-030-43066-5_21

there existed another Smedslund than the restricted picture that had come from our initial exposure to his work. Our experiences as therapists and researchers have brought us closer to Smedslund's ideas, at the same time as his expanding body of writing seems to have moved in the direction of engaging more explicitly with our clinical concerns and interests. We have now reached a position where reading Smedslund invigorates and energises our thinking about key aspects of our work.

Although his published work is wide-ranging, we have specifically found great practical value in Smedslund's argument that working as a psychotherapist relies on three sources of knowledge: (1) What we know as human beings due to the fact that we are humans; (2) the knowledge we have due to the fact that we are participants in a culture and language; and, (3) knowledge about the specific unique persons that we meet and their life circumstances and prior experiences (Smedslund and Ross 2014, p. 368). His further description of a bricoleur model of psychotherapeutic practice (Smedslund 2012, 2016b) based on these three sources of knowledge, and presented by him as an alternative to the currently prevailing scientist–practitioner model, resonates with our experiences as therapists and counsellors. The practical context for the ideas and reflections explored in this chapter is the therapeutic work carried out by Rolf Sundet and his colleagues within the Mental Health for Children and Adolescents (MHCA) services in Norway, and the practices and understandings developed by Mick Cooper and John McLeod in their pluralistic approach to psychotherapy (Cooper and McLeod 2011; McLeod 2018).

The Challenge of Doing Psychotherapy

The position that is being offered in this chapter draws on experience in a family therapy service that offered many opportunities to engage with stuckness. Part of the Norwegian specialist healthcare within Vestre Viken Health Trust, the Family Team, formerly referred to as the Family Unit, was part of what, in the period 2012–2018, was named the Ambulant Family Section. As part of MHCA, this team offered treatment and help to children, adolescents and their families who had received therapy elsewhere, most often from the outpatient clinics within MHCA, without being helped. Many of these families also reported experiencing violations in these prior treatments most often connected to the lack of being heard, respected, taken seriously and believed in what they were bringing forth about their predicament, sufferings and perspectives on these. This means that these families had long and strong experiences of stuckness, lack of change and also detrimental developments regarding the themes and problems that had brought them to therapy. We believe that the work of the Family Unit and pluralistic practices highlights a key challenge for any psychotherapeutic practice, that is, how to respond to stuckness, lack of change and evidence of not being on track (Lambert 2010).

In the psychotherapy literature, and in psychotherapy training, the occurrence of lack of client progress or change is generally addressed by using generalised knowledge from theory and research. Clinical supervision is conceived as an activity that helps the struggling therapist to find the most appropriate conceptualisation of a case to choose the most appropriate evidence-based intervention that will enable the client or family to shift in the direction of a positive trajectory of change. The work of Smedslund makes it possible to understand how and why these strategies have limited effectiveness or may even run the risk of being detrimental. The difficulty in using RCT evidence as a guide to practice has been widely discussed in the psychotherapy literature (Bohart et al. 1998). A key aspect of this debate has been the observation that, on the whole, therapists practicing a flexible approach that is responsive to client needs and preferences, record results that are equivalent to or better than those found in therapists who have adhered to treatment manuals based on empirically validated models of therapy (Budge et al. 2013; Hoyer et al. 2017; Shedler 2015). In addition, it has become clear that the effectiveness of therapy is influenced by a range of factors, such as therapist personal qualities and the organisational culture of the therapy agency within which treatment is provided. Our view is that there exists a complex relationship between research and practice (McLeod 2016). Research knowledge is only valuable when it is considered alongside other sources of knowledge, such as understanding based on everyday culture and language, and information derived from personal interaction between client and therapist (Smedslund and Ross 2014).

Using Theory

Originally, when we started as counsellors and psychotherapists, the solution advocated by our teachers was to rely on theory: "when you do not know what to do, follow the theory". Thus, the theory was not only a guide but a master to obey as it allegedly provided the correct answers around how to get out of any negative predicament. The big question for any student of psychology then became "which theory to choose and on what grounds?"

However, it became apparent that there were many problems with this strategy. One problem that we not only experienced as relevant for ourselves but also for several of our colleagues was that we chose a theory based on ideas about what it is like to be human, as well as about the culture and meaning systems we came from. For example, for both authors of this chapter, our working-class backgrounds, with its particular cultural values and manners of giving meaning to life events could, in retrospect, be seen as the source of our theoretical choices. The relationship between psychological theories and the broader philosophical or political meta-theories within which they are embedded, opens up major difficulties in respect of the task of resolving clinical dilemmas through reference to therapy theory. For example, differences between theories, or areas of convergence, with regard to what to do with a client or family, could not be addressed through rational reflection or dialogue because they depended to a large extent on personal and social factors that were never acknowledged. Also, it was not at all clear how to proceed in situations in which one's theory, or way of making sense of problems differed from that of the client or family.

In addition, there were so many theories, and they all had suggestions that seemed useful in many situations and for many persons, but never for everybody. There were always those who fell on the outside, whose lives did not fit the theory. For us, these experiences clearly illustrate the limitations of using theory as a master discourse for deciding how to practice counselling and psychotherapy. We find that this fits well with the "therapist-as-bricoleur" model of Smedslund (2012, 2016a, b) and is a great part of why we have been inspired by him.

A particularly troubling aspect of theory was, for us, the way that theories could provide explanations that attributed the cause of stuck therapy processes to aspects of the person's problem, condition, disorder or state. Our stuckness as therapists, our inability to promote change and development was suddenly moved away from us and over to the patient, client and/or family. Concepts like "lack of motivation", "readiness to change", "resistance", "hard to treat", "inaccessibility to treatment" and "lack of ability for mentalization", gave the answer to why we got stuck as therapists. This sets up a circular argument: for the client to change, he or she had to change.

For instance, in working with individuals with issues around addiction, we learned that for the person to receive treatment for his drug problem, he or she had to stop using drugs, to show us that she or he was motivated for change. If they used drugs when in the treatment, treatment was terminated, on the grounds again as a sign of lack of motivation. Similarly, if an anxious patient did not agree to engage in systematic exposure training, treatment was either not started or terminated until the person was motivated to engage with exposure activities that were basically what he or she was anxious about. It could be argued that both these examples must be nuanced. To stop using drugs is much more than just not using drugs; often it is to develop a different manner of living, and creating other solutions to difficult predicaments and emotional states instead of using drugs, solutions that could best be worked with when not on drugs. With anxious patients, exposure is often done in a gradual manner that is responsive to the pace of change of the patient. However, for us, the interesting question is what we are doing when we use theory to explain a lack of change. What we came to realise was that, when we relied on theory, we were stopping ourselves from acknowledging or investigating the possibility that lack of change could be connected to the fact that our way of working was not helping this specific client. We came to see that if we could sit down with the client and come up with a different way of working together, the "motivational" problem or "inability to mentalise" might disappear.

Over the years it has become clear to us that therapy based on a single theory establishes a context of acceptability and constraint. For better or worse, the client is being socialised into a particular cultural practice and understanding of which the first step is to make sure that the patient accepts the perspective, understanding and meaning offered by the theory. The second step is for the patient to act according to the demands of the theory. A particularly clear example of this process can be found in the research into client socialisation to the treatment model in cognitive-behavioural therapy (Daniels and Wearden 2011). As a means of making sense of this aspect of the role of theory in psychotherapy, we found it helpful to talk about theory-driven psychotherapies as situations in which the client says "yes" to the rationale of the therapy: "yes-oriented" therapies (Sundet 2017). There is nothing wrong with yes-oriented therapies as such; a great deal of empirical evidence appears to demonstrate that many people get help from such therapy processes. Rather, the problem is when someone is not helped and when this is explained within the theory, rather than taking account of other relevant factors.

As a consequence of these reflections, we have tried to become better at creating situations in which clients can say "no", for example through using feedback tools and metacommunication to facilitate dialogue around what their refusal or reluctance might mean in relation to how we might best work together (McLeod 2018; Sundet 2017). Our underlying assumption was that what we were looking for at these moments was opportunities for building a more collaborative approach, that made it possible to combine the knowledge and experience of both client and therapist. While we still believe that this is important, we have also found it necessary to remain sensitive that we might be running the risk of creating our own "yes-oriented" therapy, based on our own theoretical assumptions that collaboration, dialogue and equalisation of power relationships are necessary for therapeutic learning and change to occur. It has taken us some time to appreciate that Smedslund's ideas (described later) offer valuable additional ways of understanding these issues.

Using Research

As therapists trained in the 1970s and 1980s, we were taught that being theoretically informed was the touchstone of effective practice. Gradually, from the end of the 1990s, a new source of guidance became dominant: research-based knowledge, or so-called *evidence-based methods* or *empirically supported or validated practices* (Wampold and Imel 2015). In many ways, we live in an age of evidence. Within healthcare–research as a whole, as in psychotherapy–research, the main driver of this process has been the randomised control trial (RCT). The use of RCTs and other statistical methods can be contested on the grounds that although evidence is central, it is restricted to a certain type of evidence. First, as argued by Smedslund (2009), it is based on a flawed belief in the overall relevance of statistical averages. For example, in Norway, the government has introduced the so-called patient`s healthcare system ("pasientens helsetjeneste"). This policy reflects the laudable intention that adapting to the needs and preferences of each patient represents a core principle around which a healthcare service should revolve. However, the problem is that this policy is implemented through allocating the patient to a treatment package based on RCT-based knowledge around which intervention is most likely to be effective for their condition. Thus, what is talked about as a "patient's healthcare system" is really not about unique patients, but rather "the *average* patients' healthcare system". What then happens is that a significant source of stuckness emerges: a system based on averages has the effect of eradicating difference and variation, and struggles to be responsive to unique configurations of individual life experience represented by each individual.

Smedslund (2009, 2012, 2016b) has consistently argued that mainstream approaches to psychological research using statistical and experimental methods to test hypotheses on large samples of participants, are unable to provide knowledge that can be applied in individual cases. We have increasingly come to recognise the significance of his work as providing a means of making sense of the reasons why knowledge that is grounded in averages has little relevance for clinical practice,

The Challenge of Psychotherapy: Bringing Together the Work of Smedslund and Pluralistic Practice

Beyond his critique of mainstream research, there are three aspects of Smedslund's work that have been helpful to us in relation to making sense of how to handle the challenge of doing psychotherapy: the critique of generalised knowledge: the image of the therapist as bricoleur, and: the importance of alterations to the environment.

The Critique of Generalised Knowledge: One Family or Client at a Time

Smedslund (2009, 2012, 2015, 2016a, b) draws our attention to the extent to which the shared experience of being human, along with participation in a common language and culture and willingness to learn about the specific life experience of the other, provides a basis for allowing the uniqueness of the individual to be taken into consideration. Moreover, this perspective also brings to the fore a fundamental scepticism and rejection of the place that inductively generalised knowledge, in the form of RCT-produced knowledge, has been given within the field of psychotherapy and counselling. We find his arguments in both of these regards to be compelling as they emphasise a practice built on the attitude of relating to "one family or client at a time". The uniqueness of the individuals means that in every person and in every family we meet, we will also meet something new. As such, Smedslund's arguments seem related to the concept of plurality in Hannah Arendt's work (Arendt, 1958/1998) that we have found relevant for our work discussing the use of service user participation and feedback in psychotherapy (McLeod 2018; Sundet 2017) now referred to as Routine Outcome Monitoring (Tilden and Wampold 2017).

When working from an idea of the importance of generalised knowledge we look for similarities across cases (Sundet 2015; Smedslund 2009, 2015). One way of looking at getting stuck is that we pursue or look at our predicament in a way that is locked into a pre-prepared manner of understanding, that is, based on some accepted generalised knowledge such as a theory or a research finding generated through the use of an RCT. Moi (2017) has pointed out that Ludwig Wittgenstein's interest was the opposite of this. Rather than looking for similarities, looking for what is different in what seems to be the same. We are also here brought to the importance of a single instance.

In therapy, our explanatory practices rely on presumed generalised knowledge that aggregates the similarities of the many: what one does can be explained by what characterises the many. These explanatory practices may be complex: when you have one individual, you can always ask for explanations of aspects of the explanation given. For instance, consider the following scenario: Question 1: "Why doesn`t the person change?" Explanation 1: "It is due to his lack of mentalisation capacity": mentalisation as the ability to understand ourselves and others in terms of mental states (Fonagy et al. 2014). Question 2: "How come there is a lack of mentalisation capacity?" Explanation 2: "Epistemic trust was not established early in life due to the development of disorganised attachment": epistemic trust as trust in the authenticity and personal relevance of interpersonally transmitted knowledge (Fonagy et al. 2014). This could go on and on. From a Wittgensteinian point of view sooner or later explanations will meet a dead end where we have to resort to explanations like "the law of nature" and such "... utterances do the same work as talk about God and Fate. Explanations only take us so far. This is why Wittgenstein thinks that the task of philosophy is to provide not explanations, but descriptions" (Moi 2017, p. 36). Moi (2017) points to Wittgenstein's diagnosis of what is the problem here. It is "the craving for generality" (Wittgenstein 1958 in Moi 2017, p.92), wherein one can find contempt for the particular case.

Consider a situation in which we meet a single family. Our generalised knowledge can suggest actions that may be helpful. For instance, we may decide to offer the family a therapy package that has been shown to be effective with other families who report similar difficulties. However, generalised knowledge is of limited value around the question of how to get out of the situation when things get stuck. Along with many other therapists, we have discovered that the best way out of stuckness is to relate to actual descriptions of the life, perspectives, ideas, actions and predicaments of the family. The narrative practices developed by Michael White exemplify one strategy for accomplishing this task, by drawing on the concept of "unique outcomes": descriptive accounts of specific moments or episodes during which the client's problem has not dominated the life of the person. In narrative practice, this kind of description is used to open up possibilities for telling new stories and retelling old stories (White 2007). The general relevance of this strategy of attending to apparently incidental, non-theorised "innovative moments" has been further articulated by Gonçalves et al. (2011).

This is why our "being stuck" is important. We believe that taking stuckness seriously forces us to pay attention to differences, uniqueness and the significance of the client's "no", and instead work more purposively to start building a description of the life of the family, not generalised explanations. A description is based on shared language and culture, and always seeks to be close to the life of the family. The closer the therapists are to the family, and the more they are able to engage them in a process of collaborative inquiry, the more it becomes possible to co-create nuanced and diverse descriptions. We have found that this involves examining sharing the stuckness of the therapist: on many occasions, when the therapists experience stuckness themselves it may be because they are close to the stuckness of the family.

Therapist as Bricoleur

Smedslund (2012, 2016b) has suggested what he calls a bricoleur model of clinical practice: "a bricoleur is a resource person who is enlisted when ordinary established procedures in daily life fail to work, and who utilizes whatever is at hand in the given situations to effect a solution" (Smedslund 2012, p. 644). He adds that the bricoleur is " … a jack-of-all-trades, relying on what is at hand and, if necessarily, on conventional means, to solve problems that resist conventional solutions" (Smedslund 2016a, b, p. 50). At the same time, this unconventionality and possible creativity are not ascribed to the therapist alone: "(t)he creativity is equally on the side of the client, and the psychologist`s ideas are of value only when they trigger or nourish the client`s imagination" (Smedslund 2012, p. 652).

The concept of the psychotherapist as a bricoleur is consistent with and has the potential to inform and enrich significant strands of contemporary psychotherapeutic practice. For example, it offers a new perspective on the concept of the "not-knowing position" (Anderson 1990; cf. Smedslund 2016b) that advocated therapist openness to the experience and lived reality of the client or family. In words of Smedslund:

> When encountering a new client, the psychologist knows that it is, in principle, impossible to know anything detailed about the person in advance, except for what follows from being human, and except for his or her mastery of a certain language and certain culture. (Smedslund 2012, p. 647)

Working with families who had tried different treatment programs, the experience of the Family Team is that a majority of these families had experienced violation due to not being listened to, heard, taken seriously and believed (Sundet 2011). The lesson learned for the team was always to start by adopting a "not-knowing" stance that followed the family and the different preferences, aims and intentions of the family members. Our generalised knowledge easily became our enemy if we let this knowledge base override the perspectives of the family.

In Smedslund's bricoleur model a trusting relationship is central, and the main component in its creation is the therapist's openness. The metaphor of "getting a taste of it" (Sundet 2011) points to situations and events where the therapist may experience and feel something similar to what the family members feel. This idea offers a more down-to-earth, phenomenological equivalent to theory-laden constructs such as countertransference or emotional transport between persons. "Getting a taste of it" offers a point of departure where everybody can take a step back, reflect and search together in finding new manners of relating and acting in order to move on and beyond the predicaments that ground the experiences. For Smedslund (2012), it is here that trust becomes essential, in the sense of the therapist establishing oneself as a caring, respectful and understanding person who at the same time has her or his independent perspectives with relevant generalised knowledge that can be put to play, but only in a tentative manner, in the conversations between family and therapies. The family-based practice values these same attitudes and with similar reluctance to overvalue the therapist's ability to understand the other. This because to put oneself in a position of stating that "I understand you" can all too easily be confused with the therapist knowing something more about the client than the client knows. This kind of understanding can all too easily establish a top–down relationship of power with the therapist on top. In the family-based practice what is valued is to understand something together. Central here is a lingering conversation; conversations that do not aim at too quickly to fall down on concluding understandings and conclusions (Sundet 2011). From the perspective of Smedslund (2012), it is about retaining wondering. To be stuck then is an invitation to start to wonder, to linger in conversations where the therapist is open to and seek to notice what it is that moves and touches the family members. It is also to notice what touches and moves the therapists and let these experiences be known to the family. How are we in resonance with each other about what part of the life of the family?

We have found that it is within what individually and mutually moves both family members and the therapist that we find the themes and stories that need to be further investigated. These stories contain both the pain and suffering of the family, but also their history of success and creativity in meeting challenges in their life. It is about finding the hidden exceptions, values, principles, dreams and aims that have gotten lost when suffering pain and hardship have dominated the life of the family. Mental health, both lack of it and the development of it are about the life experiences, predicaments and existential issues and challenges that every person sometimes meets in their life. Working together on issues of mental health will always be a collaborative process between persons, never between therapists and members of a diagnostic group. Mental health is always about unique, irreplaceable individuals in joint action and living.

The concept of a therapist as bricoleur has the potential to both complement and extends the pluralistic framework for counselling and psychotherapy that has been developed in recent years (Cooper and Dryden 2016; Cooper and McLeod 2011; McLeod 2018). This is an approach to therapy that emphasises the importance of client–therapist collaboration and dialogue to enable shared decision-making around the direction of therapy, and the accomplishment of therapeutic tasks using a combination of the professional skills and knowledge of the therapist, and the life experience, preferences and personal and cultural resources of the client. In pluralistic practice: "therapeutic change is not something that therapists do to clients, but something that clients actively work to bring about" (Cooper and McLeod 2011, p. 17).

Both pluralistic practices, and the bricoleur model, are grounded in a re-conceptualisation of how therapeutic change takes place. In the language of mainstream psychotherapy, what therapists do is often referred to as an "intervention": something is done by the therapist that causes an effect in the patient (Dreier 2011). However, from an alternative perspective, what therapists do can be understood as an "invitation to respond" rather than as a linear causal factor. The therapist is active in offering invitations and being responsive to the invitations made by the client (e.g. to explore a particular topic); on the other side, the client is equally active and responsive (Bohart 2004, 2015).

For the therapists in the Family Team, and also those working pluralistically, the image of the bricoleur or jack-of-all-trades finds its partner in the idea that, in order to be responsive to the client, the practitioners needs to have a big toolbox or repertoire (Sundet 2011), based on curiosity and a commitment, through one's career, to be a collector of therapeutic ideas about working, collaborating, learning, understanding and making a difference in the sphere of problems in living (McNamee 2004). This resourcefulness, in the sense of familiarity with a plurality of theories, concepts, methods and manners of being together, is what our clients expect us to bring to the table when they meet us (Sundet 2009, 2011).

The kind of flexibility and capacity for creative improvisation that is inherent in the vision of therapy that we are outlining here is informed by a relational ethic of care in which uniqueness is understood as "irreplaceability" (Biesta 2010). When working as therapists, we are touched and moved by unexpected, new, non-anticipated events and happenings and are thrown into the existential aspects of living with others. There is a personal dimension to participating in another person's life, which we believe is a necessary part of working as a therapist. Without closeness and the lived experience of feeling or sensing something of what the other is going through, there is nothing to reflect upon. The big question in clinical work will always be: what matters to and for the other – the client, patient and family.

Modifying the Client's Surroundings or Environment

For Smedslund (2012) modification of the client's surroundings is at the core of therapy. For the Family Team, over the years, it became clear that however mental health problems are conceptualised and explained, the context and life circumstances of the client and family were central to our work. In many instances, the therapeutic work is about the family modifying their own environment and surroundings. At the same time, we experienced that contemporary society put pressure on families, which meant that we as therapists needed to attend to what created this pressure. One example was that in our society the greatest worry of parents today is for their child or adolescent to drop out of school. School and education are the key to a healthy life in the future is the message from our politicians. At the same time, children and adolescents fall out of school. Often this is accompanied by a psychiatric diagnosis. Especially ADHD has become a very popular diagnosis that is used to explain why children and adolescents fail at school.

From our perspective, this story is much more complex than a mental health disorder. It is about a society that on the one hand preaches the gospel of individuality, and on the other hand increases the pressure towards falling within group-based, standardised manners of learning and acting. Therefore, an important therapeutic task for the Family Team was to attend to the school situation and seek to increase the possibilities for an educational context that fitted the children and adolescents. Diversifying the educational context became a central task of the therapist, at the same time to retain an empathic relationship with the school and teachers who often were put in an impossible position, between the demands of our politicians and legislators and the realities of the children and adolescents in their particular school. Stuckness, lack of change and falling out of school were just as much related to lack of the educational system to include the diversity that each youngster represented, as the child's behaviour was a sign of pathology and lack of family functioning. Working for a change of our educational system concerning single children and adolescents turned therapy into political activity in the everyday life of the families, wherein securing the rights of and access to resources for the youngsters became a clear therapeutic agenda. To modify the clients' surroundings, as Smedslund states as a necessity, is not a trivial activity; it is about raising our political awareness about the predicaments of our children and adolescents and their families.

Broadening the Reach of Smedslund's Ideas: Some Links with Other Theorists

We have found that the work of Jan Smedslund has provided us with a basis for appreciating the value for psychologists and psychotherapists of ideas that have been developed by important contemporary thinkers within other academic disciplines.

The idea that uniqueness and irreplaceability are two significantly different aspects of the same coin can be found in the work of Biesta (2006, 2010) and Arendt (1958). In an interview by Winter (2011) Biesta explicates some of his ideas. One is the concept of "coming into the world" based on an idea by Nancy (1991) about "coming into presence". For Biesta, identity is about identification as a third-person perspective. It is about "identification by someone or identification with something" (Winter 2011). His ideas of "to come into presence" and "coming into the world" point to identity as a process or event and rather than identity as an essence. For Biesta, this "turned traditional education on its head by not starting from what the child is to become, but by articulating an interest in that which announces itself as a new beginning, as newness, as natality, to use Arendt's term" (Winter 2011, p. 538). Arendt states that: "Plurality is the condition of human action because we are all the same, that is, human, in such a way that nobody is ever the same as anyone else who ever lived, lives or will live" (Arendt 1958/1998, p. 8). Natality has to do with "the birth of new men and the new beginning" (Arendt 1958/1998, p. 247). This does point to the fact that at the moment of birth, there are choices, even for the newborn. From developmental psychology, we know that the newborn has volition, actions of choice. Laying on her or his back the child can voluntarily turn the head towards something out there that comes to attention. It can suck the thumb or pacifier by will, and direct his or her gaze (Stern 1985). Birth then is both to be new, a beginning and a place where choice enters. From, that on natality points to the fact that every encounter and event in our life has the potential of being the "birth of something new".

For Biesta, "coming into presence" is not something that can be done in isolation: "(t)o come into presence is always to come into presence of others ... " (Winter 2011, p. 539). When we are born, we step into life as something that affords multiple possibilities; we all are the same in our own specific way. We are all human in a unique manner. Again, going back to developmental psychology, we see that that in the first communicative event, directly after birth, there is a show of both autonomy and dependency. For sociologist Stein Bråten this has led to hypothesising that the child is born with a "'virtual other' ... that offers a participant (....) space in which others may be included in felt immediacy" (Bråten 1998, p. 106). We are born ready for the other with preferences for the human face and voice (Stern 1985), and we know now that without a response from the other, caregiver or other humans, death is imminent. No one is ever alone, although loneliness might certainly be a predicament for many of us. Maybe the worst part of loneliness is that we are never alone. The other becomes unachievable and we know and feel it.

We are born to dependency and autonomy. For Arendt (1958), it is in this double predicament that our possibilities for the new lies. Natality points away from death and the end of our life. It points to every encounter with oneself and others as an opportunity for something new (to be born), for furthering the plurality we are and are part of. In our dependency lies the great possibility of being met and responded to by others, and in our autonomy, we can make choices and respond back. As Smedslund (2009) suggests, this predicament is similar for all humans, so the others also have this relationship with us. This mutuality invites solidarity and taking responsibility for each other at the same time making this possible by taking responsibility for ourselves: the human condition means that we all may matter to each other.

Biesta states that we need "an argument for why the subjectivity of each single subject who comes into the world might matter. This is why the idea of 'coming into the world` needs to be complemented by a notion of uniqueness'" (Winter 2011, p. 539). He goes on to differentiate between "uniqueness-as-difference" and "uniqueness-as-irreplaceability". The first concerns "identity and questions about knowledge about the subject, and one which brings us to an existential argument" (Winter 2011, p. 539). This has to do with how I can be described; that is, what characterises me and how am I different from others? Biesta characterises here the relationship with others as instrumental; as to how I differ from others given different characteristics that can be ascribed a person. "Uniqueness-as-irreplaceability, on the other hand, brings in a different question: not what *makes* me unique, but *when does it* matter that I am who I am? With this move from characterisation of me/us through the use of some descriptive or explanatory tool (i.e. diagnostic system, theory) to how I matter for both others and myself is a move into the first-person perspective and the existential. With "uniqueness-as-difference" I am locked in some kind of pre-existing system of description and explanation, like a "yes-oriented" therapy. In "uniqueness-as-irreplaceability" experience is not necessarily locked into a pre-given category or theory. What arises in relation to others matters, but is never seen or met before and as such without description when it emerges. Irreplaceability, therefore, resides in the continuous production of life as a plurality.

Smedslund's bricoleur model, emphasising the uniqueness of the individual – emerged in the experience of being a human among humans using a shared language and being part of a shared culture – is compatible with a practical application of the philosophical ideas of Arendt and Biesta. Thus, Arendt and Biesta's thoughts cannot only be understood as bringing support to Smedslund's work, but they also open up avenues that liberate the bricoleur model, as well as pluralistic practices, from an understanding of psychotherapy as dependent upon generalised knowledge generated by RCTs.

There are many other sets of ideas, from other disciplines, that complement to work of Smedslund. For example, his critical understanding of the limitations of mainstream psychological research aligns with the ideas Stephen Mumford and Rani Lill Anjum, who are philosophers of science. Their analysis of underlying logic of causality that informs randomised controlled trials proposes that "inferences from frequencies to propensities comprise an ecological fallacy, which is a logically invalid inference from group average to the individual" (Anjum 2016, p.422). They carefully identify the ontological assumptions that make it impossible for RCTs to accommodate the complexity and multifactorial aspects of different illnesses (Anjum 2016). For practitioners of psychotherapy, one of the most relevant aspects of their work is their conceptual analysis is the failure of the medical model and RCT evidence to deal with Medically Unexplained Symptoms (MUS) (Eriksen et al. 2013).

Another influential theorist whose ideas complement Smedslund is the anthropologist Ingold (2013). Although his work incorporates a wide range of relevant insights, a particularly relevant aspect comprises his critique of hylomorphism, the assumption that skills and tasks are controlled by a pre-existing cognitive plan. Using examples from art, architecture and craftwork, Ingold shows that making things fundamentally involves a process of being guided by the medium itself. For example, splitting logs to make firewood follows the grain of the wood, or making pottery depends on the feel and properties of the clay. This perspective opens up further ways of making sense of the notion of the bricoleur and the importance of curiosity about the detail of the client's everyday life. It points to a sense of psychotherapy as emergent and flexible, which is entirely consistent with the writings of Smedslund.

Closing Remarks

Our chapter has sought to use the phenomenon of stuckness as a platform for acknowledging the importance of everyday language and cultural experience, and the value of engaging clients in a process of collaborative inquiry around building detailed descriptions of relevant aspects of their everyday lives. Our aim has been to stimulate an enhanced appreciation of the writings of Jan Smedslund as a key source of knowledge and understanding for therapists, and to promote further dialogue that reinforces the possibilities of a philosophically informed dialogue around the nature and further development of psychotherapy. Smedslund offers powerful arguments against building empirically based psychological practices. As we have argued, RCT does not help us in finding how to get out of stuckness, lack of change and detrimental development. Knowledge of the group does not give us sufficient help in contributing to the individual patient being able to move on. It only leads us from the acceptability and the constraint of theories to the acceptability and constraints of RCT-based research findings. The predicament, but also the hope, for counsellors and psychotherapists, is to take the person seriously as an irreplaceable individual that invites us into a process of getting to know each other as such individuals. This is a journey with unexplored paths of practice, with the possibilities of discovering new landscapes and lines of living. This is the gift of Smedslund to us all.

References

Anderson, H. (1990). Then and now: A journey from "knowing" to "not knowing". *Contemporary Family Therapy, 12*, 193–197.

Anjum, R. L. (2016). Evidence-based or person-centered? An ontological debate. *European Journal for Person-Centered Healthcare, 4*(2), 421–429.

Arendt, H. (1998). *The human condition* (2nd ed.). Chicago: The University of Chicago Press.

Biesta, G. J. J. (2006). *Beyond learning. Democratic education for a human future*. New York: Routledge.

Biesta, G. J. J. (2010). *Good education in an age of measurement. Ethics, politics, democracy*. New York: Routledge.

Bohart, A., O'Hara, M., & Leitner, L. (1998). Empirically violated treatments: Disenfranchisement of humanistic and other psychotherapies. *Psychotherapy Research, 8*(2), 141–157.

Bohart, A. C. (2004). How do clients make empathy work? *Person-Centered & Experiential Psychotherapies, 3*(2), 102–116.

Bohart, A. C. (2015). From there and back again. *Journal of Clinical Psychology, 71*(11), 1060–1069.

Bråten, S. (1998). Infant learning by altercentric participation: the reverse of egocentric observation in autism. In S. Bråten (Ed.), *Intersubjective communication and emotion in early ontogeny* (pp. 105–124). Cambridge: Cambridge University Press.

Budge, S. L., Moore, J. T., Del Re, A. C., Wampold, B. E., Baardseth, T. P., & Nienhuis, J. B. (2013). The effectiveness of evidence-based treatments for personality disorders when comparing treatment-as-usual and bona fide treatments. *Clinical Psychology Review, 33*(8), 1057–1066.

Cooper, M., & Dryden, W. (Eds.). (2016). *Handbook of pluralistic counselling and psychotherapy*. London: Sage.

Cooper, M., & McLeod, J. (2011). *Pluralistic counselling and psychotherapy*. London: Sage.

Curran, J., Parry, G. D., Hardy, G., Darling, J., Mason, A. M., & Chambers, E. (2019). How does therapy harm? A model of adverse process using task analysis in the synthesis of service users' experience. *Frontiers in Psychology, 10*, 347.

Daniels, J., & Wearden, A. (2011). Socialization to the model: The active component in the therapeutic alliance? A Preliminary Study. *Behavioural and Cognitive Psychotherapy, 39*(2), 221–227.

Dreier, O. (2011). Intervention, evidence-based research and everyday life. In P. Stenner, J. Cromby, J. Matzuka, J. Yen, & Y. Haosheng (Eds.), *Theoretical psychology. Global transformations and challenges* (pp. 260–269). Ontario: Captus Press.

Eriksen, T. E., Kerry, R., Mumford, S., Noer Lie, S. A., & Anjum, R. L. (2013). At the borders of medical reasoning: Aetiological and ontological challenges of medically unexplained symptoms. *Philosophy, Ethics and Humanities in Medicine, 8*, 11. http://www.peh-med.com/content/8/1/11.

Fonagy, P., Luyten, P., Campbell, C., & Allison, L. (2014, December). *Epistemic trust, psychopathology and the great psychotherapy debate*. [Web Article]. Retrieved from http://www.societyforpsychotherapy.org/epistemic-trust-psychopathology-and-the-great-psychotherapy-debate.

Gonçalves, M. M., Ribeiro, A. P., Mendes, I., Matos, M., & Santos, A. (2011). Tracking novelties in psychotherapy process research: The innovative moments coding system. *Psychotherapy Research, 21*, 497–509.

Hoyer, J., Čolić, J., Pittig, A., Crawcour, S., Moeser, M., Ginzburg, D., & Stangier, U. (2017). Manualized cognitive therapy versus cognitive-behavioral treatment-as-usual for social anxiety disorder in routine practice: A cluster-randomized controlled trial. *Behaviour Research and Therapy, 95*, 87–98.

Ingold, T. (2013). *Making. Anthropology, archaeology, art and architecture*. New York: Routledge.

Lambert, M. J. (2010). Prevention of treatment failure. In *The use of measuring, monitoring, and feedback in clinical practice*. Washington, DC: American Psychological Association.

McLeod, J. (2016). *Using research in counselling and psychotherapy*. London: Sage.

McLeod, J. (2018). *Pluralistic therapy. Distinctive features*. Oxon: Routledge.

McNamee, S. (2004). Promiscuity in the practice of family therapy. *Family Process, 26*(3), 224–244.

Moi, T. (2017). *Revolution of the ordinary. Literary studies after Wittgenstein, Austin, and Cavell*. Chicago and London: The University of Chicago Press.

Nancy, J.-L. (1991). Introduction. In E. Cadava, P. Connor, & J.-L. Nancy (Eds.), *Who comes after the subject* (pp. 1–8). New York: Routledge.

Safran, J. D., & Muran, J. C. (2000). *Negotiating the therapeutic alliance: A relational treatment guide*. New York: Guilford Press.

Shedler, J. (2015). Where is the evidence for "evidence-based" therapy? *The Journal of Psychological Therapies in Primary Care, 4*(1), 47–59.

Smedslund, J. (1988). *Psycho-logic*. Heidelberg: Springer-Verlag.

Smedslund, J. (2009). The mismatch between current research methods and the nature of psychological phenomena. *Theory & Psychology, 19*(6), 778–794.

Smedslund, J. (2012). The bricoleur model of psychological practice. *Theory & Psychology, 22*(5), 643–657.

Smedslund, J. (2015). The value of experiments in psychology. In J. Martin, J. Slugarman, & K. Slaney (Eds.), *The Wiley handbook of theoretical and philosophical psychology: Methods, approaches, and new directions for social sciences* (pp. 359–373). Nueva York: Wiley.

Smedslund, J. (2016a). Why psychology cannot be an empirical science. *Integrative Psychological and Behavioral Science, 50*(2), 185–195.

Smedslund, J. (2016b). Practicing psychology without an empirical evidence-base: The bricoleur model. *New Ideas in Psychology, 43*, 40–56.

Smedslund, J., & Ross, L. (2014). Research-based knowledge in psychology: What, if anything, it its incremental value to the practitioner? *Integrative Psychological and Behavioral Science, 48*, 365–383.

Stern, D. N. (1985). *The interpersonal world of the infant: A view from psychoanalysis and developmental psychology*. New York: Basic Books.

Sundet, R. (2009). *Client directed, outcome informed therapy in an intensive family therapy unit – A study of the use of research generated knowledge in clinical practice*. Oslo: Department of Psychology, Faculty of Social Science, University of Oslo.

Sundet, R. (2011). Collaboration: Family and therapists' perspectives of helpful therapy. *Journal of Marital and Family Therapy, 37*(2), 236–249.

Sundet, R. (2015). Kunnskap i evidensens tid: Mot en kunnskapsforståelse for praktiserende familieterapeuter. *Fokus på familien, 43*(1), 6–25.

Sundet, R. (2017). Feedback as means to enhance client-therapist interaction in therapy. In T. Tilden & B. E. Wampold (Eds.), *Routine outcome monitoring in couple and family therapy. The empirically informed therapist* (pp. 121–142). Cham: Springer.

Tilden, T., & Wampold, B. E. (2017). *Routine outcome monitoring in couple and family therapy. The empirically informed therapist*. Cham: Springer.

Wampold, B. E., & Imel, Z. E. (2015). *The great psychotherapy debate. The evidence for what makes psychotherapy work*. New York: Routledge.

Werbart, A., von Below, C., Brun, J., & Gunnarsdottir, H. (2015). "Spinning one's wheels": Nonimproved patients view their psychotherapy. *Psychotherapy Research, 25*, 546–564.

White, M. (2007). *Maps of narrative practice*. New York: W.W. Norton & Company.

Winter, P. (2011). Coming into the world, uniqueness, and the beautiful risk of education: An interview with Gert Biesta by Philip Winter. *Studies in Philosophy and Education, 30*(5), 537–542.

Wittgenstein, L. (1953/2009) *Philosophical investigations*. The German text, with an English translation. 1953. Rev. 4th ed., translated by G. E. M. Anscomb, P. M. S. Hacker, and Joachim Schulte. Oxford: Wiley.

Wittgenstein, L. (1958/1965). *The Blue and Brown books: Preliminary studies for the philosophical investigations*. New York: Harper Tourchbooks.

Chapter 22
The Pragmatic Status of Psychoanalytic Theory: A Plea for Thought Models

Erik Stänicke and Tobias G. Lindstad

The development of knowledge within the psychoanalytic tradition has similarities not only with research in academic psychology but also with the hermeneutic sciences. However, it also has its own distinctive character. We argue that the concepts, notions and assertions of psychoanalytic theory often constitute *thought models* that might be practically relevant. These models are thus theoretically anchored regulative principles that may be relevant for practice, although the aspects and relations they refer to are not always manifested. As such, they may contribute to ground psychotherapy as a practice where one strives to meet persons as openly and unprejudiced as possible. As this aim is also shared by Smedslund (2009, 2012b, 2016) in relation to his proposal of a so-called bricoleur model of clinical practice, it is pivotal to discuss the extent to which the perspectives are compatible and may join forces or not.

With respect to the bricoleur model, we acknowledge the critique of Salvatore and Valsiner (2010) and argue that Smedslund's related efforts to advance Psychologic (PL) must be broadened so as to include the relevance not only of deductive reasoning but also of abductive reasoning. However, pace Smedslund (2012c) and Valsiner (2014b), we argue that these reasoning capacities may reveal not only conceptual relations but also causal relations between dispositional properties of persons. On the other hand, we also extend upon Green's (2003, 2005) idea of psychoanalysis as consisting of at least two forms of *clinical thinking*. As he writes: "One of the main characteristics of clinical thought is that it is dialogical, that is, it deals not only with the patient who suffers, but also with the analyst who has the

E. Stänicke (✉)
Department of Psychology, University of Oslo, Oslo, Norway
e-mail: erik.stanicke@psykologi.uio.no

T. G. Lindstad (✉)
Asker, Norway

T. G. Lindstad et al. (eds.), *Respect for Thought*, Theory and History in the Human and Social Sciences, https://doi.org/10.1007/978-3-030-43066-5_22

task of listening to the suffering in the couple they form …" (Green 2003, p. 29, see also Stänicke et al. 2019). The other aspect of clinical thinking requires that the traditional understanding of psychoanalytic perspectives as solely based upon experiences of clinical encounters must be broadened so as to acknowledge theoretical elaborations that may be removed from direct clinical experience (Green 2005, p. 9).

Psychology has benefitted tremendously from both of these aspects through its history. Thus, not only do we call for a revival of the importance of theoretical elaborations in line with the pioneers of modern psychology (cf. Valsiner 2012; Danziger 1990; Toulmin and Leary 1985), but psychoanalytic theory development must be acknowledged for having planted the seeds for many prospering fields of psychological research, such as developmental psychology, attachment theory, mentalization and models of short-term psychodynamic therapy. Even its often-considered rival, cognitive therapy, was developed from a psychoanalyst, such as Aaron Beck who densified psychoanalytic theory to models of relevance for short-term consultation.

Psychoanalytic Thought Models

Our proposal of characterizing psychoanalytic theory as comprising *thought models* mirrors our aim of demonstrating that these aspects of the theory are developed by *thinking* about possible dispositions of persons and that the models are thus *potentially relevant for practice*. Extending on recent advancements of causal dispositionalism (Mumford and Anjum 2011; Anjum and Mumford 2018a) the term "model" suits these aims as it opts for demonstrating that significant aspects of psychoanalytic theories are concerned with dispositional properties of persons whose causal manifestations may not always be manifested. However, although the properties and relations accounted for by the thought models are not necessarily manifested, they might emerge in the course of psychotherapy, and might be relevant to understand as significant parts of the psyche of unique individuals.

It should also be noted that psychoanalytic notions are models also in the sense of being metaphoric or building on analogies, and as such psychoanalytic thought models may be considered to be scientifically idealized ways of representing psychological phenomena. Of course, speaking of thought models as idealized does not mean that they concern anything ideal. On the contrary, as clinically relevant they are often concerned with properties that may dispose towards unwanted suffering. For example, we have the well-known model of psychodynamic defence mechanism that models the dispositional need of persons to secure their well-being from overwhelming anxieties in ways that might lead to more suffering.

A common response towards psychoanalytic theories, models and notions is the surprise, or sometimes even contempt, about having a theory of anything like, for instance, the Oedipus complex. This may stem from disparaging theoretical language that puts the dynamics of the human psyche up in analogy with the narratives of non-scientific imaginary literature, or it may come from being suspicious about modelling nearly all human action as if it was sexually oriented at its base.

Responding to this critique, a common reply from psychoanalysts has been that the Oedipus complex is differently understood today with the current advancements of self-psychology, relational psychoanalysis and modern object-relation theory. However, it should be noticed that psychoanalysts rarely trash their old concepts, models or theories. Rather, it is as if they are hoarding them, stacking them all up in a closet available for future use. If one complies with a Popperian research paradigm, one may argue that this is unscientific; after all, when a model is not in use anymore, and its actual applicability in the present even falsified, should not the theory be discarded? It is not that psychoanalytic concepts and theories have never been abandoned. However, traditionally, this is understood as something that ought to happen only when clinical experience, conceptual analysis and/or empirical research convincingly demonstrate the incoherency of concepts. A good example of this is the suggestion of Mahler et al. (1975) that infants normally develop through an autistic phase. That suggestion is contrary to every empirical finding in academic developmental psychology, and furthermore, it has also been difficult to demonstrate as a clinically viable interpretation. However, this example is not the typical case in psychoanalysis. More typically analysts do not discard their theoretical notions but let them rest in latency.

A typical example of psychoanalysts keeping their theories and terms is found in Christopher Bollas (1989) when he looks upon all the various psychoanalytic concepts, models and theories as living side-by-side. Accordingly, psychoanalytic theory, all the way from Freud and up to today's advancements, can, according to Bollas (1989, p. 104), for illustrative purposes be tentatively placed within a periodical system. In this table, one finds psychoanalytic notions, concepts, models and theories like the Oedipal complex side-by-side with the models of defence mechanisms, Bion's theory of alpha function, projective identification, bi-logic, potential space, mentalization, attachment, narcissistic needs, drive affects and death work – just to name some examples. As such, Bollas writes that psychoanalysis outnumbers any other therapeutic perspective by its repertoire of "valuable ideas", and we concur with him. Over its history, psychoanalytic notions and models have been formed by therapists trying to put their own and their patients' experiences as truthfully as possible into words, and by further abductive reasoning, this has been generalized into the current theories. Abductive reasoning will be explained in a bit more detail bellow when differentiating it from both deduction and induction. Importantly, this academic emphasis on conceptualizing clinical experiences as truthfully as possible supports the clinical aim of enabling oneself to recognize the same or similar phenomena if one happens to encounter them again in later phases or with another patient.

The Legacy of Sophocles and Melanie Klein

It has been 100 years ago since Freud conceptualized his feelings in a way he referred to as an Oedipal complex, and there is no reason to discard the model. Importantly, this is so even if you seldom, or never again, come across patients with the same or similar conflict. The model of the Oedipal complex is still available and may thus not only be potentially useful for future generations of clinicians but is also relevant for psychological science as part of a coherent theory of the dispositional properties of the human psyche. Thus, even in the lack of any current empirical data supporting its existence, it may still be psychologically relevant. However, we are prone to argue that the way Freud (1900, 1910) described the Oedipus complex, it became too much marked by the socio-demographic context of his upbringing. Today the Oedipus complex is more recognizable in line with Ronald Britton's (1989) arguments that the traumatic part of being a child in a triangulated family is the experience of being left out from what the parents have together. Hence, today many analysts will find the emotional toll of the Oedipal triangular situation for the child is not so much a question of guilt and castration anxiety, but more of jealousy, envy and loneliness. Furthermore, the analyst today, in contrast to traditional psychoanalysis, will not be so much concerned with the infantile trauma of the Oedipal complex, but more on how the patient is currently managing new triangular situations, which reactivates jealousy, envy and loneliness in her contemporary life. Thus, the early constellation with parents are better thought of as a model for how these feelings are dealt with today, and accordingly, the treatment process is not so much focused on the early traumas in the past than with how to understand and deal with, and possibly accept that one may have such feelings.

Another compelling example of a psychoanalytic thought model that has been developing since several decades is the theory of projective identification. The model was first launched by Klein (1946) who characterized it not only as a defence mechanism by which children when playing with each other projected parts of themselves into others but also as the further process of identifying with this split of part of themselves. Decades later Bion (1962) described projective identification not only as a defence mechanism that could be manifested in children's play, but also as an interpersonal dynamic, typically the analyst being like a container for split of parts of a patients personality and, hence, the analyst's possible tendency to act out these parts towards the patients. Several decades went before Gabbard (1995) described how this interpersonal mechanism of projective identification is happening through the analyst's vulnerability: As if the analyst carried "personal hooks" that the patient may, possible through nonverbal communication, activate in such a way that the analyst becomes the bearer of the patient's issue. However, extending on the arguments of Lindstad (2020a) that the recent advancements of causal dispositionalism (Mumford and Anjum 2011, 2017a, b) are relevant for psychotherapy and psychotherapy research the model can be developed further. Thus, we suggest that the model of projective identification accounts for *mutually manifested* relational phenomena that *might emerge* in clinical encounters when dispositional properties of therapists and clients come together. Thus, a therapist may have properties that dispose her towards acting in ways that a patient, because of his properties, *may* react upon by interpreting the therapist as having properties that are actually features of himself.[1] Additionally, the therapist may be vulnerable in the sense that she is disposed to feel inclined to identify with the properties the patient interprets her as having and thus act as if these properties were originally hers.[2] Of course, if she also acts this way the attributes actually manifest as the therapist's own, but they could not have emerged as such without meeting this particular patient. Thus, the model of projective identification accounts for the emergence of certain kinds of changes of the therapist and patient mutually manifesting from their encounter.

There are several other psychoanalytic thought models that could be discussed, but the two earlier examples will do to illustrate that psychoanalytic theories develop over time and by thinking about possible dispositions of persons. In the following, we will characterize psychoanalytic thought models a bit further and discuss its relevance in relation to Smedslund's notion of the therapist as a bricoleur.

The Elasticity of Thought Models

Firstly, extending on the dispositionalist account of causality developed by Mumford and Anjum (2011) and Anjum and Mumford (2018a), we argue that psychoanalytic thought models are often about relations between causal dispositions of persons. This has already been demonstrated with regards to the model of projective identification but can be extended also to other models. For instance, the model of the Oedipal complex refers to potentially unmanifested dispositions of persons. For instance, a patient's report of problems with triangulated situations may have to do with feelings of jealousy or loneliness, and together with the thought model of transference, one may consider whether the patient is also disposed of for feeling that she is neglected by the therapist. Thus, the model of the Oedipus complex may aid the therapist to formulate interpretations, however – and this is of utmost importance – such interpretations can only be tentative; if they do not facilitate the patient's association, or are of no help, they must be discarded like any other misunderstanding.

Secondly, the models that refer to therapeutic interventions are characterized by not being constitutive, in the sense that they are not strict rules, but *idealized* regulative principles. For example, Killingmo (1997) has argued that the concept of neutrality does not imply that an analyst shall behave according to an ideal of being

[1] … for instance, as part of a defence mechanism; if the properties the client interprets the therapist as having are actually properties that the patient for some reason experiences as unwanted parts of himself.

[2] This is not to deny that the therapist could feel inclined to act this way without the patient ever having interpreted her as having these properties, but this is not projective identification. The scenario could also be turned around so that the therapist interprets the patient as having properties that are actually the therapist's.

cold and inhuman. Rather, neutrality is a regulative principle that provides the therapist with an idea of an ideal*ized* encounter that she can assess her behaviour and interventions up against. If the patient asks the therapist a personal question and the therapist answers the question on face value, this may actually be what is most feasible to do when encountering some specific patient in some particular context, although it represents deviance from neutrality. Still, the concept of neutrality helps the therapist to think through why she answered the question from the patient and why it may have been correct, which may also provide a further understanding of the patient's thoughts and feelings, and it may even be beneficial to provide this interpretation explicitly.

Thirdly, it must be stressed that psychoanalytic thought models are characterized by various kinds of *elasticity*. Building on earlier contentions by Sandler (1983) and Wallerstein (1984), first author (Stänicke and Stänicke 2014) has argued that psychoanalytic concepts must be elastic in the sense that the adept clinician should not be required to immediately search for a fit between the patients' properties and the thought models but should entrust an open-minded attitude towards the patient and the psychotherapy process. Indeed, this clinical strength of elasticity must not be discarded in order to instantly meet scientific ideals. However, this collaborative chapter gives the opportunity for discussing the relevant kinds of elasticity a bit further. Although it is an apt scientific ideal for our discipline to advance as precise concepts as possible, it should also be uncontroversial that elasticity is important regarding how we speak about what the thought models are about as well as how we use the terms that name these models. If it is required to be scientifically precise in any clinical setting both therapists and patients will probably be exhausted, and the opportunity to flexibly and gradually adjust towards a common understanding will be lost.

However, there is also an important sense in which psychoanalytic thought models must be considered elastic with regards to scientific aims: As our human minds are undeniably fallible, we must be open for the possibility of having to advance our models and concepts even further in order to improve our conceptual grip on the world. This is a bit like the child's discovery that her ideas of birds did not sufficiently differentiate them from butterflies, and is exemplified earlier (section "The Legacy of Sophocles and Melanie Klein") both by psychoanalysts abandoning Mahler's notion of children necessarily developing through an autistic phase and the openness for developing thought models of the Oedipus complex and projective identification further. Thus, admitting this scientifically relevant elasticity is not in conflict with striving for scientific precision. On the contrary, it encourages and facilitates curiosity. We should remind ourselves of Adorno's (1973) argument that stubbornly setting our conceptual schemes in stone exemplifies nothing but a form of identity thinking that only reproduce already established ideologies.

Encountering Uniqueness: Statistics Don't Get It!

In order to explain the pragmatic relevance of psycho-analytic thought models, it is also important to situate it in relation to the predominant reliance on statistical approaches in psychotherapy. This is also relevant in relation to Smedslund's intriguing critique of this paradigm. Thus, a dominant assumption in psychotherapy research has been that clinically oriented psychological perspectives must be evaluated by testing whether they have come up with interventions that can be proven successful on an average level via statistically supported empirical experiments in the form of randomized controlled trials (RCTs). However, as argued by Smedslund (2009, 2012b, 2015, 2016), it is not only questionable whether the RCT design is equal to this task, but it is also questionable whether there is any need for setting such a task: As no person makes sense of things from the exact same position as any other, any complete set of human experiences is inevitably unique. Also, as nothing can ever become not experienced once it is experienced, all experiences are irreversibly unique, and cannot really be experimentally replicated. Moreover, as persons are continuously susceptible to change by attaching new meanings to things from within ever-evolving unique contexts, it cannot be taken for granted that persons will react in the same or similar ways on neither the same event nor similar events.

Hence, searching for context-transcending, regular and/or lawful causal relations between therapy interventions and outcome via RCTs is at best of limited value. Nonetheless, this kind of research is still predominant, and a plethora of psychotherapy perspectives have been thrown into rivalry competing for the best result on an average level, presumably because it is thought possible to circumvent the difficulties via statistical randomization procedures. By randomly assigning a high number of persons to groups subjected to different conditions, say, some are offered psychotherapy and others are not, and estimating whether the groups subsequently show statistically significant differences, one may conclude that the differences have been caused by the therapy. The viability of this conclusion depends on the two groups being similar in all other relevant respects, and it is held that this is taken care of by the randomization. However, although characteristics that are possible for people to share, say, nationality, may spread evenly in large-sized random groups, unique characteristics, say, memories, cannot. Thus, if it cannot be precluded that unique experiences are influential, and indeed, they always are, we cannot know whether the groups are as similar as required. Hence, the randomization procedure effectively throws the baby out with the bathwater. At their best RCTs can only indicate statistically whether therapists and patients have interacted in ways that happened to be relevant in the various research contexts (Cartwright and Hardie 2012; Anjum and Mumford 2018b). However, *what* was done and understood by the persons involved in these contexts, and *how* this led to this or that result, as well as *how* it may be done elsewhere, in the future, with the same, or with any other person, is simply left obscure. Accordingly, we comply with Smedslund's (2009, 2016) arguments that practitioners cannot ever gain much from relying on theories tested by RCTs. However, we also revive Smedslund's earlier argument (1991) that empirical research may provide relevant food for thought, and as such we argue that his persistent denial of the relevance of causal explanation for psychology (2004, 2012c, 2015) is off the mark.

Don't Throw Causality Out Along with Humeanism

As discussed in more detail by the second author (Lindstad 2020a), the problem is not that psychologists have emphasized causal explanation, but that the prevailing conceptions of causality have been misleading. As such, the resurgent philosophical interest in understanding the relevance of dispositional properties for causality (Groff and Greco 2013) and the related arguments that the Humean conceptions of causality must be replaced by dispositionalism (Mumford and Anjum 2011; Anjum and Mumford 2018a) have already been offered on behalf of medicine and the health sciences in general (Anjum 2016; Kerry et al. 2012). However, it remains to clarify its implications for psychotherapy and psychotherapy research, and although this is not our main aim here, these implications are relevant for our account of psychoanalytic thought models.

According to the theory of causality presented by Hume (1739, 1748), causal relations consist of no more than that one can observe that events regularly conjoin or follow one another. Hume also presented influential ideas of a related counterfactual difference-making account on which causes are events without which their effects would not happen. On these conceptions, all we may know is that events of one kind can be observed as regularly conjoined or followed by events of another kind. Thus, the prevailing idea that RCTs is the best way to demonstrate relevant causal effects of psychotherapy (e.g. Roth and Fonagy 2005; Hollon 2006) fits the Humean conceptions like a glove as they imply that causal links must either be demonstrated by statistical evidence of correlation or by comparing the average outcome of exposure by stimuli with the average outcome of no exposure. Unfortunately, this inapt standard is not only uncritically upheld in the statement on evidence-based practice (EBPP) provided by the American Psychological Association (APA) (2006, p. 274), but probably, something very much alike the Humean conceptions is also what Smedslund (2012c, 2015) has had in mind when denying the psychological relevance of causal explanation. This would at least be reasonable in relation to his arguments about the limited clinical value of RCTs (2009, 2016), as well as his commitment (2009, 2015) to Dilthey's (1894) valuable distinction between explaining via causal laws (Erklärung) and understanding agents' points of view (Verstehen).

However, as argued by Lindstad (2020a), there are better ways to pave the way for an emphasis on human meaning-making than to deem causality irrelevant, not the least when there are accounts of causality that are radically opposed to Humean conceptions. Thus, though Valsiner (2014c, p. 19) is right that sticking to search for linear causality has led psychology to ignore alternative accounts of causality, it is not quite right that psychological phenomena exist in conditions where catalytic, *rather than* causal, processes dominate (Valsiner 2014b, p. 113, Valsiner and Brinkmann 2016, p. 83, our italics). Rather, Valsiner (2017, p. 16, our italics) is right that talk about causality must take *a new form*, and as such, we consider the recent advancements of causal dispositionalism (Mumford and Anjum 2011; Anjum and Mumford 2018a) a compelling substitute. In contrast to Humeanism, various accounts of dispositionalism have revived a view of causality on which causal relations rest upon the powers of dispositional properties to produce changes (Marmodoro 2010; Groff and Greco 2013). Thus, on the view developed by Mumford and Anjum (2011), rather than to think of causal relations as constituted by events that simply happen to succeed one another, causal relations are constituted by real properties that dispose towards other properties as their effects. Causal properties may thus only tend towards their effects so that these effects may never be manifested in any observable regularity (Anjum and Mumford 2018a). Thus, repeated measures of the same repeatable events are no royal road to know about causal relations. Although we may come to accept claims of causal relations on the basis of observed regularities, isolating variables is neither the only nor the best way to gain an understanding of causal relations. Rather, we need more thorough inquiries aiming to explain how and why causal effects emerge. Interestingly, these arguments are not only compatible with the abovementioned arguments of Smedslund about the limited value of RCT's for clinical practice, but as hinted earlier, like ourselves we guess Mumford and Anjum (2018b) will join in with Valsiner's (2014a, p. 18) outburst that "correlational data do not explain – they need explanation themselves!".

Hence, to advance an account of psychoanalytic notions as practically relevant thought models we extend upon the arguments of Lindstad (2020a) that an apt emphasis on human meaning-making does not exclude causal explanations from *Verstehen*. Rather, understanding what something may mean for someone is more often than not to get to know about their causally powerful dispositional properties. For instance (in relation to Smedslund's (2012b, 2016) frequently presented clarifications of the conditions for trust), thinking of your father as both understanding and caring when offering an old lady his seat on a crowded bus, may dispose you towards thinking that he has the disposition of being trustworthy. Although RCTs may indicate the existence of psychologically relevant causal relations, we fully agree with Smedslund (2016, p. 54) that predictions of the performance of one individual based on the average score of many individuals are less correct than predictions based on acquaintance with one individual. Even so, we agree with Smedslund that basing one's practice on RCTs may stand in the way for engaging relevantly with unique patients here and now. What is needed instead are notions that enable clinicians to grasp relevant parts of the everchanging unique set of properties of patients in unique surroundings. However, pace Smedslund, this does not make causal explanations of what may emerge in psychotherapy irrelevant. Accordingly, the working models traditionally categorized as belonging to various psychotherapy perspectives (cognitive behavioural therapy, emotion-focused therapy, person-centred therapy, etc.) was probably not originally born out of considering any results from RCTs, but was rather based on more or less systematic reasoning on why various unique patients observed in therapy was suffering, and on how to relieve that suffering. This is also what psychoanalytic thought models are about. As such, rejecting Humean conceptions of causality does not rule out the relevance of causal explanation.

The Bricoleur and the Psycho-logician

From all appearances, psychoanalytic perspectives are clearly different from Smedslund's. Where psychoanalytic theories offer conceptual innovations, analogies and intriguing metaphors sometimes even inspired by non-scientific imaginative literature, Smedslund have, as part of his efforts to advance Psycho-logic (PL) (Smedslund 1988, 1995, 1997, 2012c), argued that psychologists must strive for cooperationally precise conceptualizations, rigorous conceptual analysis and clarification of common sense. Relatedly, while Freud continues to inspire psychoanalytic scholars to inquire into irrational aspects of the human psyche, such as primary processes and dreams, Smedslund (1970, 2012c) has persistently argued that understandable aspects of the human mind are inherently logical. Although this implies that none of the perspectives can be reduced to the other without loss, their shared aim of grounding psychotherapy as a practice where one strives to meet persons as openly and unprejudiced as possible makes it vital to clarify their joint potential.

Towards this aim Smedslund (2009, 2012b, 2016, p. 50) has attempted to formulate a consistent position he has called the bricoleur model. In this model, the psychotherapist is regarded as a jack-of-all-trades who relies on whatever is at hand that might contribute to solving problems encountered. As Smedslund has argued that the clinical value of RCTs is limited, he has proposed three alternative resources for the bricoleur. *First*, like Smedslund (2016, p. 55), we regard it as uncontroversial that human beings come to know much about persons by sharing language, customs and practices, and that without sufficient knowledge in this regard psychotherapeutic processes could not get off the ground. *Second,* also uncontroversial, is that the aim of getting a sufficient understanding of unique others and their conditions are necessary for every psychotherapy process. However, Smedslund's *third* resource is not only far more controversial but largely unheeded, that is, Psycho-logic (PL).

The two former resources are also highlighted in the definition of EBPP provided by APA (2006, p. 273), apparently to ensure that therapists consider the extent to which research evidence is relevant in the context of patient characteristics, culture and preferences. However, APA also declares that the purpose of the statement is to promote *empirically* supported principles and interventions (p. 273, our italics). Moreover, though APA endorses the integration of multiple types of research evidence, not only RCTs (p. 273–274), not only are all examples of approved alternatives in the statement still only empirical (quantitative and/or qualitative), but APA also upholds RCTs as the standard for drawing causal inferences about the effect of psychotherapy. Smedslund's arguments about the limited value of RCTs, as well as his efforts to advance PL, are simply ignored. As we do not only agree with Smedslund's abovementioned arguments about the limited practical value of RCTs but also reject the Humean misconception of RCTs like the royal road to clinically relevant causal explanation, we will discuss the relevance of this proposal of PL as a *third* knowledge base for the bricoleur in relation to psychoanalytic thought models.

In presenting the bricoleur model, Smedslund (2012b, c, 2016) has taken departure in his advancements of PL, characterized as an attempt to explicate a conceptual system allegedly implicit in ordinary language and common sense. He also characterizes this knowledge as something that we all know because we are human and have persistently characterized these explications as amounting to a priori knowledge. This latter aspect relates to his notorious claim that the great mass of empirical research conducted to test and validate psychological theories, perspectives and models have been *pseudo-empirical*, that is, the theories can be known as true without empirical testing (e.g., see Smedslund 1995). Instead, Smedslund has emphasized conceptual analysis and reflection on what we as persons take for granted about being a person in the world. Although one may not fully subscribe to this account of PL we do consent to his notion of pseudo-empirical research.

As described by Smedslund, PL seems relevant for the bricoleur for two main reasons. First, the abovementioned arguments against the emphasis on RCTs in psychotherapy research are already part of PL, and thus also the conclusion that the first and the second source of knowledge is relevant for the bricoleur. Since experiences are irreversible and persons are unique the bricoleur must get to know about the unique properties of persons and their circumstances. As demonstrated by Smedslund's abovementioned arguments (section "Encountering Uniqueness: Statistics Don't Get It!") we can know this from reflecting on the properties that our psychologically relevant concepts refer to, that is, from reflecting on what it is like to be a person. There is no need for testing these assertions through empirical research. However, there is more to PL than this, which amount to the second reason PL is relevant for the bricoleur; that is, as the third source of knowledge about general characteristics of persons.

Can the Bricoleur NOT Make Use of Psychoanalytic Thought Models?

Smedslund has pushed his arguments towards two radical positions. On the one hand, he has presented PL as representing knowledge that everyone has of the general characteristics of persons (Smedslund 1995, 2016, p. 55).[3] On the other hand,

[3] A more moderate account is suggested by Lindstad (2020b) on which it is neither warranted nor necessary to take for granted that everyone takes all assertions of PL for granted to defend their status as a priori knowledge. This account is no less relevant for the bricoleur as it is similarly concerned with general properties of persons.

Smedslund's bricoleur model invokes an utmost wariness for overgeneralizations, and we are eager to discuss whether psychoanalytic thought models are compatible with the bricoleur model in this regard.

Given the uniqueness and importance of context in every clinical encounter, Smedslund (2016, p. 54) has argued that the bricoleur must be maximally open. Thus, citing Anderson and Goolishian's (1992) proposal of a not-knowing position, he has argued that …

> [t]he attitude of initial openness or not-knowing is necessary since there are no sufficiently reliable regularities and, therefore, all fixed advance hypotheses about a particular case will most likely be at least partly incorrect. In other words, all attempts to apply the psychologist's way of seeing the world to the problems of the individual client will most probably be at least partly wrong. The reason is that despite similarities that might be found, the unique features of a case must also always be taken into account in looking for possible solutions. Since the unique cannot by definition be known in advance, initial openness is the only realistic approach. (Smedslund 2016, pp. 54 and 56)

As such, Smedslund (2016) has argued not only that psychological practice must go on without relying on statistically based empirical research but also that since what persons do cannot be predicted by any general theory or dealt with by any fixed techniques, a professional approach to psychological phenomena must remain a-theoretical and a-technical (2004, pp. 8–9). As such he has even confessed that if asked by other clinicians what theories he uses for dealing with the clinical encounter his honest answer is "*none*" (2004, p. 45)!

However, as the term "theory" is ambiguous, one may wonder what an a-theoretical stance implies. In ordinary parlance, the term often is used to refer to non-scientific, unwarranted and loose ideas, as in the expression "it was just something I came up with at the moment that might as well be wrong". Smedslund may appear to have been suspicious also about what this rather deflated use of the term concerns when having argued that the ethical commitments of the bricoleur …

> necessitates an effort to lay aside stereotypes, prejudices, theories, ready-made categories, and predictions. This comparative openness and attempt *not* to jump to conclusions is, by definition, necessary, in order to encounter and assimilate the uniqueness of the other individual. (2009, p. 791)

However, this is probably not what Smedslund had in mind when promoting an a-theoretical stance. Directly following the last cited sentence, he writes:

> Therefore, what characterizes the competent practitioner is *not* the possession of vast amounts of general knowledge applicable to each new case. It is, on the contrary, an ability to discard and push into the background previous experiences and to listen to what does *not* fit into one's pre-existing categories. (2009, p. 791)

Thus, the a-theoretical stance does not seem to be, at least not primarily, about the abovementioned deflated use of the term "theory". Rather, Smedslund (2016, p. 55) seems primarily to have raised his voice against the prevailing idea that prefabricated recipes of psychotherapy interventions are generally applicable, paradigmatically exemplified by the claim of Kennair et al. (2002, p. 9) that "[though] there are variations between humans, … there also is a relatively uniform human nature [which] means that interventions that work on large groups of humans will probably work for random individuals".

Thus, though Smedslund has argued that the bricoleur must take as little as possible for granted, and patiently retain maximal openness in talking with clients, his point is hardly to ban any act of forming ideas. Rather, the initial open attitude of not knowing is for letting new impressions organize into a coherent tentative picture in subsequent cooperative explorations of possible solutions with the client (Smedslund 2012b, p. 649; Smedslund 2016, p. 55). Thus, whenever a therapist's focus is committed to a pre-construed theory promoting certain interpretations or procedures, whether this comes from aesthetic preferences (e.g. from preferring the metaphors psychoanalytic theory rather than the simplicity of cognitive therapy models, or opposite), from clinical experience with earlier clients, from clinical guidelines of governmental authorities or from inductive generalizations from accumulations of empirical data showing statistical differences between groups (RCTs), the therapists (Smedslund 2012b, p. 649) are concerned that this will distort the possibility of getting to know the individual person and the unique circumstances in sufficient detail. Described as such, we are not only in sympathy with Smedslund's a-theoretical stance, but a similarly open attitude on behalf of the therapists has already been an explicit ideal for psychoanalysts for decades. At least, it seems closely related both to the notion of elasticity discussed earlier (section "The Elasticity of Thought Models") and Bion's (1967) notorious call to "listen without memory and desire". However, there is also a third way of understanding Smedslund's a-theoretical stance that we think is problematic.

As mentioned, Smedslund has not only persistently presented PL as common sense, but he has also argued that this implies that PL is a priori knowledge (Smedslund 2012b, p. 643 & 655, Smedslund 2009, p. 791), and thus that psychotherapy must involve a maximal reliance on what we all allegedly know about being human (Smedslund 2009, p. 791). Although one may (cf. Lindstad 2020b) argue that the question of whether PL is a priori knowledge must not be conflated with the question of whether PL is common sense, this issue is not in question here.[4] The relevant question here is rather why Smedslund does not regard a maximal reliance on PL as reliance on theory. Probably, he will reply that theories that are built from empirical data or in need of empirical testing are significantly different from knowledge that is valid whether or not it is empirically based (cf. Smedslund 2012b, p. 655). However, if this is true, then what are we to make of the myriad of established models, theories and perspectives of psychotherapy? Must the bricoleur reject these approaches (e.g. cognitive behavioural therapy, emotion-focused therapy, psychodynamic theory, etc.) as having come up with anything of practical value? Will psychoanalytic thought models then be of no value for the bricoleur? However, there is another option that may pop out for anyone acknowledging the

[4] Notice that the notion of a priori knowledge suggested by Lindstad (2020b), may not only depart from the one Smedslund has had in mind, but it may also be considered a somewhat deflated notion of a priori knowledge.

notion of pseudo empirical research, highlighted by the following tripartite set of questions:

(1) Could it be that the plethora of psychotherapy perspectives are often mislabelled as theories, as any research aiming to test the assertions of these perspectives will be pseudo empirical? (2) If most assertions of most psychotherapy perspectives can be justified independently of empirical research by being deduced from the axioms, theorems and corollaries of PL, must they not be considered as valuable parts of PL? (3) If that is true, and if it is also correct that the bricoleur must rely on PL to a maximal degree, must the bricoleur not also then rely on psychoanalytic thought models to a maximal degree?

However, though we think that a direct positive answer to any of these questions is too quick, we also think they are on to something relevant. Interestingly, Smedslund seems to have hinted at similar ideas when arguing not only that in so far as treatments can be generally characterized at all, they involve features that can be derived from PL (2012c, p. 301), but also that as both the assertions of PL and the assertions of psychoanalytic theories are couched in the intentional idiom of wants, beliefs and feelings, psychoanalytic descriptions are often merely slightly more complicated formulations of the assertions of PL (2004, p. 21). Putting aside the questions of which formulations are most complicated, the psychoanalytic models, or semi-formal axioms and theorems, we believe that both perspectives might be relevant for recognizing practically relevant relations between the properties of the person and the relevant circumstances.

However, before explaining how and why we think the three abovementioned questions cannot be answered positively without further qualifications, it would be inappropriate not to mention Smedslund's Norwegian colleague Waldemar Rognes (1996) whose significant work on PL is unfortunately not accessible for readers unfamiliar with Norwegian. However, it is relevant for our purposes for two reasons. Firstly, because Rognes' seminal arguments that conducting empirical research to test the validity of several clinically relevant psychological models and perspectives will be no less pseudo-empirical than testing many other psychological theories. Secondly, for his seminal demonstrations of how various assertions of already established psychotherapy perspectives may be deductively derived from the axioms of (PL), e.g. Well's (Wells 1997) cognitive model of social phobia (Rognes 2007a), as well as Killingmo's (1999) psychoanalytic listening perspective (Rognes 1999) and Killingmo's (1997) suggestions of a so-called rule of abstinence (Rognes 2006).

Thinking About Non-Lawful Phenomena

However, though we agree with Rognes and Smedslund that assertions of psychoanalytic theories are not always in need of empirical validation from statistically based research designs, we also think that they are not thereby necessarily common sense. Moreover, though empirical inquiry may not be needed for the justification of these theories, we do think that empirical inquiry may have a role to play for improving and enriching our thoughts, and perhaps even initiate our very first thoughts about what the theories describe. This seems to be in line with Smedslund's claim that empirical research may provide relevant food for thought, and perhaps, needless to say, qualitative research with case studies has as such been the backbone of psychoanalytic theory. Interestingly, Smedslund (2012a, p. 668) has raised the related question: "Is it possible that some persons do not rely on all the axioms [of PL] in some situations?" Yes, we do not only think that this is possible but pace Smedslund (cf. Lindstad 2020b), we also think that it is possible that some persons (psychotherapists and patients alike) will never come to take all of PL for granted (i.e. all assertions derivable from the axioms of PL). This may be because one has simply not thought of this yet, either because it has not yet been *deduced* from what one already knows, or because it has not yet been needed to think of these aspects for explaining something, for instance, something one has observed in a clinical setting. This latter kind of reasoning is often called *inference to the best explanation* or *abduction* (Douven 2017).

Relatedly, what the psychoanalytic thought models are about, may never be taken for granted by anyone, although they are true descriptions of the dispositional properties of persons. As such, what these models account for may only rarely be manifested again, if ever manifested. Arguably, this is also the case for many assertions of PL. For instance, though Smedslund (2012b, p. 649) has relied on his analysis of the concept of trust for arguing that it is necessary for the bricoleur to build a trusting relationship with clients, and that part of this must involve *caring* for the clients, he has also been clear that this is not enough. Allegedly, the client must also experience the therapist as *understanding*, as having relevant *know-how*, as having *control* and as being *autonomous*. However, as argued by Lindstad (2020a, b), also when these further conditions are not yet in place, experiencing the therapist as caring still disposes of the clients towards trusting the therapist. Thus, that such a trusting relationship is not (yet) established, does not mean that the client's experience of the therapist as caring is psychologically impotent, and knowing about this could be helpful for the bricoleur trying to put the other relevant conditions in place so that the relevant trust could emerge. Probably, Smedslund had something similar in mind when arguing that this is knowledge of strategy rather than of laws governing the psychological content (Smedslund 2009, p. 792). However, as noted earlier (section "Don't Throw Causality Out Along with Humeanism") there is a crucial difference between his understanding and ours at this point. We agree with Smedslund (2004, p. 90) that the idea of psychological laws is incompatible with an apt emphasis on Dilthey's notion of Verstehen, and thus that the idea that everyone must act in the same way under given circumstances as if by some natural law, is flawed. However, pace Smedslund, that there are no causal laws for the bricoleur to fall back on, does not mean (cf. Lindstad 2020a) that knowledge about causal relations is psychologically irrelevant. It only means that the Humean conceptions of causality must be replaced by dispositionalism.

Interestingly, this point is anticipated by Smedslund's frequent use of ceteris paribus clauses ("all else being equal"), e.g. "if no other wants and beliefs intervene"

(Smedslund 1997, p. 25–26) and "and no other factors intervene" (p. 33–40). The point is also anticipated in several assertions suggested by Rognes' (1996) when he spoke of *tendencies* in relation to his seminal work on "The Psycho-logic of Self-esteem", e.g. "Any person has a *tendency* to avoid describing and talking about the negative aspects of one's self-concept" (p. 303, our translation and italics). The two features may even be aptly combined, e.g. "If a person (P) has a negative self-concept, *and no other circumstances intervene*, then P will *tend* to perceive and think about those aspects of other's behaviour that concern whether or not they care for P, and/or respect P, and/or understand P, and/or allow for P's autonomy, and this *tendency* will increase in proportion to the negative valency of P's self-concept" (p. 208–211, our italics[5]). These conditional claims are certainly about "Verstehen" and human meaning-making, as they concern the way P may understand and make sense of herself. However, though the use of the ceteris paribus phrases indicate that the Humean causal paradigm of "if A then always B" is inappropriate because the conditionals describe features of P and her surroundings that may be prevented, this does not mean that the conditionals defy a causal reading. Rather, that the conditionals describe something that might be prevented, shows the dispositional character of the causes involved. Thus, that the causes have a *tendential* nature (Mumford and Anjum 2011) is perfectly compatible with Smedslund's (2004, p. 54) argument that the traditional understanding of causality as characterized by the paradigm of "if A then always B" is unfit for psychology.

If these arguments are up to something, they may have substantial implications for the understanding of what clinically relevant competency is. On the one hand, we agree with Smedslund (2009, 2015, 2016) that the prevailing portrayal of psychotherapy as the systematic use of psychological knowledge in such a way as it is with statistical probability leads to expected change (e.g. Kennair et al. 2014; Baker et al. 2008) is utterly misleading. Relatedly, we also agree with Rognes (1996, p. 98, our translation) that to the extent that practice may improve by increased clinical experience, this cannot be the result of precarious *induction* from the unavoidably limited and biased experience of any individual therapist. Indeed, one does not necessarily get wiser from having more experience. Rather, we agree with Rognes that clinical experience may provide a relevant "food for thought", that is, it may be a resource for further relevant reflection. However, Smedslund's and Rognes' insistence that such reflection can only be concerned about conceptual relations and not causal ones are too limited, and furthermore, as we have argued earlier, it depends upon a flawed Humean conception of causality. Thus, practically relevant reflection may also, and perhaps more often, be concerned with clarifying possible relations between the general dispositions of persons, unique dispositional properties emerging from individual experiences, and the properties of the unique and complex contexts that persons are part of.

---

[5] The translation was suggested by Rognes as part of his plans to publish a book in English extending on his doctoral thesis (Rognes 1996). The translation combines Theorem 11.3, 11.5, 11.7, 11.10 and 11.11 in the thesis which contains an extensive summary in English.

Moreover, though we acknowledge Smedslund's and Rognes' efforts to demonstrate the possibility that such assertions (theorems) may be *deduced* from other such assertions (axioms and/or theorems), we also acknowledge the earlier critique of Smedslund by Salvatore and Valsiner (2010, see also Valsiner 2012; Salvatore 2020), invoking the relevance of *abductive* reasoning. The abductive inference is often thought of as attempts to find the best explanation for some unexplained specific phenomenon either by adding and/or by modifying one's assumptions with the aim of preserving consistency. Thus, abduction can be seen as an extension of induction in the direction of hypothesized deductions (if something is observed, but cannot be explained, thinking about a new feature could explain it). For instance, if the trust is not found, and the experience of care is in place, the lack of trust may be may explained by the lack of experiencing understanding. Or if P's excessive concern about whether other persons are respectful or not, cannot be explained by actual disrespect, it might be because P's negative self-concept involves the belief that he is not respectable, and that other people will also think so. Such a disposition could in other contexts perhaps also explain why P sometimes avoids other people and in other circumstances furiously expresses that he hates them etc. (Rognes 1996).

Indeed, this possibility of abductive reasoning from unique cases to general principles that could help explain the emergence of unique psychological phenomena does not only seem compatible with Rognes' (1996) abovementioned critique of the prevailing emphasis on precarious empirical induction, but it also agrees with his proposal that clinical experience may provide practically relevant "food for thought". As mentioned, this is also in line with the traditional understanding of psychoanalytic theories as based on psychoanalysts' reflections on experiences from clinical work with unique patients: Psychoanalytic theory building has almost always begun with single-case studies (McLeoud 2010). However, as may have become clear from our discussions, the meta-theoretical understanding of what kind of models the psychoanalytic ones are, and thus of their scientific and pragmatic status, need further advancement. Despite the growing concern among psychoanalysts to tests their models via RCTs, quasi-experiments and other statistically supported empirical research methods, and notwithstanding that several psychoanalytic models now have been put to such test (de Maat et al. 2013; Leichsenring et al. 2015; Steinert et al. 2017), the nature of the properties that the notions and assertions of psychoanalytic theories refer to imply not only that it is more complex to test them via quantitative empirical research, but it is not needed.

There is now a lot of research that has aimed to test psychoanalytic notions and theories empirically (for an overview see Andersen et al. 1995; Westen 1999; Bornstein 2005; Solms 2018). However, such testing is complex both because the metaphoric quality of many psychoanalytic concepts are not easily converted into operational definitions needed for replicated empirical estimates, and because the terminology (vocabulary) that is used to express the concepts of the theory are meant to describe individual and unique features of persons rather than matters relevant on an average group level. Our conjecture, however, is that revealing the dispositional nature of many of the properties that the psychoanalytic concepts and thought models refer to, may also reveal that many attempts to test psychoanalytic theories empirically will be pseudo-empirical. As argued by Lindstad (2020a) this is in line with dispositionalism as it implies not only that RCTs and other kinds of correlational studies are rarely sufficient, but they are also not necessary for clarifying causal relations. Even before any causal effects have emerged, we may gain knowledge of relevant causal relations and mechanisms by reflecting systematically on the possible and impossible interplay of various dispositional properties. Statistical evidence is thus not needed if we already understand the mechanisms involved (cf. Anjum and Mumford 2018b). For example, we may know that windows *might* break when, say, books are thrown at them, simply by reflecting upon the possible interplay of the properties of books, throwing and windows. And if we already know about human vulnerability, there is no need to test empirically whether someone *may* become anxious when together with someone they experience as unpredictable. However, we also know that these are only tendencies. There is no unpreventable law to be found that windows break whenever books are thrown at them, or that all children having unpredictable parents will become anxious; say, the children may feel safe in the context of their grandparents, they may believe they are stronger or more competent than their parents, etc. Nevertheless, we may know independently of correlational studies that we should avoid being unpredictable if we want to deserve our children's trust.

To the extent that these considerations are up to something, the prevailing attempts to generalize by statistically based inductive generalization are unwarranted, and the need for deductive and abductive alternatives is urgent. This implies that the traditional understanding of psychoanalytic perspectives as based upon experiences of clinical encounters must be broadened so as to acknowledge the relevance of theoretical elaborations that can be pushed to a level of reflection that may become removed from direct clinical experience (Green 2005, pp. 9–10). According to Green (2005), psychoanalytic theory cannot invoke experience as a raw fact to be reported naively, and thus, a mode of *clinical thinking* is needed that consider psychological phenomena from the angle of a specific causality that gives meaning to the movements, developments and transformations that offer themselves to psychoanalytic listening (p. 9). We are inclined to agree, but think the point can be made more precise: Psycho-analytic thought models are pragmatically relevant in the sense that they are concerned with dispositional relations that might be, but are not necessarily, manifested, and might be clarified by deductive and/or abductive reasoning.

Recognizing and Clarifying Misunderstandings

However, how does this relate to Smedslund's so-called a-theoretical stance? How to ensure that such theoretical elaborations will not stand in the way and distort the necessary process of getting to know about the relevant unique properties of persons? As the only way to get to know a unique client is to enter the interaction with him or her with an open, maximally unprejudiced attitude (Smedslund 2012b,

p. 649), how could clinical thinking ever become practically relevant? Moreover, one may wonder how much time psychotherapists should spend on getting to grips with thought models that concerns dispositional properties that may only rarely be manifested (if ever). The answer is twofold: Not too much, and not too little. Not so much that we do not get out of our armchairs to meet real people, and not so little that we never pull back to check for other possibilities than that our first impressions are correct.

Smedslund's (2012c, p. 299) characterization of PL as a kind of "subjective unconscious" seems related to his understanding of PL as a shared common sense. He has even considered it likely that part of this knowledge reflects a shared inborn disposition to understand persons in a certain way (2012a, p. 658), as if PL was a kind of implicit and unreflective grammar that people rarely knew about, but that they could not avoid taking for granted. However, Smedslund has also wondered whether it is possible not to rely on all the axioms of PL in some situations (2012a, p. 668). We are glad he did, because, if the bricoleur's reliance on PL is nothing more than acting by way of a human inborn habit we cannot evade, how can we know whether this purportedly shared habitus is really in touch with what is actually true about persons? The epistemological ramifications of this issue are discussed by Lindstad (2020b). Here, our focus is rather the clinically related question of whether the bricoleur relies on the axioms of PL simply because he cannot help it. However, it is one thing to demand (Smedslund 2012c, p. 300) that what PL describes should be correct about persons, it is quite another to demand that they refer to how any person automatically conceives of persons (p. 297). We have no quarrels with the former requirement, but though we (cf. Lindstad 2020b) do not deny the possibility that PL may amount to common sense, neither do we deny the possibility that persons do not always rely upon all of it. For all we know, people may never have experienced these aspects directly, nor have they ever thought of them as the best possible explanation for anything (abduction), nor as something that follows from something else they take for granted (deduction). However, though this may not always have happened, does not mean that it cannot happen.

Thus, we are reluctant about Smedslund's description of the bricoleur as someone who automatically relies upon all PL axioms in all situations and who, simply by being a person, takes the entire system of PL (axioms and theorems) for granted as common sense. This is also why we think the tripartite set of questions presented (in section "Can the Bricoleur NOT Make Use of Psychoanalytic Thought Models?") cannot be answered positively. What matters is not whether PL is common sense, but whether it makes sense to rely upon it, and if so, in what sense. However, in line with Smedslund's (1988p. vii; 2012c, p. 301) characterization of PL as the result of a process of explicating, systematizing and organizing psychologically relevant information, we think Rognes (1996, pp. 406–408) was up to something when arguing that the bricoleur may gain *interpretational degrees of freedom* through such a process of clarifying the relations between psychologically relevant phenomena. In line with Smedslund's (2009, p. 791) apt reminder of not jumping to conclusions in clinical settings and to patiently let new impressions organize into a coherent picture (2012b, p. 649), Rognes differentiated the bricoleur's reliance on PL from blind, spontaneous, immediate and unreflective interpretations and interventions. Accordingly, he argued that such an explication process may provide the bricoleur with a reflective overview of various possibilities that might become actualized in concrete situations, and even sometimes of possibilities for change that must be followed for reaching certain goals. We would like to add that such a clarification process may also strengthen an apt attitude of not knowing and a related sensitivity for considering more relevant possibilities than one's immediate first impressions. As such, the kind of explicatory process emphasized by Smedslund and Rognes may contribute to calibrate our human capacity for understanding, by strengthening our abilities to clarify misunderstandings.

To the extent that Smedslund's and Rognes' presentations can be reconciled in line with our synoptic discussion earlier, we are prone to argue that their views are compatible with our account of psychoanalytic thought models. However, in line with our abovementioned discussions, there are some aspects of Smedslund's and Rognes's accounts that we have deliberately left out in the presentation earlier, as we think they must be revised and supplemented. First, cf. Salvatore and Valsiner (2010), the process of explicating, systematizing and organizing psychologically relevant information about possible (and impossible) relations between properties of persons must not only include deductions but also abductive reasoning. Moreover, cf. Lindstad (2020a), many of these relations are not conceptual, but causal in the sense that they concern dispositions. Also, cf. Lindstad (2020b), it is not so relevant that the knowledge in question is common sense as that it makes sense.

Conclusions and Questions for Future Research

To the extent that psychoanalytic thought models can be supported either by deductive or abductive reasoning, they might provide valuable resources for the bricoleur's proclaimed openness to use whatever is at hand. This point may be extended to most, if not all, psychotherapy perspectives, models and theories. The prevailing idea that the proper way to uncover relevant causes is to observe their regular effects, has thrown hundreds of clinically relevant perspectives, models and theories into rivalry, needlessly competing for the best results on an average level. However, as randomization procedures do not take individual experiences sufficiently into account, information about aspects that are relevant in each case is inevitably lost. Thus, in the ever-evolving unique and vastly complex contexts of psychotherapy, rather than to misconstrue psychotherapy models as competing hypotheses of regular causal relations between isolated variables, they are better characterized as compatible and/or overlapping attempts to put possible relations between individual and general dispositions of persons into words. At present, Bernardi (2003, p. 126) is still right that it is not clear to what extent the wide varieties of psychoanalytic theories coincide, are incommensurable, or contradict or complement each other. However, this seems to be no less the case for psychotherapy perspectives that are not of a psychoanalytic origin. If this is correct, a great amount of integrative theoretical work remains to be done, and for this aim, projects similar to or related to Smedslund's seminal work on PL are highly relevant (cf. Rognes 2007b; Bergner 2004). The further upshot is that such integrative work will highlight the relevance of a capacity that is not only pivotal for psychological research, but also vital for any psychotherapy process: To take part in, and to study unique psychotherapy processes, requires that we take advantage of *our capacity for critically calibrating our knowledge of possible and impossible relations* between the properties of persons through thorough reflection.

References

Adorno, T. W. (1973) Negative Dialectics. New York: Seabury Press.

American Psychological Association APA Task Force on Evidence Based Practice. (2006). Evidence-based practice in psychology. *American Psychologist, 61*, 271–285.

Andersen, S. M., Glassman, N. S., Chen, S., & Cole, S. W. (1995). Transference in social perception: The role of chronic accessibility in significant-other representations. *Journal of Personality and Social Psychology, 69*(1), 41–57.

Anderson, H., & Goolishian, H. (1992). The client is the expert: A not-knowing approach to therapy. In S. McNamee & K. Gergen (Eds.), *Social construction and the therapeutic process Newbury Park* (pp. 25–39). CA: Sage.

Anjum, R. (2016). Evidence based or person centred? An ontological debate. *Journal of Evaluation in Clinical Practice: Special Issue on the Philosophy of Medicine and Health Care*, 421–429.

Anjum, R. L., & Mumford, S. (2018a). *What tends to be: The Philosophy of dispositional modality*. London: Routledge.

Anjum, R. L., & Mumford, S. (2018b). *Causation in science: On the methods of scientific discovery*. USA: Oxford University Press.

Baker, T. B., McFall, R. M., & Shoham, V. (2008). Current status and future prospects of clinical psychology: Toward a scientifically principled approach to mental and behavioral health care. *Psychological Science in the Public Interest, 9*, 67–103. https://doi.org/10.1111/j.1539-6053.2009.01036.x.

Bergner, R. (2004). An integrative framework for psychopathology and psychotherapy. *New Ideas in Psychology, 22*, 127–141.

Bernardi, R. (2003). What kind of evidence makes the analyst change his or her theoretical and technical ideas. In M. Leuzinger-Bohleber, A. U. Dreher, & J. Canestri (Eds.), *Pluralism and unity: Methods of research in psychoanalysis*. London: The International Psychoanalytical Association.

Bion, W. (1962). *Learning from experience*. London: Heinemann.

Bion, W. (1967). Notes on memory and desire. In E. R. Spillius (Ed.), *Melanie Klein today* (Vol. Vol. 2). London: Routledge.

Bollas, C. (1989). *Forces of destiny: Psychoanalysis and human idiom*. London: Free Association Press.

Bornstein, R. F. (2005). Reconnecting psychoanalysis to mainstream psychology: Challenges and opportunities. *Psychoanalytic Psychology, 22*(3), 323–340.

Britton, R. (1989). The missing link: parental sexuality in the Oedipus complex. In R. Britton, M. Feldman, E. O'Shaughnessy, & J. Steiner (Eds.), *The Oedipus complex today*. London: Karnac Books.

Cartwright, N., & Hardie, J. (2012). *Evidence-based policy: A practical guide to doing it better*. Oxford: Oxford University Press.

Danziger, K. (1990). *Constructing the subject: Historical origins of psychological research.* New York: Cambridge University Press.
deMaat, S., de Jonghe, F., de Kraker, R., Leichsenring, F., Abbass, A., Luyten, P., Barber, J. P., Van, R., & Dekker, J. (2013). The current state of the empirical evidence for psychoanalysis: A meta-analytic approach. *Harvard Review of Psychiatry, 21*(3), 103–137.
Dilthey, W. (1894). Ideen über eine beschreibende und zergliedernde Psychologie. In *Gesammelte Scriften, Band V. Die geistige Welt.* Göttingen, Germany: Vandenhoeck and Rupert.
Douven, I (2017) Abduction. In Edward N. Zalta (Ed.) *The Stanford Encyclopedia of Philosophy.* (Summer 2017 Edition). https://plato.stanford.edu/archives/sum2017/entries/abduction/.
Freud, S. (1900). The interpretation of dreams. *The Standard edition of the complete psychological works of Sigmund Freud* (Vol. V). The Hogarth Press and the Institute of Psychoanalysis, London.
Freud, S. (1910). A special type of choice of object made by men (contributions to the psychology of love I). The standard edition of the complete psychological works of Sigmund Freud (Vol. XI). The Hogarth Press and the Institute of Psychoanalysis. London.
Gabbard, G. (1995). Countertransference: The emerging common ground. *The International Journal of Psychoanalysis, 76*(3), 475–485.
Green, A. (2003). The pluralism of sciences and clinical thinking. In M. Leuzinger-Bohleber, A. U. Dreher, & J. Canestri (Eds.), *Pluralism and unity: Methods of research in psychoanalysis* (pp. 26–44). Abingdon: Routledge.
Green, A. (2005). *Psychoanalysis: A paradigm for clinical thinking.* London: Free Association Books.
Groff, R., & Greco, J. (Eds.). (2013). *Powers and capacities in philosophy: The New Aristotelianism.* New York: Routledge.
Hollon, S. D. (2006). Randomized controlled trials. In J. C. Norcross, L. Beutler, & R. F. Levant (Eds.), *Evidence-based practices in mental health: Debate and dialogue on the fundamental questions* (pp. 96–105). Washington, DC: American Psychological Association.
Hume, D. (1739/1978). In L. A. Selby-Bigge & P. H. Niddich (Eds.), *A treatise of human nature.* Oxford: Oxford University Press/Clarendon Press.
Hume, D. (1748/1993). An enquiry concerning human understanding. In E. Steinberg (Ed.), *Human nature* (2nd ed.). Indianapolis/Cambridge: Hackett Publishing Company.
Kennair, L.E.O., Aarre, T. F., Kennair, T. W., & Bugge, P. (2002). Evidence-based mental health—The scientific foundation of clinical psychology and psychiatry. Scipolicy™ The Journal of Science & Health Policy, 2(1).
Kennair, L. E. O., Hagen, R., & R. (Eds.). (2014). *Psykoterapi.* Gyldendal Norsk Forlag: Tilnærminger og metoder.
Kerry, R., Eriksen, T., Andersen, S. A., Lie, N., Mumford, S. D., & Anjum, R. L. (2012). Causation and evidence-based practice: An ontological review. *Journal of Evaluation in Clinical Practice: Special Issue on the Philosophy of Medicine and Health Care, 18*(5), 1006–1012.
Killingmo, B. (1997). The so-called rule of abstinence revisited. *The Scandinavian Psychoanalytic Review, 20*(2), 144–159.
Killingmo, B. (1999). A psychoanalytic listening perspective in a time of pluralism. *The Scandinavian Psychoanalytic Review, 22*(2), 151–171.
Klein, M. (1946). Notes on some schizoid mechanisms. In *Envy and gratitude and other works 1946–1963.* New York: Delacorte Press.
Leichsenring, F., Leweke, F., Klein, S., & Steinert, C. (2015). The empirical status of psychodynamic psychotherapy—An update: Bambi's alive and kicking. *Psychotherapy and Psychosomatics, 84*(3), 129–148.
Lindstad, T. G. (2020a). The relevance of dispositionalism for psychotherapy and psychotherapy research. In R. L. Anjum, S. Copeland, & E. Rocca (Eds.), *Rethinking causality, complexity and evidence for the unique patient.* Springer Publ. (forthcoming).
Lindstad, T. G. (2020b). A priori afterthoughts: Continuing the dialogue on psycho-logic (Chapter 12, this volume). In T. G. Lindstad, E. Stänicke, & J. Valsiner (Eds.), *Respect for thought: Jan Smedslund's legacy for psychology* (pp. 195–220). New York: Springer.

Mahler, M., Pine, F., & Bergman, A. (1975). *The psychological birth of the human infant*. New York: Basic Books.

Marmodoro, A. (Ed.). 2010. *The metaphysics of powers. Their grounding and their manifestations*. Routledge.

McLeod, J. (2010). *Case study research in counselling and psychotherapy*. London: Sage Publishing.

Mumford, S., & Anjum, R. L. (2011). *Getting causes from powers*. Oxford University Press.

Mumford, S., & Anjum, R. L. (2017a). Mutual manifestation and Martin's two triangles. In J. Jacobs (Ed.), *Putting powers to work: Causal powers in contemporary metaphysics*. 92–109. https://www.oxfordscholarship.com/view/10.1093/oso/9780198796572.001.0001/oso-9780198796572-chapter-6

Mumford, S., & Anjum, R. L. (2017b). Emergence and demergence. In M. P. Paoletti & F. Orilia (Eds.), *Philosophical and scientific perspectives on downward causation*. Routledge.

Rognes, W. (1996). Selvfølelsens Psykologikk. Doktoravhandling. [The Psychologic of Self-esteem. Doctoral Thesis.] SV-fakultetet, Universitetet i Oslo.

Rognes, W. (1999). Klinisk kommunikasjon og psykologikk [Clinical communication and psychologic]. *Impuls. Tidsskrift for psykologi, 53*(1), 20–33.

Rognes, W. (2006). Abstinens og uavhengighet. [Abstinence and independency]. *Impuls. Tidsskrift for psykologi, 60*(1), 74–79.

Rognes, W. (2007a). Well's kognitive modell for sosial fobi: En analyse. [Well's cognitive model of social anxiety; an analysis]. *Psykologisk Tidsskrift, 1*, 40–48.

Rognes, W. (2007b). Terapimangfold og psykologikk, Psykologisk Tidsskrift., *3*, 52–58.

Roth, A., & Fonagy, P. (2005). *What works for whom: A critical review of psychotherapy research* (Sec. ed.). New York: The Guilford Press.

Salvatore, S. (2020). How to avoid throwing the baby out with the bathwater: Abduction is the solution to pseudo-empiricism (Chapter 11, this volume). In T. G. Lindstad, E. Stänicke, & J. Valsiner (Eds.), *Respect for thought: Jan Smedslund's legacy for psychology* (pp. 181–194). New York: Springer.

Salvatore, S., & Valsiner, J. (2010). Between the general and the unique: Overcoming the nomothetic versus idiographic opposition. *Theory & Psychology, 20*(6), 817–833.

Sandler, J. (1983). Reflections on some relations between psychoanalytic concepts and psychoanalytic practice. *International Journal of Psycho-Analysis, 64*, 35–45.

Smedslund, J. (1970). Circular relation between understanding and logic. *Scandinavian Journal of Psychology, 11*, 217–219.

Smedslund, J. (1988). *Psycho-logic*. Heidelberg: Springer-Verlag.

Smedslund, J. (1995). Psychologic: Commonsense and the pseudoempirical. In J. Smith, R. Harre, & L. Van Langenhove (Eds.), *Rethinking psychology* (pp. 196–206). London: Sage.

Smedslund, J. (1997). *The structure of psychological common sense*. Mahwah, NJ: Lawrence Erlbaum Associates.

Smedslund, J. (2004). *Dialogues about a new psychology*. Chagrin Falls, OH: Taos Institute Publications.

Smedslund, J. (2009). The mismatch between current research methods and the nature of psychological phenomena: What researchers must learn from practitioners. *Theory & Psychology, 19*(6), 778–794.

Smedslund, J. (2012a). What follows from what we all know about human beings. *Theory & Psychology, 22*, 658–668.

Smedslund, J. (2012b). The bricoleur model of psychotherapeutic practice. *Theory & Psychology, 22*, 643–657.

Smedslund, J. (2012c). Psycho-logic: Some thoughts and after-thoughts. *Scandinavian Journal of Psychology, 55*, 295–302.

Smedslund, J. (2015). The value of experiments in psychology. In J. Martin, J. Slugarman, & K. Slaney (Eds.), *The Wiley handbook of theoretical and philosophical psychology:*

Methods, approaches, and new directions for social sciences (pp. 359–373). Nueva York: Wiley-Blackwell.

Smedslund, J. (2016). Practicing psychology without an empirical evidence-base. *New Ideas in Psychology, 43*, 50–56.

Solms, M. (2018). The neurobiological underpinnings of psychoanalytic theory and therapy. *Frontiers in Behavioral Neuroscience*. https://doi.org/10.3389/fnbeh.2018.00294.

Stänicke, E., & Stänicke, L. I. (2014). Psykoanalytisk terapi. In L. E. O. Kennair & R. Hagen (Eds.), *Psykoterapi – tilnærminger og metoder*. Oslo: Gyldendal Akademiske.

Steinert, C., Munder, T., Rabung, S., Hoyer, J. & Leichsenring, F. (2017). Psychodynamic therapy: As efficacious as other empirically supported treatments? A metaanalysis testing equivalence of outcomes. Am J Psychiatry 1;174(10):943–953.

Stänicke, E., Strømme, H., Krisitiansen, S., & Stänicke, L. I. (2019). *Klinisk tenkning i et psykoanalytisk perspektiv*. Oslo: Gyldendal Akademiske.

Toulmin, S., & Leary, D. (1985). The cult of empiricism in psychology, and beyond. In S. Koch & D. Leary (Eds.), *A century of psychology as a science*. New York: McGraw-Hill Book Company.

Valsiner, J. (2012). *A Guided Science: History of psychology in the mirror of its making*. New Brunswick, NJ: Transaction Publishers.

Valsiner, J. (2014a). Needed for cultural psychology: Methodology in a new key. *Culture & Psychology, 20*(1), 3–30.

Valsiner, J. (2014b). *An invitation to cultural psychology*. London: Sage.

Valsiner, J. (2014c). Breaking the arrows of causality: The idea of catalysis in the making. In K. R. Cabell & J. Valsiner (Eds.), *The catalyzing mind: Beyond models of causality* (pp. 17–32). New York, NY: Springer.

Valsiner, J. (2017). *From methodology to methods in human psychology*. Springer.

Valsiner, J., & Brinkmann, S. (2016). Beyond the "Variables": Developing metalanguage for psychology. In S. H. Klempe & R. Smith (Eds.), *Centrality of history for theory construction in psychology* (Annals of Theoretical Psychology) (Vol. 14, pp. 75–90).

Wallerstein. (1984). Second day. *Bulletin of the Anna Freud Centre, 7*(3), 186–212.

Wells, A. (1997). *Cognitive therapy for anxiety disorders. A practice manual and conceptual guidelines*. New York: Wiley.

Westen, D. (1999). The scientific status of unconscious processes: Is Freud really dead? *Journal of American Psychoanalytic Association, 47*(4), 1061–1106.

A Smedslund Bibliography

1952

– A critical evaluation of the current status of learning theory. *Nordisk Psykologi's Monografiserie*, 2.

1953

– The problem of "What is learned?" *Psychological Review, 60*, 157–158.

1954

– Om valideringen av dybdepsykologiske tester. (On the validation of depth-psychological tests.) *Nordisk Psykologi, 6*, 113–115.

1955

– The epistemological foundations of behaviorism. A critique. *Acta Psychologica, 11*, 412–431.
– *Multiple-probability learning. An inquiry into the origins of perception*. Oslo: Universitetsforlaget, (Doctoral thesis)

1959

– Apprentissage des notions de la conservation et de la transitivite du poids. *Etudes D'Epistemologie Genetique*, *9*, 85–124.

T. G. Lindstad et al. (eds.), *Respect for Thought*, Theory and History in the Human and Social Sciences, https://doi.org/10.1007/978-3-030-43066-5

1960

- Review of: K. B. Madsen: Theories of motivation. A comparative study of modern theories of motivation. Copenhagen: Munksgaard, 1959. *Nordisk Psykologi, 12,* 319–321.
- Transitivity of preference patterns as seen by preschool children. *Scandinavian Journal of Psychology*, *1*, 49–54.

1961

- Intuitive accuracy at the verbal level. *Acta Psychologica, 18*, 306–316.
- The utilization of probabilistic cues after 1100 and 4800 stimulus presentations. *Acta Psychologica*, *18*, 383–386.
- The acquisition of conservation of substance and weight in children. I. Introduction. *Scandinavian Journal of Psychology*, *2*, 11–20.
- The acquistion of conservation of substance and weight in children. II. External reinforcement of conservation of weight and of the operations of addition and subtraction. *Scandinavian Journal of Psychology, 2*, 71–84.
- The acquisition of conservation of substance and weight in children. III. Extinction of conservation of weight acquired "normally" and by means of empirical controls on a balance. *Scandinavian Journal of Psychology, 2*, 85–87.
- The acuisition of conservation of substance and weight in children. IV. Attempt at extinction of the visual components of the weight concept. *Scandinavian Journal of Psychology, 2*, 153–155.
- The acquisition of conservation of substance and weight in children. V. Practice in conflict situations without external reinforcement. *Scandinavian Journal of Psychology, 2*, 156–160.
- The acquisition of conservation of substance and weight in children. VI. Practice on continuous vs. discontinuous material in problem situations without external reinforcement. *Scandinavian Journal of Psychology, 2*, 203–210.

1962

- The acquisition of conservation of substance and weight in children. VII. Conservation of discontinuous quantity and the operations of adding and taking away. *Scandinavian Journal of Psychology, 3*, 69–77.

1963

- The effect of observation on children's representation of the spatial orientation of a water surface. *Journal of Genetic Psychology, 102*, 195–201.
- The acquisition of transitivity of weight in five-to-seven-year-old children. *Journal of Genetic Psychology, 102*, 245–255.
- The development of concrete transitivity of length in children. *Child Development*, *34*, 389–405.
- The concept of correlation in adults. *Scandinavian Journal of Psychology, 4*, 165–173.
- Patterns of experience and the acquisition of conservation of length. *Scandinavian Journal of Psychology, 4*, 257–264.

1965

- The development of transitivity of length: a comment on Braine's reply. *Child Development,* 36, 577–580.

1966

- Constancy and conservation: A comparison of the systems of Brunswik and Piaget. In Hammond, K. R. (Ed.) *The psychology of Egon Brunswik. New York:* Holt, Rinehart and Winston. 382–404.
- The social origins of decentration. In Bresson, F. and Montmolin. M. de (Eds.) *Psychologie et Epistemologie Genetiques: Themes Piagetiens.* Paris: Dunod.
- Performance on measurement and pseudomeasurement tasks by five- to seven-year-old children. *Scandinavian Journal of Psychology, 7,* 81–92.
- Note on learning, contingency, and clinical experience. *Scandinavian Journal of Psychology, 7,* 265–266.
- Microanalysis of concrete reasoning. I. The difficulty of some combinations of addition and subtraction of one unit. *Scandinavian Journal of Psychology, 7,* 145–156.
- Microanalysis of concrete reasoning. II. The effect of number of transformations and non-redundant elements, and some variations in procedure. *Scandinavian Journal of Psychology, 7,* 157–163.
- Microanalysis of concrete reasoning. III. Theoretical overview. *Scandinavian Journal of Psychology, 7,* 164–167.

1967

- Determinants of performance on double classification tasks. I. Effect of covered vs. uncovered materials, labelling vs. perceptual matching, and age. *Scandinavian Journal of Psychology, 8,* 88–96.
- Determinants of performance on double classification tasks. II. Effects of direct perception, and of words with specific, general, and no reference. *Scandinavian Journal of Psychology, 8,* 97–101.
- Noen refleksjoner om Rorschachtesten. (Some reflections about the Rorschach-test). *Nordisk Psykologi, 19,* 203–209.
- Psykologi (Psychology). Oslo: *Universitetsforlaget.*

1968

- Mental processes involved in rapid logical reasoning. *Scandinavian Journal of Psychology, 9,* 187–205.
- Conservation and resistance to extinction: a comment on Hall and Simpson's article. *Merrill-Palmer Quarterly of Behavior and Development, 14,* 211–214.

1969

- Psychological diagnostics. *Psychological Bulletin, 71,* 237–248.
- Meanings, implications and universals: towards a psychology of man. *Scandinavian Journal of Psychology, 10,* 1–15.

1970

- Kan man utdanne psykologer ? (Can one train psychologists?). *Nordisk Psykologi, 22,* 14–22.
- Circular relation between understanding and logic. *Scandinavian Journal of Psychology, 11,* 217–219.

1971

- Diagonal between Bruner and Piaget. Review of Olson, D. R. Cognitive Development: The Child's Acquisition of Diagonality. New York: Academic Press. *Contemporary Psychology.*

1972

- *Becoming a Psychologist. Theoretical Foundations for a Humanistic Psychology.* Oslo: Oslo University Press.

1973

- Eine humanistische Position in der Psychologie. In Edelstein, W. und Hopf, D. (Eds.) *Bedingungen des Bildungsprozesses.* Stuttgart: Ernst Klett Verlag. 489–501.

1974

- Om arbeidsmåter i grupper. (On ways of working in groups). *Tidsskrift for Norsk Psykologforening, 1974, 11,* No 6, 3–17.

1975

- Are the technical rules in group work valuable? In Uchtenhagen, A., Battegay, R. and Friedemann, A. (Eds.) *Group Therapy and Social Environment. Proceedings of the 5th International Congress for Group Psychotherapy, Zurich August 19 to 24, 1973.* Bern, Stuttgart, Wien: Verlag Hans Huber. 435–440.

1976

- Hvorfor jeg ikke vil bruke tester. (Why I do not want to use tests.) *Tidsskrift for Norsk Psykologforening, 1976, 13,* 25–28.
- Om forholdet mellom teori og empiri i psykologien. (On the relationship between theory and data in psychology). *Tidsskrift for Norsk Psykologforening, 1976, 13,* 2–10.

1977

- Piaget's psychology in practice. *British Journal of Educational Psychology, 1977, 47,* 1–6. The same article has also appeared in Norwegian as: Piagets psykologi i praksis. *Norsk Pedagogisk Tidsskrift, 61,* 52–59., and in French as: La psychologie de Piaget et la pratique. *Bulletin de Psychologie, 30,* 364–368.
- Språk og psykologi (Language and psychology). In *Språkvitenskapens forhold til samfunnsvitenskapene.* Konferanserapport. NAVF.

1978

- Bandura's theory of self-efficacy: a set of common sense theorems. *Scandinavian Journal of Psychology, 19*, 1–14.
- Some psychological theories are not empirical: reply to Bandura. *Scandinavian Journal of Psychology, 19, 101–102.*
- Measurement sequences, logical necessity and common sense. *The Behavioral and Brain Sciences, 2, 203–204.*

1979

- Between the analytic and the arbitrary: a case study of psychological research. *Scandinavian Journal of Psychology, 20, 1–12.*

1980

- Analyzing the primary code: from empiricism to apriorism. *In D. R. Olson (Ed.) The social foundations of language and thought: Essays in honor of Jerome S. Bruner*. New York: Norton. 47–73.
- From ordinary to scientific language: reply to Jones. *Scandinavian Journal of Psychology, 21*, 231–233.

1981

- The logic of psychological treatment. *Scandinavian Journal of Psychology, 1981, 22*, 65–77.
- Rationality is a necessary presupposition in psychology. *The Behavioral and Brain Sciences, 4*, 352.

1982

- Common sense as psychosocial reality: a reply to Sjoberg. *Scandinavian Journal of Psychology, 23*, 79–82.
- Seven common sense rules of psychological treatment. *Journal of the Norwegian Psychological Association, 19*, 441–449.
- Men allikevel finnes det grunnregler for behandling: Svar til Hartmann og Havik. (But, nevertheless, there are ground rules for treatment: reply to Hartmann and Havik) *Tidsskrift for Norsk Psykologforening, 19*, 622–625.
- Revising explications of common sense through dialogue: Thirtysix psychological theorems. *Scandinavian Journal of Psychology, 23*, 299–305.

1983

- Er møtet med oss selv en vitenskap? Svar til Asle Hoffarth. (Is meeting with ourselves a science? Reply to Asle Hoffarth). *Tidsskrift for Norsk Psykologforening, 20*, 278–279.
- Reflections of a dialectical existentialist: Two books by Anne-Lise Løvlie on the self and on psychotherapy. *Scandinavian Journal of Psychology, 24*, 251–253.
- Praktisk Psykologi (Practical Psychology). Oslo: *Universitets-forlaget*. Swedish translation, same title, Lund: Studentlitteratur, 1984.

1984

- The invisible obvious: culture in psychology. In Lagerspetz, K. M. J. & Niemi, P. (Eds.) *Psychology in the 1990's*. Amsterdam: Elsevier Science Publishers B. V. 443–452.
- What is necessarily true in psychology ? In J. R. Royce & L. P. Mos (Eds.) *Annals of Theoretical Psychology, 2*, 241–272.
- Psychology cannot take leave of common sense: reply to Tennesen, Vollmer and Wilkes. In J. R. Royce & L. P. Mos (Eds.) *Annals of Theoretical Psychology, 2*, 295–302.

1985

- Necessarily true cultural psychologies. In K. J. Gergen & K. E. Davis (Eds.) *The Social Construction of the Person*. New York: Springer, 73–87.

1986

- The explication of psychological common sense: Implications for the science of psychology. In Barcan Marcus et al., (Eds.) *Logic, Methodology and Philosophy of Science VII*. Elsevier Science Publishers B.V. 481–494.
- How stable is common sense psychology and can it be transcended? Reply to Valsiner. *Scandinavian Journal of Psychology, 27*, 91–94.
- Arbeidsnotater fra et behandlingshjem for ungdom som har misbrukt rusmidler. I. Skjerming vs. behandling. (Work notes from a treatment home for young former drug addicts. I. Sheltering versus treatment.) *Tidsskrift for Norsk Psykologforening, 23*, 645–648.
- Arbeidsnotater fra et behandlingshjem for ungdom som har misbrukt rusmidler. II. To hovedtrekk ved klientenes væremåte. (Work notes from a treatment home for young former drug addicts. II. Two main characteristics of the clients' way of being.) *Tidsskrift for Norsk Psykologforening, 23*, 716–720.
- Arbeidsnotater fra et behandlingshjem for ungdom som har misbrukt rusmidler. III. Samspillet mellom personale og klienter. (Work notes from a treatment home for young former drug addicts. III. The interaction between the staff and the clients.) *Tidsskrift for Norsk Psykologforening, 23*, 721–724.
- Arbeidsnotater fra et behandlingshjem for ungdom som har misbrukt rusmidler. IV. Samspill i forbindelse med brudd på regler. (Work notes from a treatment home for young former drug addicts. IV. Interaction in connection with the breaking of rules.) *Tidsskrift for Norsk Psykologforening, 23*, 785–788.

1987

- Arbeidsnotater fra et behandlingshjem for ungdom som har misbrukt rusmidler. V. Psykologens rolle. (Work notes from a treatment home for young former drug addicts. V. The role of the psychologist.) *Tidsskrift for Norsk Psykologforening, 24*, 28–34.
- Das Beschreiben von Beschreibungen, Erklaeren von Erklaerungen und Vorhersagen von Vorhersagen: paradigmatische Faelle fuer die Psychologie.

Describing descriptions, explaining explanations, and predicting predictions: paradigmatic cases for psychology. In J. Brandtstaedter (Ed.) *Struktur und Erfahrung in der psychologischen Forschung*. Berlin: W. de Gruyter. 159–168.
- Ebbinghaus the illusionist: How psychology came to look like an experimental science. In *Passauer Schriften zur Psychologiegeschichte, 5*, Ebbinghaus-Studien 2., Passau: Passavia Universitaetsverlag. 225–239.
- The epistemic status of interitem correlations in Eysenck's Personality Questionnaire: the a priori versus the empirical in psychological data. *Scandinavian Journal of Psychology, 28*, 42–55.

1988

- *Psycho-Logic*. Heidelberg: Springer-Verlag.
- Fagetiske momenter i forbindelse med psykologers opptreden i media. (Professional-ethical aspects of psychologists' behavior in the media). *Tidsskrift for Norsk Psykologforening, 25,* 242–244.
- Fritz Heider misinterpreted. *Contemporary Psychology, 33*, No. 3, 275.
- Holdning versus handling i fagetikken (Attitude versus action in professional ethics). *Tidsskrift for Norsk Psykologforening, 25*, 770–772.
- What is measured by a psychological measure? *Scandinavian Journal of Psychology, 29*, 148–151.

1989

- The hall of mirrors in psychological theorizing. In I. A. Bjørgen (Ed.) *Basic issues in psychology. A Scandinavian contribution*. Søreidgrend and London: Sigma. 255–261.

1990

- Psychology and psychologic: characterization of the difference. In K. J. Gergen and G. R. Semin (Eds.) *Everyday understanding: social and scientific implications*. London: Sage. 45–63.
- A critique of Tversky & Kahneman's distinction between fallacy and misunderstanding. *Scandinavian Journal of Psychology, 31*, 110–120.

1991

- The psychologic of forgiving. *Scandinavian Journal of Psychology, 32*, 164–176.
- Å sette ord på opplevelser: Forholdet mellom teori og praksis i psykologien. (To label experiences: The relationship between theory and practice in psychology). *Impuls, 45*, 48–52, 62.
- What is psychologic? In Baker, Wm J., van Hezewijk, R., Hyland, M.E., & Terwee, S. (Eds.). *Recent advances in theoretical psychology. Volume 2.* New York: Springer-Verlag, 453–457.
- The pseudoempirical in psychology and the case for psychologic. *Psychological Inquiry, 2*, 325–338. (Target article)

– Psychologic: a technical language for psychology. *Psychological Inquiry, 2,* 376-382. (Author`s response).

1992

– Are Frijda's "Laws of Emotion" empirical? *Cognition and Emotion, 6,* 435–456.
– Psykologikk er et teknisk språk for psykologien: Svar til Sigmund Elgarøy. (Psychologic is a technical language for psychology: reply to Sigmund Elgarøy) *Impuls, 46,* 68–71.

1993

– How shall the concept of anger be defined? *Theory and Psychology, 3,* 5–33.

1994

– Nonempirical and empirical components in the hypotheses off five social psychological experiments. *Scandinavian Journal of Psychology, 35,* 1–15.
– What kind of propositions are set forth in developmental research? Five case studies. *Human Development, 37,* 259–276

1995

– The psycho-logic of action: Reply to Vollmer. *Scandinavian Journal of Psychology, 36,* 232–234.
– Psychologic: Commonsense and the Pseudoempirical. In J. Smith, R. Harre, and L. Van Langenhove (Eds.) *Rethinking Psychology*. London: Sage. 196–206.
– Auxiliary versus theoretical hypotheses and ordinary versus scientific language. *Human Development, 1995, 38,* 174–178.

1996

– Psykologi som vitenskap—dilemmaer og løsninger. (Psychology as science—dilemmas and solutions). *Det Norske Videnskaps-Akademi. Årbok 1995.* 139–151.

1997

– Logikk, virkelighet og generaliserbarhet. (Logic, reality and generalizability). *Tidsskrift for Norsk Psykologforening, 34,* 2, 98–102.
– Is the "psychologic" of trust universal? In S. Niemeier and R. Dirven (Eds) *The language of Emotions: Conceptualization, expression, and theoretical foundation*. Amsterdam: Benjamins, 3–13.
– The ambiguity of covariation: A conceptual note. *Scandinavian Journal of Psychology, 38,* 35–38.
– The forgotten variable of understanding. *Cahiers de Psychologie Cognitive/ Current Psychology of Cognition, 16,* 217–221.
– *The structure of psychological common sense*. Mahwah, NJ: Lawrence Erlbaum.

- Book review: Geir Overskeid og Frode Svartdal (red.) Det ubevisste og moderne vitenskap. Oslo: Ad Notam Gyldendal, 1997. *Tidsskrift for Norsk Psykologforening, 34*, 1016–1017.

1998

- Social representations and psychologic. *Culture & Psychology, 4*, 349–368.
- Hvorfor klinisk forskning og praksis ikke går hånd i hånd. (Why clinical research and practice do not meet). *Tidsskrift for Norsk Psykologforening, 35*, 1090–1095.

1999

- Psykologikk, forskning og praksis. Svar til Geir Overskeid. (Psychologic, research and practice. Reply to Geir Overskeid). *Tidsskrift for Norsk Psykologforening, 36*, 228–231.
- Target article. Psychologic and the study of memory. *Scandinavian Journal of Psychology, 40*, Suppl, 3–17.
- Author's response. Psychologic in dialogue: reply to commentaries. *Scandinavian Journal of Psychology, 40, Suppl*, 123–138.

2001

- Psykoanalyse og psykologikk: kommentar til Killingmo. (Psychoanalysis and psychologic: a commentary to Killingmo). *Tidsskrift for Norsk Psykologforening, 38*, 838–841.
- Amsterdam-symposiet om "Feeling and Emotion": Noen tanker (The Amsterdam symposium on "Feeling and Emotion": Some thoughts.) *Tidsskrift for Norsk Psykologforening, 38,* 1050–1052.

2002

- Følelser er ikke underlagt generelle lover! (Feelings are not governed by general laws!) Svar til Joar Vittersø. *Tidsskrift for Norsk Psykologforening, 39*, 225–227.
- From hypothesis-testing psychology to procedure-testing psychologic. *Review of General Psychology, 6*, No.1, 51–72.
- Selvrefererende inkonsistens (self-referential inconsistency): Sluttreplikk til Vittersø. *Tidsskrift for Norsk Psykologforening, 39*, 633–634.

2003

- Fra psykologi til psykologikk: Vårt fag i forandring. (From psychology to psychologic: Our changing discipline.) *Psykologisk Tidsskrift – NTNU, 6*, 12–14.

2004

- *Dialogues about a New Psychology.* Chagrin Falls, OH: Taos Institute Publications, 2004.

2007

- Kan psykologi være en erfaringsvitenskap? (Can psychology be an empirical science?) *Impuls, 61,* 2, 60–67.

2008

- Har du sluttet å slå din kone? Ja/Nei. Kan psykologisk praksis være evidens-basert? Ja/Nei. (Have you stopped beating your wife? Yes/No. Can psychological practice be evidence-based? Yes/No.) *Tidsskrift for Norsk Psykologforening, 45,* 455–459.
- From Heider to Psycho-Logic. *Social Psychology, 39, 3,* 157–162.

2009

- Fire grunnproblemer for psykologi som erfaringsvitenskap. (Four fundamental problems in psychology as empirical science.) I Gullestad, Killingmo og Magnussen (Eds). *Klinikk og Laboratorium. Psykologi i hundre år.* Oslo: Universitetsforlaget. 75–84.
- I revolusjonens tid. (In the time of revolution). I jubileumsbok for Psykologisk Institutt. I Gullestad, Killingmo og Magnussen (Eds.) *Klinikk og Laboratorium. Psykologi i hundre år.* Oslo: Universitetsforlaget. 251–266.
- The mismatch between current research methods and the nature of psychological phenomena: What researchers must learn from practitioners. *Theory and Psychology, 19,* 6, 1–17.

2011

- Meanings of words and the use of axiomatics in psychological theory. *Journal of Theoretical and Philosophical Psychology, 31,* no. 2, 126–135.

2012

- The bricoleur-model in psychological practice. *Theory & Psychology, 22*, 643–657.
- What follows from what we all know about human beings. *Theory & Psychology, 22*, 658–668.
- Psycho-Logic: Some Thoughts and After-Thoughts. *Scandinavian Journal of Psychology, 53*, 295–302.

2014

- With Ross, L. Research-Based Knowledge in Psychology: What, if anything, is its Incremental Value to the Practitioner? *Integrative Psychological and Behavioral Science, 50*, 185–195. "Nevro"

2015

- Forstavelsen "Nevro"; Pseudoempiri og ideologi? (The Prefix "Neuro"; Pseudoempiricism and Ideology. *Tidsskrift for Norsk Psykologforening, 52,* 6, *2015,* 524–525.

2016

- Why Psychology cannot be an Empirical Science. *Integrative Psychological and Behavioral Science, 50*, 185–195.
- Practicing Psychology without an Empirical Evidence-base. *New Ideas in Psychology, 43,* 50–56.

2017

- Det kommer an på. (It all depends). *Tidsskrift for Norsk Psykologforening, 54,* 3, 403–407.
- Psykologisk empiri er som virvlene i en bekk. (Empirical findings in psychology are like whirls in a stream.) *Tidsskrift for Norsk Psykologforening, 54,* 6, 575.
- Unngår den enkleste forklaringen (Ignoring the most basic explanation). *Tidsskrift for Norsk Psykologforening, Vol 54,* 860–861.
- Ingen katastrofe for psykologien. (No catastrophy for psychology.) *Tidsskrift for Norsk Psykologforening, 54,* 10, 1022–1023.
- Vi prøver igjen: Hvordan arbeider egentlig psykologer? (We try again: How do psychologists really work?) *Tidsskrift for Norsk Psykologforening, 54*, 12, 1202–1203.

2018

- Det vi alle vet. (What we all know.) *Tidsskrift for Norsk Psykologforening, 55,* 6, 534–535.

2019

- Språkanalyse må erstatte empirisk forskning. (Linguistic analysis must replace empirical research.) *Tidsskrift for Norsk Psykologforening, 56*, 8, 585–590.
- Atferdsanalysens styrke og begrensning. (The strengths and limitations of behaviour analysis). *Tidsskrift for Norsk Psykologforening, 56*, https://psykologtidsskriftet.no/debatt/2019/09/a

Index

T. G. Lindstad et al. (eds.), *Respect for Thought*, Theory and History in the Human and Social Sciences, https://doi.org/10.1007/978-3-030-43066-5

D

E

The manufacturer's authorised representative in the EU is Springer Nature Customer Service Centre GmbH, Europaplatz 3, 69115 Heidelberg, Germany. If you have any concerns regarding our products, please contact ProductSafety@springernature.com

Printed and bound by CPI Group (UK) Ltd, Croydon, CR0 4YY
05/10/2026
02228126-0013